Fundamentals of Canadian Income Tax
Volume 1: Personal Tax

Vern Krishna, CM, QC, LL.M. (Harvard), DCL (Cantab), FRSC, FCPA, FCGA

Barrister at Law
Professor of Common Law, University of Ottawa
Of Counsel: TaxChambers LLP (Toronto)

CARSWELL®

A cataloguing record for this publication is available from Library and Archives Canada

ISBN 978-0-7798-6406-5

Printed in Canada by Thomson Reuters

TELL US HOW WE'RE DOING
Scan the QR code to the right with your smartphone to send your comments regarding our products and services. Free QR Code Readers are available from your mobile device app store. You can also email us at carswell.feedback@thomsonreuters.com

THOMSON REUTERS

CARSWELL, A DIVISION OF THOMSON REUTERS CANADA LIMITED

One Corporate Plaza
2075 Kennedy Road
Toronto, Ontario
M1T 3V4

Customer Relations
Toronto 1-416-609-3800
Elsewhere in Canada/U.S. 1-800-387-5164
Fax 1-416-298-5082
www.carswell.com
Contact www.carswell.com/contact

To Savitri, Linda, Nicola,
Sacha, Vivian, and Biggie

PREFACE

It is 30 years since the publication of the first edition of this text, and tax law has not become any easier in that time. If anything, the law has become more complex, and obtuse. Tax law must now address increasingly complicated transactions — domestic and international — that involve exchanges of goods, services or intellectual property between business entities and family members. Indeed, even as I write this preface, the government has announced its intentions to change the rules in respect of family taxation and permit limited income splitting and other child care benefits. The *Income Tax Act* is now the single most important economic statute in Canada, and its influence as an instrument of public policy cannot be overstated.

Students, practitioners, and citizens dread tax law because of its complexity and tortured style of drafting. To be sure, tax law is complicated. Some endure it with resentment, whilst others simply ignore its existence, hoping that it will go away.

Students have been known to develop narcotaxis, a medical ailment that, within thirty seconds of hearing their professors begin to explain the law, causes glassy eyes, loss of bodily feeling, and a shallow coma, which can last for ninety minutes or more. Fortunately, the condition is not enduring, and students recover completely by the end of class.

Although some lawyers manage to go through entire careers without recognizing a tax issue, it is difficult to escape the tentacles of tax in corporate, commercial, securities, family, property, estates, trusts, and (white-collar) criminal law. Given the ever-increasing bulk and complexity of the *Act*, the only way to cope with it is to understand its fundamental principles and the underlying economic and regulatory policies. As a dynamic legislative enactment, we must analyze and interpret it according to the slowly evolving rules of purposive statutory construction.

I hope that this text will assist law students and practitioners in understanding the fundamental principles of tax law. We start in this Volume 1 with the basic structure of the statute, primarily in the context of personal tax law. There are, however, many aspects of the principles discussed herein that also affect corporations and other entities and relationships. We superimpose technical detail on the fundamentals, but only to the extent necessary for an enduring understanding of law and practice.

I assume that readers of this text have no prior knowledge — at least not from a legal perspective — of tax law. Hence, we commence by examining fundamental concepts. In Chapter 1 (Introduction), for example, we look at federal and provincial powers to tax under constitutional doctrines and bi-lateral agreements. We also look at the key concepts of tax systems and the basic principles of tax policy that influence the structure and politics of the law. We then move on to examine each of the sources of income, which apply across the entire statute.

Tax law makes difficult compromises between competing social and economic values: revenue requirements, administrative efficiency, a sense of fair play and the costs of effective fiscal administration. To be sure, the primary function of tax statutes is to raise revenue. However, governments also use the law to achieve social and political goals -for example, to dispense benefits, provide economic incentives, hide indirect trade subsidies and, sometimes, to buy votes.

Preface

The text addresses five fundamental questions common to all fiscal statutes:

- Who is taxable?
- What is taxable?
- How much do we tax?
- When is income taxable? And
- What are the processes to ensure compliance, and resolve disputes?

We answer each of these questions in the context of the underlying policies, statutory and treaty authorities, administrative practices and judicial decisions relevant to the federal income tax system. Although comprehensive, the text is not intended be encyclopedic.

The *Income Tax Act* continues to grow and we expect it will double in size during the next generation. The statute is poorly drafted, and written in a style that would make our high school teachers of English cringe with embarrassment. Nevertheless, we fervently cling to the doctrine that every person is presumed to know the law. Hence, taxpayers endure tax audits, which, like opera, the revenue authorities conduct in a language that few understand and that usually end in tragedy. Tax law can be a fun course in law school. It provides a better understanding of how society functions. Parliament legislates, and taxpayers — many with limited resources — must assert their rights under difficult rules against increasingly bigger government with mega resources. How should a student learn tax law in such an environment of technical complexity? By focusing on the basic principles, structure, and topography of the subject.

The text references relevant statutory provisions, administrative publications, Advance Rulings, Information Circulars and significant income tax treaties. These additional references allow the reader to move into greater levels of detail as circumstances warrant.

Dr. Johnson said that the only end of writing is to enable readers to enjoy life better or to better endure it. I have always been somewhat skeptical that this text-or, indeed, any text on income tax law can satisfy his first criterion. I hope, however, that the text will allow students to better endure their narcotaxis attacks and reduce anxiety in income tax courses. I also hope that it will make it easier for practitioners to adapt to the ever changing challenges of the operatic world of income tax law.

The law in the text is as enacted as of November 8, 2014.

Vern Krishna, CM, QC

Please send your comments by e-mail to: *vkrishna@uottawa.ca*

http://www.vernkrishna.com

ACKNOWLEDGEMENT

I wish to acknowledge the generous assistance and support of The Fellows and Life Fellows of the Foundation of Legal Research in the preparation of this text.

The art of taxation is so to pluck the goose
that the maximum number of feathers are obtained
with the minimum amount of hissing.

Jean Colbert (1665)

TABLE OF CONTENTS

Table of Contents

Table of Contents

Chapter 4 — The Meaning of Income

xi

Chapter 5 — Measurement of Income

Table of Contents

Chapter 7 — Business Income

Table of Contents

Table of Contents

Table of Contents

Table of Contents

Table of Contents

Chapter 12 — Other Income and Deductions

Table of Contents

Table of Contents

Chapter 14 — Taxable Income

Table of Contents

Chapter 15 — Computation of Tax

Table of Contents

Table of Contents

TABLE OF CASES

Table of Cases

Table of Cases

Table of Cases

Table of Cases

Table of Cases

Table of Cases

Table of Cases

Table of Cases

Table of Cases

Table of Cases

Table of Cases

Table of Cases

Table of Cases

Table of Cases

xlv

Table of Cases

Table of Cases

Table of Cases

Table of Cases

Table of Cases

Table of Cases

Chapter 1 — The Fiscal Landscape

Table of Contents

Table of Contents

Why is it important to know a thing or two about taxes? "Because you can do something about them."[1]

I. — General Comment

Income tax is the involuntary expropriation of property without direct compensation to the person from whom the government takes the property. Thus, income tax is the compulsory contribution that the government levies on transactions in goods, services and intellectual property to finance public expenditures that society considers to be for the public good.

Income tax law has a reputation of being a difficult and dry subject. To be sure, tax law is difficult, but it is neither dry nor unpleasant. Yes, tax law is replete with difficult, obtuse language, has a great deal of technical detail and is often incomprehensible. Even Albert Einstein conceded: "The hardest thing in the world to understand is the Income Tax."

Nevertheless, taxpayers must live with the statute as it is and not with the one that they wish had been written. We must comply with the law or face severe sanctions. Advisors must advise on, litigators litigate, and judges adjudicate, uncertain, changing, complex, and poorly drafted provisions. Thus, tax litigation is long and expensive and well beyond the reach of middle-income taxpayers.

All laws are ultimately behavioral. Tax laws invite behavioral responses from taxpayers. At the top end of the rate scale, where governments take one-half of one's earned income, it is understandable that individuals expend considerable energy and resources trying to minimize the tax bite. Corporations, which are more mobile than individuals, seek to improve their return on equity (ROE) by minimizing their tax exposure to the Canadian tax and moving income to low tax jurisdictions.

Frustrated by the creativity of taxpayers in legally avoiding tax, legislators respond by drafting provisions that are ever longer and more complex in order to reduce tax leakage and

---

[1]William L. Raby, Victor H. Tidwell & Richard A. White, *Introduction to Federal Taxation*: 1991 Edition xvii (1990).

revenue loss. The *Income Tax Act* (and related law) takes up 3000 printed pages and grows every year.

The raising of revenue is the imperative justification of tax law. However, governments also use tax law to implement social policies and redistribute income. Hence, the individual tax return form is labeled "Income Tax and Benefit Return". Nearly one-third of Canadians who file personal tax returns do not pay any income tax at all. They file primarily to receive income-tested benefits from the government. Thus, we use our tax law to balance different objectives: funding of public expenditures, economic policies, regional disparities and redistribution of income. No other statute serves so many diverse — and often, conflicting — purposes.

To be sure, the *Income Tax Act* is badly drafted. The statute violates almost every principle of good grammatical construction. For example, our drafting tradition requires that each section of the Act — no matter its length — should be a single self-contained sentence. Single sentence drafting of complex provisions that can contain several hundred words causes interpretational difficulties.

The comments of a member of the British Parliament speaking about the Irish Home Rule bill in 1889 would fairly describe the Canadian *Income Tax Act* today:

> . . . it sweats difficulties at every paragraph; every provision breeds a dilemma; every clause ends in a cul-de-sac; dangers lurk in every line; mischiefs abound in every sentence and an air of evil hangs over it all.

The notion that only Parliament enacts tax legislation is the bedrock of our constitutional history. It does not mean, however, that parliamentarians read and understand the legislation that they enact. That is left to the bureaucrats, who advise the Minister of Finance, to explain what the legislation is intended to achieve. They do so in obscure language. As Judge Mogan of the Tax Court of Canada described a definition in the *Act*:[2]

> The definition is prolix in the extreme. The persons who drafted that definition did not practise any economy of words or language. One may well ask how many members of parliament understood the definition when it was made law by amendment to the Act.

. . . . .

Shorn of its technical language, however, the statute is a policy document that reflects the social, political, economic and moral values of society at any particular time. There is a reason or purpose underlying every provision. Although the policy of provisions may not be

---

[2]*Citibank Canada v. R.*, [2001] 2 C.T.C. 2260 (T.C.C. [General Procedure]); affirmed [2002] 2 C.T.C. 171 (Fed. C.A).

obvious on first reading, the rationale is there for those who search for it. As Justice Frankfurter said:[3]

> Legislation has an aim: it seeks to obviate some mischief, to supply an inadequacy, to effect a change in policy, to formulate a plan of Government. That aim, that policy is not drawn, like nitrogen, out of the air; it is evinced in the language of the statute as read in the light of other external manifestations of purpose.

Thus, we need to ask five basic questions:

1. What is the law?

2. Why is the law?

3. How does it work?

4. How do the courts interpret it?

5. How will taxpayers respond to the law?

---

[3]Frankfurter, Felix, "Some Reflections on the Reading of Statutes" (1947) 47 Colum. L. Rev. No. 4, 527 at 538-39.

ANALYTICAL FRAMEWORK

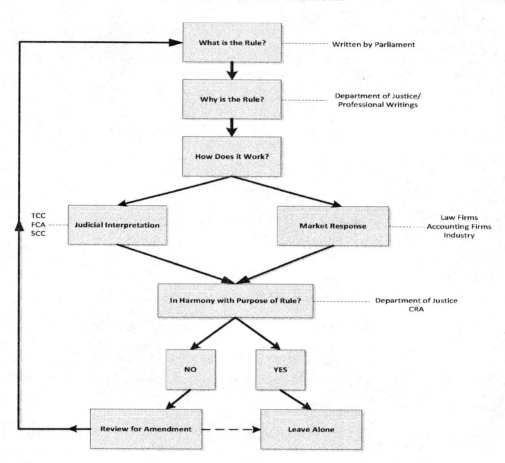

The first step requires us to read the statute slowly and carefully. The next two steps are closely related. We apply the plain meaning of words where the language is "clear and un-ambiguous". The meaning of words in tax law, however, is rarely as plain as its authors anticipate when they draft the legislation. Where the language is not clear, we should look to the purpose or policy (its object and spirit) of the provision to determine its rationale.

To be sure, judges are deferential, at least on the surface, to the words that Parliament has enacted. However, every judicial interpretation has policy implications. Judges should look at legislative history and engage in purposive analysis when the words of the statute are capable of different meanings. In *Hewlett-Packard (Canada) Co. v. R.*,[4] for example, the Tax Court had to wrestle with whether the word "lodge" included "luxury hotels". If it did, the taxpayer could not deduct expenses to entertain its employees in the particular hotels. The purpose of the rule prohibiting deduction of lodge expenses is to prevent expense account living on the public purse. Although dictionaries sometimes use the word "hotel" to describe "lodge", the Tax Court did not think that most Canadians would describe large resort hotels with a range of modern amenities as "lodges". Thus, the Court allowed the taxpayer to deduct its substantial expenses and, in doing so, sideswiped the underlying policy of the provision against the deduction of such expenses.

Purposive analysis requires an understanding of the principles and policies underlying tax law. Judges, consciously or unconsciously, may inject their own policy perspective in interpreting the statute and apply their own normative beliefs of the appropriate policy. As Justice Benjamin N. Cardozo said in his classic work, *The Nature of the Judicial Process* (1949):

> Deep below consciousness are other forces, the likes and the dislikes, the predilections and the prejudices, the complex of instincts and emotions and habits and convictions, which make the man, whether he be litigant or judge.

Ultimately, judges are lawmakers. Hence, in tax litigation, it is important to "know" your judge and his or her judicial history before arguing a case.

II. — Historical Background

Most modern income tax systems were born of the need to finance wars. Before World War I, the principal sources of revenue in Canada were customs duties and excise taxes. Sir Robert Borden, Prime Minister of Canada, introduced the federal income tax on business profits in 1916, and a tax on personal income in 1917. The government introduced both taxes as temporary measures to finance World War I.

Sir Thomas White, Minister of Finance, introduced the *Income War Tax Act* in the House of Commons with conviction:

> I have placed no time limit upon this measure . . . a year or two after the war is over, the measure should be definitely reviewed.

---

[4] 2005 CarswellNat 1765, 2005 TCC 398, [2005] 4 C.T.C. 2274, 2005 D.T.C. 976 (T.C.C. [General Procedure]).

Both statements proved to be politically accurate. There will never be a time limit on taxation; and governments do review our taxes annually. Louis St. Laurent finally made income taxes permanent on January 1, 1949.

The *Income War Tax Act* was all of ten pages. It has since grown through several reincarnations of "tax reform" into the *Income Tax Act* of today — over 3000 pages and expanding at a healthy pace.[5] Of course, the nature of the Canadian income tax system has changed significantly since its introduction. In 1917, the *Income War Tax Act* exempted the first $1,500 of income — about $24,000 in 2004 dollars — from any tax whatsoever. The highest rate of 72 percent applied to income of $107 million in 2004 dollars!

The most significant reform followed the *Carter Commission*, culminating in the current version of the *Income Tax Act*, which came into effect on January 1, 1972. Since then, there have been various attempts at reform and simplification of the statute, all with minimal success. As the Joint Committee on Taxation of the Canadian Bar Association and the Canadian Institute of Chartered Accountants, in addressing the House of Commons Committee on Finance and Economic Affairs, said:

> For any taxpayer to pick up some of this legislation we are looking at today and understand how these rules are going to impact on him when he sits down to fill out his tax return is almost impossible.

> There is no quick fix to the complexity issue. It is a very long-term problem, but I fear that the Government's priority for tax simplification has fallen down to the bottom of the various objectives set out for tax reform.

In 1997, the Report of the Technical Committee on Business Taxation reported in a similar vein:[6]

> [I]n a complex society that is part of a world economy, where the form and processes of business activities are increasingly sophisticated, and where the tax system is also used for purposes other than raising revenue, it is unrealistic to expect our tax system to be simple.

Bureaucrats always write complex laws. Taxpayers must live with the complexity of the statute and pay for professional advice to comply with the law. Resolving tax disputes is a slow, arduous and expensive process. Hence, we speak of the "unpleasant subject of taxes".

III. — The Meaning of "Tax"

The *Income Tax Act* (Canada) ("Act") does not define either "income" or "tax". The courts have developed the meaning of the terms in case law. Although there are several sources

---

[5]Up from 2,000 pages since 2004.

[6]Report of the Technical Committee on Business Taxation (December 1997), A Report to the Minister of Finance, at 1.2.

that define "tax" in various contexts, their common theme is that taxes are an enforced contribution that a state levies by virtue of its sovereignty to support its operations and public needs. Legislatures sometimes describe taxes as "charges", "exactions", or "duties". However, the common element of all taxes is that they are mandatory and coercive.[7] They "operate *in invitum* — against an unwilling person.[8]

The meaning of "tax" is important because of constitutional limits on the power to tax. The Canadian Constitution divides the authority to impose taxes between the federal and provincial governments. The federal parliament has the power to raise money by *any* mode or system of taxation. In contrast, the provinces can impose income taxes only through direct taxation within the province and then only for raising revenue for provincial purposes. Thus, it is important for constitutional reasons to identify whether a levy is a user fee, licence, penalty, or tax and on whom the burden falls.[9]

All taxes are painful. Hence, politicians like to attach soft labels to taxing statutes to lessen their pain. For example, in 1996 Premier Dalton McGuinty of Ontario introduced the Fair Share Health Care Levy (FSHCL), and in 2004, a health care "premium". Both the levy and the premium were in substance "taxes". Similarly, President Obama of the United States introduced the *Patient Protection and Affordable Care Act* (2012) ("Obama Care") as health insurance coverage. Individuals must pay a "penalty" to the Internal Revenue Service if they do not purchase the insurance.

The statutory label of a levy is important for political purposes. However, it is irrelevant in determining the legal character of the levy. Courts have held exactions not to be taxes even when labeled as such, and to be taxes when not so labeled. A licence or user fee, for example, may be an indirect tax and, if so, outside of the provincial constitutional authority to levy taxes.

There are several criteria to determine whether a levy is in fact a tax or a penalty. A tax raises revenue for public expenditures by attaching to an event — for example, earning income, buying goods and services, or engaging in an activity. In contrast, a penalty is a punitive sanction for doing something that is considered harmful and, in most cases, requires the actor to have knowledge of the wrongful act.

To be sure, both taxes and penalties affect conduct, but they do so in different ways. Tax provisions are often used for purposes other than to raise revenue. For example, taxes on cigarettes not only raise substantial revenues for governments but are also intended to en-

---

[7]*Eurig Estate, Re*, [1998] 2 S.C.R. 565, [2000] 1 C.T.C. 284 (S.C.C.).

[8]*Meriwether v. Garrett*, 102 U.S. 472 (U.S. Sup. Ct., 1880) at 514.

[9]Black's Law Dictionary: "A charge, usu. Monetary, imposed by the government on persons, entities, transactions, or property to yield public revenue." See, generally: Thomas M. Cooley, *The Law of Taxation* 62 (Clark A. Nichols ed., 4th ed. 1924). Cooley was a professor at the University of Michigan and served as Chief Justice of the Supreme Court of Michigan.

courage people to give up smoking for health reasons. In contrast, governments use liquor taxes primarily to raise revenues without excessive concern for health.

Thus, every tax is in some measure regulatory in that it poses an economic impediment to the activity taxed as compared with others that are not taxed. In contrast, penalties imply punishment for an unlawful act or omission — such as, for example, failure to secure a motor vehicle permit or a dog licence.

Taxpayers do not receive specific measurable benefits from their taxes. A tax is simply an enforced contribution pursuant to constitutional legislative authority to raise revenue for public purposes and not as a payment for some special benefit or service. Taxpayers do, however, indirectly derive benefits from government services — such as, national defense, health care, public schools, judicial services, and public roads, etc. As Justice Holmes said: "Taxes are what we pay for civilized society."[10]

IV. — Taxpayers

A significant element of tax complexity is the multitude of types of entities and relationships to which different rules apply. A tax system must identify each type that it shall tax and specify the rules that apply to each group. For example, the Canadian income tax system identifies:

- Individuals (natural persons);[11]
- Corporations (artificial entities);[12]
- Trusts (relationships);[13] and
- Partnerships (flow through relationships).[14]

Each individual is a taxpayer in his or her own right and must file a tax return in respect of tax payable for the year. Corporations, trusts and estates are also taxpayers in their own right and must file separate returns. A partnership is not a taxpayer in its own right, but we determine its income at the partnership level *as if* it were an entity and partners then declare their share of income in their tax returns. The rules that govern the flow of income between vari-

---

[10]*Compania General de Tabacos de Filipinas v. Collector of Internal Revenue*, 275 U.S. 87 (1927) at 100 (Holmes J. dissenting).

[11]§ 248(1) "individual".

[12]§ 248(1) "person".

[13]§ 248(1) "trust" and § 104(1).

[14]§ 96(1)(a).

ous types of taxpayers require complex provisions in order to prevent double taxation and tax leakage.

V. — The Incidence of Taxes

Tax law is a combination of constitutional, statutory and case law. The Constitution allocates the power to tax based on the legal incidence of the tax.

The legal incidence of a tax is on the taxpayer who is required to pay the tax. The Act identifies who is liable to pay tax,[15] the income[16] on which the tax is payable and the time for payment.[17]

The economic incidence of a tax is on the person who ultimately bears the economic cost of the tax — that is, the person who endures the financial burden. The economic incidence of a tax may be quite different from its legal incidence because the cost may be passed on. For example, the Harmonized Sales Tax (HST) is legally levied on the person who collects and remits the tax, but its economic impact is on the ultimate consumer who buys the goods or services. Similarly, since corporations are artificial entities, they do not bear the ultimate financial burden of taxes. The ultimate economic incidence of corporate taxes is passed on to shareholders (reduced dividends), employees (reduced wages), and customers (higher prices).

It is difficult to measure the economic incidence of taxes because of the complexities of the underlying supply and demand conditions (including elasticity), contractual arrangements (labour contracts) and other factors. Nevertheless, it is important for policy makers and legislators to evaluate both the legal and economic incidence of the taxes that they enact to ensure that they are efficiently targeted.

VI. — The Authority to Tax

A. — Division of Powers

Democratic societies cherish the rule of law and accountability for the collection of taxes for public purposes. Under Canadian law, the federal Parliament and provincial legislatures can impose taxes based on their constitutional authority. We trace the origin of the rule — no taxation without representation — as far back as the *Magna Carta* (1215).

---

[15]Ss. 2(1).

[16]Ss. 2(2).

[17]See generally: Division I, Section 153 and following.

Under the doctrine of parliamentary supremacy, the Constitution and legislative traditions determine the power to tax and the passage of money bills. Section 53 of the *Constitution Act*, (1867) is a constitutional imperative:[18]

> Bills for appropriating any Part of the Public Revenue, or for imposing any Tax or Impost, shall originate in the House of Commons.

The Constitution[19] divides the authority to impose taxes between the federal and provincial governments. The federal Parliament has the power under subsection 91(3) to raise money by *any* mode or system of taxation. Subsection 92(2) allows the provinces to impose income taxes, but only through *direct* taxation within the province and only for raising revenue for provincial purposes. This division of the taxing power gives the federal government considerable power over the national economy and the distribution of income.

The legislative body must clearly express its will to levy a tax in the first instance. Although the legislative body can delegate the details of taxation to another body, it must do so in unambiguous language that clearly expresses its intention.[20] However, neither the Dominion nor a province may delegate to the other its power to legislate on taxation.[21]

This dual authority to levy income taxes results in differential income tax burdens in various regions in the country. The income tax burden for Ontario residents, for example, is substantially higher (49 percent in 2013) than the equivalent tax in Alberta (39 percent). Nova Scotia had the highest tax rate in 2013 at 50 percent (all 2013 rates).

The *Income Tax Act*, the primary source of income tax law, authorizes the enactment of *Income Tax Regulations* ("Regulations"). Parliament can amend the Act but only through a Bill introduced in the House of Commons. In contrast, Regulations are enacted by Orders-in-Council, which are essentially determined by the Cabinet.

The rationale for limiting provincial legislatures to direct taxation is to contain their powers within their boundaries. Thus, the provincial taxing power is limited in law to direct taxes, imposed within the province, and for provincial purposes. This prevents a province from using its taxing power for colorable purposes by concealing its real objectives. In economic

---

[18]See, for example, *SNEAA c. Canada (Procureur general)*, (sub nom. *Confédération des syndicats nationaux v. Canada (Procureur général)*) 2008 SCC 68 (S.C.C.), Date: 20081211; Docket: 31809, 31810, for modern application of the principle.

[19]*Constitution Act, 1867* (U.K.), 30 & 31 Vict., c. 3.

[20]*O.E.C.T.A. v. Ontario (Attorney General)*, 2001 SCC 15, (sub nom. *Ontario English Catholic Teachers' Assn. v. Ontario (Attorney General)*) [2001] 1 S.C.R. 470 (S.C.C.) (provincial legislation authorizing the Minister of Finance to prescribe tax rates for school purposes was constitutional. The legislation set out the structure of the tax, the tax base and the principles for imposing the tax).

[21]*Constitutional Validity of Bill No. 136 (Nova Scotia), Re* (1950), (sub nom. *Nova Scotia (Attorney General) v. Canada (Attorney General)*) [1951] S.C.R. 31, 50 D.T.C. 838 (S.C.C.).

terms, however, we cannot contain provincial taxes within a province. Taxpayers can pass on direct taxes to persons (for example, consumers) outside the province.

The distinction between direct and indirect taxes is more rigid and formalistic in legal analysis. In 1848, John Stuart Mill stated the distinction between the two forms of taxation as follows:[22]

> A direct tax is one which is demanded from the very persons who it is intended or desired should pay it. Indirect taxes are those which are demanded from one person in the expectation and intention that he shall indemnify himself at the expense of another, such as the excise or customs.

In the final analysis, the constitutional validity of a tax depends upon its pith and substance.[23] Thus, the crucial inquiry is the object and primary purpose of the scheme and not simply its formal or superficial characteristics.[24] The pith and substance approach contrasts with blanket categorizations whereby certain categories of taxes — such as property and income taxes — are considered as direct taxes.[25]

In *Atlantic Smoke Shops Ltd. v. Conlon*, Lord Simonds emphasized the need for analysis of the real nature of the tax:[26]

> Their Lordships are of opinion that Lord Cave's reference in his judgment in the Fairbanks' case to "two separate and distinct categories" of taxes, "namely those that are direct and those which cannot be so described", should not be understood as relieving the courts from the obligation of examining the real nature and effect of the particular tax in the present instance, or as justifying the classification of the tax as indirect merely because it is in some sense associated with the purchase of an article.

---

[22]See: *Cotton v. R.* (1913), [1914] A.C. 176 (Quebec P.C.) at 193; see also *Atlantic Smoke Shops Ltd. v. Conlon*, [1943] C.T.C. 294 (New Brunswick P.C.); see generally La Forest J., "The Allocation of Taxing Power under the Canadian Constitution", Can. Tax Paper No. 45 (Can. Tax. Foundation, 1967) at 81.

[23]See, for example, the majority of the Supreme Court in *Reference re Questions set out in O.C. 1079/80, Concerning Tax Proposed by Parliament of Canada on Exported Natural Gas* (1982), 136 D.L.R. (3d) 385 (S.C.C.) at 438: "The essential question here is no different than in any other constitutional case: what is the 'pith and substance' of the relevant legislation?"

[24]*Ontario Home Builders' Assn. v. York (Region) Board of Education* (1996), 137 D.L.R. (4th) 449 (S.C.C.).

[25]See *Halifax (City) v. Fairbanks Estate*, [1927] 4 D.L.R. 945 (Nova Scotia P.C.).

[26][1943] A.C. 550, [1943] C.T.C. 294 (New Brunswick P.C.) at 565 [A.C.], quoted with approval by Justice Iacobucci at 492 of Ontario Home Builders' Assn.

Hence, we look at the *legal* incidence of a tax, not its label, to determine its constitutional validity.[27]

The categories approach does not always provide an unequivocal answer to the nature of a tax. For example, a land tax would usually be a direct tax; it may, however, also be an indirect tax under the legal incidence test. As Justice Iacobucci said in *Ontario Home Builders' Association*:[28]

> The hallmarks of a land tax are that the tax is, of course, imposed on land against the owner of the land, and that the tax is assessed as a percentage of the value of the land, or a fixed charge per acre. The tax may be an annual, recurring assessment, or a one-time charge . . . Although landowners, like everyone, may wish to pass on their tax burden to someone else or otherwise avoid taxation, this desire or ability does not transform the direct nature of the tax into an indirect one . . . the case law reveals that land taxes are generally direct taxes; but I do not believe the case law prevents a tax on land by itself from being treated as an indirect tax.

Most economists consider Mills' definition of direct and indirect taxes as narrow and rigid. Indeed, the question as to who actually bears the burden of any tax ("incidence of taxation") is an unsettled economic issue that engenders considerable debate. Nevertheless, in constitu-

---

[27]*Ontario Home Builders' Assn.* at 476:

> Of course, it is the general tendency of the tax that is of concern, rather than the ultimate incidence of the tax in the circumstances of a particular case . . . the test of incidence is based on a legal, rather than an economic distinction . . . When determining the incidence of a tax, it is important to bear in mind the context within which the tax operates as well as the purpose of the tax.

See John Stuart Mill "Principles of Political Economy, Book V", (London: John W. Parker & Son, 1852).

[28]*Ontario Home Builder's Assn.* above note 27.

tional law, Mills' distinction between the two forms of taxes provides a finite answer[29] and is now the accepted test.[30]

B. — Restraint on Powers

Section 125 of the *Constitution Act*, (1867) provides that no lands or property belonging to Canada or any province shall be liable to taxation. This provision provides inter-governmental immunity from taxation in respect of "lands or property" owned by the federal or provincial Crown. The restriction also extends to Crown agents such as Crown corporations.[31]

What is the extent of this protection? The first question we must determine is whether a particular statutory measure is a "taxation" measure or the exercise of regulatory power under some other legislative head, for example, the commerce clause. On its surface, it appears as though section 125 exempts only provincial "lands or property" from federal taxation. The restraint on the federal government is, however, broader: section 125 applies not only to provincial lands or property but also to taxes levied on persons and transactions in

---

[29]See *Lambe v. North British & Mercantile Fire & Life Insurance Co.* (1887), (sub nom. *Bank of Toronto v. Lambe*) L.R. 12 App. Cas. 575, [1917-27] C.T.C. 82 (Quebec P.C.) at 582 [L.R. 12 App. Cas.] per Lord Hobhouse:

> Taxes are either direct or indirect. A direct tax is one which is demanded from the very persons who it is intended or desired should pay it. Indirect taxes are those which are demanded from one person in the expectation and intention that he shall indemnify himself at the expense of another; such as the excise or customs.

> The producer or importer of a commodity is called upon to pay a tax on it, not with the intention to levy a peculiar contribution upon him, but to tax through him the consumers of the commodity, from whom it is supposed that he will recover the amount by means of an advance in price.

[30]*Eurig Estate, Re*, [1998] 2 S.C.R. 565, [2000] 1 C.T.C. 284 (S.C.C.) (taxpayer challenged Ontario's estate probate fees as being an indirect tax beyond the power of the provincial government. Applying Mills' definition, the tax would be indirect if the executor was personally liable for payment of probate fees, as the intention would clearly be that the executor would recover payment from the beneficiaries of the estate. However, the legislation did not make the executor personally liable for the fees. The executor would pay only in his or her representative capacity. The majority of the Supreme Court held that amounts collected in respect of grants of letters probate constituted a tax rather than a regulatory fee. The probate fee was a direct tax and, therefore, *intra vires* the Province of Ontario.)

See also, *Hudson's Bay Co. v. Ontario (Attorney General)* (2000), [2000] O.J. No. 2203, 49 O.R. (3d) 455 (Ont. S.C.J.); affirmed (2001), 2001 CarswellOnt 540 (Ont. C.A.).

[31]See, e.g., *Nova Scotia Power Inc. v. R.*, 2004 SCC 51, [2006] 5 C.T.C. 266 (S.C.C.) (NSPC acting within its purposes as a Crown agent and thus entitled to immunity from legislation, including the *Income Tax Act*, as provided by s. 17 of the *Interpretation Act*).

respect of Crown property. Thus, section 125 overrides the express powers of taxation contained in subsections 91(3) (the federal power) and 92(2) (the provincial power) of the *Constitution Act*, (1867) and provides a constitutional guarantee of immunity from federal taxation of provincial property.[32] The Supreme Court of Canada has stated:[33]

> This immunity would be illusory if it applied to taxes "on property" but not to a tax on the Crown in respect of a transaction affecting its property or on the transaction itself. The immunity would be illusory since, by the simple device of framing a tax as "*in personam*" rather than "*in rem*" one level of government could with impunity tax away the fruits of property owned by the other. The fundamental constitutional protection framed by section 125 cannot depend on subtle nuances of form.

Hence, once we determine that the "pith and substance" of a measure are "taxation", section 125 restrains the federal government from imposing the tax on provincial lands, property, Crown agents, and transactions directly involving provincial property. This appears to be the case whether or not the province is involved in commercial activity. In Professor Hogg's words:[34]

> Section 125 probably covers taxation of all property belonging to Canada or a province, regardless of whether the property is acquired for or employed in a commercial activity or a governmental activity. The section is not limited to non-commercial property.

The determination of whether the substance of legislation constitutes taxation or the exercise of a regulatory power can be a difficult question and, in some cases, produces dubious results.[35]

C. — Responsibility for Taxation

The Department of Finance determines the policy of financial affairs that fall within the authority of the federal power.[36] The Minister of National Revenue is responsible for administering the *Income Tax Act*.[37] Thus, unlike most other countries, Canada places the responsibility for enacting fiscal legislation and its administration in different ministries. The responsibility for tax litigation is with the Minister of Justice.

---

[32]*Reference re Questions set out in O.C. 1079/80, Concerning Tax Proposed by Parliament of Canada on Exported Natural Gas*, [1982] 1 S.C.R. 1004 (S.C.C.).

[33]*Ibid.*, at 1078.

[34]Hogg, *Constitutional Law of Canada*, loose-leaf (Toronto: Carswell, 1997) at 30–32.

[35]See *British Columbia (Attorney General) v. Canada (Attorney General)*, [1924] A.C. 222 (Canada P.C.).

[36]*Financial Administration Act*, R.S.C. 1985, c. F-11.

[37]*Canada Customs and Revenue Agency Act*, S.C. 1999, c. 17.

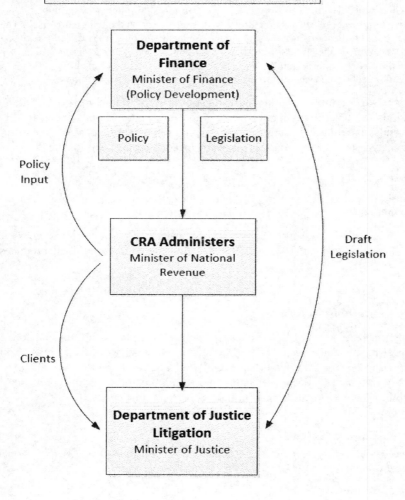

D. — Federal-Provincial Agreements

The *Federal-Provincial Fiscal Arrangements Act* governs federal-provincial income tax arrangements.[38]

The structure of the arrangement between the federal and provincial governments is governed by the *Federal-Provincial Fiscal Arrangements Act (1961)*, under which the federal Parliament unilaterally vacates a portion of the income tax field to the provinces, which allows the provinces to impose their own taxes.

The federal government has tax collection agreements (TCAs) with most of the provinces, under which the federal government collects the provincial income tax on behalf of the provinces. To facilitate tax collection and assessment, the agreements require the provinces to levy their tax by reference to a taxable base that is identical to that used for federal income tax purposes.

Prior to 2000, this was accomplished through the "tax on tax" method of income tax collection. Under this method, provincial income tax payable by individuals was calculated as a percentage of their federal tax payable. The disadvantage of this method is that it restricts the provinces' ability to raise revenues and to create tax policies based on their own evolving social and economic priorities.

In response to the provinces' desire for increased control and flexibility in setting tax policy, the federal government agreed to amend the TCAs to change the basis on which the provinces levy provincial income taxes.[39] Following the amendment, the participating provinces could continue to use the old "tax on tax" method of calculating provincial income taxes or elect to use the new "tax on income" method. The new tax on income method calculates provincial income tax payable by individuals as a percentage of their *taxable income* rather than of their federal tax payable.

The new method allows the provinces to determine their own unique income tax brackets and rates and to create their own distinct block of non-refundable tax credits,[40] which gives the provinces greater flexibility in setting tax policy. However, the provinces must still use the federal definition of "taxable income" in order to ensure a common tax base.

Ensuring a common tax base facilitates tax collection and assessment, and also mitigates the problems that can arise where there are significant discrepancies in tax policy from one province to the next. For example, a province may wish to establish a very low tax rate on capital income, compared with other sources of income, in order to attract the highly mobile capital from other provinces. If this was permitted, it could negatively impact the national economy.

---

[38] *Federal-Provincial Fiscal Arrangements Act*, R.S.C. 1985, c. F-8.

[39] See generally the Department of Finance's Federal Administration of Provincial Taxes, October 1998, Report prepared by the Federal-Provincial Committee on Taxation for Presentation to Ministers of Finance, online: http://www.fin.gc.ca/fapt/fapt3e.html.

[40] Subject to restrictions on minimums; see ibid. at Design and Operation.

E. — The Executive Process

The responsibility for fiscal policy rests with the Minister of Finance. The Department of Finance advises the Minister on changes to income tax legislation and prepares substantive tax policy papers and drafts tax legislation.

The responsibility for administering the *Income Tax Act* lies with the Canada Revenue Agency (CRA), which also has a division concerned with tax policy. Finance and the Canada Revenue Agency (the "CRA")[41] liaise closely on income tax legislation.

F. — The Legislative Process

Legislation in respect of income tax originates in the House of Commons on the recommendation of the Governor General.[42] Income tax legislation may not be introduced in the Senate. Nor is it possible for a private member to introduce a tax Bill in the House of Commons.

---

[41] In December 2003, the Canada Customs and Revenue Agency became the Canada Revenue Agency. The Customs program is now part of the new Canada Border Services Agency.

[42] *Constitution Act, 1867* (U.K.), c. 3, ss. 53, 54.

G. — The Budget

Budget Process

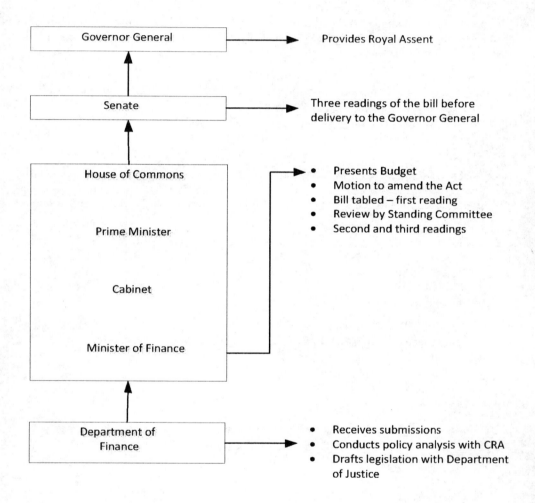

As a matter of parliamentary tradition, the Minister of Finance presents a Budget[43] to the

---

[43]"Budget" (contrary to the understanding of the term by accountants who view it as a financial statement) is a derivation from the old French "bougette", meaning "a little bag". In British parliamentary

House of Commons, following which he tables a Notice of Ways and Means Motions to introduce amendments to the *Income Tax Act*. The Budget allows the government of the day an opportunity to review the state of the economy and to announce policies in respect of its economic and fiscal programs. Following the Budget, there is a debate in the House. The debate cannot exceed six sitting days of the House of Commons.

The parliamentary tradition that the Minister of Finance should announce tax changes only in the House of Commons has softened somewhat with some Ministers unfortunately announcing proposed tax changes by press release.

Sometime after the Budget debate, the Minister of Finance introduces amending legislation in the form of a Bill to implement the proposals set out in the Notice of Ways and Means Motions. The Bill is given a first reading in the House to make it a public document and is then debated in principle during second reading. Following second reading, income tax Bills are debated by the Committee of Ways and Means, which sits as a committee of the whole House.[44]

Specialized committees, such as the Committee on Finance, Trade and Economic Affairs, may also consider the Bill and suggest amendments. Following detailed examination of the Bill by the Committee of the Whole House, it is given third reading and sent to the Senate.

The Senate does not have the power to initiate income tax legislation. It does, however, have the constitutional authority to debate tax Bills that are referred to it by the House of Commons. The Senate Committee on Banking, Trade and Commerce is an influential committee whose deliberations may have a substantial impact on such a Bill. As a practical matter, with the exception of purely technical changes, the Senate does not amend income tax legislation without the approval of the Minister of Finance.

Finally, the Bill is sent for Royal Assent and becomes law the day that it receives Assent. Amendments enacted through a Bill, however, are generally effective as of the date that the legislation stipulates.

VII. — Tax Policy

Taxation involves a transfer of resources from the private to the public sector. Tax policy concerns the efficiency with which we implement the transfer and the value and benefit that society derives from the process.

---

tradition, the "little bag" was replaced by a "little box" (14 1/2" by 10") made for Gladstone in about 1860. The box was replaced by a new one in 1996.

[44]Unlike bills dealing with non-tax matters, it is the entire House which constitutes the Committee. The public may not make representations directly to the Committee of the Whole House.

A tax system should raise sufficient revenue to finance government operations. A good tax system, however, is also concerned with the manner in which we collect the revenue. It should be neutral and efficient, fair and equitable, certain, administratively simple, and easy to comply with. These are often conflicting goals, and all the more so if we use tax law to implement economic, social and political objectives. Thus, tax law is a compromise of competing values. Tax policy analysis should evaluate the effectiveness and efficiency of the compromises.

A. — Revenue Generation

a) — The Tax Base

Income taxes are levied to generate revenues. A tax system must raise sufficient revenues to finance government operations. In concept, the amount of revenue that a tax system raises is a simple mathematical function:

$$\text{Revenue} = \text{Tax Base} \times \text{Tax Rate}$$

Thus, there are really only two variables that directly determine the amount of revenue that a tax system can raise. The interplay between these two variables, however, is complex and influences the manner in which we achieve other non-revenue objectives. The size and character of the tax base and tax rates affect the fairness of the system, economic efficiency, certainty, and the costs of compliance.

The size of the tax base also has an effect on other aspects of the tax system. A system with a broad base is usually more certain and simpler than a system with a narrowly constrained base. This is because a broad-based system requires fewer lines of demarcation between classifications of income, expenditures and exclusions than a narrowly based system. For example, a system that taxes all forms of gains, regardless of from where they derive, requires fewer rules than a system that distinguishes between different sources of economic gains, each with its own rules.

We can generate the same amount of revenue from a broadly based system as we can from a narrow base by adjusting tax rates. The trade-off between the two, however, affects the economic efficiency of the system and its complexity, which in turn affects the cost of compliance and tax administration.

The tax base for federal purposes is "taxable income". The provinces can elect to use one of two bases for the purposes of provincial tax: (a) federal "taxable income", or (b) "federal tax payable".[45] Thus, the provincial tax (except in Quebec) piggybacks on the federal tax base. Hence, any changes to the federal taxable base almost invariably affect provincial revenues.

---

[45]See Chapter 1, Part I, s. 2(d).

b) — Tax Rates

The second element in determining revenue is the tax rate that one applies to the tax base. All other things being equal (and they rarely are), the higher the tax rate, the greater the revenue collected from the tax base. Thus, ignoring behavioral responses to tax rates, a rate of 40 percent will in theory produce a greater amount of revenue than a tax rate of 20 percent.[46] However, there are many economists who maintain that a reduction in tax rates stimulates economic growth and enhances revenues, which, in turn, leads to additional tax collections.

There are three different tax rates: marginal, average, and effective. The marginal tax rate is the level of tax that applies on the last dollar of taxable income. Hence, as marginal rates rise, the total tax payable increases by a rate that is more than proportional to the increase in income.

For example, an individual who earns $30,000 taxable income will pay basic federal tax at a federal marginal rate of 15 percent. In contrast, an individual who earns taxable income of $150,000 will pay at a federal marginal rate of 29 percent (2013 rates).

We obtain the "average rate" of tax by dividing the total tax payable by the tax base. The average rate reflects the weighted average of all of the marginal tax rates. For example, the average federal tax rate of an individual who earns $30,000 is $4,500 or 15 percent. In this case, the average and the marginal rates are equal because only one marginal rate (15 percent) applies to all of the income. Where an individual earns taxable income of $140,000 in 2013, however, total tax is $30,145, which makes the average rate of tax 22 percent — that is, 7 percent lower than the individual's federal marginal rate of 29 percent.

The "effective rate" of tax is the total tax payable divided by *net income* before exclusions and exemptions. In the above example, assume that an individual who has taxable income of $140,000 earned $60,000 of capital gains in the year. By excluding one-half of the capital gains from taxable income, the individual has, in effect, reduced his or her economic income by $30,000. The individual's effective tax rate is the actual tax payable of $30,145 divided by his "real" net economic income of $170,000. Thus, the effective tax rate is 18 percent.

Effective tax rates are the only meaningful yardstick for comparing taxes in different countries. In international comparisons, marginal and average rates of tax are not helpful because they do not take into account the differences in calculating the taxable base to which one applies the actual rate. For example, assume that Country A taxes net income at 40 percent whereas Country B taxes net income at 35 percent. On the surface, it appears that Country A has higher tax rates. If, however, Country A allows generous deductions (for example, mort-

---

[46]This assumes a static model under which human behavior does not respond to a change in tax rates. In contrast, in a dynamic model, human behavior will respond to changes in tax rates and produce more or less than the directly proportional mathematical result.

gage interest and property tax deductions) in computing income that Country B does not permit, the effective rate of tax in Country A may actually be lower than in Country B.[47]

c) — Provincial Taxes

The provinces apply tax as a percentage of the federal taxable income or tax payable. A taxpayer's total tax liability is the aggregate of his federal *and* provincial taxes payable. Provincial rate schedules vary between provinces. Hence, Canadian residents pay different taxes on identical amounts of income depending upon their province of residence.

B. — Neutrality

Neutrality means that a tax system should not draw artificial distinctions between identical transactions merely on the basis of the legal form of transactions or their source. Thus, neutrality implies a level playing field that does not favour or unfairly discriminate against taxpayers merely on the basis of their choice of entities or relationships to structure their business and personal transactions. For example, in a perfectly neutral system the tax consequences would be the same regardless of whether an individual earned income personally or through a corporation.

In fact, as we will see, the Canadian tax system is far from neutral and invites behavioral responses from taxpayers who are often motivated purely by tax considerations. This is inevitable. Taxpayers faced with choices respond to the system and attempt to minimize their tax burden. To do otherwise would be irrational. For example, a Canadian corporation pays federal tax at a rate of 11 percent [2013] on the first $500,000 of its active business income.[48] In contrast, an individual in the top bracket would pay federal tax at 29 percent on the same income. Since the reduced rate of tax is not available to individuals, the system is biased in favour of the corporate form of business.[49] Taxpayers respond to this systemic bias, which is an intrinsic part of the tax system, by opting to conduct their Canadian businesses in the corporate form in order to save tax.

---

[47]See, for example, Martin F. Feldstein, James Poterba & Louis Dicks Mireaux, "The Effective Tax Rate and the Pre-Tax Rate of Return" (Working Paper 740) (*National Bureau of Economic Research Working Paper Series*, August 1981).

[48]Subs. 125(2).

[49]See generally subs. 125(1).

C. — Efficiency

The efficient allocation of resources to maximize production and economic growth is an important policy of the tax system. A policy is efficient if it promotes the optimal allocation of capital. A tax system can distort economic efficiency and capital flows by causing persons to make business decisions solely on tax considerations. Thus, we should evaluate tax measures intended to stimulate or encourage economic activities based on their cost effectiveness in the light of the objectives of the provision.

Similarly in the international arena, tax provisions can distort economic decisions and cause a non-optimal allocation of capital. The principle of capital export or international neutrality, for example, suggests that a taxpayer's choice between investing at home or abroad should not be affected by the pattern of taxation.[50] A Canadian corporate tax rate that is significantly higher than international norms stimulates export of capital and jobs to countries with lower rates in order to enhance domestic after-tax returns. For example, if Canada taxes the Royal Bank of Canada (RBC) at 30 percent on its Canadian income and the United Kingdom taxes its U.K. profits at 25 percent, the tax system will be neutral only if it taxes RBC at a net rate (after foreign credits) of 5 percent on its foreign income.

D. — Fairness and Equity

A tax system must be fair. An unfair system of taxation stimulates blatant tax avoidance and evasion. Thus, we speak of tax equity as a system that treats similarly situated taxpayers in a similar manner (horizontal equity) and promotes a fair distribution of income (vertical equity). That said, however, it is not always easy to settle upon a common understanding of fairness, which is a value that incorporates social, political and moral values.

a) — Horizontal Equity

Most people agree that taxpayers in similar financial circumstances should pay similar amounts of tax. At its simplest level, an individual who earns $100,000 from employment should be taxed at the same rate as an individual who earns $100,000 from rental income. We refer to this aspect of fairness as horizontal equity: equal treatment of those with equal ability to pay.

The accurate measurement of "income" is integral to the fairness of the tax system. For example, consider two individuals, Jane and Harry, both in a 50 percent tax bracket. Jane earns $150,000 as a public servant in government; Harry is employed in the private sector,

---

[50]See, for example, P. Musgrave, *United States Taxation of Foreign Investment Income: Issues and Arguments*, 109 (1969); L. Krause & K. Dam, Federal Tax Treatment of Foreign Income, 46–52 (1964).

earns $100,000 in salary, but also gets free accommodation valued at $50,000. The principle of horizontal equity requires that we tax both Jane and Harry in a similar manner because they earn equal amounts of economic income, albeit in different forms. But what if Jane trades off $10,000 of her salary in exchange for her employer providing on-site child care services that previously cost her $20,000 (after-tax) a year? Should Jane be taxed on $140,000, $150,000, $160,000 or $180,000?

Equity also requires that we recognize a taxpayer's ability to pay, which may be quite different from the taxpayer's "income" in an accounting sense. Assume, for example, that Harry, a single father with four infant children, looks after his elderly mother who suffers from an expensive and chronic disease. Jane is single, in good health, and spends her money on sailing. Thus, taxpayers with the same numerical income may have different capacity to pay tax. Equity suggests that we recognize these personal elements in the taxpayer's "ability to pay" to pay tax.

There is also general agreement that individuals with higher incomes should pay "more tax" than individuals with lower incomes. Most people will agree that an individual who earns $100,000 in a year should pay more tax than an individual who earns $30,000. This principle of vertical equity, which is based on the theory that a taxpayer should pay according to his or her ability to pay, does not, in itself, provide a ready answer to the more difficult question: *how much more* should the rich pay than the poor? For example, the lowest federal tax rate is 15 percent on taxable income up to $43,561 and 29 percent on taxable income exceeding $135,054 [2013]. Is this increase in marginal tax rates equitable? In technical terms, what should be the optimum slope of the tax rate curve?

Is it sufficient to pay proportionately more tax, or does vertical equity require higher income earners to pay progressively more than lower income earners? And if progressively more, what is the appropriate rate of progression?

b) — Proportional Tax Rates

In a proportional rate system we would tax the entire taxable base at a constant or flat rate. For example, if three taxpayers A, B and C with taxable incomes of $20,000, $40,000 and $60,000 respectively are each taxed at a flat rate of 17 percent, they would pay taxes commensurately proportionate with their income as follows:

Taxpayer	Taxable Income	Tax	Rate (%)
A	$20,000	$3,400	17
B	$40,000	$6,800	17
C	$60,000	$10,200	17

The total tax revenue collected would be $20,400.

Thus, in a proportional rate system, higher income levels bear a heavier tax burden. In the above example, C pays three times, and B pays twice, the total tax that A would pay. The description "flat tax" refers to the shape of the curve or line when plotted on a graph that displays the tax rate on the vertical axis and income on the horizontal axis. A true flat tax takes the same percentage of everyone's income — a family with twice the income of another must pay twice the tax.

Sales and consumption taxes (such as the HST) are levied as proportional taxes — that is, at a flat rate applied to all sales regardless of the amount expended. The shape of the tax rate curve should not be confused with the incidence of a tax. The HST, for example, is a flat tax on consumption, but has a regressive effect when measured against *income*. It takes a higher percentage of income from lower income levels than it does from higher income levels. *All* flat taxes (for example, gasoline, airline, alcohol, tobacco, entertainment, gaming and fishing, excise, environmental, energy, etc.) on use or consumption have a regressive incidence when measured against income. The real policy issue is whether the incidence and degree of regressivity of a tax properly reflects the economic and social values of society. If it does not, how should we rectify the situation — rebates or credits?

c) — Progressive Taxation

Most Canadians agree with the principle that individuals with higher incomes should pay more tax than individuals who earn less. The underlying premise is that higher income individuals have a greater ability to pay taxes and, therefore, it is fair that they pay more tax. But how much more is "fair"? The difficulty is that many believe that a tax system is fair if it taxes the other person.

Canada has a progressive tax system. The adjective "progressive" refers not to the quality of our Byzantine tax law, but to the aspect of our system by which the marginal rate of tax increases at various levels of taxable income. For example, in 2013, the four basic federal rates of tax on taxable income for individuals were as follows:

Taxable Income	Federal Rate (%)
On first $43,561	15
On next $43,562	22
On next $43,562	26
Over $135,055	29

Thus, a person who earns $135,000 pays not only more tax in absolute dollars than an individual who earns $30,000, but the rate of federal tax progresses from 15 percent to 29 percent as taxable income rises.

We justify progressivity on the principle that an individual's ability (though not enthusiasm) to pay tax increases as his or her income rises. This assumption, however, only starts the debate. One-third of Canadian taxpayers (of which there are approximately 22 million) do not pay any income tax at all. The non-payers file tax returns primarily to receive benefits paid out as income redistribution under the HST and child-tax benefits.

Progressivism kicks in at the $50,000 income level and accelerates thereafter until it peaks at the top federal marginal rate of 29 percent, which works out to approximately 50 percent in combined federal and provincial (Ontario) taxes. Thus, contrary to popular opinion, the rich in Canada do pay substantial taxes. However, there is no consensus, and likely never will be, on the meaning of what is fair in taxation.

d) — Marginal Tax Rates

Marginal tax rates play a crucial role in government tax policy analysis and tax planning. Let us consider a simple example: suppose that your employer offers you a salary increase of $10,000 to match a competitive bid for your services. How much better off will you be after the increase? The answer depends upon your marginal rate of tax. Assuming that you are in the 40 percent bracket, the salary increase is worth $6,000 after taxes. If, however, you are in a 50 percent marginal tax bracket, the increase is worth only $5,000.

In a 50 percent bracket you would be better off getting a $7,000 non-taxable benefit, which would be a pre-tax equivalent of $14,000. Thus, the benefit of any increase in income or saving in tax payable is a function of the applicable marginal tax rate. The higher the marginal rate of tax, the greater the tax payable, the greater the value of tax savings, and the greater the loss of tax revenue for the government.

Marginal tax rate analysis is also important in tax deduction decisions. A deduction of $500, for example, saves an individual in the 50 percent bracket $250 and reduces his or her net after-tax cost to $250. In contrast, the same deduction for a person in the 40 percent bracket saves only $200 and leaves an after-tax cost of $300. Thus, the lower income taxpayer has a higher after-tax cost for deductions than a higher marginal rate taxpayer. This inverted effect plays an important role in determining whether we should grant taxpayers deductions or credits for their personal expenditures — such as charitable donations and political contributions.

In contrast with individuals, corporate income taxes are for the most part flat. The basic federal rate is 25 percent. The basic rate, however, is adjusted for certain types of income and corporations. For example, in 2013, the basic federal rate of tax on a Canadian-controlled private corporation (CCPC) is 11 percent on the first $500,000 of its active business income (ABI) and 25 percent on amounts in excess of $500,000.[51] Thus, the federal marginal rate of tax rises for corporations with more than $500,000 ABI and is flat for corporations with less than $500,000 income. This sudden step-up in the marginal rate of tax is an important consideration in tax planning.

---

[51]The small business rates are adjusted periodically.

E. — Certainty and Simplicity

A good tax system is one that can be administered economically and should not impose unreasonable compliance costs on taxpayers. The more complex a tax system, the higher the compliance costs. Thus, a good system is one that is certain and simple.

A tax system must be certain so that taxpayers can plan their affairs and business transactions secure in the knowledge that the consequences that attach to the transactions are predictable. On the other hand, business transactions in a complex economy are inherently uncertain and some degree of complexity is inevitable.

A tax system should also be simple. This is particularly important in the case of personal taxes, where the majority of individuals should be able to comply with the law without being put to unnecessary professional fees for expert advice.

F. — Compromise of Values

Tax law is a compromise between competing values. Tax policy objectives of revenue generation, neutrality, efficiency, fairness and administrative feasibility pull in different directions. At any required level of revenues, a neutral tax system will generally be less complex than one that has multiple distinctions between classes of taxpayers and types of income. However, a neutral system will also be less sensitive to the objective of fairness, which implies distinctions based on ability to pay.

For example, income taxes are levied both on individuals and on corporations at different rates. This creates two tensions. First, there is an incentive to choose the form of organization that attracts the lowest rate of tax. As previously noted, there is a substantial difference between taxes imposed on Canadian corporate small business and the top marginal rate of tax on individuals. This makes it attractive to use the corporate form which makes the system less neutral, but is intended to stimulate economic activity.

Second, the levy on corporations results in double taxation of income, once at the corporate level and then again at the personal shareholder level when net profits are distributed. Double taxation is inefficient and unfair to taxpayers. The mechanism to minimize double taxation through shareholder credits for corporate taxes makes the system fairer, but also more complex.

VIII. — Retrospective Effect

Constitutional law and tradition dictate that taxes may be imposed and collected only by an Act of Parliament.[52] There is no legal authority to collect taxes before the Budget imposing

---

[52]See, e.g., *Bowles v. Bank of England*, [1913] 1 Ch. 57.

the tax is enacted and receives Royal Assent. In fact, federal income taxes are usually collected based on the Notice of Ways and Means Motions, sometimes many months before Parliament actually approves the tax.[53] When enacted, the legislation is generally retrospective to the Budget date. This process, in effect, whitewashes any potential constitutional illegality of collecting taxes prior to their legislation. Canadian taxpayers and their professional advisers have resigned themselves to this practice.

Litigation to establish the constitutional illegality of the practice would end in a pyrrhic victory since most budgets have retrospective effect.[54] Indeed, our courts have gone even further. In *Air Canada v. British Columbia*, [1989] 1 S.C.R. 1161 (S.C.C.), for example, the Supreme Court held that even if an Act imposing a tax was ultra vires, a subsequent amendment could retroactively impose the tax and authorize the government to retain any monies unconstitutionally withheld.[55]

IX. — Declaration of Taxpayer Rights

The role of taxation in history is dramatic. King John's penchant for increasing feudal taxation in England without consultation with his lords precipitated the greatest constitutional document in the common law world, the *Magna Carta*, in 1215.

Similarly, the methods of tax enforcement have provoked revolutions. The underlying grievance of the Peasant's Revolt of 1381 was a poll tax on all males and females over the age of 15. The drama of the event is recorded in Hume's *History of England*:

> The first disorder was raised by a blacksmith in a village of Essex. The tax-gatherers came to this man's shop while he was at work; and they demanded payment for his daughter, who he asserted to be below the age assigned by the statute. One of these fellows offered to produce a

---

[53]For example, there was a 16-month delay between the November 1981 budget speech and its eventual legislative enactment.

[54]See, e.g., *Swanick v. Minister of National Revenue*, [1985] 2 C.T.C. 2352, 85 D.T.C. 630 (T.C.C.) (taxpayer filed return on basis of existing law; Minister assessed return on basis of law enacted 14 months later but made retrospective to earlier period; taxpayer not deprived of property without due process of law); see also *Gustavson Drilling (1964) Ltd. v. Minister of National Revenue*, [1977] 1 S.C.R. 271, [1976] C.T.C. 1 (S.C.C.) at 279 [S.C.R.] per Dickson J.:

> First, retrospectivity. The general rule is that statutes are not to be construed as having retrospective operation unless such a construction is expressly or by necessary implication required by the language of the Act. An amending enactment may provide that it shall be deemed to have come into force on a date prior to its enactment or it may provide that it is to be operative with respect to transactions occurring prior to its enactment. In those instances the statute operates retrospectively.

[55]See also: *Huet c. Ministre du Revenu national* (1994), [1995] 1 C.T.C. 367 (Fed. T.D.).

very indecent proof to the contrary, and at the same time laid hold of the maid: which the father resenting, immediately knocked out the ruffian's brains with his hammer.

The image of the modern tax collector has improved, but only slightly. The Report of the Conservative Task Force on Revenue Canada (1984) commented on the tax collectors' proclivity towards oppressive conduct and insensitive behavior. Concerning the Canada Revenue Agency's tax collection methods, the Task Force stated:

1. What we heard disturbed us deeply. We were distressed by the fear with which ordinary Canadians greet a call from the tax department, a fear that is sometimes cultivated by Revenue Canada.

2. Another impression that was deeply instilled in us during our tour was that the tax burden is falling disproportionately on Canadians of modest means, as a result of Revenue Canada's actions.

3. The complexity of the many provisions affecting lower income Canadians often causes serious resentment. This is also the group that is most likely to be audited by less-experienced employees who may make serious errors. These taxpayers can least afford the costly professional assistance needed to defend their rights.

4. Another factor that undermines the rights of ordinary Canadians is the sweeping powers given to the Department. In some cases, they are even greater than the powers of the police.

The Conservative Government later issued a declaratory statement, impressively entitled the "Declaration of Taxpayer Rights", which addressed some of the Task Force's concerns. However, the government did not enact the Declaration into law. Hence it does not have any legal status.

In 2013, the CRA announced that it was amending the so-called "Bill of Rights" to enable taxpayers to make service complaints against the Agency without fear of reprisals. The CRA announced that the amendment will ensure that taxpayers "will be treated impartially, receive the benefits, credits, and refunds to which they are entitled and pay no more and no less than what is required by law." Most taxpayers would have expected nothing less from the agency responsible for tax collection without any such amendment!

Since the *Charter of Rights* does not protect property rights, taxpayers have few constitutional protections against the tax collector. A notable exception is with search and seizures that the government uses to prosecute tax evasion. Apart from this narrow exception for criminal investigations, the courts interpret the *Income Tax Act* as a regulatory statute. Hence, for example, the reverse onus clause, which presumes the Minister's assessment of a taxpayer to be proper and correct unless the taxpayer proves it is not, applies in tax disputes.

X. — Tax Expenditures

A government can achieve its social and economic policies in several ways. It can spend directly on programs by providing grants and subsidies through its annual budget process. Such expenditures are generally referred to as "budgetary expenditures" because their estimates are tabled in Parliament as part of the annual budget process. A government can also pursue its social and economic policies indirectly by using the tax system to provide incentives for particular initiatives or activities. Thus, a government can implement policies by providing an exemption, deduction, credit or deferral through the tax system. We refer to the costs of exemptions, deductions, credits and deferrals as "tax expenditures".

Tax expenditures, which are an alternative form of government expenditures, are real and substantial. They differ from budgetary expenditures because they are not tabled as direct outgoings and, therefore, do not require parliamentary spending approval. Instead, tax expenditures are approved indirectly through the legislative process that enacts income tax law.

We define tax expenditures as deviations from a "benchmark" tax system. A benchmark tax system refers to a normative system that measures income without reference to special incentives to achieve social, economic, and other policy objectives.

The definition and measurement of income is crucial to the benchmark because any deviation from the benchmark is considered a tax expenditure. For example, the deduction of salaries and wages from income is considered a normal expenditure that is intrinsic to the measurement of *net* business income or "profit". Thus, the deduction of such expenditures in determining business income is "normal" and is not a tax expenditure.

In contrast, a tax credit for donations to political parties is not intrinsic to the proper measurement of net income. The *Act* allows the credit to encourage support for a democratic system of government and to engage Canadians in the political process. Hence, the cost of the political contributions credit is a tax expenditure outside the benchmark tax system. Similarly, a gain on the sale of one's home would normally be "income" in the sense of economic gain and accretion of wealth. We exempt such gains, however, for social and political considerations.

It is useful for a government to disseminate information on its budgetary and tax expenditures. Budgetary expenditures receive closer scrutiny and media attention because it is easier to see the numbers in the budget estimates placed before Parliament. The media understands budget spending. Tax expenditures, which represent equally real costs, are often ignored because they are not clearly visible in the annual estimates. Thus, the cost of tax expenditures buried deep in the detail of the *Income Tax Act* escape public scrutiny.

A tax expenditure represents a loss of revenue that would otherwise be available to the government if it used a benchmark tax system. In 2000, for example, the non-taxation of lottery and gambling winnings was expected to cost the Federal Treasury approximately $1.56 billion in lost revenues. Stated another way, the federal government foregoes $1.56 billion by exempting lottery winnings from taxation, money that it would otherwise have collected if it had a benchmark tax system.

The identification of what constitutes a proper benchmark tax structure is difficult and controversial. A benchmark necessarily implies value judgments that are subjective. The debate is not on the usefulness of tax expenditure analysis, but upon what goes into the list of "tax expenditures" that require analysis. Take, for example, the deduction for child-care expenses. If child-care expenses are personal and living expenses of parents, the deduction for such expenses in computing income is a tax expenditure because they are not part of the normal benchmark of income. On the other hand, if child-care expenses are necessary expenditures incurred for, and intrinsic in, the process of earning income, deductions for such expenses are not tax expenditures. In either case, the forgone revenue from the deduction for child-care expenses, whether as part of the benchmark determination of income or as a tax expenditure, represents a financial cost to the public treasury. The controversy is not so much about the fact that child-care expenses cost the federal treasury, but whether we should identify such expenses as "tax expenditures" for analytical purposes.

The definition of income is central to the determination of what is a tax expenditure. Tax provisions that provide for the deduction of normal current costs incurred to earn income are considered to be part of the benchmark system and, therefore, not tax expenditures. Tax provisions that fall outside of what are considered to be "normal" deductions are tax expenditures.

The benchmarks for the personal income tax and corporate income tax systems are as follows:

Personal Income Tax

- Existing tax rates and income tax brackets are taken as given;
- The tax unit is the individual;
- Taxation is imposed on a calendar year basis;
- Nominal income unadjusted for inflation is used to define income; and
- Structural features such as the dividend tax credit to avoid double taxation of corporate income are normal.

Corporate Income Tax

- The existing general tax rate is taken as given;
- The tax unit is the corporation;
- Taxation is imposed on a fiscal year basis;

- Nominal income unadjusted for inflation is used to define income; and
- Structural features such as the non-taxation of inter-corporate dividends are normal.

XI. — Structure of the Act

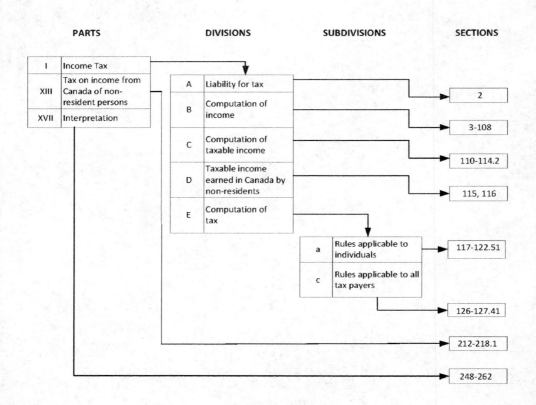

A tax system must address five basic questions:

- Who is taxable?
- What is taxable?

- At what rate is tax payable?

- When is tax payable? and

- What are the procedures for administrative compliance and judicial review?

The *Income Tax Act* answers each of these questions in a systematic arrangement. The statute is initially divided into Parts, each of which deals with distinct subject matter. The Act divides the Parts into Divisions; the Divisions into subdivisions. Each subdivision is made up of sections.

Part I contains most of the provisions of the Act. Parts I.01 through to XV deal with special situations and taxes. Parts XV and XVI deal with administration, enforcement and tax evasion. Part XVII is concerned with interpretation and includes most of the general definitions used in the Act.

XII. — The Tax Process

The tax process, outlined in the chart below, starts with the taxpayer voluntarily (subject to serious penalties for non-compliance) filing a return and self-assessing his, her or its taxes. Thereafter, the Minister assesses the return and issues a Notice of Assessment. If the taxpayer disagrees with the Assessment, he must trigger an appeal process, which proceeds through various administrative and judicial steps. From start to finish the process (except for the Informal Procedure) can take up to ten years, or longer in complex cases.

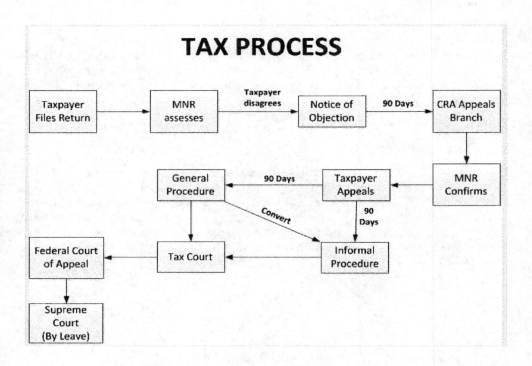

The Informal Procedure is limited to appeals to a maximum of $25,000 in taxes and $50,000 in losses.[56]

---

[56]Bill C-60, Royal Assent June 26, 2013, effective June 27, 2013.

XIII. — Conclusion

Tax law is concerned not only with generating sufficient revenue to finance government operations but also seeks to achieve other goals and objectives. Tax policy is concerned with evaluating the effectiveness with which these principles are implemented in the design of the tax structure.

To be sure, the ultimate structure of a system is a compromise of various competing values and political considerations.

Since an income tax statute expropriates private property for public purposes, it is almost inevitable that taxpayers will attempt to resist, or at least minimize, the effect of expropriation. The tension between the taxpayer and the tax collector necessitates complex provisions to prevent undue leakage of tax revenues. The scope of coverage and the changing nature of domestic and international economies require frequent changes as taxpayers adapt and adopt new techniques of tax minimization.

Selected Bibliography

History

Bale, G., "The Individual and Tax Reform in Canada" (1971) 49 Can. Bar Review 24.

Ballentine, J.G., "Broadening our Approach to Income Tax Reform" (Spring 1986) 5:1 Amer. Journal of Tax Policy 1.

Bittker, B., "A Comprehensive Tax Base as a Goal of Income Tax Reform" (1967) 80 H.L.R. 925.

Blum, W.J., "Federal Income Tax Reform — Twenty Questions" (November 1963) 41 Taxes 672.

Bossons, John, "Tax Reform and International Competitiveness", in *Proceedings of 39th Tax Conf.* 5:1 (Can. Tax Foundation, 1987).

Break, G.F., and J.A. Pechman, *Federal Tax Reform: The Impossible Dream* (Washington: 1975).

Brooks, W. Neil, *The Quest for Tax Reform* (Carswell: Toronto, 1988).

Cohen, Marshall A., and Stephen R. Richardson, "Fifteen Years After Tax Reform: A Retrospective" (1986) Special Lectures LSUC 1.

Dodge, David A., "New Directions in Canadian Tax Policy" (1989) 41 Tax Exec. 111.

Drache, A.B.C., "Introduction to Income Tax Policy Formulation: Canada 1972–76" (1978) 16 Osgoode Hall L.J. 1.

Gibson, "Tax Policy for the Long and Short Run" (1963) 11 Can. Tax J. 58.

Goodman, W.D., "Tax Reform — The Continuing Challenge" (1978) 16 Osgoode Hall L.J. 147.

Grady, Patrick, "Real Effective Corporate Tax Rates in Canada and the United States After Tax Reform" (1989) 37 Can. Tax J. 647.

Harris, "What Should Canada Do with the Carter Report?" (1967) 21 Bull. Int'l. Fisc. Doc. 531.

Head, J.G., "The Carter Legacy: An International Perspective" (1987) 4:2 Australian Tax Forum 143.

Krever, "The Origin of Federal Income Taxation in Canada" (Winter 1981) Can. Tax. 170.

Krishna, Vern, "A Law that Taxes our Understanding" (1986) 10:9 Can. Law

Chapter 1 — The Fiscal Landscape

Constitutional Authority for Taxation

Hogg, *Constitutional Law of Canada*, loose-leaf edition. (Toronto: Carswell, 1997).

La Forest, G.V., "The Allocation of Taxing Power under the Canadian Constitution", *Can. Tax Paper No. 45* (Can. Tax Foundation, 1967).

Moull, William D., "Intergovernmental Immunity From Taxation: The Unsolved Issues" (1984) 32 Can. Tax J. 54.

The Legislative Process

Canadian Tax Foundation Committee on the Budget Process, "The Canadian Budget Process" (1986) 34 Can. Tax J. 989.

The Executive Process

Edwards, S.E., "Drafting Fiscal Legislation" (1984) 32 Can. Tax J. 727. Jackett, W.R., "Too Much Income Tax Law?", Can. Tax J. 54.

The Income Tax Process

Davidson, "The Reorganization of the Legislation Branch of Revenue Canada Taxation" (1978) 26 Can. Tax J. 429.

Drache, Arthur B.C., "Income Tax Policy Formulation in Canada, 1972–76" (1978) 16 Osgoode Hall L.J. 1.

Thorson, "Formulation, Enactment and Administration of Tax Changes", in *Proceedings of 24th Tax Conf.* 14 (Can. Tax Foundation, 1972).

Thorsteinsson, P., "How to Settle an Income Tax Controversy, through Litigation and Before", *1978 Conference Report* (Can. Tax Foundation, 1979).

Tax System Objectives

"Anatomy of a Tax System", in *Proceedings of 20th Tax Conf.* 7 (Can. Tax Foundation, 1967).

Andrews, W.D., "A Consumption Type or Cash Flow Personal Income Tax" (April 1984) 87:6 H.L.R. 1113.

Bale, G., "Temporary Equity in Taxation" (1977) 55 Can. Bar Rev. 1.

Ballantyne, Janet L., "The Tax Burden of the Middle-Class Canadian" (1986) 34 Can. Tax J. 671–680.

Bird, "Income Redistribution and Ability to Pay", in *Proceedings of 20th Tax Conf.* 242, 256–64 (Can. Tax Foundation, 1967).

Bradford, D.F., "The Case for a Personal Consumption Tax", in *What Would be Taxed: Income or Expenditure?* (Washington: The Brookings Institution, 1980) at 75–113.

Bruce, Neil, "Ability to Pay and Comprehensive Income Taxation: Annual or Lifetime Basis?" as found in Brooks, W. Neil, ed., *The Quest for Tax Reform* (Toronto: Carswell, 1988) at 157.

Chapman, S.J., "The Utility of Income and Progressive Taxation" (1913), 23 Econ. J. 25.

Crowe, Ian, "Taxation: Uncertain Incentives" (March 1991) 124 CA Magazine 51.

Drache, Arthur B.C., "A Fair Tax System?" (1994) 16 Can. Taxpayer 9.

Drache, Arthur B.C., "Unfairness in Taxation" (1993) 15 Can. Taxpayer 19.

Howard, R., G. Ruggeri and Van D. Wart, "The Progressivity of Provincial Personal Income Taxes in Canada" (1991) 39 Can. Tax J. 288.

Kesselman, Jonathan R., *Rate Structure and Personal Taxation: Flat Rate or Dual Rate?* (Wellington, New Zealand: Victoria University Press for the Institute of Policy Studies, 1990).

Salyzyn, Vladimir, "Canadian Income Tax Policy: An Economic Evaluation" (1987) 66 Can. Bar Rev. 405. *Question of Incidence Analysis* (Department of Economics, University of Western Ontario, 1984).

System Characteristics

Atkeson, T.C., "Tax Simplification from the Viewpoint of a Professor of Taxation", in *Essays on Taxation* (New York: Tax Foundation Inc., 1974) at 93–109.

Audie, Suphan, "Does the Personal Income Tax Discriminate Against Women?" (1981) 1 Pub. Fin. 1.

Cassidy, Michael, "Fairness and Efficiency: Can Tax Reform Do the Job?", in *Proceedings of 39th Tax Conf.* 2:1 (Can. Tax Foundation, 1987).

Daly, Michael J., Jack Jung and Thomas Schweitzer, "Toward a Neutral Capital Income Tax System" (1986) 34 Can. Tax J. 1331.

Drache, Arthur B.C., "Flat Taxes Emerging Again" (1993), 15 Can. Taxpayer 45.

Eustice, James S., "Tax Complexity and the Tax Practitioner" (Fall 1989) 45 The Tax Lawyer 7.

Gillespie, W. Irwin et al., "Tax Incidence in Canada" (1994) 42 Can. Tax J. 348.

Howard, R. et al., "The Redistributional Impact of Taxation in Canada" (1994) 42 Can. Tax J. 417.

Hugget, Donald R., "E Pluribus Unum (The Single Tax)" 18 Can. Tax News 1.

McCaffery, Edward J., "The Holy Grail of Tax Simplification" [1990] 5 Wis. L. Rev. 1267.

Mills, Dennis, *The Single Tax — Fair and Simple for All Canadians* (Toronto: Hemlock Press, 1990).

Mills, W.D., "Tax Simplification from the Viewpoint of the Legislator", in *Essays on Taxation* (New York: Tax Foundation Inc., 1974) at 74–92.

Peterson, C.R., "Tax Simplification From the Viewpoint of the Tax Attorney", in *Essays on Taxation* (New York: Tax Foundation Inc., 1974) at 110–117.

Prebble, John, "Why is Tax Law Incomprehensible?", (1994) British Tax Rev. 380.

Roberts, S.I., et al., "Report on Complexity and the Income Tax" (1971-72), 27 Tax Law Review 325.

Ruggeri, G.C., et al., "The Redistributional Impact of Taxation in Canada" (1994) 42 Can. Tax J. 417.

"Simplification" (Summary of Recommendations of the Commons Standing Committee on Finance and Economic Affairs Report Entitled "Tax Simplification") (1986) 14 Can. Tax News 25.

Sherbaniuk, D.J., "Tax Simplification — Can Anything Be Done About It?", in *Proceedings of 40th Tax Conf.* 3:1 (Can. Tax Foundation, 1988).

Strain, William J., David A. Dodge and Victor Peters, "Tax Simplification: The Elusive Goal", in *Proceedings of 40th Tax Conf.* 4:1 (Can. Tax Foundation, 1988).

Other

Allen, R.I.G. and D. Savage, "The Case for Inflation Proofing the Personal Income Tax" (1974) Br. Tax Rev. 299.

Alter, Dr. A., "Different Techniques for Adjusting Taxable Income Under Inflationary Conditions" (1986) Br. Tax Rev. 347.

Andrew, W.D., "Personal Deductions in an Ideal Income Tax" (December 1972) 86 H.L.R. 2:309.

Arnold, B.J., *Timing and Income Taxation: The Principles of Income Measurement for Tax Purposes* (Toronto: Can. Tax Foundation, 1983).

Barry, David B., "The Relative Importance of Personal and Corporation Income Tax" (1986) 34 Can. Tax J. 460–67.

Beale, "The Measure for Income Taxation" (1911) 19 Journal of Political Economy 655, 661.

Bird, "The Tax Kaleidoscope" (1970) Can. Tax J. 444.

Blais, André and François Vaillancourt, *The Political Economy of Taxation: The Corporate Income Tax and the Canadian Manufacturing Industry* (Montreal: Université de Montréal, 1986).

Blum, "Tax Lawyers and Tax Policy" (March 1961) Taxes 247.

Bradford, D.F., *Untangling the Income Tax* (Cambridge: Harvard University Press, 1986).

Brean, Donald S., "International Influences on Canadian Tax Policy: The Free Trade Agreement and U.S. Tax Reform" (1988) Corporate Management Tax Conference 13:1.

Broadway and Kitchen, "Canadian Tax Policy", *Can. Tax Paper No. 63* (Can. Tax Foundation, 1980).

Broadway and Kitchen, "Canadian Tax Policy", *Can. Tax Paper No. 76* (Can. Tax Foundation, 1984).

Carver, "The Minimum Sacrifice Theory of Taxation" (1904) 19 Political Science Quarterly 66.

Colley, G.M., "Is Indexing a Necessary Evil/L'indexation: un mal nécessaire?" (1986) 119:9 CA Magazine 52.

Douglas, P.H., "The Problem of Tax Loopholes" (Winter, 1967-68) 37 Amer. Scholar 21.

Drache, Arthur B.C., "Towards a New Tax Philosophy" (1993) 15 Can. Taxpayer 185.

Dulude, Louise, "Taxation of the Spouses: A Comparison of Canadian, American, British, French and Swedish Law" (1985) 23 Osgoode Hall L.J. 67.

Eaton, A.K., "Essays in Taxation", *Can. Tax Paper No. 44* (Can. Tax Foundation, 1966).

Eisenstein, L., "Some Second Thoughts on Tax Ideologies" 20 Tax Law Rev. 453.

Goode, R., *The Individual Income Tax* (Washington: The Brookings Institution, 1976).

Groves, N.M., *Tax Philosophers: Two Hundred Years of Thought in Great Britain and the United States* (Madison: 1974).

Haig, R.M., "The Concept of Income — Economic and Legal Aspects", in *Federal Income Tax* (New York: Columbia University Press, 1921) at 1–28.

Chapter 1 — The Fiscal Landscape

Hellerstein, J.R., *Taxes, Loopholes and Morals* (New York: McGraw Hill, 1963).

Heyding, "Legislation by Formula" (1959) Can. Tax J. 366.

Huggett, Donald R., "A Minimum Income Tax", in *Proceedings of 37th Tax Conf.* 10:1 (Can. Tax Foundation, 1985).

Huggett, Donald R., "Dear Mike" (fictitious letter to Minister of Finance Michael Wilson) (1986) 14 Can. Tax News 17.

Johnson, Calvin H., "Why Have Anti-Tax Shelter Legislation? A Response to Professor Zelenak" (February 1989) 67 Texas Law Rev. 591.

Jones, R., *The Nature and First Principles of Taxation* (1914).

Kaldor, N., *An Expenditure Tax* (London: George Allen & Unwin Ltd., 1955).

Klein, W.A., *Policy Analysis of the Federal Income Tax Text and Readings* (New York: The Foundation Press, 1976).

Lahey, Kathleen, "The Tax Unit in Income Tax Theory" in *Women, the Law and the Economy* (Toronto: Butterworths, 1985) at 277–310.

Perry, David B., "Government Reliance on Personal Income Taxes in Canada" (1994), 42 Can. Tax J. 1145.

Perry, David B., "Individual Tax Burdens in the OECD" (1994) 42 Can. Tax J. 288.

Perry, Harvey J., "Taxation in Canada", *Can. Tax Paper No. 74* (Can. Tax Foundation, 1984).

Simons, H.C., *Personal Income Taxation* (Chicago: University of Chicago Press, 1938).

Verchere, Bruce, and Jacques Mernier, "Rights and Freedoms in Tax Matters", in *Proceedings of 38th Tax Conf.* 39 (Can. Tax Foundation, 1986).

Chapter 2 — Statutory Interpretation

Table of Contents

Table of Contents

The difficulties of so-called interpretation arise when the Legislature has had no meaning at all; when the question which is raised on the statute never occurred to it; when what the judges have to do is, not to determine what the legislature did mean on a point which was present to its mind, but to guess what it would have intended on a point not present to its mind, if the point had been present.[1]

I. — Introduction

The interpretation of tax law is evolutionary. In an earlier era, courts saw tax statutes as penal enactments to be strictly and literally interpreted without benefit of policy analysis into the purpose of its provisions. We have moved from that approach, but still have some distance to go before we fully embrace purposive analysis. In this chapter, we set out the rules of the road in interpreting tax law.

The primary purpose of statutory interpretation is to unlock legislative intent. In addition to the ordinary rules of interpretation, constitutional traditions also play an important role in tax law. Tax legislation is the product of elected legislatures. The language of the *Act* reflects the constitutional will of the people through its elected representatives. Thus, we carefully review the words that Parliament uses in the statute. There is a lesser role for judicial rulemaking in tax law than in other areas, such as constitutional law.[2]

II. — Historical Approaches

A. — The Mischief Rule

The techniques of statutory interpretation have evolved over time. In the middle ages, courts interpreted legislation to suppress the mischief that the legislature sought to remedy. Thus, the common law would interpret the law in a purposive manner to remedy the perceived problem.

---

[1]John Chipman Gray, *Nature and Sources of the Law: Statutes*, 2d ed (New York: Macmillan, 1921).

[2]See *Stewart v. R.*, 2002 SCC 46, [2002] 3 C.T.C. 439 (S.C.C.) [*Stewart*]; *Entreprises Ludco ltée c. Canada*, 2001 SCC 62, [2002] 1 C.T.C. 95 (S.C.C.) [*Ludco*].

B. — The Literal or Strict Rule

In the 20th century courts moved to the literal or strict construction of fiscal statutes, which were perceived as "penal" in nature. The judiciary deferred to Parliamentary supremacy. Thus, courts interpreted tax statutes in context. However, they excluded the admission of extrinsic aids including, ironically, statements in Hansard.

As a "penal" statute, charging provisions were construed strictly against the Crown and exemptions construed narrowly against the taxpayer. There is no room for equity in taxing statutes.

The doctrine of strict interpretation produced some absurd results. In *Witthuhn v. Minister of National Revenue*, 17 Tax ABC 33 (1957), for example, the taxpayer Mrs. W, who was severely suffering from pulmonary tuberculosis, was confined by her doctor to her bed or her rocking chair. Section 27(1) of the *Income Tax Act* read as follows:

... There may be deducted from income for the year ...

> (iv) as remuneration for one full-time attendant upon the taxpayer, his spouse or any such dependant who was throughout the whole of a 12 months' period ending in the taxation year necessarily confined by reason of illness, injury or affliction to a bed or wheelchair.

The Tax Appeal Board denied Mrs. W the deduction because she did not have a wheelchair, which would have been much more expensive than a rocking chair. The Board said she was "... not legally entitled to the deduction claimed . . .. There is, unfortunately, no equity in a taxation statute." Could it possibly have been the intention of Parliament to deny the expense deduction to those who could not afford a wheelchair and allow it only for those who could?

Similarly, in a series of decisions[3] involving section 62 — which allows a deduction for moving expenses if the distance between the taxpayer's old residence and his new work location is not less than 40 kilometres greater than the distance between his new residence and his new work location — the Tax Court held that the distance was to be measured "as the crow flies". As A.P. Herbert said: "If Parliament does not mean what it says, it must say so."

The Federal Court of Appeal finally reversed the decisions saying that the courts below had interpreted "distance" out of context. The court appears to give some weight to the purpose of the moving expenses deduction in the statute:

> A realistic measurement of travelling distance is necessary in order to give effect to the purpose of the provision. The straight line method bears no relation to how an employee travels to

---

[3]*Cameron v. Minister of National Revenue*, [1993] 1 C.T.C. 2745 (T.C.C.); *Haines v. Minister of National Revenue*, [1984] C.T.C. 2422 (T.C.C.); *Bracken v. Minister of National Revenue*, [1984] C.T.C. 2922 (T.C.C.); *Bernier Estate v. Minister of National Revenue*, [1990] C.T.C. 2535 (T.C.C.).

work. It is illogical to apply this technique to a provision which exists to recognize work related relocation expenses. It leads to absurd results where the old residence and the new workplace are separated by a body of water.

III. — The Modern Approach

A. — The Interpretation Act

Section 12 of the *Interpretation Act* states:[4]

> Every enactment is deemed remedial, and shall be given such fair, large and liberal construction and interpretation as best ensures the attainment of its objects.

Thus, we should interpret tax law in a fair and liberal manner as best ensures the attainment of its purpose as articulated in the statute. However, there is tension in interpreting the language of a provision as expressed by Parliament according to its context and the purpose (often unarticulated) underlying the provision.

B. — The Modern Rule

The doctrine of strict interpretation works well if the statute captures legislative purpose precisely. In these circumstances, we implement the purpose simply by applying the words of the Act. Experience, however, has taught us that legislation is not susceptible to such precise drafting. As early as 1936, in an era of comparatively simple tax legislation, the *Income Tax Codification Committee* in England realized the futility of attempting to anticipate every situation with comprehensive legislative drafting:

> The imagination which can draw an income tax statute to cover the myriad transactions of a society like ours, capable of producing the necessary revenue without producing a flood of litigation, has not yet revealed itself.

Literal interpretation contributes to the complexity of tax legislation. There is impressionistic evidence to suggest that as the courts interpreted the Act strictly, the legislative draftsman responded with ever more complex and comprehensive statutory language in an attempt to provide for, and anticipate, every conceivable factual nuance and circumstance.

---

[4]*Interpretation Act*, RSC 1985, c. I-21, as amended. Section 3 reads:

> (1) Every provision of this Act applies, unless a contrary intention appears, to every enactment, whether enacted before or after the commencement of this Act.
>
> (2) The provisions of this Act apply to the interpretation of this Act.
>
> (3) Nothing in this Act excludes the application to an enactment of a rule of construction applicable to that enactment and not inconsistent with this Act.

In *Stubart Investments Ltd. v. Canada (Stubart)*[5] we see the first breach in the doctrine of strict construction. The Supreme Court of Canada shifted from six decades of literal interpretation by looking at the "object and spirit" of the Act.[6] Following *Stubart*, the Supreme Court expanded on more specific aspects of interpretative methodology in *Golden*,[7] *Bronfman Trust*,[8] *Johns-Manville Canada*,[9] *Antosko*,[10] *Corporation Notre-Dame de Bon-Secours*,[11] *Friesen*,[12] *Shell Canada*,[13] *Ludco*,[14] and *Stewart*.[15]

The difficulty is in balancing the literal meaning of words with contextual and purposive analysis. However, we must be careful of purposive interpretation that puts a gloss on legislative language that was not contemplated by the legislator. If the words of the statute are clear and plain, they should be given their effect and not altered by legislative purpose or object.[16] Purposive interpretation should not alter the result of commercial transactions

---

[5]*Stubart Investments Ltd. v. R.*, [1984] 1 S.C.R. 536, [1984] C.T.C. 294 (S.C.C.) [*Stubart*].

[6]See also *Irving Oil Ltd v. R.*, [1988] 1 C.T.C. 263 (Fed. T.D.); affirmed [1991] 1 C.T.C. 350 (Fed. C.A.); leave to appeal refused (1991), 136 N.R. 320 (note) (S.C.C.); *Indalex Ltd. v. R.*, [1986] 2 C.T.C. 482 (Fed. C.A.); *Consolidated Bathurst Ltd v. R.*, [1985] 1 C.T.C. 142 (Fed. T.D.); affirmed in part [1987] 1 C.T.C. 55 (Fed. C.A.); *Orr v. Minister of National Revenue*, [1989] 2 C.T.C. 2348 (T.C.C.); *Hickman Motors Ltd. v. R.*, [1993] 1 C.T.C. 36 (Fed. T.D.); affirmed [1995] 2 C.T.C. 320 (Fed. C.A.); reversed [1998] 1 C.T.C. 213 (S.C.C.); *Earlscourt Sheet Metal Mechanical Ltd. v. Minister of National Revenue*, [1988] 1 C.T.C. 2045 (T.C.C.); *Montgomery v. Minister of National Revenue*, [1987] 2 C.T.C. 2023 (T.C.C.); *R. v. Vivian; R. v. Parsons*, [1984] C.T.C. 354 (Fed. C.A.); *Bastion Management Ltd. v. Minister of National Revenue*, [1988] 1 C.T.C. 2344 (T.C.C.); affirmed [1994] 2 C.T.C. 70 (Fed. T.D.); affirmed [1995] 2 C.T.C. 25 (Fed. C.A.); *Daggett v. Minister of National Revenue*, [1992] 2 C.T.C. 2764 (T.C.C.); *454538 Ontario Ltd. v. Minister of National Revenue*, [1993] 1 C.T.C. 2746 (T.C.C.); *Goulard v. Minister of National Revenue*, [1992] 1 C.T.C. 2396 (T.C.C.).

[7]*R. v. Golden*, [1986] 1 S.C.R. 209, [1986] 1 C.T.C. 274 (S.C.C.).

[8]*Bronfman Trust v. R.*, [1987] 1 C.T.C. 117 (S.C.C.) [*Bronfman Trust*].

[9]*Johns-Manville Canada Inc. v. R.*, [1985] 2 S.C.R. 46, [1985] 2 C.T.C. 111 (S.C.C.).

[10]*Antosko v. Canada*, [1994] 2 S.C.R. 312, [1994] 2 C.T.C. 25, 94 D.T.C. 6314 (S.C.C.).

[11]*Québec (Communautéurbaine) c. Notre-Dame de Bonsecours (Corp.)*, [1994] 3 S.C.R. 3, [1995] 1 C.T.C. 241 (S.C.C.).

[12]*Friesen v. R.*, [1995] 2 C.T.C. 369 (S.C.C.) [*Friesen*].

[13]*Shell Canada Ltd. v. R.*, [1999] 4 C.T.C. 313, 99 D.T.C. 5669 (S.C.C.) [*Shell Canada*].

[14]*Ludco*, above note 2.

[15]*Stewart*, above note 2.

[16]*Antosko*, above note 10.

where the words of the Act are clear and plain and where the legal and practical effect of the transaction is undisputed. As the Supreme Court has said:

> In the absence of evidence that the transaction was a sham or an abuse of the provisions of the Act, it is not the role of the court to determine whether the transaction in question is one which renders the taxpayer deserving of a deduction. If the terms of the section are met, the taxpayer may rely on it, and it is the option of Parliament specifically to preclude further reliance in such situations.[17]

And:

> Where the words of the section are not ambiguous, it is not for this Court to find that the appellants should be disentitled to a deduction because they do not deserve a "windfall" . . . . In the absence of a situation of ambiguity, such that the Court must look to the result of a transaction to assist in ascertaining the intent of Parliament, a normative assessment of the consequences of the application of a given provision is within the ambit of the legislature, not the courts.[18]

And again in *Friesen*:

> [T]he clear language of the *Income Tax Act* takes precedence over a court's view of the object and purpose of a provision . . . . The object and purpose of a provision need only be resorted to when the statutory language admits of some doubt or ambiguity.[19]

We draw the line between strict and literal construction and pedantic application of the purposive approach in the face of clear and unambiguous legislative language. Courts apply the teleological approach only when the words of the statute are not clear.[20] As McLachlin J (as she then was) stated in *Shell Canada*:

> Finding unexpressed legislative intentions under the guise of purposive interpretation runs the risk of upsetting the balance Parliament has attempted to strike in the Act. . . . The courts' role is to interpret and apply the Act as it was adopted by Parliament. *Obiter* statements in earlier cases that might be said to support a broader and less certain interpretive principle have therefore been overtaken by our developing tax jurisprudence.[21]

However, the Act does not operate in a commercial vacuum, but draws upon the meaning of words in their broader commercial context. Thus, in applying the plain meaning rule, we should interpret words in the context of the general commercial law and settled legal defini-

---

[17]*Ibid.* at para 29.

[18]*Ibid.* at para 34.

[19]*Friesen*, above note 12 at paras 59-60.

[20]See *Notre-Dame de Bon-Secours*, above note 11.

[21]*Shell Canada*, above note 13 at paras 43 and 45.

tions therein.[22] Thus, purposive analysis must be temperate, rooted in the statutory text and must not circumvent the intention of the legislature.[23]

C. — Tax Treaties

Interpretation of tax treaties is more expansive than for domestic fiscal statutes and courts consider the purpose of provisions even in the absence of ambiguity. The Supreme Court has stated the rule as follows:

> In interpreting a treaty, the paramount goal is to find the meaning of the words in question. This process involves looking to the language used and the intentions of the parties.[24]

D. — Ambiguity

Where statutory language is clear and unambiguous, we apply the language of the statute in its proper context. To do otherwise would have the judiciary usurp the function of the legislature. This is an easy rule to state, but difficult to apply. However, even simple words are susceptible to misunderstanding and must be read in context.[25] Thus, when Justice Holmes was asked to determine whether an aircraft was a "motor vehicle" for the purposes of a motor vehicle theft statute, he disposed of the question as follows:

> No doubt etymologically it is possible to use the word to signify a conveyance working on land, water or air, and sometimes legislation extends the use in that direction . . .. But in everyday speech "vehicle" calls up the picture of a thing moving on land.[26]

---

[22]*Will-Kare Paving & Contracting Ltd. v. R.*, 2000 SCC 36, [2000] 3 C.T.C. 463 (S.C.C.) (the word "sale" has an established meaning that the *Income Tax Act* should not broaden without clear parliamentary intention). See also *Re Rizzo & Rizzo Shoes Ltd*, [1998] 1 S.C.R. 27 [*Rizzo*] and *65302 BC Ltd*, [1999] 3 S.C.R. 804, [2000] 1 C.T.C. 57, 99 D.T.C. 5799 (S.C.C.).

[23]*Bastien (Succession de) c. R.*, 2011 SCC 38, [2011] 5 C.T.C. 111 (S.C.C.) at para 25.

[24]*Crown Forest Industries Ltd. v. R.*, [1995] 2 S.C.R. 802, [1995] 2 C.T.C. 64 (S.C.C.).

[25]As Cardozo J explained in *Panama Refining Co. v. Ryan*, 293 U.S. 388 (1935) at 439: "The meaning of a statute is to be looked for, not in any single section, but in all the parts together and in their relation to the end in view."

[26]*McBoyle v. US*, 283 U.S. 25 (1931) at 26.

Harmonious interpretation requires that we interpret words and phrases in the context of the statutory provision in which they appear and in the context of the *entire Act*. In *Colquhoun v. Brooks*, for example:[27]

> It is beyond dispute, too, that we are entitled and indeed bound when construing the terms of any provision found in a statute to consider any other parts of the Act which throw light upon the intention of the legislature and which may serve to show that the particular provision ought not to be construed as it would be if considered alone and apart from the rest of the Act.

Where words are ambiguous and capable of various meanings, however, courts should select the interpretation that best promotes the smooth working of the system[28] and avoid interpretations that produce absurd, unjust, anomalous or inconvenient results.[29] In Lord Esher's words:

> If the words of an Act are clear, you must follow them, even though they lead to a manifest absurdity. The court has nothing to do with the question whether the legislature has committed an absurdity. In my opinion, the rule has always been this — if the words of an Act admit of two interpretations, then they are not clear; and if one interpretation leads to an absurdity, and

---

[27]*Colquhoun v. Brooks* (1889), 14 App Cas 493 (HL) at 506 per Lord Herschell; cited with approval by Pratte J in *R. v. Cie Immobilière BCN Ltée*, [1979] C.T.C. 71 (S.C.C.). See also *Highway Sawmills Ltd. v. Minister of National Revenue*, [1966] C.T.C. 150 (S.C.C.): at 157-58

> The answer to the question what tax is payable in any given circumstances depends, of course, upon the words of the legislation imposing it. Where the meaning of those words is difficult to ascertain it may be of assistance to consider which of two constructions contended for brings about a result which conforms to the apparent scheme of the legislation.

See also *R. v. Canada Sugar Refining Co.*, [1898] A.C. 735 (Canada P.C.) at 741, Lord Davey: "Every clause of a statute should be construed with reference to the context and the other clauses of the Act, so as, so far as possible, to make a consistent enactment of the whole statute or series of statutes relating to the subject-matter"; *R. v. Cadboro Bay Holdings Ltd*, [1977] C.T.C. 186 (F.C.T.D.) ("active business" defined as any quantum of activity giving rise to income); *Noranda Mines Ltd. v. R.*, [1982] C.T.C. 226 (Fed. T.D.); affirmed [1984] C.T.C. 659 (Fed. C.A.) (words claimed to be ineffectual or surplusage).

[28]*St-Michel (Ville) v. Shannon Realties Ltd.*, [1924] A.C. 185 (Quebec P.C.).

[29]*R. v. London (City) Court Judge*, [1892] 1 Q.B. 273 (C.A.) (whether amount received from employer for completing course constituted a "prize"). See also *Gill v. Donald Humberstone & Co.*, [1963] 1 W.L.R. 929 (H.L.) (roofer not in "working place" when he fell off ladder); *Railton v. Wood* (1890), 15 App Cas 363 (P.C.) ("distress for rent" includes holder of bill of sale taking back goods from bailiff); *Fry v. Inland Revenue Commissioners*, [1959] 1 Ch. 86 (C.A.) (estate tax on reversionary interest in possession but not indefeasibly vested); *Arrow Shipping Co. v. Tyne Improvement Commissioners*, [1894] A.C. 508 (H.L.) (interpretation of "possession" at time of salvage and destruction of vessel); *R. v. Tonbridge Overseers* (1884), 13 Q.B.D. 339 (C.A.) (dispute over jurisdiction to levy rates by opposing burial boards; ordinary meaning conflicted with other Act).

the other does not, the court will conclude that the legislature did not intend to lead to an absurdity, and will adopt the other interpretation.[30]

The case for avoiding absurd interpretation is easy to make. The more difficult case is resolving ambiguity to promote statutory purpose and harmony. As the Supreme Court said in *Canada Trustco*: "The relative effects of ordinary meaning, context and purpose on the interpretative process may vary, but in all cases the court must seek to read the provisions of an Act as a harmonious whole."[31] Faced with ambiguity, we can use purposive interpretation to avoid harsh results.[32]

IV. — Summary of Rules of Interpretation

A. — Contextual Interpretation

The fundamental rule of statutory construction is that a provision should be interpreted in a textual, contextual and purposive way giving all sections of a related group of provisions a coherent meaning if at all possible.[33] The meaning of an ambiguous word or phrase should derive from its context in the document and other provisions or segments of the statute in which it appears. Thus, one should read the entire document and not just the particular provision that is at issue.

---

[30]*R. v. London (City) Court Judge, ibid* at 290; see also *R. v. Savage*, [1980] C.T.C. 103 (F.C.T.D.); reversed on other grounds [1981] C.T.C. 332 (Fed. C.A.); affirmed [1983] C.T.C. 393 (S.C.C.) (whether $500 exemption applicable to "prize" from employer); *Victoria (City) v. Bishop of Vancouver Island*, [1921] 2 A.C. 384 (British Columbia P.C.) (should exemption for house of worship include land upon which building erected); *Inland Revenue Commissioners v. Hinchy*, [1960] A.C. 748 (H.L.) (whether fine of "treble the tax" owed should include surtax); *Cartledge v. E. Jopling & Sons*, [1963] A.C. 758 (H.L.) (statutory limitation period expired before workers aware noxious dust caused injury to lungs); *Mersey Docks & Harbour Bd v. Henderson Bros* (1888), 13 App Cas 595 (H.L.) (dues in port payable when "trading inwards" or "trading outwards"; interpretation in respect of voyage with several ports); *Clerical, Medical & General Life Assurance Society v. Carter* (1889), 22 QBD 444 (C.A.) (interpretation of "profits or gains" and "interest of money"); *Warburton v. Loveland* (1832), 2 Dow & Cl 480 (H.L.); *Corp. d'administration & de placements Ltée v. Castonguay* (1970), 3 N.B.R. (2d) 278 (Co. Ct.) (two interpretations of *Creditor's Relief Act*, one avoided injustice).

[31]*Canada Trustco Mortgage Co. v. R.*, [2005] 5 C.T.C. 215 (S.C.C.) at para. 10.

[32]See, for example, *Québec (Communauté urbaine) c. Notre-Dame de Bonsecours (Corp.)*, [1994] 3 S.C.R. 3, [1995] 1 C.T.C. 241 (S.C.C.) [*Notre-Dame de Bon-Secours*].

[33]See, for example, *Redeemer Foundation v. Minister of National Revenue*, 2008 SCC 46, [2008] 5 C.T.C. 135 (S.C.C.); *Canada Trustco*, above note 31 at para 10, McLachlin CJ and Major J:

The interpretation of a statutory provision must be made according to a textual, contextual and purposive analysis to find a meaning that is harmonious with the Act as a whole.

a) — Ordinary Meaning of Words

Words are presumed to bear their ordinary meaning unless specifically defined. Commercial words or phrases are interpreted according to their usage in normal commercial practice.

b) — Consistent Meaning

A word or phrase is presumed to have the same meaning throughout a document, provision or statute unless there is a clear contrary indication.

c) — Harmonious Interpretation

A statutory provision should be interpreted to render it harmonious, and not contradictory with the other provisions of the enactment.

d) — No Superfluous Provisions

If at all possible, a provision should not be interpreted so as to render it — or any other provision — superfluous, unlawful or invalid.

e) — No Surplusage

Every word should, if possible, be given effect; no word should be read as surplusage.

f) — Criminal Provisions

A legislative provision that defines a criminal offence or has a criminal sanction should, in cases of ambiguity, be interpreted to favour the person accused of the offence.

g) — Ut Magis Valeat Quam Pereat ("So that It May Survive Rather than Perish")

An ambiguous provision should be interpreted in a way that makes it valid rather than invalid. Parliament does not intend to enact pointless legislation.[34]

---

[34]See, for example, *Rizzo*, above note 22 at para 27: ". . . a label of absurdity can be attached to interpretations which defeat the purpose of a statute or render some aspect of it pointless or futile."

h) — Inclusio Unius Est Exclusio Alterius ("The Inclusion of One Implies the Exclusion of Others")

For example, a provision that provides benefits to a person up to the age of eighteen necessarily implies that the benefit is not available to any person over the age of eighteen.

i) — Ejusdem Generis ("Of the Same Kind")

A general residual category following a list of other items refers to items of the same sort.

V. — Form and Substance

It is trite to suggest that substance should take precedence over form to the extent that it is consistent with the wording and objective of the statute. This chestnut of interpretational technique is easier to state than it is to apply. We start with the following questions:

- What does the transaction or arrangement achieve?
- Does it fit within the plain meaning of the provision?
- Does the result fit within the purpose of the statutory provision(s)?
- If it does not fit within the purpose of the provision(s), should the taxpayer be allowed the benefit of the provision or be subject to the avoidance strictures of the Act?

The difficulty with the substance doctrine is that, despite its intuitive appeal, it does not offer any objective yardstick to measure against particular facts. If applied on an *ex-post* basis, the doctrine leaves commercial transactions in an uncertain state. It is an unpredictable doctrine of varying reach. In 1936, Lord Tomlin referred to it disparagingly as the "so-called doctrine" in *CIR v. The Duke of Westminster*:

> [I]t is said that in revenue cases there is a doctrine that the Court may ignore the legal position and regard what is called "the substance of the matter" . . .. [The] supposed doctrine . . . seems to rest for its support upon a misunderstanding of language used in some earlier cases. The sooner this misunderstanding is dispelled, and the supposed doctrine given its quietus, the better it will be for all concerned, for the doctrine seems to involve substituting "the incertain and crooked cord of discretion" for "the golden and streight metwand of the law." Every man is entitled if he can to order his affairs so as that the tax attaching under the appropriate Acts is less than it otherwise would be . . .. This so-called doctrine of "the substance" seems to me to be nothing more than an attempt to make a man pay and notwithstanding that he has so ordered his affairs that the amount of tax sought from him is not legally claimable.[35]

---

[35]*Inland Revenue Commissioners v. Duke of Westminster*, [1936] A.C. 1 (H.L.) at 19.

Notwithstanding these early reservations, the doctrine has had a pervasive, but uncertain, effect in tax law. In 1984, the Supreme Court knocked it down in *Stubart*,[36] but it rose three years later under the guise of the "commercial reality" test in *Bronfman Trust*,[37] where Dickson CJ stated:

> I acknowledge, however, that just as there has been a recent trend away from strict construction of taxation statutes . . . so too has the recent trend in tax cases been towards attempting to ascertain the *true commercial and practical nature of the taxpayer's transaction*. There has been, in this country and elsewhere, movement away from tests based on the form of transactions and towards tests based on what Lord Pearce has referred to as a "common sense appreciation of all the guiding features" of the events in question . . .. This is, I believe, a laudable trend *provided it is consistent* with the text and purposes of the taxation statute.[38]

Thus, for a limited period, we see the pendulum swinging from form towards a looser standard, a common sense appreciation of "commercial reality".

However, by 1999, the Supreme Court realigns the doctrine of statutory construction in tax law:

> Unless the Act provides otherwise, a taxpayer is entitled to be taxed on what it actually did, not on what it could have done, and certainly not based on what a less sophisticated taxpayer may have done.[39]

And:

> [I]n the absence of a specific statutory bar to the contrary, taxpayers are entitled to structure their affairs in a manner that reduces the tax payable . . .. An unrestricted application of an "economic effects" approach does indirectly what this Court has consistently held Parliament did not intend the Act to do directly.[40]

What do "substance", "commercial reality" and "common sense view" really mean? How do we accurately measure the substance of transactions in the context of a tax structure premised upon artificial distinctions of different sources of income? For example, a taxpayer who needs a capital asset for business use can acquire it in one of three ways. He can:

* Purchase the asset outright and acquire legal title to it immediately, but pay for it over time;

* Lease the asset and pay rent for its use, but without acquiring title in the property; or

---

[36]*Stubart*, above note 5.

[37]*Bronfman Trust*, above note 8.

[38]*Ibid.*, at paras 36-37 [emphasis added].

[39]*Shell Canada*, above note 13 at para 45.

[40]*Ibid.*, at para 46.

- Lease the asset with an option to purchase the property for a token amount of, say, $1 when the lease expires.

In the first case, the taxpayer clearly acquires title and ownership of the property. If the property is depreciable property, the taxpayer can write off the capital cost of the asset as capital cost allowance (tax depreciation).[41]

In the second case, the taxpayer does not acquire title to the property but has a user interest in exchange for rental payments, which may or may not coincide with the amount deductible as capital cost allowance or tax depreciation. The write-off would depend upon the term of the lease, the underlying cost of financing, etc. If the lease is for ninety-nine years, is it transformed into an outright purchase in fee simple? In legal terms, the lease remains a lease with no change in title. In terms of economic substance the lease is the equivalent of an outright sale.

In the third case, the economic substance of the transaction is that the taxpayer purchases the property, but with delayed transmission of legal title. The commercial reality of the transaction is identical to an outright purchase of the asset in the first case. As a matter of legal substance, however, the taxpayer is a lessee during the tenure of the lease and acquires legal title only when the lease expires and she pays the token sum of $1. Thus, the legal substance of the transaction is that it is a lease until the lessee acquires title to the property by exercising the option.

Although courts may be sensitive to the economic realities of a particular transaction, rather than being bound to what first appears to be its legal form,[42] the doctrine is subject to at least two important caveats. First, absent a specific provision of the Act to the contrary or a finding that they are a sham, the taxpayer's formal legal relationships should be respected in tax cases. Second, where the provision at issue is clear and unambiguous a court should apply its terms.[43]

VI. — Burden of Proof

The burden of proof in civil tax cases is on a balance of probabilities. In criminal tax cases of tax evasion, the burden is on the Crown to establish its case beyond a reasonable doubt.

---

[41] See Chapter 8.

[42] *Shell Canada*, above note 13.

[43] *Ibid.*

A. — *Presumption of Validity*

Subsection 152(8) of the Act addresses the onus in civil cases:

> An assessment shall . . . be *deemed* to be valid and binding notwithstanding any error, defect or omission in the assessment or in any proceeding under this Act relating thereto. [Emphasis added.]

The taxpayer carries the onus to establish on a balance of probabilities that the factual findings and the assumptions of fact upon which the minister based the assessment are wrong.[44] The minister must disclose the findings of fact upon which he bases an assessment. He does this in his Reply to the Notice of Appeal. The taxpayer's onus of proof lies in rebutting the facts disclosed by the minister in the assessment. This burden tilts the scale in favour of the minister.

B. — *Reversal of Onus*

Subsection 163(2) of the Act authorizes the minister to impose a penalty on a person who has either "knowingly" or "under circumstances amounting to gross negligence" made a false statement or omission in an income tax return. In these circumstances, where the minister imposes a penalty on the basis of the taxpayer's gross negligence, the Act reverses the burden of proof and puts it on the minister to show the gross negligence on the basis of the particular facts.[45]

Subsection 163(2) requires that the minister show not only that there has been an act of omission or misstatement by the taxpayer (or his or her agent), but also that the taxpayer (or agent) had a state of mind that justifies a finding of gross negligence. In *Udell v. Minister of National Revenue*,[46] for example, the court stated: "In my view the use of the verb 'made' in the context in which it is used also involves a deliberate and intentional consciousness on the part of the principal to the act done."

---

[44] *Johnston v. Minister of National Revenue*, [1948] C.T.C. 195 (S.C.C.); *R. v. Anderson Logging Co.* (1924), [1925] S.C.R. 45, [1917-27] C.T.C. 198 (S.C.C.); affirmed [1917-27] C.T.C. 210 (British Columbia P.C.). See, however, *Anchor Point Energy Ltd. v. R.*, 2006 TCC 424, [2006] 4 C.T.C. 2353 (T.C.C. [General Procedure]); reversed 2007 FCA 188, [2007] 4 C.T.C. 5 (F.C.A.); leave to appeal refused [2007] S.C.C.A. No. 368 (S.C.C.).

[45] *Income Tax Act*, R.S.C. 1985, c 1 (5th Supp.), subs. 163(3).

[46] *Udell v. Minister of National Revenue*, [1969] C.T.C. 704 (Can. Ex. Ct.) at 714 (Cattanach J).

VII. — The General Anti-avoidance Rule (GAAR)

The interpretation of GAAR in section 245 involves a broader analysis of the taxpayer's motive, the purpose of provisions, and the effect of a series of transactions on the purpose. The section specifically requires purposive interpretation.

The Supreme Court of Canada's decision in *Copthorne*[47] was a shot across the bow of tax professionals — lawyers and accountants — who spend long hours buried in the detail of the *Income Tax Act*. There is a danger of not seeing the forest for the trees. The message of the decision is clear: step back from the technical and convoluted detail of transactions to see whether an arrangement or scheme abusively undermines the object, spirit and purpose of the tax statute. The sword of Damocles hangs by a single horse's hair over the head of every lawyer rendering tax opinions.

The case involved companies controlled by Li Ka-Shing and his son, Victor Li, non-residents of Canada, who invested $97 million in a Canadian company, which then used $67 million of the money to purchase shares in its subsidiary. The subsidiary lost money on its investments and the family sought to utilize the losses through other more profitable investments in other companies with the family group.

Under the tax rules, if the parent and subsidiary amalgamated, the inter-company investment of $67 million would disappear. Instead, however, in order to preserve the invested capital, there followed a complex series of amalgamations and reorganizations, the net effect of which was to convert the relationship of the companies into affiliated corporations, rather than the parent and subsidiary companies that they had been initially.

The *Income Tax Act* permits shareholders to withdraw their capital tax free from a corporation. In a vertical amalgamation of a parent and its subsidiary corporation, the capital of the intercompany invested is cancelled because it represents the investment of the parent in the subsidiary. In *Copthorne* the total investment was only $97 million, of which $67 million was down-streamed into the subsidiary.

However, where affiliated corporations (that is, sister and brother corporations) owned by a common parent are amalgamated, their capital is aggregated and becomes the capital of the new corporate amalgamated entity. Thus, a horizontal amalgamation creates a much larger capital pool that can be withdrawn tax-free.

By using a horizontal amalgamation the non-residents sought to extract $164 million tax-free even though its cash investment was only $97 million. The Minister of National Revenue disagreed.

None of the transactions in the series of reorganizations technically offended the provisions of the Act. In aggregate, however, they resulted in an arrangement that circumvented the underlying policy of the amalgamation rules and "abusive" of the statute.

---

[47]*Copthorne Holdings Ltd. v. R.*, 2011 SCC 63, [2011] 3 S.C.R. 721, [2012] 2 C.T.C. 29 (S.C.C.).

The Supreme Court took pains to emphasize that "abusive" does not imply moral opprobrium concerning the taxpayer's efforts to minimize its taxes. Indeed, the court endorsed the *Westminster* principle — a 1930's English decision — that taxpayers are entitled to select courses of action or enter into transactions that minimize their tax liability.

GAAR superimposes a purpose test in determining the validity of transactions, which blunts the *Westminster* doctrine of literal interpretation by focusing on the object, spirit and purpose of tax provisions.

Purposive analysis does not depend on whether the words of the statute are clear or ambiguous. Even where the words of the Act are clear, a court can determine the rationale or purpose of the words to determine whether transactions abuse the statute. Thus, GAAR analysis requires balancing between two competing interests: the interest of the taxpayer in minimizing his or her taxes through technically legitimate means and the legislative interest in ensuring the integrity of the income tax system.

An arrangement is abusive where the transaction (or series of transactions) culminates in an outcome that defeats the purpose of the statutory provisions used to implement it. It is trite to say that GAAR creates uncertainty. Of course it does. It is only when the Minister cannot rely on specific provisions that he will rely on GAAR if the transactions undermine the rationale or purpose of the statute.

GAAR was enacted for the very purpose of attacking transactions that escaped the literal meaning of words in provisions, but had the overall effect of frustrating and undermining the purpose of the Act read as a whole. As Justice Frankfurter said:

> Legislation has an aim: it seeks to obviate some mischief, to supply an inadequacy, to effect a change in policy, to formulate a plan of Government. That aim, that policy is not drawn, like nitrogen, out of the air; it is evinced in the language of the statute as read in the light of other external manifestations of purpose.

We have moved a long way from the penal philosophy of tax interpretation. As professionals giving opinions on structures, we need to assess business plans from a broad perspective of purposive analysis. To adapt Cicero: Does not *Copthorne* seem to make it sufficiently clear that there can be nothing happy for the person over whom some fear of GAAR always looms?

VIII. — Conclusion

We see from the above that the rules of statutory construction of tax law are not as definitive as one might have anticipated. Unlocking legislative intention is an uncertain process. Taxpayers crave certainty and are entitled to know the legal consequences of their transactions and arrangements. However, we must also balance the needs of taxpayers for certainty with the role that Parliament has assigned the Act as a fiscal and socio-economic statute. The *Interpretation Act* contemplates remedial, fair and liberal interpretation for *every* enactment.

The line between legitimate and abusive tax avoidance also shifts as the courts to develop new approaches to statutory construction of fiscal legislation. The courts have shifted away from interpreting the Act as a penal statute. Nevertheless, we continue with problems of statutory construction. Sometimes we lean towards the "plain meaning" rule and, at other times, in favour of "purposive" interpretation. This tension in statutory construction leads to uncertainty and legislative complexity in tax law.

Finally, the introduction of the General Anti-Avoidance Rule[48] into our tax law raises additional interpretational uncertainty. The broad language of section 245 of the *Income Tax Act* stands in contrast to the other detailed provisions of the statute[49] and creates (or at least, adds to) uncertainty. To be sure, tax law is difficult, but it is not dry. On the contrary, its influence on human behaviour is probably greater than that of any other statute.

---

[48]See Chapter 19.

[49]See, for example, *Lipson v. R.*, [2009] 1 C.T.C. 314 (S.C.C.).

Chapter 3 — Taxable Nexus

Table of Contents

Fundamentals of Canadian Income Tax Vol 1: Personal Tax

Table of Contents

I. — General Comment

The first question we must answer when designing a tax system is: Who is taxable? The answer to this question shapes the substantive and administrative structure of the statute. A state must have taxable nexus with the person whom it seeks to tax. Even the most rudimentary tax system based on head count (for example, a poll tax) raises the question whose heads one should count. The following table outlines some options for taxable nexus.

Connecting Factor	Theory of Connection	Comment
1. Citizenship	• Political affiliation • Entitlement to state's protection	United States is primary example
2. Domicile	• Physical presence • Intention to reside indefinitely • Economic and social affiliation	Difficult to establish intention; can circumvent easily; U.K. "non-doms"
3. Residence	• Economic and social affiliation • Intention not required • Can be involuntary presence	Generally used in combination with one of the other options, e.g. source or citizenship

Connecting Factor	Theory of Connection	Comment
4. Source	• Territorial affiliation	Easy to escape if sole criterion; useful with residence

There are several options for asserting taxable nexus with a person: the legal status of the person; the territorial source of income; or the place where the person manages his or her activities. For example, in the case of individuals, we could use citizenship, domicile, or residence to determine whether the person has a nexus with Canada. Similarly, we could use source of income. Place of management as a connecting factor is an option for artificial entities, such as corporations. Regardless of the option, taxable nexus is central to the administration of the tax system.

We can justify citizenship or nationality as a connecting factor on the theory that citizenship confers a legal status that is not constrained by geographical boundaries. One can argue that the citizens of a country should pay their taxes to it regardless of where they reside because they derive benefits from their citizenship. Even non-resident citizens of a state are entitled to its political protection and, therefore, should bear some of the costs to reflect the benefits of citizenship. The United States is the most prominent country that uses citizenship as one of the basis for taxation.

Citizenship implies duties and responsibilities that require a balancing of the costs and benefits of national belonging. During the Israeli incursion into Lebanon in 2006, for example, Canadian, American, British and Scandanavian governments evacuated their citizens from the war zone. Canada evacuated 15,000 of its citizens from Lebanon at a cost of $85 million. Approximately 7,000 of the evacuees returned to Lebanon after hostilities ceased.

However, citizenship, as the sole connecting factor, creates problems. Citizenship is a political nexus between an individual and a country, and has little bearing upon economic activities. There are also administrative difficulties in asserting claims against non-resident citizens and measuring the value of the benefits they derive during their absence from their country of citizenship. Canada decided early on that it would not use citizenship as a connecting factor for tax purposes. Indeed, even those countries (and there are very few[1]) that use citizenship or nationality to establish a taxable nexus usually couple it with other factors, such as residence. The United States, for example, asserts full tax liability on the worldwide income of its citizens and resident aliens.

Domicile is another form of legal status. Unlike citizenship, however, domicile uses different criteria, namely, physical presence and an intention to reside indefinitely in the country.

---

[1]Few countries (United States, Philippines and Korea Vietnam and Eritrea, for example) use citizenship as a basis of personal taxation.

65

We premise taxation based upon domicile on the theory that an individual should pay tax commensurate with the individual's economic and social association with the country.

Domicile depends upon intention and free choice. Every person has a domicile of origin at birth, usually the father's domicile. An individual may adopt a domicile of choice, which entails physical presence in a country coupled with an intention to reside there indefinitely. Depending as it does on physical presence and intention, domicile is fraught with substantial uncertainty and is not easy to administer for tax purposes. Britain, for example, uses residence and domicile in their tax system.

Residence is still another type of legal status connecting a taxpayer to a country. The theory underlying residence as a connecting factor is that a person should owe economic allegiance to the country with which he, she or it most closely connected in economic and social terms. The obligation to pay tax based on residence derives from the principle that persons who benefit from their economic and social affiliation with a country have an obligation to contribute to its public finances. Residence as a connecting factor is also administratively practical and convenient. It is generally easy for a country to ensure compliance with its tax laws if the person over whom it asserts the law has close economic links with the country and has assets within its administrative reach.

Taxation based upon source of income is territorial taxable nexus. It is administratively practical and easily enforceable if one can pinpoint the source of income. The use of source of income as the primary connecting factor for taxation is, however, contrary to tax equity because it does not accurately measure a taxpayer's ability to pay. Corporate taxpayers in particular may derive all the economic, political, and legal benefits of residence in a country and arrange their international transactions that they earn their income in low-tax countries or tax havens. The development of electronic commerce, which can assign the source of transactions to locations that have little bearing on the economic substance of the transactions, will increase the problems of source taxation. Hence, most developed economies (including Canada) use source taxation only as an adjunct to full tax liability based on some other connection — such as, citizenship, domicile or residence.

A. — Who Is Taxable?

Section 2 is the charging provision for determining who is liable for tax. Canada uses residence as its primary connecting factor to exercise domestic taxable jurisdiction on the theory that a person who enjoys the legal, political and economic benefits of association with the country should bear the appropriate share of the costs of association. Subsection 2(1) states:

> An income tax shall be paid . . . on the taxable income for each taxation year of every person[2] resident in Canada at any time in the year.

---

[2]Subsection 248(1) defines a "person" to include individuals and corporations.

The subsection is quite clear: a resident of Canada is taxable on his or her worldwide income. In addition to residence, however, Canada also uses territorial nexus to tax non-resident persons. Thus, subject to tax treaty provisions,[3] Canada also taxes non-residents, but only on their Canadian-source income.

Canadians are taxable on their worldwide income, regardless of where they earn the income. "Resident" includes a person who is "ordinarily resident" in Canada.[4] Full tax liability on worldwide income promotes horizontal equity. For example, assume that A and B, of Canada, each earn $100,000, but B earns half of her income from investments in a foreign country. The principle of horizontal equity requires that A and B should pay an equal amount of tax. Since they are Canadian, we can apply the principle only if both are fully liable to tax in Canada on their worldwide income. However, to prevent double taxation of B, who might also pay tax at source on her foreign investment income, Canada grants a tax credit for some or all of her foreign taxes. As we will see, taxable nexus based upon source of income require countries to negotiate their taxable jurisdiction through tax treaties.

Canada taxes non-residents only on their Canadian-source income. Subsection 2(3) states that a non-resident is taxable in Canada only if he or she is employed in Canada, carries on business in Canada or derives a capital gain from the disposition of taxable Canadian property. This rule, however, is also subject to Canada's bilateral tax treaties, which can limit the right to tax a non-resident's income from Canadian sources. For example, tax treaties generally limit the right to tax Canadian business income if the taxpayer does not have a "permanent establishment" in Canada.

The concept of residence for tax purposes is quite different from residence for immigration purposes. A Canadian resident for immigration purposes may be non-resident for tax purposes and *vice versa*.

Nor is residence for tax purposes synonymous with physical presence in Canada. Residence for tax purposes refers to the legal and economic *nexus* that an individual has with Canada. Although physical presence is an important criterion for residence for tax purposes, it is not necessarily conclusive in establishing taxable nexus. A person who is physically present in Canada, for example, a transient visitor, is not necessarily a Canadian resident.[5] Conversely, a person who is absent from Canada for a considerable period (for example, a Canadian diplomat) may be a Canadian resident for income tax purposes.

---

[3]See, for example, Article 7, *OECD Model Convention*.

[4]See subs. 250(3); *Laurin v. R.*, [2007] 2 C.T.C. 2048 (T.C.C. [General Procedure]); affirmed [2008] 3 C.T.C. 100 (F.C.A.) (Air Canada pilot living in Turks & Caicos and flying out of Canada not ordinarily resident in Canada); *R. v. Reeder*, [1975] C.T.C. 256, 75 D.T.C. 5160 (Fed. T.D.) (employee can be ordinarily resident in Canada even if he is out of the country for extended period).

[5]See, however, the 183-day rule in subs. 250(1).

B. — Individuals

An individual may be a resident, non-resident or part-time resident of Canada. Each of these categories marks the boundary of Canada's jurisdiction to tax. A resident of Canada is taxable on his or her worldwide income, regardless of where it is earned.[6] A non-resident is subject to Canadian income tax only if he or she is employed in Canada, carries on business in Canada, or disposes of taxable Canadian property.[7] A part-year resident of Canada is also subject to tax on his or her worldwide income, but only while he or she is resident in Canada.[8]

We determine an individual's residence in one of three ways — under statutory rules, case law rules, or international tax treaty rules. The statutory rules deem individuals with substantial economic connections with Canada to reside in Canada, regardless of their physical presence in the country. The case law rules are essentially facts and circumstances tests that apply in the absence of statutory provisions to determine whether an individual has a taxable nexus with Canada. Tax treaty rules may apply to prevent double taxation of individuals when two countries both claim taxable jurisdiction over the taxpayer.

C. — Statutory Rules

The Act deems an individual to be a resident of Canada if he or she:[9]

- Sojourns in Canada for 183 days or more in a year;

- Is a member of the Canadian Forces;

- Is a member of the Canadian diplomatic or quasi-diplomatic service;

- Performs services in a foreign country under a prescribed international development assistance program of the Canadian government;

- Is a member of the Canadian Forces school staff; or

- Is a child of a person holding a position referred to in the above categories (other than a sojourner), if he or she is wholly dependent upon that person for support.

---

[6]Subs. 2(1). A resident taxpayer is, within limits, entitled to a credit for foreign taxes paid by him or her; see s. 126.

[7]Subs. 2(3).

[8]S. 114.

[9]Subs. 250(1). An individual cannot, however, be deemed to be resident in Canada by virtue of subsection 250(1) if he or she is considered resident in Canada on the basis of the case law rules. In certain circumstances, subs. 250(1)(g) may deem spouses of Canadian diplomats to be resident in Canada if the diplomat marries a non-resident.

A deeming provision is a conclusive presumption of law. Thus, the above deeming rules ensure that individuals who have substantial economic connections with Canada are subject to Canadian tax despite their absence from the country for extended periods of time.

a) — Sojourners

The Act *deems* an individual who sojourns in Canada for 183 days or more in a year to reside in Canada *throughout the taxation year*.[10] The term "day" means a 24-hour period or part thereof.[11]

This rule is the most elusive of the deeming rules in subsection 250(1). The concept of sojourning is not easy to grasp and the term is not defined in the Act. Sojourning implies a temporary stay in a place, as opposed to ordinary residence. As Estey J. said, "One sojourns at a place where he unusually, casually or intermittently visits or stays."[12] "Sojourning", which is something less than establishing a permanent abode in Canada, has the effect of deeming the individual to be resident in Canada *throughout* the particular taxation year.

The fact that an individual is present in Canada for less than 183 days does not, *by itself*, mean that he or she is not a Canadian resident. An individual who is in Canada for less than 183 days may be considered a resident under the "facts and circumstances" common law test[13] (factual residence). Thus, an individual may be a Canadian resident for tax purposes even though he or she has only "visitor status" under the immigration rules.[14]

"Sojourning" is different from permanent residence. For example, an individual who ceases to be a Canadian resident after 183 days in the year cannot be deemed to reside in Canada throughout the year by virtue of the sojourning rule. Rather, the individual becomes a part-

---

[10]Para. 250(1).

[11]See IT-221R3 for similar reference under the *Canada-U.S. Treaty*.

[12]*Thomson v. Minister of National Revenue*, [1946] S.C.R. 209, [1946] C.T.C. 51, 2 D.T.C. 812 (S.C.C.) at 70 [C.T.C.] and 813 [D.T.C.].

[13]This rule is subject to treaty provisions to the contrary. See, e.g., Article XV of the *Canada-United States Income Tax Convention*, 1980 re exemption of employment income where an individual spends fewer than 183 days in Canada.

[14]*Lee v. Minister of National Revenue*, [1990] 1 C.T.C. 2082, 90 D.T.C. 1014 (T.C.C.) (individual considered resident prior to obtaining landed immigrant status on basis of marriage to Canadian resident and purchase of matrimonial residence).

time resident for the particular year and a non-resident thereafter.[15] Thus, part year residence is transitional between full time and non-resident status.

b) — Government Personnel

Subsection 250(1) also deems members of the Canadian Forces, certain development workers, Canadian Forces school staff, and officers and employees of the Government of Canada or a province to be Canadian, regardless of where they are posted and the length of time they are out of the country. A person who ceases to hold a position described above is considered to have been resident in Canada for the part of the year during which he or she held that position.[16]

c) — Prescribed Agencies

Individuals who perform services at any time in the year in a foreign country under a "prescribed international development assistance program of the Government of Canada" are *deemed* to be resident in Canada during the period of their absence from Canada if they were resident in Canada at any time in the three-month period immediately prior to commencing their service.[17]

D. — "Common Law" Rules

The "common law" rules determine an individual's factual residence by her links with Canada. Where the links are sufficiently strong, we consider the individual to have taxable nexus with Canada and she is a resident for tax purposes.[18] The sufficiency of connecting

---

[15]The Agency accepts this position in IT-221R3 "Determination of an Individual's Residence Status" (Oct. 4, 2002); but see *Truchon v. Minister of National Revenue* (1970), 70 D.T.C. 1277 (T.A.B.) (incorrectly decided and rule not followed).

[16]Subs. 250(2).

[17]Para. 250(1)(d); Reg. 3400. See *Petersen v. Minister of National Revenue*, [1969] Tax A.B.C. 682, 69 D.T.C. 503 (Can. Tax App. Bd.); *Bell v. R.*, [1996] 2 C.T.C. 2191, 97 D.T.C. 484 (T.C.C.) (Shifting of onus to Minister to prove that program qualifies).

[18]*Weymyss v. Weymyss's Trustees*, [1921] Sess. Cas. 30.

factors is a question of fact[19] that depends upon several criteria, including the presence in Canada of:

- Property or dwelling;

- Spouse or common-law partner;

- Dependants;

- Social interests;

- Business interests; and

- Life and family ties.

Also taken into account are:

- Physical presence;

- Nationality and background; and

- Social connections by reason of birth or marriage.

Although the relative weight that one attaches to each of these factors is a question of fact,[20] the CRA considers the first three (dwelling place, matrimonial ties, and dependants) to be significant residential ties.[21] These factors should be considered in the context of certain generally accepted legal propositions:

- A taxpayer must reside somewhere;[22]

- A taxpayer need not have a fixed place of abode to be resident in the jurisdiction;[23]

---

[19]As Lord Buckmaster observed in *Lysaght v. Inland Revenue Commissioners*, [1928] A.C. 234 (H.L.) at 247-248:

> . . . it may be true that the word "reside" . . . in other Acts may have special meanings but in the *Income Tax Acts* it is, I think, used in its common sense and it is essentially a question of fact whether a man does or does not comply with its meaning . . . the matter must be a matter of degree.

[20]See, e.g., *MacLean v. Minister of National Revenue*, [1985] C.T.C. 2207, 85 D.T.C. 169 (T.C.C.); affirmed [1990] 1 C.T.C. 16 (Fed. T.D.) (taxpayer resident on the basis of continued connections with Canada despite the CRA's waiver of source deductions).

[21]IT-221R3 (Consolidated). "Determination of an Individual's Residence Status".

[22]*Rogers v. Inland Revenue Commissioners* (1897), 1 Tax Cas. 225 (Scot. Ct. of Ex.).

[23]*Reid v. Inland Revenue Commissioners* (1926), 10 Tax Cas. 673 (Scot. Ct. of Sess.).

- Residence requires more than mere physical presence within the jurisdiction;[24]

- Residence does not require constant personal presence;[25]

- A taxpayer may have more than one residence;[26]

- The number of days that[27] a taxpayer spends within Canada is not determinative;

  - Residence may be established by presence within Canada even though the presence is compelled by the authorities, business necessity or otherwise;[28]

- "Residing" and "ordinarily resident" do not have special or technical meanings, and the question whether a person is "residing or ordinarily resident in Canada" is a question of fact;[29] and

- Intention and free choice, which are essential elements in domicile, are not necessary to establish residence; residence is quite different from domicile of choice.[30]

"Residing" is not a term of invariable elements. As Rand J. said in *Thomson v. Minister of National Revenue*:[31]

> . . . [it] is quite impossible to give it a precise and inclusive definition. It is highly flexible, and its many shades of meaning vary not only in the contexts of different matters, but also in different aspects of the same matter. In one case it is satisfied by certain elements, in another by others, some common, some new.

---

[24]*Levene v. Inland Revenue Commissioners* (1928), 13 Tax Cas. 486 (H.L.).

[25]*Young, Re* (1875), 1 Tax Cas. 57 (Scot. Ct. of Ex.).

[26]*Lloyd v. Sulley* (1884), 2 Tax Cas. 37 (Scot. Ct. of Ex.).

[27]*Reid v. Inland Revenue Commissioners*, above note 23.

[28]*Lysaght v. Inland Revenue Commissioners*, [1928] A.C. 234 (H.L.).

[29]*Ibid.*

[30]*Schujahn v. Minister of National Revenue*, [1962] C.T.C. 364, 62 D.T.C. 1225 (Can. Ex. Ct.) (change of domicile depends on will of individual).

[31]*Thomson v. Minister of National Revenue*, [1945] C.T.C. 63, 2 D.T.C. 684 (Can. Ex. Ct.); affirmed [1946] S.C.R. 209, [1946] C.T.C. 51, 2 D.T.C. 812 (S.C.C.) at 63-64 [C.T.C.] and 815 [D.T.C.]. See also *Beament v. Minister of National Revenue*, [1952] 2 S.C.R. 486, [1952] C.T.C. 327, 52 D.T.C. 1183 (S.C.C.) (taxpayer not resident where he was physically absent from Canada, did not maintain any dwelling place in Canada, and maintained matrimonial home in U.K.); *Russell v. Minister of National Revenue*, [1949] C.T.C. 13, 49 D.T.C. 536 (Can. Ex. Ct.) (examination of indicia of residence during active service overseas); *Schujahn v. Minister of National Revenue*, [1962] C.T.C. 364, 62 D.T.C. 1225 (Can. Ex. Ct.) (taxpayer not resident though family remained in Canada for purpose of selling home); *Griffiths v. R.*, [1978] C.T.C. 372, 78 D.T.C. 6286 (Fed. T.D.) (established residence was yacht in Caribbean despite spouse, assets and income in Canada).

Chapter 3 — Taxable Nexus

The following is a comprehensive list of relevant indicia in determining Canadian residence:

- Past and present habits of life;

- Regularity and length of visits to Canada;

- Ties within Canada;

- Ties elsewhere;

- Purpose of stay;

- Ownership of a home in Canada or rental of a dwelling on a long-term basis (for example, a lease for one or more years) (significant factor);

- Residence of spouse, children and other dependent family members in a dwelling that the individual maintains in Canada (significant factor);

- Memberships with Canadian churches or synagogues, recreational and social clubs, unions and professional organizations;

- Registration and maintenance of automobiles, boats and airplanes in Canada;

- Credit cards issued by Canadian financial institutions and commercial entities, including stores, car rental agencies, etc.;

- Local newspaper subscriptions sent to a Canadian address;

- Rental of a Canadian safety deposit box or post office box;

- Subscriptions for life or general insurance, including health insurance, through a Canadian insurance company;

- Mailing address in Canada;

- Telephone listing in Canada;

- Business cards showing a Canadian address;

- Magazine and other periodical subscriptions sent to a Canadian address;

- Canadian bank accounts other than a non-resident bank account;

- Active securities accounts with Canadian brokers;

- Canadian driver's licence;

- Membership in a Canadian pension plan;

- Frequent visits to Canada for social or business purposes;

- Burial plot in Canada;

- Will prepared in Canada;

- Legal documentation indicating Canadian residence;

- Filing a Canadian income tax return as a Canadian resident;

- Ownership of a Canadian vacation property;

- Active involvement in business activities in Canada;

- Employment in Canada;

- Maintenance or storage in Canada of personal belongings, including clothing, furniture, family pets, etc.;

- Landed immigrant status in Canada; and

- Severing substantially all ties with former country of residence.

An individual who is out of Canada, even for an extended period, may, nevertheless, be considered "ordinarily resident in Canada" if they have sufficient ties with Canada.[32] A graduate student, for example, who goes away to study for five years, but who intends to return to Canada and maintains ties with Canada would be ordinarily resident in Canada.

E. — Administrative Rules

The CRA focuses on three principal factors: (1) dwelling place; (2) family connections; and (3) personal property and social ties. The most important of these factors in determining residence for tax purposes is whether the individual maintains a home or dwelling in Canada that is available to him.[33]

To be considered a significant connecting factor, the home must be readily available to the taxpayer. For example, where a taxpayer leases out his home to an arm's length third party for twelve months, or longer, the home is not considered sufficiently available to him to establish residence.[34]

---

[32]See subsections 250(3).

[33]IT-221R3, "Determination of an Individual's Residence Status" (Oct. 4, 2002).

[34]See, for example, *Salt v. R.*, [2007] 3 C.T.C. 2255, 2007 D.T.C. 520 (Eng.) (T.C.C. [General Procedure]).

Facts to Consider When Determining Residence Status of an Individual (IT-221R3)		
Factor	**Resident**	**Non-Resident**
Significant residential ties a) Dwelling place b) Spouse or common-law partner c) Dependants		
Secondary residential ties a) Personal property in Canada b) Social ties with Canada c) Economic ties with Canada d) Landed immigrant status or appropriate work permits e) Hospitalization and medical insurance coverage from Canada f) Driver's licence from Canada g) Vehicle registration in Canada h) Seasonal dwelling place in Canada i) Canadian Passport j) Memberships in Canadian Union or professional organization		
Other residential ties of limited importance a) Retention of Canadian mailing address b) Canadian post office box c) Canadian safety deposit box d) Personal stationery or business cards showing Canadian address e) Telephone listing in Canada f) Canadian newspaper and magazine subscriptions		

Facts to Consider When Determining Residence Status of an Individual (IT-221R3)		
Factor	**Resident**	**Non-Resident**
Nature of absence from Canada a) Evidence of intention to permanently sever ties with Canada b) Regularity and length of visits to Canada c) Residence ties outside of Canada		

F. — International Treaty Rules

An individual may be taxable in more than one country in the same year. For example, a Canadian resident who is a U.S. citizen is potentially liable to taxation by both Canada and the United States. Similarly, an individual with international investments may be liable to tax in multiple jurisdictions. For example, a U.S. resident who sojourns 200 days in the year in Canada and receives dividends from a United Kingdom corporation would be liable for tax on his or her gross dividend income both in Canada and the United States under the domestic rules of both countries. In addition, the individual would also be liable for any taxes the U.K. government withholds at source on the dividends. Thus, without specific relief, the individual would be potentially liable for tax on the same income in three countries.

Multiple taxation of income is unfair and economically inefficient. Thus, Canada has negotiated numerous bilateral tax treaties to prevent double taxation of income and capital. Bilateral tax treaties resolve dual residency claims on individuals by two countries by allocating the jurisdiction to tax to one or other of the countries.

Tax treaties allocate taxable jurisdiction by applying a series of tie-breaker rules so that only one of the countries will have the primary right to tax the individual as its resident. The other country may retain a secondary right to tax income based on its source. The rules determine the degree of attachment that an individual has with a country, and are ranked in descending order of significance as follows:

- Location of permanent home;

- Centre of vital interests;

- Habitual abode; and

- Nationality.

Article 4(2) of the *OECD Model Double Taxation Convention on Income and on Capital*, which Canada uses as the model for most of its treaties, states the hierarchy of tie-breakers as follows:

> Where . . . an individual is a resident of both Contracting States, then his status shall be determined as follows:
>
>> (a) he shall be deemed to be a resident of the State in which he has a permanent home available to him; if he has a permanent home available to him in both States, he shall be deemed to be a resident of the State with which his personal and economic relations are closer (centre of vital interests);
>>
>> (b) if the State in which he has his centre of vital interests cannot be determined, or if he has not a permanent home available to him in either State, he shall be deemed to be a resident of the State in which he has a habitual abode;
>>
>> (c) if he has a habitual abode in both States or in neither of them, he shall be deemed to be a resident of the State of which he is a national;
>>
>> (d) if he is a national of both States or of neither of them, the competent authorities of the Contracting States shall settle the question by mutual agreement.

If one cannot resolve the issue of dual residency through the application of any of the above criteria, we refer the matter to the revenue authorities of each of the countries concerned for administrative resolution.

a) — Permanent Home

Treaties typically deem a dual resident individual to reside in the country in which he or she has a permanent home. Permanence implies that the individual must have arranged and retained the home for his or her permanent use.

A "home" includes any form of residential establishment, for example, a house, apartment, or even rented furnished rooms. It is the permanence of the home, rather than its size or nature of ownership or tenancy, that is the measure of attachment to the country.

b) — Centre of Vital Interests

Where an individual has a permanent home in both of the countries that consider the individual a resident under their domestic laws, the treaty deems the individual to reside in the country with which he or she has closer personal and economic relations ("centre of vital interests").[35] One determines personal and economic relations by family and social relations, occupation, political and cultural activities, place of business, and the place of admin-

---

[35]Article 4(2), OECD Model Convention.

istration of property. The OECD Commentary describes the centre of vital interests as follows:[36]

> The circumstances must be examined as a whole, but it is nevertheless obvious that considerations based on the personal acts of the individual must receive special attention. If a person who has a home in one State sets up a second in the other State while retaining the first, the fact that he retains the first in the environment where he has always lived, where he has worked, and where he has his family and possessions, can, together with other elements, go to demonstrate that he has retained his centre of vital interests in the first State.

c) — Habitual Abode

If one cannot determine an individual's centre of vital interests or if the individual does not have a permanent home in either country, the model treaty deems the individual to reside in the country in which he or she maintains a habitual abode. Alternatively, where an individual has a permanent home available to him or her in both countries, a habitual abode in one, rather than in the other, will tip the balance towards the country where he or she stays more frequently.[37]

Where, however, an individual does not have a permanent home in either country, all of his or her stays in the country should be considered without reference to the reason for the stay. For this purpose, it is necessary to determine whether the individual's residence in each of the two countries is sufficiently "habitual" to provide a meaningful answer.

d) — Nationality

If none of the above criteria are sufficient to break the deadlock, treaties typically deem the individual to reside in the country of which he or she is a national.[38]

e) — Competent Authorities

Finally, if one cannot resolve dual residency through the application of any of the specific attachment criteria, we refer the matter to the "competent authorities". The CRA is the designated competent authority in Canada's bilateral treaties.

---

[36]Para. 15, Commentary on Article 4(2).

[37]*Allchin v. R.*, [2004] 4 C.T.C. 1, 2004 D.T.C. 6468 (F.C.A.) (Resident of both Canada and the United States had her "habitual abode" in the U.S.A. under Article IV(2)(b) Canada-United States Income Tax Convention (1980). Hence, not subject to tax under subs. 2(1) of the ITA).

[38]See, for example, Article IV of the *Canada-U.S. Tax Treaty*.

II. — Part-Year Residents

An individual is a part-year resident if he or she gives up or takes up Canadian residence part way through the year. For example, a Canadian resident may emigrate during the year and take up residence elsewhere. In these circumstances, the individual would be a resident of Canada until his or her departure and a non-resident for the remainder of the year. As a resident, the individual would be taxable on his or her global income. As a non-resident, the individual would be taxable in Canada only if he or she was employed, or carrying on a business, in Canada or if he or she realized a capital gain from taxable Canadian property.[39]

A resident who gives up residence during a taxation year may claim deductions for that year but only on a proportional basis.[40] We determine an individual's non-refundable tax credits for the period of residency based on reasonableness, such as the number of days of residency. For example, an individual who becomes a Canadian resident on September 1 of a year is liable for Canadian tax on his or her global income earned during the period of September 1 to December 31 of the year. The individual's personal exemptions may be calculated on the basis of 122/365 (122 being the number of days out of the year spent in Canada) of the annual deductions otherwise available. An individual may also claim — subject to annual maximums — additional NRTCs for the period of non-residency if he earns at least 90 percent of his income for the period of non-residency in Canada.[41]

A. — Giving Up Residence

An individual who wishes to give up her Canadian residence should minimize her ties with Canada.[42] It is not easy to relinquish Canadian residence. An individual must produce convincing evidence that she has severed ties with Canada on a fairly permanent basis in order to cease residence. The CRA looks at four principal factors to determine whether an individual has given up Canadian residence:

- Permanence and purpose of stay abroad;

- Residential ties within Canada;

- Residential ties elsewhere; and

- Regularity and length of visits to Canada.

---

[39]Subs. 2(3) and subject to any treaty provisions.

[40]Ss. 114, 118.91.

[41]S. 118.94.

[42]See, e.g., *Ferguson v. Minister of National Revenue*, [1989] 2 C.T.C. 2387, 89 D.T.C. 634 (T.C.C.) (Canadian in Saudi Arabia for five years considered Canadian resident because he retained Ontario driver's licence and union membership, and his spouse remained in Canada).

Thus, at the very least, an individual who wishes to give up residence should:

- Sell or lease her dwelling in Canada;

- Sell her motor vehicle;

- Cancel any lease in respect of a dwelling in Canada that she occupies, or sublease the dwelling for the period of her absence; and

- Cancel bank accounts, club memberships and similar social and business connections within Canada.

There is no bright-line factual test to determine the minimum length of time that an individual should be out of Canada to claim non-resident status.

B. — Becoming a Resident

It is much easier for an individual to become a Canadian resident than to relinquish residence. An individual who takes up residence in Canada is taxed as a part-year resident for the portion of the year after her arrival and as a non-resident prior to her arrival.

Thus, it is generally advantageous for an individual to deliberately establish residence in Canada rather than be deemed a "sojourner" in Canada in the year of arrival. The Act deems a sojourner to be a Canadian resident for the *entire year* and taxable on her worldwide income.[43] In contrast, an incoming resident is taxable on his or her worldwide income only after arrival in Canada. Thus, timing of immigration is important. An immigrant can minimize tax by splitting income between Canada and the country of his departure.

Residence for immigration purposes is different from residence for tax purposes. An individual can establish permanent residence status for immigration purposes without becoming a resident for tax purposes. "Landed immigrant" status is determined on the basis of selection standards that are quite different from those used to determine residence for tax purposes. For immigration purposes, a landed immigrant must spend 183 days in Canada in a *12-month period*. For tax purposes, the Act deems an individual to be a resident of Canada if he or she spends 183 days or more in Canada in a *calendar year*. Thus, an individual can become a landed immigrant in Canada in a particular year and maintain his non-resident status for income tax purposes in the same year.

III. — Corporations

A corporation is a legal entity, a person, and a taxpayer in its own right regardless of whether its shareholders have limited or unlimited liability for its debts. A corporation resi-

---

[43]Para. 250(1)(a); subs. 2(1).

dent in Canada is taxable on its worldwide income. Non-resident corporations are taxable in Canada on their Canadian-source income. As with individuals, we determine the residence of a corporation in one of three ways — under statutory rules, at "common law" (factual residence), or by virtue of international tax treaty provisions.

A. — Statutory Rules

Many countries — for example, Canada, Australia, Germany, the Netherlands and the United States — use two tests of corporate residence: the place of incorporation (the statutory rule) and the place of central mind and management (factual residence).

The statutory rule is simple. The Act deems a corporation incorporated in Canada to be resident in Canada for tax purposes.[44] This rule applies to all corporations incorporated in Canada after April 26, 1965, regardless of where they are managed or controlled.[45]

The Act also deems a corporation incorporated in Canada prior to April 26, 1965 to be resident in Canada in a taxation year but only if after that date it:[46]

- Becomes resident in Canada at any time under the "common law" rules; or

- Carries on business in Canada.[47]

A corporation incorporated in Canada is also considered a "Canadian corporation".[48] This concept is important because of special incentive provisions that apply only to Canadian corporations.

Finally, the Act deems a corporation that is continued into or outside Canada to have been incorporated in that jurisdiction.[49] Thus, a corporation that is incorporated in Canada and continued outside Canada escapes the deemed residence rules,[50] which are based on the jurisdiction of incorporation. For example, the Act deems a corporation that is initially incorporated in the United States and then continued under federal or provincial corporate law in Canada, but which remains resident in both countries because of the "central management and control" test, to be a resident of Canada. Thus, U.S. corporations continued into Canada

---

[44]Para. 250(4)(a). This deeming provision only applies to corporations incorporated in Canada after April 26, 1965.

[45]Para. 250(4)(a).

[46]Para. 250(4)(c).

[47]See meaning of "carrying on business in Canada" in s. 253.

[48]Subs. 89(1) "Canadian corporation".

[49]Subs. 250(5.1).

[50]Subs. 250(4).

acquire "Canadian corporation" status, even if they are effectively managed from the United States. Such U.S. corporations are eligible for favorable treatment under the Act.[51]

B. — The "Common Law" Rules

The determination of corporate residence at "common law" is essentially a question of fact and circumstances. A corporation is resident where its "central management and control" resides.[52] The factual test originated in the Court of Exchequer in 1876 in *Calcutta Jute Mills v. Nicholson* (1876), 1 T.C. 83 (Eng. Ex. Div.) and *Cesena Sulphur Co. Ltd. v. Nicholson* (1876), 1 T.C. 88 (Eng. Ex. Div.). The House of Lords adopted the test thirty years later in *De Beers*, which is now considered the seminal authority on corporate residence. As Lord Loreburn said:[53]

> In applying the conception of residence to a company, we ought, I think, to proceed as nearly as we can upon the analogy of an individual. A company cannot eat or sleep, but it can keep house and do business. We ought, therefore, to see where it really keeps house and does business. . . . [A] company resides for purposes of income tax where its real business is carried on. . . . I regard that as the true rule, and the real business is carried on where the central management and control actually abides.

We identify central management and control with the control that a company's board of directors has over its business and affairs — generally in the jurisdiction where the board meets. Thus, corporate residence is different from corporate capacity. One determines residence by *de facto* "central management and control"; we determine corporate capacity

---

[51]For example, for tax-deferred rollovers on transfers of property to the corporation on a merger with another taxable Canadian corporation.

[52]*De Beers Consolidated Mines Ltd. v. Howe*, [1906] A.C. 455 (H.L.) at 458 (central management and control determined through scrutiny of course of business and trading); *United Construction Co. v. Bullock (Inspector of Taxes)*, [1959] 3 All E.R. 831 (H.L.) (three wholly-owned African subsidiaries of English corporation resident in U.K. because parent corporation exercised *de facto* control of subsidiaries from U.K.). The English common law test of "central management and control" is part of Canadian tax law: see *British Columbia Electric Railway v. R.*, [1946] C.T.C. 224, 2 D.T.C. 839 (Canada P.C.) (corporation was resident where whole of business carried on, all directors resident, and all shareholders meetings held in Canada). See also *Bedford Overseas Freighters Ltd. v. Minister of National Revenue*, [1970] C.T.C. 69, 70 D.T.C. 6072 (Can. Ex. Ct.) (management and control of business exercised by Canadian directors though instructed by non-resident shareholder owner); *Zehnder & Co. v. Minister of National Revenue*, [1970] C.T.C. 85, 70 D.T.C. 6064 (Can. Ex. Ct.) (management of company and attention to company's interests and affairs exercised in Canada); *Birmount Holdings Ltd. v. R.*, [1978] C.T.C. 358, 78 D.T.C. 6254 (Fed. C.A.) (company "keeping house" and "doing business" in Canada; see list of factors considered).

[53]*De Beers Consolidated Mines Ltd. v. Howe*, ante at 458.

through the legal documents used to create the corporation and the law of the jurisdiction of incorporation.

a) — General Propositions

The following propositions apply to corporate residence:

- A corporation can have more than one residence if its central management and control is located in one jurisdiction and it is incorporated in another.[54]

- Central management and control refers to the exercise of power and control by the corporation's board of directors and not to the power of the corporation's shareholders. Thus, the residence of shareholders is irrelevant for the purposes of determining corporate residence.[55]

- The residence of a subsidiary corporation, even a wholly-owned subsidiary, is determined independently of its parent corporation — the subsidiary's residence is determined by its central management and control.

- A subsidiary corporation may have the same residence as its parent corporation if the parent exercises effective control over the subsidiary's activities and management.[56]

In corporate law, parent and subsidiary corporations are separate entities each with its own board of directors. Parent corporations can influence management of their subsidiaries without effect on the latter's residence. Where, however, the parent's board effectively usurps the subsidiary's management, the residence of the subsidiary is determined by its *de facto* control.

There is no bright-line factual test that determines corporate residence in every case. To determine the central management and control of a corporation one must carefully evaluate all the surrounding factors, including:

- The location of meetings of its directors;

- The degree of independent control that the directors exercise; and

- The relative influence and power that its Canadian directors exercise, as compared with foreign directors (the "rubber stamp" test).

---

[54]*Swedish Central Railway v. Thompson*, [1925] A.C. 495 (H.L.) (company resident in location of registered office and where controlled and managed); *Minister of National Revenue v. Crossley Carpets (Can.) Ltd.*, [1969] 1 Ex. C.R. 405, [1968] C.T.C. 570 (Can. Ex. Ct.) (paramount authority for businesses divided between two countries).

[55]*Gramophone & Typewriter Ltd. v. Stanley*, [1908] 2 K.B. 89 (C.A.).

[56]*United Construction Co. v. Bullock (Inspector of Taxes)*, above note 52.

Ultimately, each case depends upon an evaluation of where the corporation is factually managed.

Viewed from the opposite perspective, a corporation that desires non-resident status should incorporate outside Canada and conduct all of its board meetings, banking, and corporate policy outside the country. Where there are several directors, the majority should be non-residents. Annual shareholders meetings should also be held outside Canada.

b) — Dual Residence

Since different countries use different connecting factors to assert taxable jurisdiction over corporations, a corporation may be considered resident in more than one country. For example, a corporation that is incorporated in the United States and managed and controlled in Canada would be resident in both countries.

The *OECD Model Convention* uses the "place of effective management" as a tie-breaker to determine the residence of companies. Article 4(3) of the Convention states:

> Where . . . a person other than an individual is a resident of both Contracting States, then it shall be deemed to be a resident of the State in which its place of effective management is situated.

Both Canada and the United States, however, reserve the right to use place of incorporation as the determinative test for corporate residence. Thus, Article IV(3) of the *Canada-U.S. Treaty* provides that:

> Where . . . a company is a resident of both Contracting States, then if it was created under the laws in force in a Contracting State, it shall be deemed to be a resident of that State.

Some jurisdictions allow local incorporation of an entity that is already organized and incorporated under the laws of another country. Under the *Canada-U.S. Treaty*, however, the determinative factor is the location of the corporation's original creation.[57]

c) — "Permanent Establishment"

A Canadian resident corporation is taxable in Canada on its worldwide income. A non-resident corporation is taxable in Canada only if it carries on business in Canada or disposes taxable Canadian property.[58]

---

[57]See Revised Technical Explanation — Canada-U.S. Income Tax Convention 1980 (U.S. Treasury Department).

[58]Subs. 2(3) and s. 253.

However, a non-resident enterprise of a country with which Canada has a bilateral tax treaty is taxable only if it carries on business in Canada through a "permanent establishment". Thus, the threshold test for determining liability of a non-resident from a treaty country is higher than the simple test of carrying on business in Canada. To be liable for Canadian tax, the non-resident must be carrying on business *through a permanent establishment* in Canada. A "permanent establishment" provides sufficient taxable nexus for source taxation of non-resident corporations.

The term "permanent establishment" is a tax treaty concept. Tax treaties typically provide that a "permanent establishment" means a ". . . *fixed* place of business in which the business of the enterprise is wholly or partly carried on."[59] But what does this mean? A fixed place implies more than mere formal presence in a country. In *Consolidated Premium Iron Ores, Re*, for example, the United States Tax Court outlined some of the considerations:[60]

> The term "permanent establishment", normally interpreted, suggests something more substantial than a licence, a letterhead and isolated activities. It implies the existence of an office, staffed and capable of carrying on the day-to-day business of the corporation and its use for such purpose, or it suggests the existence of a plant or facilities equipped to carry on the ordinary routine of such business activity. The descriptive word "permanent" in the characterization "permanent establishment" is vital in analysing the treaty provisions. . . . It indicates permanence and stability.

Thus, in determining whether a corporation has "an office" in a particular place, one traditionally looked at:

- Presence of permanent physical premises;
- Presence of directors or employees;
- Bank accounts and books of account;
- Telephone listings; and
- Employees or agents established with the general authority to contract for the taxpayer in that jurisdiction.

However, the U.S. Tax Court decided *Consolidated Premium Iron Ores* in 1957 before the advent of the Internet. It remains to be seen whether the tests in the decision are entirely relevant in the context of electronic commerce.

---

[59]Article 5, OECD Model Convention.

[60]*Consolidated Premium Iron Ores, Re* (1957), 28 T.C. 127 at 152; affirmed S. (2d) 230 (6th Circuit, 1959).

d) — Treaty Shopping

Corporate taxpayers can quite easily arrange their affairs to take advantage of the rules that determine residence by virtue of specific statutory and treaty provisions.[61] A corporation can be incorporated in a country (for example, the United States) solely to locate its residence in that jurisdiction. This might allow the corporation to take advantage of U.S. bilateral tax treaties that it might not otherwise be able to invoke. There is increasing concern in the international community that treaties should restrain tax planning motivated solely by tax avoidance through treaty shopping. There is little doubt that the trend in international communities is towards placing greater restrictions on the "improper" use of tax treaties. We see statutory provisions (for example, GAAR[62]) restricting the application of the *Westminster*[63] principle in international planning. We are also seeing specific restrictions appearing in bilateral tax treaties that are intended to curtail tax avoidance. Article XXIX(A) of the *Canada-U.S. Treaty*, for example, limits the benefits of the treaty to "qualifying persons", a phrase that the Treaty defines restrictively. The Article also allows the authorities to deny the benefits of the Treaty where taxpayers use it in an abusive manner.

The Commentary on Article 1 of the *OECD Model Convention* considers the improper use of bilateral tax conventions:

> True, taxpayers have the possibility, double tax conventions being left aside, to exploit the differences in tax levels as between States and the tax advantages provided by various countries' taxation laws, but it is for the States concerned to adopt provisions in their domestic laws to counter possible manoeuvres. Such States will then wish, in their bilateral double taxation conventions, to preserve the application of provisions of this kind contained in their domestic laws. . . . For example, if a person . . . acted through a legal entity created in a State essentially to obtain treaty benefits which would not be available directly to such person. Another case would be one of an individual having in a Contracting State both his permanent home and all his economic interests, including a substantial participation in a company of that State, and who, essentially in order to sell the participation and escape taxation in that State on the capital gains from the alienation . . . transferred his permanent home to the other Contracting State, where such gains were subject to little or no tax. . . . It may be appropriate for Contracting States to agree in bilateral negotiations that any relief from tax should not apply in certain cases, or to agree that the application of the provisions of domestic laws against tax avoidance should not be affected by the Convention.

The Commentary goes on to discuss various approaches that member countries may consider in combatting the problem of tax avoidance through, for example, the use of conduit companies. One approach is to use "look-through" provisions to disallow treaty benefits to

---

[61]*MIL (Investments) S.A. v. R.*, [2006] 5 C.T.C. 2552, 2006 D.T.C. 3307 (Eng.) (T.C.C. [General Procedure]); affirmed [2007] 4 C.T.C. 235 (F.C.A.).

[62]S. 245.

[63]*Inland Revenue Commissioners v. Duke of Westminster*, [1936] A.C. 1 (H.L.) (taxpayer entitled to order affairs so as to minimize tax payable).

corporations that are not owned, directly or indirectly, by of the country in which the corporation is a resident. The Commentary suggests the following wording for such a provision:

> A company which is a resident of a Contracting State shall not be entitled to relief from taxation under this Convention with respect to any item of income, gains or profits unless it is neither owned nor controlled directly or through one or more companies, wherever resident, by persons who are not of the first-mentioned State.

The use of such provisions in Canadian bilateral tax treaties would prevent third party countries from incorporating in Canada in order to take advantage of Canada's treaty network with other countries. Similar anti-treaty shopping provisions have been negotiated by the United States in all of its recent treaties.[64]

Canada's anti-treaty shopping rules vary in scope. Article 27(3) of the *Canada-Mexico Income Tax Convention* (1991), for example, states:[65]

> The Convention shall not apply to any company, trust or partnership that is a resident of a Contracting State and is beneficially owned or controlled directly or indirectly by one or more persons who are not of that State, if the amount of the tax imposed on the income or capital of the company, trust or partnership by that State is substantially lower than the amount that would be imposed by the State if all of the shares of the capital stock of the company or all of the interests in the trust or partnership, as the case may be, were beneficially owned by one or more individuals who were of that State.

In other cases, Canada's treaties state that treaty benefits may not apply to certain corporations established in particular jurisdictions. Article XXX(3) of the *Canada-Barbados Income Tax Agreement*,[66] for example, states that it ". . . shall not apply to companies entitled to any special tax benefit under the Barbados *International Business Companies (Exemption from Income Tax) Act* . . . or to companies entitled to any special tax benefits under any similar law enacted by Barbados in addition to or in place of that law.".

---

[64]See, for example, Article 28 of the *U.S.-Germany Treaty* and Article 17 of the *U.S.-Mexico Treaty*.

[65]Article 27(3), *Canada-Mexico Income Tax Convention*, 8 April 1991, [1992] Can. T.S. No. 15.

[66]*Canada-Barbados Income Tax Agreement*, 22 January 1980, [1980] Can. T.S. No. 29.

Framework for Analysis of Residence

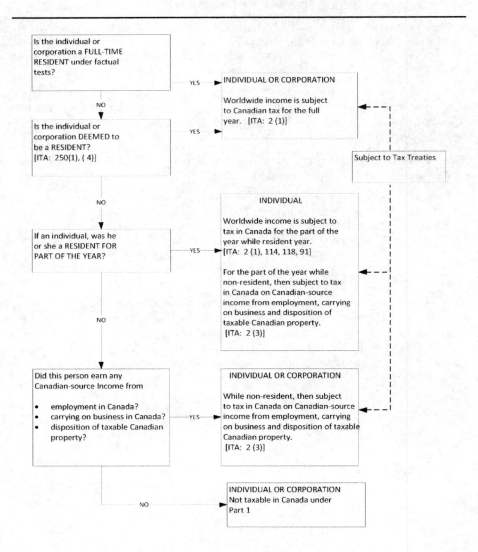

e) — Deemed Non-Resident By Treaty

A person may be a resident in Canada, but also be deemed to be resident in another country by virtue of the "tie-breaker" rules in a treaty. For example, a corporation may be incorporated in Canada and, hence, deemed to be resident in Canada. The corporation may also be resident in another country because its mind and management is in that country (see, for example, Article 4(3) of the Canada — U.K. Tax Convention).

In these circumstances, the corporation might, absent subsection 250(5), escape paying Part I tax in Canada and also not be subject to withholding tax under Part XIII of the *Act*. Subsection 250(5), which is essentially an anti-avoidance rule, would deem the corporation to be a non-resident of Canada and subject to withholding tax.

IV. — Trusts

A trust is a legal relationship that arises when a person (the trustee) is compelled by law to hold property for the benefit of some other person (the beneficiary). The property is to be held in such a manner that the real benefit of the property accrues to the beneficiary, not the trustee.

A trust is *not* a separate legal entity in private law. For tax purposes, however, a trust is taxable as a separate person.[67] The residence of a trust for tax purposes is a question of fact determined according to the common law rules applicable to individuals.

Because of the unique legal character of trusts, determining a trust's residence has been a troublesome issue in Canadian tax law. The conventional view was that the residence of a trust followed the residence of its trustees, regardless of their active involvement in managing the trust. The CRA acquiesced in this approach for nearly thirty years. This led to taxpayers gaming the system by emphasizing form over substance and creating offshore trusts in friendly jurisdictions under the control of nominal trustees. The rule allowed accounting firms to set up factories to create offshore trusts that they administered. Barbados, in particular, is a popular location because of its generous treaty with Canada.

The fiscal landscape changed with the Supreme Court's decision in *Fundy Settlement*,[68] which involved a non-resident individual in the Caribbean settling an irrevocable trust for beneficiaries resident in Canada. An accounting firm's corporation purported to manage the trust in Barbados. When the trust disposed of shares that it owned in two Ontario corporations for more than $450 million, the purchaser prudently remitted $152 million to the Minister of National Revenue as withholding tax on account of Canadian capital gains realized by the trusts on the sale of shares. The trustee sought return of the withheld amount based on an exemption from capital gains tax in the *Canada-Barbados Tax Treaty*, under which tax is payable only in the country in which the seller is resident. The trustee claimed that because it was resident in Barbados, the trusts were also resident in Barbados.

---

[67]Subs. 104(2).

[68]*Garron Family Trust (Trustee of) v. R.*, 2012 SCC 14, [2012] 3 C.T.C. 265 (S.C.C.).

The trial judge found that the Barbados corporate trustee, an entity owned by an accounting firm, was selected merely to provide administrative services.[69] Its role was to execute documents as required. It was generally not expected that the corporate trustee would have responsibility for decision-making beyond that. Although the accounting firm had significant expertise in accounting and tax matters, it was questionable whether they had expertise in managing trust assets. The beneficiaries of the trust exercised actual management and control in Canada. Hence, the trust was resident in Canada for tax purposes. The Supreme Court upheld the trial judge. As with corporations, the residence of a trust is determined by the principle that it resides where it carries on its real business and is actually controlled and managed.

Thus, a trust resides where its trustee resides only if the trustee is also the mind and management of the trust.[70] Where a trust has more than one trustee, it is resident where a majority of its trustees reside if the trust instrument permits majority decisions on all matters within the discretion of the trustees and the trustees actually control and manage the trust.[71] Under the mind and management test, a trust may have dual residence if the duties of the trustees are split between them and the trust allows for majority decisions. However, this proposition has not been tested.

In the event that a trust has multiple trustees, some of whom are individuals and others corporations, one must determine the residence of each of the trustees according to the common law and statutory rules. For example, we might determine the individual trustee's factual residence according to the common law tests and the residence of a corporate trustee by reference to its place of incorporation. The determination of a trust's residence is more complicated if its trustees reside in different jurisdictions, each with bilateral tax treaties with Canada.

---

[69]2009 TCC 450, [2010] 2 C.T.C. 2346 (T.C.C. [General Procedure]); affirmed 2010 FCA 309, [2011] 2 C.T.C. 7, 411 N.R. 125 (F.C.A.).

[70]*McLeod v. Canada (Minister of Customs & Excise)*, [1917-27] C.T.C. 290, 1 D.T.C. 85 (S.C.C.) (taxation of accumulated income in hands of trustee); *Royal Trust Co. v. Minister of National Revenue*, [1928-34] C.T.C. 74, 1 D.T.C. 217 (Can. Ex. Ct.) (trust with non-resident beneficiaries but resident trustee taxable); *Holden v. Minister of National Revenue*, [1928-34] C.T.C. 127, 1 D.T.C. 234 (S.C.C.); varied on other grounds [1928-34] C.T.C. 129, 1 D.T.C. 243 (Canada P.C.) (trust taxed on undistributed income whether beneficiaries resident or not); *Williams v. Singer*, [1921] 1 A.C. 65 (H.L.) (trust not taxed on foreign dividends received for non-resident beneficiary); *I.R.C. v. Gull*, [1937] 4 All E.R. 290 (English charitable trust exempt where one trustee non-resident).

[71]*Thibodeau Family Trust (Trustee of) v. R.*, [1978] C.T.C. 539, 78 D.T.C. 6376 (Fed. T.D.); see also IT-447, "Residence of a Trust or Estate" (May 30, 1980).

V. — Partnerships

A partnership is the relationship that subsists between persons carrying on business in common with a view to profit.[72] The liability of partners for partnerships may be unlimited (general partnerships) or limited (limited liability partnerships). Whether liability is limited or unlimited, a partnership is *not* a separate legal entity. For tax purposes, however, partnership income is calculated *as if* the partnership were a separate person.[73] A partnership's income is calculated as if the partnership was an entity, and the income is then allocated to the partners according to the terms of their agreement. Thus, a partnership is a conduit, and its income flows through to the partners. Individual partners are taxed as individuals; corporate partners are taxed as corporations.

A "Canadian partnership" is a partnership in which all the members are resident in Canada.[74]

VI. — Provincial Residence

Canadians are liable for federal income tax on their worldwide income. In addition to federal tax, however, a Canadian resident may also be liable for provincial tax. Provincial income tax liability is generally calculated in a way similar to that of federal tax liability.

For the purpose of determining provincial income tax liability, an individual resides in a province throughout the taxation year if he or she resides in the province on December 31 of the year. For example, an individual who emigrates from Ontario to Alberta on December 30 is taxable on his or her income for the entire year in Alberta. This rule, although somewhat imperfect in its technical accuracy, is easy and convenient for individuals to apply and for the provinces to administer. Thus, the rule trades off a minor revenue loss for the province from which the individual emigrates in exchange for administrative simplicity and certainty.

In the case of corporations, the calculation of provincial tax is more complex. A corporation must allocate its Canadian source income to each of the provinces in which it maintains a permanent establishment.[75] The allocation is made in accordance with a formula based on the proportion of revenue and payroll attributable to a province.

---

[72]*Partnerships Act*, R.S.O. 1990, c. P.5, s. 2.

[73]Para. 96(1)(a).

[74]Subs. 102(1).

[75]S. 124; *Income Tax Regulations*, C.R.C., c. 945, s. 400.

VII. — Non-Residents

Non-residents are taxable in Canada only on their Canadian-source income. Thus, Canada exercises source or territorial jurisdiction over non-residents who earn income in Canada. There are two broad categories of Canadian-source income — active and passive. Active income is taxable under Part I of the Act; passive income is subject to withholding tax under Part XIII.

A non-resident person has active Canadian source income if he or she:

- was employed in Canada;

- carried on business in Canada; or

- disposed of taxable Canadian property

at any time either in the current year or in a previous year.

An individual is considered to be employed in Canada if he or she performs the duties of an office or employment in Canada. This rule applies whether or not the individual's employer resides in Canada.

A non-resident person carries on business in Canada if he or she engages in any business activity, solicits orders, or offers anything for sale in Canada.[76] Subsection 248(1) defines a "business" to include a profession, calling, trade, manufacture or undertaking of any kind whatever, and an adventure or concern in the nature of trade.

Taxable Canadian property includes real property in Canada, shares of resident Canadian corporations (other than most public corporations), and capital property used in carrying on a business in Canada.[77]

The liability of a non-resident person for Canadian income tax also depends upon whether the taxpayer resides in a country with which Canada has a tax treaty. A bilateral tax treaty can modify the scope of a non-resident's liability for Canadian tax.[78] The general treaty rule is that business profits earned by a non-resident in Canada are taxable only if the non-resident has a "permanent establishment" in Canada and the profits are attributable to the establishment. A "permanent establishment" (PE) means a ". . . fixed place of business in which the business of the enterprise is wholly or partly carried on."[79]

A PE requires a degree of permanence and stability to the place of business in Canada. The effect of this rule is that the threshold for determining a non-resident's liability for Canadian

---

[76] S. 253.

[77] Subs. 248(1) "taxable Canadian property".

[78] Subs. 2(3).

[79] See, for example, Art. 5, s. 1 of the *OECD Model Convention*.

income tax on business profits is higher in the case of the countries with which Canada has a tax treaty than it is for non-residents from non-treaty countries.

A non-resident who earns passive Canadian-source income (for example, dividends, interest, or royalties) is liable for Canadian withholding tax under Part XIII of the Act. The general rate of withholding tax is 25 percent. This rate is reduced, however, in Canada's tax treaties. There is no withholding on interest income under the *Canada-U.S. Treaty*.

VIII. — Exempt Persons

The Act exempts certain persons from tax under Part I of the Act:[80]

- Persons holding diplomatic and quasi-diplomatic positions in Canada, members of their families and their servants;

- Municipal authorities;

- Corporations owned by the Crown;

- Registered charities;

- Labour organizations;

- Non-profit clubs, societies or associations ("NPOs");[81]

- Prescribed small business investment corporations;[82]

- Registered pension funds and trusts;

- Trusts created for:

  - Employee profit-sharing plans;

  - Registered supplementary unemployment benefit plans;

  - Registered retirement savings and income plans;

  - Deferred profit-sharing plans; and

  - Registered education savings plans;

- Retirement compensation arrangements.

---

[80]S. 149. The persons listed in this section are exempt from Part I tax. Subs. 227(14) extends the exemption for taxes under other parts to corporations exempt under s. 149.

[81]An election by an NPO for the purposes of GST legislation does not, in and of itself, adversely affect its tax-exempt status for income tax purposes: Technical Interpretation (August 27, 1990), CRA.

[82]Para. 149(1)(o.3); Reg. 5101(1).

The rationale for exempting the above persons varies. Some are exempt under international law (diplomats); others for social policy (charities); others for political reasons (labour organizations); and others to facilitate retirement planning (pensions, RRSPs, etc.).

IX. — Aboriginals

Aboriginals are subject to all of the responsibilities of Canadian citizens except for those excluded by treaties or the *Indian Act*.[83] Thus, aboriginals resident in Canada are liable for taxes on their worldwide income unless they are specifically exempted from taxation. (Note: The Federal statute is entitled the *Indian Act* and refers to aboriginals as Indians. Hence, the terminology used in this section.)

The tax status of Aboriginals is determined for the most part by two statutes: the *Indian Act*[84] and the *Income Tax Act*. The principal provision is section 87 of the *Indian Act*, which provides as follows:

> Notwithstanding any other Act of the Parliament of Canada or any Act of the legislature of a province . . . the following property is exempt from taxation, namely:
>
> > (a) the interest of an Indian or a band in reserve or surrendered lands; and
> >
> > (b) the personal property of an Indian or band situated on a reserve; and no Indian or band is subject to taxation in respect of the ownership, occupation, possession, or use of any property mentioned in paragraph (a) or (b) or is otherwise subject to taxation in respect of any such property. . . .

Paragraph 81(1)(a), of the *Income Tax Act* exempts from taxation "an amount that is declared to be exempt from income tax by any other enactment of the Parliament of Canada." The exemption from taxation is available only if:

- The taxpayer claiming the exemption qualifies as an "Indian or a band";

- The property is either an interest in a reserve or surrendered lands or is personal property; and

- The property is *situated* on a reserve.

Subsection 90(1) of the *Indian Act* deems to be situated on a reserve:

> For the purposes of ss. 87 and 89, personal property that was
>
> > (a) purchased by Her Majesty with Indian monies or monies appropriated by Parliament for the use and benefit of Indians or bands, or

---

[83]*Nowegijick v. R.*, [1983] 1 S.C.R. 29, [1983] C.T.C. 20, 83 D.T.C. 5041 (S.C.C.).

[84]*Indian Act*, R.S.C. 1985, c. I-5.

(b) given to Indians or to a band under a treaty or agreement between a band and Her Majesty,

shall be deemed always to be situated on a reserve.

The exemption of Aboriginals from taxation is rooted in Canadian history and has no connection whatsoever with income tax policy. Section 87 of the *Indian Act* is more than sufficient authority for the exemption ("Notwithstanding any other Act of the Parliament of Canada. . . ."). It does not need to be bolstered by section 81 of the *Income Tax Act*.

The original purposes of the exemptions from tax were to preserve the entitlement of Aboriginals to their reserve lands and to ensure that property on their lands is not eroded through taxation or seizure.[85] The exemption is a recognition by the Crown, as expressed in the *Royal Proclamation of 1763*, that Aboriginals should not be dispossessed of their property that they hold *qua* Indians. The exemption was intended to shield Aboriginals from the white man, who might otherwise be inclined to dispossess Aboriginals of their land base and personal property on their reserves.

The exemption clearly violates the principle of horizontal equity that similarly situated taxpayers should pay similar amounts of tax. Since, however, the exemption is a provision of the *Indian Act*, we should interpret it in the context and policy of that statute, rather than in terms of tax policy. Hence, the exemption must be read in the light of Canadian history, British colonial philosophy, and the intended purposes of protection of Aboriginal reserve lands and personal property situated on such lands.

X. — Conclusion

Canadian taxable jurisdiction depends upon a variety of legal, economic, international, and political concepts. Clearly, the concept of residence as the primary determinant of taxable nexus can create problems of double taxation of income. We use residence as the primary basis of asserting jurisdiction to tax, and source of income as the secondary basis. However, we elaborate the concept of residence in various provisions of the Act and in bilateral tax treaties for different entities and relationships. Thus, we answer the question — who should be taxable? — in a variety of ways, depending upon the nature of the particular entity or relationship, its economic links with Canada, international trade and treaty considerations, and mindful of principles of fairness and economic efficiency.

---

[85]*Mitchell v. Sandy Bay Indian Band*, [1990] 2 S.C.R. 85 (S.C.C.).

Selected Bibliography to Chapter 3

General

Bale, "The Basis of Taxation", in *Canadian Taxation*, Hansen, Krishna and Rendall, eds., (Toronto: Richard De Boo, 1981).

McGregor, Gwyneth, "Deemed Residence" (1974) 22 Can. Tax J. 381.

Residence — Individuals

Halpern, Jack V., "Residence or Domicile: A State of Mind" (1993) 41 Can. Tax J. 129.

Hansen, "Individual Residence", in *Proceedings of 29th Tax Conf.* 682 (Can. Tax Foundation, 1977).

Jackel, Monte A., "Canadian/U.S. Treaty: Dual Status Aliens Torn Between Two Nations" (March 1989) 47 Advocate 269.

McGregor, "Deemed Residence" (1974) 22 Can. Tax J. 381.

Sherbaniuk, D., et al., "Liability for Tax — Residence, Domicile or Citizenship?", in *Proceedings of 15th Tax Conf.* 325 (Can. Tax Foundation, 1963).

Smart, P. St.J., "Ordinarily Resident" (January 1989) 38 Int. & Comp. L. Q. 175.

Smith, "What Price Residence?" (1961) 9 Can. Tax J. 381.

Wosner, "Ordinary Residence, The Law and Practice" (1983) Br. Tax Rev. 347.

Residence — Corporations

Farnsworth, The Residence and Domicile of Corporations (London: Butterworth, 1939).

Flannigan, Robert, "Corporate Residence at Common Law" (1990) 5 Securities and Corporate Regulation Rev. 42.

Ilersic, "Tax Havens and Residence" (1982) 30 Can. Tax J. 52.

Kaufman, "Fiscal Residence of Corporations in Canada" (1984) 14 R.D.U.S. 511.

Lanthier, Allan R., "Corporate Immigration, Emigration and Continuance" (1993) Corp. Mgmt. Tax Conf. 4:1.

Pyrcz, "Corporate Residence" (1973) 21 Can. Tax J. 374.

Raizenne, Robert, "Corporate Residence, Immigration and Emigration", in *Special Seminar on International Tax Issues 1993* (Toronto: Carswell, 1994).

Sarna, "Federal Continued Corporations and the Deemed-Resident Provisions of subsection 250(4) of the *Income Tax Act*" (1979) McGill L.J. 111.

Ward, "Corporate Residence as a Tax Factor", *Corporate Management Tax Conf.* 3 (Can. Tax Foundation, 1961).

Residence — Trusts

Cooper, "Canadian Resident Inter Vivos Trusts with Nonresident Beneficiaries" (1982) 30 Can. Tax J. 422.

Green, "The Residence of Trusts for Income Tax Purposes" (1973) 21 Can. Tax J. 217.

Residence — Partnerships

Witterick, Robert G., "The Partnership as a Modern Business Vehicle", in *Proceedings of 41st Tax Conf.* 21:1 (Can. Tax Foundation, 1989).

Chapter 4 — The Meaning of Income

Table of Contents

Table of Contents

A word is not a crystal; transparent and unchanged, it is the skin of a living thought and may vary in colour and content according to the circumstances and the time in which it is used.

(Justice Holmes in *Towne v. Eisner*, 245 U.S. 418 and 425, 38 S.Ct. 158 and 159, 62 L.Ed. 372 and 376)

I. — Introduction

The *Income Tax Act* taxes income. Hence, we must distinguish income from other potential taxable bases such as capital, wealth, and consumption. The accurate measurement of income determines the size of the base, the structure of the tax system, and its fairness.

In this chapter we address three questions:

1. What is income?

2. When do we recognize income? and

3. What is the source of the income?

The Act does not define "income" for tax purposes. Although the Act sometimes speaks of what we include in or exclude from income, it neither identifies nor describes the legal characteristics of income.[1] Thus, the initial step in determining whether a receipt is taxable as *income* is to determine its nature and character. We include a receipt in the taxable base if it is income *unless*, even though of an income nature, the Act specifically excludes it. Section 81 excludes a long list of items from income.[2]

The following figure presents an overview of the Act's characterization of receipts into taxable and non-taxable components.

---

[1]For example, paragraph 6(1)(a) specifies that the value of board and lodging is *included* in employment income; section 7 *deems* certain stock option benefits to be employment income; subsection 6(9) *deems* imputed interest from an interest-free loan to be income, etc.

[2]Subsection 81(1).

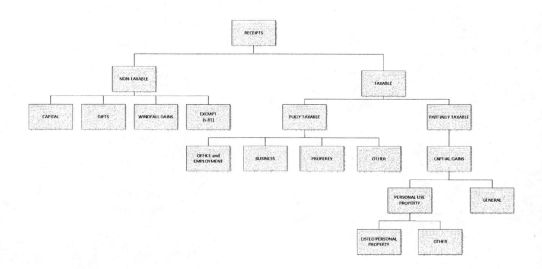

The seemingly simple task of identifying and characterizing receipts creates considerable difficulty. For example: suppose an employer gives his or her employee $1,000 at Christmas. Is the $1,000 income or a gift to the employee? The distinction is crucial to the employee who will be subject to tax if the $1,000 is remuneration, but will not be taxable if it is a gift. What if the employer gives his employee $25,000? We can determine taxability only after we draw the line between remuneration and gifts. As we shall see, tax law involves a lot of lines that distinguish between forms and sources of income and expenses. These distinctions make tax law complex because they induce behavioral responses in taxpayers to minimize their taxes.

II. — Concepts of Income

OVERVIEW OF CONCEPTS OF INCOME

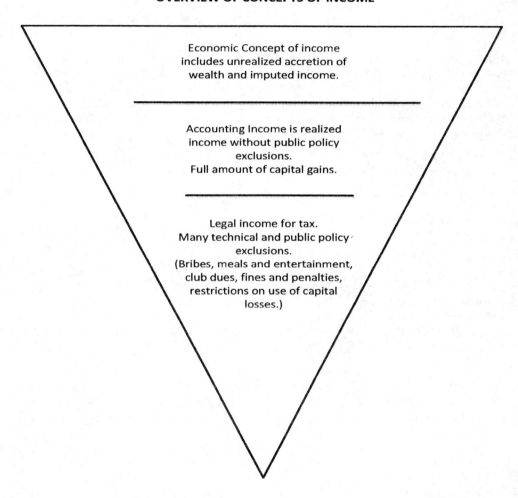

Economic Concept of income includes unrealized accretion of wealth and imputed income.

Accounting Income is realized income without public policy exclusions.
Full amount of capital gains.

Legal income for tax.
Many technical and public policy exclusions.
(Bribes, meals and entertainment, club dues, fines and penalties, restrictions on use of capital losses.)

The term "income" literally means "incoming" or "what comes in" to a person. The literal meaning is not very helpful because the "incoming" may be either capital or income. However, it is useful to start with the generic concept of the term before we look at the different types of income and their sources.

Webster's Dictionary defines "income" as "a gain which proceeds from labour, business, property, or capital of any kind, as the produce of a farm, rent of houses, proceeds of professional business, the profits of commerce, or of occupation, or the interest of money or stock in funds."

The *Oxford Dictionary* describes income as "periodical (usually annual) receipts from one's business, lands, work, investments, etc."

Thus, in many situations, income is a recurring gain derived from labour or capital. These definitions, which are useful starting points, provide an intuitive response that income represents an increment ("incoming") to wealth over a period of time. This view was influential in the early thinking on the nature of income. In *Eisner v. Macomber*,[3] for example, the U.S. Supreme Court said that "income may be defined as the gain derived from labour, from capital, or from both combined."

Thirty five years later, the U.S. Supreme Court broadened the concept of income to include "realized accession to wealth over which the taxpayer has complete dominion."[4]

A. — The Economic Concept

The concept of accession to wealth has its origins in economic thought. Economists use the term "income" to mean net *accretion* of wealth, or increase in economic power, during a period of time. Two tax theorists, Haig and Simons, formulated the most famous economic definition of income. Robert M. Haig was a professor at Columbia University; H.C. Simons a professor of economics at the University of Chicago. Working independently in the 1920s and the 1930s, they developed what has become the standard economic definition of income as "the algebraic sum of (1) the market value of rights exercised in consumption and (2) the change in the value of the store of property rights between the beginning and end of the period in question."[5]

Thus, Haig-Simons saw income as the accretion in the *value* of assets on hand at the end of the period over the *value* of assets on hand at the beginning of the period after adjustments for the value of goods consumed. The concept refers to the increment or "incoming" in the

---

[3]*Eisner v. Macomber* (1920), 252 U.S. 189.

[4]*CIR v. Glenshaw Glass Company*, 348 U.S. 426 (1955) (punitive two-thirds portion of treble damage anti-trust award taxable as income. Stock dividend did not constitute a realized gain, but was merely a change of form of stockholder's capital investment.)

[5]In Haig's language, income is "the increase or accretion in one's power to satisfy his wants in a given period in so far as that power consists of (a) money itself or, (b) anything susceptible of valuation in terms of money." Simons equates personal income with the algebraic sum of consumption and change in net worth. See "The Concept of Income C Economic and Legal Aspects" in R.M. Haig (ed.), *The Federal Income Tax* (New York, 1921).

value of wealth over time. For example, if an individual begins a year with $1,000, spends $20,000 on personal expenditures during the year and has $5,000 in net assets at the end of the year, his or her income for the year would be $24,000.

We emphasize two aspects of the Haig-Simons formulation of income: (1) the formula does not distinguish between sources of income; and (2) net *accretion* of wealth includes unrealized gains, imputed income, and even increases in human capital resulting from education or acquired skills.[6] Thus, the Haig-Simons concept of income is broad, all inclusive, and without preferences.

Although the Haig-Simons formulation of income may appear bizarre to some, it is generally accepted as gospel among tax theorists and used extensively by economists in the development of tax policy. To be sure, the definition is politically explosive. For example, few politicians would dare to embrace the theory that one should tax imputed income from owner-occupied housing or housework.

Nevertheless, tax policymakers view the Haig-Simons formula as the ideal to which we should aspire. Hence, they regard any deviation from the definition as inherently unjustifiable. Indeed, the Department of Finance publishes these deviations from the norm as "tax expenditures". The debate intensifies when we come to discuss the capital gains preference that excludes one-half of such gains from income.

There are also other definitions of "income". For example:

- R. Haig, "The Concept of Income," in *The Federal Income Tax* 1, 7 (Columbia University, 1921): "Income is the money value of the net accretion to one's economic power between two points of time."

- C. Plehn, "Income as Recurrent, Consumable Receipts," 14 Amer. Econ. Rev. 1, 5 (1924): "Income is essentially wealth available for recurrent consumption, recurrently (or periodically) received. Its three essential characteristics are: receipt, recurrence and expendability."

- W. Hewett, *The Definition of Income and its Application in Federal Taxation*, (1925), pp. 22-23: "Net individual income is the flow of commodities and services accruing to an individual through a period of time and available for disposition after deducting the necessary cost of acquisition."

- R. Posner, *Economic Analysis of Law*, (1973), pp. 231-32: "The broadest definition of income would be all pecuniary and non-pecuniary receipts, including leisure and gifts."

---

[6]We speak of imputed income as the benefit that we derive from consumption or use of our own assets.

- Professor Irving Fisher, of Yale, considered income to be "a flow of benefits during a period of time."[7]

- Professor Ely, of Wisconsin, distinguished between wealth and income:[8] "Wealth refers to the stock of goods on hand at a particular time. Real income, on the other hand, has reference to the satisfaction we derive from the use of material things or personal services during a period of time."

- Sir John Hicks, the Oxford economist and Nobel laureate, defined income as the maximum amount an individual could spend in a period and still expect to be *as well off* at the end of the period as he or she had been at the beginning.

The common feature of these definitions is that they are comprehensive and inclusive, characteristics that the Carter Commission adopted in its report on the Canadian tax system:[9]

> We are completely persuaded that taxes should be allocated according to the changes in the economic power of individuals and families. If a man obtains increased command over goods and services for his personal satisfaction, we do not believe it matters, from the point of view of taxation, whether he earned it through working, made it through operating a business, received it because he held property, made it by selling property, or was given it by a relative. Nor do we believe it matters whether the increased command over goods and services was in cash or in kind. Nor do we believe it matters whether the increase in economic power was expected or unexpected, whether it was a unique or recurrent event, whether the man suffered to get the increase in economic power, or it fell in his lap without effort.

However, the implementation of abstract concepts (such as benefits, utilities, and satisfactions) into a working formula that provides a simple and accurate measure of income is difficult in practice. The concept of income for tax purposes must be one that we can administer at a reasonable cost. As Professor Taussig, of Harvard, said:[10]

> . . . for almost all purposes of economic study, it is best to content ourselves with a statement, and an attempt at measurement, in terms not of utility but of money income. . . . The reason

---

[7]Fisher, Irving, *Elementary Principles of Economics* (New York: The MacMillan Company, 1911) at 34.

[8]Ely, *Outlines of Economics* (New York: The MacMillan Company, 1908) at 98. See also Professor Alfred Marshall, of Cambridge, *Elements of Economics of Industry* (London: MacMillan, 1901) at 51:

> . . . a woman who makes her own clothes, or a man who digs in his own garden or repairs his own house, is earning income just as would the dressmaker, gardener, or carpenter who might be hired to do the work. . . . For scientific purpose, it would be best if the word income when occurring alone should always mean total real income.

[9]*Report of the Royal Commission on Taxation* (Ottawa: Queen's Printer, 1966) (Chair: K.M. Carter), vol. 1, at 9; see also Simons, *Personal Income Taxation: The Definition of Income as a Problem of Fiscal Policy* (Chicago: University of Chicago Press, 1938).

[10]Taussig, *Principles of Economics*, Vol. X (New York: The MacMillan Company, 1916) at 134.

for this rejection of a principle which is in itself sound lies in the conclusion . . . regarding total utility and consumer's surplus: they cannot be measured.

The Haig-Simons formulation of income as the net accretion of wealth between two points in time would be difficult and expensive to administer. The cost, for example, of measuring the "value" of assets at the end of every fiscal year would be prohibitive. In determining whether a taxpayer is "as well off" at the end of a year as he or she was at its beginning, would one measure income in terms of "real" or nominal dollars? Even assuming that it is possible to track one's expenditures accurately for a given period, the periodic valuation of assets would present great difficulties and, in some cases, create considerable uncertainty leading to disputes and litigation. The measurement of all forms of imputed income — for example, the value of a homeowner's vegetable garden — would be unworkable.

B. — The Legal Concept

Economic theory is helpful in understanding the concept of income, but does not provide an easy working formula. Since the *Income Tax Act* does not define "income", we rely on judicial decisions to formulate the basic concept.

Income in tax law is a measure of *gain*, but does not include the realized value of the *source* of the gain itself.[11] For example, if a taxpayer buys goods at a cost of $10 per unit and sells the goods for $30 per unit, his income is $20 per unit. He merely recovers his capital investment from the first $10 from the sale. The income tax is a tax on income and not a tax on capital or wealth.

In the absence of specific statutory rules, "income" means *net* income determined in accordance with ordinary commercial principles. In *Dominion Natural Gas*, for example:[12]

> The generally recognized rule as regards trade expenses is that a deduction is permissible when it is justifiable on business and accountancy principles, but this principle is subject to certain specific statutory provisions which prohibit the allowance of certain expenses as deductions in computing the net profit or gain to be assessed. To the extent that ordinary business and accountancy principles are not invaded by the statute, they prevail.

---

[11]This principle underlies the oft-quoted statement that income is the fruit only and never the tree; see e.g., *Straighten's Independence Ltd. v. Howbeit*, 213 U.S. 399; *Ryall v. Hoare* (1923), 8 Tax Cas. 521. This principle is modified by statutory provisions in certain circumstances; e.g., para. 12(1)(g) taxes as income any amounts paid that are calculated by reference to production, regardless of whether or not the payment actually represents an instalment of the sale price of the property.

[12]*Minister of National Revenue v. Dominion Natural Gas Co.*, [1940-41] C.T.C. 144, 1 D.T.C. 499-81 (Can. Ex. Ct.) at 147-48 [C.T.C.] and 499-83 D.T.C.]; reversed on facts [1940-41] C.T.C. 155, 1 D.T.C. 499-133 (S.C.C.).

Thus, even where the Act does not use the adjective "net" to qualify "income", we read the term as "net income".[13] For example, assume that an individual buys merchandise for $10 per unit and pays $1 per unit on account of freight to have the goods delivered to her business premises. The taxpayer then sells the goods for $30 per unit and pays shipping costs of $2 per unit. The taxpayer's *gross* revenue is $30 per unit, but her "income" for tax purposes is only $17 per unit — that is, the net *realized accretion* to the taxpayer's wealth. The taxpayer is entitled to recover his capital investment of $10 and expenses of $3 in calculating her gain.

a) — Characteristics of Income

Courts have developed a judicial concept of income for tax purposes, which the *Act* embellishes with statutory inclusions and exclusions based upon social, political, cultural and other considerations. The general characteristics of the judicial concept are that income involves:

  (i) flow of receipts;

  (ii) periodicity;

  (iii) ownership of the gain;

  (iv) receipt by the taxpayer;

  (v) a gain in money or convertible into monies worth; and

  (vi) realization of the gain.

i) — The Flow of Receipts

The legal concept of income has its origins in trust law, which distinguishes between income and capital. Income flows from the capital of a trust. The income and capital of a trust may belong to different persons. Capital belongs to the capital beneficiaries and the flow of gains from the capital belongs to income beneficiaries. For example, a parent may set up a trust created upon death (a testamentary trust) and provide that her children are to receive the capital assets of the trust, but that the surviving spouse is entitled to all of the income of the trust during his lifetime (a life interest). In this situation, the surviving spouse is the income beneficiary; the children are capital beneficiaries.

Tax law developed long after trust law. William Pitt, the Younger (Prime Minister at the age of 24) introduced income tax in Britain as a war measure to fight Napoleon in 1799. The tax

---

[13]See Chapter 7 "Business Income".

was repealed in 1802 upon the cessation of hostilities with France. By that time, trust law was already well developed.

ii) — Periodical Receipts

A common characteristic of the judicial concept of income is that it is usually recurring and regular. In contrast, capital receipts are usually not recurring. For example, payments on account of salary, wages, interest and royalties occur regularly and are easily identified as income. In other cases, however, the recurrence may be less frequent, but nevertheless have the character of income. For example, annual payments are periodic and, therefore, of an income nature. Payments may be considered periodic even if the interval between successive payments is longer than one year. This can be an important issue in alimony and support payments.[14]

iii) — Ownership of the Gain

For an amount to be considered as income in the hands of a taxpayer, the amount that the taxpayer received must belong to him or her. An amount that the taxpayer receives as an agent or conduit to be held on behalf of, or expended for, another person is not income. For example, a trust may pay an amount to a person who has the responsibility to expend the amount for an infant beneficiary. The receipt is not income to the agent.

iv) — Income in the Hands of the Taxpayer

In order to be taxable the amount that a taxpayer receives must be income in his or her hands. The character of a payment by the payor does not necessarily determine the nature of the payment to the payee. For example, a corporation may pay $20,000 to promote and advertise its cosmetic product by making gifts to a target audience. The $20,000 is not income in the hands of the payee even though the corporation may deduct the expense on account of promotion and advertising.

v) — Income Must be a Money Gain or Convertible into Money's Worth

A gain that a person receives that is not convertible into money or money's worth is not income under the judicial concept of income. In the classic decision of the House of Lords in *Tennant v. Smith*[15] the issue was whether the yearly value of the benefit of free residence in

---

[14]See subsection 56.1(4) "support amount" and subsection 60.1(4).

[15][1892] A.C. 150 (H.L.).

a house that the employee's bank conferred upon the taxpayer to the employee was income. The employee was required to occupy the residence that the bank provided while employed by the bank and he was not entitled to sublet the residence. The money that the employee saved from not renting his own home was not considered income as the employee did not actually receive any money or anything that was convertible into money. Thus, the receipt of a benefit that cannot be turned to pecuniary account is not income. Note, however, because of the decision in cases such as *Tennant v. Smith* the *Income Tax Act* specifically provides in paragraph 6(1)(a) that the value of board lodging and other benefits *of any kind whatever* that an employee receives or *enjoys* is taxable as income. As we shall see later, the issue comes down to who benefits from the supplied housing, the employer or the employee.

vi) — Income Must be a Realized Gain

The judicial concept of income recognizes only nominal legal gains and does not consider the economic value of the gain. For example, a taxpayer may deposit $1000 in his bank savings account and receive interest at five percent per year. At the end of the first year, he will receive $50 as interest. Assuming a three percent rate of inflation, his economic gain is only two percent or $20. Nevertheless, the taxpayer is taxable on his nominal ($50) gain for the year.

On the flipside, the judicial concept of income has a narrow view of "gain". In *Hochstrasser (Inspector of Taxes) v. Mayes*,[16] for example, the taxpayer was an employee who was transferred to another town by his employer. The employer paid the taxpayer's moving expenses and, under its housing scheme, agreed to reimburse the taxpayer for any loss that he might incur on the sale of his residence if he was transferred to another location. The taxpayer purchased a house at his new location and was transferred again three years later. The taxpayer sold his house at a loss and the employer reimbursed him his personal loss. The taxpayer used the payment to pay off his loans, but did not make a net gain. However, he did not suffer a loss. The House of Lords unanimously held that the amount was not taxable as income. Lord Denning said:

> My Lords, tried by the touchstone of common sense — which is, perhaps, rather a rash test to take in a revenue matter — I regard this as a plain case. No one coming fresh to it, untrammelled by cases, could regard this [amount] as a profit from employment. Mr. Mayes did not make a profit on the resale of the house. He made a loss. And even if he had made a profit, it would not have been taxable. How, then, can his loss be taxable simply because he has been indemnified against it? . . .

> Why, then, if this case is as plain as I think it is, how has it got so far as to reach your Lordships' House? Only, I suggest, because of a broad proposition the Crown advanced about "profits". This proposition was put forward as if it were a definition of what the law regards as the "profits" of employment. . . . I need hardly say, if there were available to your Lordships a

---

[16][1960] A.C. 376 (H.L.).

definition of "profits", it would be a pearl of great price. But I am afraid that this pearl turned out to be cultivated and not real. It was culled from the cases and not from the statute. It did not survive the critical examination of your Lordships. When subjected to close scrutiny, it was found to be studded with ambiguities and defaced by exceptions. It would, if accepted, put a greater burden on the taxpayer than ever the statute warrants, and it would introduce more confusion into a subject where enough already exists.

b) — Compensatory Payments

Compensatory payments pose special problems in distinguishing between income and capital. Under the judicial concept of income, payments that a taxpayer receives as compensation for a revenue asset are considered income; compensation for capital assets is considered capital. For example, if a person receives compensation for the breach of his employment contract, the severance amount is on account of income because it substitutes for his employment income. If, however, the taxpayer receives a payment for the destruction of his capital (for example payments under an insurance policy for the complete destruction of a building by fire), the amount is considered to be a replacement of capital. Hence, the first question is: What is the payment replacing? If the payment replaces income, it should be considered income. If it replaces capital, it should be considered capital. Thus, the compensation payment is characterized by the nature of the payment that it replaces or the hole that it fills.

A difficulty arises, however, where the compensatory payment in a lump sum merely substitutes a series of payments that were due to the taxpayer. In other words, the payment may be the net capitalized value of a series of periodic payments that are of an income nature. For example, the value of a rental building is the discounted net present value of its future cash flows from rentals. If the building is completely destroyed, the compensation paid in one lump sum should equal the discounted net present value of its future cash flows, which would have been rental income to the landlord. However, the courts consider compensation for the destruction of the entire capital capacity of an individual as a capital payment even though, mathematically speaking, the value of the capital asset is equal to the discounted net present value of future income flows from the property.

c) — Realization

We recognize income only when we realize or crystallize it in a market transaction, such as a sale, exchange or disposition of goods and services. Realization may be actual or deemed. In contrast, the economist refers to income as an "accretion" to wealth, regardless of whether the taxpayer realizes the increased value in a market transaction. For example, assume that an individual purchases shares at a price of $10 per share and the shares increase in value to $25 per share by the end of the year. Under the Haig-Simons concept of income, the individual's income for the year is $15 per share. This amount represents the net accretion in the *value* of the shares and, therefore, measures the increase in his or her wealth. For tax purposes, however, the taxpayer does not need to report any income until he or she sells, or is deemed to sell,[17] the shares and actually realize the gain.

However, there are some special statutory rules that deviate from the realization principle. For example, financial institutions must use unrealized changes — "mark-to-market" — from certain shares and debt to measure income.[18] These are, however, exceptions from the general requirement of realization.

The realization requirement is a compromise between the economic theory of income and the administrative feasibility of applying the theory in practice. Taxation on the basis of annual valuations to determine the net *accretion* of one's wealth would be financially inconvenient, create uncertainty, and cause disputes over valuations. Thus, for most purposes, we are content to tax only realized gains.

In effect, the realization requirement makes the income tax a tax on transactions, rather than a tax on income in the pure economic sense. As well, the realization principle creates problems, such as the bunching of income in the year of sale. A taxpayer who receives "bunched income" can be bumped up into a higher marginal tax bracket in the year that she realizes the investment. For example, assume that Jennifer buys shares for $10,000, which appreciate in value at 20 percent (compounded) per year for 5 years. When she sells the shares for approximately $25,000, she will be taxed on a gain of $15,000, which may put her into a higher tax bracket. In some circumstances (for example, death) the Act deems the realization of assets in order to trigger gains and prevent prolonged tax deferral.

The realization requirement raises two subsidiary questions: (1) when do we realize income? and (2) what are the consequences of not taxing income until we realize it?

Generally, we realize income when we complete a transaction, that is when we sell or dispose of an asset[19] or complete a service. For example, if Harry buys shares at a cost of $1,000 and the shares appreciate in value to $3,000, Harry generates economic income of $2,000 — the amount of the appreciation. On paper, Harry is $2,000 wealthier. For tax purposes, however, the gain is not taxable because he has not realized it. In contrast, if Jane purchases shares at a cost of $10,000 and the shares pay a dividend of $2,000, the dividend is taxable because Jane realizes it in cash. Thus, although both Harry and Jane are wealthier by $2,000, only Jane is taxable on her gain. Harry defers the tax until he disposes of the

---

[17]See, for example, subsection 70(5) (deemed disposition on death).

[18]Sections 142.2 to 142.6.

[19]See generally: Shaviro, "An Efficiency Analysis of Realization and Recognition Rules under the Federal Income Tax", 48 Tax L. Rev. 1 (1992); Strand, "Periodicity and Accretion Taxation: Norms and Implementation", 99 Yale L. J. 1817 (1990); Fellows, "A Comprehensive Attack on Tax Deferral", 88 Michigan Rev. 722 (1990); Shakow, "Taxation Without Realization: A Proposal for Accrual Taxation", 134 U. Pa. L. Rev. 1111 (1986).

appreciated shares. Thus, the tax is on the transaction and not on the economic gain. This is an important consideration in tax planning, where we seek to defer tax.

The realization rule trades off equity against administrative convenience. Although both Harry and Jane are equally able to pay, taxing Harry on his unrealized appreciation might cause him a cash flow problem. Of course, Harry could sell a portion of his shares to meet any tax obligation. This would work well with publicly traded shares. It might not be as easy, however, to realize their value in the absence of a public market. The problem of liquidity would be exacerbated if, for example, the asset was land instead of shares.

What are the consequences of the realization requirement in tax law? First, we see that realization converts the tax system from a tax on income to a tax on transactions. This affects the timing of the tax payable on the transaction. Thus, the realization requirement allows us to defer our tax liabilities and, apart from certain events such as death, we can generally control when we will recognize income from appreciated property. The value of the tax deferral depends upon the prevailing interest rate and the length of time that we delay realization.

From the treasury's perspective, tax deferral is a revenue loss. As between taxpayers who are similarly well off, the requirement allows some to delay paying taxes. However, tax law is a compromise between competing values; in this case, a compromise between administrative convenience and equity.

C. — Income by Source

Economic theory is not concerned with the source of income: net accretions of wealth are income, regardless of their source. Source is irrelevant as a measure of economic well-being. After all, a taxpayer's ability to pay depends not upon his or her source of income but the measure of his or her enrichment. Equity requires that we tax all gains equally, regardless of their source. The Canadian income tax system, however, relies solidly on the source concept. We calculate income from each source separately and aggregate income according to the rules applicable to that particular source.[20]

a) — Origin of the U.K. Source Doctrine[21]

Britain introduced its first income tax to finance its war against France. Prior to 1798, the English revenue system relied primarily on customs and excise duties. The medieval system of taxes on property was by then a very small proportion of general revenues. After the declaration of war with France in 1793, the British needed to increase their revenues to fight

---

[20]Section 3.

[21]See, generally, Edwin Robert Anderson Seligman, *The Income Tax: A Study of the History, Theory and Practice of Income*, The Lawbook Exchange Ltd. (1914).

their great struggle. Customs, excise, and stamp duties provided most of the revenues, which were increased and imposed on a wider range of produce — such as, tea stone and salt. In 1797, the system was further extended from carriages, servants, and horses to include taxes on hair powder, dogs, watches and clocks. However, none of these provided sufficient revenues to conduct the war.

In his budget speech of November 24, 1797, Pitt introduced a new scheme: "a general tax on persons possessed of property commensurate as far as practical with their means".[22] Even then, Pitt was concerned with tax avoidance and conceded that the "Assessed Taxes (on goods and property) are often eluded by men of large property who, by denying themselves many of the enjoyments of life, hoard up money and exclude themselves from assessment".[23]

On December 14, 1797, Pitt made a brilliant speech in defense of his proposed new tax bill. Mallet Du Pan, a contemporary observer, said:

> From the time that the deliberative assemblies have existed, I doubt whether any man ever heard a display of this nature, equally astonishing for its extent, it precision, and the talents of its author. It is not a speech spoken by the minister; it is a complete course of public economy; a work, and one of the finest works, upon practical and theoretical finance, that ever distinguished the pen of a philosopher and statesman.[24]

The Act was called *The Aid and Contribution Act*. It divided taxpayers into three categories, each to pay taxes at a progressively higher rate. The highest category included the wealthy taxpayers, who owned carriages, men-servants, horses and who, in Pitt's words, "paid on optional consumptions and luxuries."[25]

The next lower category included persons who had houses, windows, clocks, or watches. The lowest category comprised the poorest individuals, who paid taxes only on their lodgings or shops.

Here we also see the beginnings of the progressive income tax structure. The second category paid twice the taxes as the lowest category and the highest category paid five times as much as the lowest. The appropriate degree of progressivity was fiercely debated, as it is today.

The tax was not popular and there was rampant avoidance and evasion from the outset. Instead of the four and one-half million pounds sterling that it was supposed to yield, it actually brought in only two million pounds sterling. Pitt attributed this to "the difficulties

---

[22] The Speeches of the Right Honourable William Pitt in the House of Commons, Second Edition, London, 1808, Vol. II, page 353.

[23] Quoted in The Financial Statements of 1853, 1860–1863.

[24] *Ibid.*

[25] Pitt's Speeches Vol. II, page 348.

which the measure encountered from the shameful evasion, or rather the scandalous frauds by which its effects were counteracted."[26] An early lesson that higher taxes do not automatically and inevitably bring in more revenues.

On December 8, 1798, Pitt introduced another new scheme of taxation to prevent the frauds that he complained of with his earlier tax statute. He proposed to set aside the old system and impose a general tax upon the leading sources of income for the purpose of obtaining, by an efficient and comprehensive tax upon real ability, every advantage which flourishing and invigorating resources can confer upon national efforts.[27]

A direct tax on all income was novel for the times. Pitt maintained that all incomes, *from whatever source derived*, should be taxed, and be taxed alike. For example, defending the tax on government securities, which had been exempt from tax, he said:

> I should say to the stockholders, as one of the public, if you expect from the state the protection which is common to us all, you ought also to make the sacrifice which we are called upon to make. It is not peculiar to you, it does not belong to the quality of your income, but it is made general and required from all; you could not embark your capital in any other species of security in which it would not be subject to the same charge. I do not know what objection the stockholder could make to this appeal.[28]

Pitt's Bill was enacted into law on January 9, 1799, and became effective on April 5, which has remained Britain's budget day ever since. Here we also see the thread between Pitt's law and the proposals of the Carter Commission in 1967 that "a buck is a buck".

The Act was comprehensive and contained 124 sections, covering 152 pages (The *Canadian Income War Tax Act (1917)* was a mere ten pages). The Act imposed a tax upon all residents of Great Britain in respect of their entire income, irrespective of whether the income originated in Great Britain or elsewhere, and also on all absentees — that is, British subjects not resident in Great Britain, in respect of income from property in Great Britain. This was the origin of the concept of taxation of worldwide income based upon residence, and on source taxation for property within the taxing jurisdiction. These two principles are the foundation of the Canadian tax system to this day. Thus, the tax moved away from being calculated according to one's expenditures and was payable directly upon the entire income of the individual.

As with all taxes, the income tax was unpopular and criticized by many. Some fought the tax arguing that it was inherently unequal and that it would discourage industry. There was a debate about the incidence of the tax, which some argued shifted from the tradesman to his customers and from the farmer to his landlord. Others objected to the inquisitional nature of the tax, and one, with the remarkable foresight, writing under the *nom de plume* of Hour-

---

[26]Speeches, Vol. II, page 429.

[27]Speeches, Vol. II, pages 431–433.

[28]Speeches, Vol. II, page 444.

glass predicted how the tax would be administered in the year 2000, referring to the tax collectors as "merciless mercenaries" and the "brutes at the head of the inquisitorial band, or banditti, with all the rudeness that insolence and self-important ignorance could suggest, either to distress the feelings of the indigent, or glut the bloated importance of a jack in office."[29]

b) — Addington's Act of 1803

By 1803, Britain was at war with France and needed money to fight. Addington, in his budget speech of June 13 of that tax year, proposed a tax on property saying: "I wish it to be distinctly understood that I consider these duties as applicable to war only, and I intend to propose that they should cease within six months after the restoration of peace."[30]

The Act entitled "An Act for Granting to His Majesty until the sixth day of May next year after the ratification of a definitive treaty of peace, a contribution of the profits arising from property, professions, trades and offices" became law on August 11, 1803.[31]

The Act moved away from a comprehensive tax on all income and introduced the source concept in assessing income. Instead of taxing an individual on his total worldwide income as a single amount, the new regime divided income into a number of categories or schedules. Each schedule was taxed as a separate source of income. Initially, the tax was payable by the person who paid the sum that constituted the income of the recipient. Thus, the tax was stopped at its source.

The law provided for a series of taxes rather than for a single income tax. The official exposition stated: "The act comprehends four different sources of profit, applicable to four principal classes of individuals, under different modes of taxation, each of which must receive a distinct consideration, as if they had formed the subject of four distinct acts of Parliament."[32]

The four categories were landed property, funded property, produce of industry, and offices held under government.

Landed property was divided into two categories: "landlord's duty"; and "tenant's duty". The landlord's duty in Schedule A was on the annual value of all lands; the tenant's duty in

---

[29]The Mouse — Trap Maker and the Income Tax; a Tale, supposed, by, Anticipation, to be written in the Year 2000; by Humphrey Hourglass. London, n.3d [1799 page 12].

[30][Sir Thomas White echoed a similar sentiment when he introduced the *Canadian Act in 1917*]. Parliamentary History, Vol. XXXVI, page 1596.

[31]Forty-three George III, 122.

[32]An Exposition of the Act, etc. page 5.

Schedule B also dealt with lands, with some exceptions for dwellings with no income and for farms.

"Funded property" was all "profits arising from annuities, dividends and shares of annuities" and was taxable under Schedule C. In an early example of tax reporting at source, the Bank of England, the South Sea Company and the Exchequer furnished an annual account of the dividends paid, although the shareholders were liable for and paid the tax.

Schedule E comprised income from public office or employment profit and from salaries, annuities, pensions, or stipends payable by the Crown or out of the public revenue. This category included income from any corporation, company or society. The tax was assessed to the payer of the income and was deducted from the sums receivable by the payee.

Schedule D was a sweeping clause that included the profits arising from all property not taxed in Schedules A, B and C. It also included the annual profits or gains from any profession, trade, employment, or vocation not chargeable under Schedule E. This schedule also applied to non-residents of Great Britain who owned property in the country (source taxation).

Schedule D was subdivided into six categories, each for a particular type of income. For example, the first case included income from any trade or manufacturer, which was taxable on an average of three years' profit. The second case included professions, employments, or vocations, and the tax was assessed on the profits, gains, and emoluments within the preceding year, and so on. The sixth case included a "sweeping" clause — that is, annual profits or gains not charged anywhere else.

The scheduler system was supposed to counter tax evasion and ensure taxpayer privacy by placing the responsibility for each schedule in the hands of different Commissioners of Taxation. The tax was not popular but eventually gained patriotic support. Some said that it would be wiser to declare part of one's profits to the income tax commissioners than to give up all to Napoleon.

There were several changes made in each of the schedules and some property was transferred from one schedule to another for various administrative and enforcement reasons. An interesting adjustment was the abolition of the deduction for children, which had led to an astounding official increase of large families.

The statute also introduced the concept of residence and liability for tax after residence of six months in Britain. Thus, if a person resided in England for a short time, then departed, and again returned, he was liable for tax, if during the year he had resided in total for a period of six months. This was the origin of the modern 183 day rule, which is part of the Canadian and international tax system today.

With the defeat of Napoleon at Waterloo in 1815, Britain abolished its income tax in 1816 by a slight majority in the House of Commons. Lord Brougham, the leader of the opposition, fueled the debate and read the wording of the law that introduced the income tax: "Be it enacted that this act shall continue in force during the present war and until April 6 next and after the definite signing of a treaty of peace, *and no longer*." The tax was abolished and Brougham moved that all of the records of the tax be destroyed. The motion was carried overwhelmingly.

The repeal of the income tax left a huge gap in Britain's revenues, which it had to fill by imposing new taxes, essentially on personal property of any kind. Thus, Britain moved once again towards a system of indirect taxes, which were also unpopular. Sydney Smith described the system in the 1820 edition of the *Edinburgh Review*:

> We can inform Brother Jonathan what is the inevitable consequence of being too fond of glory. Taxes upon every article which enters into the mouth or covers the back or placed under the foot. Taxes upon everything which it is pleasant to see, hear, feel, smell or taste. Taxes upon warmth, light and locomotion. Taxes on everything on earth or under the earth, on everything that comes from abroad or is grown at home. Taxes on the raw material, taxes on every fresh value that is added to it by the industry of man. Taxes on the sauces which pamper man's appetite and the drug which restores him to health; on the ermine which decorates the judge, and the rope which hangs the criminal; on the poor man's salt and the rich man's spice; on the brass nails of the coffin and the ribbons of the bride; at bed or board, couchant or levant, we must pay. The school boy whips his taxed top; the beardless youth manages his taxed horse with a taxed bridle, on a taxed road, and the dying Englishman, pouring his medicine, which has paid seven percent, into a spoon which has paid fifteen percent, flings himself back upon a chintz bed, which has paid twenty two percent, and expires in the arms of an apothecary who has paid a license of one hundred pounds for the privilege of putting him to death. His whole property is then immediately taxed from two to ten percent, besides the probate judge's fees demanded for burying him in the channel; his virtues are handed down to posterity on taxed marble, and he will then be gathered to his fathers to be taxed no more.

Britain reintroduced the income tax in *Peel's Act of 1842* popularly called the *Property and Income Tax Act* with the scheduler system (albeit modified). The country supported the income tax, not so much because it loved the tax more, but because it loved the indirect taxes less.

John Stuart Mill, in *Principles of Political Economy* (London, 1848, ii, pp. pages 376, 377) described his opposition to the income tax and the difficulties associated with its avoidance. He stated his objection to be "in the present low state of public morality, the impossibility of ascertaining the real incomes" of individuals. He conceded that flagrant fraud is unavoidable but, "the tax, on whatever principles of equality it may be imposed, is in practice unequal in one of the worst ways, falling heaviest on the most conscientious . . . The unscrupulous succeed in evading a great proportion of what they should pay; even persons of integrity in their ordinary transactions are tempted to palter with their consciences: while the strictly veracious may be made to pay more than the state intended, by the powers of arbitrary assessment necessarily entrusted to the commissioners . . . It is to be feared, therefore, that the fairness which belongs to the principle of an income tax cannot be made to attach to it in practice: and that this tax, while apparently the most just of all modes of raising a revenue, is in effect more unjust than many others which are *prima facie* more objectionable. This consideration would lead us to concur in the opinion which, until of late, has usually prevailed — that direct taxes on income should be reserved as extraordinary resources for great national emergencies."

c) — Canadian Source Doctrine

There is an important difference between the English scheduler system and the Canadian source doctrine. Under the English tax system,[33] a receipt is not taxable as income unless it comes within one of the named schedules, which are mutually exclusive.[34] Thus, the schedules mark the outside boundaries of the tax net.[35]

In Canada, however, the language of income tax statutes has been more expansive. In Section 3(1) of the *Income Tax War Act*, for example:

> For the purposes of this Act, "income" means the annual net profit or gain or gratuity, whether ascertained and capable of computation as being wages, salary, or other fixed amount, or unascertained as being fees or emoluments, or as being profits from a trade or commercial or financial or other business or calling, directly or indirectly received by a person from any office or employment, or from any profession or calling, or from any trade, manufacture or business, as the case may be; and shall include the interest, dividends or profits directly or indirectly received from money at interest upon any security or without security, or from stocks, or from any other investment, and, whether such gains or profits are divided or distributed or not, and also the *annual profit or gain from any other source. . . .. (emphasis added)*

Under the *Income Tax Act* (Canada), the named sources of income (office, employment, business, property and capital gains) in section 3 are not exhaustive and income can arise from *any* other unnamed source. Income from *any* source inside or outside Canada is taxable.[36] This is justifiable both on the basis of the statutory language, principle and the history of the source doctrine under a different statutory regime. To the extent that horizontal equity, as measured by the ability to pay, is an important objective of the tax system, all income should be taxable, regardless of its particular source. Thus, the touchstone of income

---

[33]*Income and Corporation Taxes Act, 1970* (Eng.), c. 10.

[34]S. 1. As Lord Radcliffe said in *Mitchell v. Ross*, [1961] 3 All E.R. 49, 40 Tax Cas. 11 at 55 [All E.R.]:

> Before you can assess a profit to tax you must be sure that you have properly identified its source or other description according to the correct Schedule; but once you have done that, it is obligatory that it should be charged, if at all, under that Schedule and strictly in accordance with the Rules that are there laid down for assessments under it. It is a necessary consequence of this conception that the sources of profit in the different Schedules are mutually exclusive.

[35]There are six schedules, some of which are subdivided into cases. Each schedule deals with a particular type of income.

[36]*Income Tax Act*, para. 3(a) requires income "from a source inside or outside Canada" to be included in income.

in law is realized enrichment, regardless of its source. To be sure, section 61 of the U.S. *Internal Revenue Code* is clearer on this point than section 3 of the *Canadian Act*. Section 61 states ". . . gross income means all income from whatever source derived . . .".

The scope of the source doctrine, however, remains unsettled. Canadian courts have excluded many payments as not constituting income from a source even though the payment enhances the taxpayer's wealth. Understandably, taxpayers make every effort to have their receipts classified as something other than income from a source. In *Fries*,[37] for example, the Supreme Court held that strike pay is not taxable as income. The Court did not, however, address the fundamental underlying question: was the strike pay not taxable because it was not "income" in the sense of realized enrichment or because it did not flow from a named "source" in section 3?

Fries highlights the inadequacy of source concept. Fries, an employee of the Saskatchewan Liquor Board and a member of the Saskatchewan Government Employees' Union ("Union"), went on strike and received strike pay equal to his normal net take-home pay. The Union's strike fund was formed out of the tax-deductible dues contributed by its members. The usual "strike stipend" paid to members on strike was $10 a week. The Union's provincial executive, however, had the sole right to determine the amount to be paid. They generally authorized strike stipend payments of up to 80 percent of gross pay. In this case, however, they authorized stipends equal to the full amount of the members' normal take-home pay. The employees of the Liquor Board voted in favour of supporting the strike, and the members knew there would be a recommendation that they would be reimbursed their full loss of pay as a result of the strike support.

The Supreme Court, which was heavily backlogged with reserved decisions at the time, disposed of the appeal in a terse decision excluding strike pay from income because the Act does not *specifically* provide for its inclusion in the taxable base:[38]

> The board need express no opinion on the principle involved — whether "strike pay" should or should not be taxable even though that principle was vigorously contested by the parties. It is only required that the Board express an opinion on whether the Act as it now stands provides for the taxation of the amount in question as well as it can be identified and described. *The Act does not provide for such taxation.* [Emphasis added.]

Thus, the Supreme Court bypassed the fundamental issue: should section 3 be read expansively on a global, or narrowly on a schedular, basis[39] Fries realized his gain from his strike pay, which derived from his (and others') deductible contributions to his tax exempt union.

---

[37]*R. v. Fries*, [1990] 2 S.C.R. 1322, [1990] 2 C.T.C. 439, 90 D.T.C. 6662 (S.C.C.).

[38]Adopting the decision of the Tax Review Board, *R. v. Fries*, [1983] C.T.C. 2124, 83 D.T.C. 117 (T.R.B.) at 2128 [C.T.C.] and 121 [D.T.C.].

[39]See, in contrast, the United States Supreme Court in *Commissioner v. Glenshaw Glass Co.*, 348 US 426 (1955), where Warren C.J. gave a broad interpretation.

In *Schwartz*,[40] the Supreme Court reviewed, once again, paragraph 3(a). The taxpayer, a lawyer, received damages as compensation for the cancellation of his employment contract. The taxpayer had accepted an offer of employment from a company and, as a consequence thereof, resigned his partnership in a law firm. The parties agreed that the taxpayer would start working only on completion of an interim assignment he had undertaken to perform for the government of Ontario. Before he could commence his assignment, however, the company advised the taxpayer that it would not require his services. The parties reached a settlement under which the company agreed to pay $360,000 as damages plus $40,000 on account of costs.

The Supreme Court held that the damages in respect of the intended employment were not taxable as a "retiring allowance" and disposed of the case on that basis. Four of the seven judges maintained in *obiter*, however, that paragraph 3(a) should be read in an expansive manner:

> . . . when Parliament used the words "without restricting the generality of the foregoing," great care was taken to emphasize that the first step in calculating a taxpayer's "income for the year" was to determine the total of all amounts constituting income inside or outside Canada and that the enumeration that followed merely identified examples of such sources. The phrasing adopted by Parliament, in paragraph 3(a) and in the introductory part of subsection 56(1) is probably the strongest that could have been used to express the idea that income from *all* sources, enumerated or not, expressly provided for in subdivision d or not was taxable under the Act.

The *obiter* reflects the underlying policy of paragraph 3(a) and the principle of equity that equates the burden of tax with the ability to pay. However, we must wait to see whether the principle of horizontal equity is subsumed in the historical development of the source theory. As Major J. noted: "If paragraph 3(a) was applied literally to provide for taxation of income from any source, then again it is arguable the existing jurisprudence would be placed in jeopardy." To be sure, that is the case anytime the Supreme Court shifts its position in law. The evolution of jurisprudence towards a more equitable interpretation would accord with modern principles of tax policy. However, until the court moves off its narrow interpretation of paragraph 3(a), taxpayers are entitled to the benefit of tax-free strike pay.

III. — Recovery of Capital

The income tax is a tax on *net* gains or the increment in realized value. The accurate measurement of gains is essential to a fair and efficient tax system. There are two components to the measurement of net gain: (1) the recovery of basis (costs), and (2) the matching of income flows against recovery of capital.

---

[40]*Schwartz v. R.*, [1996] 1 S.C.R. 254, [1996] 1 C.T.C. 303, 96 D.T.C. 6103 (S.C.C.). See generally, IT-426R, "Shares sold subject to an earnout agreement".

The net gain from the sale of an asset can be straightforward or complicated, depending upon the number of assets that one holds and the period over which one acquires the assets. In the simplest case, a gain or loss from the sale of an asset is the difference between its selling price and its cost or "basis". For example, where an individual buys 100 shares for $10,000 and later sells the shares for $15,000, the gain on the sale is $5,000. If the individual also incurs $20 in selling costs, the *net* gain is $4,980. The first $10,000, that is, the cost basis of the shares, is not taxable because it represents the recovery of capital. The $20 is the expense to earn the gross gain of $5,000.

The situation is more complicated, however, where an individual acquires several batches of shares over a period of years and then disposes of only a part of her shareholding. In these circumstances, we need a method for determining the cost basis of the shares sold so as to obtain a fair and accurate measure of the taxpayer's net gain. We need rules for scheduling the recovery of the capital in the shares. The rules determine whether the taxpayer pays tax on the full amount of her economic net gain or on some lesser portion. Assume in the above example that the individual purchases additional 200 shares at a cost of $30,000 before she sells any shares. If the taxpayer then sells 100 shares for $15,000, we must determine the cost basis of her shares in order to calculate the gain. There are at least four possibilities. For example, we can assume that the taxpayer sells:

1. The first batch of 100 shares;

2. Half of the second batch of 200 shares;

3. Half from the first batch (50) and half from the second batch (50); or

4. One-third from the first batch (33) and two-thirds from the second batch (67).

Each of these assumptions produces a different deductible cost basis and, hence, a different net income.

OPTION	COST BASIS	SALES	GAIN	EXPENSES	NET GAIN
1	$10,000	$15,000	$5,000	$20	$4,980
2	$15,000	$15,000	NIL	$20	$(20)
3	$12,500	$15,000	$2,500	$20	$2,480
4	$13,350	$15,000	$1,650	$20	$1,630

There is no absolute logic for selecting one basis over the other for tax purposes. The important point is that each method of cost recovery produces a different result. Each method produces a different allocation between the amount of tax currently payable and the tax deferred. The definitive accounting must wait until the final disposition (for example, on death) of the remaining 200 shares. In the interim, all we can do is estimate a fair measure of income (net gain) for the year.

A second, and more subtle, aspect of cost recovery arises if we attempt to match income flows against the recovery of capital. Say that in the above example the shares yield an annual dividend of 5 percent, or $500 on the first batch of 100 shares. Should the shareholder be taxed on the $500 on a current basis or should the shareholder be taxable only after she recovers the entire capital cost of the investment (say in 20 years if the dividend rate remains unchanged)? If the current annual dividend is taxable on a current basis, the full recovery of capital is delayed until the shareholder sells her shares in 20 years.

Under the latter option, the annual dividend would reduce the basis of the capital invested in the shares until such time as it was zero. Of course, when the shareholder ultimately disposes of the shares, the net gain would be that much higher because the cost base of the shares would have been reduced to zero. If the shareholder sold her shares in 20 years for $40,000, the entire $40,000 would be the realized net gain. Although the ultimate nominal result under both options is the same, the timing of the net gain is significantly different. The net present value of the tax payable under the second option is considerably less than the amount payable under the first. As we will see in subsequent chapters, the Act generally prefers current basis taxation of annual income flows but, in a few rare cases, permits cost basis reduction.

	Original Cost	$ 10,000
YR1	Dividend Received	(500)*
	Cost Basis	9,500
YR2	Dividend	(500)*
	Cost Basis	$ 9,000
...		
	Cost Basis	$ 500*
YR20	Dividend	(500)*
	Cost Basis	0
	Proceeds for Sale	40,000
	Gain (ignoring expense)	40,000

Notes:

* The dividend is used to reduce the cost basis (i.e., treated as a recovery of capital) rather than being taxed as current income.

IV. — Imputed Income

"Imputed income" refers to income that an individual derives from the personal use of one's own assets and from the performance of services for one's own benefit. For example, assume that Harry, a lawyer, earns $80,000 a year from his law practice. Joseph, a farmer, earns $70,000 from his farming operations and consumes $10,000 of the meat and produce that he farms. Both Harry and Joseph earn the same amount of income, albeit in different forms. Harry earns all of his income in the marketplace and must buy his meat and produce in the market. Joseph earns less cash income, but has the advantage that he consumes what he grows and cultivates. Thus, Joseph enhances his economic well-being and his ability to pay by consuming his own produce. The principle of horizontal equity suggests that, other things being equal, the two taxpayers should each pay the same amount of tax.

The Canadian income tax system does not generally impute income to a taxpayer. Consumption of personal services, home repairs, home-grown food, owner-occupied home occupancy, and the like are not taken into account in measuring income for tax purposes. There are several reasons for excluding imputed income from the taxable base. First, it is clear that the valuation of imputed goods and services would be a substantial problem for taxpayers. One would need to obtain the value of "equivalent market" transactions under comparable circumstances. It would be a nightmare for taxpayers.

Second, the nightmare for taxpayers would soon translate into an administrative nightmare for the CRA, which would have prolonged debates with taxpayers on the appropriate imputed value of goods and services. In many cases, it is more than likely that there would be substantial non-declaration of imputed goods and services. This would ultimately undermine the credibility of the entire tax system.

To be sure, the exclusion of imputed income from the taxable base offends the principle of tax neutrality and equity. The exclusion encourages taxpayers to engage in non-market transactions such as home improvements. For example, assume that Jennifer and Lorrie each own homes. Jennifer, an accountant and an accomplished carpenter, does her own home repairs, thereby saving herself $6,000 each year that she would otherwise pay to a professional. In contrast, Lorrie, a hairdresser, is completely incompetent when it comes to home repairs and must pay $6,000 annually to have someone come in and do her home repairs. If Jennifer and Lorrie each earn $50,000 cash income per year, they have equal economic income, but in different forms. Lorrie must first earn her marketplace income, pay tax on that income, and use her after-tax income to pay for her home repairs. If Lorrie has a tax rate of 40 percent, she must earn an additional $10,000 (in order to have an after-tax amount of $6,000) with which to pay for her home repairs.

Hence, the tax advantage inherent in owning a home rather than renting. Assume that two individuals, Martha and Larry, each inherit $200,000 from their parents. Martha invests her $200,000 in a home that she occupies. Larry takes his $200,000 and purchases bonds that yield 8 percent. Assume further that both individuals have a marginal tax rate of 50 percent. In these circumstances, Larry earns $16,000 interest income, on which he pays tax of $8,000. He can use his after-tax income of $8,000 to rent a home or an apartment. In contrast, Martha derives the economic benefit of owner-occupancy and uses her $200,000 without any intervention from the tax system. In other words, Martha derives the benefit of pre-tax investment in her home occupancy, while Larry must pay for equivalent accommodation with after-tax dollars. The tax system makes it very attractive (even ignoring considerations of potential appreciation in property values) for taxpayers to own and occupy their own homes. This bias, which is enhanced by the principal residence exemption, affects the allocation of resources between rental housing and owner-occupied homes.

V. — Section 3

Section 3 is the anchor provision that dictates the basic rules for determining income for a taxation year. Unavoidably, the definition of income in the section is tautological: "The *income* of a taxpayer for a taxation year . . . is the taxpayer's *income* for the year . . .". The section then sets out a sequence for the aggregation of the different sources of income and losses. The sequence is rigid and causes a good deal of complexity in the tax system. The inflexibility of section 3 is also the impetus for tax planning by taxpayers who seek to maneuver their transactions from higher taxed sources of income to take advantage of lower tax rates on other sources. For example, a taxpayer will generally prefer to have gains characterized as capital gains (only one-half taxable) rather than business income (fully taxable).

Section 3 identifies at least six major categories for the classification of income and losses. Some of the categories (such as capital gains) are divided into subcategories. The rules in respect of the computation of income and losses from each source are then set out neatly, but not simply, in separate subdivisions of the Act.

The rigid scheme by which income and losses are segregated according to source contributes more than any other single factor to the complexity of the tax system. Taxpayers, understandably, make every effort to reclassify income from high-rate sources into income that is either tax-exempt or taxed at a lower rate. Thus, income conversion and tax deferral are two of the cornerstones of tax planning. The distinction between business income and capital gains, for example, has been the subject of hundreds of litigated cases because of the lower effective tax rate on capital gains. Equally difficult, and sometimes even more subtle, is the distinction between business and investment income, which can be taxed at different rates.[41]

---

[41]See, for example, sections 125 and 129.

The following is an overview of Section 3:

Paragraph		
3(a)	Employment income	$ +
	Business and property income	+
	Other income (excluding taxable capital gains)	+
	ADD	
3(b)	Taxable capital gains	
	(including taxable *net* gains from LPP)*	+
	Exceeds:	
	Allowable capital losses	
	(other than LPP losses) in excess of allowable busi-ness investment losses	- +
	EXCEEDS	
3(c)	The remaining subdivision deductions	-
	(negative number is deemed equal to zero)	
	EXCEEDS	
3(d)	Office and employment losses	-
	Business and property losses	
	Allowable business investment losses	-
	INCOME FOR THE YEAR	
		$
	(negative number is deemed equal to zero)	
	Notes:* Listed personal property.	

Each class of income in section 3 is referred to as "income from a source" and the income from each source must be calculated separately.[42] For example, employment income is a category of income separate from income from business or investments, which, in turn, are

___

[42]Subs. 4(1). The source concept derives from the United Kingdom's tax system under which income is taxable if it falls into one of the Schedules of the *Income and Corporation Taxes Act, 1970* (Eng.), c. 10.

different from capital gains. Different rules apply to the computation of income from each of these sources.

We determine the income from each source in the following sequence:

1. Characterize receipts as being on account of income or capital;

2. If income, classify it by source;

3. Deduct expenses applicable to each source to determine net income from that source; and

4. Aggregate the various sources of net income in the sequence in section 3.

A. — The Named Sources of Income

The Act specifically identifies the following sources of income:

- Office;

- Employment;

- Business;

- Property; and

- Capital gains.

This is not an exhaustive list. Apart from the named sources, section 3 states that income from *any* other source is also taxable. Thus, the policy underlying the section is to tax all income if it has a source, whether inside or outside Canada. As we saw earlier, however, judicial decisions relying on English history and a different statute have constrained the meaning of "income" for tax purposes.

Some of the named sources of income are divided into subsources. For example, capital gains are divided into personal use property gains, which are further subdivided into listed personal property (LPP) gains. Business investment losses are a subsource of capital losses. Each of these subsources of income is subject to additional rules that apply only to the particular source. For example, an individual can offset LPP losses, but only against LPP gains and not against any other types of capital gains. The compartmentalization of income into segregated sources requires a vast number of special rules to prevent the leakage of income and losses from one source into another.

Example
The following data applies to an individual. All amounts shown are net of deductions in each category.

Employment income $ 30,000

Example

Business (No. 1) income		12,000
Business (No. 2) loss		(6,000)
Property income		6,000
Taxable capital gains (shares)		1,500
Taxable LPP net gain		1,500
Allowable capital losses (*including* allowable business investment losses)		(4,900)
Moving expenses		(800)
Allowable business investment losses		(4,000)

Then the individual's income for the year is as follows:

Paragraph 3(a)

Employment income		$ 30,000
Business income		12,000
Property income		6,000
		48,000

ADD Paragraph 3(b)

Taxable capital gains	$ 1,500	
Taxable *net* LPP gain	1,500	
	3,000	
Exceeds:		
Allowable capital losses in excess of allowable business investment losses ($4,900 - 4,000)	(900)	2,100
		50,100

EXCEEDS Paragraph 3(c)

Moving expenses		(800)
		49,300

EXCEEDS Paragraph 3(d)

Business loss	$ (6,000)	
Allowable business investment losses	(4,000)	(10,000)

Example	
Income for the year	$ 39,300

B. — Losses by Source

The characterization of losses by source is also important. For example, business losses are fully deductible against any source of income; capital losses are only partially deductible from income and then only against net taxable capital gains. Unused business losses may be carried forward 20 years and back three years; unused capital losses may be carried forward indefinitely and back for three years. Similarly, listed personal property losses are deductible only against net gains from listed personal property and not from other types of capital gains.

We have already seen that income from each source must be calculated separately. A taxpayer must compute income as though *each* source of income was his *only* source of income. Deductions from income are similarly limited: a deduction may be taken against a source of income only if it may be regarded as applicable to that source.[43]

Note, however, that the Act does not identify certain amounts — for example, moving expenses, with specific sources. Therefore, we account for them separately.[44] The following example illustrates the operation of the source doctrine and its impact on net income.

Example			
Assume that the following data applies to three corporations:			
		Corporation	
	A	B	C
Business income	$ 1,000	$ 2,000	$ 6,000
Property income (loss)	(1,000)	$ 2,000	—
Taxable capital gains (losses)	2,000	(2,000)	(4,000)*
Aggregate accounting income	$ 2,000	$ 2,000	$ 2,000
Income for tax purposes is:			
Business income	$ 1,000	$ 2,000	$ 6,000
Property income	—	2,000	—
Taxable capital gains	2,000	—	—
	3,000	4,000	6,000
Exceeds:			

---

[43]Subs. 4(1).

[44]Subs. 4(2).

Example			
Assume that the following data applies to three corporations:			
		Corporation	
	A	B	C
Property or business losses	(1,000)	*	*
Income for the year	$ 2,000	$ 4,000	$ 6,000

Notes:

* Capital losses may only be offset against capital gains.

The above example illustrates how accounting income differs from net income for tax purposes. Although each corporation has the same realized economic income, corporation C will pay three times the amount of tax that corporation A pays.

VI. — Structure of the Act

A person may be liable for tax under different Parts of the *Income Tax Act*. For example, residents, and non-residents who are employed or carry on a business in Canada, are taxable under Part I of the Act. Non-residents are also subject to withholding tax on certain forms of passive income (such as dividends, interest) under Part XIII of the Act. There are also special taxes imposed under Part IV on certain types of investment income and under Part II.1 on dividend-like payments. For the present we focus on Part I of the Act; we discuss the other Parts of the Act later.

Determining the amount of tax payable involves multiple steps. First, we determine the taxpayer's liability under Part I by reference to "taxable income".[45] We apply the applicable tax rate to taxable income to determine the amount of basic federal tax payable. Then, we apply tax credits and, if applicable, surcharges to determine the net *federal* tax payable. Finally, we add the provincial tax payable to arrive at the total tax payable.

The following chart sets out the general scheme for determining tax payable under Part I.

---

[45]S. 2; Part I, Division C.

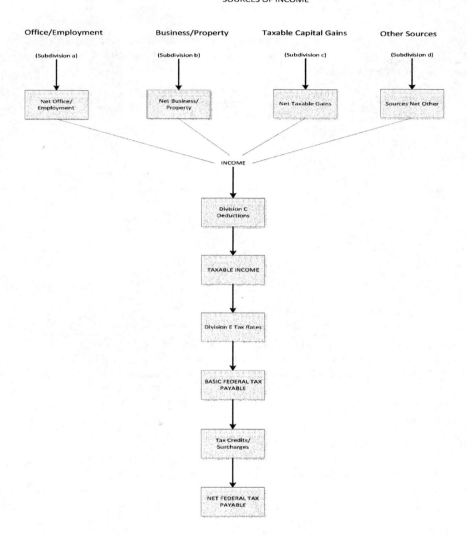

TAXATION OF CANADIAN RESIDENTS

SOURCES OF INCOME

VII. — Deductions vs. Credits

The income tax is a tax on income *net* of deductions and credits. The amount of tax initially payable on net income is reduced through tax credits, thereby lowering the effective rate of tax. The difference between a deduction from income and a tax credit is that a deduction has

131

the effect of reducing income, which indirectly reduces the amount of tax payable, whereas a tax credit directly reduces the amount of tax payable without reducing income.

Example		
Assume that an individual with a marginal tax rate of 50 percent earns $100,000. The following example illustrates the effect of a $20,000 deduction from income compared to a credit of $20,000 against tax.		
	Deduction from income	**Tax credit**
Income	$ 100,000	$ 100,000
Less: deduction	(20,000)	—
Taxable income	$ 80,000	$ 100,000
Basic tax at 50%	$ 40,000	$ 50,000
Tax credit	—	(20,000)
Net tax payable	$ 40,000	$ 30,000

The above example illustrates that a dollar of tax credit is worth more to a taxpayer than a dollar deduction from income. The reason for this is that a deduction is only worth its face value multiplied by the taxpayer's marginal rate of tax. For instance, a $100 deduction to an individual with a marginal rate of 50 percent is worth $50 tax savings; at a marginal rate of 25 percent, the saving is only $25. The value of a deduction increases as an individual's marginal rate rises.

Thus, we use marginal rate analysis in tax planning because we want to maximize savings on the top dollar. In contrast, the value of a tax credit remains constant through all marginal tax rates. This distinction is important in determining the distributional effect of taxes, exemptions and credits. To equalize the value of deductions and credits, the value of the credit should be lower than its deduction equivalent. In the above example, the credit should be reduced to $10,000.

VIII. — Exclusions from Income

A. — General Comment

Income for tax purposes is not synonymous with the economist's or accountant's understanding of income. Taxable income is a far less comprehensive measure of wealth (adjusted by consumption) than that contemplated in economic theory. Economists measure income by reference to the net accretion of wealth between two points in time.

The tax measure of income is based on realized gains from sources and a judicial understanding of what constitutes "income". The Act also has numerous *ad hoc* statutory inclusions[46] and exclusions based upon various policy considerations.[47] As Professor Rendall said:[48]

> . . . the fact is that our notions of income have been intuitive rather than logical and that our jurisprudence has developed on a case-by-case basis and has often reflected primarily a gut feeling about the characterization of a particular amount. What this means is that "income", for tax purposes, is not at all a single, consistent, concept.

There are several exclusions from income, but the most prominent common law exclusions are:

- Gambling gains;
- Gifts and inheritances; and
- Windfall gains.

The rationale for each of these exclusions varies.

B. — Gambling Gains

There are three types of gambling gains: (1) casual or pleasurable; (2) as an adjunct to a business; and (3) professional.

---

[46]See, e.g., s. 12.

[47]See, e.g., s. 81.

[48]Rendall, "Defining the Tax Base," in Hansen, Krishna, Rendall eds., *Canadian Taxation* (Toronto: DeBoo, 1981).

Winnings from casual betting and incidental gambling are not income, even if the individual is a compulsive gambler.[49] Some judges explain this exclusion on the theory that gambling is an irrational activity:[50]

> What is a bet? A bet is merely an irrational agreement that one person should pay another person something on the happening of an event. A agrees to pay B something if C's horse runs quicker than D's or if a coin comes down one side up rather than the other side up. There is no relevance at all between the event and the acquisition of property. The event does not really produce it at all. It rests, as I say, on a mere irrational agreement.

The rationale is not entirely persuasive. Games of chance rely on probability theory and distributions. A horse race is hardly more irrational than the trading on commodities futures on a stock exchange. In any event, they are all realized accretions to wealth, as the winner of any Lotto 649 will confirm.

English courts said that such gains do not flow from a source and, hence, are not included under any of the U.K. schedules of income. This interpretation, however, is less helpful in the Canadian context. It ignores the statutory language of section 3, which includes income from *any* source inside or outside Canada.[51]

We can better justify the exclusion of gambling gains from income on administrative and revenue considerations. Accounting for casual betting for pleasure would impose an unreasonable burden on individuals. One can only speculate how many individuals would voluntarily comply and declare their winnings from an evening at the casino. Probably as many as servers who declare their cash tips! Any attempt to tax such gains would result in flagrant disregard of the rule and bring the administration of tax into disrepute.

Further, if losses were deductible, the revenue gains would be minimal or negative since more people lose than win. Thus, we exclude gambling gains from income where the taxpayer realizes the gain in pursuit of a hobby and is not engaged in the business of gambling.[52] Similarly, losses from gambling are not deductible unless they are incurred in the conduct of a gambling *business*.

---

[49]*Leblanc v. R.*, [2007] 2 C.T.C. 2248, 2007 D.T.C. 307 (Eng.) (T.C.C. [General Procedure]).

[50]*Per* Rowlatt, J., in *Graham v. Green (Insp. of Taxes)*, [1925] 2 K.B. 37 at 39-40; *Graham v. Green Minister of National Revenue v. Morden*, [1961] C.T.C. 484, 61 D.T.C. 1266 (Can. Ex. Ct.).

[51]See, e.g., *Rumack v. Minister of National Revenue*, [1992] 1 C.T.C. 57, 92 D.T.C. 6142 (Fed. C.A.) at 59 [C.T.C.] and 6144 [D.T.C.]; leave to appeal refused (1992), 143 N.R. 393 (note) (S.C.C.).

[52]See, e.g., *Minister of National Revenue v. Walker*, [1951] C.T.C. 334, 52 D.T.C. 1001 (Can. Ex. Ct.) (gambling winnings taxable when achieved by taxpayer who himself owned and raced horses, had inside information, and could not afford to lose).

The exclusion of gains from income, however, applies only to the capital sum of the gambling gain and not to any income earned when the gambler invests his winnings. The exclusion does not extend to "cash for life" lotteries.[53]

A gambling gain is taxable if the individual gambles as an adjunct to his or her business — for example, a race horse owner who bets on the races.

Similarly, a professional gambler's gains are taxable. A professional is a person who uses his expertise and skill to earn a livelihood from gambling — for example, a pool shark or river boat gambler.

C. — Gifts and Inheritances

Gifts and inheritances are not income for tax purposes, but are transfers of capital. "Gift" is defined in *Halsbury* as follows:

> A gift *inter vivos* may be defined shortly as the transfer of any property from one person to another gratuitously while the donor is alive and not in expectation of death. . . .

Black's Law Dictionary defines a "gift" as:

> A voluntary transfer of personal property without consideration. . . . A parting by owner with property without pecuniary consideration.

The *Shorter Oxford Dictionary* defines "giving" as:

> A transfer of property in a thing, voluntarily and without any valuable consideration. . . .

A "gift" is a voluntary and gratuitous transfer of property from one person to another. It may be subject to a pre-condition, but, this apart, it is not revocable or terminable. Thus, a transfer of property qualifies as a gift only if the transfer is both voluntary and made without any expectation of reward or return. A payment that requires a *quid pro quo* is not a gift.

In common law, a gift is a transfer of "capital" from one person to another. A gift represents an accretion to the recipient's wealth and, as such, would be considered income in economic theory. For tax purposes, however, gifts and inheritances are not income, but are considered capital transfers.[54]

---

[53]*Rumack v. Minister of National Revenue*, [1992] 1 C.T.C. 57, 92 D.T.C. 6142 (Fed. C.A.); leave to appeal refused (1992), 143 N.R. 393 (note) (S.C.C.).

[54]The Carter Commission proposed that, subject to a minimum exemption, gifts and inheritances should be included in the income of the recipient; see *Report of the Royal Commission on Taxation* (Ottawa: Queen's Printer, 1966) (Chair: K.M. Carter), vol. III, chapter 17.

Since Canada does not have gift or inheritance taxes, gifts and inheritances are entirely free of tax. The exclusion of gifts and inheritances from the taxable base clearly impinges on the principle of fairness as measured by ability to pay.

D. — Windfall Gains

The exclusion of "windfall gains" from income is problematic. Windfall gains are clearly realized accretions to wealth that enhance the taxpayer's ability to pay. Windfalls are not usually capital transfers. The only unusual feature of a windfall is that it is unexpected. If the policy of the income tax is to impose similar taxes on those in similar financial circumstances, there is little merit in distinguishing between increments to wealth based on their source or expectations of return.

It is also difficult to identify a "windfall". The phrase generally implies a gain that is unexpected or unplanned and one that we cannot link to one of the named sources (office, employment, business, property, and capital gains) of income. In fact, "windfall gains" represent nothing more than an unarticulated, and irrational, bias against taxing certain types of gains. The implication is that income can arise only from *expected* returns, and "unexpected" gains are windfalls and are not taxable as income.

In *The Queen v. Cranswick*, for example:[55]

> In the absence of a special statutory definition . . . income from a source will be that which is typically earned by it or which typically flows from it as the *expected* return.

This harks back to the *Macomber* concept that income is the expected return from labour or capital, but, in this case, coupled with the source doctrine.

Thus, a windfall gain represents an unexpected and unplanned gain that cannot be directly linked to one of the named sources of income — office, employment, business, property, and capital gains. More specifically, a windfall gain is a gain that:

• Does not result from a legally enforceable claim;

• Is not expected, either specifically or customarily;

• Is not likely to recur;

• Is not customarily a source of income for the recipient of the gain;

• Is not given as consideration for services rendered, to garner favour, or anything else provided; and

---

[55]*R. v. Cranswick*, [1982] C.T.C. 69, 82 D.T.C. 6073 (Fed. C.A.) at 73 [C.T.C.] and 6076 [D.T.C.]; leave to appeal refused (1982), 42 N.R. 355 (S.C.C.); *Frank Beban Logging Limited v. R.*, [1998] 2 C.T.C. 2493, 98 D.T.C. 1393 (T.C.C) (*Ex gratia* payment of $800,000 by government to logging company was windfall as taxpayer did not expect the payment.) See IT-334R2 (February 21, 1992) para. 3.

• Is not earned as a result of an activity or pursuit of gain.

To summarize: a windfall gain is a gain that is unexpected, unplanned, and unrelated to any of the named sources of income.[56]

IX. — Barter Transactions

A barter transaction is one in which two or more persons agree to a reciprocal exchange of goods or services without the use of money. In its simplest form, bartering involves market transactions where the medium of exchange is goods or services instead of legal tender.[57]

Barter payments are governed by the same principles applicable to payments in cash. A payment or benefit in kind is a realized accretion to wealth and enhances the taxpayer's ability to pay. Payments in kind may involve bilateral or multilateral exchanges of property. For example, a lawyer who renders legal services to a farmer may accept a cow in settlement of the account. Alternatively, the lawyer may accept a non-cash credit which can be exchanged in a barter "pool" for other goods and services, e.g., the cow credit may be exchanged for plumbing services. The essence of barter is that they involve market transactions, whether bilateral or multilateral, of goods and services without the use of money.

Barter transactions have special valuation problems. Should the payment in kind be valued based on its *value in use* to the recipient or its *value in exchange* for the goods or services sold or rendered? For example, suppose a lawyer renders legal services for which she would usually charge $2,000 in exchange for a cow that has a market value of $1,600. How much should the lawyer include in her income, $2,000 (value of the services) or $1,600 (value of the exchange)? The CRA says that the recipient's income is increased by the price that she would "normally have charged" for the goods or services provided,[58] in this example, $2,000. Where, however, the goods or services given up cannot readily be valued but the

---

[56]*MacEachern v. Minister of National Revenue*, [1977] C.T.C. 2139, 77 D.T.C. 94 (T.R.B.) (proceeds from sale of gold and silver coins found by three deep-sea divers was income from organized activity that was more than a hobby); *Charles R. Bell Ltd. v. R.*, [1992] 2 C.T.C. 260, 92 D.T.C. 6472 (Fed. C.A.); leave to appeal refused (1993), 156 N.R. 239n (S.C.C.) (lump sum payment to corporate taxpayer upon termination of exclusive distributorship agents was income); *Johnson & Johnson Inc. v. R.*, [1994] 1 C.T.C. 244, 94 D.T.C. 6125 (Fed. C.A.) (unexpected refund was business income and not windfall when looked at in context); *Federal Farms Ltd. v. Minister of National Revenue*, [1959] C.T.C. 98, 59 D.T.C. 1050 (Can. Ex. Ct.) (voluntary payments to help taxpayer whose farm was flooded during hurricane was gift, not income); *R. v. Cranswick, ante* (majority shareholder paid minority shareholder sum to avoid controversy over reorganization; unexpected and unusual payment was windfall).

[57]IT-490, "Barter Transactions" (July 5, 1982).

[58]*Ibid.*

goods or services rendered can, the value of the latter can be used to set the price of the transaction.

In multilateral barter schemes with restrictions on exchange of barter credits, the value of consideration received may be considerably less than the "theoretical" value of goods and services sold or rendered. Since barter credits are a substitute medium of exchange, it is the value of the medium that should determine the price. In effect, a taxpayer who renders services for credits that have a restricted exchange value discounts the price normally charged for such services.[59]

X. — Exempt Income

The Act exempts certain forms of income from tax. It is important to note the distinction between a taxpayer who is exempt from tax[60] and income that is tax-exempt.[61] In the former case, the recipient is exempt from tax regardless of the nature of the income that it earns. For example, labor unions are exempt from tax. In the latter case, specific types of income are exempt from tax, regardless of who receives it.

Examples of Exempt Income

Payment	ITA	Comments
Amounts declared by any other federal statute to be exempt from income tax: *Indian Act* exemptions.*	para. 81(1)(a)	Other than amounts exempted by virtue of a treaty. See: *Williams* [1992] 1 CTC 225 (SCC)
Amounts from War Savings Certificates	para. 81(1)(b)	
Income of a non-resident earned in Canada from operation of a ship or aircraft in international traffic	para. 81(1)(c)	only if the individual's country of residence grants a similar exemption

---

[59]*Linett v. Minister of National Revenue*, [1985] 2 C.T.C. 2037, 85 D.T.C. 416 (T.C.C.).

[60]S. 149.

[61]S. 81.

Examples of Exempt Income

Payment	ITA	Comments
Pension, payment, allowance or compensation received under *Pension Act, Civilian War-related Benefits Act, Gallantry Awards Order* or section 9 of the *Aeronautics Act*	para. 81(1)(d)	Regular (non-disability) pensions are taxable — *Chiasson*, 2010 CarswellNat 916 (TCC)
Payments received on account of death or disability incurred in service from an allied country (includes civilian casualties).	para. 81(1)(e)	only if the country grants similar relief with respect to pensions paid in Canada
Any payments with respect to death or injury sustained in the 1917 Halifax explosion	para. 81(1)(f)	
Compensation paid by Federal Republic of Germany to victims of Nazi persecution (Holocaust survivors).	para. 81(1)(g)	if amount is exempt from tax by German law
Income or taxable capital gains from property or from disposition of property received as compensation for physical or mental injury	paras. 81(1)(g.1), 81(1)(g.2), 81(5)	if income or gain is earned or received before taxpayer becomes 21; taxpayer may elect deemed disposition of capital property in the year he or she attains age of 21

Examples of Exempt Income

Payment	ITA	Comments
Receipt of income-tested social assistance payment by taxpayer on behalf of individual other than spouse, common law partner or relative (foster care).	para. 81(1)(h)	if individual resides in taxpayer's principal residence
Amount for injury, disability or death under *RCMP Pension Continuation Act* or *RCMP Superannuation Act*	para. 81(1)(i)	Also exempt from withholding tax if paid to non-resident — subsection 212(1)(h)(iii).
Certain payments from an employee profit-sharing plan	para. 81(1)(k); s. 144	
Receipts of a share of a corporation by prospector or grubstaker	para. 81(1)(l); s. 35	to extent provided by s. 35
Interest accrued, receivable or received by resident corporation on an obligation received as consideration for the disposition before June 18, 1971 of a business of a public utility or service nature	para. 81(1)(m)	if the obligation is guaranteed by the government or one of its agencies of the country where the business is carried on
Income (other than salary) from the office of Governor General of Canada	para. 81(1)(n)	Salary is taxed effective 2013. Salary increased to compensate for tax.
Amount paid to an individual as prescribed indemnity under provincial law	para. 81(1)(q); Pt. LXV. Reg. 6501	

Examples of Exempt Income

Payment	ITA	Comments
Amounts credited to foreign retirement arrangement account	para. 81(1)(r)	
Allowances paid to an elected member of legislative assembly (MLA's) for expenses incidental to the duties of office	subs. 81(2)	to extent that allowance is not more than 1/2 of the maximum of the member's salary. Federal MP allowances exempt under subsection 6(1)(b)(i).
Allowances paid to elected officers of municipal utilities board, commission or corporation; public or separate school board for expenses incidental to the duties of office	subs. 81(3)	to extent that allowance is not more than 1/2 of the officer's salary
Amount received by a part-time employee as an allowance or reimbursement of travelling expenses incurred during a period when he had other employment or carried on a business	subs. 81(3.1)	so long as amounts are reasonable and duties are performed at least 80 kms from his or her principal place of employment or business and residence
Payments for volunteer emergency services	Subs. 81(4)	See also subsection 118.06 for option of tax credit.

Notes:

* See, e.g., *Indian Act*, R.S.C. 1985, c. I-5; *Foreign Missions and International Organizations Act*, S.C. 1991, c. 41; *Visiting Forces Act*, R.S.C. 1985, c. V-2.

Example

Facts		
Harry Schmidt is a Canadian resident to whom the following data applies. INCOME:		
Net salary	$	54,000
Deductions from salary:		
CPP		(445)
EI		(648)
Income tax		(8,000)
Pension plan (registered)		(3,500)
Premiums to group health plan		(50)
Commissions from employment		7,000
Interest on bonds		5,000
Net rental income		12,420
Taxable capital gain on listed personal property		12,000
Allowable capital loss on listed personal property		13,000
Taxable capital gain		5,500
Allowable capital loss (incl. ABIL)		3,000
Allowable business investment loss (ABIL)		1,500
EXPENSES:		
Alimony support payments		6,500
Charitable donations		2,000
Tuition fees		1,500
Accounting fees for preparation of personal tax return		500
Legal fees to purchase rental property		1,500
Income tax instalments		5,000
Calculate Mr. Schmidt's income according to section 3.		

Income determined under Section 3:			
para. 3(a):			
Gross salary*	$	66,643	
Commissions from employment		7,000	
Less: pension contributions		(3,500)	
Net employment income			$ 70,143
Income from property:			
Net rental income	$	12,420	
Interest on bonds		5,000	
			17,420
			87,563
para. 3(b):			
Taxable capital gain			5,500
Taxable gain on LPP	$	12,000	
Allowable loss on LPP		(13,000)	
Net gain on LPP			0
Allowable capital loss (incl. ABIL)	$	3,000	
Less ABIL		1,500	
			(1,500)
			91,563
para. 3(c):			
Alimony payments			(6,500)
			85,063
para. 3(d):			
Allowable business investment loss			(1,500)
Income			$ 83,563

Notes:

* Net salary ($54,000) plus all deductions from salary (CPP, E.I., etc.) added back in.

XI. — Conclusion

We have seen in this chapter that there is no definitive definition of income. The measure of income, which is central to the determination of the taxable base, has been substantially influenced by the jurisprudence. Thus, starting with a "pure" economist's concept of income as represented by the Haig-Simons formulation, we have adapted it to more closely accommodate the needs of taxpayers in daily life and commerce. For example, we modify the economic concept of income to include only realized gains and to exclude imputed income completely. However, the source theory and judicial exclusions of windfall gains pose difficult questions that need to be addressed. Finally, the list of statutory exclusions in section 81 should be re-evaluated to ensure that the policies reflected therein are as valid today as they were when the exemptions were introduced.

Selected Bibliography to Chapter 4

General

Bittker, "Income Tax Reform in Canada: The Report of the Royal Commission on Taxation" (1968) 35 U. Chi. L. Rev. 367.

Bossons, "The Value of a Comprehensive Tax Base Reform Goal" (1970) 13 J. Law & Econ. 327.

Bruce, Neil, "Ability to Pay and Comprehensive Income Taxation: Annual or Lifetime Basis" in *The Quest for Tax Reform: The Royal Commission on Taxation Twenty Years Later* (Toronto: Carswell, 1988) at 157.

Haig, R.M., ed., *The Federal Income Tax* (New York, 1921).

Perry, Harvey, "Federal Individual Income Tax: Some General Concepts" *Tax Paper No. 89* 42 (Can. Tax Foundation, 1990).

Rendall, "Defining the Tax Base", in *Canadian Taxation*, Hansen, Krishna, Rendall eds., (Toronto: De Boo, 1981).

Royal Commission on Taxation, Study No. 19B, pp. 88–157 (1957).

Simons, H.C., *Personal Income Taxation* (Chicago: The University of Chicago Press, 1938).

Stone, "A Comprehensive Income Tax Base for the U.S.?: Implications of the Report of the Royal Commission on Taxation" (1969) 22 Nat. Tax J. 24.

The Meaning of "Income"

La Brie, "The Meaning of Income in the Law of Income Tax" (1953) U.T.L.J. 81.

Exclusions from Income

Comment, "Taxation of Found Property and Other Windfalls" (1953) 20 U. Chi. L. Rev. 748.

Duff, David G., "Taxing Inherited Wealth: A Philosophical Argument" (1993) 6 Can. J. of Law and Jurisprudence 3.

Krishna, Vern, "Windfall Gains and Inducement Payments" (1986) 1 Can. Current Tax J-163.

Barter Transactions

Krishna, Vern, "Payments in Kind and Barter — Inclusion in Income — Valuation" (1985) 1:20 Can. Current Tax J-93.

Exempt Income

Drache, A.B.C., "Tax Exempt Expenses for Moonlighting Employees" (1991) XIII Can. Taxpayer 159.

Chapter 5 — Measurement of Income

Table of Contents

Fundamentals of Canadian Income Tax Vol 1: Personal Tax

Table of Contents

Chapter 5 — Measurement of Income

Table of Contents

I. — General Comment

A fair tax system requires an accurate measure of the taxable base. Sales taxes, for example, must identify taxable sales of goods and services. Usage taxes, such as highway tolls, must identify the consumer's use of the particular facility. Thus, the key to a good income tax system is the accurate measurement of the income.

"Income" is a measure of gain over some defined period. Thus, measuring income requires that we identify the amount of the gain and relate it to the appropriate period when we should recognize the gain for tax purposes. Both of these aspects of measurement involve processes influenced by law, economics and accounting. The measurement of income is as much an art as it is a science.

Accounting is the art of measuring and presenting financial information in an organized manner. As such, accounting is the language of financial transactions. Users of financial information need to understand this language, regardless of whether they act for business or represent interests that are adverse to business. Lawyers, for example, must deal with accounting problems in the same way they address other issues, with judgment and analysis. For example, lawyers need to understand accounting to draft financial clauses in contracts to structure negotiated settlements, for advocacy in litigation, for tax purposes, and to negotiate damage awards.

As with all languages, accounting has rules of structure and composition. We refer to these rules as accounting principles. Contrary to popular conceptions and, perhaps, most fortunately, accountants did not devise the fundamental structural rules of recording financial data. In 1494, a Renaissance monk named Luca Pacioli devised the basic process of recording financial data through a system of double entry bookkeeping, which he published in a text "Summa Arithmetica". This process allows us to record information in a methodical manner for analysis and decision-making.

It is important to note, however, that the principles of accounting are neither rigid nor uniform. Variations in accounting principles make comparisons of financial information difficult. For present purposes, however, we confine our attention to the basic principles of Canadian accounting.

II. — Accounting Principles and Reporting Standards

The phrase "generally accepted accounting principles" (GAAP) is an intrinsic and fundamental component of financial language. Auditors' Reports specifically refer to GAAP in their opinions. Since January 1, 2011, public companies must also report using International Financial Reporting Standards (IFRS).

GAAP and IFRS refer to broad principles and conventions that apply generally in accounting. They also refer to specific rules to determine accounting practices at particular times. In Canada, the authoritative source of GAAP and IFRS is the *Handbook* of the Canadian Institute of Chartered Accountants, which states (at para 1000.60):

> GAAPs encompass not only specific rules, practices and procedures relating to particular circumstances but also broad principles and conventions of general application.

However, GAAPs are not universal and identical. The United States has its own set of GAAPs. The International Accounting Standards Board (IASB) has other GAAPs. Canada has adopted international GAAPs as articulated by the IASB, and known as IFRS, for public companies.

A. — Where Do GAAPs and IFRS Come From?

GAAPs and IFRS are *generally accepted* principles developed by accounting bodies after study and research in consultation with academics, business, and government. Accounting bodies develop GAAPs and IFRS by exercising professional judgment and analyzing the advantages and disadvantages of alternative methods of accounting and reporting. Since accounting does not produce precise answers to every question, GAAPs and IFRS provide rules and guidelines that are generally acceptable. GAAPs and IFRS may offer choices between allowable alternatives or may be entirely silent on the particular point.

GAAPs and IFRS also have an important role in the calculation and disclosure of net income for income tax purposes. However, they are not determinative. The *Income Tax Act* of Canada is the statutory source of law for tax purposes and it will, in many cases, specify methods that do not necessarily accord with commercial GAAPs.

Legal contracts often refer to GAAPs in the preparation of financial statements. For example, contracts that contain negative covenants relating to financial status or ratios, such as working capital or debt/equity ratios, frequently state that the relevant financial statements must be prepared in accordance with GAAP.

B. — The Hierarchy of GAAP Sources

There are various sources for GAAP. At the top of the hierarchy, however, are the official statements from organizations that the accounting profession designates as the official body to determine appropriate accounting treatment for financial transactions. In Canada, the Institute of Chartered Accountants of Canada is the official source of GAAP, which are discussed in its *Handbook*.

In the United States, the official body for determining the appropriate accounting treatment of transactions is the Financial Accounting Standards Board (FASB), an independent body created to establish and improve standards for financial accounting and reporting. It is made up of a cross-section of accountants, academics, and users of financial statements. In order to enhance the independence of the board, the seven members of FASB cannot hold private employment during their tenure of service on the board.

In the United States, the Securities and Exchange Commission (SEC) regulates the sale of securities and securities markets. Therefore, publicly listed companies must file regular financial statements according to specified criteria with the SEC.

The SEC does not routinely develop accounting principles, but leaves the development of such principles to the independent accounting bodies, such as FASB. Nevertheless, the SEC will, on some occasions, promulgate accounting principles if it is of the opinion that the accounting profession or bodies are not acting fast enough on their own.

C. — GAAP & Tax Law

Tax accounting is quite different from financial statement accounting because the objectives of the two processes are quite different. The policies and objectives of an income tax system are quite different from the policies that underlie the preparation of general purpose financial statements. To be sure, both tax accounting and general financial accounting share a common overarching objective: the preparation of financial statements that produce a meaningful and fair measure of net income for the taxpayer or accounting entity. Hence, they start from the same premise that "net income" is the base upon which one should pay income taxes.

However, tax law also has other policy objectives — social, cultural, political, and economic — that can distort the accounting measure of net income. For example, the tax system generally requires an entity to include unearned revenues in income. For accounting purposes, unearned revenues would not be included in the current year's net income, but would show as deferred liabilities revenue on the balance sheet until the entity actually earns the revenue. The government, however, prefers to tax receipts sooner rather than later and taxes the unearned revenue because the taxpayer has use of the money.

Similarly, although a Canadian business can use the last-in, first-out (LIFO) system of accounting for inventories, it cannot use LIFO for income tax purposes. In the United States, a slightly different rule applies: if a business elects to use LIFO for income tax purposes, it must also use the same method for its financial statement reporting to shareholders. IFRS does not approve of LIFO for income measurement.

D. — Auditing & Professional Standards

Before the *Sarbanes-Oxley Act* (SOX) (2002), the American Institute of Certified Public Accountants (AICPA) used to set auditing and professional standards. Since SOX, however, the Public Company Accounting Oversight Board (PCAOB) is responsible for setting standards for public companies and the AICPA for private companies. Similarly, in Canada, IFRS applies to public companies and Canadian GAAP for private companies.

E. — Role of Management in Selecting GAAPs

Management has a key role in determining the nature, format, and underlying principles of its financial statements. Indeed, the Representation Letter that corporate management must submit to its auditors will usually state in the first paragraph:

> We are responsible for the fair presentation in the financial statements of financial position, results of operations and changes in financial position in conformity with generally accepted accounting principles.

To discharge its responsibility, management must select accounting principles; determine asset life; and decide reporting policy if there is no existing principle.

F. — Is GAAP Good for You?

GAAP and IFRS are rules of content that deal with compiling and disclosing information in the financial statements. The first item in the Notes to the financial statements will describe the principles that the particular enterprise applies in the preparation of its financial statements. GAAP and IFRS provide considered and properly researched principles that accountants can adhere to and readers can use with reasonable confidence in understanding financial statements. They also make financial statements more comparable if the underlying GAAP are the same for all statements. As noted above, tax law may vary from GAAP for many reasons peculiar to the fiscal system and to prevent tax avoidance.

Given the variety of GAAPs that one may apply to measure or report upon the same situation, we can have many net income figures, each of which is equally valid and according to GAAP. This is an important consideration in drafting legal agreements. It can also be an important issue in tax law.

G. — Accounting Standards

The two key accounting standards — setting bodies in the world are the International Accounting Standards Board (IASB) and the Financial Accounting Standards Board (FASB) of the United States. The two bodies do not have identical standards. Indeed, they differ quite significantly in some areas such as "fair value" accounting.

Broadly speaking, fair value accounting standards value a firm's assets and liabilities based upon market value rather than historical cost. The difference is particularly important in the valuation of financial instruments and property, plant, and equipment on the balance sheet.

Canada adopted International Financial Reporting Standards (IFRS) for public companies in 2011 even though our economy is more closely linked to the United States, which primarily uses FASB.

H. — Framework of IFRS

IFRS refers to the body of authoritative literature of the International Accounting Standards Board (IASB) designed principally for use by profit-oriented entities. The IFRS Foundation oversees the IASB. The IASB developed a *Conceptual Framework* for the development of IFRS and for guidance to accountants in preparing public entity financial statements. The objective of the IASB is to narrow the differences among accounting standards, procedures, and regulations that apply in the preparation of financial statements in different countries. Harmonization will facilitate economic decision making and international comparisons of companies. Reporting entities must comply with all of the standards and interpretations (including disclosure requirements) and make a positive statement of explicit and unreserved compliance in the audit opinion.

The framework recognizes that the overall objective of general purpose financial reporting is to provide financial information about the reporting entity that is useful to existing and potential investors, lenders and other creditors in making decisions about providing resources to the entity.[1] General purpose financial reports are not designed to show the value of a reporting entity. However, they provide useful information to help existing and potential investors, lenders, financial analysts, and other creditors to estimate the value of the reporting entity. For tax purposes, the primary objective of financial statements is to provide information on the entity's net earnings for revenue generation according to the law. There is no requirement for a taxpayer to pay more than the law demands.

Financial statements for corporate entities prepared according to IFRS involve:

- Accounting policy choices;

- Professional judgment in making estimates;

- Fair value measures in the financial statements; and

- Disclosures in the Notes.

---

[1]Canadian Institute of Chartered Accountants, *CICA Handbook — Accounting*, loose-leaf (Toronto: Canadian Institute of Chartered Accountants, 2010), Part I (2012) OB 2 [*CICA Handbook*].

The overall objective of IFRS is fair presentation in the financial statements. In this aspect, there is no underlying difference in principle between IFRS and Canadian GAAP. However, absent specific prohibition, IFRS admits deviation and provides for a "true and fair" override if complying with IFRS would produce misleading information. In contrast, there is no such concept of a true and fair view override in Canadian GAAP.

Financial reports are based on estimates, judgments, and models rather than exact depictions. The Conceptual Framework of IFRS establishes the concepts that underline those estimates, judgments, and models.[2] The fundamental qualitative characteristics of useful financial information are relevance and faithful representation.[3] For tax purposes, they must also comply with the statute and developed jurisprudence. For example, although LIFO inventory valuation may provide a fair measure of income, taxpayers cannot use the method because of the decision of the Privy Council in *Anaconda Brass*.

Financial statements, *per se*, are not predictions or forecasts. However, relevant and faithful representations of material financial information are the foundation for making predictions and forecasts by investors, management, financial analysts. They are also the basic information for regulatory compliance.

Faithful representation or fair measure of income does not imply perfect accuracy in all respects, but the information should be relevant and faithfully represented. Information in financial reports should be material. Materiality means that omission or misstatement of the information could influence decisions that users make based on the information about a specific reporting entity. In tax law, however, the requirement for compliance is more rigid and financial statements are tested by the letter of the law, at least where the law is specific.

I. — Who Is Affected by IFRS?

The underlining objective of the IFRSs is to produce global accounting standards that are transparent and provide comparable information on financial statements. By having a single set of global standards, public corporations can eliminate multiple GAAP reconciliations between countries.

Both IFRS and Canadian GAAP are comprehensive sets of principles-based standards that have a similar form and structure and share similar basic concepts of income recognition and measurement principles. However, IFRS requires more professional judgment and a greater volume of disclosures.

Canadian Accounting Standards are simpler to apply and, therefore, less costly. They also have fewer disclosure requirements than IFRS. However, Canada adopted IFRS for "publicly accountable enterprises" (PAE), which include "profit-oriented" enterprises with pub-

---

[2] *Ibid.*, OB 11.

[3] See *ibid.*, QC 5.

licly issued securities and enterprises that hold assets in a fiduciary capacity for a broad group of outsiders. PAE also includes government business enterprises, such as the Ontario Securities Commission. Not-for-profits are not required to adopt IFRS.

Part I of the *CICA Handbook* deals with IFRS. Entities that prepare their financial statements in accordance with the part must state in their audit opinion that they have been prepared in accordance with IFRS. Such entities may also state that its financial statements are in accordance with Canadian GAAP.

IFRS and Canadian GAAP require that management account for financial transactions based upon their substance, rather than their legal form. Thus, accountants should recognize transactions with shareholders in their capacity as shareholders directly in the equity portion of the financial statements rather than through the income statement.

However, there are differences between IFRS and Canadian GAAP. Generally, there are fewer bright lines and rules in IFRS. Hence, there are more accounting policy choices and fewer interpretative matters. In particular, there are substantial differences in valuation and disclosure of impaired assets and securitizations.

J. — Fair Value Measurement

Most items are disclosed in the financial statements based on their historical costs. In some circumstances (such as inventories), historical cost may be reduced to reflect a loss if fair market value is less than cost (International Accounting Standard (IAS) 2). In other cases, such as property, plant, and equipment, an entity may reduce or increase amounts to reflect their fair value (IAS 16). IFRS 13 defines fair value and has a framework for measuring and disclosing it in the financials.

Fair value is the price that an entity would receive if it sold an asset or paid to transfer a liability in an orderly transaction between market participants as at the measurement date. Thus, fair value is a market-based measurement, not an entity-specific measurement. When measuring fair value, an entity uses the assumptions that market participants would use to price the asset or liability under current market conditions. As such, the entity's intention to hold the asset is not relevant when measuring fair value. The measure is what the buyer will pay for the benefit that it expects to generate from the use (or sale) of the assets, regardless of the entity's actual intentions.

An entity measuring fair value must determine:

- The particular asset or liability that is to be measured;
- For a non-financial asset, the highest and best use of the asset and whether it will be used in combination with other assets or on a stand-alone basis;
- The market in which the orderly transaction would take place for the asset or liability; and

- The appropriate valuation technique to use.

To increase consistency and comparability in the fair value measurements, IFRS 13 establishes a fair value hierarchy that categorizes the inputs used in valuation techniques.

Level 1: Inputs are quoted prices in active markets for identical assets or liabilities that the entity can access at the measurement date.

Level 2: Inputs are inputs (other than quoted prices included within Level 1) that are observable for the asset or liability, either directly or indirectly.

Level 3: Inputs are non-observable inputs for the asset or liability. Such inputs must reflect the assumption that market participants will use when pricing the asset or liability, including assumptions about risk.

In order to measure fair value, management must identify the characteristics of an asset or liability that market participants will take into account when pricing that asset or liability. They must also determine whether a principal market for an asset or liability exists and whether the entity has access to that market. In the absence of a principal market, it will be necessary to identify the most advantageous market for the asset or liability, which is likely to be that which maximizes the amount that would be received to sell the asset or minimize the amount that would be paid to transfer the liability.

For non-financial assets, management must determine the highest and best use of the asset from the perspective of market participants. This is so even if the entity intends to use the asset for a different purpose. Management must exercise judgment in determining the appropriate valuation technique to measure fair value.

The rationale of the input disclosures is to provide users with information so they may assess the valuation techniques and inputs used to develop fair value measurements, their effect on profit or loss or on other comprehensive income for the period.

K. — Profits

A taxpayer's income for a taxation year from a business or property is his *profit* therefrom for the year.[4] The term "profit" means *net* profit, that is, the amount of revenue remaining after the deduction of expenses incurred for the purpose of earning the revenue.[5]

Most recently, since 2012, Canada has adopted International Financial Reporting Standards (IFRS) as a supplement to Canadian GAAP in certain cases.

---

[4]Subs. 9(1); subs. 9(2) defines "loss".

[5]*Montreal Light, Heat & Power Consolidated v. Minister of National Revenue*; *Montreal Coke & Mfg. Co. v. Minister of National Revenue*, [1940-41] C.T.C. 217, 2 D.T.C. 506 (Can. Ex. Ct.); affirmed [1942] C.T.C. 1, 2 D.T.C. 535 (S.C.C.); affirmed [1944] C.T.C. 94, 2 D.T.C. 654 (Canada P.C.).

Chapter 5 — Measurement of Income

Net income or profit essentially comprises two components, namely, revenue and expenses during a period of time. We calculate net profit or net income according to the formula:

$$NI = R - E$$

where:

NI = Net Income

R = Revenues

E = Expenses

The measurement of income for commercial purposes begins with this basic formula, the essence of which is matching revenues and expenses over a period of time. For tax purposes, the period is usually one year.

The first step in the calculation of net profit is to look to accounting and commercial principles. In *Daley v. Minister of National Revenue*, for example:[6]

> . . . the first inquiry whether a particular disbursement or expense is deductible should not be whether it is excluded from deduction by [paragraph 18(1)(a) or (b)] but rather whether its deduction is permissible by the ordinary principles of commercial trading or accepted business and accounting practice. . . .

---

[6]*Daley v. Minister of National Revenue*, [1950] C.T.C. 254 at 260, 4 D.T.C. 877 at 880 (Can. Ex. Ct.) (fee for call to Bar not deductible expense as preceding commencement of the practice of law). See also, *R. v. Metropolitan Properties Co. Ltd.*, [1985] 1 C.T.C. 169, 85 D.T.C. 5128 (Fed. T.D.) (in absence of specific statutory provisions, generally accepted accounting principles applied); *Imperial Oil Ltd. v. Minister of National Revenue*, [1947] C.T.C. 353, 3 D.T.C. 1090 (Can. Ex. Ct.) (damages paid on negligence settlement incurred as consequence of operations by which business income earned; damages deemed deductible expenses); *Royal Trust Co. v. Minister of National Revenue*, [1957] C.T.C. 32, 57 D.T.C. 1055 (Can. Ex. Ct.) (club fees allowed executives to meet new clients; expenses need not be directly related to income); *Frankel Corp. v. Minister of National Revenue*, [1958] C.T.C. 314, 58 D.T.C. 1173 (Can. Ex. Ct.); reversed [1959] C.T.C. 244 (S.C.C.) (sale of capital assets of one of four of taxpayer's businesses not taxable as inventory sales but, oddly, taxable as deemed receipt because of diversion tactics); *Canadian General Electric Co. v. Minister of National Revenue* (1961), [1962] S.C.R. 3, [1961] C.T.C. 512, 61 D.T.C. 1300 (S.C.C.) (debts decreased due to change in foreign exchange rate; profit apportioned amongst tax years rather than upon actual payment of note); *Irwin v. Minister of National Revenue*, [1964] S.C.R. 662, [1964] C.T.C. 362, 64 D.T.C. 5227 (S.C.C.) (concept of profit for tax purposes clarified); *Quemont Mining Corp. v. Minister of National Revenue*, [1966] C.T.C. 570, 66 D.T.C. 5376 (Can. Ex. Ct.) (disagreement in formula used to calculate mining taxes paid to province); *Minister of National Revenue v. Atlantic Engine Rebuilders Ltd.*, [1967] S.C.R. 477, [1967] C.T.C. 230, 67 D.T.C. 5155 (S.C.C.) (valuation of inventory consistent and coincidentally correct though original basis of evaluation flawed); *Sherritt Gordon Mines Ltd. v. Minister of National Revenue*, [1968] C.T.C. 262, 68 D.T.C. 5180 (Can. Ex. Ct.) (generally accepted business and commercial principles used in respect of capitalization of interest expenses during construction period).

See also, *Dominion Taxicab Assn. v. Minister of National Revenue*:[7]

> The expression "profit" is not defined in the Act. It has not a technical meaning and whether or not the sum in question constitutes profit must be determined on ordinary commercial principles unless the provisions of the *Income Tax Act* require a departure from such principles.

Commercial principles are the first step in determining profit, but they are not necessarily conclusive. Ultimately, the profit for tax purposes is a question of law.[8]

III. — Accounting Concepts

There are three basic concepts in the preparation and interpretation of financial statements: (1) historical cost accounting, (2) stable dollar value, and (3) the going concern assumption. As we will see in subsequent chapters, these concepts also determine tax results.

A. — Historical Cost Accounting

We prepare financial statements using historical and original costs to record transactions. Thus, except on the date when we acquire an asset, its cost does not represent the price for which we can replace (replacement cost) or sell it (fair market value). For this reason, historical cost statements, which trade-off relevance for reliability, are of limited value in interpretation. They are, however, useful for reporting to the tax authorities, who are concerned with compliance and not with interpretation.

Although accountants generally report assets at either historical or depreciated cost, they do adjust some assets, such as temporary investments, for upward and downward swings in market values. In other cases, such as inventories, we write down assets when their historical cost exceeds their realizable or fair market values. The theory underlying such adjustments is that we expect to realize (sell) inventories in the current term and, therefore, their market value is more relevant than historical cost. With the introduction of IFRS, there is a greater emphasis on fair value reporting.

B. — Stable Dollar Value

GAAP treats the dollar as a stable unit of measure. Therefore, if a company owns land that it purchased in 1970 for $25,000 and in 2013 it purchased an identical adjacent tract for

---

[7]*Dominion Taxicab Assn. v. Minister of National Revenue*, [1954] S.C.R. 82, [1954] C.T.C. 34 at 37, 54 D.T.C. 1020 at 1021 (S.C.C.).

[8]*Canderel Ltd. v. R.*, [1998] 1 S.C.R. 147, [1998] 2 C.T.C. 35 (S.C.C.); *Toronto College Park v. R.*, [1998] 1 S.C.R. 183, [1998] 2 C.T.C. 78 (S.C.C.).

$500,000, the lands will appear as $525,000 on the balance sheet. This completely overlooks the fact that during the 43-year period the purchasing power of the dollar has substantially declined. Similarly, if the company sold the first plot of land in 2013 for $500,000, we would record a gain of $475,000 on the income statement, even if the $500,000 has no more purchasing power than the $25,000 in 1970. In other words, historical balance sheet values can be meaningless and we need to evaluate them with care. The rationale for continuing to use a constant dollar as a unit of measure is that historical costs are objective. In contrast, financial statements adjusted for changes in purchasing power require subjective judgments in their preparation. This compromises their reliability. Thus, every balance sheet trades off relevance for reliability. This has important implications in tax law where we pay taxes based on nominal profits without regard to purchasing power.

C. — The Going Concern Assumption

The going concern assumption means that the entity expects to continue in operation into the indefinite future and, therefore, will realize its assets and discharge its liabilities in the normal course of its business. This assumption supports the historical cost basis of accounting because the business can reasonably expect cost recovery of its assets during the course of their useful life. If the assumption is not valid, some other model of accounting, for example, the liquidation basis, may be more appropriate. Thus, the basis of valuing assets (historical cost or liquidation value) on the balance sheet must be consistent with expectations for the entity.

IV. — Accounting Principles and Tax Law

Having determined the appropriate treatment of a receipt or expenditure according to commercial and accounting practice, the next step is to determine whether the Act or case law prescribes a different treatment for tax purposes. The Minister cannot insist on a taxpayer using a specific method if the method that the taxpayer uses is permissible under well-accepted business principles and is not prohibited by the Act or by some specific rule of law.[9] Although accounting principles assist in interpreting tax law, they cannot be used where the Act prescribes otherwise.[10]

Where the Act specifically prohibits the deduction of an expenditure, the statute prevails over commercial and accounting principles and the expenditure is not deductible in computing profit. For example, under generally accepted accounting principles permit, indeed mandate the deduction of depreciation as an expense in calculating income. Depreciation is the allocation of the historical cost of an asset over its useful life in a going concern business.

---

[9]*Canderel Ltd. v. R.*, [1998] 1 S.C.R. 147, [1998] 2 C.T.C. 35, 98 D.T.C. 6100 (S.C.C.).

[10]*Consumers' Gas Co. v. R.*, [1987] 1 C.T.C. 79, 87 D.T.C. 5008 (Fed. C.A.).

However, since the Act specifically prohibits the deduction of depreciation, any depreciation calculated for financial statement purposes is not deductible as an expense for tax purposes.[11] Thus, for tax purposes, we add back depreciation to financial net income. However, the Act allows a taxpayer an alternative deduction to allocate asset costs over their useful life. We refer to this statutory deduction as capital cost allowance.[12]

Similarly, case law may also prohibit the use of a particular method of calculating income that is otherwise acceptable in commercial practice. For example, although the last-in, first-out (LIFO) method of valuing inventory is generally acceptable for financial statement purposes, we cannot use LIFO to calculate income for tax purposes.[13]

The Act can, however, also specifically override a general prohibition against the deduction of a type of expenditure.[14] For example, interest payable on indebtedness would be a non-deductible payment on account of capital[15] were it not for paragraph 20(1)(c), which specifically allows for its deduction in computing income from a business or property. This simply reflects the rule of statutory construction that a specific rule prevails over a general rule.

V. — Measurement and Timing

Although measurement and timing of income are two different concepts, they are closely linked. For example, suppose a business started up in 1900 and closed down in 2014. There might be a number of difficulties involved in measuring the aggregate income of the enterprise over the 114 years. If all we need to know is the net income figure for the 114 years, there is no issue of timing. Serious problems of timing arise, however, if we need to measure income for 2014 only. Then, we need to match 2014 revenues and expenses. Thus, we need to know when we earn revenues, when we recognize the revenues in our financial statements, and the principles of matching of revenues and expenses.

---

[11] Para. 18(1)(b).

[12] Para. 20(1)(a).

[13] *Minister of National Revenue v. Anaconda American Brass Ltd.*, [1955] C.T.C. 311, 55 D.T.C. 1220 (Canada P.C.).

[14] See, e.g., the general prohibitions in paras. 18(1)(a) (expenditure must be incurred for the purpose of earning income), 18(1)(b) (expenditure cannot be on account of capital), 18(1)(h) (expenditure cannot be on account of personal or living expenses).

[15] *Canada Safeway Ltd. v. Minister of National Revenue*, [1957] S.C.R. 717, [1957] C.T.C. 335, 57 D.T.C. 1239 (S.C.C.) (use of borrowed money important in characterization of interest expense as business or property; acquisition of shares of subsidiary complicated issue); *Interprovincial Pipe Line Co. v. Minister of National Revenue*, [1967] C.T.C. 180, 67 D.T.C. 5125 (Can. Ex. Ct.); affd. [1968] S.C.R. 498, [1968] C.T.C. 156, 68 D.T.C. 5093 (S.C.C.) (tax loophole in treaty cured; incidental interest earned deducted from interest expense to determine loss); *Sherritt Gordon Mines Ltd. v. Minister of National Revenue*, above note 6.

We can illustrate these problems by examining the accounting concepts of "realization", "recognition", "accrual", "matching", and "conservatism".

A. — Realization

The measurement of income requires one to calculate gain and relate it to the appropriate time period. Generally, we measure gain at the point that we realize the revenue that triggers the gain.

A simple definition of "realization" would refer to the point of sale, the time at which X parts with property and receives a real gain in the form of cash. The following examples illustrate the inadequacy of this simple definition. If X sells Black Acre and takes back a mortgage, X realizes a gain that should be recognized for tax purposes. Similarly, we treat an exchange of Black Acre for White Acre, a property of equal value, or for stock in Black Acre Developments Ltd., as a realization. Even if X gives Black Acre away, she will realize a gain. In all these cases the rationale is the same: X has parted with her investment in Black Acre, and for tax purposes, we treat X as if she sold the property for cash.

The fundamental question is *when* do we "realize" a gain or loss. Suppose, for example that X buys Black Acre for $50,000. By the end of the year the property is worth $60,000. Does X experience a $10,000 gain? Certainly she has a potential gain, a "paper gain", an accrued gain in the Haig-Simons sense. Traditional accounting practice, however, ignores the gain as unrealized.

In the following year, X's property might decline in value to $45,000 or might rise to $70,000. Suppose, in either case, that X then sells the property. According to traditional practice, X is treated as "realizing" a $5,000 loss or a $20,000 gain in the year that she sells the property. In the first case, the $5,000 loss represents a $10,000 paper gain in Year 1 combined with a paper loss of $15,000 in Year 2. In the second case, X had a paper gain of $10,000 in each of the years 1 and 2.

B. — Recognition

The second aspect of measurement is to identify the appropriate period in which we wish to recognize the gain for tax purposes. Some accounting systems (for example, mark-to-market) would recognize all the "paper" gains and losses in a year even though they are "unrealized". For the most part, however, the Act does not recognize "unrealized" amounts for tax purposes.

There are good reasons for not recognizing paper gains. Accountants, true to the axiom of their conservatism in estimating income, normally disregard such gains because they may prove illusory if values decline in a subsequent period. From the perspective of a taxpayer, the recognition of unrealized gains could prove a hardship. If X was required to recognize a $10,000 paper gain on Black Acre, and to pay tax on it, she would be required to find the money to pay the tax at the end of Year 1. Attempts in the past to tax unrealized gains on certain corporate shares were strongly resisted.[16]

On the other hand, deferring the recognition of the entire gain to the point of realization creates problems of irregularity and "lumping" of income. Delayed realization also allows taxpayers to defer their taxes. This is an important principle in tax planning.

There are some cases in which the Act recognizes unrealized gains. For example, the Act deems a taxpayer who ceases to be a Canadian resident to have disposed of any capital property and realized any accrued gain or loss for tax purposes. In other situations, the Act does not recognize a gain even though it has been realized through an actual disposition. For example, the Act does not recognize realized gains when a person transfers appreciated capital property to his spouse. These exceptions reflect other policy considerations in the tax system that override the accurate measurement of income.

Accountants are not as reluctant to recognize unrealized losses as they are to recognize unrealized gains. Consistent with accounting conservatism in estimating income, and depending upon the nature of the asset concerned, it is sometimes considered good accounting practice to recognize a "paper" loss. Understandably, the revenue authorities usually do not agree that this principle of conservatism should apply to calculations of income for tax purposes. To forestall the possibility of complete accounting doom and gloom in such matters, the Act does not recognize most paper losses for tax purposes.

We have explored, in a very simple way, the concept of realization of gain. There remain a number of slightly more sophisticated problems concerning the time when gains should be recognized.

Suppose that X starts a business of manufacturing and selling widgets. The business cycle can be broken down into the following steps:

1. Acquisition of inventory of raw metal;

2. Fabrication of metal into an inventory of widgets;

3. Sales activity that results in orders for widgets;

4. Delivery of widgets to customers;

5. Invoicing of customers; and

6. Payment of invoices.

An argument could be made for X choosing any one of the last five steps as the point at which he should recognize his gain for the purposes of calculating income. Our earlier discussion would probably suggest that he should not recognize his gain at any point before step 4. Standard accounting would lead to a choice of step 5 as the point at which X should

---

[16]See, for example, *Proposals for Tax Reform* (Ottawa: Finance Canada, 1969), ss. 1.30 and 3.36.

recognize a gain. In any event, as a matter of usual business practice, steps 4 and 5 are usually merged. Commonly, the invoice accompanies the delivery of widgets. As we shall see below, if X's business adopts a cash basis of accounting, he will not recognize his gain until step 6, when the business actually receives payment.

Thus, the timing of revenues is the first decision in the measurement process. For accounting purposes, we generally recognize revenues at the point when the entity's earning process is substantially complete — usually when we pass title to the product to the purchaser, or when we complete the service. At this point, we have sufficient information to measure revenues objectively.

The important point to observe here is that revenue does not necessarily relate in the earnings cycle to when we receive cash for the product or service. For example, if a company sells merchandise on credit (payable in 30 days), we recognize the full sales value when we ship the goods to the customer. The fact that the cash may not come in for 30 days or later does not matter. Indeed, in some cases, the customer might even pay in advance for the purchase of the goods. Nevertheless, we recognize revenues only when we ship the goods and title passes from the company to its customer. Until then, we consider the advance to be a debt owing to the customer. At the point of sale, we transform the debt into revenues.

To be sure, this principle of recognizing revenues at the time of sale and shipment does not make a great deal of difference in most cases, except at the end of the accounting cycle. For example, it matters little to a company with a December 31 year-end whether it takes its revenue for July sales into account in July, August, or September when it collects its cash from sales. Since all of the revenue falls in the same accounting period, it matters little for measurement purposes so long as the revenue falls in the current year.

The principle, however, is critical at the year-end. It makes a great deal of difference whether revenues from sales for merchandise shipped out in mid-December are taken into the current year's income or in the income of the year following. In this case, the timing of revenues affects the company's bottom-line profit for commercial purposes. Of course, it also affects the company's net income for tax purposes and, therefore, the amount of tax payable in the current year. Thus, it is imperative that we match revenues and related expenses in the same period.

C. — Accrual

The principles of accrual accounting are central to the matching of revenues and expenses. Accrual accounting requires that we recognize revenues in the period to which they relate, rather than when we collect the cash. Similarly, we recognize expenses in the period when we incur the expense, rather than when we pay for them. For example, assume we purchase merchandise on December 20 of the current year and pay for it on January 10 of the following year. Accrual accounting requires us to recognize the purchase in the current year, even though we did not pay for it until the following year.

As we will see, recognizing expenses in the appropriate period depends upon the nature of the expense. We recognize time-related expenses such as salaries and wages, utilities, interest, etc. at the end of the accounting period to which they relate. This is so even though we have not paid the expenses. Again, this may not make a great deal of difference to expenses we incur in the middle of an accounting period, but it can be important in terms of year-end accounting. Here also, accounting principles do not rely upon the outgoing of cash to determine when we take the expenditure into account in the financial books. The essential concept is matching the expense with revenues in the period in which we derive the benefit of the expense to earn the revenues.

D. — Matching

So far we have been discussing the appropriate time to recognize gains and losses. In an accounting sense, we measure gains and losses by reflecting expenditures and receipts. "Gains" or "losses" in themselves are net concepts, as is the "income" of a business, since it reflects all expenditures and all receipts.

Accrual and matching are related. The matching principle requires us to deduct expenses (E) in the same period as they contribute to the earning of revenues (R). Hence, if we incur expenses in one time period but the expenses will benefit several periods, we allocate the expense in some reasonable manner between the various periods. This principle lies at the core of the income equation. In other words, the "R" and "E" in the formula must match each other. The "E" must track the "R" so that both match for accounting purposes. For example, assume that a company orders and receives merchandise on December 15, 2014. We allocate the cost of the merchandise to 2014 or beyond depending upon when we sell the goods and pass title. Hence, if we sell the merchandise and recognize revenues in 2014, we also recognize the expenses (cost of goods sold) of the sale in the same year. If, however, the merchandise remains on hand as inventory, we recognize the cost as an asset in the current year. We then recognize the expense when we sell the merchandise in the following year. Thus, expenses are merely consumed assets.

Matching is essentially an allocation process between time periods. We recognize expenses that benefit the current time period in that period. Expenses that will benefit future time periods are "held" in asset accounts. We recognize them in subsequent time periods when we match them against revenues.

Mismatching of revenues and expenses distorts the net income figure and can seriously mislead readers of financial statements. For tax purposes, mismatching can lead to tax deferral if we delay recognizing revenues or accelerate recognizing expenses. The most extreme scenario is one where the taxpayer delays recognizing revenues and concurrently accelerates the time when he charges off the expenses. This might occur, for example, if the taxpayer receives a lump sum for two years' rental that he does not recognize until the second year, but recognizes the associated rental expenses in the first year.

The following example illustrates how we resolve the problem of matching.

Assume that City Dairy Ltd. delivers milk door to door and for this purpose requires 100 trucks costing $6,000 each. The trucks will have a useful life of approximately five years and will be disposed of for $1,000 each at the end of that time. Thus, over the course of five years, each truck represents a $5,000 expense of City Dairy's business. If, however, City Dairy bought and expensed 100 trucks in its first business year, it would dramatically distort its income for the year by recognizing the entire cost of $600,000 as an expenditure for that year. This particular problem is resolved by applying the notion of "depreciation" in order to allocate the cost of such assets over an appropriate number of years.

Although "matching" is a well-accepted business principle, it is simply an interpretive aid that assists, but is not determinative, in arriving at an accurate picture of the taxpayer's income.[17] We do not need to match if an expenditure does not directly relate to future revenues, or if it relates to future revenues but also refers to benefits realized in the year of expenditure.

E. — Conservatism

Conservatism is attitude. Conservatism refers to the accounting profession's approach to measuring profits. Measuring income means allocating costs and values to time periods and then matching revenues and expenses in the periods. Since we do not always know how much to allocate with absolute certainty, measuring profits requires professional judgment. Conservatism requires a cautious approach in allocating values and recognizing revenues and losses. In effect, conservatism means that an enterprise should not recognize revenues before earning them, but should recognize all anticipated losses even before they actually occur. Some call this a pessimistic approach; others say it is merely being prudent. Regardless of the label, conservatism implies caution and prudence. Recognize no gains in advance of realization, but recognize all losses at the earliest signal of trouble.

Conservatism and matching can conflict. For example, should we write off research and development costs over time to match revenues through increased sales? The matching principle requires that we recognize research and development as capital costs that we allocate over time as the new products generate revenues. The concept of conservatism, however, dictates prudence. Should we recognize the research expenditures as early as possible with-

---

[17]*Canderel Ltd. v. R.*, [1998] 1 S.C.R. 147, [1998] 2 C.T.C. 35, 98 D.T.C. 6100 (S.C.C.) (tenant inducement payment paid to secure 10 year lease from key tenant deductible entirely in year paid rather than over the period of the lease since sufficient benefit (preserved reputation, ensured future income stream, satisfied interim financing requirements) realized in first year to match expense); *Ikea Ltd. v. R.*, [1998] 1 S.C.R. 196, [1998] 2 C.T.C. 61, 98 D.T.C. 6092 (S.C.C.) (tenant inducement payment received for signing a 10 year lease taxable as income entirely in year received); *Toronto College Park Ltd. v. R.*, [1998] 1 S.C.R. 183, [1998] 2 C.T.C. 78, 98 D.T.C. 6088 (S.C.C.) (tenant inducement payment paid to secure lease deductible entirely in year made since amortization over period of lease would not present a more accurate picture of income).

out waiting for future revenues that might never materialize? Thus, measuring profit according to accounting principles is fraught with judgment calls that can materially affect an enterprise's bottom line. Indeed, it is entirely possible for two accountants to look at the same set of numbers and arrive at completely different conclusions on net income. Those responsible for the development of tax policy are fully aware of the variances that occur from discretionary judgments. Thus, we see many provisions in the Act that provide for a particular and specific method of measuring profit, regardless of accounting principles. In almost all cases, the Act prescribes a method of measuring profit that is more onerous than that allowed under accounting principles. This is understandable. Given a choice, why would the tax collector prescribe a method of accounting that produces a better result for the taxpayer?

VI. — Accounting Statements

Financial statements provide information about an economic entity's financial performance, economic resources and legal obligations to investors, creditors, management, tax authorities, and other regulators. Thus, we can use financial statements to assess management's performance, predict the entity's ability to generate future cash flows to meet obligations, assess the return to shareholders, measure tax liabilities, and regulatory compliance.

There are four different financial statements:

- The Balance Sheet;
- The Income Statement, including Statement of Comprehensive Income);
- The Statement of Retained Earnings; and
- The Statement of Changes in Financial Position.

The explanatory notes to financial statements are also an integral part of the statements.

The two most common accounting statements for tax purposes are the balance sheet and the income statement (sometimes called a statement of profit and loss).

A balance sheet reflects, *as at a particular date*, the condition of the business as it may be judged by a statement of what the business owns (assets) and a statement of its obligations (liabilities) and equity.

The liabilities side of the balance sheet is divided into two parts: (1) a statement of indebtedness to outsiders, and (2) a statement of the owner's equity. All business financing must come from these two sources — capital and debt. The owner may contribute capital to the business and the business may borrow money from a bank or purchase goods on credit. The traditional balance sheet equation:

$$A = L + E$$

(assets = liabilities + owner's equity)

is true because owner's equity is a constantly shifting amount that represents the difference between assets and liabilities. Hence:

$$E = A - L$$

Regardless of its legal status, a business is a distinct entity for accounting purposes. City Dairy Ltd., for example, is both an accounting entity and a legal entity separate from its incorporators. If X conducts his business as X Widgets, a sole proprietorship, X Widgets is not a distinct entity in law. It is, however, an entity in terms of accounting treatment. These rules also apply for tax purposes.

An income statement is a summary of the revenues and expenses of a business *for a stated period of time.*

The two statements, the balance sheet and the income statement, are closely inter-related and must be read together in order to present a complete and meaningful picture of the profitability and solvency of a business.

As an illustration, assume that A and B opened a retail business on January 1, Year 1 with each person contributing $2,500, and a bank loan of $10,000. The opening balance sheet *as at* January 1, Year 1, would appear as follows:

BALANCE SHEET

As at January 1, Year 1

ASSETS			LIABILITIES and EQUITY		
Cash	$	15,000	Bank loan	$	10,000
			Owner's equity:		
			Capital A		2,500
			Capital B		2,500
	$	15,000		$	15,000

Note: This is the historical format for balance sheets. Modern balance sheets use an up and down format or show assets and liabilities on separate pages. Regardless of the particular format, the accounting equation always applies.

The first point to observe is that the balance sheet balances: the left side of the statement that lists all the property that the business owns is *exactly equal* to the right side of the statement that lists its sources of financing. In other words, the left side of the statement informs the reader as to *what* the business owns (assets), and the right side discloses *how* the assets were financed (liabilities and equity). Hence, the above balance sheet informs any reader without further explanation of the statement that the business entity (the retail business) owned $15,000 of property (assets) as at January 1, Year 1, and that it held it in the form of cash.

Further, it informs the reader that the firm was financed from two sources, one external (bank loan $10,000) and the other internal (owner's equity $5,000).

The following transactions illustrate the operation of the fundamental accounting equation A = L + E:

On January 2, Year 1, the business leased office space at an annual rent of $6,000 and pays two months' rent on that date.

BALANCE SHEET
As at January 2, Year 1

ASSETS		LIABILITIES and EQUITY	
Cash	$ 14,000	Bank loan	$ 10,000
Pre-paid rent	1,000	Owner's equity:	
		Capital A	2,500
		Capital B	2,500
	$ 15,000		$ 15,000

On January 4, Year 1, the business acquired office furniture at a cost of $3,000, paying $1,500 in cash with a promise to pay the balance in 90 days.

BALANCE SHEET
As at January 4, Year 1

ASSETS		LIABILITIES and EQUITY	
Cash	$ 12,500	Accounts payable	$ 1,500
Pre-paid rent	1,000	Bank loan	10,000
Office furniture	3,000	Owner's equity:	
		Capital A	2,500
		Capital B	2,500
	$ 16,500		$ 16,500

On January 15, Year 1, the business hired two employees at a monthly salary of $1,000 each, and paid their salaries on January 31, Year 1.

BALANCE SHEET
As at January 31, Year 1

ASSETS		LIABILITIES and EQUITY		
Cash	$ 11,500	Accounts payable	$	1,500
Pre-paid rent	500	Bank loan		10,000
Office furniture	3,000	Owner's equity:		
		Capital A		1,750
		Capital B		1,750
	$ 15,000		$	15,000

During the month of February Year 1, the business provided services and collected $6,000 in cash, again paying its staff $2,000 in salary.

BALANCE SHEET
As at February 28, Year 1

ASSETS		LIABILITIES and EQUITY		
Cash	$ 15,500	Accounts payable	$	1,500
Office furniture	3,000	Bank loan		10,000
		Owner's equity:		
		Capital A		3,500
		Capital B		3,500
	$ 18,500		$	18,500

Each of the transactions described has been recorded using the fundamental equation: $A = L + E$. The reader sees that the business owns property (assets) that cost $18,500, now held in two forms, cash and office furniture, and that the firm is financed, as at February 28, Year 1, by outsiders to the extent of $11,500, with insiders (owner's equity) providing the balance of $7,000. The balance sheet does not, however, disclose any information as to *how* and *why* the owners' interest in the business increased from $5,000 to $7,000 during the two months of operations. Based on the balance sheet alone it would be difficult, if not impossible, for any user to assess the profit of the business.

Should the owners, A and B, be required to pay income tax on the increase in their equity of $2,000, or on some other amount? We find the answer in the income statement. The purpose of the income statement is to disclose *how* a business has performed between two successive points in time. In this sense, it is a connecting link between successive balance sheets. Whereas a balance sheet informs a reader *where* a business stands as at a given time, an income statement reveals *how* the business moved from the opening balance sheet to the closing balance sheet.

Continuing with the previous illustration, the income statement reveals the following information:

INCOME STATEMENT
For the Two Months ended February 28, Year 1

REVENUE			$	6,000
EXPENSES				
Wages	$	3,000		
Rent		1,000		
NET INCOME:				(4,000)
			$	2,000

ALLOCATION OF NET INCOME
To A at 50% of $2,000 = $1,000
To B at 50% of $2,000 = $1,000

This statement now informs the reader *how* the owner's equity increased by $2,000. Specifically, the business generated revenues of $6,000 and expended $4,000 in the process of generating those revenues, leaving an excess of revenues over expenses of $2,000. Thus, the purpose of the income statement is to match revenues earned with expenses incurred to generate the revenue. The statement can usually explain the change in the owners' equity between successive points in time.

The net income figure derived from the matching process provides a starting point in calculating a taxpayer's income tax liability. One observes this starting point in subsection 9(1) of the *Income Tax Act*: ". . . a taxpayer's income for a taxation year from a business or property is the taxpayer's *profit* from that business or property for that year." The terms "income" and "profit" are often used interchangeably, and it is now established that in the absence of specific statutory provisions or judicial doctrine, "profit" is to be computed in accordance with well-accepted commercial principles.

VII. — Accounting Methods

To this point, the term "income" has been used to denote the excess of revenues earned over expenses incurred to generate those revenues. Hence, in one sense income is an increase in net wealth; conversely, a loss is a decrease in net wealth. This definition is terse and obvious but mathematically demonstrable. The essence of the concept is thereby reduced to "gain during an interval of time". Thus, "gain" is the *sine qua non* of income. While this definition satisfies the purpose of conceptual explanation, it is necessary to adapt it for use in the preparation of financial statements.

A. — Time Intervals

As a preliminary matter, it is essential to select the appropriate "interval of time" between successive financial statements. For no other reason than that of administrative convenience, it has been conventionally established that financial statements should be prepared at least on an annual basis. Thus, annual financial statements for external reporting and tax purposes are now, with limited exceptions, the general statutory rule. It is this statutory requirement of annual reporting that gives rise to several income measurement problems.

B. — Cash vs. Accrual Accounting

The first of these measurement problems is to determine whether financial statements should be prepared on a "cash basis" or on an "accrual basis". The principal distinction between the cash and accrual methods of accounting arises in connection with the timing and the treatment of accounts receivable and payable. Accounts receivable from customers are not included in income under the cash method until the taxpayer is actually paid. In contrast, accrual method taxpayers must report their income when services are completed and billed, regardless of when the customer actually pays the account. Thus, the distinction between the two is essentially one of time and recognition.

In cash basis accounting, transactions are recorded at the time, and in the accounting period, when the business receives or disburse cash. Assuming an accounting period of January 1 to December 31 and the sale of merchandise on December 15, YEAR 1 for $3,000 with payment received on January 15, YEAR 2, a cash basis business would record and report the $3,000 revenue earned in YEAR 2. Further assume that the cost of the merchandise to the business was $1,000, paid in cash at time of purchase on December 1, YEAR 1. A cash basis business would record and report the cost of merchandise sold in YEAR 1. The effect of the purchase and sale of merchandise would be reflected in the Income Statements of the business as follows:

(Cash Basis)

	YEAR 1	YEAR 2	COMBINED
Sales Revenue	$ 0	$ 3,000	$ 3,000
Cost of Merchandise Sold	(1,000)	0	(1,000)
Net Income (Loss)	$ (1,000)	$ 3,000	$ 2,000

It is worthy of emphasis that, regardless of the accounting method, the *combined* net income of the business in the circumstances described would always amount to $2,000. The disadvantage of the cash basis method lies, however, in the mismatching in a particular accounting (fiscal) period of revenues earned and expenses incurred to earn those revenues. Thus, YEAR 1 shows a net loss of $1,000 due to the combined effect of early expense recognition and delayed revenue recognition. A year later the statement shows net income of $3,000 by ignoring the earlier expense write-off. Each of years 1 and 2 viewed in isolation presents a distorted result of the underlying business transaction: an economic increase of $2,000 in net wealth.

We said earlier that net income can only be determined with absolute accuracy when the reporting period for financial statements covers the entire life of a business. By selecting a shorter period of time than the life of the business, we change the task from income determination to estimation of net income. The sacrifice in mathematical accuracy, however, is well justified by the enhanced administrative and business convenience that results from timely financial statements.

The fact that, in most situations, cash basis accounting distorts the financial statements of an entity and more readily conceals the true impact of business transactions has, with limited exceptions, led to its rejection as an appropriate method of financial reporting. A notable exception is in the reporting of employment income, which individuals must report on a cash basis. This requirement results from a balancing of the enhanced administrative convenience to the employee, employer, and the CRA, and the minimal distortion that occurs in measuring employment income on a cash basis.

In contrast with the cash basis of accounting, accrual accounting recognizes revenue when it is realized, and expenses are reported in the same time period as the revenues for which they were incurred. The accrual basis is premised on the rationale that reporting revenues earned and expenses incurred in the same accounting period provides a better "matching", and that such "matching" more accurately depicts the underlying business transaction. Using the same figures as in the previous example, an income statement prepared on an accrual basis would disclose the following:

(Accrual Basis)

	YEAR 1	YEAR 2	COMBINED
Sales Revenue	$ 3,000	$ 0	$ 3,000
Cost of Merchandise Sold	(1,000)	0	(1,000)
Net Income (Loss)	$ 2,000	$ 0	$ 2,000

Although the ultimate combined net incomes of the two years is the same in both the cash basis and accrual basis methods of reporting, the latter method more accurately reflects the increase in net wealth in each period. (The outstanding accounts receivable of $3,000 as at December 31, YEAR 1, represents a customer's debt that increased net wealth.)

The accrual method also prevents tax deferral. For example, if a person pays five years' worth of lease payments in advance, the lump sum is capitalized and written off over a five-year period. Similarly, the lessor will treat the prepaid rents as an asset and recognize only 20 percent of the lump sum in each of the five succeeding years. Unfortunately, tax and commercial accounting do not always arrive at the same solution. Tax accounting puts the lessor on the cash method and compels him to recognize the full five-year lump sum payment in the year that he receives it. The lessee, however, is not entitled to deduct the lump sum in the year that he pays it, but must spread it out over five years. This asymmetric policy works to the advantage of the government and against the taxpayer.

C. — Revenue Recognition

There are two tests to select the appropriate time period to recognize revenue. First, the major economic activity concerned with the earning process must have been substantially completed. Second, there should be some objective measurement available. Thus, we should recognize revenues only when major uncertainties in respect of its measurement have been substantially resolved.

Applying these criteria, it is easy to see the rationale for selection of point of sale as the most usual time of revenue recognition. In most merchandising and service businesses, the point of sale represents completion of the major portion of economic activity. In these situations the point of sale is assumed to be the primary economic event and it provides an objective measurement yardstick, namely, sale price.

At the same time a sale generates a flow of assets that converts inventory into accounts receivable or cash. Concurrently with the objective measurement of revenue, related expenses are determinable with reasonable certainty, and any remaining uncertainty is reduced, for pragmatic purposes, to an acceptable level. Finally, the point of sale is clear and determinable. For all these reasons, time of sale is the point of revenue recognition in most business transactions.

D. — Accounting Adjustments

Let us assume that X Widgets is preparing its accounting statements for its fiscal year ending October 31, YEAR 1. Some special accounting entries are required to implement the system of accruing expenses incurred and revenue earned, in order to comply with the matching principle. In the preceding section we saw that entries are made when an invoice is received or rendered, even though no cash changes hands. At the year-end, some special entries are required to reflect expense or income that has accrued but as to which no transaction is currently taking place. These entries are designed to adjust the "timing" and recognition of expenses and revenue. A further group of entries may also be made to adjust the "measurement" of revenues or expenses.

a) — The "Timing" Adjustments

Some transactions that give rise to normal accounting entries represent expense or revenue for a period that straddles the year-end. Assume the following about X Widgets:

1. On July 1, YEAR 1 it paid a $900 premium for insurance for one year to June 30, YEAR 2;

2. Its employees are paid monthly on the 15th of the month and the monthly salary expense is $8,000;

3. It holds a Bond that pays $1,200 interest each November 30;

4. It rents an unused part of the land adjacent to its building to a company that parks its trucks there. The annual rent is $1,200, paid each January 31 and July 31 in advance.

To avoid a misstatement of the expenses and revenues for the year ending October 31, YEAR 1, four adjustments are necessary:

1. A reduction in insurance expense to reflect the fact that 2/3 of the insurance benefit paid for in July still remains;

2. An increase in salary expense to reflect the 1/2 month's labor already enjoyed by the business, but which will not be paid for until November 15;

3. An increase in investment income to reflect the 11/12 of the bond interest accrued to October 31; and

4. A decrease in rental income to reflect the receipt of three months' rent not yet earned.

The following four adjusting entries will be made:

1. Insurance expense will be reduced by $600 and a balance sheet asset, "prepaid expense", will be set up;

2. Salary expense will be increased by $4,000 and a balance sheet liability, "salary expense payable", will be set up;

3. Investment income will be increased by $1,100 and a balance sheet asset, "accrued bond interest", will be set up; and

4. Rental income will be reduced by $300 and a balance sheet liability, "rent received in advance", will be set up.

b) — The "Measurement" Adjustments

It is consistent with accounting conservatism to recognize, at the year-end, that the value of some of the business assets may be overstated and therefore, that business profitability may be exaggerated.

One of the most obvious adjustments to correct for this danger is an allowance for doubtful debts. If X Widgets shows $20,000 in accounts receivable at the year-end, it may well be realistic to predict that some of the debts will never be collected. On that assumption, the balance sheet asset, "Accounts Receivable", would be reduced by an amount (referred to as an allowance for doubtful accounts) that would also reduce the current year's income.

A business may face many contingencies and hazards that a careful accountant and a prudent business manager would like to provide for by making similar "allowances". All of them will have the effect of reducing the statement of current profitability. It may be obvious that the revenue authorities are not prepared to be as gloomy in their forecasting of business hazards, and that the Act will not permit, for the purpose of reporting income for taxation, all of the allowances that the accountant and the business manager might wish.

One adjustment that must be mentioned is the allowance for depreciation. In our earlier hypothetical situation, City Dairy will experience, over five years, a cost of $500,000 in respect of its fleet of trucks. To allocate this cost appropriately in order to match expense and revenue, it may reflect a depreciation expense of $100,000 at the end of each year. This is essentially a "timing" adjustment designed to spread a large cost over the appropriate accounting periods. There is, however, an element of measurement involved: both the assumed useful life of the trucks and their assumed salvage value are based on estimates.

VIII. — Basic Income Tax Accounting

A. — Accounting Period

The division of a business lifetime into arbitrary segments gives rise to problems in calculating accurate income. A taxpayer's lifetime is similarly segmented into annual periods and this segmentation also gives rise to some special problems.

For individuals, the Act prescribes a tax year coincident with the calendar year. Corporations are allowed to choose their own fiscal periods for tax purposes.[18]

Businesses carried on in partnership or as a sole proprietorship, although distinct accounting entities, do not have a separate legal personality and are not taxpayers as such. The income from such businesses must be reported by the partners or the proprietor in their personal capacity. The business may, however, use a fiscal period that is different from the calendar

---

[18]Subs. 249(1) and 249.1.

year. For example, X Widgets will calculate its income for its fiscal year ending October 31, 2014; that income will be included in X's income for the 2014 taxation year.[19] This means that any income earned in 2014 by X Widgets, after November 1, need not be reported until X files a 2015 tax return in the spring of 2016.

B. — Accounting Methods

a) — General Comment

While employees must report their income according to the cash basis of accounting, businesses are generally required to use the accrual method. The accrual method is considered particularly appropriate for a trading business.[20] There are, however, other methods of accounting that may be more appropriate for some businesses, particularly businesses with peculiar or unique cash flow patterns.

i) — Instalment Sales

Some businesses involve such unusual features that the standard accrual basis of accounting fails to achieve an appropriate matching of expenses and revenues. For example, some businesses involve a high volume of sales on terms that call for instalment payments over an extended period of time. Such a business may have significant costs associated with the selling activity but, notionally, a large "profit margin" as judged by the difference between selling price and cost of sales. The incidence of uncollectible accounts in such a business, however, is usually higher than for most other businesses. At best, the accounts are not "receivable" on a current basis, but are going to be received over a much longer period than is usual for businesses generally. This kind of business might adopt the instalment method of accounting which does not recognize the accounts receivable in revenue. In effect, the business uses a hybrid accounting system, which recognizes all expenses except the cost of goods sold on an accrual basis, but recognizes revenue on a cash basis by ignoring its accounts receivable.[21]

---

[19]S. 11.

[20]*Ken Steeves Sales Ltd. v. Minister of National Revenue*, [1955] C.T.C. 47, 55 D.T.C. 1044 (Can. Ex. Ct.).

[21]*Minister of National Revenue v. Publishers Guild of Can. Ltd.*, [1957] C.T.C. 1, 57 D.T.C. 1017 (Can. Ex. Ct.).

ii) — Completed Contract

Other businesses carry on long-term projects that may involve several years' work to complete. Payment for work completed may be by way of advances or there may be significant delay in receiving payment; and there may be a holdback to satisfy liens or to give the payer a guaranteed opportunity to judge whether the work is satisfactory. Again, because of the difficulty of appropriately matching expenses and revenues, such a business may use a "completed contract" method of accounting.

The completed contract method of accounting has been rejected for tax purposes although it might be an appropriate accounting method. Under this method, the taxpayer defers recognition of all expenses and all revenues in respect of long-term contracts until the contract is complete.[22]

iii) — Cash

Individuals report income from office or employment on a cash basis. This is confirmed by the use of the words "received" and "enjoyed" in sections 5 and 6 of the Act.

The decision to allow certain taxpayers to use the cash method of accounting is based primarily on a concern for administrative convenience. It would be quite difficult, if not impossible, for millions of employees to prepare their annual income tax returns on an accrual basis of accounting. The accrual basis requires at least some rudimentary knowledge of accounting principles (realization, timing, etc.) that is beyond the inclination of most non-accountants.

It is also important to remember that accrual basis statements require more careful auditing by the tax authorities. Since employee income tax returns represent approximately 80 percent of all tax returns filed, mandatory accrual basis returns from all taxpayers would place an intolerable burden on the CRA's resources. The incremental auditing and accounting fees incurred by both taxpayers and the CRA as a result of accrual accounting cannot be justified by the marginal improvement in the accuracy of annual net income calculations. Once again, we see that tax law is a compromise between competing values.

Having said that, it is important to note that the requirement of cash accounting for employees does allow for some modest amount of tax planning. Employees can, within limits, reduce their immediate tax liabilities by accelerating payment of their expenses and delaying receipt of their income.

It is also important to note, however, that in determining income for tax purposes under the cash method, an individual must include not only the *cash* that he or she receives in the year,

---

[22]*Wilson & Wilson Ltd. v. Minister of National Revenue*, [1960] C.T.C. 1, 60 D.T.C. 1018 (Can. Ex. Ct.).

but also any other payments that the individual *constructively* receives in the year. Thus, the cash method of accounting includes in income both actual and constructive receipts. The essence of the constructive receipts doctrine is that an individual cannot postpone recognizing income simply by failing to exercise his power to collect it. For example, although an individual can delay actual payment beyond the year-end, he cannot avoid including an amount in income merely by waiting until the next year to pick up his pay cheque.

The distinction between the two situations is subtle but significant. In the first case, the taxpayer does not have the power to cash, or otherwise control, the cheque because he does not receive it until after the year-end. In the second case, the taxpayer constructively possesses the cheque, but chooses not to exercise his power of possession in order to delay including the amount in income.

These distinctions are important in closely-held corporations. Where an owner-manager of a corporation performs services for the corporation, he is entitled to payment for services. Although the owner exercises discretion as to the timing of the payment, the salary is not considered to be paid until the owner has the corporation's cheque in his possession. Thus, merely because the owner controls the timing of the cheque does not mean that payment to him or her is accelerated to a point in time before the corporation actually issues the cheque.

To be sure, this allows owner-managers of corporations considerable flexibility in arranging their annual compensation through salary and bonuses. Depending upon the prevailing rates of tax for a particular year, an owner can elect to accelerate or defer salary payments in order to maximize his after-tax returns. This form of tax avoidance is a small price to pay for what would otherwise become an impossibly complex accounting system for employees. Similarly, the owner-manager may choose to forego some or all of his salary in a year. The amount forgone, however, is not imputed to the individual merely because he or she was entitled to the amount. We do not impute taxable salaries to controlling shareholders.

iv) — Accrual

In contrast with the requirement of cash basis accounting for employment income, the Act requires business and property income be reported on an accrual basis. The Act does not specifically stipulate a particular method for calculating business or property income. Section 9 merely says that a taxpayer's income from a business or property is his *profit* therefrom. The term "profit", however, has been judicially interpreted to mean profit calculated in accordance with commercial practice, and commercial practice favours accrual accounting for most businesses. Hence, the accrual method is indirectly mandated through the requirement to adhere to generally accepted accounting principles.

v) — Modified Accrual

There are some departures from the usual rule that business and property income is calculated in accordance with the rules of accrual accounting. First, there is an important exception in the case of farmers and fishers; these two categories of taxpayers are specifically authorized to use the cash basis method of accounting.[23] The theoretical justification for this particular variation is that, in most circumstances, the distortion of net income when using the cash basis method is minimal and, hence, justifiable in that it is easier for these taxpayers to maintain cash basis books of account.

More pragmatically, one recognizes that it would be politically inconvenient to withdraw a tax concession that has been available to farmers for so long. If anything, the pull is in the opposite direction. Until 1980 only farmers could use the cash basis of accounting; in that year the cash basis of accounting was extended to fishers, a practice that had been administratively tolerated by the CRA for many years.

A second exception from the accrual basis of accounting is found in the "modified accrual method" applicable to professionals. Professionals, like their business counterparts, are required to calculate income on an accrual basis. Professionals can, however, elect to exclude their work-in-progress in calculating net income for tax purposes.[24]

vi) — Holdbacks

We have already stated that, in applying the accrual basis of accounting, the time of sale of goods and services is usually the most convenient time to recognize revenue. The time of sale is not, however, the only time for revenue recognition. Certain businesses may deviate from the norm and recognize revenue at some other time. For example, contractors (persons engaged in the construction of buildings, roads, dams, bridges and similar structures) can, by administrative grace, defer recognition of their income until such time as "holdback payments" become *legally* receivable.[25] This rule varies from the usual accrual accounting test, which does not use legal entitlement as the determining criterion for recognizing revenue. Contractors may, however, also accelerate the recognition of profit by bringing into income amounts that may not be legally receivable by virtue of a mechanics' lien or similar statute.

vii) — Net Worth

To this point, we have discussed the more conventional methods of income determination — cash basis, accrual accounting and modified accrual. There remains one other technique for calculating income, which can be particularly painful to a taxpayer and particularly useful to the CRA. This technique is the "net worth" method of calculating income.

---

[23] S. 28.

[24] Para. 34(a).

[25] See IT-92R2.

The CRA usually issues a net worth assessment when a taxpayer does not file a return or, in some cases, when it does not accept the taxpayer's figures.[26] The theoretical principle underlying the calculation of income using the net worth basis is simple: Income is equal to the difference between a taxpayer's wealth at the beginning and at the end of a year, plus any amount that the taxpayer consumes during the year. There can also be adjustments for capital transfers, such as gifts. This principle derives from the Haig-Simons definition of income.

Algebraically, the basic principle is stated as follows:

$$\text{Income} = (\text{WE} - \text{WB}) + \text{C}$$

where:

WE = Wealth at end of year,

WB = Wealth at beginning of year, and

C = Consumption

Note, however, that, unlike the Haig-Simons formulation of income, the formula does not take into account any accrued but unrealized gains in the value of property.

Assume that a taxpayer started out a year owning $100,000 in property — such as, a house, car, clothing, furniture, cash, etc. At the end of the year it is estimated that the taxpayer owns $105,000 in property. It is also estimated that the taxpayer spent $45,000 during the year on food, clothing, mortgage payments, vacations, children's education, etc. If the taxpayer has not engaged in any borrowing or repayment of loans, his net income for the year is $50,000, i.e., ($105,000 - $100,000) + $45,000. If in fact, the taxpayer borrowed $8,000 during the year, his wealth at the end of the year is only $97,000 and his income for the year would be only $42,000.

Notice the resemblance between the net worth basis of determining income and the Haig-Simons concept of income. When a taxpayer does not, or cannot, use conventional accounting records to calculate his income and the CRA does not have any other way of assessing the delinquent taxpayer's income, the system must rely on fundamental concepts: income is the money value of the net realized accretion of economic power between two points of time.

---

[26]Subs. 152(7).

b) — Section 9

The Act determines income from business or property by reference to subsection 9(1):

> Subject to this Part, a taxpayer's income for a taxation year from a business or property is the taxpayer's profit from that business or property for that year.

At one time there was a tentative proposal to incorporate into the Act a general statement to the effect that business profits should be calculated according to GAAP. The proposal was never implemented because of the difficulty in establishing just what GAAP means in all cases. The absence of a statutory provision requiring the computation of profits according to GAAP did not, however, inhibit the development of a comparable, but not identical, doctrine in case law.

Although there may be disagreement among accountants concerning the best practice in respect of certain matters, it is now well established that section 9 imports into the Act, at least *as a starting point*, the standard commercial methods used in the business world. Thorson P. dealt with this matter in *Imp. Oil v. Minister of National Revenue*,[27] in *Daley v. Minister of National Revenue*[28] and in *Royal Trust Co. v. Minister of National Revenue*[29] In this last case, dealing with the deductibility of a claimed expenditure, he said:[30]

> . . . it may be stated categorically that . . . the first matter to be determined . . . is whether it was made or incurred by the taxpayer in accordance with the ordinary principles of commercial trading or well accepted principles of business practice.

The important point remains, however, is that the determination of "net profit" is a question of law and not a matter of generally accepted accounting principles.[31] Although a court may look at the treatment of particular items by reference to GAAP, they are at best only representative of the principles used for preparing financial statements. GAAP may influence the calculation of income only on a case-by-case basis.[32] To be sure, GAAP may well be influential in determining what is deductible, but they are not the operative *legal* criteria. Thus, subsection 9(1) represents a starting point and normal accounting practices for tax purposes

---

[27]*Imperial Oil v. Minister of National Revenue*, [1947] C.T.C. 353, 3 D.T.C. 1090 (Can. Ex. Ct.).

[28]*Daley v. Minister of National Revenue*, [1950] C.T.C. 254, 4 D.T.C. 877 (Can. Ex. Ct.).

[29]*Royal Trust Co. v. Minister of National Revenue*, [1957] C.T.C. 32, 57 D.T.C. 1055 (Can. Ex. Ct.); see also *R. v. Metropolitan Properties Ltd.*, [1985] 1 C.T.C. 169, 85 D.T.C. 5128 (Fed. T.D.) (GAAP normal rule for measuring income).

[30]*Royal Trust Co. v. Minister of National Revenue, ibid.*, at 42 [C.T.C] and 1060 [D.T.C.].

[31]*Symes v. R.* (1993), [1993] 4 S.C.R. 695, [1994] 1 C.T.C. 40, 94 D.T.C. 6001 (S.C.C.); *Neonex International Ltd. v. R.*, [1978] C.T.C. 485, 78 D.T.C. 6339 (Fed. C.A.).

[32]*Canderel Ltd. v. R.*, [1998] 1 S.C.R. 147, [1998] 2 C.T.C. 35, 98 D.T.C. 6100 (S.C.C.).

may be overborne by specific statutory provisions, judicial precedent, or commercial practice.[33]

i) — Tax Profits

What is the relationship between accounting profit and profit as determined for income tax purposes? For tax purposes, the starting point requires an examination of generally accepted commercial practice. Is a particular expenditure deductible in computing income according to the rules of general commercial and accounting practice? Or is a particular receipt included in computing income according to commercial rules? Once these preliminary questions are answered, other factors may come into play in determining the appropriate tax treatment.

Take depreciation as an example.[34] The general commercial and accounting rule is that, in calculating net income, a reasonable amount of depreciation can be deducted from revenues. Indeed, commercial practice recognizes many different methods of calculating depreciation (for example, straight-line, declining balance, sum of the years, etc.). Provided that the method is acceptable and the amount is reasonable, depreciation expense is a deductible expense in determining net income for financial statement purposes.

The Act, however, *specifically* prohibits a deduction for depreciation[35] and, therefore, such an expense cannot be taken into account in calculating net income for tax purposes. In lieu of depreciation, the Act allows a deduction for Capital Cost Allowance ("CCA") in an amount that may or may not be related to accounting depreciation. In many cases, CCA is based on social, economic or cultural considerations. Thus, tax profits and accounting income may be substantially different.

ii) — Statutory Deviations

The Act deviates from accounting principles in many areas. We discuss three important deviations from standard accounting practice are discussed below.

---

[33]See generally: *Associated Investors of Canada Ltd. v. Minister of National Revenue*, [1967] C.T.C. 138, 67 D.T.C. 5096 (Can. Ex. Ct.); *Neonex International Ltd. v. R.*, [1978] C.T.C. 485, 78 D.T.C. 6339 (Fed. C.A.); *R. v. Metropolitan Properties Co. Ltd.*, [1985] 1 C.T.C. 169, 85 D.T.C. 5128 (Fed. T.D.); *MHL Holdings Ltd. v. R.*, [1988] 2 C.T.C. 42, 88 D.T.C. 6292 (Fed. T.D.); *Coppley Noyes & Randall Ltd. v. R.*, [1991] 1 C.T.C. 541, 91 D.T.C. 5291 (Fed. T.D.); varied (1992), 93 D.T.C. 5508 (Fed. C.A.); and *West Kootenay Power & Light Co. v. R.*, [1992] 1 C.T.C. 15, 92 D.T.C. 6023 (Fed. C.A.).

[34]Numerous other examples may be found in Subdivision b of Division B, Part I of the Act.

[35]Para. 18(1)(b).

1. — Reserves and Allowances

Accountants sometimes prefer to anticipate certain contingencies by setting up an allowance that has the effect of reducing income in the current period. The Act seriously inhibits this conservative and quite normal accounting practice by denying, as a deduction, "an amount transferred or credited to a reserve, contingent account or sinking fund except as expressly permitted by this Part."[36] Instead, the Act sets out a specific and rigid regime in respect of accounting for reserves. Thus, there can be a significant difference between accounting reserves and tax reserves.

2. — Depreciation

At one time, depreciation expense was recognized as a legitimate deduction for tax purposes, subject to showing a sound accounting basis for the deduction. It is indisputable that many capital assets depreciate with use, but the amount of depreciation and the rate at which it occurs are frequently quite speculative. To control the speculations, and to minimize disputes, the Act details a Capital Cost Allowance (CCA) system, which imposes limits on the amount of depreciation deductible in calculating income for tax purposes.

Although, in general, CCA rates are designed to be reasonably realistic, the system is Procrustean. There is no attempt to guarantee that the rates for tax purposes conform to depreciation for accounting purposes. The rates are the same for all taxpayers although their depreciation experience may differ greatly. Further, we can use the CCA system to achieve other socio-economic objectives. It may, for example, be used to stimulate economic activity in depressed regions of the country or stimulate cultural activities such as Canadian art. Thus, income for tax purposes can differ quite significantly from income reported to shareholders or creditors, and there is nothing unusual or improper in this.

3. — Inventory

A major component of the expenses of some businesses, and thus a major factor in determining income, is the cost of goods sold. To calculate the cost of goods sold, a business must establish its inventory of goods on hand at the year-end, and determine its value. There are a number of accounting approaches to inventory valuation. One method that is commonly used by accountants for financial statement purposes, the last-in, first-out ("LIFO"), has been judicially rejected for tax purposes as being inappropriate.[37] Here, once again, the use of one method for accounting and another for tax purposes can cause a significant difference in the final net income figure.

---

[36]Para. 18(1)(e).

[37]*Minister of National Revenue v. Anaconda Amer. Brass Ltd.*, [1955] C.T.C. 311, 55 D.T.C. 1220 (Canada P.C.).

c) — Conformity of Methods

A taxpayer can use one generally accepted accounting method for financial statement purposes and another for income tax purposes. In the absence of any statutory requirement that a taxpayer use the same method of accounting to calculate income both for tax and financial statement purposes, a taxpayer can select the most appropriate method of accounting for tax purposes.

The purpose for which income is calculated determines the appropriate method of accounting. An accounting method that is suitable for a particular purpose is not necessarily the appropriate measure of income for tax purposes.[38]

What is appropriate for tax purposes? The general rule is to apply that principle or method which provides the proper picture of net income. In MacGuigan J.'s words:[39]

> ... it would be undesirable to establish an absolute requirement that there must always be conformity between financial statements and tax returns and I am satisfied that the cases do not do so. *The approved principle* is that whichever method presents the "truer picture" of a taxpayer's revenue, which more fairly and accurately portrays income, and which "matches" revenue and expenditure, if one method does, is the one that must be followed. [Emphasis added.]

d) — A "Truer Picture" of Income

It is not always easy to apply the rule that a taxpayer may adopt whichever accounting method presents the "truer picture" of revenues and expenses. There are cases where a particular accounting principle presents a "truer picture" for income statement purposes at the expense of some accuracy or relevance in the balance sheet. In other cases, the adoption of a particular accounting method more accurately summarizes a taxpayer's closing balances while sacrificing accuracy on the income statement. *West Kootenay*[40] rightly emphasized a proper matching of revenues and expenses and accuracy of the net income figure for tax purposes. Ultimately, however, the computation of profit and choice of method for tax purposes is a question of law.[41]

---

[38]*Friedberg v. R.*, [1993] 4 S.C.R. 285, [1993] 2 C.T.C. 306, 93 D.T.C. 5507 (S.C.C.).

[39]*West Kootenay Power & Light Co. v. R.*, [1992] 1 C.T.C. 15, 92 D.T.C. 6023 (Fed. C.A.) at 22 [C.T.C.] and 6028 [D.T.C.]. See also: *Maritime Telegraph and Telephone Company v. R.*, [1992] 1 C.T.C. 264, 92 D.T.C. 6191 (Fed. C.A.) ("earned method" of reporting income for accounting and tax purposes produced "truer picture" of taxpayer's income).

[40]*West Kootenay Power & Light Co. v. R.*, ante.

[41]*Canderel Ltd. v. R.*, [1998] 1 S.C.R. 147, [1998] 2 C.T.C. 35, 98 D.T.C. 6100 (S.C.C.); *Ikea Ltd. v. R.*, [1998] 1 S.C.R. 196, [1998] 2 C.T.C. 61, 98 D.T.C. 6092 (S.C.C.); *Toronto College Park Ltd. v. R.*, [1998] 1 S.C.R. 183, [1998] 2 C.T.C. 78, 98 D.T.C. 6088 (S.C.C.).

A classic example of the conflict between income statement and balance sheet values is seen in accounting for inventory values. Under the last-in, first-out ("LIFO") method of inventory accounting, the cost of goods most recently purchased or acquired is the cost that is assigned to the cost of goods sold. Hence, the inventory on hand at the end of an accounting period is valued at the cost that was attributed to the inventory at the beginning of the period (first-in, still here). Any increases in quantity during a period are valued at the cost prevailing during the time the accumulations are deemed to have occurred. Any decreases in quantities are considered to have first reduced the most recent accumulations.[42]

Under the first-in, first-out ("FIFO") method, the process is reversed: the cost of goods first acquired is assigned to the first goods sold. The closing inventory comprises the cost of the most recent purchases (last-in, still here).

The use of the FIFO method of accounting for the flow of inventory costs tends to overstate net income during inflationary periods, but more accurately reflects the current value of closing inventory on the balance sheet. In contrast, the LIFO method more realistically measures "real" net income, while sacrificing some accuracy in year-end balance sheet values.

Most accountants and business people argue that the use of LIFO for inventory accounting during inflationary periods results in a more meaningful and "truer picture" of business income during inflationary periods. The Privy Council in *Anaconda Brass*,[43] however, rejected the use of the LIFO method of inventory valuation for tax purposes. Their Lordships were concerned that the method would permit the creation of hidden reserves:[44]

> . . . the evidence of expert witnesses, that the LIFO method is generally acceptable, and in this case the most appropriate, method of accountancy, is not conclusive of the question that the Court has to decide. That may be found as a fact by the Exchequer Court and affirmed by the Supreme Court. The question remains whether it conforms to the prescription of the *Income Tax Act*. As already indicated, in their Lordships' opinion it does not.

The accounting principle for selecting the proper method of inventory valuation is clear: the most suitable method for determining cost is that which results in charging against operations those costs that most fairly match the sales revenue for the period. The *CICA Handbook* states the principle as follows:[45]

> The method selected for determining cost should be one which results in the fairest matching of costs against revenues regardless of whether or not the method corresponds to the physical flow of goods.

---

[42]See *CICA Handbook* §3030.07.

[43]*Minister of National Revenue v. Anaconda American Brass Ltd.*, [1955] C.T.C. 311, 55 D.T.C. 1220 (Canada P.C.).

[44]*Minister of National Revenue v. Anaconda American Brass Ltd.*, ibid., at 321 [C.T.C.] and 1225 [D.T.C.].

[45]See *CICA Handbook* §3030 and the virtually identical language of *AICPA*, ARB 43, Ch. 4.

Anaconda Brass was an unfortunate decision based upon a misunderstanding of accounting methods. The decision rests on two notions: (1) the physical flow of inventory determines values; and (2) the potential for creation of "hidden" reserves. Both premises are fundamentally flawed. The determination of cost does not depend upon the physical flow of goods, but on the fairest matching of revenues and expenses. The "fairest" matching of costs against revenues is, presumably, also the method that presents the "truer picture" of income for tax purposes. Thus, the question is: which method of accounting produces the best and fairest picture of annual profits? Equally, the hidden reserve argument ignores the primary purpose of the method, namely, the determination of a fair measure of an enterprise's annual income.

e) — Non-Arm's Length Transactions

The Act contains stringent anti-avoidance rules to govern transfers of property between persons who do not deal with each other at arm's length. The purpose of these rules is to discourage taxpayers who have close social, family, or economic relationships with each other from artificially avoiding tax through the manipulation of transaction values.

Related persons are deemed not to deal with each other at arm's length.[46]

It is a question of fact whether unrelated persons deal with each other at arm's length. Parties are not considered to be dealing with each other at arm's length if one person dictates the terms of the bargain on both sides of a transaction.[47]

The anti-avoidance rules are as follows:[48]

- Where, in a non-arm's length transaction, a purchaser acquires anything for a price in *excess* of its fair market value, he or she is deemed to have acquired the property at its fair market value. Consequently, notwithstanding that the purchaser actually paid a price higher than fair market value, the purchaser is *deemed* to acquire the property at a cost equal to fair market value.

---

[46]S. 251.

[47]*Swiss Bank Corp. v. Minister of National Revenue*, [1971] C.T.C. 427, 71 D.T.C. 5235 (Can. Ex. Ct.); affirmed (1972), [1974] S.C.R. 1144, [1972] C.T.C. 614, 72 D.T.C. 6470 (S.C.C.) (parties acted in concert, exerting considerable influence together; money transactions merely moved funds from one pocket to another); *Millward v. R.*, [1986] 2 C.T.C. 423, 86 D.T.C. 6538 (Fed. T.D.) (members of law firm who dealt with each other at less than commercial rates of interest not at arm's length); *Noranda Mines Ltd. v. Minister of National Revenue*, [1987] 2 C.T.C. 2089, 87 D.T.C. 379 (T.C.C.) (existence of arm's length relationship excluded where one party has *de facto* control over both parties).

[48]S. 69.

Example

A taxpayer buys land from his mother at a cost of $70,000 when, in fact, the land has a fair market value of $50,000 (this may happen if the mother deliberately wants to trigger a higher capital gain to offset unused capital losses). The Act deems the son to have acquired the land at a cost of $50,000. The mother calculates her gain on the basis of her *actual* proceeds of $70,000.

- Where, in a non-arm's length transaction, a vendor has disposed of anything at *less* than its fair market value, the vendor is deemed to have received proceeds equal to fair market value. Thus, notwithstanding that she actually received a lower price, the vendor is taxed on the basis of her deemed proceeds.

Example

A taxpayer sells land that has a fair market value of $50,000 to his daughter for $40,000. Paragraph 69(1)(b) *deems* the father to have received $50,000. His daughter, however, acquires the property for her *actual* cost of $40,000, leaving her with the potential of a larger gain when she sells the property.

The overall effect of these rules is that taxpayers can be liable to double taxation in non-arm's length transactions. Section 69 is designed to be punitive to discourage family members and other non-arm's length parties from dealing with each other at prices other than fair market value.

Example

Assume: An individual owns a property to which the following applies:

Cost	$ 1,000
FMV	$ 5,000

She sells the property to her son for $4,000.

Then:

Tax consequences to mother:

Deemed proceeds of sale	$	5,000
Cost		(1,000)
Gain	$	4,000

If the son sells the property at its fair market value of $5,000, he also realizes a gain of $1,000:

Actual proceeds of sale	$	5,000
Actual cost of property		(4,000)
Gain	$	1,000

Example		
Total gain:		
Realized by mother	$	4,000
Realized by son		1,000
	$	5,000

Thus, an asset with an accrued gain of $4,000 triggers an actual gain of $5,000. The $1,000 that is exposed to double taxation represents the shortfall between the fair market value of the property ($5,000) and the price at which it is sold ($4,000).

C. — Timing of Income

We saw earlier that employment income is generally taxed on a cash basis. In contrast, with a few important exceptions, business and property income are normally calculated on an accrual basis. Thus, generally speaking, income from business and property are recognized for tax purposes when services are performed or goods are sold, rather than when payment for the goods or services is actually received. In other words, although a taxpayer may have to wait for some time to receive payment for goods sold or services rendered, she will be taxed on income in the year in which it is earned.

The accrual method of accounting is the appropriate method of determining profit in most circumstances. It warrants emphasis, however, that this is *not* the only acceptable method for tax purposes. Since subsection 9(1) is silent on the method of accounting that one can use to calculate "profit", a taxpayer is free to use generally accepted accounting principles appropriate to her circumstances if the method is not prohibited by the Act or by judicial precedent.[49]

a) — Payments in Advance

The accrual method is modified by the Act for certain payments. For example, payments received in advance of rendering a service or sale of goods are included in income even though the payments represent unearned amounts that would usually be excluded from income for accounting purposes. Under accounting principles, unearned revenue is considered a liability. For tax purposes, unearned revenue is included in income in the year the payment

---

[49] *Oxford Shopping Centres Ltd. v. R.*, [1980] C.T.C. 7, 79 D.T.C. 5458 (Fed. T.D.); affirmed [1981] C.T.C. 128, 81 D.T.C. 5065 (Fed. C.A.).

is received, rather than when the revenue is earned. A taxpayer may, however, claim a reserve for goods and services to be delivered in the future.[50]

b) — Receivables

A taxpayer is to include in income all amounts *receivable* by the taxpayer in respect of property sold or services rendered in the course of business carried out during the year.[51]

"Receivable" means that the taxpayer has a clearly established *legal right* to enforce payment at the particular time under consideration:[52]

> In the absence of a statutory definition to the contrary, I think it is not enough that the so-called recipient have a precarious right to receive the amount in question, but he must have a clearly legal, though not necessarily immediate, right to receive it.

For example, in the construction industry, it is usual practice, when work is performed under a contract extending over a lengthy period of time, for interim payments to be made to the contractor. These payments, which are based on progress reports, are usually subject to a percentage holdback to ensure satisfactory completion of the project. In these circumstances, holdbacks need not be brought into income as "receivables" until such time as the architect or engineer has issued a final certificate approving the completion of the project.[53]

An amount is deemed to be receivable on the earlier of the day the account is actually rendered and the day on which it *would have been* rendered had there been "no undue delay" in rendering the account.

c) — Professionals

i) — Modified Accrual

The rules in respect of the computation of income of certain professionals (accountants, dentists, lawyers, medical doctors, veterinarians and chiropractors) vary somewhat from the normal accrual basis of accounting. These professional businesses may report income on a so-called modified accrual basis by electing to exclude work in progress in the computation

---

[50]Paras. 12(1)(a) and 20(1)(m).

[51]Para. 12(1)(b).

[52]*Minister of National Revenue v. John Colford Contracting Co.*, [1960] C.T.C. 178 at 187, 60 D.T.C. 1131 at 1135 (Can. Ex. Ct.); affirmed without written reasons [1962] S.C.R. viii, [1962] C.T.C. 546, 62 D.T.C. 1338 (S.C.C.).

[53]*Minister of National Revenue v. John Colford Contracting Co.*, [1962] S.C.R. viii, [1962] C.T.C. 546, 62 D.T.C. 1338 (S.C.C.).

of income.[54] On the sale of the professional business, any work in progress previously excluded is brought into the income of the vendor.[55]

ii) — Work in Progress

Generally, if a professional elects to exclude work in progress in the computation of income, his income is computed on the basis of fees billed, subject to any adjustment for undue delay in billing. The election is binding on the taxpayer for subsequent years unless it is revoked with the consent of the Minister.[56]

iii) — Advance Payments

Amounts received in advance of performance of services are included in income unless the funds are deposited in a segregated trust account.[57] For example, a lawyer who obtains a retainer that must be returned to the client in the event of non-performance of services may exclude the retainer from income if the funds are deposited in a trust account.[58] The taxpayer may, however, claim a deduction in respect of services that will have to be rendered after the end of the year.[59]

iv) — Farmers and Fishers

Income from a farming or fishing *business* may be calculated on a cash basis. Thus, the income of a taxpayer from a farming or fishing business is computed by aggregating amounts *received* in the year and deducting therefrom amounts *paid* in the year. Accounts receivable are included in income only when they are collected by the taxpayer.[60]

---

[54]Para. 34(a).

[55]Para. 10(5)(a) and s. 23.

[56]Para. 34(b); see IT-457R, "Election by Professionals to Exclude Work-In-Progress from Income" (July 15, 1988).

[57]Para. 12(1)(a).

[58]IT-129R, "Lawyers' Trust Accounts and Disbursements" (November 7, 1986).

[59]Para. 20(1)(m).

[60]S. 28.

IX. — Prohibition against Reserves

The term "reserve" is now in disfavour among accountants because it has been applied so widely as to lose any specific meaning. Nevertheless, the term continues to be employed in commercial jargon. The Act specifically sets its face against "reserves".[61]

The general prohibition in paragraph 18(1)(e) of a deduction for any reserve, "contingent account" or "sinking fund", except as specifically permitted by the Act, not only causes accounting for tax purposes to deviate significantly from accounting for other purposes, but it also produces inconsistencies within the system of income tax accounting.

Whether we refer to "reserve", "allowance", "contingency fund" or some other expression, accountants recognize that a simplistic presentation of accrual basis financial statements fails to estimate profitability accurately. The failure results from overlooking *future* risks or obligations that affect *present* profitability. An obvious example is depreciation of capital assets. It would be foolish and poor accounting, to fail to recognize an asset's ultimate obsolescence or exhaustion over a period of time. As already noted, the *Income Tax Act* concedes the wisdom of depreciating capital assets and provides for cost allocation through capital cost allowance or tax depreciation.

A clear line must, however, be drawn between depreciation and a decline in the market value of an asset. Although an accountant might think it is prudent for financial statement purposes to recognize a paper loss on investments, the tax system does not allow such an accounting practice for the purpose of determining net income. In *Minister of National Revenue v. Consolidated Glass Ltd.*,[62] for example, the taxpayer attempted to deduct as a capital loss an amount that reflected the decline in value of the shares of its subsidiary company. A majority of the Supreme Court of Canada held that the taxpayer could not claim a loss in respect of assets of a fluctuating value until such time as the assets were sold (realized) or became worthless so that the loss was irrevocable. This rule is merely the flip side of the realization principle in tax law. No doubt, the taxpayer would have preferred the Haig-Simons formula recognizing the net reduction in its wealth.

A. — Doubtful and Bad Debts

Accounts receivable is a major balance sheet asset for many businesses. Receivables are normally recorded on the books at face value, i.e., at the value stated on the invoice. As with depreciation, it would be foolish to ignore the obvious risk that all of the accounts of a business are not collected. Every business that sells on credit suffers some credit risk. Although this is the sort of contingent risk that the Act is careful to prevent taxpayers from

---

[61]Para. 18(1)(e).

[62]*Minister of National Revenue v. Consolidated Glass Ltd.*, [1957] S.C.R. 167, [1957] C.T.C. 78, 57 D.T.C. 1041 (S.C.C.).

exploiting, it specifically authorizes a deduction for a reserve for doubtful debts[63] and bad debts.[64]

A taxpayer's doubtful debt reserve may be based on an analysis of the likelihood of collection of individual accounts. Alternatively, it may be stated as a percentage of total accounts receivable. The CRA, however, does not consider percentage based reserves to be reasonable.[65] The deduction must be reasonable. The mere fact that a debt has remained unpaid for a considerable time does not mean that it is bad.[66] There must be some additional analysis to support the conclusion. The deduction is in respect of debts "that are established by the taxpayer to have become bad debts in the year."[67]

B. — Prepaid Income

We can make an adjusting entry to reduce current income by setting up a balance sheet liability to reflect the fact that some amount received was unearned. For example, X Widgets sets up a liability, "rent received in advance", for the purpose of moving $300, received in its fiscal period ending October 31, into the following accounting period. If the prepayment was a deposit and subject to refund on demand, it could be said that X Widgets had not "realized" the amount and should not recognize it in income at that time.

Assuming, however, that X Widgets can retain the $300 even if the payer discontinues use of the rented property, it is nevertheless incorrect, from an accrual accounting point of view, to recognize the $300 in the period ending October 31.

There are two ways of expressing the accountant's concern that current income is being overstated. One is to say that revenue is overstated because the $300, though received, has not yet been earned. The other is to say that income is overstated as a result of failure to recognize a business liability in the next accounting period, i.e., the obligation to make the rented property available for three months. Although these two ways of expressing the

---

[63]Para. 20(1)(l).

[64]Para. 20(1)(p).

[65]See para. 24 IT-442R.

[66]See *No. 81 v. Minister of National Revenue* (1953), 8 Tax A.B.C. 82, 53 D.T.C. 98 (Can. Tax App. Bd.) (factors to consider are time element, history of account, finances of client, taxpayer's past experiences with bad debts, business conditions in locality and in country, and relative sales volume); *No. 409 v. Minister of National Revenue* (1957), 16 Tax A.B.C. 409, 57 D.T.C. 136 (Can. Tax App. Bd.) (delay in payment not sufficient to justify reserve after two months, in circumstances); *Atlas Steels Ltd. v. Minister of National Revenue* (1961), 27 Tax A.B.C. 331, 61 D.T.C. 547 (Can. Tax App. Bd.) (reserve of three percent of accounts receivable allowed in circumstances despite unfavourable comparison with company's history of collections). See also CRA Rulings doc. 9238377.

[67]Para. 20(1)(p).

matching concept boil down to the same thing in accounting terms, they are not at all alike for income tax purposes.

C. — Inclusion in Income

Paragraph 12(1)(a) reads as follows:

> There shall be included in computing the income of a taxpayer for a taxation year as income from a business or property such of the following amounts as are applicable:
>
>> (a) any amount received by the taxpayer in the year in the course of a business
>>
>>> (i) that is on account of services not rendered or goods not delivered before the end of the year or that, for any other reason, may be regarded as not having been earned in the year or a previous year, or
>>>
>>> (ii) under an arrangement or understanding that it is repayable in whole or in part on the return or resale to the taxpayer of articles in or by means of which goods were delivered to a customer. . . .

This requires X Widgets to bring the $300 into income, whether or not it has been earned. The question then arises whether X Widgets can make an entry to reflect the overstatement of income. The reference in paragraph 12(1)(a) to amounts "regarded as not having been earned" confirms that the adjustment cannot be made directly to the statement of revenues. In any event, normal accrual accounting practice would recognize the receipt and make the adjustment by setting up the liability (unearned income) to reflect the future obligation to provide the rental property.

a) — Deduction from Income

This brings us back to paragraph 18(1)(e), which prohibits all reserves except those that the Act expressly permits. Fortunately for X Widgets, subparagraph 20(1)(m)(iii) expressly allows "a reasonable amount as a reserve in respect of . . . periods for which rent or other amounts for the possession or use of land or chattels have been paid in advance."

X Widgets is a simple example of future obligations that affect current income and can easily be accommodated because the future obligation can be precisely quantified and its occurrence can be precisely predicted. Thus, there are no problems of measurement or timing. Other examples may be found in the publishing business, which receive prepaid subscriptions for which the publisher must provide magazines for a determined future period, and the entertainment business, which sells tickets for future performances with each ticket referable to a specified seat on a specified date.

b) — Uncertainty

In some circumstances, businesses may legitimately claim future obligations, but the amount of the obligation may be uncertain both in respect of quantum and timing. Contrast the sale of season tickets to hockey games with the sale by a movie theatre chain of gift books of tickets for cinema performances. In the first case, the hockey club knows the date of each performance for which it has received ticket revenue. Whether or not the seats are occupied, the revenue is earned, and the club's obligation is satisfied on a game-by-game basis as each game is played. In the second case, the theatre company knows neither when the gift tickets will be used, nor how many will go forever unused.

There is also an intermediate situation, in which a business cannot accurately predict the amount of its future obligation, but it can at least predict the timing within reasonable limits. An example would be the dinner-of-the-month arrangement under which a group of restaurants participate in a promotional scheme of selling books of tickets for free dinners at participating restaurants. Each book contains 12 tickets; each ticket is usable at a specified restaurant during a specified month. As each ticket entitles the user to a free meal equal in value to another purchased at the same time by the user's dinner partner, Restaurant A cannot be certain of its maximum obligation. Perhaps it can make a reliable estimate based on past experience. In any event, each month, the obligation for that month is determined, and at the end of 12 months the entire obligation has been quantified and satisfied.

c) — Reserve for Future Goods and Services

Paragraph 20(1)(m) authorizes a reserve for a "reasonable amount" for goods or services "that it is reasonably anticipated will have to be delivered [or rendered] after the end of the year."[68] The same provision allows a reasonable reserve for anticipated refunds of deposits made on containers or other "articles in or by means of which goods were delivered to a customer."[69] The uncertainty involved in determining the amount of these future obligations is apparent from the requirement of the provision that the reserve be a "*reasonable* amount" and that the obligation be "*reasonably* anticipated".

A special problem of future obligations arises from a certain promotional technique used by some retailing businesses. A customer making a purchase at a Canadian Tire Store, for example, receives some "funny money", a form of scrip that can be applied to future purchases at Canadian Tire. Other businesses have used trading stamps that, after a sufficient quantity were accumulated, could be redeemed for merchandise. For a time, some of the major oil companies issued a card in which a hole was punched on the occasion of a purchase from one of the company stations. When the prescribed number of holes had been punched, the card could be redeemed for a set of dishes or cutlery. In all of these cases, the business is

---

[68]Subparas. 20(1)(m)(i) and (ii).

[69]Subparas. 20(1)(m)(iv) and 12(1)(a)(ii).

being carried on in such a way that current profitability will be overstated unless the future obligation to redeem the scrip, the trading stamps, or the cards is recognized. The problems inherent in any attempt to determine the amount and the timing of future obligations generated by such promotional schemes are, however, very difficult. The proportion of the trading stamps thrown away or lost is probably high, just as it is very likely that the "funny money" will be carried around in the wallets of Canadian Tire customers for years.

In *Dominion Stores Ltd. v. Minister of National Revenue*,[70] the Minister argued that the taxpayer was not entitled to a deduction under paragraph 20(1)(m), which is conditional upon showing that the reserve is in respect of amounts that have been included in the taxpayer's income pursuant to paragraph 12(1)(a). The Minister argued that the "green stamps" given to customers were free, as they were advertised to be, and that the entire payment by the customer was referable to the food and other items being purchased at the time. Accordingly, Dominion Stores had no income in respect of the green stamps and was not entitled to any reserve to recognize the future obligation to redeem them. Cattanach J. held that the price paid at the check-out desk was a combined price for both the goods being purchased and the green stamps that accompanied them. The taxpayer was, therefore, entitled to take a reserve. It is interesting to note that only this narrow legal issue was submitted to the Court. The parties had, by agreement, fixed the appropriate amount of the reserve if the taxpayer was permitted to take it. Obviously, the determination of a "reasonable reserve" would require careful analysis of past experience with green stamp redemptions, and some speculative estimate as to the proportion that would never be redeemed.

X. — Conclusion

The arbitrary division of a business lifetime into annual segments produces numerous accounting problems. These problems are greatly exacerbated because of the annual accounting for income tax purposes. Under a progressive rate structure, an individual whose income fluctuates widely over a number of years will pay more tax than another taxpayer with the same aggregate income over the period but with little annual fluctuation.

Further, a serious problem occurs when income falls below zero in some years. Without a system of negative income tax and refunds, there is no automatic solution for a taxpayer with a net loss tax year. Some relief is available in section 111 for the carryover of losses from one tax year to another.

Ultimately, the accurate measurement of annual income is, regardless of allocation issues, the *sine qua non* of a fair and equitable tax system.

The measurement of income or profit, which is the foundation of the taxable base on which we impose taxes, is an imperfect art that involves many estimates, assumptions and judg-

---

[70]*Dominion Stores Ltd. v. Minister of National Revenue*, [1966] C.T.C. 97, 66 D.T.C. 5111 (Can. Ex. Ct.).

ment calls. To be sure, ultimately, net taxable income is a single number on which we impose taxes. The number itself, however, is at best an educated estimate of properly matched revenues and expenses, accounting principles, judicial doctrines, political and tax policy considerations. To understand the measurement of income one must understand law, economics and accounting principles.

Selected Bibliography to Chapter 5

Measurement of Income

Arnold, Brian J., "Timing and Income Taxation: The Principles of Income Management for Tax Purposes," in *Proceedings of 35th Tax Conf.* 133 (Can. Tax Foundation, 1983).

Harris, Edwin C., "Measuring Business Income", in *Proceedings of 19th Tax Conf.* 78 (Can. Tax Foundation, 1967).

Drobny, Sheldon, "Inventory and Accounting Methods: Controversy and Paradoxes" (October 1990) 68 Taxes 764.

Kaplow, L. and A.C. Warren, "The Bankruptcy of Conventional Tax Timing Wisdom is Deeper Than Semantics: A Rejoinder to Professors Kaplow and Warren, [Discussion of An Income Tax By Any Other Name — A Reply to Professor Strand]" (1986) 38 Stan. L. Rev. 399.

Robertson, D.A., "Timing is Everything" (1988) 121:3 CA Magazine 32.

Strand, J., "Tax Timing and the Haig-Simons Ideal: A Rejoinder to Professor Popkin [Discussion of Tax Ideals in the Real World: A Comment on Professor Strand's Approach to Tax Fairness]" (1986) 62 Ind. L.J. 73.

White, Robert, "Profits and Prophets — An Accountant's Afterword" (1987) 8 Br. Tax Rev. 292.

Basic Income Tax Accounting

Cooper, Graeme S., "Some Observations of Tax Accounting" (1986) 15 Aust. Tax Rev. 221.

Knight & Knight, "Recent Developments Concerning the Completed Contract Method of Accounting" (1988) 41 Tax Exec. 73.

Roberts, J.R. and William Leiss, "Technological and Accounting Innovation: Can They Mesh?" (1986) 36 Can. Tax Foundation Conf., Report of Proceedings 25:1.

Strand, J., "Tax Timing and the Haig-Simons Ideal: A Rejoinder to Professor Popkin [Discussion of Tax Ideals in the Real World: A Comment on Professor Strand's Approach to Tax Fairness]" (1986) 62 Ind. L.J. 73.

Generally Accepted Accounting Principles

Drobny, Sheldon, "Inventory and Accounting Methods: Controversy and Paradoxes" (October 1990) 68 Taxes 764.

McDonnell, T.E., "Falling Between the GAAP's?" (1991) 39 Can. Tax J. 1313.

Murray, K.J. and Nicole Mondou, "The Relevance of GAAP in Cyprus Anvil Mining Corporation v. The Queen" (1990) 3 Can. Current Tax P5.

Padwe, Gerald W., "The Death of G.A.A.P. Reporting — A Tale from the Folks Who Brought You U.S. Tax Reform", *Corporate Management Tax Conf.* 11:1 (Can. Tax Foundation, 1987).

Strain, William J., "Now You See It, Now You Don't: The Elusive Relevance of G.A.A.P. in Tax Accounting", in *Proceedings of 37th Tax Conf.* 38 (Can. Tax Foundation, 1985).

Realization and Recognition of Income

Callard, Rosalind M., "When to Recognize Revenue" (1986) 119 CA Magazine 67.

Durnford, John W., "If it Is Payable, Is it Due?" Can. Tax Letter, June 3, 1983 (De Boo).

Freedman, Judith, "Profit and Prophets — Law and Accountancy Practice on the Timing of Receipts — Recognition Under the Earnings Basis (Schedule D, Cases 1 and 11)" (1987) Brit. Tax Rev. 61 and 104.

Realization of Income: Timing

Arnold, Brian J., "Timing and Income Taxation: The Principles of Income Management for Tax Purposes", in *Proceedings of 35th Tax Conf.* 133 (Can. Tax Foundation, 1983).

Grower, Kenneth W., "Tax Reform and Farmers", in *Proceedings of 40th Tax Conf.* 24:1 (Can. Tax Foundation, 1988).

McNair, D.K., "The Taxation of Farmers and Farming" (1986) Special Lectures LSUC 77.

McNair, D.K., *Taxation of Farmers and Fishermen* (Toronto: Richard De Boo, 1986).

O'Brien, M.L., "Taxation of Profits Derived From Criminal or Illegal Activities" (1988) 2 Can. Current Tax J-85.

Robertson, D.A., "Timing is Everything" (1988) 121:3 CA Magazine 32.

Tiley, John, "More on Receivability and Receipt" (1986) Br. Tax Rev. 152.

Turner, Paul E., "The Reform Down On The Farm'" (July 1990) 24 CGA Magazine 25.

Turner, Paul E., "Restricted Farm Losses" (December 1990) 24 CGA Magazine 47.

Reserves and Allowances

Cadesky, Michael, "Corporate Losses", in *Proceedings of 42nd Tax Conf.* 19:1 (Can. Tax Foundation, 1990).

Frankovic, Joseph V., "Taxing Times: Foreclosures, Default Sales, Debt Forgiveness, Doubtful and Bad Debts" (1991) 39 Can. Tax J. 889.

Krishna, Vern, "Meaning of Allowance" (1986) 1 Can. Current Tax J-144.

Land, Stephen B., "Contingent Payments are the Time Value of Money" (1987) 40 Tax Lawyer 237.

Lokken, Lawrence, "The Time Value of Money Rules" (1986) 42 Tax Rev. 1.

Accounting for Inventory

Arnold, Brian J., "Conversions of Property To and From Inventory: Tax Consequences" (1976) 24 Can. Tax J. 231.

Arnold, Brian J., "Recent Developments in the Tax Treatment of Inventory", in *Proceedings of 31st Tax Conf.* 865 (Can. Tax Foundation, 1979).

Cadesky, Michael, "Corporate Losses", in *Proceedings of 42nd Tax Conf.* 19:1 (Can. Tax Foundation, 1990).

Innes, William I., "The Tax Treatment of Accrued Gains on Inventory at Death" (1992) 12 Estates and Trust J. 122.

Looney, Steve R., "Using L.I.F.O. to Value Costs Under the Completed Contract Method: A Tale of Two Accounting Methods" (1986) 39 Tax Lawyer 235.

McDonnell, Thomas E., "An Inventory Adventure" (1993) 41 Can. Tax J. 965.

McQuillan, Peter E., "Real Estate Inventory Valuation" (1992) Canada Tax Foundation 5:35.

Chapter 6 — Employment Income

Table of Contents

Table of Contents

Chapter 6 — Employment Income

Table of Contents

Classification is the beginning of wisdom.

(Seligman, Double Taxation and International Fiscal Cooperation (1928))

I. — General Comment

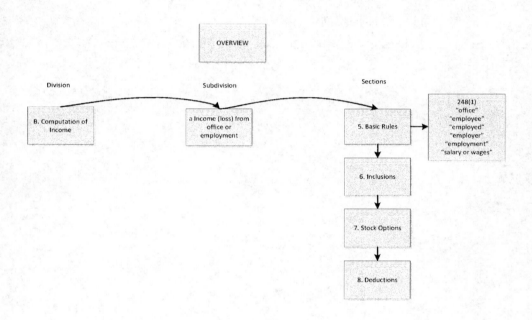

A distinguishing characteristic of the Canadian income tax system is the rigid classification of income by source. Section 3 of the Act determines the manner and sequence in which income from each source is brought into the computation of income. The section names the following sources of income:

- Office;
- Employment;
- Business;
- Property;
- Capital gains; and
- Other income.

The rules and sequence of section 3 are mandatory and rigid. The Act neatly compartmentalizes each source in distinct subdivisions. The segregation of income into distinct sources contributes to the complexity in the statute.

Employment income is the single largest source of government revenues and has a critical role in government financing. Nearly fifteen million taxpayers file as employees every year. Even a small leak in the employment income tax system can have substantial revenue consequences to federal and provincial treasuries.

The employment income rules also affect a large number of individuals, each of whom is a potential voter. Thus, although tax law is sensitive to the need for government revenues, it must be seen as fair.

There are three basic issues in the taxation of employment income:

1. Characterization: what is the nature of the income?

2. Timing: when do we tax it?

3. Scope: what is included?

Four aspects of employment-source income distinguish it from other types of income. First, the statute strictly limits deductions from employment income. Subsection 8(2) prohibits the deduction of any employment-related expense unless it is *specifically* authorized by the Act. This rule keeps a tight rein on employment deductions. In contrast, we presume that deductions from business or investment income are acceptable if they comply with commercial and accounting principles. The presumption is that business expenses are deductible unless the statute specifically prohibits it.[1] Thus, deducting expenses against business income is

---

[1]Subs. 9(1); *Royal Trust Co. v. Minister of National Revenue*, [1957] C.T.C. 32, 57 D.T.C. 1055 (Can. Ex. Ct.) (payment of dues and memberships in community and social clubs on behalf of employees deductible where employees expected to make contacts and generate business); *Dominion Taxicab Assn. v. Minister of National Revenue*, [1954] S.C.R. 82, [1954] C.T.C. 34, 54 D.T.C. 1020 (S.C.C.) (fees to company contracting with taxicab owners not deductible; funds contingently received not in-

much easier than against employment income. This difference between business and employment income is a powerful incentive for taxpayers to characterize their income as business income.

Second, a taxpayer must calculate employment income on a calendar-year basis.[2] Thus, an employee cannot choose any other fiscal year in respect of employment-source income. In contrast, we determine business income based on a fiscal period. This distinction allows some flexibility in tax planning with business income.

Third, we withhold tax on employment income at source,[3] and hold the tax in trust for the Crown.[4] In contrast, there is no systematic withholding at source on business income. Taxpayers who earn business income must make instalment payments on account of their estimated tax payable.[5]

Fourth, employment income is generally taxable on a cash basis.[6] Business and investment income are taxable on an accrual, or as-earned basis, no matter when the taxpayer receives the income.

Because of these restrictions in calculating employment income, individuals generally prefer independent contractor status for tax purposes. This can cause some legal tension in the characterization of employment relationships.

We must address six issues:

- Is the taxpayer an employee?

- Does the taxpayer hold an office?

- Has the taxpayer received remuneration or taxable benefits?

- What is the value of the remuneration or benefit?

---

come); *R. v. Bank of Nova Scotia*, [1980] C.T.C. 57, 80 D.T.C. 6009 (Fed. T.D.); affirmed [1981] C.T.C. 162, 81 D.T.C. 5115 (Fed. C.A.) (value of foreign tax credit determined in accordance with ordinary commercial principles, taking weighted rate of exchange at time tax payable).

[2]Subs. 5(1) and para. 249(1)(b).

[3]Para. 153(1)(a).

[4]Subs. 227(4). Failure to withhold tax on employment income renders the employer liable to a civil penalty of 10 percent plus interest at a prescribed rate (subs. 227(8)) and to criminal penalties (subs. 238(1)). Directors of a corporation who fail to withhold and remit taxes may be personally liable (subs. 227.1(1)).

[5]Subs. 156(1).

[6]Subs. 5(1). There is an important exception for "salary deferral arrangements"; see para. 6(1)(i), subs. 248(1)"salary deferral arrangement" and subs. 6(11).

- When did the taxpayer receive the remuneration or benefit?
- Is the taxpayer entitled to any statutory deductions from employment income?

II. — Nature of the Employment Relationship

There is a fair volume of litigation concerning the nature of working relationships. The issue occurs in different contexts — tax law, Canada Pension Plan claims, Employment Insurance, and labour law. The doctrine of employee relationship has evolved, and will continue to do so, as working conditions and workplace relationships adapt from bricks and mortar commerce to electronic commerce.

The first point to observe is that the label that a person attaches to a contract does not determine the nature of the relationship of the parties. An employment relationship means the position of an individual in the service of some other person. The term "employee" includes an officer. Thus, the key is to determine the substantive nature of the relationship between the service provider and the person to whom he provides the services. This is not always an easy question to answer.

The Act defines "employment" as the position of an individual in the service of some other person.[7] This is not a very helpful definition. Thus, the first step in the characterization of employment income is to determine whether there is a contract of service between the taxpayer and the source of his or her income.

In traditional contract of service relationships, characterization depends on the degree of control and supervision that a person exercises over another in the provision of the services. In an employment relationship, the employee is under the direct control and supervision of the employer and is obliged to obey that person's lawful orders. The employer controls not only what the employee does but also how he or she does it. Hence, older cases refer to a contract of employment as a master-servant relationship.

In an independent contract for services, a person engages another to perform services in order to achieve a prescribed objective. The manner of achieving the objective is not prescribed. An independent contractor offers his or her services for a fee. The distinction between the two types of contracts has been described as follows: "It seems to me that the difference between the relations of master and servant and of principal and his agent is this: a principal has the right to direct what the agent has to do; but a master has not only that right, but also the right to say how it is to be done."[8]

---

[7]Subs. 248(1).

[8]*R. v. Walker* (1858), 27 L.J.M.C. 207 (Eng. Q.B.) at 208, Baron Bramwell (C.C.R.).

Thus, we must evaluate the elements of a relationship to distinguish a contract of employment from a contract for service. The traditional elements are:

• The degree of supervision and control between the parties;

• The method of remuneration for services;

• Arrangements for holidays;

• Provisions for sick leave;

• Opportunities for outside employment;

• Provision of medical coverage;

• Compensation for work-related travel; and

• The nature of termination clauses.

Determining an employment relationship is essentially a question of fact. There is no absolute formula or bright-line test by which one conclusively determines whether a person is an employee or an independent contractor. No single test invariably yields a clear answer.[9] Indeed, in some situations, an employee may also provide independent contractor services to his employer outside the scope of his regular employment relationship.[10]

A. — Supervision and Control

The classic test to determine whether a person retains another as an employee or as an independent contractor is to look at the degree of control over the service provider. This is the test Baron Bramwell used in 1858[11] and that the Supreme Court of Canada adopted in 1978 in *Hôpital Notre-Dame*.[12] However, the Supreme Court has since shifted to a more flexible approach that looks at the total relationship of the parties.[13]

---

[9] *671122 Ontario Ltd. v. Sagaz Industries Canada Inc.*, [2001] 2 S.C.R. 983, 2001 SCC 59, [2001] 4 C.T.C. 139 (S.C.C.); reconsideration / rehearing refused (2001), 10 C.C.L.T. (3d) 292 (S.C.C.).

[10] See, for example, *Criterion Capital Corp. v. R.*, [2001] 4 C.T.C. 2844 (T.C.C. [General Procedure]). See also *Wolf v. R.*, [2002] 3 C.T.C. 3, 2002 D.T.C. 6853 (Fed. C.A.).

[11] *671122 Ontario Ltd. v. Sagaz Industries Canada Inc.*, above note 9.

[12] *Hôpital Notre-Dame de l'Espérance c. Laurent* (1977), [1978] 1 S.C.R. 605, 17 N.R. 593 (S.C.C.).

[13] See, for example, *671122 Ontario Ltd. v. Sagaz Industries Canada Inc.*, 2001 SCC 59, [2001] 4 C.T.C. 139 (S.C.C.); reconsideration / rehearing refused (2001), 10 C.C.L.T. (3d) 292 (S.C.C.); *Royal Winnipeg Ballet v. Minister of National Revenue*, [2008] 1 C.T.C. 220, 2006 D.T.C. 6323 (Eng.), 2006 FCA 87 (Fed. C.A.) (expressed intention of parties in contractual arrangement given weight).

We evaluate control by four principal criteria:[14]

1. Power to select the person who renders the service;

2. Mode and time of payment;

3. Evaluation of the method and performance of work; and

4. Right to suspend or dismiss the person engaged to perform the work.

In a conventional employment relationship the employer selects his or her employee, sets the amount of wages and benefits and the time of payment, evaluates the employee's performance and the work done, and can terminate the relationship with appropriate notice. Further, depending on the employer's policies, he or she may provide supplementary medical coverage and set out policies in respect of travel, sick leave, disability, outside employment, and vacations.

To be sure, each of these facets of the "control test" is useful in characterizing conventional employment relationships. They are, however, only of limited value in characterizing the working relationships of technical persons and skilled professionals. As MacGuigan J. said in *Wiebe Door Services Ltd.*: ". . . the test has broken down completely in relation to highly skilled and professional workers, who possess skills far beyond the ability of their employers to direct."[15] Thus, for professionals, we supplement the control test with the "organization and integration" test.

B. — Organization and Integration

Characterizing the working relationships of skilled professionals involves more than merely identifying who has the power to dictate how one is to work. In relationships involving

---

[14]See *Gould v. Minister of National Insurance*, [1951] All E.R. 368, [1951] 1 K.B. 731 (K.B.) (contract for services of a music hall artist contained restrictions and elements of control but only those necessary for proper working of the theatre); *Bell v. Minister of National Revenue* (1952), 52 D.T.C. 8 (Can. Tax App. Bd.) (physician to rural villages contracted to provide services; still maintained private practice); *Fainstein v. Minister of National Revenue* (1952), 52 D.T.C. 102 (Can. Tax App. Bd.) (physician and others setting up health departments). See also: *Hôpital Notre-Dame de l'Espérance c. Laurent*, [1978] 1 S.C.R. 605 at 613 (S.C.C.) where Pigeon J. quoted with approval the following passage from *Traité pratique de la responsabilité civile délictuelle* by André Nadeau (translation):

> The essential criterion of employer-employee relations is the right to give orders and instructions to the employee regarding the manner in which to carry out his work.

[15]*Wiebe Door Services Ltd. v. Minister of National Revenue*, [1986] 2 C.T.C. 200, 87 D.T.C. 5025 (Fed. C.A.) at 203 [C.T.C.]; *671122 Ontario Ltd. v. Sagaz Industries Canada Inc.*, [2001] 2 S.C.R. 983, [2001] 4 C.T.C. 139 (S.C.C.) at para. 33; reconsideration / rehearing refused (2001), 10 C.C.L.T. (3d) 292 (S.C.C.).

skilled persons, the user of services usually does not have the technical expertise or "know-how" to dictate how the service provider is to work. Hence, any power or control that does exist is more illusory than real. After all, the very reason for hiring a professional person is so he or she can instruct management in the performance of complex and technical tasks that are beyond the competence of the user of the service. We hire professionals to provide expertise, not to tell them how to do the job.

Thus, the question becomes: is the person an intrinsic part of the organization or merely an adjunct to it? This question is sometimes described as the organization or integration test. But there is no simple formula or single test that supplies the answer. One looks to the whole scheme of operations to elicit the nature of the relationship between the parties. Here, too, the mode and manner of compensation (vacations, sick leave, disability policies, medical coverage, etc . . .) provides an indication of the nature of the relationship. The greater the number and value of ancillary benefits, the greater the likelihood of an employment relationship.

C. — Total Relationship

Although the control and the organization/integration tests are useful in appropriate situations, they are not determinative in all circumstances. They have an overly narrow focus. The better approach is a broader examination of the "total relationship" between the parties,[16] including:

- Supervision and control;

- Ownership of assets;

- Chance of profit; and

- Risk of loss.

No single test is conclusive.[17] These are not four separate and independent tests. They are different aspects of the same test. We determine the nature of the relationship of persons on an analysis of the whole scheme of operations.

Although the extent of control may vary from case to case, an employment relationship implies at least some supervision and control over the employee. Further, in an employment relationship the employer usually owns the assets, carries the risk of the enterprise or working relationship, and derives the benefits of profit.

---

[16]See *Montreal (City) v. Montreal Locomotive Works Ltd.* (1946), [1947] 1 D.L.R. 161 (Quebec P.C.) at 169-70, Lord Wright.

[17]For a good synthesis see *Market Investigations v. Minister of Social Security*, [1968] 3 All E.R. 732, [1969] 2 Q.B. 173 (Eng. Q.B.); *Sang v. Chi-Keung*, [1990] 2 A.C. 374 (Hong Kong P.C.).

The shared intention of the parties to the contract, whilst not determinative, is important if the objective evidence supports their view of the relationship. In the final analysis, the determination of a relationship depends upon the nature of the evidence. There may be clear evidence of shared intention between the parties or other contractual and control indicia that prevail. The onus is on the individual to establish the nature of her particular relationship.[18]

As in most cases of characterization of relationships, the extremes of the spectrum are always easy to identify. The bank teller is an employee of the bank and under its stringent supervision and control. A partner in a law firm serves clients, but is not an employee of any client. What of the lawyer with only one large client, who provides all the lawyer's revenue, reimburses all his expenses, and permits the lawyer to participate in a bonus arrangement that depends on profits?

D. — Office

Section 5 brings into income a taxpayer's income from an office or employment.[19] The Act defines "office" as a position that entitles an individual to a fixed or ascertainable stipend or remuneration.[20] If the stipend is pre-determined in amount, it is fixed. If it is not pre-determined in amount, but may be determined by reference to some formula, it is ascertainable.

The distinction between an "office" and "employment" is that the former does not require the individual to be in the service of some other person, which would imply an employment relationship. For example, judges, ministers of the Crown, and members of a Legislative Assembly or Parliament are "officers" and are not employees. The distinction between an "officer" and an "employee" is not particularly significant for tax purposes because both categories are taxable on their remuneration and benefits on a cash basis.

E. — CRA Views

The CRA does not have a general administrative position on employment contracts.[21] Interpretation Bulletin IT-525R, "Performing Artists," considers limited aspects of relationships involving musicians and other performing artists. The bulletin does, however, address the

---

[18]*Lang v. Minister of National Revenue*, 2007 TCC 547, 2007 D.T.C. 1754 (Eng.) (T.C.C. [Employment Insurance]) (shared intention of parties determined they were independent contractors).

[19]Subs. 248(1) "employment".

[20]Subs. 248(1) "office".

[21]The CRA published guidelines on the employed or self-employed issue in RC4110 available on http://www.cra-arc.gc.ca.

particular problems of persons who have special skills and expertise.[22] For example, it considers an artist is self-employed if she:[23]

- Has a chance of profit or risk of loss;

- Provides instruments and other equipment;

- Has a number of engagements with different persons during the course of a year;

- Regularly auditions or makes applications for engagements;

- Retains the services of an agent regularly;

- Selects or hires employees or helpers, fixes their salary, directs them, etc.;

- Arranges the time, place, and nature of performances; or

- Earns remuneration that is directly related to particular rehearsals and performances.

. . . . .

F. — International Dimensions

Employment status is also an important issue in international tax treaties. For example, under Article XIV of the *Canada-U.S. Tax Treaty*, Canada has the primary right to tax an independent contractor's income that he earns in the United States. The U.S., however, can also tax the income if the individual has a fixed base in that country. This may result in double taxation for which we provide relief under other provisions.[24]

III. — Timing

We calculate employment income on a cash-basis. Thus, we tax an individual on his earnings in the year that he receives payment[25] and credit any taxes withheld at source. These are rules of administrative convenience that allow employees to comply with the tax system with minimum accounting records.

---

[22]*Ibid.*, at para. 4.

[23]*Ibid.*, at para. 7.

[24]See Chapter 15.

[25]Subs. 5(1); but see *Blenkarn v. Minister of National Revenue* (1963), 32 Tax A.B.C. 321, 63 D.T.C. 581 (Can. Tax App. Bd.) (voluntary deferment of salary due and payable to employee held to be taxable in year amount due, not when actually received); *Ferszt v. Minister of National Revenue*, [1978] C.T.C. 2860, 78 D.T.C. 1648 (T.R.B.) ($5,000 advance against commissions included in income). Farming and fishing businesses also permitted to use cash method of accounting; see s. 28.

To be sure, cash-basis accounting allows employees some flexibility in tax planning. For example, an owner-manager of a corporation is taxable on her salary in the year that she receives payment, whereas the corporation may deduct the salary payable on an accrual basis.[26] This imbalance between deduction and inclusion permits modest tax deferral. If the corporation accrues the deduction on December 31 of a year and pays the employee on January 1 of the year following, the employee can defer her tax on the income for an entire year. The Act tolerates this minor mismatch of deductions and inclusions in the interests of administrative convenience. It does, however, limit the deferral advantage from mismatching income and expenses by requiring payment within 180 days after the end of the employer's fiscal period.[27]

IV. — Salary and Wages

An employee (or a person who holds an office) is taxable on his or her salary, wages, and any other remuneration (including gratuities) that he or she receives in the year.[28] Of course, what constitutes "salary or wages" depends on whether there is an employment relationship between the parties. "Remuneration" is compensation for services from an employment relationship, whether past, present, or future.[29]

V. — Benefits & Perks

A. — General Comment

Section 5 brings into a taxpayer's office and employment income amounts that he or she receives as salary, wages, or other remuneration. However, employment income must also

---

[26]*Earlscourt Sheet Metal Mechanical Ltd. v. Minister of National Revenue*, [1988] 1 C.T.C. 2045, 88 D.T.C. 1029 (T.C.C.).

[27]Subs. 78(4).

[28]S. 5; subs. 248(1) "salary or wages".

[29]Note that the definition of "salary or wages" in subs. 248(1) does not apply for the purposes of calculating employment income under s. 5. See *Adam v. Minister of National Revenue*, [1985] 2 C.T.C. 2383, 85 D.T.C. 667 (T.C.C.) (mere bookkeeping entries not capable of converting salary into something else, e.g., dividends); *Hochstrasser (Inspector of Taxes) v. Mayes*, [1959] Ch. 22 (C.A.) at 33; *Brumby v. Milner*, [1976] 3 All E.R. 636 (H.L.); *Tyrer v. Smart (Inspector of Taxes)*, [1979] 1 All E.R. 321, [1979] S.T.C. 34 (H.L.); *Nicoll v. Austin* (1935), 19 Tax Cas. 531 (employer requested continued residence of director in costly manor, but paid stipend to compensate for expenses); *Jaworski v. Inst. of Polish Engr. in Great Britain Ltd.*, [1951] 1 K.B. 768, [1950] 2 All E.R. 1191 (C.A.) (oral contract for foreign national stipulated deductions and taxes borne by "employer"; held to be contract for services).

include non-cash benefits in income if the tax system is to be equitable among taxpayers. Section 6 reinforces the equitable principle and brings into income the value of any benefits that the taxpayer receives or enjoys in the year.

A benefit is an economic advantage, measurable in monetary terms, that an employer (or related person) confers on an employee in his or her capacity as an employee.

Benefits constitute compensation and are taxable because their inclusion in income reflects the taxpayer's ability to pay. The principle of horizontal equity requires taxpayers in comparable financial circumstances to bear comparable burdens of tax. The appropriate treatment of benefits is important to the principle of fairness in taxation. Exclusion of benefits from income would distort the tax system, undermine its integrity, and erode taxpayer confidence in the self-assessment and compliance system. Thus, we should be particularly careful in considering the effect of excluding benefits from income on the tax system.

It is not always easy, however, to determine what is a taxable benefit and how much of it we should tax. Consider, for example, the tax status of three individuals: A works for X company, which pays A $4,000 per month and provides him with low-cost meals in its cafeteria, dental coverage for his entire family, access to a club that provides social and recreational facilities, and discount purchases on its goods. The fringe benefits cost X company $400 per month per employee. B is employed by Y Company, a competitor, and receives $4,400 per month in salary. Y company does not give its employees any fringe benefits. C is paid $4,200 per month to work at Z Company, which also does not pay any fringe benefits, but has a better and a more comfortable working environment than either X Company or Y Company. Z Company's premises have better lighting, air conditioning, and are surrounded by attractive parks and green space. These environmental facilities cost Z Company an average of $200 per month per employee. Should A, B, and C pay tax only on their cash income or on their cash income and benefits? If they should pay tax on benefits, which of the advantages should we consider "taxable" and which, if any, should we exclude from income? If we consider all the benefits to be "taxable", what value should we attach to them — market value, cost to the employer or value to the employee? What if C suffers from allergies that are aggravated by Z Company's green surroundings: Should C be taxable on any portion of her environmental "benefits"?

a) — Meaning of Benefits

Subsection 6(1) is quite clear: a taxpayer must include in his income ". . . the value of board, lodging and other *benefits* of *any* kind whatever received or *enjoyed* . . ." by the taxpayer in the year in respect of, in the course of, or by virtue of his or her office or employment. A benefit is an economic advantage or material acquisition, measurable in monetary terms, that one confers on an employee in his or her capacity as an employee. Thus, there are several questions:

- Did the employee receive or enjoy an economic advantage?

- Is the economic advantage measurable in monetary terms?

- Was the economic advantage for the benefit of the employee or for the benefit of his employer? and

- Did the employer confer the economic advantage on the employee in respect of, in the course of, or by virtue of the employment relationship with the employee?

If we answer all these questions in the affirmative, the economic advantage or material acquisition is a taxable benefit from employment *unless* the statute specifically exempts it from tax.[30]

The interpretation of "benefit" under the Act is broader than under its counterpart in the United Kingdom. In the U.K., a benefit in kind was considered income only if it was readily convertible into cash.[31] For example, rent-free accommodation was considered to be a non-taxable benefit because the employee could not readily convert his accommodation into cash. As the House of Lords said in *Tennant v. Smith*: "A person is chargeable for income tax . . . not on what saves his pocket but what goes into his pocket."[32] Paragraph 6(1)(a) clearly displaces the principle in *Tennant v. Smith* (also described as the "money's worth" principle).

The first question in the analysis is whether the taxpayer derives an economic advantage.[33] Benefits come in all sorts of varieties and guises. Some, such as payment of an individual's personal vacation and living expenses by an employer, are obvious. Others are more subtle: for example, the payment of a grievance settlement to a unionized employee,[34] the discharge

---

[30]See, *R. v. Savage*, [1983] 2 S.C.R. 428, [1983] C.T.C. 393 at 399, 83 D.T.C. 5409 at 5414 (S.C.C.) approving the judgment of Evans, J.A. in *R. v. Poynton*, [1972] C.T.C. 411, 72 D.T.C. 6329 (Ont. C.A.) at 420 [C.T.C.] and 6335-56 [D.T.C.]:

> I do not believe the language to be restricted to benefits that are related to the office or employment in the sense that they represent a form of remuneration for services rendered. If it is a material acquisition which confers an economic benefit on the taxpayer and does not constitute an exemption, e.g., loan or gift, then it is within the all-embracing definition of s. 3. A gift is a gesture of goodwill and is made without regard to services rendered by the recipient of the gift. For example, if an employer distributes turkeys to all employees at Christmas, the value of the turkey is not considered to be a benefit which must be included in an employee's income.

[31]*Tennant v. Smith*, [1892] A.C. 162 (HL).

[32]The law in the U.K. has been changed by statute, which now requires all payment of expenses, including reimbursements, to be included in income.

[33]*Schroter v. R.*, [2010] 4 C.T.C. 143, 2010 D.T.C. 5062 (Fed. C.A.) (free parking pass was taxable economic advantage).

[34]*Norman v. Minister of National Revenue*, [1987] 2 C.T.C. 2261, 87 D.T.C. 556 (T.C.C.).

of a mortgage upon dismissal from employment,[35] or the issuance of stock options by a person other than the employer.[36]

Canadian tax law has wrestled inconclusively with the concept of what constitutes an economic advantage. *Ransom*[37] was the first of many decisions to distort the equity of the tax system. The taxpayer sold his residence at a loss of approximately $4,000 when his employer relocated him from Sarnia to Montreal. The employer compensated the taxpayer for his loss. The Exchequer Court held that the reimbursement for the loss was not taxable because the taxpayer did not benefit from the payment — it did not put any money in his pocket, but merely saved his pocket. In effect, the Court applied the money's worth principle despite the unequivocal language of paragraph 6(1)(a).

Ransom clearly offends the principle of horizontal equity. A taxpayer who receives compensation for his capital loss on the sale of a home is clearly better off than an individual who is not so compensated. Nevertheless, many courts applied *Ransom* to relocation expenses. In *Hoefele v. R.*,[38] for example, the taxpayer moved from Calgary to Toronto, and purchased a house in Toronto that was more expensive than the one he had left in Calgary. His employer picked up the increased mortgage interest on the differential between the two houses, thereby reducing his personal living expenses. The Federal Court of Appeal held that the mortgage interest subsidy was not taxable because the taxpayer was not enriched, but merely restored to his original economic position. The Court said:[39]

> If, on the whole of a transaction, an employee's economic position is not improved, that is, if the transaction is a zero-sum situation when viewed in its entirety, a receipt is not a benefit and, therefore, is not taxable under paragraph 6(1)(a).

However, the courts said that compensation for the higher cost of a new home in a new location is a taxable benefit because it increases the taxpayer's net worth. In *Phillips*,[40] for example, the taxpayer moved from Moncton to Winnipeg. His employer paid him $10,000 to compensate for his increased housing costs in Winnipeg. The $10,000 subsidy was a taxable benefit because it "did more than save his pocket — it put money into it." Thus, the

---

[35]*Galanov v. Minister of National Revenue*, [1987] 2 C.T.C. 2353, 87 D.T.C. 647 (T.C.C.).

[36]*Robertson v. R.*, [1988] 1 C.T.C. 111, 88 D.T.C. 6071 (Fed. T.D.); affirmed [1990] 1 C.T.C. 114, 90 D.T.C. 6070 (Fed. C.A.); leave to appeal refused (1990), 113 N.R. 319 (note) (S.C.C.).

[37]*Ransom v. Minister of National Revenue*, [1967] C.T.C. 346, 67 D.T.C. 5235 (Can. Ex. Ct.).

[38][1996] 1 C.T.C. 131, 95 D.T.C. 5602 (Fed. C.A.); leave to appeal refused (1996), 204 N.R. 398 (note) (S.C.C.).

[39]See also *Splane v. R.*, [1991] 2 C.T.C. 224, 91 D.T.C. 5549 (Fed. C.A.).

[40]*Phillips v. Minister of National Revenue*, [1994] 1 C.T.C. 383, 94 D.T.C. 6177 (Fed. C.A.); leave to appeal refused (1994), 179 N.R. 320 (note) (S.C.C.).

Court applied the money's worth principle to arrive at the right decision for the wrong reasons.

It is difficult to rationalize the difference between enhancing one's wealth through employer-subsidized financing[41] and subsidized capital costs.[42] Thus, subsection 6(20) provides special tax treatment for eligible housing losses. Generally, one-half of employer reimbursements in excess of $15,000 in respect of eligible housing losses is taxable as an employment benefit to the taxpayer.[43] The one-half exclusion is an accommodation or compromise for those who move from one city to another and incur a loss as a consequence of their move.

The law on the taxation of reimbursements on relocation is neither clear, consistent, nor rational. In *Gernhart v. Minister of National Revenue*,[44] for example, the Tax Court of Canada refused to extend the reasoning of *Ransom* to reimbursements of income tax to accommodate a differential tax burden between Canada and the United States. The taxpayer, an employee of General Motors, moved from Ohio to Windsor. Her employer compensated her for Canada's higher income tax rates by paying her the tax differential between Canadian and U.S. rates in order to equalize her net after-tax income. The Court rightly characterized the reimbursement as a form of salary compensation. It is difficult in principle to distinguish *Gernhart* from *Hoefele*. In both cases, the taxpayer was not enriched, but merely restored to his original position. Nevertheless, the principle in *Gernhart* is preferable, in that the taxpayer was taxed on her benefit based on her enhanced ability to pay.[45]

Thus, the taxability of a benefit depends on the answers to several questions. First, has the taxpayer received or enjoyed an economic advantage? If so, was the economic advantage measurable in monetary terms? We tax an employee on monetary benefits that he derives from his office but not on the pleasure of pleasant working conditions. Thus, for example, psychic income (such as job satisfaction, pleasant work environment) is not taxable.

The second question is whether the advantage is measureable in monetary terms. In this context, although somewhat dated, Kleinwachter's conundrum illustrates the difficulty with taxing working conditions as income to the employee.

---

[41]*Hoefele v. R.*, [1996] 1 C.T.C. 131, 95 D.T.C. 5602 (Fed. C.A.); leave to appeal refused (1996), 204 N.R. 398 (note) (S.C.C.).

[42]*Phillips v. Minister of National Revenue*, [1994] 1 C.T.C. 383, 94 D.T.C. 6177 (Fed. C.A.); leave to appeal refused (1994), 179 N.R. 320 (note) (S.C.C.).

[43]Subs. 6(20).

[44]*Gernhart v. R.* (1997), [1998] 2 C.T.C. 102, 98 D.T.C. 6026 (Fed. C.A.); affirming [1996] 3 C.T.C. 2369, 96 D.T.C. 1672 (T.C.C.); leave to appeal refused (1998), 227 N.R. 397 (note) (S.C.C.).

[45]Amount treated as income under subs. 5(1). See also: subs. 6(20) for eligible housing losses.

Let us consider here another of Kleinwachter's conundrums. We are asked to measure the relative incomes of the ordinary officer serving with his troops and a *Flugeladjutant* to the sovereign. Both receive the same nominal pay; but the latter receives quarters in the palace, food at the royal table, servants, and horses for sport. He accompanies the prince to the theatre and opera, and, in general, lives royally at no expense to himself and is able to save generously from his salary. But suppose, as one possible complication, that the *Fluge-ladjutant* detests opera and hunting.

> The problem is clearly hopeless. To neglect all compensation in kind is obviously inappropriate. On the other hand, to include the perquisites as a major addition to the salary implies that all income should be measured with regard to the relative pleasurableness of different activities — which would be the negation of measurement. There is hardly more reason for imputing additional income to the *Flugeladjutant* on account of his luxurious wardrobe than for bringing into account the prestige and social distinction of a (German) university professor. Fortunately, however, such difficulties in satisfactory measurement of relative incomes do not bulk large in modern times; and, again, these elements of unmeasurable psychic income may be presumed to vary in a somewhat continuous manner along the income scale. . . .[46]

Now, substitute for the *Flugeladjutant* an executive assistant to the Governor General or Prime Minister.

The third question to consider is whether the economic advantage was for the benefit of the taxpayer or for the benefit of the employer who conferred it. A payment that is primarily for the convenience of the employer is not taxable to the employee.[47] Thus, the key is: who is the *primary* beneficiary of the payment? For example, where an employer requires an employee to take computer courses so that he or she is better trained for his or her job, the cost of the job training is not a taxable benefit to the employee even though he or she becomes a better qualified and a more valuable person. The benefit to the employee is incidental to the benefits that the employer derives.[48]

Similarly, where an employer sends her employee for second language training, the expenses are primarily for the benefit of the employer even though the employee is better trained and marketable. What if the Government of Canada sends one of its senior executives on a fully reimbursed basis to Paris for a year to study French? Would it make a difference if the executive was 45 years of age or 70 years?

---

[46]H. Simons, Personal Income Taxation 53 (1938).

[47]*Lowe v. R.*, [1996] 2 C.T.C. 33, 96 D.T.C. 6226 (Fed. C.A.) (trip to New Orleans with wife not taxable as it was for employer's benefit).

[48]*Dhillon v. R.*, [2002] 4 C.T.C. 2648, 2002 D.T.C. 2083 (T.C.C. [General Procedure]) (to be taxable the benefit must be for benefit of employee).

There is no bright-line test to determine what constitutes a benefit to the employee and convenience-to-the-employer, particularly where there are mutual benefits.[49] The convenience-to-the-employer test does not imply that the employee cannot derive pleasure from the task entrusted to him or her. For example, a hotel manager who is "compelled" to live in a luxury suite in a resort hotel is not taxable on the value of the suite if the manager's job requires him or her to be on the premises for the benefit of the employer.[50]

The fourth question to consider is whether the economic advantage was conferred in respect of, in the course of, or by virtue of the employment relationship between the taxpayer and his or her employer. Did the employer confer the economic advantage on his or her employee *qua* employee or in his or her personal capacity? The former may be taxable; the latter is not taxable as employment income. For example, a gift to an employee in his or her personal capacity is not a benefit for tax purposes.[51]

---

[49]See, e.g., *Cutmore v. Minister of National Revenue*, [1986] 1 C.T.C. 2230, 86 D.T.C. 1146 (T.C.C.) (employees taxed on fees paid for preparation of personal tax returns despite employer's policy requiring such preparation).

[50]*Benaglia v. C.I.R.* (1937), 36 B.T.A. 838 (U.S. B.T.A.).

[51]See, e.g., *Busby v. R.*, [1986] 1 C.T.C. 147, 86 D.T.C. 6018 (Fed. T.D.); *Phaneuf v. R.*, [1978] C.T.C. 21 at 27, 78 D.T.C. 6001 at 6005 (Fed. T.D.), *per* Thurlow, A.C.J.:

> Is the payment made "by way of remuneration for his services" or is it "made to him on personal grounds and not by way of payment for his services"? It may be made to an employee but is it made to him as an employee or simply as a person? Another way of stating it is to say is it received in his capacity as employee, but that appears to me to be the same test. To be received in the capacity of employee it must, as I see it, partake of the character of remuneration for services. That is the effect that, as it seems to me, the words "in respect of, in the course of, or by virtue of an office or employment" in paragraph 6(1)(a) have.

See also *Seymour v. Reed*, [1927] A.C. 554 (H.L.) at 559, where Viscount Cave L.C. expressed the question in the following manner:

> . . . the question, therefore, is whether the sum . . . fell within the description, contained in r. 1 of Sch. E. of "salaries, fees, wages, prerequisites or profits whatsoever therefrom" (i.e., from an office or employment of profit) "for the year of assessment", so as to be liable to income tax under that Schedule. These words and the corresponding expressions contained in the earlier statutes (which were not materially different) have been the subject of judicial interpretation in cases which have been cited to your Lordships and it must now (I think) be taken as settled that they include all payments made to the holder of an office or employment as such, that is to say, by way of remuneration for his services, even though such payments may be voluntary, but that they do not include a mere gift or present (such as a testimonial) which is made to him on personal grounds and not by way of payment for services. The question to be answered is, as Rowlatt, J. put it: "Is it in the end a personal gift or is it remuneration?" If the latter, it is subject to the tax; if the former, it is not.

The characterization of capacity can be difficult.[52] *Savage*[53] is the classic scenario. The taxpayer, a junior employee of a life insurance company, took three courses offered by the Life Office Management Association that were designed to provide a broad understanding of insurance company operations. She undertook the courses of her own volition and without pressure from her employer. Nevertheless, pursuant to its enlightened corporate policy, which was well known to employees, the employer reimbursed the taxpayer $100 for each course that she successfully completed. The reimbursements were taxable benefits. The phrase "in respect of an office or employment" in paragraph 6(1)(a) has wide scope.[54] Thus, the payments were taxable as benefits from employment because they were paid to the taxpayer in her capacity as an employee and primarily for her advantage.[55]

---

[52]*Ball v. Johnson* (1971), 47 Tax Cas. 155; *Hochstrasser (Inspector of Taxes) v. Mayes*, [1960] A.C. 376 (H.L.) (Court must be satisfied that the service agreement was *causa causans* and not merely *causa sine qua non* of receipt of benefit); *Bridges v. Hewitt*, [1957] 2 All E.R. 281 (C.A.).

[53]*R. v. Savage*, [1980] C.T.C. 103, 80 D.T.C. 6066 (Fed. T.D.); reversed on other grounds [1981] C.T.C. 332, 81 D.T.C. 5258 (Fed. C.A.); affirmed [1983] C.T.C. 393, 83 D.T.C. 5409 (S.C.C.).

[54]*R. v. Savage*, [1983] C.T.C. at 399, 83 D.T.C. at 5414. The Court endorses its earlier decision in *Nowegijick v. R.*, [1983] 1 S.C.R. 29, [1983] C.T.C. 20, 83 D.T.C. 5041 (S.C.C.) at 25 [C.T.C.] and 5045 [D.T.C.]:

> . . . the words "in respect of" are, in my opinion words of the widest possible scope. They import such meanings as "in relation to", "with reference to" or "in connection with". The phrase "in respect of" is probably the widest of any expression intended to convey some connection between two related subject matters.

The Court also distinguishes earlier English jurisprudence on benefits:

> Our Act contains the stipulation not found in the English statute referred to, "benefits of any kind whatever . . . in respect of, in the course of, or by virtue of an office or employment". The meaning of "benefit of whatever kind" is clearly quite broad.

See also: *Jex v. R.*, [1998] 2 C.T.C. 2688, 98 D.T.C. 1377 (T.C.C.) (CRA employee taxed on reimbursement of professional course fees in the absence of any requirement by employer to take courses); *Faubert v. R.*, 98 D.T.C. 1380 (T.C.C.).

[55]Dickson, Ritchie, Lamer and Wilson JJ. specifically addressed the question with reference to para. 6(1)(a)); McIntyre J. left the issue open by excluding payment from income under para. 56(1)(n) and not addressing para. 6(1)(a). According to their Lordships (*R. v. Savage, ante*, [1983] C.T.C. at 398, 83 D.T.C. at 5413:

> . . . the *Hochstrasser* case and *Ball v. Johnson* are of little assistance. The provisions of s. 156 of the *Income Tax Act, 1952* of England are not unlike s. 5(1) of the Canadian *Income Tax Act* but our Act goes further in s. 6(1)(a). In addition to the salary, wages and other remuneration referred to in s. 5(1), s. 6(1)(a) includes in income the value of benefits "of any kind whatever . . . received or enjoyed . . . in respect of, in the course of, or by virtue of an office or employment".

b) — Timing

Timing and valuations of benefits are inextricably linked to each other. An employee is taxable on benefits that he or she *receives or enjoys* in the year. The word "enjoys" enlarges the rule beyond actual receipt of the benefit.

Section 6 does not distinguish between cash and "in kind" benefits. To illustrate: assume that on September 1 a corporation confers 100 shares of capital stock on its employee. The shares are trading at $100 per share at the time. On December 31 the shares are trading at $125. The employee sells the shares on March 1 for $160 per share and derives an economic gain of $16,000. This raises two issues: (1) how much should we include in the employee's income in the first year when she receives the stock? and (2) what should be the employee's gain when she sells the stock? The answer to the first question is that paragraph 6(1)(a) taxes "in kind" and cash benefits equally in the year of receipt. The only issue is the value of the shares, which, in this case, we can easily determine. The employee is taxable on $10,000, the market value of the shares. In effect, the shares are the equivalent of a cash bonus. If the taxpayer's marginal tax rate is 50 percent, she must pay tax of $5,000 even though she did not receive cash. Thus, the taxpayer must either come up with the $5,000 or sell sufficient shares to raise the cash.

The answer to the second question depends upon the answer to the first. If we tax the employee on the $10,000 benefit in the year that she receives the shares, we must allow the employee to bump up her cost basis in the shares from zero to $10,000. Otherwise we would tax her twice on the same amount when she sells the shares in Year 2. The gain when the employee sells the shares is only $6,000, even though she did not pay anything for the shares. Thus, the employee must recognize $10,000 of her total economic gain in the first year and can defer recognizing $6,000 until she sells the shares.

The difference in timing is important. The present value of the $5,000 tax liability in the first year is $5,000. The present value of the $3,000 tax liability in Year 2 is only $2,778 if we assume an interest rate of 8 percent. Thus, the employee's decision to delay selling the shares affects not only the timing of her liability but also its net present value.

If we assume for a moment that the employee is not taxable in the year that she receives the shares but only when she sells them, the results are quite different. The employee's income inclusion in the first year is nil and does not trigger any tax. In the subsequent year, however, her gain on sale is $16,000, the difference between the cost and selling price. At a tax rate of 50 percent, she is liable to pay $8,000. The present value of the tax at an interest rate of 8 percent is now only $7,407. Thus, the delay of only one year results in a tax saving of $371. Deferring taxes means saving taxes. This is a repeating concern in tax law.

Where an employee acquires a right to acquire property from his employer and the right depends upon the fulfillment of a condition or contingency, the right is not a benefit until the condition or contingency is satisfied.

Similarly, a benefit is taxable only when it vests in the employee.[56] There are considerable difficulties in determining when rights vest in an employee and, if they have vested, the present value of benefits that are payable in the future. For example, how do we determine when an employee "receives or enjoys" a benefit from his employer's contribution to his pension plan? Should the employee be taxable on the present value of his employer's contribution in the year that the employer contributes it or when it vests in the employee? To circumvent these difficulties of timing and value, the Act has a detailed scheme for the taxation of deferred income plans.[57] For example, employer contributions to an employee's registered pension plan are not taxable upon payment into the plan, but are taxable only when the plan makes pension payments to the employee.[58]

c) — Valuation

Having determined that a particular "in kind" benefit or "perk" is taxable as employment income, the next question is: what is the taxable amount? Should the employee pay tax on the fair market value of the benefit, the cost of the benefit to the employer, or on its exchange value? For example, suppose an airline allows its employees to travel free of charge on its planes on a space-available basis. Should an employee who takes advantage of the facility be taxable on the equivalent of full-fare, advanced booking fare, or standby fare? What is the value of the trip if the employee is "bumped up" into first class because that is the only available space on the flight?

---

[56]*Hogg v. R.*, [1987] 2 C.T.C. 257, 87 D.T.C. 5447 (Fed. T.D.).

[57]See "Deductions from Business and Investment Income".

[58]Subpara. 6(1)(a)(i) and para. 56(1)(a).

There is no single formula for the valuation of all benefits. We value some benefits at their cost to the employer,[59] others according to market prices for similar products,[60] and others by their opportunity cost.[61]

The valuation of benefits is almost always a contentious issue between taxpayers and revenue authorities. Thus, in the interests of administration and certainty, the Act prescribes valuation formulas for some of the more contentious benefits, such as those from automobiles, stock options and low-cost loans.[62] In other cases, the CRA simply ignores the value of certain perks. The result is that the tax system is riddled with benefits rules and exceptions that distort comparative tax burdens between similarly situated taxpayers. Understandably, employees with negotiation leverage will try to maximize their no-tax or low-tax perks.

As a matter of administrative practice and political expediency, the CRA does not tax a benefit unless it can easily measure the value of the benefit in monetary terms. For example, it does not attribute an amount to an employee who is given free scramble parking on his employer's premises if such facilities are available to the public and all employees *and* it is not possible to appraise the value of the benefit. It will, however, attribute tax benefits if the perk is selective and it can value it by commercial standards. There are also special rules for individuals who are blind or have severe mobility impairments.[63]

Similar considerations apply to employer-provided child care facilities. These exclusions are premised more on administrative convenience than on principles of tax equity. Why, for

---

[59]See, e.g., *Rendell v. Went* (1964), 41 Tax Cas. 654 (H.L.) (assumption by employer of costs of employee's criminal defence taxable benefit equal in value to amount of cost assumed).

[60]See, e.g., *Wilkins v. Rogerson* (1961), 39 Tax Cas. 344 (C.A.) (second-hand value, rather than cost, of suits supplied by employer to employees was amount of taxable benefit); *per* Harman L.J.:

> . . . the only controversy was whether he was to pay tax on the cost of the prerequisite to his employer, or on the value of it to him. It appears to me that this prerequisite is a taxable subject-matter because it is money's worth. It is money's worth because it can be turned into money, and when turned into money the taxable subject-matter is the value received. I cannot myself see how it is connected directly with the cost to the employer. . . . The taxpayer has to pay on what he gets. Here he has got a suit. He can realize it only for £5. The advantage to him is therefore, £5. The detriment to his employer has been considerably more, but that seems to me to be irrelevant. The validity of the Court's reasoning is dubious. Had His Lordship asked the question "what is the value in use?" instead of "what is the value in exchange?", he may have arrived at a different conclusion.

[61]*Youngman v. R.*, [1986] 2 C.T.C. 475, 86 D.T.C. 6584 (Fed. T.D.); reversed [1990] 2 C.T.C. 10, 90 D.T.C. 6322 (Fed. C.A.) (shareholder benefit measured by reference to capital cost of house supplied by corporation rather than by reference to its rental value).

[62]See, e.g., subs. 6(2) (formula for automobile benefits), s. 7 (formula for stock option benefits), s. 80.4 (formula for benefit of low-cost loans).

[63]Para. 6(16)(a) overrides Subsection 6(1).

example, should we exclude a benefit from income merely because similar benefits are extended to all employees? Why not tax all the employees on the same value of the benefit?

B. — Taxable Benefits

Benefits come in various forms and guises. For example, travel rewards are taxable as benefits, but only if the reward mileage was accumulated by virtue of the frequent flyer's employment relationship and the employer paid for the trips. Reward miles are taxable in the year in which the individual uses the miles for airline travel or other personal expenditures. Thus, the benefit is recognized at the time of utilization and not when the miles are credited to the frequent flyer's account. An individual is taxable on the fair market value of the benefit derived from free (or reduced cost) airline travel.

Other common forms of taxable benefits include:

- Board and lodging furnished at an unreasonably low rate (except for the value of board and lodging at special worksites);

- Rent-free or low-rent housing provided by the employer;

- Personal use of employer's automobile;

- Gifts in cash or in kind, including Christmas gifts (with minor exceptions), if the gift is disguised as remuneration;

- Holiday trips, prizes, and incentive awards in recognition of job performance;

- Premiums paid by an employer under provincial hospitalization and medical care insurance plans, and certain Government of Canada plans;

- Tuition fees paid for, or reimbursed to, employees in respect of their private education;

- Travelling expenses of employee's spouse; and

- Interest-free or low-interest loans.

C. — Excluded Benefits

Paragraph 6(1)(a) excludes as taxable benefits any economic advantage derived from:

- Employer contributions to a registered pension plan, group sickness or accident insurance plan, private health services plan, supplementary unemployment benefit plan, deferred profit-sharing plan, or group term life insurance policy;

- A retirement compensation arrangement, an employee benefit plan, or an employee trust;

- A benefit in respect of the use of an automobile (taxed under other provisions);

- Benefits derived from counselling services; and

- Benefits under a salary deferral arrangement (taxed under other provisions).

These exclusions are justified on varied considerations, such as stiming, valuation or social policies.

Also, as a matter of administrative policy, the CRA does not generally consider the following as taxable benefits:

- Discounts on merchandise for employees of merchandising businesses;

- Subsidized meals to employees, staff lunchrooms, and canteens;

- Uniforms and special protective clothing supplied by employers, including cost of laundry and dry-cleaning;

- Subsidized school services for families of employees in remote areas;

- Transportation to the job in a vehicle supplied by the employer free or for a nominal charge;

- Social or athletic club fees where it is to the employer's advantage for the employee to be a member;

- Moving expenses of an employee paid or reimbursed by the employer;

- Premiums under private health services plans paid on the employee's behalf by the employer; and

- Contributions by employers to provincial hospitalization and medical care insurance plans to the extent that the employer is required to pay amounts to the plan.

D. — Allowances

Employment income includes all amounts that an individual receives in the year "as an allowance for personal or living expenses or as an allowance for any other purpose. . . ."[64] An "allowance" is a limited and pre-determined sum of money paid to an individual that he is not required to account for. In contrast, a "reimbursement" is a payment to indemnify an individual against actual expenses and is usually accounted for by providing receipts to substantiate the expenditure.[65] The taxability of allowances and reimbursements is fundamental to the fairness of the tax system.

---

[64]Para. 6(1)(b).

[65]*Gagnon v. R.*, [1986] 1 S.C.R. 264, [1986] 1 C.T.C. 410, 86 D.T.C. 6179 (S.C.C.) ("allowance" linked to spouse's ability to dispose of it for own benefit regardless of restriction that it be applied to

There is no consistent rationale for the taxation of allowances. Most allowances are taxable as income.[66] There are some, however, that the Act *specifically* excludes. For example, salespeople who are employed for the purpose of selling property or negotiating contracts may exclude a reasonable allowance paid for travelling expenses. Employees (other than salespeople) may exclude a reasonable allowance paid to them to cover travelling expenses if the allowance is calculated by reference to time spent by the employee travelling away from the municipality where he ordinarily works. Hence, employees in receipt of a *per diem* travelling allowance are not taxable on the allowance if the amount of the allowance is reasonable. Parliamentary expense allowances are not taxable even if paid on a non-accountable basis.

a) — Personal and Living Expenses

Unless specifically excluded, allowances for personal or living expenses are taxable as income. Reimbursement of personal or living expenses is also taxable as income as a benefit under paragraph 6(1)(a). For example, if an employer reimburses her employee's credit card bills for personal travel and entertainment, the amount of the reimbursement is a taxable benefit under paragraph 6(1)(a). If, instead, the employer provides her employee with an allowance of $5,000 per month for personal and living expenses, the allowance is taxable under paragraph 6(1)(b). Thus, it makes little difference whether a payment to an employee on account of personal or living expenses is an allowance or a reimbursement. In either case, the amount is taxable unless there is an exemption that specifically excludes the allowance from income.

The Act excludes the following allowances for personal and living expenses from income:

- Allowances fixed by an Act of Parliament or by the Treasury Board;

- Travel and separation allowances paid to members of the Canadian Forces;

- Representation or other special allowances paid to diplomats and Canadian officials posted abroad;

- Reasonable allowances for travel expenses paid to an employee who is employed to sell property or negotiate contracts for his or her employer;

- Reasonable allowances for travel expenses paid to an employee where the employee is required to travel away from the municipality where his or her employer's establishment is located; and

---

particular purpose); *R. v. Pascoe*, [1975] C.T.C. 656, 75 D.T.C. 5427 (Fed. C.A.) (Court defines "allowance" and "payable on periodic basis"; note C.T.C. editorial note at 656).

[66]Para. 6(1)(b).

• Reasonable allowances for the use of motor vehicles received by an employee from the employer for travelling in the performance of the duties of an office or employment.

b) — Special Work Sites

Allowances for personal living expenses are usually taxable as employment income. In certain narrowly prescribed circumstances, however, the Act permits tax fee allowances for employees who must work in remote locations or must commute long distances. This exclusion is justified on the basis of the especially high costs of living in remote locations and to encourage part-time employment. An employee who receives an allowance for transportation, board or lodging at a special work site may exclude the allowance from income if he also maintains a principal residence at another location.[67] Thus, only employees who actually maintain two residences, one where they regularly live and the other at the temporary work site, can exclude the allowance. Thus, the tax system subsidizes the high cost of living and working in remote locations rather than making employers bear the cost in the form of higher wages.

The cost of commuting to and from a place of employment is considered a personal expense. It follows, then, that commuting expenses are not generally deductible from income. A special rule applies, however, with respect to part-time employees who travel substantial distances to their part-time jobs. A part-time employee who receives an allowance for, or reimbursement of, travelling expenses may exclude the amount received from income if:[68]

• He or she deals at arm's length with the employer;

• He or she is employed or carries on business elsewhere throughout the period of part-time employment;

• The part-time employment is located not less than 80 kilometres from his or her residence and principal place of employment or business; and

• The amount of the allowance or reimbursement does not exceed a reasonable amount and is not on account of other non-travel-related expenses incurred in the performance of the part-time employment.

This rule encourages individuals to seek part-time employment by reducing their taxable costs.

---

[67]Subs. 6(6).

[68]Subs. 81(3.1).

VI. — Advances and Loans

We saw earlier that employees are taxable on a cash basis on their employment income. Thus, advances against salary are taxable in the year in which the employee *receives* the advance.[69] An "advance" is a payment on account of future salary or wages. Typically, the employee is not expected to repay the advance, but to work off his or her financial obligation by rendering service to the employer.[70]

In contrast, a loan is a capital transfer and, therefore, is not income. A loan is a debt with provision for repayment within some reasonable time. Thus, the distinction between an advance and a loan is in the mode in which the employee will discharge the obligation.

VII. — Automobiles

A. — General Comment

Employees are generally taxable on the benefit that they derive from employer-supplied automobiles. Taxable benefits from employer-supplied automobiles come in two forms: (1) operating expenses, and (2) standby charges. An "automobile" is a motor vehicle that is designed primarily to carry individuals on highways and that has a maximum seating capacity, including the driver, of nine persons.[71]

B. — Operating Costs

An employee is taxable on the value of any personal net operating costs that his employer pays on his behalf. Thus, employees must allocate gas, oil, maintenance, and insurance costs to determine their personal component.[72] Payments to an employee to compensate for the operating expenses of a personally owned automobile are also taxable as a benefit.

C. — Standby Charge

The purpose of the standby charge is to tax employees on the benefit that they derive from the availability of their employer's car for personal use. The employee must pay the charge

---

[69]*Randall v. Minister of National Revenue*, [1987] 2 C.T.C. 2265, 87 D.T.C. 553 (T.C.C).

[70]CAIXIT IT-421R2.

[71]Subs. 248(1).

[72]Para. 6(1)(l).

if he has access to the car for personal use, regardless whether he actually uses it. The benefit derives from availability, not from use.[73]

The amount of the standby charge is set by formula. The essence of the formula is that the benefit is equal to 2 percent of the original cost (including HST) of the automobile for every month that it is available to the employee. The word "reasonable" in the phrase "reasonable standby charge" is entirely misleading. The formula is a deeming provision that dictates the *exact* amount to be included in the employee's income. The calculation, which has little to do with the value of the benefit, is precise for administrative convenience and to avoid litigation.

The basic standby charge in respect of an employer-owned automobile is equal to:

$$(\text{cost} \times 2\% \times (\text{no. of days available}))/30$$

The number of days divided by 30 is rounded to the next whole number.

Example
Assume:

Personal use		24,000 kms
Basic cost of automobile	$	20,354
Taxes @ 13%		2,646
Total cost of automobile	$	23,000
Number of days available		365 days
Expenses reimbursed by employee		NIL

Then, a reasonable standby charge is:

2% × $23,000 × 12[*]	$	5,520

Notes::

*   365/30 is rounded to 12

Example
Assume that an employer pays $3,600 toward his employee's *personal*-use operating expenses, for which the employee reimburses the employer $1,600.
Then:

(1)	Benefit under para. 6(1)(l) —	$	3,600
	Amount		(1,600)
	reimbursed		
	Inclusion in	$	2,000

---

[73]*Adams v. R.*, [1998] 2 C.T.C. 353, 98 D.T.C. 6266 (Fed. C.A.) (mere right of usage is sufficient to trigger standby charge).

Example

	income	
(2)	Standby charge	
	2% × $23,000 × 12	5,520
	Taxable benefits	$ 7,520

To simplify record keeping, however, an employee who uses his or her automobile primarily (that is, more than 50 percent) for employment purposes can opt to include an additional one-half of the automobile standby charge in income in lieu of his share of operating costs.[74] Hence, the employee might include 3, instead of 2, percent of the cost of the automobile as a taxable benefit.

The standby charge for automobile salespeople is calculated somewhat differently. The rate applicable is 75 percent of the rate applicable to all other employees.[75] Also, the charge is calculated by reference to the *average* cost of *all* automobiles that the employer purchases in the year.

The benefit from leased automobiles is calculated as two-thirds of the cost of leasing the automobile (excepting any portion related to insurance) for the period that the automobile is available to the employee. The cost of the automobile, in the formula, is its actual cost and not the cost that the employer is entitled to depreciate for tax purposes.[76]

D. — Employee-Owned Cars

Where an employee is compensated for the personal use of her own car in the course of employment, the nature and amount of compensation determines the tax treatment of the employee. Generally, an amount paid to reimburse an employee for her business use of a personally owned car is not included in income. Similarly, a reasonable allowance from an employer as compensation for the business use of a personal automobile is not taxable. Allowances calculated by reference to something other than kilometres driven are deemed not to be reasonable. Where an employee is reimbursed for expenses in addition to being paid a per-kilometre allowance, the Act deems the allowance to be in excess of a "reasonable amount". In these circumstances, the full amount of the unreasonable allowance is taxable to the employee.[77]

---

[74]Subpara. 6(1)(k)(iv).

[75]Subs. 6(2.1).

[76]See Class 10.1, Sch. II, Regulations. The maximum is updated from time to time per Reg. 7307(1)(b).

[77]Subparas. 6(1)(b)(x) and (xi).

VIII. — Imputed Interest

Low cost loans are another popular employment perk. The Act taxes employees on the imputed benefit that they derive from low cost loans by virtue of their employment.[78]

The Act deems a benefit to the employee where it is reasonable to conclude that, but for the employment, the employer would not have made the loan to the employee.[79] A loan to the employee's spouse is also taxable to the employee if she obtains it by virtue of her employment. The taxable benefit is equal to the interest imputed on the loan[80] at a rate that is determined quarterly. The rate is based on the average Treasury Bill rate of the first month during the preceding quarter.[81]

The value of low-interest loans should not be underestimated as a benefit or perquisite of office. A low-interest loan may produce a taxable benefit, but it is only taxable at the marginal rate. Thus, the *effective* after-tax cost of a low-cost loan is considerably lower than the cost of commercial loans.

Example
Assume that a taxpayer with a marginal tax rate of 50 percent receives an interest-free loan of $100,000 from her employer when the prescribed rate is 8 percent. The imputed interest is calculated as follows: Taxable benefit (8% × $100,000) $ 8,000 Tax thereon (50% × $8,000) $ 4,000 *Effective* after-tax cost of loan ($4,000 / $100,000)   4%

---

[78]Subs. 6(9).

[79]S. 80.4(1.1).

[80]S. 80.4(1).

[81]Reg. 4301.

Example

Assume that an individual receives a loan of $150,000 by virtue of her employment. She pays $8,000 interest on the loan and a corporation related to the employer pays $3,000 interest on her behalf. The prescribed rate of interest is 12 percent and the loan is outstanding throughout the year.

Then:

Prescribed rate × loan amount

(12% × $150,000)	$	18,000
Add amounts paid by third party		3,000
		21,000

Less amounts paid on loan

($8,000 + $3,000)		(11,000)
Taxable benefit	$	10,000

A. — Exclusions

The imputed interest rules do not apply if the rate at which an employee borrows from his employer is equal to, or greater than, the prevailing commercial rate for parties dealing with each other at arm's length.[82] Thus, an employee who borrows from his employer at a commercial market rate is not subject to imputed interest if the commercial rate increases after the loan is taken out, provided that the other terms and conditions of the loan are no more advantageous than those available in the commercial marketplace.

B. — Deemed Payments

An employee deemed to receive imputed interest is also deemed to have paid an equivalent amount pursuant to a legal obligation.[83] Hence, any interest imputed on a loan or indebted-

---

[82]Subs. 80.4(3).

[83]S. 80.5.

ness used for the purpose of earning income (for example, the purchase of shares) is deductible as interest expense.[84]

C. — Forgiveness of Loan

Where an employer forgives a loan to an employee, the principal amount of the loan is included in the employee's income at the time that the employer forgives the loan.[85] An imputed interest benefit is not included in income in the year that the employer forgives the loan.[86]

IX. — Stock Options

A. — General Comment

Stock options are a popular form of compensation for employees and senior executives, particularly for employees in the high technology industries. Companies such as Microsoft, Apple and Google made many secretaries into millionaires through their stock option plans. Stock options are attractive both from the employer's and the employee's perspective. They preserve the corporation's cash for capital investment and link its well-being to the employee's remuneration. This gives the employee an ownership interest in his or her employer.

The taxation of stock options, however, raises special problems of timing and valuation. Suppose, for example, that a corporation grants its executive an option to purchase 1,000 shares of its stock at $10 a share at any time in the next three years. The shares trade at $12 on the day that the employer grants the option. The shares are non-transferable. The executive can exercise the options only if he is an employee of the corporation when he triggers the options. The executive exercises the option in Year 2 when the shares are trading at $50 a share and sells the shares in Year 3 for $60 a share. Clearly, the executive makes an overall profit of $50,000 over the three years.

This gives rise to three questions: (1) should we treat all of the gain as employment compensation? (2) when should we tax the profit? and (3) how much of the profit, if any, should we tax?

---

[84]Subpara. 20(1)(c)(i).

[85]Subs. 6(15).

[86]Para. 80.4(3)(b).

We can break down the $50,000 profit into at least three components:

Year 1 profit on the day the option is granted	$ 2,000
Year 2 profit when the option is exercised	$ 38,000
Year 3 profit when the shares are sold	$ 10,000

The corporation does not give its executive the option for nothing.[87] The stock option is compensation from employment, which the corporation gives to the employee in exchange for her services and as an incentive for future performance and loyalty. Thus, stock options are in a sense "golden handcuffs".

The common law rule is that stock option benefits are taxable in the year in which the employer grants the option.[88] This is so regardless that the taxpayer has not sold the stock and realized a gain. The option represents compensation for personal service and accretion of wealth, albeit only on paper. Hence, any benefit should be taxable as employment income.

The second question is more troublesome and raises issues of timing and value. To be sure, the executive theoretically increases his net wealth in Year 1 when he acquires a contractual right of $12,000 value. At that time, however, there are various uncertainties. The options have value, but only if the executive continues as an employee with the corporation, and that the price of the stock may decline before he exercises the options. Thus, the common law rule has several problems. It is difficult to value benefits from unexercised options, particularly where the company restricts the right to dispose of the underlying shares ("golden handcuffs").

Of course, we can tax the employee immediately on the $2,000 gain and then allow for retroactive adjustments for price declines etc., or discount the value of the benefit to take the uncertainties into account. Both of these choices create uncertainty and are prone to valuation disputes. Alternatively, we can delay taxation until the employee exercises the options and crystallizes his profit of $40,000. There is a trade-off in both solutions. If we delay the tax, the taxpayer defers his liability and benefits therefrom. If we tax the employee in Year 1, we must discount the value of the benefits for risk and uncertainty, which will likely stimulate litigation concerning valuation.

The third question raises separate policy issues. Clearly, the final $10,000 gain derives from holding the shares that the taxpayer acquires in Year 2. This portion of the gain derives from the taxpayer's investment decision to hold the shares, rather than from his employment. Thus, we tax this amount as a gain from the sale of capital assets and not as employment income.

---

[87]*Commissioner v. LoBue* (1956), 351 U.S. 243.

[88]See *Abbott v. Philbin*, [1961] A.C. 352 (H.L.); *Commissioner v. LoBue* (1956), 351 U.S. 243.

B. — The Statutory Scheme

Section 7 of the Act addresses each of the above questions and sets out a complete code for the taxation of option benefits.[89] The basic stock option rule is simple enough: option benefits are taxable as employment income because they are, in effect, an alternative to cash compensation. The statutory scheme, however, is more complex, because the rules also serve as an incentive for other economic objectives, such as equity ownership in Canadian corporations and employee equity participation. The statutory rules, which also apply to mutual fund units,[90] specify both the method of valuation and the timing of inclusion in income.[91]

We must answer three questions:

(a) Does the option benefit derive from employment?

(b) When is the benefit taxable?

(c) What is the value of the benefit?

a) — "By Virtue of Employment"

An employee is taxable on stock option benefits only if she derives the benefits by virtue of employment.[92] Subject to tax treaty provisions, non-residents are also taxable on stock options in respect of employment in Canada, regardless of where they exercise the options.[93] Thus, the first question is: does the employee derive the benefit in respect of, in the course of, or by virtue of her employment relationship? Stock options issued for other considerations (for example, as a gift or in return for guaranteeing a loan) are not a benefit from employment.[94]

---

[89]Subsection 7(3).

[90]Subsetion 7(7).

[91]S. 7.

[92]Subs. 7(5).

[93]*Hale v. R.*, [1992] 2 C.T.C. 379, 92 D.T.C. 6473 (Eng.) (Fed. C.A.); leave to appeal refused (1993), 151 N.R. 159 (note) (S.C.C.).

[94]*Busby v. R.*, [1986] 1 C.T.C. 147, 86 D.T.C. 6018 (Fed. T.D.) (options granted by virtue of taxpayer's "special" relationship with principal shareholder and for guaranteeing corporation's loans were not taxable as employment income). See also IT-113R4.

b) — Timing

The benefit of an option is recognized when shares are acquired at a price less than their value. Thus, timing is the key. We determine the time of acquisition by reference to general principles of commercial practice, as modified by statute. For example, a federal corporation may not issue shares until they are fully paid for in money or in property.[95] Thus, under federal corporate law, a taxpayer cannot acquire shares in a corporation until she pays for the shares. In some jurisdictions, however, an individual may purchase shares on an install-ment basis. In these circumstances, shares are acquired at the time the contract is completed, even though the shares are not paid for until a later date.

c) — Valuation

We determine the fair value of the benefit when the employee acquires the shares or exer-cises the option.[96] The benefit is equal to the difference between the cost of the option to the employee, any amount paid for the shares, and the value of the shares at the time that the employee acquires them from the plan.[97] For example, if an individual acquires 100 shares at a cost of $10 per share when the shares have a value of $15 per share and he pays $1 per share for the option, the intrinsic value of the taxable benefit is $4 per share or $400. At a tax rate of 50 percent, the net cost of the benefit is $200. The individual would be in the same financial position if the employer paid him an additional $400 in salary.

"Value" means "fair market value" or the price at which a willing seller and buyer would trade.[98] In the case of publicly traded securities, stock market prices are usually indicative of fair market value. Since listed stock prices inherently reflect the value of minority share-holdings, there is no need to further discount their value for minority interests. The valuation of shares of private corporations is a more difficult matter. Shares of private corporations are generally valued by reference to estimated future cash flows and the adjusted net value of assets. Thus it is appropriate to discount the *pro rata* value of the corporation to reflect a discount for minority interests and lack of liquidity. The employer is not allowed to deduct as an expense any costs pertaining to the issuance of the shares to the employee.[99]

---

[95]*Canada Business Corporations Act*, R.S.C. 1985, c. C-44, subs. 25(3); see also *Business Corpora-tions Act*, R.S.O. 1990, c. B.16, subs. 23(3).

[96]*Steen v. R.*, [1988] 1 C.T.C. 256, 88 D.T.C. 6171 (Fed. C.A.). (Value is the freely established price on the stock market.)

[97]Para. 7(1)(a).

[98]See, e.g., *Steen v. R.*, [1986] 2 C.T.C. 394, 86 D.T.C. 6498 (Fed. T.D.); affirmed [1988] 1 C.T.C. 256, 88 D.T.C. 6171 (Fed. C.A.).

[99]See, for example, *Minister of National Revenue v. Chrysler Canada Ltd.*, [1992] 2 C.T.C. 95 (Fed. T.D.) and para. 7(3)(b).

C. — Incentive Provisions

The general stock option rule is that option benefits are taxable as employment income. In addition to the general rule, however, there is a special rule for options that a Canadian-controlled private corporation ("CCPC") issues to its employees. These special rules are essentially incentive provisions to promote equity participation in Canadian corporations.

a) — Options Issued by CCPCs

The taxable benefit from shares acquired from a CCPC's stock plan in an arm's length transaction is reduced if the taxpayer holds the shares for at least two years.[100] This is so whether the shares are issued by the employer corporation or by another CCPC with which the employer does not deal at arm's length. The employee can defer recognizing any benefit that he derives from the stock options until he or she disposes of the shares. This rule, which delays income recognition and permits tax deferral, is intended to promote share ownership in Canadian companies. The longer the employee holds the shares, the greater the value of the tax deferral.

Second, when the employee disposes of the shares, he is taxable on only 1/2 of the value of the benefit derived.[101] Thus, the employee turns one-half of the benefit into exempt income.

An employee who disposes of his shares in a CCPC within two years from the date that he or she acquires them is usually taxable on the full value of any benefit derived in the year that the employee disposes of the shares.[102] An exchange of options or of shares as a consequence of an amalgamation or a share-for-share exchange is not a disposition for the purposes of the two-year rule.[103]

The Act deems shares that are identical properties to be disposed of in the order they are acquired.[104]

D. — Comparison of Option Plans

The effect of the three different types of stock option plans is set out below:

---

[100]Subs. 7(1.1) and para. 110(1)(d.1).

[101]See subs. 7(1.1) and para. 110(1)(d.1).

[102]Subpara. 110(1)(d.1)(ii). But see IT-113R4 (para. 19).

[103]Subss. 7(1.4) and 7(1.5).

[104]Subs. 7(1.3).

Example

Assume that Jennifer, an employee, acquires shares from her employer in the following (alternative) circumstances:

Case (A)   General
                        Rules

Shares with a fair market value (FMV) of $100 for $76. She sells the shares for $100.

Case (B)   CCPC

Share with FMV of $100 for $76 from a CCPC and she holds the shares for at least two years.

Then:	(A) General Rules		(B) CCPC	
Acquisition of shares:				
FMV at acquisition	$	100	$	100
Cost of acquisition		(76)	$	76
Stock option benefit		24 =	=	Nil
Adjusted cost base (ACB) of shares:				
Cost of acquisition	$	76	$	76
Add:				
Stock option benefit		24		—
ACB of shares	$	100	$	76
Disposition of shares:				
Sale price	$	100	$	100
ACB		(100)		(76)
Capital gain		—		—
Stock option benefit		—		24
50% deduction		—		(12)
Net inclusion as employment income			$	12
Inclusions in employment income:				
Upon acquisition	$	24	$	—
Upon disposition		—		12
Total	$	24	$	12

E. — Disposition of Rights

The Act deems an employee who disposes of stock option rights to a person in an arm's length transaction to have received a benefit equal to the value of the consideration received for the shares, less any amount that he paid to acquire the rights.[105] Similarly, any consider-

---

[105]Para. 7(1)(b).

ation that the employee receives for the surrender of stock option rights is taxable as a benefit from a disposition of the rights, less any amounts paid.[106]

F. — Adjusted Cost Base of Shares

The inclusion of stock option benefits in income would lead to double taxation if the full gain was taxed again when the employee disposed of the shares. Hence, in order to prevent double taxation, the full value of any benefit included in the employee's income is added to the cost base of the shares acquired.[107] Thus, any subsequent gain or loss on the disposition of the shares is calculated by reference to the stepped-up cost base of the shares. For example, where an employee of a public company acquires shares at $12 per share when the shares have a market value of $18 per share, the full benefit of $6 is added to the cost base of his shares. Hence, the adjusted cost base of the shares increases to $18. If the employee later sells the shares for $30 per share, he will have a capital gain of $12 per share.

G. — Effect on Employer

Opportunity costs are not usually deductible for tax purposes. Hence, from the employer's perspective, the opportunity costs associated with a stock option plan should not be deductible, because the corporation does not incur any outlay or expense by issuing its shares at less than their market value.[108] The employer corporation merely foregoes capital proceeds that it would have received had it issued the shares at their fair market value. Hence, unless one of the special incentive provisions[109] applies, a corporation that is taxable at full rates may be better off paying its employees an equivalent bonus, which they can then use to purchase shares at full fair market value. There are special rules in section 143.3 that permit the employer limited deductions.

---

[106]*Greiner v. R.*, [1984] C.T.C. 92, 84 D.T.C. 6073 (Fed. C.A.).

[107]Para. 53(1)(j).

[108]Para. 7(3)(b); *Placer Dome Inc. v. R.*, [1992] 2 C.T.C. 99, 92 D.T.C. 6402 (Fed. C.A.); leave to appeal refused (1993), 151 N.R. 392 (note) (S.C.C.).

[109]Subs. 7(1.1) or para. 110(1)(d).

SUMMARY OF SELECTED BENEFITS

	ITA	CASE LAW
Value of board and lodging	6(1)(a); 6(6)	*Cockerill* 65DTC 525 *Savage* 83 DTC 5409 (SCC) *Poynton* 72 DTC 6329
Statutory exceptions	6(1)(a)	
Flexible benefit programs	IT 529	
Indirect benefits	6(1) j IT 470 R	*Jowe*, 96 DTC 6226 *Huffman* 90 DTC 6405 (FCA) *Hale* 68 DTC 5326 (Ex. Ct.)
Housing loss and housing costs	6 (19–23)	
Employee loans	6(9); 80.4(1)	
Allowances	6(1)(b)	*Ransom* 67 DTC 5235 *Splane*, 92 DTC 6021
Director's or other fees	6(1)(c); 248(1)	
Employment insurance benefits	6(1)(a); 6(1)(f)	
Payments by employer to employee	5; 6(3)	*Curran*, 59 DTC 1247 (SCC) *Blanchard*, 95 DTC 5479 (FCA) *Ballard*, 87 DTC 157 (TCC)
Restrictive covenants	6(3.1); 56 (4)	
Stock options	7, 153 (1.01)	

X. — Salary Deferral Arrangements

A. — General Comment

The general rule is that employment income is taxed on a cash basis, that is, when the employee receives payment. This rule opens the door to employees to defer receipt of their salary to suit their personal circumstances. For example, a taxpayer in a high tax bracket might defer receipt of a portion of her annual salary until such time as she is in a lower tax bracket.

Example		
Assume that Levonia Hargreaves defers her bonus of $10,000 payable on January 1 for three years and is credited with the indicated rates of return. Alternatively, the bonus is paid on January 1 and the after-tax amount is invested in a GIC at the indicated rates of return. The income from the investment is reinvested for the remainder of the term at the same rate of return. Levonia has a marginal tax rate of 50 percent.		
Rate of return	8%	4%
FV of bonus deferred three years	$ 12,600	
FV of bonus paid on current basis		$ 11,200
Tax @ 50%	(6,300)	(5,600)
Net after-tax bonus	$ 6,300	$ 5,600
Percentage increase in after-tax return	12.5%	

To prevent employees from taking advantage of such arrangements, there are special rules that prevent tax deferral and rate shifting by taxing parties to salary deferral agreements on an accrual basis.[110]

A "salary deferral arrangement"[111] ("SDA") is a plan or arrangement (whether funded or not) *one of the main* purposes of which is to permit a taxpayer to postpone tax on his salary in a year to a subsequent taxation year. Arrangements that are contingent upon the deferred amount being paid on the occurrence of some event or transaction are also SDAs unless there is a "substantial risk" that the condition will not be satisfied. Thus, a salary deferral arrangement has three components:

- A plan or arrangement;

- A legal right to defer receipt of salary or wages; and

- An intention to defer receipt for tax reasons.

---

[110]See subpara. 6(1)(a)(v), para.6(1)(i), subss. 6(11)–(14).

[111]Subs. 248(1) "salary deferral arrangement".

The employer's deduction of the payment is synchronized with the inclusion of the amount in the employee's income.[112]

B. — Exclusions

The following plans are excluded from salary deferral arrangements:

- Registered pension funds or plans;
- Disability or income-maintenance insurance plans with an insurance corporation;
- Deferred profit-sharing plans;
- Employee profit-sharing plans;
- Employee trusts;
- Group sickness or accident insurance plans;
- Supplementary unemployment benefit plans;
- Vacation pay trusts;
- Education or training plans for employees;
- Plans for deferring salary or wages of professional athletes;
- Plans under which a taxpayer has a right to receive a bonus in respect of services rendered in the taxation year, to be paid within three years following the end of the year;
- Leave-of-absence arrangements,[113] and
- Prescribed plans or arrangements.

An SDA is a plan where tax deferral is *one* of the *main* purposes of the plan or arrangement. Thus, tax deferral does not have to be the only purpose, but it must be one of the *main* purposes. It is difficult to conceive how a plan can have more than one main purpose. If main means "chief" or "principal",[114] is it ever possible to have more than one chief or principal purpose? Can a plan have five *main* purposes?

[112]Paras. 18(1)(o.1), 20(1)(oo) and 20(1)(pp).

[113]Reg. 6801.

[114]Oxford Dictionary.

C. — Contingent Arrangements

Contingent plans and deferral arrangements that are at substantial risk that one of the conditions triggering the contingency will not be satisfied are not SDAs. What constitutes a substantial risk of forfeiture sufficient to exclude a plan or arrangement from the definition of SDA? There is a substantial risk of forfeiture if the condition imposes a significant limitation or duty that requires a meaningful effort on the part of the employee to fulfil, and the limitation or duty creates a definite and substantial risk that forfeiture may occur. The Act does not consider the following types of conditions sufficient to exempt a plan or arrangement as an SDA:[115]

- Non-competition clauses following retirement or termination;

- Restraints on the employee's transferring, or encumbering the employee, or the employee's interest in the deferred amount;

- Restraints that make payment contingent on the employee's not being dismissed for cause or the commission of a crime; or

- Receipt of the deferred amount being contingent on the employee's remaining with the employer for a minimum period of time.

D. — Leave of Absence Plans

The Act excludes certain leave of absence plans from salary deferral arrangements. Thus, an employee can use a leave of absence plan to defer tax on income that would otherwise be taxable on a current basis. An employee can self-fund a leave of absence and defer receipt of up to a maximum of one-third of his regular annual salary. Although the employee defers the tax that would otherwise be payable on the salary, any investment income earned on the deferred salary remains taxable on a current basis.[116]

A leave of absence plan must satisfy the following conditions:[117]

- The arrangement must provide for a leave of absence from employment of not less than six consecutive months (it cannot be used to fund retirement benefits);

- The leave must commence within six years from the beginning of the commencement of the salary deferral;

---

[115]See Department of Finance Technical Notes (Bill C-23) November 7, 1986.

[116]The Department of Finance issued a comfort letter (June 30, 2000) where they agree that any allocated income that is re-contributed to the plan is not taxable.

[117]Reg. 6801; ATR-39 "Self-funded leave of absence".

- The employee must undertake to return to the employer for a further period of employment of at least equal length to that of the leave;

- The amount of salary deferred in any year must not exceed one-third of the employee's regular annual salary; and

- During the leave of absence the employee must not receive any salary, other than the deferred amounts, from his employer.

Hence, an employee can defer tax on a portion of his salary for up to six years and use the accumulated savings to finance a leave of absence from the employer.

XI. — Counselling Benefits

Employer-provided counselling services for employees are not taxable as benefits from employment if the counselling is in respect of:[118]

- The employees' (or related individual's) physical or mental health;

- Re-employment for employees whose employment has been terminated; or

- Retirement.

These exclusions from employment income are accommodations for hardship cases and are intended to facilitate re-employment.

XII. — Directors' Fees

A director of a corporation holds an "office".[119] Thus, fees received by virtue of a directorship are taxable as income from an office.[120] Where a director's fees are paid directly to a third party or are turned over by the director to a third party (for example, to a partnership of which he or she is a member), the CRA administratively permits the fees to be taxable as the income of the ultimate recipient and not the director.[121]

---

[118]Subpara. 6(1)(a)(iv).

[119]Subs. 248(1).

[120]Subs. 5(1) and para. 6(1)(c).

[121]See IT-377R and rulings document 2006-0193141 E5.

XIII. — Strike Pay

The taxation of strike pay is a politically contentious issue. As a matter of administrative policy, the CRA exempts certain types of financial assistance paid by unions to their members during the course of a strike.

Political considerations aside, it is not at all clear why strike pay should not be taxable. "Income" in section 3 is the realized accretion to wealth from any source. The concept of income in section 3 is clearly not restricted to the specifically named sources. Income from *any* source inside or outside Canada is taxable under paragraph 3(a) of the *Income Tax Act*. In the only (brief) decision on point, the Supreme Court adopted a narrow concept of source and held that strike pay is not income. Although strike pay is not taxable as income, union dues are deductible as expenses from employment income.[122]

XIV. — Deductions from Employment Income

A. — General Comment

Employment income is generally taxable on a "gross" basis without deductions. Subsection 8(2) limits the deduction of expenses from employment income to those that the Act specifically authorizes. The limitation on deductions is tightly controlled and enforced in order to protect the government's revenue base, which relies heavily on income from personal taxation.

In contrast, business income is much more generously treated and is taxable on a "net" basis — that is, net of deductions. Because of this difference in the treatment of deductions, most individuals would prefer to be considered as independent contractors rather than employees for tax purposes. When it comes to employee compensation schemes, however, individuals prefer employee status.

B. — Salesperson's Expenses

A travelling salesperson may deduct expenses from employment income if she is:[123]

- Employed to sell property or negotiate contracts;

---

[122]Subpara. 8(1)(i)(iv). See *R. v. Fries*, [1989] 1 C.T.C. 471, 89 D.T.C. 5240 (Fed. C.A.); reversed [1990] 2 S.C.R. 1322, [1990] 2 C.T.C. 439, 90 D.T.C. 6662 (S.C.C.).

[123]Para. 8(1)(f) and subs. 8(9).

- *Required* to pay her own business expenses (that is, not reimbursed);[124]

- *Ordinarily* required to carry out her duties away from the employer's regular place of business;

- Remunerated, at least in part, by commissions related to the volume of sales; and

- Not in receipt of a tax-free allowance for travelling expenses that is excluded from income.[125]

The employee must file a prescribed form where the employer certifies that the employee has satisfied the above conditions.[126]

a) — Limits

The maximum amount of the deduction is limited to the commission income that he or she receives in the year. The employee must file a prescribed form where the employer certifies that the employee has satisfied all the above conditions.[127]

b) — Capital Cost Allowance

A salesperson may also deduct capital cost allowance ("CCA") and interest expense in respect of a motor vehicle or aircraft that he uses in the performance of employment-related duties.[128] The claim for CCA and interest expense is not limited to commission income and may be used to reduce income from other sources. Here, as elsewhere in the Act, any expenses claimed must be reasonable in the circumstances.[129]

---

[124]See *Slawson v. Minister of National Revenue* (1984), [1985] 1 C.T.C. 2075 (T.C.C.); *Goldhar v. Minister of National Revenue*, [1985] 1 C.T.C. 2187 (T.C.C.); *Bowman v. Minister of National Revenue*, [1985] 1 C.T.C. 2380 (T.C.C.).

[125]Subpara. 6(1)(b)(v). *Cossette v. Minister of National Revenue* (1955), 13 Tax A.B.C. 170, 55 D.T.C. 365 (Can. Tax App. Bd.) (Where the allowance is unreasonably low, the taxpayer may include the allowance in income and deduct his actual expenses.).

[126]Subs. 8(10).

[127]*Laliberté v. Minister of National Revenue* (1953), 9 Tax A.B.C. 145, 53 D.T.C. 370 (Can. Tax App. Bd.) (traveling salesman allowed to deduct rent for sample rooms); *Sherman v. Minister of National Revenue*, [1970] Tax A.B.C. 618, 70 D.T.C. 1409 (Can. Tax App. Bd.) (advertising expenses by securities salesman allowed as deduction).

[128]Para. 8(1)(j); Reg. 1100(1).

[129]S. 67. *Niessen v. Minister of National Revenue* (1960), 60 D.T.C. 489, 25 Tax A.B.C. 62 (Can. Tax App. Bd.) (claim for CCA on Cadillac disallowed as excessive).

C. — Travelling Expenses

Employees who:

- are ordinarily required to carry on their employment duties away from their employer's regular place of business,

- are required to pay their own travelling expenses, and

- do not receive a tax-free allowance,

may deduct their travelling expenses[130] to the extent that they are not reimbursed by their employer.[131] In this context, "ordinarily" means as a matter of regular occurrence.[132] The deduction is available to all employees and is not restricted to commissioned salespeople.

A salesperson who claims a deduction for expenses under paragraph 8(1)(f), however, cannot also claim travelling expenses under paragraph 8(1)(h). The salesperson may, however, claim the deduction under whichever of the two provisions is most advantageous to him or her.

a) — Inadequate Compensation

An employee who is not fully reimbursed for her employment-related expenses may be able to claim the shortfall as an expense deduction. For example, an employee who spends 50 cents a kilometre to run a motor vehicle and is reimbursed only 40 cents a kilometre may claim an expense deduction equal to 10 cents per kilometre travelled on the employer's business if he can establish that the allowance was unreasonably low.[133]

b) — Requirement of Travel

Deductibility of travelling expenses depends upon the employee being required to travel away from her employer's place of business. This requirement need not be expressly stated

---

[130]Paras. 8(1)(h) or (h.1).

[131]Subparas. 6(1)(b)(v), (vi), (vii).

[132]*Healy v. R.*, [1978] C.T.C. 355, 78 D.T.C. 6239 (Fed. T.D.); reversed [1979] C.T.C. 44, 79 D.T.C. 5060 (Fed. C.A.) (jockey club employee not "ordinarily" reporting for work at Fort Erie but spending 1/3 of his time there); *R. v. Patterson*, [1982] C.T.C. 371, 82 D.T.C. 6326 (Fed. T.D.) (school principal who made 56 trips to other schools "ordinarily" required to carry out duties in different places; expenses deductible).

[133]*Peters v. Minister of National Revenue*, [1986] 2 C.T.C. 2221, 86 D.T.C. 1662 (T.C.C.). But see *Gauvin v. Minister of National Revenue*, [1979] C.T.C. 2812, 79 D.T.C. 696 (T.R.B.) and *Hudema v. R.*, [1994] C.T.C. 42, 94 D.T.C. 6287 (Fed. T.D.) and IT-522R.

in the employment contract, but may be implied from the surrounding circumstances, such as employer expectations, industry practice, etc.[134] The employer must, however, certify that the employee meets all of the statutory requirements.[135]

c) — Motor Vehicles and Aircraft

Subject to the restrictions in respect of travelling expenses, an employee may also deduct motor vehicle and aircraft expenses incurred in the course of employment.[136] Any interest paid on money borrowed to purchase, and capital cost allowance resulting from the ownership of, a motor vehicle or aircraft is deductible to the extent that the vehicle or aircraft is used in the course of employment.[137]

d) — Meals

An employee may claim 50 percent of meal expenses as part of travel costs if he consumes the meal while away for at least 12 hours from the municipality in which his employer is located.[138]

e) — Legal Expenses

Nearly fifteen million employees file income tax returns annually and are the largest source of government revenues. The law presumes every individual to know the tax law in all its exacting detail and imposes severe penalties for misinterpretation.

An employee can deduct legal expenses that he pays to collect an amount owed to him if the amount would, if received, be taxable as income from employment. Legal expenses subse-

---

[134]*Moore v. Minister of National Revenue*, [1987] 1 C.T.C. 319, 87 D.T.C. 5217 (Fed. T.D.); reversed [1990] 1 C.T.C. 311 (Fed. C.A.); leave to appeal refused (1990), 121 N.R. 322 (note) (S.C.C.) (principal would have received unfavorable performance reviews had she not attended meetings; expenses allowed); *Rozen v. R.*, [1986] 1 C.T.C. 50, 85 D.T.C. 5611 (Fed. T.D.) (requirement to use automobile in course of employment implied term of contract); *R. v. Cival*, [1983] C.T.C. 153, 83 D.T.C. 5168 (Fed. C.A.); leave to appeal refused (1983), 52 N.R. 155 (S.C.C.) (deduction denied where taxpayer not required to use own car under contract of employment).

[135]Subs. 8(10).

[136]Paras. 8(1)(f) and (h).

[137]Para. 8(1)(j) and subs. 8(9).

[138]Subs. 8(4) and s. 67.1.

quently reimbursed are taxable as employment income under para. 6(1)(j) except to the extent that they were previously included in income or reduced the legal expense deduction.[139]

Legal expenses associated with establishing a right to a pensions benefit or retiring allowance (including payments for wrongful dismissal) are also deductible.[140]

However, employees are not allowed to deduct any professional fees that they pay for tax advice and return preparation. The law also deems the Canada Revenue Agency's assessment of a taxpayer to be correct unless the taxpayer can prove otherwise, usually through expensive and protracted litigation. Employees may, however, deduct their legal fees after they get into trouble with the CRA. The government's policy to deny a deduction for fees spent on prevention of litigation, but allow it for legal fees after the dispute arises, may be good for revenue collection and tax administration. However, it is not fair for taxpayers who must comply with a complex statute.

Legal fees and expenses are deductible on a cash basis — that is, in the year that the taxpayer pays them. The fees are deductible even if the objection or appeal relates to the taxpayer or some other person in whom the taxpayer has an interest. For example, fees that a director or shareholder pays to contest a corporate assessment may be deductible. Similarly, a tax shelter investor who funds another person's appeal in order to protect his own interest may deduct the legal fees that he or she incurs. The law is uncharacteristically generous here and allows taxpayers to deduct fees and expenses paid to non-lawyers — for example, to accountants, consultants, and even paralegals!

An employee can deduct legal fees to collect salary and wages from her employer or former employer, insurance benefits under a sickness or accident insurance policy that the employer provides, or payments under the Canada Pension Plan.

The interpretation of what constitutes deductible legal fees is not always easy. In the context of fees paid to collect salary or wages, for example, the jurisprudence is beset with subtle distinctions. In one case, fifty-five Department of Justice lawyers in Vancouver brought an action for damages against their employer claiming that they were entitled to the higher salaries that the department paid to their counterparts in Toronto — in effect, a legal action for equal pay for equal work. The Federal Court of Appeal allowed the lawyers to deduct their legal fees regardless of the substantive merits of the litigation and the nature of the taxpayers' claim. In another case, however, the court did not allow employees to claim a

---

[139]Para. 8(1)(b). See, e.g., *Loo v. R.*, [2004] 3 C.T.C. 247, 2004 FCA 249, 2004 D.T.C. 6540 (Fed. C.A.) (plaintiff one of 55 B.C. lawyers suing their employer, the federal Dept of Justice, because they are paid less than Justice lawyers in Toronto; legal fees deductible; not relevant to determine whether claim is well founded in law or likely to succeed).

[140]Para. 60(o.1). See, e.g., *Atkinson v. R.*, 2004 TCC 445, [2004] 4 C.T.C. 2272 (T.C.C. [Informal Procedure]) (police officer allowed to deduct legal fees of $32,226.49 since he would have lost his job and pension had he not successfully defended the criminal charges made against him.)

deduction for legal fees paid to establish a right to a promotion that would entitle them to a higher salary.

The law is similarly subtle in actions against judicial or regulatory decisions that adversely affect employment, professional status, or claims for financial compensation in connection with allegations of unlawful or wrongful acts by the employer. For example, a professor who paid legal fees to protect him against complaints from students — which, if established, would have affected his career and eliminated his income — could not deduct the fees even though he was successful.

The deductibility of legal fees from employment income sometimes depends upon whether the lawsuit is successful. For example, a police officer convicted of dangerous driving could not deduct his legal fees when he was *automatically* suspended without pay. Upon his successful appeal, however, the officer could deduct his entire legal fees because his suspension changed retroactively to being with pay.

Eventually, as Benjamin Cardozo said: "The methods and subjects of taxation are matters of governmental policy." The fine legal distinctions of deductibility of legal fees and expenses for litigation but not for prevention of disputes has less to do with fundamental policies of tax law and fairness and more with revenue collection and administration.

D. — Musicians

An employed musician who must furnish his own musical instruments may deduct amounts that he or she pays on account of the maintenance, insurance or rental of such instruments.[141] The amount deductible cannot exceed his employment income as a musician. Where the musician owns the instrument used in employment, he is also entitled to depreciate it at a rate of 20 percent on a declining balance basis.[142]

E. — Canadian Residents Employed Overseas

As a general rule, Canadian residents are taxable on their global income regardless of where they earn the income.[143] Residence-based taxation ensures that individuals are taxed on an equal basis on their ability to pay tax on income without reference to its geographic source. This promotes horizontal equity.

---

[141]Para. 8(1)(p); *Royal Winnipeg Ballet v. Minister of National Revenue* (2006), [2008] 1 C.T.C. 220 (Fed. C.A.) (dancers were employees rather than independent contractors).

[142]Reg. 1100(1)(a)(viii).

[143]Subs. 2(1); s. 3.

Some residents employed outside Canada, however, are eligible for special tax credits on their overseas employment income until 2016. These concessions are provided for "competitive reasons" to allow Canadian employers to compete for international contracts by reducing their net payroll costs. The tax credits put Canadian employers on a competitive footing with foreign companies that receive similar tax subsidies from their governments. Thus, we trade-off equity for international economic competitiveness.

The overseas employment tax credit has three constraints. A Canadian resident is entitled to the credit only if:[144]

- He or she is employed by a "specified employer";[145]

- His or her employment-related duties are performed outside Canada for a period of more than six consecutive months; *and*

- The employer is engaged in the construction, exploration, engineering, or agricultural business, or in a *prescribed* activity.

The tax credit is equal to 80 percent of the employee's net overseas earnings up to a maximum of $80,000 annually. The credit is prorated over the number of days the employee works abroad in a year and is applied against the taxes that he or she would otherwise pay.

The credit will not be available after 2015.

F. — Other Deductions

Section 8 also lists other deductions from employment income. Note particularly:

Type of Expense	Statutory Reference
* Legal expenses incurred by employee in collecting or establishing right to his salary or wages.	para. 8(1)(b)
* Value of cleric's residence, or rent paid by cleric	para. 8(1)(c); IT-141R
* Contribution by a teacher to a fund established for the benefit of Commonwealth teachers present in Canada on an exchange program	para. 8(1)(d)

---

[144]Subs. 122.3(1).

[145]Para. 122.3(2).

Type of Expense	Statutory Reference
* Expenses of railway company employees employed away from ordinary place of residence	para. 8(1)(e); IC 73-21
* Expenses for meals, lodging and travel incurred by a transport business employee while carrying out duties of employment	para. 8(1)(g); IC 73-21
* Annual professional membership dues required to maintain professional status	subpara. 8(1)(i)
* Dues to a professions board required under provincial law	subpara. 8(1)(i)(vii)
* Trade union or association annual dues	subpara. 8(1)(i)(iv)
* Annual union dues	subpara. 8(1)(i)(v)
* Dues paid to a parity or advisory committee under provincial law	subpara. 8(1)(i)(vi)
* Office rent or salary paid by employee as required by contract of employment	subpara. 8(1)(i)(ii)
* Cost of supplies consumed in the performance of duties of employment	subpara. 8(1)(i)(iii)
* Interest on borrowed money for the purchase of, and capital cost allowance for the use of, a motor vehicle or aircraft used in the performance of duties of employment	subpara. 8(1)(j)(i); Reg. 1100(1)(a)(x.1)
* Canada Pension Plan contributions and employment insurance premiums paid by an employee to an individual employed as an assistant	para. 8(1)(l.1)
* Employee RCA contributions	para. 8(1)(m.2)

Type of Expense	Statutory Reference
* Amounts paid by employee as reimbursement for amounts paid to the employee as workers' compensation	para. 8(1)(n)
* Amounts forfeited under salary deferral arrangement	para. 8(1)(o)
* Employment expenses of artists	para. 8(1)(q)

Notes::

*   *Lucas v. M.N.R.*, [1987] 2 C.T.C. 23, 87 D.T.C. 5277 (F.C.T.D.).

XV. — Limitations on Deductions

A. — Overall Limitation

The deductibility of an expense from employment income depends on two criteria:

    1. Authority for the deduction; and

    2. Reasonableness of the amount claimed.[146]

In the context of employment income, subs. 8(2) limits deductions specifically unless authorized. Thus, there are no deductions from employment income under commercial principles. Further, even authorized deductions may not be deductible for tax purposes if they are unreasonable in amount. Thus, deductibility depends on both the reasonableness of the amount claimed and the legitimacy of the claim itself.

Whether an expense is reasonable in the circumstances is a question of fact. In the context of salary and bonuses paid to employees, for example, the following factors are relevant in determining whether the amount is reasonable:

• Rank or level within organization;

• Special knowledge, skills or connections;

• Comparable compensation paid to persons in similar businesses with similar responsibilities; and

• Past practices with respect to compensation in the particular business community concerned.

---

[146]S. 67.

B. — Food and Entertainment

In addition to the general rule that all expenses must be reasonable in amount, there is an additional restriction for expenses incurred for meals and entertainment, which the Act restricts to 50 percent of the amount actually paid.[147]

XVI. — Conclusion

Although there are only four sections of the Act that deal directly with employment income, the provisions affect millions of employees. Since employment income is the largest source of public revenues, the Department of Finance is ever vigilant to include employment income in the taxable base. We see, however, that even this small area of tax law is complex and subject to inconsistent legislation and judicial interpretation. This inconsistency detracts from the equitable treatment of employees. The taxation of relocation benefits, for example, produces inconsistent results for employees who move to new locations. The exemption of non-accountable allowances for legislators, for example, is an obvious distinction in the tax mosaic that differentiates between classes of taxpayers.

The presumption against the non-deductibility of employment expenses is understandable in the interests of administrative convenience. It does, however, place an unfair burden on employees who incur employment-related expenses that the Act does not specify. The substantial differences between the generous treatment of business expenses and the strict regulation of employment income are a powerful incentive to re-characterize income from one source into the other. Classification may be the beginning of wisdom, but it also makes tax law that much more complex.

---

[147]Subs. 67.1(1).

Selected Bibliography to Chapter 6

General

Atiyah, P.S., *Vicarious Liability in the Law of Torts* (London: Butterworths, 1967).

Hansen, Krishna and Rendall, eds., "The Taxation of Employees", *Canadian Taxation* (Toronto: De Boo, 1981) at 187.

Krishna, Vern, "Converting Salary into Management Fees" (1993) 4 Can. Current Tax C-1.

Krishna, Vern, "International Employment Income" (1993) 4 Can. Current Tax C-23.

Krishna, Vern, "The Scope of Employment Benefits" (1994) Can. Current Tax C-55.

McKie, A.B., "Artists and Athletes: Tax Acts" (1990) 3 Can. Current Tax C-17.

The Characterization of Employment Income

Douglas, William O., "Vicarious Liability and the Administration of Risk" (1928-29) 38 Yale L.J. 584.

Drache, A.B.C., "Employee Compensation" (1986) Special Lectures LSUC 17.

Drache, A.B.C. and Goldstein, "The Professional as an Employee", *Tax Planning for Professionals* (Toronto: De Boo, 1979) at 22.

Khan, A.N., "Who is a Servant?" (1979) 53 Austr. L.J. 832.

Inclusions in Employment Income

General

Krishna, Vern, "Employee Benefits" (1984) 1 Can. Current Tax C7.

Krishna, Vern, "Taxation of Employee Benefits" (1986) 1:35 Can. Current Tax C-173.

Krishna, Vern, "Taxation of Employee Benefits" (August 1987) 21 CGA Magazine 25.

Perry, Harvey, "Federal Individual Income Tax: Income Computation", *Tax Paper No. 89* 42 (Can. Tax Foundation, 1990).

Allowances

Beam, Robert E., and Stanley N. Laiken, "Employee Allowances" (1989) Can. Tax J. 141.

Drache, A.B.C., "Allowances or Reimbursements" (1993) 15 Can. Taxpayer 23.

Drache, A.B.C., "Tax Exempt Expenses for Moonlighting Employees" (1991) 13 Can. Taxpayer 154.

Automobiles

"Revenue Canada's Framework for Automobile Deductions" (1993) 5 Tax. of Executive Compensation and Retirement 839.

Tang & Hyatt, "Business-Use Automobiles: The Complex New Tax Rules" (1988) 36 Can. Tax J. 195.

Stock Option Plans

Bowman, S.W., "Employment Benefits — Stock Options Not Falling under S. 7" (1990) 38 Can. Tax J. 82.

Dionne, Andre, "Stock Purchase Arrangements can be Structured to Allow Deduction for Employers" (1992) 3 Tax. of Executive Compensation and Retirement 604.

Dunbar, Alisa E., "Sale of Stock Plan Shares may Produce Freely Deductible Loss" (1991) 3 Tax. of Executive Compensation and Retirement 499.

"Employment Benefits — Stock Options Not Falling Under Section 7" (1990) 38 Can. Tax J. 82.

Krishna, Vern, "Stock Options Exercised after Becoming Non-resident" (1993) 4 Can. Current Tax C-27.

Michaelson, Suzanne, "Employee Stock Options Revisited" (1992) 40 Can. Tax J. 114.

Reimbursed Legal Expenses

Dunbar, Alisa E., "Legal Services Provided to Employee Results in Tax Benefit" (1991) 2 Tax. of Executive Compensation and Retirement 403.

Krasa, Eva M., "The Income Tax Treatment of Legal Expenses" (1986) 34 Can. Tax J. 757.

Other

Billinger, Jo-anne, "Flexible Benefits a Practical Approach for Employers and Employees in the Cost-conscious '90s" (1993) 4 Tax. of Executive Compensation and Retirement 747.

Boulanger, Claude, "Disability Insurance Plans can be Structured to Avoid Taxable Payout" (1991) 2 Tax. of Executive Compensation and Retirement 435.

Bush, Kathryn M., "Executive Compensation: Supplemental Pension Plans" (1991) 8 Bus. and the Law 46.

Buyers, D.R., and D.E. Harvey, "The Cost of Terminating Employees: Tax and Unemployment Insurance Consequences" (1987) 4 Bus. & L. 9.

Dewling, Alan M., "RCA may be Used to Pre-fund Health and Other Post-Retirement Benefits" (1993) 4 Tax. of Executive Compensation and Remuneration 707.

Dionee, Andre, "RCA Cash Flow Problems may be Alleviated by Filing Early Trust Tax Return" (1990) 2 Tax. of Executive Compensation and Retirement 371.

Drache, A.B.C., "Club Memberships as a Taxable Benefit" (1993) 15 Can. Taxpayer 163.

Drache, A.B.C., "FCA Upholds Revenue Canada on Employee Reimbursement" (1994) 16 Can. Taxpayer 49.

Drache, A.B.C., "Group Life Insurance: New Interpretations" (1980) 17 Can. Taxpayer 152.

Fitzgerald, Brian A.P., "Tax-effectiveness may be Enhanced by Maximizing Ancillary Benefits" (1993) 4 Tax. of Executive Compensation and Retirement 760.

"Home Purchase Loans to Employee/Shareholder may have Extended Term" (1992) 3 Tax. of Executive Compensation and Retirement 552.

Krishna, Vern, "Retiring Allowances" (1994) 4 Can. Current Tax C-53.

Krishna, Vern, "How Will They Tax Frequent Flyer Programs?" (1985) 5:21 Ont. Lawyers Weekly 7.

Laushway, Keith, "Retiring Allowances and Future Employment by Affiliates" (1993) 4 Can. Current Tax P-15.

Maclagan, Bill, "Taxable Benefits on Employer Relocation" (1993) 3 Employment and Labour Law Rev. 25.

McKie, A.B., "Beneficial Occupation" (1994) 4 Can. Current Tax C-49.

Novek, Barbara L., "Employment Benefits may be Tax-free if Provided in Connection with Special Work Site or Remote Location" (1991) 3 Tax. of Executive Compensation and Retirement 505.

Novek, Barbara L., "Retiring Allowances are subject to Administrative Guideline" (1991) 3 Tax. of Executive Compensation and Retirement 523.

Novek, Barbara L. "RCT Expands Unpublished Guidelines in Salary Leave Plans" (1993) 4 Tax. of Executive Compensation and Retirement 715.

"Owner-managers may be Eligible for Tax-free Reimbursement of Medical Expenses" (1990) 1 Tax. of Executive Compensation and Retirement 299.

Pound, R.W., "Fringe Benefits: Management Perks'", *Corporate Management Tax Conf.* 63 (Can. Tax Foundation, 1979).

"Revenue Canada Clarifies Policy on Relocation Assistance" (1992) 3 Tax. of Executive Compensation and Retirement 559.

"Revenue Canada Clarifies Position on Temporary Accommodation" (1992) 3 Tax. of Executive Compensation and Retirement 563.

Roux, Clement, "Current Planning for Fringe Benefits", in *Proceedings of 35th Tax Conf.* 478 (Can. Tax Foundation, 1983).

Schwartz, Alan M., "Tax Considerations on Being Hired and Fired: Some Exotica", *Corporate Management Tax Conf.* 212 (Can. Tax Foundation, 1985).

Simon, Karla W., "Fringe Benefits and Tax Reform: Historical Blunders and a Proposal for Structural Change" (1984) 36 Univ. of Florida Law Rev. 871.

Solursh, John M., "Pension Arrangements can be Funded to Avoid RCA Tax" (1991) 3 Tax. of Executive Compensation and Retirement 469.

Deductions from Employment Income

General

Neville, Ralph T., "Deductibility of Automobiles, Meals and Entertainment and Home Office Expenses After Tax Reform", in *Proceedings of 40th Tax Conf.* 25:1 (Can. Tax Foundation, 1988).

New Rules on Tax Assistance for Retirement Savings (Montreal: Sobeco, 1990).

Perry, Harvey, "Federal Individual Income Tax: Income Computation", *Tax Paper No. 89* 42 (Can. Tax Foundation, 1990).

Teichman, Lyle S., "Deducting Employee Expenses: A Hard Act to Follow" (1994) 5 Tax. of Executive Compensation and Retirement 859.

Templeton, Michael D., "Employee Expenses C A Practical Approach" (1990) 38 Can. Tax J. 666.

Other

Austin, Barbara, "RRSP Implications of the New Foreign Pension Plan Rules" (1993) 1 RRSP Plan. 53.

Boulanger, Claude, "Employee Profit Sharing Plans may Provide Framework for Incentive Payments" (1991) 2 Tax. of Executive Compensation and Retirement 508.

"Can I, as an Employee, Deduct My Home-Office Expenses?" (1990), 44 D.T.C. 7028.

Corn, George, "Expense Reimbursements: Not Taxable as Employee Benefits" (1990) 3 Can. Current Tax J-24.

Expenses of Sales Representatives: Tax Treatment (Toronto: CCH Canadian, 1990).

Kingissepp, Andrew H., "Canadian Officers and Directors can Treat Indemnity Payment as Tax-free Receipt" (1993) 4 Tax. of Executive Compensation and Retirement 763.

Krasa, Eva M., "Recent Developments in Retirement Savings and Deferred Compensation: A Pot Pourri" (1992) Can. Tax Foundation 18:1.

Krishna, Vern, "A Striking Decision" (November 1989) 23 CGA Magazine 43.

Novek, Barbara L., "Part-time and Interrupted Employment Included in Computing Portion of Retiring Allowance Eligible for Rollover to RRSP" (1992) 4 Tax. of Executive Compensation and Retirement 637.

Novek, Barbara L., "Sector Specific Tax Relief for Canadian Residents Working Overseas" (1993) 5 Tax. of Executive Compensation and Retirement 808.

Roberts, David G., "Registered Retirement Savings Plans" (1989) 37 Can. Tax J. 64.

"Sec. 8(1)(f): Is the Frustration Over?" (1990), 44 D.T.C. 7021.

Thomas, Richard B., "No To Nanny Expense Deduction" (1991) 39 Can. Tax J. 950.

"Why Not Work at Home and Deduct the Home-Office Expense?" (1990), 44 D.T.C. 7014.

Chapter 7 — Business Income

Table of Contents

I. — General Comment

Income for tax purposes is calculated by determining income from each source separately. Business income and investment income are calculated according to subdivision b of Division B of Part I of the Act. In this chapter we examine how the tax system distinguishes three different sources: business, investment, and capital gains income.

The rules that distinguish between the various sources necessarily complicate the Act and cause taxpayers to characterize their transactions for maximum advantage. This in turn leads to anti-avoidance rules to prevent such positioning. Subdivision b addresses both business income and investment income,[1] but they are in fact two distinct and separate sources of income. Although most of the rules dealing with these two sources of income are the same, there are important differences in how these sources are taxed. For example:

- The attribution rules in sections 74.1 and 74.2 only apply to investment income and capital gains (losses) and do not apply to income from business; and

- The small business deduction is available only in respect of income from business and does not generally apply to investment income.

Hence, it is important to distinguish between the two sources of income.

We determine income or loss for tax purposes in two distinct steps. First, we characterize a receipt or loss as flowing from a particular source that is taxable under section 3 of the Act. Second, we measure the amount of income or loss according to the rules applicable to that particular source.

The intrinsic nature of income does not determine its source for tax purposes. The intrinsic nature of income is essentially a question of commercial law, regardless of who receives the income. Interest, rent, royalties and dividends, for example, may be investment income or business income depending upon who earns the income, the degree of activity and effort to earn the income. Thus, in the absence of a deeming rule, the source of income is essentially a question of fact.

A. — "Business"

The Act does not define "business", which is a central concept in the income tax system. Subsection 248(1) merely says that "business" *includes* a profession, calling, trade, manufacture or undertaking of any kind whatever, and, for most purposes, also includes an adventure or concern in the nature of trade. There is also an extended meaning of "carrying on business" as it relates to non-residents.[2] This raises the question: When is an "undertaking" a business for tax purposes?

Generally, "business" refers to activity — economic, industrial, commercial, or financial. The traditional common law definition of business is "anything which occupies the time and

---

[1]Technically referred to as "income from property".

[2]Subs. 248(1) "business"; see also s. 253.

attention and labour of a man for the purpose of profit."[3] As the English Court of Appeal said in *Erichsen v. Last*:[4]

> I do not think there is any principle of law which lays down what carrying on of trade is. There are a multitude of incidents which together make the carrying on [of] a trade, but I know of no one distinguishing incident which makes a practice a carrying on of trade, and another practice not a carrying on of trade. If I may use the expression, it is a compound fact made up of a variety of incidents.

A "trade" is the business of selling goods, with a view to profit, that the trader has either manufactured or purchased.[5]

The quintessential characteristics of business are activity, enterprise, entrepreneurship, commercial risk, and the pursuit of profit. To be sure, "business" implies activity and profit motive.[6] The pursuit of profit differentiates a trade or business from a hobby or pastime. Thus, the first question to determine is whether the taxpayer undertakes the activity in pursuit of profit or as a personal endeavour or hobby. Pursuit of profit, and not its actual realization, is the key element in distinguishing between commercial ventures and hobbies.

Paragraph 18(1)(a) merely restates the necessity of the profit motive test: A taxpayer is not entitled to deduct an expense unless he or she incurs the expenditure for the *purpose* of gaining or producing income from a business or property.

The purpose of the pursuit of profit test is to distinguish between commercial and personal activities. Hence, one first looks to see if there are indicia of commerciality or badges of trade. The test is relevant only if there is some personal or hobby element to the taxpayer's activity. It has no relevance if the activity is clearly commercial. If the activity is clearly commercial, then it matters not whether it actually generates income or loss. It is not for the revenue authorities to determine *ex post* whether the taxpayer had a reasonable expectation

---

[3]*Stewart v. R.*, [2002] 2 S.C.R. 645, [2002] 3 C.T.C. 439, 2002 D.T.C. 6969 (Eng.) (S.C.C.); see also *Smith v. Anderson* (1880), 15 Ch. D. 247 (Eng. C.A.) at 258; *Terminal Dock and Warehouse Co. v. Minister of National Revenue*, [1968] 2 Ex. C.R. 78, [1968] C.T.C. 78, 68 D.T.C. 5060 (Can. Ex. Ct.); affirmed [1968] S.C.R. vi, 68 D.T.C. 5316 (S.C.C.).

[4](1881), 4 T.C. 422, 8 Q.B.D. 414, 51 L.J.Q.B. 86, 45 L.T. 703, 46 J.P. 357, 30 W.R. 301 (Eng. C.A.) at 423 [T.C.].

[5]*Grainger & Son v. Gough*, [1896] A.C. 325, 3 T.C. 462 (U.K. H.L.).

[6]See *e.g.*, *Fleming v. Minister of National Revenue*, [1987] 2 C.T.C. 2113, 87 D.T.C. 425 (T.C.C.) (university professors did not have expectation of profit in publishing research); *Shaker v. Minister of National Revenue*, [1987] 2 C.T.C. 2156, 87 D.T.C. 463 (T.C.C.) (keen desire, talent and determination did not necessitate reasonable expectation of profit in an undertaking); *Kusick v. Minister of National Revenue* (1987), [1988] 1 C.T.C. 2052, 88 D.T.C. 1069 (T.C.C.) (taxpayer changed type of business, obviously realized no chance of profits); *Ianson v. Minister of National Revenue* (1987), [1988] 1 C.T.C. 2088, 88 D.T.C. 1074 (T.C.C.) (horse racing carried on as hobby); *Issacharoff v. Minister of National Revenue* (1987), [1988] 1 C.T.C. 2006, 87 D.T.C. 673 (T.C.C.).

of profit in the pursuit of a commercial venture.[7] Thus, one should not evaluate business judgment with hindsight. If the activity is not a personal endeavor or hobby, the next question is whether the source of commercial income is business or property income.[8]

If the venture has both commercial and personal elements, one must determine if the commercial element is sufficient to characterize the income as a source of income for the purposes of the Act.[9] Here one may look to see if there are sufficient commercial indicia such as adequate financing, time devoted to activity, industry norms, etc.

The profit motive test is crucial to the integrity of the tax system. It draws the line between providing limitless tax subsidies for personal pursuits with minimal economic flavour and economic enterprises conducted on a commercial basis for profit. Taxpayers should not expect other taxpayers to subsidize their personal hobbies. On the other hand, the test should not be so stringent that it discourages entrepreneurial activities that result in losses.

Prior to the Supreme Court of Canada's decision in *Stewart*[10] courts applied a "reasonable expectation of profit" test to determine whether a taxpayer's activities were of a commercial or personal nature. Courts would ask with the benefit of hindsight whether the taxpayer had a reasonable expectation of profits from his or her activities. If the taxpayer had such an expectation, the income was considered to be from a source of business or property.

Stewart effectively overruled the REOP test in most commercial contexts:

> In our view, the reasonable expectation of profit analysis cannot be maintained as an independent source test. To do so would run contrary to the principle that courts should avoid judicial innovation and rule-making in tax law . . . .. In addition, the reasonable expectation of profit test is imprecise, causing an unfortunate degree of uncertainty for taxpayers. As well, the nature of the test has encouraged a hindsight assessment of the business judgment of taxpayers in order to deny losses incurred in bona fide, albeit unsuccessful, commercial ventures (*per* Iacobucci and Bastarache JJ.).

It is important to note, however, that *Stewart* did not completely abolish the REOP test, but confined it to cases where there is some personal element to the activity in question.[11]

---

[7]As the Supreme Court of Canada said in *Stewart v. R.*, [2002] 2 S.C.R. 645, [2002] 3 C.T.C. 439, 2002 D.T.C. 6969 (Eng.), 2002 D.T.C. 6983 (Fr.): "With respect, in our view, courts have erred in the past in applying the REOP test to activities such as law practices and restaurants where there exists no such personal element."

[8]See *Stewart v. R., ibid.*

[9]*Ibid.*

[10]*Ibid.*

[11]See *Nadoryk v. R.* (2003), [2004] 2 C.T.C. 87, 2003 D.T.C. 5744, [2003] F.C.J. No. 1786 (Fed. C.A.).

B. — "Property"

Investment income is the yield from property. For example: shares yield dividends, bonds yield interest, intellectual property yields royalties, real property yields rent, and so on.

"Property" includes virtually every type of economic interest:[12]

> "[P]roperty" means property of any kind whatever whether real or personal, immovable or movable, tangible or intangible, or corporeal or incorporeal and, without restricting the generality of the foregoing, includes
>
> (a) a right of any kind whatever, a share or a chose in action,
>
> (b) unless a contrary intention is evident, money,
>
> (c) a timber resource property, and
>
> (d) the work in progress of a business that is a profession.

A right of property includes the right to possess, use, lend, alienate, consume or otherwise possess it to the exclusion of others.[13] Thus, a right of property represents a bundle of distinct rights. For example, the right of ownership is a right distinct from the right of possession. One can own without possessing and possess without owning.

There is, however, one particularly important exclusion from property income. "Income from property" does *not* include a capital gain from the property itself. Similarly, "loss from property" does not include a capital loss from the property.[14] Gains and losses from selling a property are a separate source of income to which completely different rules apply.[15]

---

[12]Subs. 248(1)"property"; see also *Fasken Estate v. Minister of National Revenue*, [1948] C.T.C. 265, 49 D.T.C. 491 (Can. Ex. Ct.); *Jones v. Skinner* (1835), 5 L.J. Ch. 87 at 90: It is well-known, that the word "property" is the most comprehensive of all the terms that can be used, inasmuch as it is indicative and descriptive of every possible interest the party can have. See also *Manrell v. R.*, [2003] 3 C.T.C. 50, 2003 D.T.C. 5225 (Fed. C.A.) (in the context of non-competition payments).

[13]*West. Electric Co. v. Minister of National Revenue*, [1969] C.T.C. 274, 69 D.T.C. 5204 (Can. Ex. Ct.) at 289 [C.T.C.] and 5212 [D.T.C.]; affirmed [1971] S.C.R. vi, [1971] C.T.C. 96, 71 D.T.C. 5068 (S.C.C.) (amounts paid to appellant claimed not to be rentals, royalties or otherwise for the use of property; Court determined that payments equivalent to royalties under treaty); *R. v. St. John Shipbldg. & Dry Dock Co.*, [1980] C.T.C. 352, 80 D.T.C. 6272 (Fed. C.A.); leave to appeal refused (1980), 34 N.R. 348n (S.C.C.) (lump sums paid for computerized information not related to use, sales or benefit derived; not within classes of property in treaty).

[14]Subs. 9(3).

[15]See subdivision c.

C. — "Capital Gains"

The importance of characterizing an amount on account of income or capital against (losses) is crucial. Capital gains are treated preferentially and taxed at lower effective tax rates. In some cases, capital gains are completely exempt from tax.[16] In other cases, capital gains are subject to an inflation penalty.

The Act does not define either "capital gain" or "income". The purported definitions in paragraphs 39(1)(a) and (b) of the Act are circular and of minimal practical value. The distinction between "capital gains" and "income" derives essentially from the case law.

The distinction between capital gains and income appears simple. Income derives from trading or the periodic yield of an investment. Capital gains derive from sale or realization of the investment. The distinction is often put in the form of an analogy.[17]

> The fundamental relation of "capital" to "income" has been much discussed by economists, the former being likened to the tree or the land, the latter to the fruit or the crop; the former depicted as a reservoir supplied from springs, the latter as the outlet stream, to be measured by its flow during a period of time.

The tree is the capital that produces a yield (the fruit), and income is the profit that derives when we sell the fruit. A gain from the sale of the tree itself is on account of capital. The answer is always easy when it is obvious. For example:

- A building is capital; rent derived from the building is income;
- Shares are capital; dividends on the shares are income; and
- Bonds are capital; interest payments on the bonds are income.

Thus, an investment in property represents capital, and the flow from the investment represents income.

Capital gains derive from a disposition of investments that constitute "capital property". Income gains derive from a sale of trading assets or as the yield from investments. Thus, the key to determining whether we have an income gain or a capital gain is in identifying whether we have traded assets or sold an investment. Therein lies the difficulty. What is an investment? What if in the above examples, the taxpayer trades in buildings, shares, or bonds? The distinctions can be subtle and appear deceptively simple.

---

[16]See, for example, the exemption for principal residences and qualified shares of small business corporations.

[17]*Eisner v. Macomber* (1920), 252 U.S. 189.

D. — "Investment"

To say that a capital gain or loss arises from the disposition of an investment is not very helpful in characterizing gains and losses. The fundamental question is: what is an "investment"? How do we recognize investments (the sale of which yields a capital gain) and trading assets (the sale of which yields income)? This characterization is more problematic than it first appears. For example, consider the following judicial statement:[18]

> It is quite a well-settled principle that where the owner of an ordinary investment chooses to realize it, and obtains a greater price for it than he originally acquired it at, the enhanced price is not profit. . . . But it is equally well established that enhanced values obtained from realisation or conversion of securities may be so assessable, where what is done is not merely a realisation or change of investment, but an act done in what is truly the carrying on, or carrying out, of a business. . . .

The statement tells us that the distinction between business income and capital gains depends upon whether the taxpayer is trading or investing. But that merely leads to another question: how do we know when a person is trading or investing?

The distinction cannot rest upon the taxpayer's desire to make a profit. Everyone wants to make a profit, whether they are trading or investing. Trading implies a profit-making scheme to earn income by buying and selling property. Investment implies acquiring and holding an asset for its potential yield, but with the possibility that the investment may, at some time, be sold for a profit.

In *Sissons*, for example:[19]

> Here the clear indication of "trade" is found in the fact that the acquisition of the securities was a part of a profit-making scheme. The purpose of the operation was not to earn income from the securities but to make a profit on prompt realization. The operation has therefore none of the essential characteristics of an investment; it is essentially a speculation.

To be sure, profit motive is the *sine qua non* of business. But, since both traders and investors search for profit, profit motive by itself is not sufficient to distinguish between business income and capital gains. The distinction rests upon the taxpayer's operative intention at the time she acquires the property. Was the taxpayer intending to trade (do business) or invest (hold property)?

---

[18]*Californian Copper Syndicate Ltd. v. Harris* (1904), 5 Tax Cas. 159 (Scot. Ex. Ct. 2nd Div.) at 165-66.

[19]*Minister of National Revenue v. Sissons*, [1969] S.C.R. 507, [1969] C.T.C. 184, 69 D.T.C. 5152 (S.C.C.) at 188 [C.T.C.] and 5154 [D.T.C.].

a) — Taxpayer Intention

An "investment" is an asset or property that one acquires with the *intention* of holding or using *to produce* income. Thus, in tax law, an investment is a means to an end. Where a taxpayer acquires property with an intention to trade — that is, to purchase and resell the property at a profit — any gain or loss from the trade is business income (loss). Hence, the distinction between an investment and trading inventory depends not upon the nature of the property, but upon the intention with which the taxpayer acquires it.

For example, suppose A registers an Internet domain name for $100 and later sells it to B for $1,000. The characterization of the $900 gain depends upon A's intention at the time A registered the name. If A's regular practice is to acquire and sell domain names, then the gain is business income. If, however, A acquires the name to use for her website and sells it to B when her plans change, the gain is a capital gain.

In most cases, the taxpayer's intention at the time he acquires the asset is the basic issue. One determines the character of the gain on the basis of evidence that provides an insight into the taxpayer's state of mind at the relevant time. The taxpayer's conduct, rather than any *ex post facto* declarations, usually provides the key to his intention. One may, however, sometimes infer a taxpayer's intention from another taxpayer's conduct. For example, one can attribute the intentions of a person to a spouse where the latter is clearly relying on the knowledge and information of the former.[20]

How do we evaluate a taxpayer's intentions? The only conclusive rule is: *No single factor is conclusively determinative*. We look at the circumstances of the transaction and balance multiple, often conflicting, indicia to determine the taxpayer's intention. As one judge stated: ". . . a common sense appreciation of *all* the guiding features will provide the ulti-mate answer."[21] This is not a very helpful statement for taxpayers who must determine the issue, but is one that judges frequently rely upon to make such decisions with the benefit of *ex post* analysis.

In addition to looking at a taxpayer's primary intention for the purpose of characterizing income or gain, the courts sometimes also look to see if the taxpayer had a secondary inten-

---

[20]See, e.g., *Darch v. R.*, [1992] 2 C.T.C. 128, 92 D.T.C. 6366 (Fed. T.D.); affirmed as Wright in [1994] 2 C.T.C. 1, 98 D.T.C. 6629 (Fed. C.A.).

[21]*B.P. Australia Ltd. v. Commissioner of Taxation of Australia*, [1966] A.C. 224 (Australia P.C.) at 264, *per* Lord Pearce, approved by the S.C.C. in *Johns-Manville Canada Inc. v. R.*, [1985] 2 S.C.R. 46, [1985] 2 C.T.C. 111 at 125, 85 D.T.C. 5373 at 5383 (S.C.C.) (thorough analysis of law; purchase of land to allow expansion of mining pit so that slope could be maintained at safe angle was an operational expense); see also *Canadian General Electric Co. v. R.*, [1987] 1 C.T.C. 180, 87 D.T.C. 5070 (Fed. C.A.); leave to appeal refused (1987), 86 N.R. 264 (note) (S.C.C.) (heavy water production "know-how" and licence sold; amount received was income because sales replaced taxpayer's business); *Paco Corp. c. R.*, [1980] C.T.C. 409, 80 D.T.C. 6328 (Eng.) (Fed. T.D.) (losses for demonstration plant constituted operating expense; determined by taxpayer's intention).

tion to trade. Where a taxpayer has a *secondary* intention to trade, any gain or loss resulting from the trade is business income (loss).[22] Therefore, a taxpayer who claims that a gain is a capital gain must show two things: (1) that his primary intention at the time of entering into the transaction was to make an investment; and (2) that he had no secondary intention at that time to trade in the particular property.

Secondary intention to trade is also a question of fact and the trier of fact may draw inferences from the taxpayer's conduct.[23] The determination is on a balance of probabilities.[24] Hence, taxpayer credibility is always in issue. The same rules apply to distinguish between business (non-capital) losses and capital losses.[25]

A taxpayer has a secondary intention to trade if the possibility of early resale at a profit was a *motivating* consideration at the time that she acquired the property. Thus, the critical times are just before, and the moment that, the taxpayer enters into a binding agreement to purchase the property in question.[26] Although motive to trade or invest is a subjective criterion, we determine its absence or presence by inference from objective evidence — that is, the taxpayer's conduct and the circumstances surrounding the particular transaction.[27]

---

[22]*Bayridge Estates Ltd. v. Minister of National Revenue*, [1959] C.T.C. 158, 59 D.T.C. 1098 (Can. Ex. Ct.) (profit one of motives in sale of raw land); *Fogel v. Minister of National Revenue*, [1959] C.T.C. 227, 59 D.T.C. 1182 (Can. Ex. Ct.) (by-laws necessitated abandonment of building plans; subsequent sale for profit found to have been alternative intention); *Regal Heights Ltd. v. Minister of National Revenue*, [1960] S.C.R. 902, [1960] C.T.C. 384, 60 D.T.C. 1270 (S.C.C.) (plans for shopping centre frustrated and parcels of land sold; profits of highly speculative venture constituted income).

[23]*Reicher v. R.*, [1975] C.T.C. 659, 76 D.T.C. 6001 (Fed. C.A.).

[24]*Factory Carpet Ltd. v. R.*, [1985] 2 C.T.C. 267, 85 D.T.C. 5464 (Fed. T.D.).

[25]*Minister of National Revenue v. Freud*, [1969] S.C.R. 75, [1968] C.T.C. 438, 68 D.T.C. 5279 (S.C.C.).

[26]*Dickson v. R.*, [1977] C.T.C. 64, 77 D.T.C. 5061 (Fed. C.A.) (resolution to sell land dated 1964 but agreement dated 1967; purchaser's financial plight at date of signing agreement relevant to intention); *Racine v. Minister of National Revenue*, [1965] C.T.C. 150, 65 D.T.C. 5098 (Can. Ex. Ct.) (to constitute "secondary intention", purchaser must have possibility of reselling as operating motivation for acquisition at moment of purchase).

[27]*Reicher v. R.*, [1975] C.T.C. 659, 76 D.T.C. 6001 (Fed. C.A.) at 664 [C.T.C.] and 6004 [D.T.C.] *per* Le Dain J.A.:

> The issue on this appeal is whether at the time they acquired the property the appellant . . . had a secondary intention, as an operating motivation for such acquisition, to sell the property at a profit should a suitable opportunity present itself.

See also *Hiwako Investments Ltd. v. R.*, [1978] C.T.C. 378, 78 D.T.C. 6281 (Fed. C.A.) (whether or not onus on taxpayer to disprove Minister's stated assumption that taxpayer primarily motivated by intention to trade); *Kit-Win Holdings (1973) Ltd. v. R.*, [1981] C.T.C. 43, 81 D.T.C. 5030 (Fed. T.D.) (Minister did not precisely allege exclusive motivation to develop property for profit).

Mere awareness at the time that one acquires a property that future events might dictate a change of investments does not *necessarily* mean that the transaction is an adventure in the nature of trade. Nor does sensitivity to the probability of capital appreciation necessarily imply a trading intention. Such sensitivity indicates no more than a prudent and informed investment decision.[28]

There is a difference, however, between a taxpayer who responds to a *changing* investment climate and a taxpayer who actively contemplates the potential of profit on resale at the time of investment. Where the potential of profit is a motivating consideration, it suggests a secondary intention to engage in an adventure in the nature of trade:[29]

> . . . an intention at the time of acquisition of an investment to sell it in the event that it does not prove profitable does not make the subsequent sale of the investment the completion of an "adventure or concern in the nature of trade". Had the alleged assumption been that there was an expectation on the part of the purchaser, at the time of purchase, that, in the event that the investment did not prove to be profitable, it could be sold at a profit, and that such expectation was one of the factors that induced him to make the purchase, such assumption, if not disproved, might (I do not say that it would) support the assessments based on "trading" if not disproved.

b) — Criteria to Determine Taxpayer Intention

A taxpayer's intention, whether primary or secondary, is always a question of fact. We look objectively at various criteria as aids in determining intention. No single criterion is conclusive. The common criteria include: (1) number of similar transactions; (2) nature of the asset; (3) related activity; (4) corporate objects and powers; and (5) degree of organization.

(i) — Number of Similar Transactions

Evidence that a taxpayer engaged in numerous similar transactions to the one at issue may suggest that the taxpayer is a trader and engages in a business. All other things being equal (although they rarely are), the greater the number of similar transactions in the past, the greater the likelihood that the gain or loss in issue is business income or loss. The converse,

---

[28]*Hiwako Investments Ltd. v. R.*, *ante*; *R. v. Bassani*, [1985] 1 C.T.C. 314, 85 D.T.C. 5232 (Fed. T.D.) (mere expectation that price of property would rise did not constitute "secondary intention" without operating motivation).

[29]*Hiwako Investments Ltd. v. R.*, [1978] C.T.C. 378, 78 D.T.C. 6281 (Fed. C.A.) at 383 [C.T.C.] and 6285 [D.T.C.].

however, does not apply. Merely because a transaction is an isolated event does not mean that it is not business income or loss. As the Exchequer Court stated:[30]

> ... while it is recognized that, as a general rule, an isolated transaction of purchase and sale outside the course of the taxpayer's ordinary business does not constitute the carrying on of a trade or business so as to render the profit therefrom liable to the income tax ... it is also established that the fact that a transaction is an isolated one does not exclude it from the category of trading or business transactions of such a nature as to attract income tax to the profit therefrom.

A gain from an isolated transaction can give rise to business income or loss if the transaction is either closely related to the taxpayer's ordinary business activities or the property disposed of is of a type characterized as a "trading" property.[31] Lord President Clyde put it succinctly:[32]

> A single plunge may be enough provided it is shown to the satisfaction of the Court that the plunge is made in the waters of trade. ...

(ii) — Nature of Asset

The nature of the asset is important in the characterization of any gain or loss from its disposition. Land, for example, *particularly raw land*, is viewed suspiciously as a trading, rather than an investment, asset if the taxpayer subdivides and develops it. This attitude also extends to the sale of shares of corporations incorporated *solely* for the purpose of holding raw land.[33] In contrast, transactions involving corporate shares are generally seen as on account of capital. As the Supreme Court observed:[34]

> ... a person who puts money into a business enterprise by the purchase of the shares of a company on an isolated occasion, and not as a part of his regular business, cannot be said to have engaged in an adventure in the nature of trade merely because the purchase was speculative in that, at that time, he did not intend to hold the shares indefinitely, but intended, if

---

[30]*Atlantic Sugar Refineries Ltd. v. Minister of National Revenue*, [1948] C.T.C. 326, 48 D.T.C. 507 (Can. Ex. Ct.) at 333-34 [C.T.C.] and 511 [D.T.C.]; affirmed [1949] S.C.R. 706, [1949] C.T.C. 196, 49 D.T.C. 602 (S.C.C.).

[31]*Minister of National Revenue v. Taylor*, [1956] C.T.C. 189, 56 D.T.C. 1125 (Can. Ex. Ct.).

[32]*Balgownie Land Trust Ltd. v. I.R.C.* (1929), 14 Tax Cas. 684 (Scot.).

[33]*Fraser v. Minister of National Revenue*, [1964] S.C.R. 657, [1964] C.T.C. 372, 64 D.T.C. 5224 (S.C.C.); see also *Mould v. Minister of National Revenue*, [1986] 1 C.T.C. 271, 86 D.T.C. 6087 (Fed. T.D.) (156 acres of land sole asset of corporation: "... the acquisition of the shares was merely a method of obtaining an interest in the land").

[34]*Irrigation Industries Ltd. v. Minister of National Revenue*, [1962] S.C.R. 346, [1962] C.T.C. 215, 62 D.T.C. 1131 (S.C.C.) at 219 [C.T.C.] and 1133 [D.T.C.].

possible, to sell them at a profit as soon as he reasonably could. I think that there must be clearer indications of "trade" than this before it can be said that there has been an adventure in the nature of trade.

Thus, a purchase of shares with an intention to resell at a profit is not, *by itself*, likely to result in the characterization of any gain or loss from their sale as resulting from an adventure in the nature of trade. An isolated transaction in shares, however, can give rise to business income or loss if there are other factors that indicate an intention to trade.[35] For example, a "quick flip" of shares may suggest a trading intention unless it can be explained on other grounds. An isolated transaction in speculative penny mining shares may well give rise to business income or loss if the taxpayer is acting like a mining promoter. *A fortiori*, speculative and highly leveraged trading in high risk, non-yielding shares and options may be seen as trading in securities.[36]

All investors hope, albeit sometimes unrealistically, that their investments will increase in value. The mere expectation of profit is not, by itself, sufficient to characterize a transaction as an adventure in the nature of trade. Certain types of assets, though — typically, commodities that cannot possibly provide any investment yield — are always suspect as "trading assets". Profits resulting from the sale of these types of assets are summarily classified as business income. As Lord Carmont stated:[37]

> ... this means that, although in certain cases it is important to know whether a venture is isolated or not, that information is really superfluous in many cases where *the commodity itself* stamps the transaction as a trading venture, and the profits and gains are plainly income liable to tax. [Emphasis added.]

In contrast, assets with a *potential, even if a somewhat remote possibility*, of yielding income, are generally seen as "investment assets" and profits resulting from transactions in these types of assets are usually, though not inevitably, characterized as capital gains. Corporate shares in particular enjoy this status. Corporate shares tend to be viewed as investment assets because they have the *potential* to yield dividends. Are corporate shares really

---

[35]*Osler Hammond & Nanton Ltd. v. Minister of National Revenue*, [1963] S.C.R. 432, [1963] C.T.C. 164, 63 D.T.C. 1119 (S.C.C.) (investment dealer sold shares arranged for during underwriting); *Hill-Clarke-Francis Ltd. v. Minister of National Revenue*, [1963] S.C.R. 452, [1963] C.T.C. 337, 63 D.T.C. 1211 (S.C.C.) (lumber dealer purchased all outstanding shares of supplier; Court looked at intention at time of acquisition and sale of shares).

[36]See, e.g., *Oakside Corp. v. Minister of National Revenue*, [1991] 1 C.T.C. 2132, 91 D.T.C. 328 (T.C.C.).

[37]*I.R.C. v. Reinhold* (1953), 34 Tax Cas. 389 (Scot.) at 392; see also *Rutledge v. I.R.C.* (1929), 14 Tax Cas. 490 (Scot. Ct. of Sess.) (isolated transaction in toilet paper characterized as adventure in nature of trade); *I.R.C. v. Fraser*, 27 Tax Cas. 502 (Scot.) (isolated transaction in whiskey gave rise to funds taxable as business income); *Minister of National Revenue v. Taylor*, [1956] C.T.C. 189, 56 D.T.C. 1125 (Can. Ex. Ct.) (isolated transaction in lead).

any different from other assets? The Supreme Court thought so in *Irrigation Industries Ltd. v. Minister of National Revenue*:[38]

> ... the nature of the property in question here is shares issued from the treasury of a corporation and we have not been referred to any reported case in which profit from one isolated purchase and sale of shares, by a person not engaged in the business of trading in securities, has been claimed to be taxable. ... *Corporate shares are in a different position because they constitute something the purchase of which is, in itself, an investment.* They are not, in themselves, articles of commerce, but represent an interest in a corporation which is itself created for the purpose of doing business. Their acquisition is a well recognized method of investing capital in a business enterprise. [Emphasis added.]

The Court adopted a more stringent approach, however, in *Freud* where Pigeon J. stated:[39]

> It is clear that while an acquisition of shares may be an investment ... it may also be a trading operation depending upon circumstances. ...

The converse is equally true. It is generally difficult, but by no means impossible, for a taxpayer to establish that she was engaged in a speculative venture or an adventure in the nature of trade in trading shares.[40] Thus, share losses are seen as capital transactions.

Assets other than "trading assets" and "investment assets" fall into some middle ground in which the nature of the asset does not play as important a role as the taxpayer's conduct in relation to the asset. Real estate, other than vacant land, falls into this middle ground.

To summarize:

- *By itself*, we cannot determine anything conclusive from the fact that a transaction is an isolated one in the taxpayer's experience;

- If there are other factors indicative of trade, a profit from an isolated transaction will be ordinary income resulting from an adventure in the nature of trade;

- Even if there are no other business attributes, a transaction may still give rise to business income if the asset traded is of a trading; and

- If the asset in question is an investment asset (e.g., corporate shares), and there are no other factors indicative of trading, the transaction will *usually* (not inevitably) be

---

[38]*Irrigation Indust. Ltd. v. Minister of National Revenue, ante* (gain from speculative mining shares purchased with short-term loan on account of capital).

[39]*Freud v. Minister of National Revenue*, [1969] S.C.R. 75, [1968] C.T.C. 438, 68 D.T.C. 5279 (S.C.C.) at 80-81[S.C.R.], 442 [C.T.C.] and 5282 [D.T.C.].

[40]*Becker v. R.*, [1983] C.T.C. 11, 83 D.T.C. 5032 (Fed. C.A.) (purchase of shares in business with intention of transforming it into profitable enterprise); *Factory Carpet Ltd. v. R.*, [1985] 2 C.T.C. 267, 85 D.T.C. 5464 (Fed. T.D.) (purchase of shares with substantial deductible non-capital losses with intention of revamping and reselling business, therefore trading).

viewed as a capital transaction. This is so even though the investment asset is acquired *for the purpose of resale at a profit.*

(iii) — Related Activity

A taxpayer's profits and losses from transactions that are closely related to his other ordinary business activities are usually characterized as business income or losses.[41] It is very difficult for a taxpayer to maintain successfully that a profit arising out of a transaction connected in any manner with ordinary business activity is a capital gain. As Thorson P. stated:[42]

> ... they were transactions in the same commodity as that which it had to purchase for its ordinary purposes. In my view, they were of the same character and nature as trading and business operations as those of its business in its ordinary course, even though they involved a departure from such course.

There is a strong, but rebuttable, presumption that a transaction connected in any way with a taxpayer's usual business is intrinsically part of that business. The presumption may be re-

---

[41]See generally: *Smith v. Minister of National Revenue* (1955), 12 Tax A.B.C. 166, 55 D.T.C. 101 (Can. Tax App. Bd.) (mortgage discounting closely related to taxpayer's business as realtor; treated as trading since so related); *Darius v. Minister of National Revenue*, [1971] Tax A.B.C. 889 (Can. Tax. App. Bd.); affirmed [1974] C.T.C. 337, 74 D.T.C. 6260 (Fed. T.D.) (shareholder in construction company sold land parcels in her own name to achieve better tax result than company able to achieve); *Morrison v. Minister of National Revenue*, [1917-27] C.T.C. 343, 1 D.T.C. 113 (Can. Ex. Ct.) (taxpayer with skill and knowledge in trade acquired through experience, who then traded privately in the same commodity, was carrying on a business); *McDonough v. Minister of National Revenue*, [1949] C.T.C. 213, 4 D.T.C. 621 (Can. Ex. Ct.) (trading not precluded by mere fact that isolated transaction; prospector became promoter of mines in one trade of over a million shares); *No. 351 v. Minister of National Revenue* (1956), 15 Tax A.B.C. 351, 56 D.T.C. 375 (Can. Tax App. Bd.) (frequent trading of grain futures); *Boivin v. Minister of National Revenue*, 70 D.T.C. 1364 (a dozen property "flips" by wife on direction of building contractor husband motivated by profit and deemed "trading"); *Kinsella v. Minister of National Revenue* (1963), 34 Tax A.B.C. 196, 64 D.T.C. 56 (Can. Tax App. Bd.) (frequency of sales and modernization of buildings indicated carefully-planned method of increasing income); *Minister of National Revenue v. Spencer*, [1961] C.T.C. 109, 61 D.T.C. 1079 (Can. Ex. Ct.) (lawyers acted as mortgagees for bonuses; although held to maturity, deemed business and not investments); *Kennedy v. Minister of National Revenue*, [1952] C.T.C. 59, 52 D.T.C. 1070 (Can. Ex. Ct.) (stated intention of taxpayer on purchase only relevant if supported by evidence; see editorial note at C.T.C. 59); *No. 13 v. Minister of National Revenue* (1951), 3 Tax A.B.C. 397, 51 D.T.C. 117 (Can. Tax App. Bd.) (real estate developer treated one property specially, holding it for 10 years as an investment apart from his ordinary business); *Everlease (Ontario) Ltd. v. Minister of National Revenue*, [1968] Tax A.B.C. 162, 68 D.T.C. 180 (Can. Tax App. Bd.) (building sold to cover lack of funds was trade due to owner's close association with real estate developers and managers).

[42]*Atlantic Sugar Refineries Ltd. v. Minister of National Revenue*, [1948] C.T.C. 326, 48 D.T.C. 507 (Can. Ex. Ct.) at 513 [D.T.C.]; affirmed [1949] C.T.C. 196, 49 D.T.C. 602 (S.C.C.).

butted through evidence that the transaction was not part of the taxpayer's ordinary business, but was an unrelated capital investment. *Actual* use of the property as an investment asset over some period of time, or a plausible explanation for selling the investment, may also rebut the presumption.

(iv) — Corporate Objects and Powers

A corporation has the capacity, rights, powers and privileges of a natural person.[43] Thus, unless specifically restricted by its articles of incorporation, a corporation may engage in any business other than those from which it is specifically precluded by statute. A corporation may restrict its scope of business activities by specifying the restrictions in its articles of incorporation or other constating documents.[44]

For tax purposes, characterization of corporate income depends upon the business that the corporation actually conducts and not on any restrictions in its incorporating documents.[45] Thus, we characterize corporate income according to the intention and secondary intention of the taxpayer and not according to any stipulations in the corporation's constating documents.

(v) — Degree of Organization

Where a taxpayer deals with property in much the same way as a dealer would with similar property, any resulting profit is likely business income. Thus, a transaction, *albeit* isolated and unrelated to the taxpayer's ordinary business activity, may have the stamp of business purpose if it is organized and carried on in the manner of a trader. As Lord Clyde said in *I.R.C. v. Livingston*:[46]

> I think the test, which must be used to determine whether a venture such as we are now considering is, or is not, "in the nature of 'trade'," is whether the operations involved in it are of the same kind, and carried on in the same way, as those which are characteristic of ordinary trading in the line of business in which the venture was made.

For example, a taxpayer who purchases undeveloped land that the taxpayer then subdivides and sells for profit, behaves as a developer would in the normal course of business. In the

---

[43]See, e.g., *Business Corporations Act*, R.S.O. 1990, c. B.16, s. 15.

[44]See, e.g., *Canada Business Corporations Act*, R.S.C. 1985, c. 44, para. 6(1)(f), and Ontario *Business Corporations Act*, R.S.O. 1990, c. B.16, subs. 3(2) and 17(2).

[45]*Sutton Lumber & Trading Co. v. Minister of National Revenue*, [1953] 2 S.C.R. 77, [1953] C.T.C. 237, 53 D.T.C. 1158 (S.C.C.).

[46]*I.R.C. v. Livingston* (1927), 11 Tax Cas. 538 at 542 (Scot.).

absence of a convincing explanation, the taxpayer's profits would constitute income from business.[47]

It is clear that dealing with an asset as a businessperson would deal with similar assets may, by itself, be sufficient to show an intention to trade. It is also clear that a taxpayer's intention at the time of acquisition can be quite different from his intention at the time of sale. For example, in *Moluch*,[48] the taxpayer did not originally acquire the lands with an intent to sell them at a profit. The taxpayer's intention to use the land as a capital asset and his actual use as such for an extended period of time were never in question. Nevertheless, the taxpayer's activities subsequent to the acquisition showed that he converted the investment property into inventory. The Court said:[49]

> . . . even if at the time of acquisition, the intention of turning the lands to account by resale was not present, it does not necessarily follow that profits resulting from sales are not assessable to income tax. If at some subsequent point in time, the appellant embarked upon a business, using the lands as inventory in the business of land subdividing for profit, then clearly the resultant profits would not be merely the realization of an enhancement in value, but rather profits from a business and so assessable to income tax. . . .

E. — Electing Capital Gains

To reduce the uncertainty associated with the troublesome question of whether a gain is on account of income or capital, the Act allows taxpayers to elect "guaranteed" capital gains or capital loss treatment on a disposition of certain types of properties.[50] The following rules apply:

- The election is available only upon the disposition of a "Canadian security".

---

[47]See, e.g., *Moluch v. Minister of National Revenue*, [1966] C.T.C. 712, 66 D.T.C. 5463 (Can. Ex. Ct.) at 720 [C.T.C.] and 5468 [D.T.C.] where the Court observed:

> . . . moreover I am unable to distinguish what the appellant did after his decision to subdivide had been reached from what a person engaged in the business of land development would do once he had acquired a parcel of property.

See also IT-218R, "Profit, Capital Gains and Losses from the Sale of Real Estate, Including Farmland and Inherited Land and Conversion of Real Estate from Capital Property to Inventory and Vice Versa" (September 16, 1986).

[48]*Moluch v. Minister of National Revenue, ibid.*

[49]*Moluch v. Minister of National Revenue, ibid.*, at 718 [C.T.C.] and 5466 [D.T.C.]; see also *Hughes v. R.*, [1984] C.T.C. 101, 84 D.T.C. 6110 (Fed. T.D.) (apartment building acquired as investment asset; converted into inventory upon application to turn it into condominium).

[50]Subs. 39(4), 39(4.1) and 39(6).

- To qualify as a "Canadian security", the issuer of the security must be a Canadian resident, and the security must be either equity or debt. Warrants and options do not qualify as "Canadian securities".[51]

- Once a taxpayer elects to have a gain deemed a capital gain, all subsequent dispositions of "Canadian securities" by the taxpayer are similarly characterized. Hence, all losses would also be considered capital losses.[52]

- The election is not available to a trader or dealer in securities.[53]

- The election must be made on a prescribed form and filed together with the tax return for the year.

Traders and dealers in securities cannot use the election. Whether a person is a trader or dealer is in itself a question of fact to be determined by the taxpayer's intentions and conduct. A person who participates in the promotion or underwriting of securities is a trader or dealer.[54] The CRA also considers corporate "insiders" who trade for a quick profit to be "traders".

F. — Conversion of Property

A taxpayer may convert capital property into inventory and vice versa. The timing of a conversion is a question of fact requiring a clear and unequivocal act implementing such a change of intention as to clearly indicate a change in the character of the property.[55]

G. — Business Income vs. Investment Income

Having drawn a line between "income" and "capital gains", we must further refine the process and distinguish between business income and investment income. The characterization

---

[51]Subs. 39(6); Reg. 6200.

[52]Subs. 39(4).

[53]Subs. 39(5).

[54]IT-479R, "Transactions in Securities" (February 29, 1984).

[55]*Magilb Development Corp. v. Minister of National Revenue*, [1987] 1 C.T.C. 66, 87 D.T.C. 5012 (Fed. T.D.)) (father made plans for development of family farm corporation; actions did not convert farm from a capital to a trading asset); *Cantor v. Minister of National Revenue*, [1985] 1 C.T.C. 2059, 85 D.T.C. 79 (T.C.C.) (townhouses purchased by law partners proved unprofitable and sold as condominiums; no change in character of investment where diversification occurred to dispose of property most profitably).

of income as resulting from business or investments (more technically, income from property) is also a question of fact.[56]

Since most businesses use property to generate income, it is not particularly helpful to ask whether the income derives from the *use* of property. The critical question is: does the income flow *from* property or *from* business?[57] It is the subtlety of this distinction that gives rise to difficulties in characterizing the source of income. There is no bright-line test that clearly answers the question.

In many, perhaps most, cases the distinction between business income and property income does not affect the end result. A taxpayer's income for a taxation year from a source that is business *or* property is his profit therefrom for the year.[58] We calculate income from both of these sources according to the same commercial and statutory rules. There are, however, circumstances in which the distinction between the two is crucial. For example:

- The attribution rules apply only to income from property and do not apply to business income;[59]

- Active business income earned by a Canadian-controlled private corporation is eligible for special tax credits that substantially reduce the effective tax rate on such income;[60]

- Corporate income from property is subject to a different scheme of taxation and at different rates for different sources of such income.[61]

Generally, income from property is the investment yield on an asset. Rent, dividends, interest, and royalties are typical examples. An investment yields income in a relatively passive process. For example, where an individual invests in land, stocks, bonds, or intangible property,[62] and collects rent, dividends, and interest without doing much more than holding the property, the income is investment income or income *from* property.

---

[56]*Canadian Marconi Co. v. R.*, [1986] 2 S.C.R. 522, [1986] 2 C.T.C. 465, 86 D.T.C. 6526 (S.C.C.) at 530-31 [S.C.R.], 470 [C.T.C.] and 6529 [D.T.C.] *per* Wilson J.: "It is trite law that the characterization of income as income from a business or income from property must be made from an examination of the taxpayer's whole course of conduct viewed in the light of surrounding circumstances."

[57]Para. 3(a); subs. 9(1); see also IT-511R, "Interspousal and Certain other Transfers and Loans of Property", February 21, 1994.

[58]Subs. 9(1).

[59]S. 74.1.

[60]Subs. 125(1); see Chapter 20, "Corporate Business Income".

[61]See Part IV of the Act.

[62]Such as, copyrights, trademarks, etc.

In contrast, business income generally implies activity in the earning process. Business generates from using property as part of a process that combines labour and capital. For example, a taxpayer may *invest* in bonds and clip the coupons to earn the interest income therefrom; alternatively, he may actively *trade* in bonds to earn a profit from trading activities. In the first case, the earnings derive from a passive process and are investment income; in the second case, the income is from business.[63]

Although the distinction between income from business and investment income is easy to state in general terms, the borderline between the two can be unclear. What is the level of activity beyond which a passive holding becomes an active process of earning income?[64] The issue is complicated because of some statements from the Supreme Court that there is a rebuttable presumption that income earned by a corporate taxpayer in the exercise of its duly authorized objects is income from a business.[65]

[63]It is important to note that profits from an isolated trade may be business income. The phrase "adventure in the nature of trade" implies an isolated transaction: see subs. 248(1) "business".

[64]*Canadian Marconi Co. v. R.*, [1986] 2 S.C.R. 522, [1986] 2 C.T.C. 465, 86 D.T.C. 6526 (S.C.C.) ($18 million invested yielded interest that was included in manufacturing and processing profits); *Wertman v. Minister of National Revenue*, [1964] C.T.C. 252 (Can. Ex. Ct.) (concerning rent from apartment units: "the concepts of income from property and income from business are not mutually exclusive but blend completely"); *Walsh v. Minister of National Revenue*, [1965] C.T.C. 478, 65 D.T.C. 5293 (Can. Ex. Ct.) (ordinary janitorial services did not convert property to business, as would maid, linen, laundry and breakfast services); *Burri v. R.*, [1985] 2 C.T.C. 42, 85 D.T.C. 5287 (Fed. T.D.) (services provided by owners incidental to the making of revenue from property through the earning of rent).

[65]*Canadian Marconi Co. v. R. ibid.*, at 529 [S.C.R.], 468 [C.T.C.] and 6528 [D.T.C.]; see also *Supreme Theatres Ltd. v. R.*, [1981] C.T.C. 190, 81 D.T.C. 5136 (Fed. T.D.) at 193 [C.T.C.] and 5138 [D.T.C.] *per* Gibson J. (F.C.T.D.); *Queen & Metcalfe Carpark Ltd. v. Minister of National Revenue*, [1973] C.T.C. 810, 74 D.T.C. 6007 (Fed. T.D.) at 817-18 [C.T.C.] and 6011 [D.T.C.] *per* Sweet D.J.; *Calvin Bullock Ltd. v. Minister of National Revenue*, [1985] 1 C.T.C. 2309, 85 D.T.C. 287 (T.C.C.) at 2312 [C.T.C.] and 289 [D.T.C.] *per* St-Onge T.C.J.; *No. 585 v. Minister of National Revenue* (1958), 21 Tax A.B.C. 56, 58 D.T.C. 754 (Can. Tax App. Bd.) at 66 [Tax AB.C.] and 759 [D.T.C.] *per* Mr. Boisvert; *Tenir Ltée v. Minister of National Revenue*, [1968] Tax A.B.C. 772, 68 D.T.C. 589 (Can. Tax App. Bd.) at 595 [D.T.C.] *per* Mr. Davis; *SBI Properties Ltd. v. Minister of National Revenue*, [1981] C.T.C. 2288, 81 D.T.C. 263 (T.R.B.) at 2297 [C.T.C.] and 270-271 [D.T.C.] *per* Mr. St-Onge; *King George Hotels Ltd. et al. v. The Queen*, [1981] C.T.C. 78 (Fed. T.D.) at 80, *per* Smith D.J.; affirmed [1981] C.T.C. 87, 81 D.T.C. 5082 (Fed. C.A.).

Traditionally, a corporation carrying on activities described in the objects clause (if any) of its constating documents is presumed to earn income from business. The presumption appears as early as 1880 in *Smith v. Anderson*:[66]

> You cannot acquire gain by means of a company except by carrying on some business or other, and I have no doubt if any one formed a company or association for the purpose of acquiring gain, he must form it for the purpose of carrying on a business by which gain is to be obtained.

But these judicial statements were born of a foreign tax system with a different structure. It is less clear whether corporations created in jurisdictions that do not require objects clauses should also be subject to this presumption.[67]

One answer is that the rebuttable presumption applies to all corporations, but that it is more readily rebuttable in the case of private corporations that pay the Part IV tax on their investment income.[68]

a) — Real Estate

The issue in characterizing rental income from real estate is whether the income results from activity and services associated with a commercial enterprise or from passive ownership of the property with only minimal ancillary activity. Income that derives from passive ownership of real estate is investment income. Income that flows from the use of real estate as an asset in a commercial endeavor is business income.[69]

The critical test in distinguishing an investment in real estate from a real estate business is the level of services provided as a supplement to the rental of the real property.[70] The greater the level of services that one provides as an adjunct to the rental of real estate, the greater the likelihood that the income therefrom is business income.[71] The distinction does

---

[66]*Smith v. Anderson* (1880), 15 Ch. D. 247 (C.A.) at 260.

[67]*Smith v. Anderson, ante*, at 530-31.

[68]See Chapter 19, "Corporate Investment Income" for a discussion of the Part IV tax and the statutory scheme in connection therewith.

[69]*Martin v. Minister of National Revenue*, [1948] C.T.C. 189, 3 D.T.C. 1199 (Can. Ex. Ct.) at 193 [C.T.C.] and 1201 [D.T.C.].

[70]The phrase "mere [sic] investment" has sometimes been used to describe a passive investment that gives rise to income from property. See, e.g., *Marks v. Minister of National Revenue* (1962), 30 Tax A.B.C. 155, 62 D.T.C. 536 (Can. Tax App. Bd.).

[71]*Fry v. Salisbury House Estate Ltd.*, [1930] A.C. 432 (H.L.) at 470 (management company operated elevators, provided porters, security guards, heating and cleaning at extra charge; property ownership, not trade); see also *Crofts v. Sywell Aerodrome Ltd.*, [1942] 1 K.B. 317 (C.A.) (activities, though

not rest on any single criterion but upon an assessment of the aggregate level of activity associated with the generation of the income. One factor may outweigh several others, but it is always a facts and circumstances test.

Here, as elsewhere in tax law, it is easy to characterize at either extreme of the spectrum. For example, a traditional hotel rents its guests more than a room. Hotels usually provide services, such as, laundry, food, cleaning, and entertainment facilities. In contrast a tenant in an apartment usually rents only space with minimal services. The distinction is less clear, however, between an apartment that provides extensive ancillary services and a hotel that makes minimal provision beyond accommodation. The provision of maid, linen, laundry and food services, for example, suggests business. In contrast, routine and necessary ancillary services, such as heating, cleaning and snow removal, are seen as mere adjuncts to the ownership of property. In either case, time spent on managing the property is not the determining factor.[72]

b) — Short-Term Investments

The characterization of income from short-term investments raises more subtle distinctions. The issue is particularly important for Canadian corporations because of the special rules in respect of the small business deduction, the manufacturing and processing credit, and the refundable dividend tax on investment income.

The small business deduction and the manufacturing and processing credit may only be claimed on Canadian "active business" income. Income must first qualify as business income before it can be characterized as "active" business income. The refundable tax on

---

varied and extensive, consisted of exercise and exploitation of property rights of aerodrome); *Malenfant v. Minister of National Revenue*, [1992] 2 C.T.C. 2431, 92 D.T.C. 2097 (T.C.C.) (income from hotel and motel rooms was income from rental property as services provided were only those required to maintain rooms).

[72]See, e.g., the comments of Thurlow J., in *Wertman v. Minister of National Revenue*, [1964] C.T.C. 252 (Can. Ex. Ct.) at 267 [C.T.C.] and 5167 [D.T.C.]:

> The nature of the services provided, in my opinion, also has a bearing on the question; some, such as maid service and linen and laundry service, being more indicative of a business operation than the heating of the building which, in my view, is so closely concerned with the property itself as to offer no definite indication one way or the other. Nor do I think that the fact that the management of the property occupies the appellant's time or the fact that he uses his car to go to and from the property indicate that the operation is a business, for, at most, these facts indicate that he renders a service to himself and to the other owners of the building which, so far as charged for, represents a proper outgoing against revenue for the purpose of ascertaining the net profit divisible among the owners regardless of whether the rentals are mere income from property or income from a business.

income from property may only be claimed on "investment income" earned by a Canadian-controlled private corporation.[73]

(i) — Integration Test

An "active business" is ". . . *any* business carried on by the taxpayer *other than* a specified investment business or a personal services business . . ."[74] and for some purposes ". . . includes an adventure or concern in the nature of trade."[75]

"Investment income" is ". . . income for the year from a source . . . that is property. . . ."

The characterization of a taxpayer's income from short-term investments involves a two-step process:

> 1. Determine whether the taxpayer's investments are an integral part of his or her business activities. If they are, income from the investments is business income; and

> 2. If they are not, determine whether the taxpayer's investment activities constitute a separate business. If they do, the income from those activities is business income. If the investment activity does not constitute a separate business, the income from those activities is income from property.

(ii) — "Employed and Risked" Test

A taxpayer's investments are considered to be an integral part of a business if his or her funds are "employed and risked" in the business.[76] Is the making of investments a part of

---

[73]See Chapter 19, "Corporate Investment Income".

[74]Subs. 248(1) "active business".

[75]Subs. 125(7) "active business".

[76]See *R. v. Ensite Ltd.*, [1986] 2 S.C.R. 509, [1986] 2 C.T.C. 459, 86 D.T.C. 6521 (S.C.C.) at 529 [S.C.R.], 468 [C.T.C.] and 6528 [D.T.C.]; (property yielding interest must be linked to some "definite obligation or liability of the business"); *Bank Line Ltd. v. I.R.C.* (1974), 49 Tax Cas. 307 (Scot. Ct. of Sess.) (no actual risk or employment of reserve funds in the company's business of owning, operating and replacing ships). In *R. v. Marsh & McLennan Ltd.*, [1983] C.T.C. 231, 83 D.T.C. 5180 (Fed. C.A.), for example, the taxpayer, an insurance broker, temporarily invested its insurance premiums in short-term paper. The taxpayer could do so because of the lag between the time that it received a premium from its customer and the time that it remitted the premium to the customer's insurer. The taxpayer's business involved two dimensions: brokerage and investment. The two activities were so interdependent that its investments were an integral part of its business; hence, its investment income was income from a business and *not* income from property. See also the speech of Lord Mersey in *Liverpool & London & Globe Ins. Co. v. Bennett* (1913), 6 Tax Cas. 327 (H.L.) at 379-80:

the mode of conducting the business? If the answer is yes, then the income from the investments is part of the income of the business.

Business income from investments represents the fruit derived from a fund "employed and risked" in the taxpayer's business. Thus, the temporary investment of working capital constitutes an intrinsic part of the business.

(iii) — Separate Business Test

Where a taxpayer's investments are not an integral part of his or her business operations, the question arises whether the investment activities constitute a separate business.[77] The answer to this question depends upon several factors:

- The number and value of transactions;
- The time devoted to investment activities;

It is said that the dividends in question are derived from investments made . . . and that such investments form no part of the "business" of the Company. In my opinion there is no foundation either in fact or in law for this contention. It is well known that in the course of carrying on an insurance business, large sums of money derived from premiums collected and from other sources accumulate in the hands of the insurers, and that one of the most important parts of the profits of the business is derived from the temporary investment of these moneys. These temporary investments are also required for the formation of the reserve fund, a fund created to attract customers and to serve as a standby in the event of sudden claims being made upon the insurers in respect of losses. It is, according to my view, impossible to say that such investments do not form part of this Company's insurance business, or that the returns flowing from them do not form part of its profits. In a commercial sense the directors of the Company owe a duty to their shareholders and to their customers to make such investments, and to receive and distribute in the ordinary course of business, whether in the form of dividends, or in payment of losses, or in the formation of reserves, the moneys collected from them.

[77]*Canadian Marconi Co. v. R.*, [1986] 2 S.C.R. 522, [1986] 2 C.T.C. 465, 86 D.T.C. 6526 (S.C.C.). The taxpayer, a manufacturer of electronic equipment, divested itself of its broadcasting division and found itself with surplus funds of approximately $20 million. While awaiting a suitable opportunity to invest in another business, the taxpayer invested these surplus funds in short-term, interest-bearing securities. During the period under assessment, the taxpayer earned substantial interest income (approximately $5 million) on which it claimed the manufacturing and processing credit on the basis that its income from its short-term investments represented "business income" and, therefore, "active business income". In deciding in favour of the taxpayer, the Supreme Court applied the presumption that income that a corporate taxpayer earns is business income. The facts fell short of supporting the Minister's contention that he rebutted the presumption. See also *Colonial Realty Services Ltd. v. Minister of National Revenue*, [1987] 1 C.T.C. 2343, 87 D.T.C. 259 (T.C.C.) (excess funds placed in investment certificates; no corporate activity or circumstances converted the yield to active business income).

- The relationship between the taxpayer's investment income and his or her total income; and

- The relationship between the value of the taxpayer's investment and the total value of his or her assets.

Is the taxpayer merely managing personal investments or carrying on an investment business? The greater the amount of time devoted to, and the greater the value of, investment activities as compared to business activities, the more likely it is that the investment segment constitutes a separate business.

II. — Conclusion

It should be clear by now that the classification of income by source causes enormous complexity in the tax system. Different rules govern each of the sources of income, each of which requires strict legislative supervision. Taxpayers, understandably, try to move income into categories that attract lower tax and losses into sources that are taxed at higher rates. Hence, the thousands of disputes that involve capital gains and business income. Conversely, and equally understandably, the Agency is likely to see losses as capital, and not as business losses, in order to protect the tax base. Throughout subsequent chapters, we will see how the Act seeks to protect the boundaries of each of the sources to prevent leakage between the various categories.

Selected Bibliography to Chapter 7

General

Anderson, William D., "A Potpourri of Elements in Computing Business Income: Part 2", *Corporate Management Tax Conf.* 6:1 (Can. Tax Foundation, 1987).

Carr, Brian R., "A Potpourri of Elements in Computing Business Income: Part 1", *Corporate Management Tax Conf.* 5:1 (Can. Tax Foundation, 1987).

Drache, A.B.C., "A Dog is Not a Horse or a Fish" (1991) XIII Can. Taxpayer 135.

Durnford, John, "The Distinction Between Income From Business and Income From Property and the Concept of Carrying on Business" (1991) 39 Can. Tax J. 1131.

Harris, Edwin C., "Measuring Business Income", in *Proceedings of 19th Tax Conf.* 78 (Can. Tax Foundation, 1967).

Khan, D. and B. Sakich, "Business Income" (1985) 13 Can. Tax News 90.

McGregor, Ian, "Another Look at First Principles" (1962) 10 Can. Tax J. 65.

Roberts, J.R. and William Leiss, "Technology and Accounting Innovation: Can They Mesh?", in *Proceedings of 38th Tax Conf.* 25 (Can. Tax Foundation, 1986).

Characterization of Income

Brayley, C.A.M., "Income or Capital — The Spin of a Coin" (1986) 8 Sup. Ct. L.R. 405.

Boyle, J. Ladson, "What is a Trade or Business?" (1986), 39 The Tax Lawyer 737.

Corn, George, "Interest Income: Business Income or Investment Income" (1992) Can. Current Tax J141.

Corn, George, "Reasonable Expectation of Profit" (1994) Can. Current Tax J61.

Corn, George, "Taxation of Gain on Appreciation of Shares — Capital Gain or Income from an Adventure in the Nature of Trade" (1994) Can. Current Tax J39.

Craig, J.D., "Other than in the Ordinary Course of Business" (1980) 54 Cost and Management 45.

Drache, A.B.C., "Opting to Be a Market Trader" (1991) XIII Can. Taxpayer 175.

Durnford, John W., "Profits on the Sale of Shares: Capital Gains or Business Income — A Fresh Look at Irrigation Industries" (1987) 35 Can. Tax J. 837.

Durnford, John W., "The Distinction Between Income from Business and Income from Property, and the Concept of Carrying on Business" (1991) 39 Can. Tax J. 1131.

Hodgson, John, "What is Income? What is Capital?" (1988) 7 The Philanthropist 24.

Karp, "Rental Income: Property or Business?" (1968) 16 Can. Tax J. 191.

Krishna, Vern, "Characterization of 'Income from Business' and 'Income from Property'" (1984) 1 Can. Current Tax C-37.

Krishna, Vern, "Sale of Franchises: Receipts on Account of Eligible Capital Property or Income from Business?" (1986) 1 Can. Current Tax J-157.

Ladson, Boyle F., "What Is a Trade or Business?" (1986) 39 Tax Lawyer 737.

McDonnell, T.E., "Interest Income: Whether Income from Active Business or Income from Property" (1986) 34 Can. Tax J. 1431.

McGregor, Ian, "Capital Gainsay" (1964) 12 Can. Tax J. 116.

McGregor, Ian, "Secondary Intention" (1961) 9 Can. Tax J. 33.

McKie, A.B., "Properly Taxing Property" (1988) 2 Can. Current Tax C-91.

McLean, Bruce M., "Sourcing of Business Income", *Corporate Management Tax Conf.* 9:1 (Can. Tax Foundation, 1987).

Morris, D. Bernard, "Capital versus Income: Loans and Real Estate" (1992) Can. Tax Foundation 26:1.

Motz, Robert, "Employee vs. Independent Contractor", (November 1990) 64 CMA Magazine 26.

Richards, Gabrielle M.R., "Quick Flips as Adventure in Nature of Trade" (1993) Can. Current Tax J9.

Richardson, Elinore J., "Holding Real Estate for the Production of Income", *Corporate Management Tax Conf.* 1 (Can. Tax Foundation, 1983).

Strother, Robert C., "Income Tax Implications of Personal-Use Real Estate", *Corporate Management Tax Conf.* 59 (Can. Tax Foundation, 1983).

Thomas, Richard B., "Reasonable Expectation of Profit: Are Revenue Canada's and the Court's Expectations Unreasonable?" (1993) 41 Can. Tax J. 1128.

Warnock, Bruce A., "Income or Capital Gains on Dispositions of Property", in *Proceedings of 42nd Tax Conf.* 48:1 (Can. Tax Foundation, 1990).

Measurement of Income

Arnold, Brian J., "Timing and Income Taxation: The Principles of Income Management for Tax Purposes", in *Proceedings of 35th Tax Conf.* 133 (Can. Tax Foundation, 1983).

Harris, Edwin C., "Measuring Business Income", in *Proceedings of 19th Tax Conf.* 78 (Can. Tax Foundation, 1967).

Drobny, Sheldon, "Inventory and Accounting Methods: Controversy and Paradoxes" (October 1990) 68 Taxes 764.

Kaplow, L. and A.C. Warren, "The Bankruptcy of Conventional Tax Timing Wisdom is Deeper Than Semantics: A Rejoinder to Professors Kaplow and Warren, [Discussion of An Income Tax By Any Other Name — A Reply to Professor Strand]" (1986) 38 Stan. L. Rev. 399.

Robertson, D.A., "Timing is Everything" (1988) 121:3 CA Magazine 32.

Strand, J., "Tax Timing and the Haig-Simons Ideal: A Rejoinder to Professor Popkin [Discussion of Tax Ideals in the Real World: A Comment on Professor Strand's Approach to Tax Fairness]" (1986) 62 Ind. L.J. 73.

White, Robert, "Profits and Prophets — An Accountant's Afterword" (1987) 8 Br. Tax Rev. 292.

Other

Beninger, Michael, J., "The Scope and Application of Section 79 of the *Income Tax Act*" (1985) 33 Can. Tax J. 929.

Bernstein, Jack, "Hotels and Motels as Tax Shelters" (1983) 116:10 CA Magazine 1972.

Burke, Harold A., "Real Estate Breakups: Tax, Valuation, and Division Issues", in *Proceedings of 38th Tax Conf.* 43 (Can. Tax Foundation, 1986).

Crawford, R.W., "Sales of Real Estate: Tax Planning for the Seller", *Corporate Management Tax Conf.* 138 (Can. Tax Foundation, 1983).

Curtis, "Isolation, Intention and Income", in *Legal Essays in Honour of Arthur Moxon* 239 (University of Toronto Press, 1953).

"Deferred Compensation: Diabolus Ex Machina", *Can. Tax Letter*, November 25, 1983 (De Boo).

Drache, A.B.C., "Renewed Attack on Management Companies" (1983) 5 Can. Taxpayer 157.

Dwyer, Blair P., "Deductibility of Tenant Inducement Payments" (1987-89) Can. Current Tax C53.

Krishna, Vern, "Does Supreme Court Expand Deductibility of Business Expenses in *Symes*?" (1994) Can. Current Tax J35.

MacInnis, Ian V., "Deduction of Rental Losses Require Reasonable Expectation of Profit" (1990) 7 Business and the Law 39.

O'Brien, Martin L., "Commodity Trading — Convertible Hedges" (1994) Can. Current Tax J31.

Popkin, W.D., "Tax Ideals in the Real World: A Comment on Professor Strand's Approach to Tax Fairness, [Discussion of Taxation of Income from Capital — A Theoretical Reappraisal]" (1986-87) Ind. L.J. 63.

Valliere, Charles E., "Both Deduction and Capitalization Treatment Denied with respect to Real Estate that Produces No Income" (1991) 39 Can. Tax J. 1033.

Chapter 8 — Inclusions in Business and Investment Income

Table of Contents

I. — General Comment

Income from business or property is the "profit" therefrom. Although profit is generally determined according to accounting principles and commercial practice, the *Income Tax Act* does not rely completely upon such principles and practice. In certain circumstances, the Act specifies the manner in which income is to be calculated for tax purposes. For example, the Act specifies in section 12 that certain amounts are to be included in income for tax purposes, regardless of the manner in which the particular item is treated in accounting practice.

There are three main areas in which the tax statute varies from accounting:

- timing adjustments;
- modification of the common law concept of income; and
- clarification of uncertain issues in accounting practice.

II. — Timing Adjustments

"Profit" from business or property is generally calculated on an accrual basis of accounting. Paragraph 12(1)(b) of the Act reinforces this concept and requires a taxpayer to include in income in a year any receivables on account of goods sold or services rendered in the year, regardless of when the amounts are due or actually collected. An amount is considered "receivable" when the taxpayer completes the sale or service so that her right to receive the amount is perfected.

Generally accepted concepts of accrual accounting require inclusion in income only of amounts that have been earned. Unearned revenue is a liability and not income. For tax purposes, however, paragraph 12(1)(a) modifies the general accounting rule: *all* receipts, whether earned or unearned, are included in income for the year. Thus, a taxpayer must include an amount received on account of services to be rendered in the future in income in the year of receipt and not in the year in which he earns the income. The taxpayer may, however, claim a reserve against unearned income.[1]

---

[1]Para. 20(1)(m).

III. — Modification of Common Law Rules

A. — *Interest Income*

"Interest" is defined as the return or material consideration given for the use of money belonging to another person. Interest must be referable to a principal sum of money or an obligation to pay money.[2] Thus:[3]

> . . . there must be a sum of money by reference to which the payment which is said to be interest is to be ascertained. A payment cannot be "interest of money" unless there is the requisite "money" for the payment to be said to be "interest of".

Interest may vary with the gross revenues or profits of the borrower.[4] Amounts payable as a percentage of profit are less likely to constitute interest.[5] Profit percentage arrangements are more usually associated with a partnership relationship between the parties.[6]

Payments on account of interest are generally considered to be for the use of money over a period. Thus, in business and commerce, interest is the equivalent of a "rental" charge for the use of someone else's money. The common law, however, considers interest as an expenditure on account of capital. To overcome the judicial characterization of interest as a payment on account of capital, the Act specifically provides for the treatment of interest as an income or expense item.

There are several ways to account for interest income for tax purposes — the cash basis, modified cash basis, receivable basis, accrual basis and modified accrual basis. Different rules apply to individuals, corporations, and partnerships.

---

[2]*Saskatchewan (Attorney General) v. Canada (Attorney General)*, [1947] S.C.R. 394 (S.C.C.) at 411; affirmed [1949] A.C. 110 (Canada P.C.); *R. v. Melford Developments Inc.*, [1982] 2 S.C.R. 504, [1982] C.T.C. 330, 82 D.T.C. 6281 (S.C.C.); see also, *Halsbury's Laws of England*, 4th ed., vol. 32 (London: Butterworths, 1980) at 53, where "interest" is defined as ". . . the return or compensation for the use or retention by one person of a sum of money belonging to or owed to another. Interest accrues from day to day even if payable only at intervals. . . ." The CRA generally accepts these criteria in defining interest. See IT-533 (October 31, 2003) para. 1.

[3]*Euro Hotel (Belgravia) Ltd., Re*, [1975] 3 All E.R. 1075 (Eng. Ch. Div.) at 1084 *per* Megarry J.

[4]*Pooley v. Driver* (1876), 5 Ch. D. 458 (C.A.); *Cox v. Hickman* (1860), 11 E.R. 431 (H.L.); see *Partnerships Act*, R.S.O. 1990, c. P.5, para. 3(1)(d).

[5]See e.g., *Balaji Apartments Ltd. v. Manufacturers Life Insurance Co.* (1979), 25 O.R. (2d) 275 (Ont. H.C.).

[6]See e.g., *Sedgwick v. Minister of National Revenue*, [1962] C.T.C. 400, 62 D.T.C. 1253 (Can. Ex. Ct.).

For tax purposes, the term "receivable" means *legally* receivable and not "receivable" in the sense that one uses it in accrual accounting.[7] An amount is "receivable" for tax purposes only when the taxpayer has a clear legal right to it. The right must be legally enforceable. For example, assume a taxpayer buys a bond for $1,000 on December 1, and the bond pays interest at a rate of 12 percent per year payable at the end of May and November of each year. By December 31, the taxpayer will have earned 1/12 of her annual interest income. In accrual accounting, the taxpayer is considered to have *earned* $10 in the month of December even though she may not have received payment. The $10 would be accrued as a receivable for general accounting purposes. For tax purposes, however, the $10 is not a "receivable" because there is no legal obligation on the issuer of the bond to pay the interest as at December 31. The legal obligation to pay the interest will arise on the date stipulated in the bond contract, namely May 31.

a) — Consistency

A taxpayer who selects a particular method of reporting interest income for a particular property must conform to that method from year to year. Although a taxpayer is required to account for interest income on a consistent basis from year to year, there is no requirement that the taxpayer follow the same basis for reporting interest income from all investment sources. For example, a taxpayer may report interest income from a rental deposit on a cash basis and, in the same year, report interest income from a mortgage on a receivable basis.[8] Paragraph 12(1)(c) merely requires that interest from the *same source* be reported on a consistent basis — that is, interest from the same debtor on the same type of obligation.

b) — Annual Reporting

As a general rule, an individual may report interest income on a cash or accrual basis.[9] There are, however, special restrictions in respect of "investment contracts". Individuals must report income from "investment contracts every year on its anniversary date, regardless of whether or not the income has been paid out in the year.[10] The rule is intended to prevent prolonged deferral of tax on investment income.

---

[7]*Minister of National Revenue v. John Colford Contracting Co.*, [1962] S.C.R. viii, [1962] C.T.C. 546, 62 D.T.C. 1338 (S.C.C.).

[8]*Industrial Mortgage & Trust Co. v. Minister of National Revenue*, [1958] C.T.C. 106, 58 D.T.C. 1060 (Can. Ex. Ct.); see also IT-396R, "Interest Income" (May 29, 1984).

[9]Para. 12(1)(c).

[10]Subs. 12(4). See also, subs. 12(3) for corporations, partnerships, and trusts.

An "investment contract" is a debt such as a note, bond, debenture, or guaranteed investment contract. An "investment contract" does not include the following:[11]

- Salary deferral arrangements;

- Income bonds and debentures;

- Retirement compensation arrangements;

- Employee benefit plans;

- Small business development bonds;

- Small business bonds; or

- Debt obligations in respect of which the taxpayer has included in his investment income at least annually.

c) — Blended Payments

A taxpayer is *not* obliged to charge interest on money loaned to another.[12] Interest, however, may be blended into principal, in which case it must be segregated and included in income for tax purposes.[13] A blended payment is a single payment in which interest and principal are blended into one amount on repayment of a loan.[14] Whether a payment is blended is a question of fact that depends upon the terms of the contract.

Interest and principal may be blended by issuing a debt instrument at a discount and redeeming it at its face value upon maturity. Government Treasury Bills, for example, do not stipulate any interest rate or amount on their face, but are issued at a discount from their face value. The discount rate is a direct function of the prevailing interest rate. The substance of the transaction is that the redemption value is, in effect, made up of principal and interest. Thus, payment on maturity must be broken down into its interest and principal components.[15]

---

[11]Subs. 12(11) definition of "investment contract".

[12]*Minister of National Revenue v. Groulx*, [1966] C.T.C. 115, 66 D.T.C. 5126 (Can. Ex. Ct.); affirmed [1967] C.T.C. 422, 67 D.T.C. 5284 (S.C.C.). Note, however, that the recipient of an interest-free loan may be taxable on the benefit imputed on the loan; see s. 80.4.

[13]Subs. 16(1).

[14]See generally, IT-265R3 "Payments of Income and Capital Combined" (October 7, 1991) (now archived by the CRA as being out of date).

[15]*O'Neil v. Minister of National Revenue* (1991), 91 D.T.C. 692 (T.C.C.); see also *Beck v. Lord Howard de Walden*, [1940] T.R. 143; *Lomax v. Peter Dixon & Sons Ltd.*, [1943] 1 K.B. 671 (Eng. C.A.).

Whether an amount represents a blended payment of interest and principal is a question of fact that is determined by the terms of the agreement, the course of the negotiation between the parties and, of particular importance, the price at which the property is sold in the context of market prices.

d) — Discounts

(i) — Rate Adjustments

It is important to distinguish between effective and nominal interest yields. A corporation can issue debt instruments at a discount to their face value. The discount plus the "coupon rate" (i.e., the nominal rate of interest on the face of the debt instrument) combine to produce the overall "effective" rate of return or "yield" of the instrument. Thus, a debt instrument issued at a discount effectively raises its rate of interest. For example, if a corporation issues a one year $1,000 bond with a nominal rate of interest of 10 percent at $960, the effective rate of interest or yield to the bondholder is 14 percent ($100 interest plus $40 discount). (See example below.) Hence, discounting the issue price of a bond is simply another way of changing the effective rate of interest on the bond.

Example

Assume that S Ltd. issued bonds on April 28, 2006 at a price of $88.38. The bonds have a coupon rate of 6.75 percent and will mature on June 4, 2020.

Then:

Nominal rate	= 6.75%	($67.50 per $1,000 bond)
Effective rate (yield)	= 8.15%	
Discount on bond	= $11.62	

The common law, however, does not consider the discount on a bond as interest. Instead, it characterizes the spread between the issue price and the face value of a bond as a capital gain.[16] Hence, the common law rules invite corporations to convert interest income into

---

[16]*Wood v. Minister of National Revenue*, [1969] S.C.R. 330, [1969] C.T.C. 57, 69 D.T.C. 5073 (S.C.C.).

capital gains. The Minister of Finance described the difficulties of this interpretation in his budget speech of December 20, 1960:

> Unfortunately, increasing use is deliberately being made of a device to pay bondholders the equivalent of interest in a form that is tax-free. If a borrower issues a one-year $100 bond for, say, $96 and the bond bears a coupon rate of 1 percent, the bondholder will receive $4 more than he paid for it when the bond matures at the end of the year. This excess over purchase price, plus the $1 in interest, will give the lender a 5.2 percent return on his investment but it has been found difficult to collect tax on more than the $1 designated as interest.

The Act modifies the common law rule. The rules in respect of bond discounts vary depending upon the tax status of the issuer of the bond.

1. — Tax-Exempt Organizations

Where a tax-exempt organization, a non-resident person not carrying on business in Canada, or a governmental body issues a bond at a "deep discount", the *entire* discount is income in the hands of the first taxable Canadian resident who holds the bond.[17] A bond has a "deep discount" if the effective rate of interest on the bond exceeds the nominal rate by more than one-third.

2. — Taxable Entities

Where a taxable entity issues a bond at a discount, a purchaser of the bond can treat the difference between the issue price and its par value as a capital gain. If the discount is a "deep discount", the taxable entity issuing the bond can deduct only one-half of the discount as interest expense. If the discount is "shallow" (i.e., the effective rate of interest does *not* exceed the nominal rate by more than one-third and it is not issued at less than 97 percent of its maturity value), the taxable entity can deduct the entire discount.[18]

Example
Assume:
A municipality issues bonds with a face value of $1,000 (coupon rate of 4.5 percent, maturity five years) at a price of $930.
Then:

---

[17]Subs. 16(3).

[18]Para. 20(1)(f).

Example

Nominal rate	4.50 %
Effective rate (yield)	(6.14)
	_____
Difference	1.64 %

Since 6.14 percent is more than 4/3 × 4.50 percent, the *entire* discount of $70 per bond is income in the hands of the first Canadian resident, taxable owner of the bond.

Example

	Shallow Discount	Deep Discount
Issue price of bond	$ 990	$ 960
Nominal rate of interest	8 %	8 %
Effective rate of interest	10 %	12 %
Discount on bond	10	40
Amount deductible by issuer &	$ 10	$ 20

IV. — Variations from Accounting Practice

A. — Payments Based on Production or Use of Property

One can determine the selling price of a property in several ways. The parties can fix the price at the time that they enter into the agreement of purchase and sale. Alternatively, parties may set the price by reference to a formula based upon production from, or use of, the property. For example, a taxpayer may sell land containing sand for a fixed amount of

$15,000 or on the basis that the purchaser shall pay 5 cents for every ton of sand extracted from the land. The fixed payment of $15,000 would be on account of capital. In the latter case, the sale price depends upon the quantity of sand taken from the land, and the total price is not determined until all of the sand is extracted. The payments would normally be considered income.

Paragraph 12(1)(g) provides that a taxpayer must include in income all amounts that he receives that depend upon the use of, or production from, property. In the above example, if the purchaser of the land extracts 300,000 tons, he will pay $15,000 to the seller, which will be income. This rule prevents taxpayers from converting what would otherwise be fully taxable rent or royalty income into capital. Subsection 12(2.01) ensures that one cannot use the paragraph to defer tax to the date of receipt if the amount would be includable in income on an accrual basis under section 9.

The rationale of the statutory structure is captured in the following analysis by Rowlatt J. in *Jones v. Inland Revenue Commissioners*:[19]

> There is no law of nature or any invariable principle that because it can be said that a certain payment is consideration for the transfer of property it must be looked upon as price in the character of principal. In each case, regard must be had to what the sum is. A man may sell his property for a sum which is to be paid in instalments, and when that is the case the payments to him are not income: *Foley v. Fletcher* (1858), 3 H. & N. 769. Or a man may sell his property for an annuity. In that case the *Income Tax Act* applies. Again, a man may sell his property for what looks like an annuity, but which can be seen to be, not a transmutation of a principal sum into an annuity, but in fact, a principal sum payment which is being spread over a period and is being paid with interest calculated in a way familiar to actuaries — in such a case, income tax is not payable on what is really capital: *Secretary of State [in Council of] India v. Scoble*, [1903] A.C. 299 (H.L.). On the other hand, a man may sell his property nakedly for a share of the profits of the business. In that case the share of the profits of the business would be the price, but it would bear the character of income in the vendor's hands. *Chadwick v. Pearl Life Assurance Co.*, [1905] 2 K.B. 507 and 514, was a case of that kind. In such a case the man bargains to have, not a capital sum but an income secured to him, namely, an income corresponding to the rent which he had before. I think, therefore, that what I have to do is to see what the sum payable in this case really is.

Examples:

- A sells land containing 300,000 tons of sand for $15,000. The purchase price is payable at a rate of $5,000 per year for three years.

  Paragraph 12(1)(g) does *not* apply to the transaction. The payments are not related to the "use of" or "production from" property.

---

[19][1920] 1 K.B. 711 (Eng. K.B.).

- B sells land containing sand to X. The sale price is determined at 5 cents per ton of sand extracted over the next three years. X extracts 300,000 tons and pays the vendor $15,000.

  Paragraph 12(1)(g) applies; the $15,000 is income to B.

- C sells land containing sand to Y. The sale price is determined at 5 cents per ton of sand extracted in the next three years, provided that the total price cannot exceed $10,000. Y extracts 300,000 tons and pays C $10,000.

  Paragraph 12(1)(g) applies; the $10,000 is income to C. The payment depends upon production from property.

- D sells land containing sand to Z. The sale price is determined at 5 cents per ton of sand extracted in the next three years but *not to be less than* $10,000. In fact, Y extracts 300,000 tons and pays $15,000.

  Paragraph 12(1)(g) does *not* apply to the $10,000 since this amount does not depend upon production; $5,000 is included in D's income by paragraph 12(1)(g).

B. — Stock Dividends

Dividends are income from property in the hands of a passive investor and income from business in the hands of a taxpayer who is in the investment business. For most tax purposes, a "dividend" includes stock dividends.[20] Stock dividends paid to a corporation or mutual fund trust by a non-resident corporation are excluded.

For accounting purposes, a stock dividend is simply the capitalization of retained earnings into share capital. It represents the transformation of one type of equity capital (retained earnings) into another type (share capital). A stock dividend does not have any income effect in accounting.

However, for tax purposes, a corporation can return capital to shareholders on a tax-free basis. Thus, section 12 includes stock dividends in income. But the tax treatment of dividend income, whether on account of investments or from business, is complicated by the potential of double taxation of such income. Thus, there is a special regime for the taxation of dividends that depends on:

- The status of the recipient;
- The source of the dividend; and
- The nature of the payer corporation.

These rules are examined later in the corporate context.

---

[20]Subs. 248(1) "dividend".

C. — Inducement Payments

An "inducement payment" is an economic incentive that is intended to lead or persuade a person to perform a particular action or decision. Examples include government subsidies to business to locate in a particular place, landlord inducements to tenants to sign a lease in a shopping plaza, etc.

An inducement may be on account of capital or on account of income. For tax purposes, however, an inducement receipt, whether from a governmental or private organization, is taxable as income.[21] This is so whether the payment is a grant, subsidy, forgivable loan, deduction from tax, or other allowance. A taxpayer may, however, elect to treat an inducement payment as a reduction in the cost or capital cost of any property that he or she acquires with the payment.[22] The effect of such an election is that it allows the taxpayer to defer recognition of the income until such time as he disposes of the property.

V. — Other Inclusions in Income

Item	Statutory Reference	Comments
Amounts received for goods and services to be rendered in the future	subpara. 12(1)(a)(i)	
Amounts received for deposits on returnable items	subpara. 12(1)(a)(ii)	IT-165R (archived)
Amounts received for property sold or services rendered, due in a future tax year	para. 12(1)(b)	IT-129R, IT-170R
Amounts received as interest (or in lieu of interest) if not previously included	para. 12(1)(c)	IT-396R
Amount deducted in preceding year as a reserve for doubtful debts	para. 12(1)(d)	IT-442R; authorization for deduction in preceding year: 20(1)(l)

---

[21]Para. 12(1)(x).

[22]Subs. 53(2.1) and 13(7.4).

Item	Statutory Reference	Comments
Amounts deducted in preceding year as reserve for guarantee	paras. 12(1)(d.1); 20(1)(l.1)	authorization for deduction: 20(1)(l.1)
Amount deducted in preceding year as a reserve for:	subpara. 12(1)(e)(i)	IT-154R; authorization for deduction in preceding year
* deposits on returnable containers	subpara. 20(1)(m)(iv)	
* goods delivered and services performed after end of year	subparas. 20(1)(m)(i), (ii); subs. 20(6)	
* a manufacturer's warranty	para. 20(1)(m.1)	
* prepaid rent	subpara. 20(1)(m)(iii)	
* policies of an insurer	para. 20(7)(c)	
Amount deducted in preceding year as unpaid amounts	subpara. 12(1)(e)(ii)	IT-154R; authorization for deduction in preceding year: para. 20(1)(n)
Insurance proceeds used to repair depreciable property	para. 12(1)(f)	costs of repairs deductible from income
Amounts received based on production or use of property disposed	para. 12(1)(g) ss. 12(2.01)	IT-426R, IT-462; exception: sale of agricultural land
Amount deducted in preceding year for quadrennial survey	para. 12(1)(h)	authorization for deduction in preceding year: para. 20(1)(o)

Item	Statutory Reference	Comments
Recovered bad debts, previously deducted	para. 12(1)(i)	IT-442R authorization for deduction in previous years: paras. 20(1)(l), (p), subs. 20(4)
Dividends from corporations resident in Canada and other corporations	paras. 12(1)(j), (k)	IT-67R3, IT-269R3
Income from partnership	para. 12(1)(l)	IT-278R2
Income from trusts	para. 12(1)(m)	
Benefits from profit-sharing plan and employee trust to employer	paras. 12(1)(n)	IT-502
Net amounts received from employee benefit plan	para. 12(1)(n.1)	IT-502
Royalties paid or payable to government authority	paras. 12(1)(o); 12(1)(x.2)	IT-438R2
Amount received under *Western Grain Stabilization Act*	para. 12(1)(p)	deduction of amount: para. 20(1)(ff)
Amount deducted for employment tax	para. 12(1)(q)	inoperative paragraph
Cost of inventory at year-end representing an allowance for depreciation	para. 12(1)(r)	
Reinsurer must include maximum amount which insurer may claim as reserve	s. 18(9.02)	insurer's reserve: para. 20(7)(c)

Item	Statutory Reference	Comments
Amount deducted as investment tax credit if not previously included	para. 12(1)(t)	IT-210R2, IC 78-4R3
Government of Canada grant for home insulation or energy income conversion	para. 12(1)(u)	for property used principally for earning income from business or property
Forfeited salary deferral amounts	para. 12(1)(n.2)	
Amounts received from retirement compensation arrangement	para. 12(1)(n.3)	
Amount of negative balance arrived at in scientific research deduction	para. 12(1)(v)	IT-151R5; calculation for research made under subs. 37(1)
Benefit received from non-interest bearing or low interest loan by virtue of services performed by corporation carrying on a personal services business	para. 12(1)(w)	IT-421R2; deemed taxable benefit by subs. 80.4(1)
Inducement or assistance payments	para. 12(1)(x); *French Shoes Ltd. v. The Queen*, [1986] 2 C.T.C. 132, 86 D.T.C. 6359 (Fed. T.D.)	all amounts received not already included in income or deducted from the cost of certain property.
Cash bonus on Canada Savings Bonds	s. 12.1	IT-396R
Certain amount in respect of fuel tax rebates under *Excise Tax Act*	para. 12(1)(x.1)	
Automobile provided to partner	para. 12(1)(y)	IT-63R5

Item	Statutory Reference	Comments
Amateur athlete trust payments	para. 12(1)(z)	required by s. 143.1 to be included in income
Proceeds of a right to receive production	s. 12(i)(g.1)	Matchable expenditures subs. 18.1(6)
Debts for disposition of eligible capital property written off and later recovered	s. 12(1)(i.1)	IT-442R subs. 20(4.2)
Amounts from foreign corporations, foreign trusts & foreign investment entities	s. 12(1)(k)	ss. 90 to 95
Amounts paid to foreign governments for oil & gas production	s. 12(1)(o.1)	Amounts treated as eligible for foreign Tax Credits subs. 126(5) & (7)
Amounts received as beneficiary of Qualifying Environmental Trust	s. 12(1)(z.1)	subs. 107.3(1)
Amounts received as consideration from the disposition of a Qualifying Environmental Trust	s. 12(1)(z.2)	subs. 107.3(1)
Certain amounts related to debt forgiveness	s. 12(1)(z.3)	subs. 80(13) to (17)
Amounts related to eligible funeral arrangements	s. 12(1)(z.4)	subs. 148.1(3)
Refund of amounts for anti-dumping duties previously deducted	s. 12(1)(z.6)	para. 20(1)(vv)

Selected Bibliography to Chapter 8

General

Freedman, Judith, "Profit and Prophets — Law and Accountancy Practice on the Timing of Receipts — Recognition under the Earnings Basis (Schedule D, Cases I and II)" (1987) Brit. Tax Rev. 61.

Freedman, Judith, "Profit and Prophets — Law and Accountancy Practice on the Timing of Receipts — Recognition Under the Earnings Basis (Schedule D, Cases I and II), Continued" (1987) Brit. Tax Rev. 104.

Harris, Edwin C., "Timing of Income and Expense Items", *Corporate Management Tax Conf.* 84 (Can. Tax Foundation, 1975).

Knechtel, Ronald C., "Role of Generally Accepted Accounting Principles in Determining Income for Tax Purposes", in *Proceedings of 31st Tax Conf.* 845 (Can. Tax Foundation, 1979).

Krishna, Vern, "Conformity of Accounting Methods for Tax and Financial Statement Purposes: A Search for the 'Truer Picture' of Income" (1992) Can. Current Tax C95.

Perry, Harvey, "Federal Individual Income Tax: Taxable Income and Tax", *Tax Paper No. 89* 58 (Can. Tax Foundation, 1990).

Pickford, Barry W., "Tax Accounting for Contract Earnings", in *Proceedings of 31st Tax Conf.* 885 (Can. Tax Foundation, 1979).

Reed, "The Dilemma of Conformity: Tax and Financial Reporting", *Corporate Management Tax Conf.* 20 (Can. Tax Foundation, 1981).

"Timing of Receivables and Expenses for Tax Purposes", *Cana. Tax Letter*, January 3, 1977 (De Boo).

Tremblay, Richard G., "The Meaning of Earned Income in Sub-Paragraph 12(1)(a)(i)" [Case Comment: *Versatile Pacific Shipyards Inc. v. R.*, [1988] 2 C.T.C. 90 (Fed. C.A.)].

Interest Income

"Discounts, Premiums and Bonuses and the Repeal of IT-114: What Happens Now?" (1994) No. 1181 Tax Topics 1.

"Income Tax Treatment of Interest — What's Happening" (1995) No. 1181 Tax Topics 2.

Kraayeveld, Serena H., "Accrual Basis of Reporting Interest Income", *Prairie Provinces Tax Conf.* 245 (Can. Tax Foundation, 1983).

Razienne, Robert, "Accrual of Interest Income", in *Proceedings of 40th Tax Conf.* 23:1 (Can. Tax Foundation, 1988).

Ulmer, John M., "Taxation of Interest Income", in *Proceedings of 42nd Tax Conf.* 8:1 (Can. Tax Foundation, 1990).

Stock Dividends

Le Rossignol, Dan G., "Stock Dividends and Stock Options" (1979) 112 CA Magazine 67.

Ware, J.G., "Public Corporations — Stock Dividends", *Corporate Management Tax Conf.* 74 (Can. Tax Foundation, 1978).

Inducement Payments

Dwyer, Blair P., "Deductibility of Tenant Inducement Payments (Income Tax)" (1987–89) 2 Can. Current Tax C-53.

Harris, Neil H., "Tax Aspects of Condominium Conversions and Lease Inducement Payments to Recipients" (1986), in *Proceedings of 38th Tax Conf.* 45 (Can. Tax Foundation, 1986).

Ward, David A., and Neil Armstrong, "Corporate Taxation: Lease Inducement Payments" (1986) 5 Legal Alert 98.

Other

Burger, George, "International Aspects of the Taxation of Discounted Securities" (1987) 35 Can. Tax J. 1131.

Haney, M.A., "Payments Dependent on Use or Production: Paragraph 12(1)(g)" (1987) 35 Can. Tax J. 427.

Lawlor, "Income Debentures and Term-Preferred Shares" (1978) 26 Can. Tax J. 200.

Sohmer, David H., "Purchase and Sale of a Closely-Held Business (2)" (1979) 112 CA Magazine 70.

Chapter 9 — Deductions from Business and Investment Income

Table of Contents

Fundamentals of Canadian Income Tax Vol 1: Personal Tax

Table of Contents

Chapter 9 — Deductions from Business and Investment Income

Table of Contents

Table of Contents

I. — General Comment

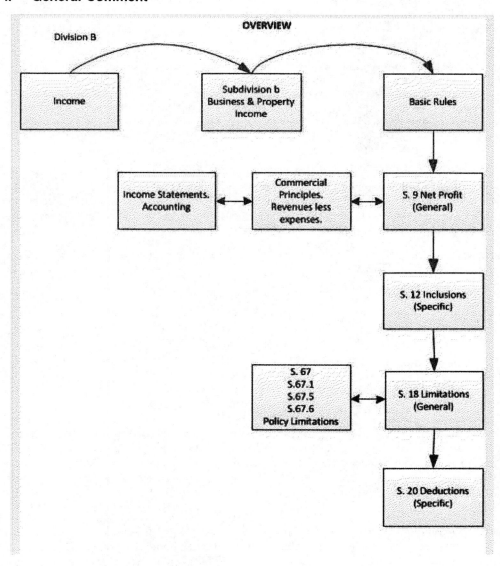

Income from business and property is taxable on a *net* basis. Thus, we need to determine which expenses are deductible from revenues in order to calculate net profit for tax purposes.

The calculation of net profit is essentially a question of law. However, we start the process by looking at commercial and accounting principles insofar as they do not conflict with specific statutory provisions or judicial decisions. *Royal Trust* explains the scheme for the deductibility of expenses as follows:

> Thus, it may be stated categorically that in a case under the *Income Tax Act* the first matter to be determined in deciding whether an outlay or expense is outside the prohibition of . . . [paragraph 18(1)(a)] of the Act is whether it was made or incurred by the taxpayer in accordance with the ordinary principles of commercial trading or well accepted principles of business practice. If it was not, that is the end of the matter. But if it was, then the outlay or expense is properly deductible unless it falls outside the expressed exception of . . . [paragraph 18(1)(a)] and, therefore, within its prohibition. . . .[1]

Thus, the analysis commences under subsection 9(1) to determine if an expense meets the threshold of deduction under commercial principles. The prohibitions in section 18 — such as, in paragraphs (a) and (h) — only come into play after the expense satisfies deduction under section 9. The Minister will often, incorrectly, assume as a fact that an expense is of a capital nature, which, in itself, is a question of law.

There are six general tests to determine whether expenditures are deductible as expenses from income. The expenditure must:

- Be of an income, and not a capital, nature (para. 18(1)(b));
- Be reasonable in amount (section 67);
- Be incurred for the purpose of earning income (para. 18(1)(a));
- Not be on account of personal expenses (para. 18(1)(h));
- Not be expressly prohibited by the Act (for example, para. 18(1)(c)); and
- Not be "abusive" tax avoidance (section 245).

Although there is no overall public policy prohibition on the deductibility of expenses,[2] there are many specific and detailed statutory provisions based on policy considerations. For example, the Act limits deductions for meals and entertainment to 50 percent incurred, even if incurred on account of business to account for the personal element of the total expense. Similarly, section 67.5 prohibits the deduction of illegal payments, section 67.6 prohibits the deduction of fines and penalties, even if incurred to earn business income.

The above limitations serve different purposes from those that generally accepted accounting and commercial principles serve. For example, the requirement that expenditures should be reasonable in amount is not an accounting rule, but a constraint to protect the govern-

---

[1]*Royal Trust Co. v. Minister of National Revenue* (1956), [1957] C.T.C. 32, 57 D.T.C. 1055 (Can. Ex. Ct.) at 42 [C.T.C.].

[2]*65302 British Columbia Ltd. v. R.*, [1999] 3 S.C.R. 804, [2000] 1 C.T.C. 57, 99 D.T.C. 5799 (S.C.C.).

ment's taxable base. The prohibition against the deductibility of expenses that the statute specifically proscribes allows the legislator to use it to foster socio-economic and public policies. The prohibition against deduction of bribes paid to foreign public officials is based more on moral values than economic considerations. The anti-abusive rule in section 245 is a broad "catch-all" clause for expenses and creative tax structures that the legislator could not think of and did not proscribe more specifically or anticipate, but which undermine the national tax base.

A. — Current Expense or Capital Expenditure?

a) — General Principles

For most purposes, the income tax is a tax on realized income from consummated transactions. The starting point is to determine whether an expenditure is on account of income or capital.

Only expenditures on account of income are currently deductible from revenues. Expenditures on account of capital are not currently deductible for tax purposes, but may be deducted in future periods.[3] This prohibition reinforces the commercial and accounting concept that income represents the excess of revenues expenses during a specified period.

Thus, an expense must satisfy two preliminary tests, purpose and timing: (1) one must incur the expenditure for the *purpose* of gaining or producing income from a business or property, and (2) the expense must be relevant to the *current* reporting period. These two requirements are interrelated:[4]

> Since the main purpose of every business undertaking is presumably to make a profit, any expenditure made "for the purpose of gaining or producing income" comes within the terms of [paragraph 18(1)(a)], whether it be classified as an income expense or a capital outlay.

> Once it is determined that a particular expenditure is one made for the purpose of gaining or producing income, in order to compute income tax liability it must next be determined whether such disbursement is an income expense or a capital outlay.

Expenditures that benefit more than one accounting period are generally capital outlays for accounting purposes. For example, expenditures on long-enduring assets — such as, goodwill, incorporation fees, patents, trademarks, buildings, and machinery are typically ex-

---

[3]Para. 18(1)(b).

[4]*British Columbia Electric Railway v. Minister of National Revenue*, [1958] S.C.R. 133, [1958] C.T.C. 21, 58 D.T.C. 1022 (S.C.C.).

penses of a capital nature. This distinction between current expenses and capital expenditures is central to the measurement of income.[5]

For tax and accounting purposes, we measure income for a finite period of time, usually annually. Thus, we must match revenues and expenses during a period. Expenditures that benefit subsequent fiscal periods are not current expenses, but capital outlays. As a statement of principle, this is straightforward enough. But how does one in law distinguish an expenditure that benefits the current period from one that benefits the future?

b) — Mixed Law and Fact

The *Income Tax Act* levies a tax on income and not on capital. The characterization of expenditures as current expenses on account of the income earning process or capital outlays is a question of mixed law and fact.[6] Characterization depends not upon the nature of property acquired[7] but upon the nature of the expenditure: what did the taxpayer actually expend the payment for?

There is no single definitive test for determining whether an expenditure is of a capital or revenue nature.[8] There are, however, several legal principles that distinguish between capital

---

[5]*Canderel Ltd. v. R.*, [1998] 1 S.C.R. 147, [1998] 2 C.T.C. 35, 98 D.T.C. 6100 (S.C.C.) (Tenant Inducement Payments constituted running expenses that could be deducted entirely in the year in which they were incurred; in attempting to assess a taxpayer's profit for tax purposes, the test is which method of accounting best depicts the reality of the financial situation of the particular taxpayer).

[6]*Johns-Manville Canada Inc. v. R.* (1985), [1985] 2 S.C.R. 46, [1985] 2 C.T.C. 111, 85 D.T.C. 5373 (S.C.C.); applied in *Gifford v. R.*, [2004] 1 S.C.R. 411, [2004] 2 C.T.C. 1, 2004 D.T.C. 6120 (Eng.) (S.C.C.) (financial advisor paid departing colleague $100,000 for his client list — i.e. goodwill with clients — and a non-compete agreement; payment on account of capital, thus interest on associated loan not deductible).

[7]*Golden Horse Shoe (New) Ltd. v. Thurgood*, [1934] 1 K.B. 548 (Eng. C.A.) at 563.

[8]*B.P. Australia Ltd. v. Commissioner of Taxation of the Commonwealth of Australia, infra.*

Chapter 9 — Deductions from Business and Investment Income

and revenue expenditures. One applies them flexibly to particular factual situations.[9] A test that may be useful in one set of circumstances may not be relevant in another.[10]

One principle has primacy:[11]

... where an expenditure is made, not only once and for all, but with a view to bringing into existence an asset or an advantage for the enduring benefit of a trade, I think that there is very good reason (in the absence of special circumstances leading to an opposite conclusion) for treating such an expenditure as properly attributable not to revenue but to capital.

The focus of the above test is on the purpose of the expenditure and not on the physical attributes of the particular property. The *purpose*, rather than the result, of an expenditure determines whether it is a capital outlay or a current expense.[12] Does one incur the expenditure for the purpose of bringing into existence an asset of enduring value? The physical

---

[9]*Johns-Manville Canada Inc. v. R.*, above note 6; *B.P. Australia Ltd. v. Commissioner of Taxation of the Commonwealth of Australia*, [1966] A.C. 224, [1965] 3 All E.R. 209 (Australia P.C.) (deductibility of amount paid to gas stations to secure monopoly of station, i.e., that it sell only B.P. gas in furtherance of marketing reorganization plan), approved by the Supreme Court of Canada in *Minister of National Revenue v. Algoma Central Railway*, [1968] S.C.R. 447, [1968] C.T.C. 161, 68 D.T.C. 5096 (S.C.C.) (Court agreed with test enunciated in *B.P. Australia Ltd.*, then decided without reasons); see also *Bowater Power Co. v. Minister of National Revenue*, [1971] C.T.C. 818, 71 D.T.C. 5469 (Fed. C.A.):

The solution, therefore, depends on what the expenditure is calculated to effect from a practical and business point of view, rather than upon the juristic classification of the legal rights, if any, secured, employed or exhausted in the process. The question of deductibility of expenses, must also, therefore, be considered from the standpoint of the company or its operations, as a practical matter.

[10]*Commissioner of Taxes v. Nchanga Consolidated Copper Mines Ltd.*, [1964] A.C. 948 (Rhodesia P.C.) at 959, per Lord Radcliffe (P.C.).

[11]*British Insulated & Helsby Cables Ltd. v. Atherton*, [1926] A.C. 205 (H.L.) at 213-14.

[12]*Hinton v. Maden & Ireland Ltd.* (1959), 38 Tax Cas. 391 (H.L.) (replacement cost of knives and lasts in shoe manufacturing machinery characterized as capital; equipment essential to functioning of plant); *MacMillan Bloedel (Alberni) Ltd. v. Minister of National Revenue*, [1973] C.T.C. 295, 73 D.T.C. 5264 (Fed. T.D.) (although fan belts and oil were operating costs deductible in maintaining fleet of trucks, tires lasting a year were not; tires comprising 10–15 percent of value of truck; truck purchased intact not in individual parts); *Oxford Shopping Centres Ltd. v. R.*, [1980] C.T.C. 7, 79 D.T.C. 5458 (Fed. T.D.); affirmed [1981] C.T.C. 128, 81 D.T.C. 5065 (Fed. C.A.) ("once and for all" payment by taxpayer to municipality to assist with road changes deductible); see also *Johns-Manville Canada Inc. v. R.*, [1982] C.T.C. 56, 82 D.T.C. 6054 (Fed. C.A.); reversed [1985] 2 C.T.C. 111 (S.C.C.) in which the Court stated:

I recognize that the regular recurrence of the acquisitions is relevant in determining whether the outlays for the lots are income or capital in nature. But it is in no way decisive. As Dixon J. (as he then was) put it in *Sun Newspapers Limited v. The Federal Commissioner of Taxation*

characteristics of the product of the expenditure do not determine its nature. For example, for General Motors the cost of manufacturing an automobile is an expense if it sells the automobile in the year (and it does not endure), but is on account of capital if it is not sold and remains in inventory at the end of the year. The recurrence of the expenditure is irrelevant.

Thus, annual expenditures are on account of capital if they are intended to bring into existence assets of enduring value — that is, if the assets have a life longer than a year. Conversely, a one-time expenditure is a current expense if it is intended that one consume the entire benefit of the expenditure in one fiscal period.

(i) — Enduring Benefit

"Enduring benefit" refers to benefits that endure in the sense that some assets have a life longer than one fiscal year. Benefits that accrue from saving payments over a number of years are not necessarily a capital asset. In *Anglo-Persian Oil Co. Ltd. v. Dale*, Rowlatt J. explained the distinction as follows:[13]

> . . . a benefit which endures, in the way that fixed capital endures; not a benefit that endures in the sense that for a good number of years it relieves you of a revenue payment. It means a thing, which endures in the way that fixed capital endures. It is not always an actual asset, but it endures in the way that getting rid of a lease or getting rid of onerous capital assets . . . endures.

The explanation is not entirely satisfactory. Note that Justice Rowlatt uses the word "endures" seven times to explain the meaning of "enduring", which suggests the difficulty of defining the concept.

One can also derive an enduring benefit from discharging a liability as from acquiring an asset.[14]

> . . . the disposition of a source of liability may be equivalent to the acquisition of a source of profit — an extension perhaps, but not an exception, to the principle that in some sense or other an asset of a capital nature, tangible or intangible, positive or negative, must be shown to be acquired.

The "enduring benefit" test is easier to state than it is to apply in practice. To be sure, it provides an answer in self-evident cases. Common sense and accounting principles tell us that a taxpayer who purchases a building for rental cannot write off its entire cost in the year

---

(1938), 61 C.L.R. 337 at page 362 ([Aust. HC]), "recurrence is not a test, it is no more than a consideration, the weight of which depends upon the nature of the expenditure".

[13]*Anglo-Persian Oil Co. Ltd. v. Dale* (1931), 16 Tax Cas. 253 (C.A.) at 262, approved by Lord Wilberforce in *Tucker v. Granada Motorway Services Ltd.*, [1979] S.T.C. 393 (H.L.) at 396.

[14]*I.R.C. v. Carron Co.* (1968), 45 Tax Cas. 18 (H.L.) at 75.

that he or she acquires it, and that the purchase price is a capital expenditure that has enduring benefits over many years. It is equally clear that the costs of heating the building are
annual operating costs and should be charged as current expenses against revenues in each
year. But what of the in-between cases? Consider the following:

- The taxpayer expends $20,000 on advertising the building for rent;[15]

- The taxpayer spends $40,000 on lobbying against rent control legislation;[16]

- The taxpayer installs a concrete lining in the basement of the building to protect it
  against an oil nuisance created by a nearby refinery.[17]

Each case involves subtle distinctions that are not easy to resolve. Some judges are quite
candid about the difficulty of characterizing expenditures. As Sir Wilfred Greene M.R.
said:[18]

> . . . there have been . . . many cases where this matter of capital or income has been debated.
> There have been many cases which fall upon the borderline: indeed, in many cases it is almost
> true to say that the spin of a coin would decide the matter almost as satisfactorily as an attempt
> to find reasons. . . .

Unfortunately, a taxpayer who makes the wrong call on the spin of the coin faces financial
sanctions.

(ii) — Direct vs. Indirect Consequences

One must decide each case on its own factual circumstances to determine if the expenditure
"brings into existence an asset of enduring value".

In determining whether an expenditure has enduring value, should one look to the direct and
immediate consequence of an expenditure, or its ultimate effect on the taxpayer's business?
We should not interpret "enduring" literally but in its commercial context. Many current
expenses have enduring benefits in the sense that advantages that accrue from the expendi-

---

[15]*Minister of National Revenue v. Tower Investment Inc.*, [1972] C.T.C. 182, 72 D.T.C. 6161 (Fed.
T.D.) (Court allowed deferral of deduction, in effect, matching expense to period when most of the
resulting revenue would accrue).

[16]*Morgan v. Tate & Lyle Ltd.*, [1955] A.C. 21, 35 Tax Cas. 367 (H.L.) (expenditure on propaganda
campaign to prevent nationalization of sugar refining industry was current expense); *Boarland v.
Kramat Pulai Ltd.* (1953), 35 Tax Cas. 1 (cost of pamphlet circulated to shareholders, critical of government policy not wholly on account of trade).

[17]*Midland Empire Packing Co. v. Commr.* (1950), 14 T.C. 635 (U.S.) (concrete lining essentially a
repair; deductible as expense).

[18]*I.R.C. v. Br. Salmson Aero Engines Ltd.* (1938), 22 Tax Cas. 29 (C.A.) at 43.

ture continue for a long time. For example, a payment to be rid of an incompetent employee is a current expense even though the payment will, hopefully, have enduring beneficial consequences.[19] An oil change is of enduring benefit to the life of an automobile, which would otherwise seize. Nevertheless, routine maintenance is a current expense even though it enhances the long-term life of an asset.

1. — Goodwill

Expenditures on account of the development or acquisition of goodwill are also difficult to classify. In *Minister of National Revenue v. Algoma Central Railway*[20] for example, the taxpayer expended funds to obtain a geological survey of the mineral potential of the area through which the railway operated. The expenditure was a once-and-for-all cost intended to stimulate its railway traffic by attracting developers to engage in mining the area. There were two issues:

(1) Did the expenditures bring into existence an asset of enduring value?

(2) Was enduring value to be tested by looking to the immediate or ultimate consequences of the expenditures?

The Exchequer Court held that the *direct* consequences of the expenditures did not bring into existence an asset of an enduring nature; the expenses were deductible as a current expense.

Clearly, *purchased* goodwill is an asset of enduring value, and the purchase price is a capital outlay.[21] For example, if one were to purchase the Coca Cola Company, there would be considerable goodwill in the brand name. In contrast, routine institutional advertising by Coca Cola that generates goodwill would be a current deductible expense. In both of these situations, however, we can clearly and directly trace the funds to the end use.

It is the intermediate case, where one expends funds to protect existing goodwill that presents the most difficulties. In *Canada Starch Co. v. Minister of National Revenue*,[22] for example, the taxpayer spent $80,000 to develop a new brand name, "Viva". The taxpayer

---

[19]*Mitchell v. B.W. Noble Ltd.*, [1927] 1 K.B. 719 (C.A.) (payment to get rid of a director was a revenue expense).

[20]*Minister of National Revenue v. Algoma Central Railway*, above note 9.

[21]See, e.g., *Gifford v. R.*, 2004 SCC 15, [2004] 2 C.T.C. 1, (sub nom. *Gifford v. R.*) 236 D.L.R. (4th) 1 (S.C.C.).

[22]*Canada Starch Co. v. Minister of National Revenue*, [1968] C.T.C. 466, 68 D.T.C. 5320 (Can. Ex. Ct.); *Border Fertilizer (1972) Ltd. v. Minister of National Revenue*, [1987] 2 C.T.C. 183, 87 D.T.C. 5391 (Fed. T.D.) (legal fees to defend a taxpayer's senior officials against criminal prosecution not deductible as expenses if cost incurred to prevent damage to taxpayer's goodwill).

faced opposition to the registration of the name as a trade mark on the grounds that "Viva" was confusing with another registered trademark. As a result, the taxpayer paid $15,000 in return for withdrawal of the opposition to registration. Jackett P. described the difference between acquiring and developing assets as follows:

- An expenditure for the acquisition or creation of a business entity, structure or organization, for the earning of profit, or for an addition to such entity, structure or organization, is an expenditure on account of capital, and

- An expenditure in the process of operation of a profit-making entity, structure or organization is an expenditure on revenue account.

Since the expenditures made *in the course of the taxpayer's operations* that gave rise to the trademark were current expenses, the $15,000 payment was part of the process of the registration of an asset that already existed. Therefore, the expenditure was deductible as an expense.

On the general question of expenditures on account of promotion, advertising, and goodwill, Jackett P. said:

> According to my understanding of commercial principles ... advertising expenses paid out while a business is operating, and directed to attract customers to a business, are current expenses. Similarly, in my view, expenses of other measures taken by a businessman with a view to introducing particular products to the market — such as market surveys and industrial design studies — are also current expenses. They also are expenses laid out while the business is operating as part of the process of inducing the buying public to buy the goods being sold.

> It remains to consider expenses incurred by a businessman, during the course of introducing new products to the market, to obtain the additional protection for his trademark that is made available by trademark legislation. A new mark adopted and used in the course of marketing a product gradually acquires the protection of the laws against passing off (assuming that it is, in fact, distinctive). This is something that is an incidental result of ordinary trading operations. Additional expenditure to acquire the additional protection made available by statute law seems to me to be equally incidental to ordinary trading operations. It follows that, in my view, the fees paid to the trade mark lawyers and to the trade mark office are deductible.

Although legal fees for commercial purposes are deductible as expenses, legal fees to defend a taxpayer's senior officials against criminal prosecution to prevent damage to the taxpayer's goodwill are not.[23]

(iii) — Preservation of Capital Assets

The distinction between a current expense and capital expenditure is even more blurred when the question arises in the context of expenditures to maintain or preserve capital assets

---

[23]*Border Fertilizer (1972) Ltd. v. Minister of National Revenue, ante.*

already in existence. Is an expenditure that one incurs for the protection or maintenance of a capital asset a capital expenditure? The answer depends more upon the *type* of property on which one incurs the expenditure than on any clear-cut, bright line rule.

2. — Legal Expenses

The deductibility of legal expenses for protecting a capital asset is unclear. The weight of the cases is against deductibility. In an early case, *Minister of National Revenue v. Dominion Natural Gas Co.*,[24] for example, the Supreme Court held that legal expenses incurred in successfully protecting the taxpayer's gas franchise were capital outlays and not deductible from income. In reaching his decision, Duff C.J.C. enlarged Lord Cave's test (bringing into existence an asset of enduring benefit to the business) as follows:

> The expenditure was incurred *both* "once and for all" and it was incurred for the purpose and with the effect of procuring for the company "the advantage of an enduring benefit".

In contrast with a decision of the English court in the same year,[25] the court did not accept that the expenses were incidental to the ordinary course of the taxpayer's business. Thus, the Court put up a two-step hurdle to establish that an expenditure is current and deductible.

The stature of *Minister of National Revenue v. Dominion Natural Gas Co.*, however, has been eroded by subsequent decisions. In *Kellogg Co. of Canada v. Minister of National*

---

[24][1941] S.C.R. 19, [1940-41] C.T.C. 155, [1920-1940] 1 D.T.C. 499-133 (S.C.C.).

[25]See *Southern v. Borax Consol. Ltd.*, [1940] 4 All E.R. 412 at 416 and 419, *per* Lawrence J.:

> ... In my opinion, the principle which is to be deducted from the cases is that where a sum of money is laid out for the acquisition or the improvement of a fixed capital asset it is attributable to capital, but *if no alteration is made* in the fixed capital asset by the payment, then it is properly attributable to revenue, being in substance a matter of maintenance, the maintenance of the capital structure or the capital assets of the company. ...

> It appears to me that the legal expenses which were incurred ... did not create any new asset at all but were expenses which were incurred in the ordinary course of maintaining the assets of the company, and the fact that it was maintaining the title and not the value of the company's business does not, in my opinion, make it any different. [Emphasis added.]

See also *Mitchell v. B.W. Noble Ltd.* (1927), 11 Tax Cas. 372 (Eng. K.B.) at 421:

> The object (of the expenditure) ... was that of preserving the status and reputation of the company which the directors felt might be imperilled ... to avoid that and to preserve the status and divided-earning power of the company seems to me a purpose which is well within the ordinary purpose of the trade.

Revenue,[26] for example, the taxpayer successfully deducted substantial legal fees incurred in defending an allegation of trademark infringement. The Supreme Court distinguished *Dom. Natural Gas Co.* on the basis that the trademark action in *Kellogg Co. of Can.* was neither a right of property nor an exclusive right. The Court held the expenses to be ordinary legal expenses and deductible in the ordinary course of business.[27]

In *Evans v. Minister of National Revenue*,[28] the taxpayer, who was entitled to one-third of an estate left to her by her husband and by her father, incurred legal fees when her right to the income of the estate was challenged. Once again, the Supreme Court held that the legal fees were a current expense and were not paid on account of capital. Cartwright J., speaking for the majority of the Court, distinguished *Dom. Natural Gas Co.* on the basis that the legal fees in that case were "expenses to preserve a capital asset in a capital aspect." In the Court's opinion, Mrs. Evans's right to the income of the estate was not a capital asset.

What is the distinction between "a capital aspect" and "a revenue aspect"?[29] This test does not likely add anything to the other tests. Ultimately, the resolution of the entire question depends on the facts and circumstances. The Privy Council identified the process in *B.P. Australia Ltd. v. Commissioner of Taxation of the Commonwealth of Australia* as follows:[30]

> [T]he solution to the problem is not to be found by any rigid test or description. It has to be derived from many aspects of the whole set of circumstances, some of which may point in one direction, some in the other. One consideration may point so clearly that it dominates other

---

[26]*Kellogg Co. of Canada v. Minister of National Revenue*, [1942] C.T.C. 51, 2 D.T.C. 548 (Can. Ex. Ct.); affirmed [1943] C.T.C. 1, 2 D.T.C. 601 (S.C.C.).

[27]*Kellogg Co. of Canada v. Minister of National Revenue*, *ante*, in which the learned Chief Justice said:

> The right upon which the (taxpayer) relied was not a right of property, or an exclusive right of any description, but the right (in common with all other members of the public) to describe their goods in the manner in which they were described.

[28]*Evans v. Minister of National Revenue*, [1960] S.C.R. 391, [1960] C.T.C. 69, 60 D.T.C. 1047 (S.C.C.); see also *Farmers Mutual Petroleums Ltd. v. Minister of National Revenue*, [1966] C.T.C. 283, 66 D.T.C. 5225 (Can. Ex. Ct.); affirmed [1968] S.C.R. 59, [1967] C.T.C. 396, 67 D.T.C. 5277 (S.C.C.) (legal expenses incurred in defending title to mineral rights were capital outlays); *British Columbia Power Corp. v. Minister of National Revenue*, [1966] C.T.C. 454, 66 D.T.C. 5310 (Can. Ex. Ct.); affirmed (1967), [1968] S.C.R. 17, [1967] C.T.C. 406, 67 D.T.C. 5258 (S.C.C.) (legal expenses incurred in preserving right to shares that had purportedly been expropriated by a provincial government were non-deductible capital expenditures).

[29]See, e.g., *R. v. Jager Homes Ltd.*, [1988] 1 C.T.C. 215, 88 D.T.C. 6119 (Fed. C.A.) (legal fees to defend action to wind up company on capital account and not deductible as current expense).

[30]*B.P. Australia Ltd. v. Commissioner of Taxation of the Commonwealth of Australia*, [1965] 3 All E.R. 209, [1966] A.C. 224 (Australia P.C.) at 264, cited with approval by the S.C.C. in *Johns-Manville Canada Inc. v. R.*, [1985] 2 C.T.C. 111, 85 D.T.C. 5373 (S.C.C.) at 5383.

and vaguer indications in the contrary direction. It is a common sense appreciation of all the guiding features which must provide the ultimate answer.

3. — Repairs, Maintenance and Alterations

The dividing line between capital expenditures and current expenses due to routine mainte-nance and repairs is also unclear. Here too, the underlying principle is easy to state, but difficult to apply. An expenditure in one fiscal period that enhances, substantially improves, enlarges, or prolongs the life of an asset beyond the period is a capital outlay. In contrast, an expenditure that merely maintains an asset or restores it to its original condition is a deducti-ble current expense.

Here, as elsewhere in tax law, it is easy to identify the correct answer in polar cases when one does not really need an answer. It is the grey areas in between that cause the problems and litigation. For example, the extension of an existing building by adding new floor space is a capital expenditure; it brings into existence an asset of enduring value. Routine mainte-nance of an existing building, for example, performance of minor repairs, replacement of light bulbs, cleaning, painting, and maintenance of heating and ventilation systems, is cur-rent expenses.

Between these extremes, however, there are cases that require one to analyze each expendi-ture *in the context of the taxpayer's activities*. For example, a taxpayer who expends money to restore a decrepit and rundown building incurs capital expenditures, even though routine deductible maintenance by the owner or previous owner would have prevented the building from deteriorating to a decrepit state. Similarly, a business that regularly expends funds to change the oil in its fleet of automobiles incurs current expenses. Neglecting to change the oil in its automobiles may, at a later date, involve substantial costs by way of engine replace-ments that would result in capital outlays.[31]

4. — "Repair" vs. "Renewal"

"Repair" and "renew" do not necessarily imply different meanings. "Repair" means "resto-ration by renewal or replacement of subsidiary parts of a whole." "Renewal" means "recon-struction of the entirety, meaning by the entirety, not necessarily of the whole."[32] The Privy

---

[31]*Better Plumbing Co. v. Minister of National Revenue* (1952), 6 Tax A.B.C. 177, 52 D.T.C. 146 (Can. Tax. App. Bd.); see also *Glenco Investment Corp. v. Minister of National Revenue*, [1967] C.T.C. 243, 67 D.T.C. 5169 (Can. Ex. Ct.) (cost of plumbing and electrical installations in a warehouse acquired and converted into a commercial building suitable for rental was capital outlay).

[32]*Lurcott v. Wakely*, [1911] 1 K.B. 905 (C.A.).

Council considered the relationship between repairs and renewals in *Rhodesia Rys. Ltd. v. Bechuanaland Collector of IT*:[33]

> The periodical renewal by sections, of the rails and sleepers of a railway line as they wear out through use, is in no sense a reconstruction of the whole railway and is an ordinary incident of railway administration. The fact that the wear, although continuous, is not and cannot be made good annually, does not render the work of renewal when it comes to being effected, necessarily a capital charge. The expenditure here in question was incurred in consequence of the rails having been worn out in earning the income of the previous years on which tax had been paid without deduction in respect of such wear, and represented the cost of restoring them to a state in which they could continue to earn income. It did not result in the creation of any new asset; it was incurred to maintain the appellant's existing line in a state to earn revenue.

5. — Replacements

Renewal costs that go beyond financing the replacement of worn-out parts, and that transform one asset into another, are capital expenditures. In *Highland Rwy. Co. v. Balderston*,[34] the taxpayer was not allowed to deduct the costs of replacing iron rails with steel rails as a current expense. The Lord President of the Scottish Court of Exchequer said:

> [T]hen when we come to the question of the alteration of the main line itself, it must be kept in view that this is not a mere relaying of the line after the old fashion; it is not taking away rails that are worn out o[r] partially worn out, and renewing them in whole or in part along with the whole line. That would not alter the character of the line; it would not affect the nature of the heritable property possessed by the Company. But what has been done is to substitute one kind of rail for another, steel rails for iron rails.

Although each type of rail is used for the same purpose — transporting trains, steel rails are a different class of asset from iron rails.

Whether replacement costs are deductible as a current expense depends on the magnitude of the replacement in the context of the complete unit of which it forms a part. The replacement of small parts in an automobile is routine maintenance; replacement of the entire engine is a capital outlay. The test in each case is: Are the expenditures on account of repair of the larger property by replacement of a component, or on account of replacement of an entire unit, complete in itself?[35] The question is often pragmatically resolved by comparing the

---

[33]*Rhodesia Rys. Ltd. v. Bechuanaland Collector of IT*, [1933] A.C. 368 (P.C.) at 374.

[34]*Highland Rwy. Co. v. Balderston* (1889), 2 Tax Cas. 485 at 488; see also *Tank Truck Transport Ltd. v. Minister of National Revenue* (1965), 1965 CarswellNat 140, 38 Tax A.B.C. 332, 65 D.T.C. 405 (Can. Tax. App. Bd.) (replacement of 12 cast iron tanks with stainless steel tanks held to be capital outlay).

[35]*Vancouver Tug Boat Co. v. Minister of National Revenue*, [1957] C.T.C. 178, 57 D.T.C. 1126 (Can. Ex. Ct.) ($42,000 replacement of tugboat engine held to be replacement of substantial part of the

cost of replacement with the cost of ordinary repairs in the context of the total unit of which the replacement is a part. The higher the cost of replacement compared to the costs of the total unit, the greater the likelihood that the costs are on account of capital.

(iv) — Discharge of Obligations

A payment to eliminate an enduring disadvantage or an onerous obligation may have enduring benefits and constitute a capital expenditure. A *surrogatum* payment to discharge a revenue expense — for example, a payment to dismiss an unsatisfactory employee — is deductible as a current expense.[36] Similarly, a payment to discharge a capital liability is a capital expenditure.[37] The intermediate cases are not as clear. Here too we look to the permanency of the advantage secured by discharging the liability.[38]

(v) — Factual Ambiguity

As the above discussion illustrates, the characterization of expenditures is largely factual in the context of broadly defined legal principles. To be sure, the process is uncertain and

---

whole, hence capital outlay); *Canada Steamship Lines Ltd. v. Minister of National Revenue*, [1966] C.T.C. 255, 66 D.T.C. 5205 (Can. Ex. Ct.) (cost of replacing boiler in ship held to be capital expenditure).

[36]*Mitchell v. B.W. Noble Ltd.*, [1927] 1 K.B. 719 (C.A.) (payment to secure retirement of director whose conduct likely to damage taxpayer's business was revenue payment).

[37]*Countess Warwick Steamship Co. v. Ogg (Inspector of Taxes)*, [1924] 2 K.B. 292 (Eng. K.B.) (payment to secure cancellation of contract to acquire capital asset was capital expense).

[38]*Whitehead (Inspector of Taxes) v. Tubbs (Elastics) Ltd.*, [1984] S.T.C. 1 (C.A.) at 3 (payment to secure release from onerous term in loan agreement, which significantly limited taxpayer's power to borrow, constituted capital payment), per Oliver L.J.:

> Here the advantage sought to be achieved was one which was permanent in the sense that the company was relieved, for the balance of the loan period, of the disadvantages arising from the restrictions and relieved of restrictions attributable to a non-recurring transaction. One cannot separate the payment made from the origins of the restrictions in respect of which it was made. In effect these restrictions — and whether they were contained in the agreement or the debenture is really immaterial, for they clearly went and were intended to go hand-in-hand — were the price or premium paid by the company for the loan, and the loan, it is not in dispute, was clearly a transaction of a capital nature.

ambiguous. We should resolve factual ambiguity in the taxpayer's favour.[39] As Mr. Justice Estey, speaking for a unanimous Supreme Court, stated:[40]

> Such a determination is, furthermore, consistent with another basic concept in tax law, that where the taxing statute is not explicit, reasonable uncertainty or factual ambiguity resulting from lack of explicitness in the statute should be resolved in favour of the taxpayer.

(vi) — Summary

There is no single test that one can apply to all circumstances. There are, however, three broad criteria that offer a useful starting point in determining whether an expenditure is on account of capital or revenue:

1. The character of the advantage or the duration of the benefit (the more enduring the benefit the more likely that the expenditure is on account of capital);

2. Recurrence and frequency of the expenditure (the more frequent the expenditure the less enduring the benefit); and

3. Identification of the payment as a *surrogatum* for expenditures that would be on account of capital or revenue (a substitute for a capital expenditure is more likely a capital expenditure).

B. — Unreasonable Expenses

A taxpayer can deduct an expense only if it is reasonable in amount. This rule, which relates only to the amount of the expense and not its nature, prevents taxpayers from artificially reducing their income through unreasonable expenses.

What is "reasonable" is a question of fact determined by comparing the expense in question with amounts paid in similar circumstances in comparable businesses. In *Doug Burns Excavation Contractor Ltd. v. Minister of National Revenue*,[41] for example, the Tax Court disallowed the taxpayer's deduction for a bonus of $100,000 that it paid to the president's wife who worked as a clerk in his office.

---

[39] *Johns-Manville Canada Inc. v. R.*, [1985] 2 C.T.C. 111, 85 D.T.C. 5373 (S.C.C.).

[40] *Ibid.*, at 5384.

[41] [1983] C.T.C. 2566, 83 D.T.C. 528 (T.C.C.).

C. — Levies, Fines, and Penalties

An expense is generally deductible if the taxpayer incurs it for the purposes of gaining or producing income. A taxpayer may usually deduct expenses incurred from illegal acts to the extent that he incurs them to earn income. However, this principle does not extend to the deduction of fines and penalties and certain types of bribes.

A taxpayer cannot deduct a fine or penalty imposed by law in *any* jurisdiction. Section 67.6 overturns the decision of the Supreme Court in *65302 B.C. Ltd.*,[42] which held that fines and penalties incurred for the purpose of gaining or producing income were deductible expenses and not caught by the prohibition in paragraph 18(1)(a).

The rationale behind the prohibition is that allowing a deduction for fines and penalties diminishes their deterrence value, and, therefore, is contrary to public policy objectives. However, the Act leaves open the door for the deduction of prescribed fines where it would be contrary to public policy to deny their deductibility.[43]

D. — Illegal Payments

As a general rule, taxpayers may deduct reasonable amounts that they incur to earn income from a business or property. There are, however, some limitations based exclusively on grounds of public policy and morality. A preeminent example is the prohibition against deducting bribes paid to foreign public officials.

Corruption of government officials is a cost of doing business in many countries, including Canada. For example, Transparency International's Corruption Perceptions Index (2012), which measures the perceived levels of public sector corruption in 177 countries, reveals that 70 percent of all countries are sufficiently corrupt to receive a failing grade. Canada ranked in ninth place with a score of 84 out of 100; China in 80th with a score of 39; and India in 94th with a score of only 36.

The *Corruption of Foreign Public Officials Act* (S.C. 1998, c. 34) features three primary offences: bribery of foreign public officials; money laundering; and possession of proceeds from money laundering and bribery. Aiding, abetting and counseling such activities are also criminal offences.

---

[42]In *65302 British Columbia Ltd. v. R.*, [1999] 3 S.C.R. 804, [2000] 1 C.T.C. 57, 99 D.T.C. 5799 (S.C.C.), an over-quota levy imposed on an egg-producing poultry farm by the B.C. Egg Marketing Board was an allowable deduction pursuant to subsection 9(1) and paragraph 18(1)(a) of the Act. The levy was incurred as part of the taxpayer's day-to-day operations. Furthermore, the business decision to produce over-quota was a deliberate decision made in order to realize income. Since the fine was imposed to remove the profit of over-quota production, it was allowable as a deductible current expense.

[43]See, for example, Reg. 7309, which prescribes fines under the *Excise Tax Act*.

The core offence, which covers individuals and corporations, is the bribery of foreign public officials at any level of government, whether international, national or local. A "bribe" — in German, "Schmiergeld" or lubrication money — is an offer or promise, either explicitly or implicitly, to give undue pecuniary or other advantage, directly or through intermediaries, in order to obtain or retain business or other improper advantage. The offence extends to all businesses, professions and trades, regardless of where they are situated or practiced. For example, it is an offence to bribe a foreign public official to obtain a contract to build an embassy in Canada.

The essence of the offence is the corruption of foreign public officials to get them to act or refrain from acting in the performance of their public duties. A bribe is a payment to obtain, directly or indirectly (such as, payment to the spouse of a foreign official) to obtain a contract or concession. For example, Griffiths Energy International Inc. of Calgary paid $2 million for energy contracts to a company controlled by the spouse of the Chad (ranked 163 out of 177 with a score of 19) ambassador, resulting in a fine plus surcharges of $10.35 million in 2013. Niko Resources Ltd. of Calgary paid benefits of nearly $200,000 by providing a luxury vehicle to an official of the Bangladesh government. The company was fined $9.5 million in 2011.

There is no bright line test for determining a payment or gift as a bribe. Each business must make its own decisions based on their judgment in the context of the particular circumstances and local culture. Unlike the United States IRS, the CRA does not provide guidelines for what constitutes a "reasonable payment" and businesses must exercise judgment. For example, a dinner gift of a bottle of single malt Scotch whiskey costing $300 may be entirely appropriate for a senior government official. However, a collector bottle valued at $128,000 (as released in China in 2013) may raise eyebrows and spark prosecutorial interest.

Not all payments to expedite performance by foreign officials are bribes. Business must go on according to the local culture. In certain societies "grease", "commissions", "facilitation fees", "agency fees" and "baksheesh" are essential to doing business. Many governments control the issuance of licences to produce, manufacture or distribute products that sometimes assure the recipient of a monopoly or protected market. Civil servants supervise the grant of such licences and, in the process, may supplement their modest income. No bribe, no licence. Canadian companies that participate, directly or indirectly, in any such bidding process are open to criminal prosecution and civil sanctions. The local culture may be "No bribe, no licence!"

"Facilitation" payments to get officials to perform acts of a "routine nature" within the scope of their public duties are not bribes under the statute. Subsection 3(4) states:

> . . . a payment is not a loan, reward, advantage or benefit to obtain or retain an advantage in the course of business, if it is made to expedite or secure the performance by a foreign public official of any act of a routine nature that is part of the foreign public official's duties or functions, including
>
> > (a) the issuance of a permit, licence or other document to qualify a person to do business;

(b) the processing of official documents, such as visas and work permits;

(c) the provision of services normally offered to the public, such as mail pick-up and delivery, telecommunication services and power and water supply; and

(d) the provision of services normally provided as required, such as police protection, loading and unloading of cargo, the protection of perishable products or commodities from deterioration or the scheduling of inspections related to contract performance or transit of goods.

[However, this law has been repealed, but not proclaimed in force as of January 1, 2014. The Canadian government is waiting to see what the Americans, who do allow facilitation payments, do under their comparable legislation, *The Foreign Corrupt Practices Act, 1977*, as amended, 15 U.S.C. §§78dd-1, et seq. ("FCPA"),]

Thus, under the current law, Canadians can pay foreign officials to perform functions that they are supposed to be performing as part of their job — issuance of a permit, licence, or visa to which one is entitled — without breaking the law. For example, it is routine, indeed expected, that one pay customs officials in some countries to ensure that there is no delay in unloading perishable food off a ship. Judges in many countries also expect supplemental consideration to release their judgments in a timely manner. Similarly, it would not be considered socially offensive to pay a tax official to issue an assessment or clearance certificate to which one would normally be entitled upon completion of certain transactions.

The real difficulty is in determining when grease crosses the line from being a facilitation payment and becomes an illegal act. The distinction is important in at least four legal aspects.

First, and most obvious, bribery of foreign officials is a criminal act and carries a maximum term of imprisonment of fourteen years.

Second, the offence carries a fine that is entirely in the discretion of the judge. The Act does not stipulate any maximum amount.

Third, the prohibition in section 67.5(1) is absolute: Bribes are not deductible as expenses for income tax purposes even if the taxpayer pays them solely for the purposes of conducting business and there is no alternative but to pay if one is to secure the contract.

Fourth, there is no limitation period and the tax authorities can reassess the taxpayer at any time in the future (section 67.5(2)).

E. — *Purpose of Expenditure*

a) — *Purpose, Not Result*

An expenditure is deductible as an expense in computing income only if one incurs it for the *purpose* of earning income and is not prohibited by specific provisions of the Act.[44] It is the *purpose*, and not the result, of the expenditure that determines deductibility. Thus, an expense for the purpose of earning income from a business is deductible, regardless of whether it actually produces income. For example, if a taxpayer incurs advertising expenses for the purpose of promoting sales, failure of the advertising program to stimulate sales does *not* disqualify the expenditure as a deductible expense. The Exchequer Court explained the statutory scheme as follows:[45]

> Thus, it may be stated categorically that in a case under the *Income Tax Act* the first matter to be determined in deciding whether an outlay or expense is outside the prohibition of paragraph 18(1)(a) of the Act is whether it was made or incurred by the taxpayer in accordance with the ordinary principles of commercial trading or well accepted principles of business practice. If it was not, that is the end of the matter. But if it was, then the outlay or expense is properly deductible unless it falls outside the expressed exception of paragraph 18(1)(a) and, therefore, within its prohibition. . . .

The essential limitation in paragraph 18(1)(a) is that the taxpayer must incur the outlay or expense "for the purpose" of gaining or producing income "from the business". Thus, the purpose must be that of gaining or producing income from the business in which the taxpayer engages. *A fortiori*, the business must exist at the time that the taxpayer incurs the expenditure.

---

[44]Para. 18(1)(a). This rule does little more than reinforce subs. 9(1), which states that the income from a business or property is the profit therefrom. To constitute an "expense", the taxpayer must be under an obligation to pay money to someone. An obligation to do something that may entail an expenditure in the future is *not* an expense; see *R. v. Burnco Industries Ltd.*, [1984] C.T.C. 337, 84 D.T.C. 6348 (Fed. C.A.).

[45]*Royal Trust Co. v. Minister of National Revenue*, [1957] C.T.C. 32, 57 D.T.C. 1055 (Can. Ex. Ct.) at 42, 44 [C.T.C.] and 1060, 1062 [D.T.C.]; see also *British Columbia Electric Railway v. Minister of National Revenue*, [1958] C.T.C. 21, 58 D.T.C. 1022 (S.C.C.) (payments made by taxpayer to enable it to become more profitable not deductible even though made for purpose of producing income on account of capital; case departing from previous law; see editorial note at [1958] C.T.C. 21).

b) — Primary Purpose

The characterization of an income-earning purpose is a question of fact. We can break down expenditures into deductible and non-deductible portions.[46] An expenditure does not have to be wholly and exclusively expended for business purposes in order to be deductible.[47]

The focus is on the *primary* purpose of the expenditure. For example, a lawyer who travels from Toronto to Paris for a business meeting can deduct her travel expenses for the trip, even though she remains there for the weekend for personal reasons. The lawyer may also deduct any *incremental* expenditures (such as additional hotel and meal charges) associated with the personal portion of her visit if the expenses are part of the cost of waiting for meetings to resume on Monday. The personal component is secondary to the primary business purpose of the visit.

c) — Legal Fees and Criminal Charges

We use the primary purpose test to evaluate the deductibility of legal fees. For tax purposes, an individual's business income is his *net* profit from the business — revenues less expenses to earn income. Thus, a taxpayer can deduct expenses for legal fees in the normal course of business.

Legal fees on account of criminal charges are a more challenging problem in tax law. Although courts look at commercial principles to determine business practice, determining net profit is essentially a question of law. One starts by asking whether the taxpayer would have incurred the particular expense "but for" the pursuit of business income. Would the need to incur the expense exist apart from the business?

Thus, characterizing criminal charges account of business or personal activities is the key to determining deductibility of legal fees, most of which occur in the context of white collar crimes. However, white-collar crimes vary considerably. Typically, such charges arise out of corporate or personal conduct in the context of illegal combines, price fixing, securities violations, insider trading, unlawful conspiracy to lessen competition, accounting fraud, and

---

[46]*Consumers' Gas Co. of Toronto v. Minister of National Revenue* (1955), 13 Tax A.B.C. 429 (Can. Tax App. Bd.) (taxpayer obtained gas export permit to improve business; permit and fees for securing permit capital in nature; remainder of fees referable to particular business difficulties, not assets); *KVP Co. v. Minister of National Revenue*, [1957] C.T.C. 275, 57 D.T.C. 1208 (Can. Ex. Ct.) (extensive aerial surveys required by province to preserve timber cutting rights; current expense to the extent of previous average survey expense).

[47]Considerable care should be taken in reading English cases on the deductibility of expenses incurred for business and personal purposes. Under the English statute, an expenditure must be *wholly and exclusively* for business purposes if it is to be deductible; see *Mallalieu v. Drummond*, [1983] 2 A.C. 861 (H.L.).

income tax evasion. We are also seeing an increasing number of prosecutions for bribery and corruption of domestic and foreign government officials.

Regardless of the context of the offence, the critical element in determining deductibility of legal fees is the primary purpose of the conduct that led to the charges. If the primary purpose of the activity is to earn business income, the expense is deductible unless the expenditure is on account of capital. To be sure, all criminal charges against individuals also have some incidental personal consequences — psychological problems, loss of job, financial problems, reputation implications, jail, etc. The key decision, however, is to determine which of the two — business or personal — is the primary reason for the charges.

If the primary purpose of incurring legal defense costs is to preserve and maintain the business, the fees are deductible even if there is a secondary personal element for the expenditures. This is essentially a question of fact in each case. The ultimate outcome of the criminal charges — guilty or not guilty verdict — should be irrelevant in assessing the purpose of legal fees.

Businesses are taxable on their income, regardless whether the income flows from lawful or unlawful practices. Hence, they should be able to deduct their legal fees even if they arise from illegal commercial operations that generate taxable income. In this context, legal fees are simply "working expenses" — one incurs them in the process of earning business income. For example, legal fees in defending violations of competition laws are usually deductible because of the close nexus between the alleged criminal act and the earning of business income through anti-competitive acts. Tax law is neutral and does not morally judge such corporate behavior. This contrasts with the statutory prohibition against the deduction of fines and penalties.

In contrast, legal fees to defend charges of income tax evasion are not deductible. Tax evasion is not a normal or ordinary incident of carrying on business. The evasion occurs after the income earning process is complete. In *Thiele Drywall*, for example, the taxpayer falsely recorded payments that it made to certain individuals as reimbursements for expenses instead of income for services. False characterization of service payments as reimbursements is not part of the process of earning business income. The Tax Court disallowed the taxpayer's claim for legal fees because of the underlying nature of the offence.

The issue of deducting legal fees cuts close to the bone if the defendant is a lawyer who faces potential disbarment from the law society. Legal fees to avoid disbarment, or secure reinstatement, as a lawyer may be deductible if they are directly on account of current expenses and not on account of securing a capital asset — the licence to practice. It is easier to defend the deduction of fees to prevent disbarment because the expenses are in respect of protecting an asset that the lawyer already has and uses directly to produce business income. Fees to defend personal charges — for example, sexual harassment — that may lead to disbarment from the Law Society are less likely deductible. The potential of disbarment is not sufficiently close to the primary purpose of the expenditure, namely, the defense of the sexual harassment allegations.

F. — Personal and Living Expenses

a) — General Comment

A taxpayer cannot deduct personal or living expenses in computing income from business or property.[48] To be deductible, an expense must be incurred for the purpose of earning income.[49] The Act allows a taxpayer to deduct expenses incurred "for profit" activities and prohibits the deduction of expenses incurred "for pleasure" activities or on account of capital. The distinction between profit, pleasure and capital expenses involves difficult classification problems in the individual's income tax. Characterization involves drawing a dividing line between categories. The line that divides deductible and non-deductible expenses should provide an accurate measure of income that is both equitable and can be administered easily.

The distinction between profit and pleasure expenses is blurred and, indeed, sometimes meaningless because it is impossible to quantify profit and pleasure at discreet intervals. Nevertheless, the distinction is important for tax purposes and taxpayers are routinely asked to determine which of the two objectives, profit or pleasure, is the predominant motive for an expenditure. The distinction between the two determines whether a taxpayer pays a dollar or 50 cents on the dollar for a particular expense. The courts are equally uncomfortable with these distinctions and often rely more upon compilations of deductible and non-deductible lists, rather than on principled formulations of policy.

Expenses can be put on a continuum. At one extreme are those expenses quite obviously of a purely business nature, and there is no serious issue of their deductibility. For example, a taxpayer who pays salaries, rent, utilities and operating expenses on account of his or her business is entitled to deduct the expenditures (subject only to quantum limitations) as routine business expenses.[50] At the other end of the continuum, we find expenses that are of a purely personal nature. Hence, for example, a taxpayer is not generally entitled to deduct his

---

[48]Para. 18(1)(h) and subs. 248(1) "personal or living expenses". The prohibition does not cover traveling expenses (including the full cost of meals and lodging) incurred on a business trip. "Personal or living expenses" include expenses incurred to maintain a property where the property is not maintained in connection with a business that is being carried on for profit or with a reasonable expectation of profit. They also include expenses incurred for purchasing a life insurance policy, the proceeds of which are payable to the taxpayer, or to a person related to the taxpayer.

[49]Para. 18(1)(h) was originally implemented as para. 2(2)(e) of c. 55, S.C. 1919, which amended s. 3 of the *Income War Tax Act, 1917*. In response to a question in the House regarding the purpose of this section, asked by a questioner who noted that it was already "quite evident that no one has the right to deduct his personal and living expenses from income before he declares it for the purposes of this Act", the Minister of Finance stated that the section was "just to make it clear that deduction must not be made" and to "make it perfectly clear that the full net income must be assessed" (Commons Debates, June 24, 1919).

[50]S. 9.

or her personal meals, clothing, cosmetics, personal grooming and the everyday costs of living. The difficulty of determining deductibility, however, lies not at the extremes of the continuum but in the middle, where the expenditure is clearly neither one nor the other, but has attributes both of business and personal. It is in this grey area that one must determine which attributes predominate.

Expenditures in the grey zone of deductibility fall into two broad categories: (1) the "special costs" of a person engaged in business, such as, child care and commuting, and (2) "personal gratification costs" that give pleasure in the pursuit of profit or bring about profit in the pursuit of pleasure, for example, travel and entertainment. Tax law deals quite easily with both of these categories of expenditures in the case of employed persons. Employees are prohibited from deducting *any* expenses *unless* the Act specifically authorizes the deduction.[51] Thus, we tax employees based on their gross income with minimal deductions. We justify this rule on the basis of administrative simplicity, without much concern for an accurate measure of net income.

The problem, however, is not so easily resolved in the case of business expenditures, where the rule is the converse: a taxpayer is entitled to deduct *any* expense incurred for the purpose of earning income *unless* the deduction is *specifically* prohibited. This inverse burden leads to tension for taxpayers who may choose between employee versus independent contractor status. Individuals often prefer independent contractor status for tax purposes and employee status under labour laws for workplace protections. Thus, they want the best of both worlds, maximum tax deductions and maximum workplace protection.

b) — Purpose Test

We determine the purpose of an expenditure by looking for the predominant reason for which one incurs the expenditure. This is a positive test and quite different from asking the converse: "what would happen if the taxpayer did *not* incur the expense?" The purpose test is not the "but for" test. The test for deductibility is *not*: "but for this expense, could the taxpayer have earned his income?" Such a broad test would completely obliterate the distinction between business and personal expenses and negate the value of the purpose test.

For example, how should we classify childcare expenses, the classic hybrid of "for profit" and "for pleasure" expenditures? In a conventional family setting with infant children, both parents cannot go out to work without some provision for the children. This raises two questions. Does the parent incur the childcare expenses primarily and predominantly for the purpose of allowing the parent (usually the mother) to engage in business? Or are the expenses a basic function of family life and, hence, of a personal nature?

---

[51] Subs. 8(2).

In *Smith*,[52] for example, the United States Board of Tax Appeals denied the taxpayer a deduction for babysitting expenses on the theory that allowing such a deduction would extend the deduction to all consumption expenditures (such as food, shelter, clothing and recreation) that allow taxpayers to carry on their day-to-day activities.

The Board was concerned with opening the floodgates for the deduction of all personal expenditures, however tenuous their connection with the income-earning process.

> The fee to the doctor, but for whose healing service, the earner of the family income could not leave his sickbed; the cost of the labourer's raiment, for how can the world proceed about its business unclothed; the very home which gives us shelter and rest and the food which provides energy, might all by an extension of the same proposition be construed as necessary to the operation of business and to the creation of income. Yet these are the very essence of those "personal" expenses the deductibility of which is expressly denied.

There is, however, an important distinction between expenses incurred primarily for personal purposes and expenses incurred predominantly for the purpose of earning income but which have only incidental and ancillary personal elements. The difficulty lies in drawing the line between the two. Certain expenditures are common to everyone, whether they are employed, engaged in a business or unemployed. The basic personal expenditures for food, shelter, clothing and the everyday necessities of life are clearly not deductible, regardless of one's working status. One does not incur such expenditures primarily for the purposes of earning income. Childcare expenses, however, pose a different conceptual problem.

Childcare expenses are a basic family consumption expenditure if we begin from the premise that at least one parent must stay at home to look after the child. Then, any childcare expenses are primarily of a personal nature. The business aspect of the expenditure on account of childcare arises if, and only if, the previously stay-at-home parent decides to enter the commercial marketplace and engage in business. Thus, one's perspective on childcare expenses depends on where one starts the analysis. To be sure, the short answer might well be that the Act has a detailed statutory framework for the deduction of childcare expenses and, hence, one cannot deduct such expenses under the general provisions[53] because of the prescribed scheme.[54] But such a response avoids the difficult question. Apart from specific statutory provisions, the theoretically correct answer is that the incremental cost of a hybrid profit/pleasure expenditure is deductible for tax purposes if the *primary and predominant* motive for incurring the expenditure is to earn business income.

The deductibility of childcare expenses also raises equity issues if some taxpayers get tax-free childcare while others are denied the same treatment. An employer, for example, can deduct the cost of childcare that it provides at its facilities if it incurs the expenses for the

---

[52]*Smith v. Commr.* (1939), 40 B.T.A. 1038, 113 F.2d 114 (U.S. 2nd Cir., 1940).

[53]S. 9.

[54]S. 63.

purposes of earning business income. Since the employer requires and needs the services of all of its employees (some of whom have young children), the cost of providing childcare on its premises is directly related to the employees' services. Parents with young children who are being well taken care of on the employer's premises are likely to work longer, and with less anxiety, than parents who need to dash off to rescue their children at pre-determined hours from day-care services. The same can be said of nanny care.[55]

Thus, a person who pays for child care services to get to her business is not entitled to deduct the cost, but her employer can deduct the same cost to obtain her services. The supposed logic of this disparate treatment is that the employer incurs the cost *after* her employees are on the business premises, whilst the parent incurs her child care expenses to get *to* the employer's premises. This invites arbitrage in salary negotiations. The obvious behavioural response is that one should (if possible) negotiate a lower salary with on-site childcare, rather than a higher salary with nanny care paid with after-tax dollars.

The question in *Smith*[56] was essentially whether the differential in childcare expenses (or any part thereof) should be allowed as business expenses incurred for the purposes of earning income. The answer, based on the floodgates theory that allowing such expenses would open the door to allowing every other personal expense as a deduction (the "but for" test as the yardstick for determining deductibility), is not entirely satisfactory. There is a difference between expenses that are incurred, regardless of whether one works or not (basic food, personal clothing, shelter, etc.), and the *incremental* expenses associated only with the process of earning income.

Scott[57] recognizes this distinction in allowing a "foot and transit courier" to deduct the cost of his incremental food and water required to perform his job. The taxpayer travelled 150 kilometers a day carrying a backpack that weighed between 20–50 pounds. He worked on foot and public transportation 10 hours per day, 5 days per week, and 52 weeks per year. He consumed an *extra* meal per day for which he sought to deduct $11 ($8 for extra food and $3 for extra bottled water and juice) as business expenses. Since the taxpayer incurred expenses on account of food and beverages, the CRA denied his deduction for the incremental expenses. The Federal Court, quite rightly, refused to deny the deduction for the expenses simply on the grounds that such expenses have always been considered "personal" and, therefore, must continue to be so.[58] Instead, the Court allowed the taxpayer to deduct his

---

[55]See *Symes v. R.*, [1993] 4 S.C.R. 695, [1994] 1 C.T.C. 40, 94 D.T.C. 6001 (S.C.C.).

[56]*Smith v. Commr.* (1939), 40 B.T.A. 1038, 113 F.2d 114 (U.S. 2nd Cir., 1940).

[57]*Scott v. R.*, [1998] 4 C.T.C. 103, 162 D.L.R. (4th) 595, 98 D.T.C. 6530 (Fed. C.A.).

[58]See, for example, Justice Iacobucci's comment in *Symes v. R.*, [1993] 4 S.C.R. 695, [1994] 1 C.T.C. 40, 94 D.T.C. 6001 (S.C.C.) at 54:

> This appeal presents a particular expense which has been traditionally characterized as personal in nature. If, in coming to a decision, this Court stated that since such expenses have

incremental food and drink expenses because the extra consumption was the direct result of his efforts to earn income. The incremental food and drink were the equivalent of the incremental gas that a person uses in his automobile for business purposes.[59]

The Court rejected arguments that the deduction for food and beverage expenses would open the floodgates to a myriad of claims for deductions for personal expenses. The floodgates argument, always a concern for tax administrators, is an argument of last resort to preserve the status quo. The deduction ". . . should in no way be interpreted as providing a basis to challenge all traditional prohibitions on the deduction of food and beverages as a business expense under the Act." The deduction for food and beverages is already tightly controlled under subsection 67.1(1) of the Act, which limits the deduction for such expenses to a maximum of 50 percent of the amount expended, even if one incurs the expense entirely for business purposes. Thus, it is unlikely that the floodgates will open on account of food and beverage expenses incurred for business purposes.

The question remains, however, as to how far tax policy can go in permitting the deduction of other personal costs that are incurred solely and incrementally for the purposes of earning business income. Can the mortician deduct his somber clothing, the lawyer her navy suit, the accountant his white shirt, the actress her designer clothes, etc.?

To summarize: Characterizing business expenses involves three questions: (1) What is the need that the expense meets? (2) Would the need exist apart from the business? (3) Is the need intrinsic to the business? The answers to these questions are questions of fact.[60]

> If a need exists even in the absence of business activity, and irrespective of whether the need was or might have been satisfied by an expenditure to a third party or by the opportunity cost of personal labour, then an expense to meet the need would traditionally be viewed as a personal expense. Expenses which can be identified in this way are expenses which are incurred

---

> always been personal they must now be personal, the conclusion could be easily and deservedly attacked. For this reason, proper analysis of this question demands that the relationship between child care expenses and business income be examined more critically, in order to determine whether that relationship can be sufficient to justify the former's deductibility.

[59]*Per* Justice McDonald:

> This result takes into account the different methods by which the same job is done and puts all couriers on an equal footing. Arguably, it also recognizes and encourages [rather than discourages as a prohibition on this expense would] new environmentally responsible ways of producing income.

[60]*Symes v. R.*, [1993] 4 S.C.R. 695, [1994] 1 C.T.C. 40, 94 D.T.C. 6001 (S.C.C.):

> In another case, the arguments might be differently balanced, since the existence of a business purpose within the meaning of s. 18(1)(a) *is a question of fact*, and that the relative weight to be given to the factors analyzed will vary from case to case. . . . It can be difficult to weigh the personal and business elements at play. [Emphasis added.]

by a taxpayer in order to relieve the taxpayer from personal duties and to make the taxpayer available to the business.

Traditionally, expenses that simply make the taxpayer *available* to the business are not considered business expenses since the taxpayer is expected to be available to the business as a *quid pro quo* for business income received.

The needs test based upon primary objective should, in the absence of specific statutory provisions, provide an unequivocal answer. But it does not. The expense must also be *intrinsic* to the business. In *Symes*, for example, the taxpayer's child care expenses met the needs test. The taxpayer could not operate her business without being present on the premises. The Supreme Court, however, said that the expenses merely made her *available* to practice her profession, rather than for any purpose intrinsic to the operation of the business itself. The expenses got her to her business, but they were not an integral part of the business. But having got to her place of business, the expenses would have been deductible *by the business* if it provided the services.

c) — Type of Expenditure

Given the subjective nature of the purpose test, we look at the nature of an expenditure to determine its purpose. Is the expenditure of a type that is ordinarily and usually a direct expenditure in the pursuit of business, or one that is primarily personal and only tenuously related to business? Consider the distinction between a businessperson who entertains an out-of-town client at home for $100 and one who takes a client out for dinner to a restaurant for $400. The expenses of entertaining at home are usually personal, even though one devotes the entire evening (much to the chagrin of our spouses) to business matters. This is because home entertainment is ordinarily and usually a personal affair. In contrast, $200 of the cost of the dinner in the restaurant would be deductible as a business expense, even if most of the evening was spent discussing personal and social affairs. Entertaining in restaurants is ordinarily and usually associated with business, and expenses in respect thereof are usually "business expenses".[61]

---

[61] *Vuicic v. Minister of National Revenue* (1960), 24 Tax A.B.C. 253 (Can. Tax App. Bd.) (tavern keeper not allowed to deduct capital cost allowance in respect of $7,000 boat); *Brown v. Minister of National Revenue* (1950), 1 Tax A.B.C. 373 (Can. Tax App. Bd.) (special clothing required by radio technician posted in north not deductible); *No. 431 v. Minister of National Revenue* (1957), 17 Tax A.B.C. 300 (Can. Tax App. Bd.) (salary paid to physician's housekeeper entirely personal or living expense notwithstanding housekeeper's answering physician's telephone); *Macquistan v. Minister of National Revenue* (1965), 38 Tax A.B.C. 23 (Can. Tax App. Bd.) (babysitter employed by physician in order to permit her to carry on practice was personal expense); *Nadon v. Minister of National Revenue* (1965), 40 Tax A.B.C. 33 (Can. Tax App. Bd.) (housekeeper engaged during illness of taxpayer's wife not deductible); *Lawlor v. Minister of National Revenue*, [1970] Tax A.B.C. 369 (Can. Tax App. Bd.) (lawyer not entitled to deduct cost of babysitters employed to permit business entertaining); *Cree v. Minister of National Revenue*, [1978] C.T.C. 2472, 78 D.T.C. 1352 (T.R.B.) (auto racing not carried

The distinction between business and personal expenses can also depend upon the tax-payer's discretionary power to incur the expense. For example, Thorson P. denied a deduction for commuting expenses on the basis that:[62]

> The personal and living expenses referred to . . . are those over which the taxpayer has a large amount of personal control, depending upon the scale of living which he may choose. Such expenses would probably not be deductible even if there were no provision in the statute relating to the matter, for if personal and living expenses were deductible from income and only the balance left for taxation purposes, the amount of net or taxable income would depend upon the taxpayer's own choice as to the scale of living that he might adopt and in many cases there would be no taxable income at all. It is obvious that the determination of what the taxable income of a taxpayer shall be cannot depend upon or be left to the taxpayer's own choice as to whether his personal and living expenses shall be up to the extent of his income or not.

The above rationale is not persuasive. Most expenses, including business expenses, are ultimately within the taxpayer's discretion. A simpler explanation is that personal expenses are not deductible against business income because they are not incurred primarily and predominantly for business purposes and, as such, they are not relevant in determining income from business.

---

on with reasonable expectation of profit; losses not deductible); *Hume v. Minister of National Revenue*, [1980] C.T.C. 2645, 80 D.T.C. 1542 (T.R.B.) ("hobby" investor denied deduction for cost of investment periodicals); *Warden v. Minister of National Revenue*, [1981] C.T.C. 2379, 81 D.T.C. 322 (T.R.B.) (high school principal denied deduction of losses from farming and other operations since no expectation of profit); *Peters v. Minister of National Revenue*, [1981] C.T.C. 2451, 81 D.T.C. 454 (T.R.B.) (bank employee denied deduction of losses from bee keeping and sheep raising); *White v. Minister of National Revenue*, [1981] C.T.C. 2456, 81 D.T.C. 457 (T.R.B.) (taxpayer's losses from breeding and racing quarter horses disallowed for lack of reasonable expectation of profit); *Beyer v. Minister of National Revenue*, [1978] C.T.C. 2026, 78 D.T.C. 1066 (T.R.B.) (car racing losses not deductible); *Payette v. Minister of National Revenue*, [1978] C.T.C. 223, 78 D.T.C. 1181 (T.R.B.) (writing and publication of books without reasonable expectation of profit; outlays not deductible); *Fluet v. Minister of National Revenue*, [1978] C.T.C. 2902, 78 D.T.C. 1657 (T.R.B.) (bank manager's cost and maintenance of guard dog for family protection not deductible); *Merchant v. Minister of National Revenue*, [1980] C.T.C. 2336, 80 D.T.C. 1291 (T.R.B.); affirmed [1984] C.T.C. 253 (Fed. T.D.) (expenses incurred in attempt to secure leadership of Saskatchewan Liberal Party not deductible); *Symes v. R.*, [1991] 2 C.T.C. 1, 91 D.T.C. 5386 (Fr.) (Fed. C.A.); affirmed [1993] 4 S.C.R. 695, [1994] 1 C.T.C. 40, 94 D.T.C. 6001 (S.C.C.) (lawyer's nanny expenses not deductible).

[62] *Samson v. Minister of National Revenue*, [1943] C.T.C. 47, 2 D.T.C. 610 (Can. Ex. Ct.) at 64 [C.T.C.].

d) — Business versus Personal Expenditures

Expenses are deductible from income only if they are on account of commercial activities, whether from business or property. Business income arises from commercial activities generally involving a combination of labour and capital.

The concept of source of income is an intrinsic part of the Canadian income tax system.[63] The distinguishing feature of the source concept is the pursuit of profit. In order to determine whether a particular activity constitutes a source of income, the taxpayer must show that he or she carries on the activity in pursuit of profit. Thus, the characterization of income as being from a commercial activity is the first step in determining business or property income.

A hobby for personal pleasure is not a named source of income. An amateur photographer, for example, who exhibits her works for pleasure but never sells any, cannot claim expense deductions for her materials and supplies.

The law presumes that an activity in pursuit of profit that does not involve any personal or hobby element — such as, the practice of law — is a commercial venture and, as such, a source of income.[64] The only question that remains is whether the source is income from business or income from property.

If the activity is clearly commercial, there is no need to further analyze the taxpayer's business decisions, even if subsequently they prove to be unsound and unprofitable. After all, many business people make bad commercial decisions. They should not be penalized by the tax system on an ex-post analysis of their commercial decisions. The objective is to determine the commercial nature of the taxpayer's activity and not his or her business acumen with hindsight.[65]

However, where there are mixed personal and commercial elements to an activity, one must determine which elements predominate. Does the taxpayer carry on the activity in a sufficiently commercial manner to constitute a source of income? In these circumstances, one must evaluate the commercial content of the undertaking by looking at the taxpayer's expectation of profit and mode of operation. For example, a serious photographer may conduct her activities with the commercial hallmarks of a professional. If on an objective analysis of the evidence it is clear that the taxpayer's predominant intention is to derive profit from her activities, the income has a source and expenses to earn the income are deductible if they otherwise satisfy the Act.

---

[63]See Chapter 4 and *Stewart v. R.*, [2002] 2 S.C.R. 645, [2002] 3 C.T.C. 439, 2002 D.T.C. 6969 (Eng.) (S.C.C.) at para. 5.

[64]*Stewart v. R.*, *ibid.*, at para. 5.

[65]See *Stewart v. R.*, *ibid.*, at para. 55.

Thus, the characterization of income and expenses involves two distinct steps. First, one must determine whether the taxpayer's undertaking is for profit or for personal purposes. If the taxpayer undertakes the activity primarily for profit, it is a source of income. The second step is to determine whether the source of income is from business or from property. The traditional common law definition of "business" is anything that occupies the time, attention and labour of a person for the purpose of profit.[66] Business income generally requires a higher level of taxpayer activity than property income. Nevertheless, regardless of the level of taxpayer activity, any commercial undertaking in pursuit of profit is a source of income, either from business or property.

A commercial activity is one that the taxpayer undertakes for profit. We determine the taxpayer's intention by looking at objective evidence to support his or her intentions. The taxpayer must establish that his or her predominant intention is to make a profit from the activity and that he or she carries on the activity in accordance with objective standards of business behavior. Thus, we look at:

1. the taxpayer's profit and loss experience in past years;

2. the taxpayer's training and expertise in the field of his or her activities;

3. the taxpayer's intended course of action; and

4. the financial viability of the venture to show a profit.

This is not an exhaustive list and the factors to be taken into account in determining intention will differ according to the facts and circumstances of each case. Thus, having a reasonable expectation in the financial viability of the venture to show a profit is only one of the factors in evaluating the taxpayer's intention, and by itself it is not conclusive.

e) — Statutory Exceptions

Some expenses that, at least in part, may be personal expenses are, nevertheless, deductible under specific statutory provisions. For example, moving expenses,[67] child care expenses,[68] and tuition fees[69] are all expenditures that are deductible from income or creditable against taxes but only in narrowly defined circumstances. The justification for the deductibility of these expenses for tax purposes is usually social or economic policy considerations, for ex-

---

[66]*Smith v. Anderson* (1880), 15 Ch. D. 247 (Eng. C.A.) at 258; *Terminal Dock & Warehouse Co. v. Minister of National Revenue*, [1968] 2 Ex. C.R. 78, [1968] C.T.C. 78, 68 D.T.C. 5060 (Can. Ex. Ct.); affirmed [1968] S.C.R. vi, 68 D.T.C 5316 (S.C.C.).

[67]S. 62; see Chapter 12, "Other Income and Deductions".

[68]S. 63; see Chapter 12, "Other Income and Deductions".

[69]S. 118.5; see Chapter 15, "Computation of Tax".

ample, mobility of labour, access to labour markets, and investment in human capital and resources.

G. — General Anti-Avoidance Rule

A taxpayer seeking to deduct expenses from income must always be mindful of the general anti-avoidance rule ("GAAR"), which applies to "abusive" income tax avoidance transactions and arrangements. The rule allows the CRA to ignore offensive "avoidance transaction" and redetermine income tax consequences in certain circumstances.[70]

An "avoidance transaction" is any transaction or series of transactions that gives rise to a tax benefit, unless the transaction is one that is undertaken for *bona fide* purposes other than that of obtaining a tax benefit. The Act defines a "tax benefit" to include, *inter alia*, a transaction to avoid taxes. Thus an avoidance transaction includes transactions in which the taxpayer seeks to avoid tax. However, even a tax-motivated transaction is not an "avoidance transaction" if it does not misuse the Act, Regulations, ITARs, or Tax Treaties.[71] Hence, the essential issue is whether the particular transactions "abuse" the underlying policy of the Act.

H. — Exempt Income

An expense to earn exempt income is not deductible for tax purposes.[72] Generally, "exempt income" is any income that is not included in computing income under Part I of the Act.[73] Thus, one cannot offset expenditures to earn exempt income against other taxable income.

I. — Specific Deductions

The starting point in computing income from business or property is to determine the *net* profit therefrom according to generally accepted commercial principles. We repeat, however, that the determination of profit is ultimately a question of law governed by legal precepts. Commercial principles assist in determining net profit, but they are not necessarily conclusive.

In addition to the deductions allowed according to commercial and accounting principles, the Act also specifically authorizes the deduction of certain expenses. The rationale for these specific deductions varies: some of the rules regulate deductions that might otherwise be

---

[70]S. 245.

[71]Subs. 245(4).

[72]Para. 18(1)(c).

[73]Subs. 248(1) "exempt income".

governed by unclear or flexible accounting principles (e.g., reserves); some (e.g., capital cost allowances) replace accounting rules with more specific and detailed tax rules; some (e.g., restrictions on financing passenger motor vehicles) reflect a concern that the tax system should not subsidize personal expenditures; and some incorporate political and cultural values (e.g., restrictions on advertising in non-Canadian periodicals). There is no single thread that connects these deductions. Each has its own rationale and the list expands annually to accommodate evolving values.

J. — *Reserves and Contingent Liabilities*

a) — *General Scheme*

As a general rule, a taxpayer cannot deduct a reserve or a contingent liability.[74] A reserve is an appropriation, as opposed to an expense that one incurs for the purpose of earning income. As we will see, however, there are many exceptions to the general rule. The Act permits reserve deductions, but only in circumscribed conditions.

The term "reserve" has a much broader meaning in tax law than it does in accounting. For accounting purposes, a "reserve" denotes an appropriation of income from retained earnings. Such appropriation may be pursuant to a contractual stipulation (for example, pursuant to a trust indenture) or at the discretion of the taxpayer.[75] For tax purposes, however, a "reserve" generally refers to an amount that one sets aside for future use.

One must distinguish between reserves and unpaid liabilities. A "reserve" represents an amount set aside as a provision against a future uncertain event. A liability is a known and existing obligation.[76] Thus, an obligation is a liability for tax purposes only if all of the conditions precedent are present to create the liability have been satisfied.[77]

In contrast, a contingent liability is only a potential liability that may become actual if, and only if, certain events occur. The generally accepted test of contingencies is events that may or may not occur. A contingent liability depends upon an event that may or may not hap-

---

[74]Para. 18(1)(e); IT-215R Archived, "Reserves, Contingent Accounts and Sinking Funds" (January 12, 1981) as amended by Special Release dated November 30, 1989.

[75]CICA Handbook, s. 3260.01.

[76]*No. 297 v. Minister of National Revenue* (1955), 14 Tax A.B.C. 100, 55 D.T.C. 611 (Can. Tax. App. Bd.) (amount set aside by taxpayer for employee bonuses not a reserve since liability to pay definite).

[77]*Kerr Farms Ltd. v. Minister of National Revenue*, [1971] Tax A.B.C. 804, 71 D.T.C. 536 (Can. Tax. App. Bd.) (conditions precedent outstanding; accrued employee bonuses not liabilities).

pen.[78] Thus, contingent liabilities are not real liabilities, but have the potential of becoming real on the happening of some future event.

Generally, a taxpayer may claim a reserve in a year only if the Act specifically authorizes the deduction. The general structure of the Act is that if a taxpayer claims a reserve in a particular year, it is added back into his or her income in the following year. The taxpayer may then claim a new reserve according to the terms and conditions of the authorizing provisions. Thus, there is an annual renewal of the reserve and one must annually justify the deduction of a reserve. This structure prevents the limitation period even applying to claims for old reserves.

b) — Deductible Reserves

Deduction allowed for	ITA Reference	To be included in income in the following year
Reserve for doubtful debts	20(1)(l)	12(1)(d)
Reserve for goods delivered and services performed after end of year	20(1)(m)(i)(ii)	12(1)(e)(i)
Reserve for deposits on return-able containers	20(1)(m)(iv)	12(1)(e)(i)
Manufacturer's warranty reserve	20(1)(m.1)	12(1)(e)(i)
Reserves for amounts not due on instalment sales contracts	20(1)(n)	12(1)(e)(ii)
Reserve for quadrennial survey	20(1)(o)	12(1)(h)
Prepaid rents	20(1)(m)(iii)	12(1)(e)(i)

---

[78]See *Winter v. Inland Revenue Commissioners* (1961), [1963] A.C. 235 (U.K. H.L.), at 262 *per* Lord Guest. See also: *Wawang Forest Products Ltd. v. R.*, [2001] 2 C.T.C. 233, 2001 D.T.C. 5212 (Fed. C.A.) (a legal obligation to pay does not become contingent because of delay).

(i) — Doubtful Debts

A taxpayer may deduct a reasonable amount for doubtful trade accounts if the amounts receivable in respect of the accounts were included in income, either in the year in which he claims the reserve or in a previous year.

A reserve may also claim a reserve for doubtful debts arising on loans or lending made in the ordinary course of business where the taxpayer is an insurer or involved in the business of lending money.[79]

A reserve for financial statement purposes is not necessarily the amount deductible for tax purposes. Whether the collectability of a debt is sufficiently "doubtful" to justify a reserve is a question of fact that requires specific analysis of each account. As a matter of practice, however, the CRA does accept reserves calculated as a percentage of doubtful accounts, provided that the taxpayer can support the percentage by reference to his or her actual loss experience. A reserve computed without reference to actual experience is not acceptable for tax purposes.

The factors that one takes into account in determining the collectibility of an account receivable are as follows:[80]

- History and age of the overdue account;
- The debtor's financial position;
- Past experience in respect of the debtor's bad debts;
- General business conditions;
- Specific business conditions in the debtor's industry;
- Specific business conditions in the debtor's locality; and
- Changes in sales and accounts receivable as compared with previous years.

A taxpayer who claims a reserve for doubtful accounts in one year must include the amount in his income in the following year.[81] The taxpayer can then evaluate the collectibility of accounts receivable in the next year and deduct a new reserve. Thus, unlike accounting practice that permits incremental additions to, and subtractions from, the previous year's reserve, we deduct the *entire* amount of the reserve in the year in which we claim it. This amount is then added to income in the following year, a new amount is deducted, and so on. This

---

[79]Para. 20(1)(l); IT-442R, "Bad Debts and Reserve for Doubtful Debts" (September 6, 1991).

[80]*No. 81 v. Minister of National Revenue* (1953), 8 Tax A.B.C. 82, 53 D.T.C. 98 (Can. Tax App. Bd.) at 98 [Tax A.B.C.].

[81]Para. 12(1)(d).

scheme allows the CRA to challenge the entire reserve in the year it is claimed, without any risk that a portion of the reserve is statute-barred. Under accounting practices, it is arguable that only the incremental portion is current. The base of the reserve could be statute-barred.[82]

The initial claim for a reserve is a tentative one that is added back to income in the following year. The taxpayer may either collect the amount in a subsequent year or claim a write-off for actual bad debts. A taxpayer may also deduct his or her actual bad debts.[83] An amount written off that is subsequently collected by the taxpayer is brought back into income in the year of collection.[84]

Example

Assume:

Year	Accounts Receivable (year-end)	Reserve for Doubtful Debts	Bad Debts Deducted	Bad Debts Recovered
1	$100,000	$10,000	—	—
2	$120,000	$12,000	$6,000	—
3	$150,000	$15,000	$4,000	$5,000

Then, the *net* deduction from income in each year is determined as follows:

Example

Year 1

Net deduction (Year 1) $ 10,000

---

[82]Subs. 152(4).

[83]Para. 20(1)(p).

[84]Para. 12(1)(i).

Year 2

Reserve for doubtful debts	$	12,000
Bad debts deducted		6,000
		18,000
Less: reserve deducted (Year 1)	(	10,000)
Net deduction (Year 2)	$	8,000

Year 3

Reserve for doubtful debts	$	15,000
Bad debts deducted		4,000
		19,000
Less: reserve deducted (Year 2))	(	12,000)
bad debts recovered		(5,000)
Net deduction (Year 3)	$	2,000

(ii) — Goods and Services

A taxpayer must include in income all payments on account of goods to be delivered or services to be rendered in the future. This rule overrides the generally accepted accounting principle that we recognize income only when we realize it and not when we receive it.[85] A taxpayer can, however, deduct a reasonable amount in respect of goods that will be delivered, or services that will be rendered, in a subsequent year.[86] This reserve is available only in computing income from a business and *not* in computing income from property.

---

[85]See "Measurement and Timing".

[86]Para. 20(1)(m).

A taxpayer can also deduct a reserve for deposits that may be refundable (excluding deposits on bottles), prepaid rent for the use of land or chattels, and for amounts that are receivable but not yet due.[87]

Both paragraphs 20(1)(m) and 20(1)(n) refer to the deduction of a reasonable amount as a reserve. What is "reasonable" is a question of fact depending upon the circumstances. A reasonable reserve is not necessarily equal to the amount included in income under paragraph 12(1)(a). For example, a taxpayer who sells tokens that are redeemable for products must include the proceeds from the tokens in income. If all the tokens have not been redeemed at the end of the taxation year, the taxpayer may claim a reserve equal to the value of the tokens that he or she expects will be redeemed by customers. Where, however, the history of the taxpayer's business indicates that some of the tokens sold will never be redeemed, the taxpayer must reduce that reserve by the amount of the tokens that are not expected to be redeemed.

(iii) — Amounts Not Due

In calculating income from a *business*, a taxpayer may deduct a reserve for the purchase price of property sold, but that is not due until sometime after the end of the year.[88]

1. — Property Other than Land

Where the subject matter of the sale is property other than land, a taxpayer may claim a reserve only if the proceeds of the sale are not due until a time more than two years after the date of sale. In effect, the taxpayer can allocate his or her profit over an extended period in much the same way as under instalment sales accounting. One calculates the reserve, which must be reasonable, by comparing the amount due as at the end of the taxation year to the gross sales proceeds. This ratio is applied against the gross profit realized on the sale, and the resulting amount is the reserve for that sale for the year.

Example

Assume:

Sale price	$ 200,000

---

[87]Paras. 20(1)(m), (n).

[88]Para. 20(1)(n); *Home Provisioners (Manitoba) Ltd. v. Minister of National Revenue*, [1958] C.T.C. 334, 58 D.T.C. 1183 (Can. Ex. Ct.) (absolute assignment of right to receive instalment payments precluded right to claim reserve).

Cost		100,000
Gross profit		$ 100,000

Cash re-
ceived:

Year 1	$ 125,000
Year 2	50,000
Year 3	25,000

Then:

Year 1:

Profit on sale			$ 100,000
Less reserve:	$ 75,000 × $ 100,000		(37,500)
	$ 200,000		
Income (A)			$ 62,500

Year 2:

Previous year's reserve			$ 37,500
Less reserve:	$ 25,000 × $ 100,000		(12,500)
	$ 200,000		
Income (B)			$ 25,000

Year 3:

Previous year's

reserve $ 12,500

Less reserve: 0   × $ 100,000   0

                              $ 200,000

        Income (C) $ 12,500

Total gain included in income

(A + B + C) $ 100,000

2. — Land

A taxpayer can claim a reserve when he or she sells land if part of the proceeds of sale are payable after the end of the taxation year in which the land is sold.[89]

c) — Limitations on Reserves

The Act limits reserves in various circumstances. The following illustrate some of the limits. Note the general limitation in para. 20(8)(b), which restricts the reserve to a three-year period.

(i) — Food, Drink and Transportation

Where a taxpayer claims a reserve in respect of food, drink or transportation that it plans to deliver or provide after the end of the year, the reserve cannot exceed the revenue from these sources included in income for the year.[90]

---

[89]Subpara. 20(1)(n); IT-152R3 "Special Reserves — Sale of Land" (June 18, 1985).

[90]Subs. 20(6).

Example

Assume:

Transportation tickets issued in year	$	60,000
Tickets unused at the end of the year	$	10,000

Then:

The reserve under paragraph 20(1)(m) and subsection 20(6) is $10,000 unless experience indicates that a portion of the tickets will never be redeemed. If experience indicates, for example, that five percent of all tickets issued are never redeemed, a reasonable reserve would be computed as follows:

Tickets unused at the end of the year	$	10,000
Tickets that will not be redeemed		
[5% × $60,000]		(3,000)
Reasonable reserve	$	7,000

(ii) — Non-Residents

A taxpayer who gives up his or her Canadian residency and does not carry on business in Canada cannot deduct a reserve in respect of unrealized receivables. Thus, since a reserve that a taxpayer claims in one year is added to his or her income in the following year, the taxpayer cannot avoid tax simply by giving up Canadian residence.[91]

(iii) — Guarantees, Indemnities and Warranties

Where a taxpayer sells property or services and provides a guarantee, indemnity or warranty for those goods or services, the cost of the guarantee is usually included in the sale price. The taxpayer cannot claim a reserve in respect of the expected liabilities under the guarantees, indemnities or warranties.[92]

---

[91] Subs. 20(8); paras. 20(1)(n) and 12(1)(e).

[92] Subs. 20(7). For obvious reasons, taxpayers computing income on a cash basis are not entitled to claim a reserve under para. 20(1)(m).

K. — Interest Expense

a) — General Comment

The cost of financing is one of the most important decisions for businesses and investors. If one starts with the financial premise that interest represents the economic rental cost of the use of other people's money, interest expense should be deductible if one incurs it to earn income. The Act, however, is not that simple, and the issue is litigated frequently.

The Act generally allows a taxpayer to deduct interest on money that he or she borrows to earn income from business or property.[93] The disputes arise primarily from source distinctions between types of income and taxpayer attempts to shift their position to minimize taxes.

The trouble begins with a Supreme Court decision that held that interest is an expenditure on account of capital. The Court held that a tax deduction for interest on borrowed money would in fairness require a similar deduction for the *imputed* cost of equity capital:[94]

> ... *in the absence of an express statutory allowance*, interest payable on capital indebtedness is not deductible as an income expense. If a company has not the money capital to commence business, why should it be allowed to deduct the interest on borrowed money? The company setting up with its own contributed capital would, on such a principle, be entitled to interest on its capital before taxable income was reached, but the income statutes give no countenance to such a deduction.

We allow taxpayers to deduct their business rent, even though we do not allow owners of their premises to deduct imputed rental expense.

The decision in *Canada Safeway* was wrong in any economic sense. Nevertheless, the law stands: the Supreme Court is never wrong, at least not until it says it is. Thus, without specific statutory authority, interest expense is a capital expenditure for tax purposes and, therefore, not deductible.[95]

Paragraph 20(1)(c) authorizes one to deduct interest in the pursuit of certain "for profit" activities. The object of section 20(1)(c) is to create an incentive to accumulate income-producing capital by allowing taxpayers to deduct interest costs associated with its acquisition. This is seen as desirable because it creates wealth and increases the income tax base.[96] Parliament formulated this provision specifically to overrule *Canada Safeway's* denial of the

---

[93]Para. 20(1)(c).

[94]*Canada Safeway Ltd. v. Minister of National Revenue*, [1957] S.C.R. 717, [1957] C.T.C. 335, 57 D.T.C. 1239 (S.C.C.) at 344 [C.T.C.] and 1244 [D.T.C.].

[95]Para. 18(1)(b).

[96]*Entreprises Ludco ltée c. Canada*, [2001] 2 S.C.R. 1082, [2002] 1 C.T.C. 95, 2001 D.T.C. 5505 (Eng.) (S.C.C.) at para. 63.

deduction of interest as an expense. The statutory rule is permissive: it allows the deduction for interest as a current expense to earn business and investment income in circumstances that judge-made law would not. Paragraph 20(1)(c) is not an anti-avoidance provision, and one should not interpret it as such without precise and specific language.[97]

b) — Tax Arbitrage

Financing decisions depend upon risk, reward, security and taxes. Two characteristics of the Canadian income tax system have a particularly important influence on financing transactions. First, there are the statutory distinctions between the various sources of income and expenses. As we will see, interest on money that one borrows for business and investment purposes is generally deductible for tax purposes. Interest on debt to earn exempt income or capital gains is not deductible.

Second, there is the distinction between debt and equity capital. Debt represents borrowed capital that creates a liability to repay according to a pre-determined schedule. Equity is capital that one invests in exchange for an ownership interest. There is generally no fixed timetable to repay equity capital to the enterprise's owners.[98]

Interest on borrowed money is an expense of earning profits. For tax purposes, dividends on shareholder equity are a distribution of profits to the owners *after* they earn the profits. Hence, dividends are not deductible as an expense of obtaining financing.

These two features of the tax system, strict segregation of income by source and the distinction between debt and equity capital, materially affect Canadian corporate financing decisions as taxpayers arbitrage to reduce taxes and maximize their economic returns.

Dividend income is double taxed: first, in the corporation that pays tax on the income from which it pays dividends; second, in the hands of the shareholder who receives the dividend. Double taxation is unfair and distorts tax structures — for example, the shift to income trust structures and away from traditional corporations (since performed) was essentially tax inspired to avoid double tax. To be sure, there are some who argue that it is not double taxation because the income is taxed to two separate persons, the corporation and the shareholder. They are legally correct, but not so in an economic sense. The corporation is an artificial person.

---

[97]*Neuman v. Minister of National Revenue*, [1998] 1 S.C.R. 770, [1998] 3 C.T.C. 177, 98 D.T.C. 6297 (S.C.C.): "We should not be quick to embellish [a] provision . . . when it is open for the legislator to be precise and specific with respect to any mischief to be avoided."

[98]There may be some exceptions in the case of redeemable preferred shares, etc. These types of shares, however, more closely resemble debt capital with an equity flavor, rather than pure equity capital.

Since interest is generally deductible only when one incurs it in the pursuit of "for profit" activities and is not deductible when one uses debt "for pleasure" or for consumption, individuals have an incentive to tax arbitrage — that is, convert non-deductible personal interest into deductible business expenses by arranging transactions to attach the interest to their "for profit" activities. For example, a lawyer with cash savings might borrow an equal amount to invest in the capital of his or her law firm and then use the savings to buy a home.[99]

Even "for profit" activities promote tax arbitrage. For example, one might use loans on which interest is fully deductible to produce income that is taxed at a lower rate. Thus, an investor might deduct interest expense taxed at 50 percent to earn Canadian-source dividend income taxed at a lower rate. With only slightly greater sophistication, an investor might borrow to earn business income, which is fully taxable, and convert the end profit into a capital gain, only one-half of which is taxable. Tax arbitrage is an economic response to a system of segregation of income into sources and categories that we tax at different rates.

c) — Statutory Requirements

"Interest" is compensation for the use of a sum of money belonging or owed to another.[100] It represents a legal obligation that one calculates by reference to the principal sum owing. The obligation to pay interest may arise from an express agreement, by legal implication, or by statute. Thus, interest expense is the rental cost for debt capital.

A taxpayer may deduct interest if it:[101]

- Is paid or payable in the year;

- Arises from a legal obligation;

- Is payable on borrowed money that one was for the purpose of earning income (other than exempt income) from a business or property; and

- Is reasonable in amount.

The Act overrides the common law restriction that interest is a capital expenditure. However, it restricts the deductibility of interest to money that one uses in "for profit" activities and denies the deduction for funds used in "for pleasure" activities. It also limits the deductibility of interest to money *used for the purpose* of earning income from business or pro-

---

[99]See, for example, *Singleton v. R.*, [1999] 3 C.T.C. 446, 99 D.T.C. 5362 (Fed. C.A.); affirmed [2001] 2 S.C.R. 1046, [2002] 1 C.T.C. 121, 2001 D.T.C. 5533 (Eng.) (S.C.C.). See also *Entreprises Ludco ltée c. Canada*, [2001] 2 S.C.R. 1082, [2002] 1 C.T.C. 95, 2001 D.T.C. 5505 (S.C.C.).

[100]*Saskatchewan (Attorney General) v. Canada (Attorney General)*, [1947] S.C.R. 394 (S.C.C.) at 411; affirmed [1949] A.C. 110 (Canada P.C.).

[101]Para. 20(1)(c).

perty. Thus, it confines the deduction to specific sources of income. If a payment blends capital and interest, the interest component is deductible if it otherwise satisfies the Act.[102] Where an interest rate is established in a market of lenders and borrowers acting at arm's length from each other, it is generally a reasonable rate.[103]

d) — Legal Obligation

What is interest is essentially a question of law. The main criterion is that interest represents payment for the use of debt capital. Hence, one calculates interest by reference to a principal sum. Some courts have grafted an additional precondition that interest must accrue daily.[104]

Interest is deductible only if the lender has *legal* rights to enforce payment of the amounts due. Thus, deductibility depends upon an unconditional and legally enforceable obligation to pay interest. The obligation must be actual and not contingent. If there is no legal obligation to pay the interest, paragraph 18(1)(e) prevents its deduction.

e) — Use of Money

A taxpayer may deduct an amount paid or payable in respect of the year ". . . pursuant to a legal obligation to pay interest on borrowed money *used for the purpose of* earning income from a business or property . . . or a reasonable amount in respect thereof, ..." The phrase ". . . used for the purpose of . . ." incorporates two separate tests: use and purpose. One applies these tests to distinguish between "for profit" and "for pleasure" activities.

A taxpayer may deduct interest as an expense only if he or she uses the borrowed money for earning income from a business or investment property. Interest is not deductible for the purposes of earning capital gains, which are a separate source of income.[105] Thus, a tax-

---

[102]Subs. 16(1).

[103]See *Mohammad v. R.*, [1997] 3 C.T.C. 321, 97 D.T.C. 5503 (Fed. C.A.) at 5509 [D.T.C.]; *Irving Oil Ltd. v. R.*, [1991] 1 C.T.C. 350, 91 D.T.C. 5106 (Fed. C.A.) at 359 [C.T.C.]; leave to appeal refused (1991), 136 N.R. 320 (note) (S.C.C.).

[104]*Ontario (Attorney General) v. Barfried Enterprises Ltd.*, [1963] S.C.R. 570 (S.C.C.).

[105]See., e.g., *Ludmer c. Ministre du Revenu national*, [1993] 2 C.T.C. 2494, 93 D.T.C. 1351 (Eng.), [1993] T.C.J. No. 1 (T.C.C.); affirmed [1998] 2 C.T.C. 104 (Fed. T.D.); affirmed [1999] 3 C.T.C. 601, 99 D.T.C. 5153 (Eng.) (Fed. C.A.); reversed [2002] 1 C.T.C. 95 (S.C.C.) (interest on money used to purchase shares not deductible if *income* from shares cannot yield profit); *Hastings v. Minister of National Revenue*, [1988] 2 C.T.C. 2001, 88 D.T.C. 1391 (T.C.C.) (interest expense on commodities trades not deductible); *R. v. Stirling*, [1985] C.T.C. 275, 85 D.T.C. 5199 (Fed. C.A.) (interest and safekeeping charges for purchase of gold bullion not deductible in determining capital gain); *R. v. Canadian Pacific Ltd. (No. 1)*, [1977] C.T.C. 606, 77 D.T.C. 5383 (Fed. C.A.) (deduction of interest

payer who borrows to buy shares can deduct interest if he or she reasonably expects that the shares will pay dividends. The *amount* of dividends expected or received is not determinative.[106] However, the taxpayer is not entitled to a deduction if she expects to earn only capital gains when she sells the shares. This distinction causes taxpayers to "hide" interest, for example, in bond discounts and premiums.

The use test traces the direct flow of funds to determine how one applies the borrowed money. It is the actual, and not the alleged, uses of borrowed money that determines the deductibility of interest payable on the funds.[107] In *Sinha v. Minister of National Revenue*,[108] for example, a student borrowed from the Canada Student Loan Plan at a low rate of interest and reinvested the borrowed funds at a higher rate. The Board rejected the Minister's argument that the purpose of the borrowing was personal (educational) and allowed the taxpayer to deduct his interest expense since he *actually* used the borrowed money for investment purposes.

f) — Purpose of Borrowing

The second test of interest deductibility is that the taxpayer must use the funds for the *purpose* of earning income from business or property. Thus, the taxpayer must have a *bona fide* intention to use the borrowed money for an income-earning purpose. Earning income from business or property need not be the primary or dominant purpose for borrowing. Absent a sham or window dressing, the taxpayer's ancillary purpose to earn income is equally capable of providing the requisite purpose.[109] In addition, whether he or she actually realizes income is irrelevant. The purpose test is concerned solely with intention. The two tests are, however, inter-related:[110]

> Eligibility for the deduction is contingent on the use of borrowed money for the purpose of earning income . . . it is not the purpose of the borrowing itself which is relevant. What is relevant, rather, is the taxpayer's purpose in using the borrowed money in a particular manner.

---

under old subs. 8(3) only allowable where corporation subject to Part I tax); *Birmingham (City) v. Barnes (Inspector of Taxes)*, [1935] A.C. 292 (H.L.) (clarification of capital costs for laying tramway lines where expenditure contributed to by another party).

[106]*Ludmer c. Ministre du Revenu national, ibid.*, at para. 59.

[107]*Bronfman Trust v. R.*, [1987] 1 S.C.R. 32, [1987] 1 C.T.C. 117, 87 D.T.C. 5059 (S.C.C.).

[108]*Sinha v. Minister of National Revenue*, [1981] C.T.C. 2599, 81 D.T.C. 465 (T.R.B.).

[109]*Ludmer c. Ministre du Revenu national*, [1999] 3 C.T.C. 601, 99 D.T.C. 5153 (Eng.) (Fed. C.A.) at para. 51; reversed [2002] 1 C.T.C. 95 (S.C.C.).

[110]*Bronfman Trust v. R.*, [1987] 1 S.C.R. 32, [1987] 1 C.T.C. 117, 87 D.T.C. 5059 (S.C.C.) at 125 [C.T.C.] and 5064 [D.T.C.].

> . . . Consequently, the focus of the inquiry must be centred on *the use to which the taxpayer put the borrowed funds.* [Emphasis added.]

Further, in *Shell Canada*,[111] the Supreme Court said:

> The issue is the use to which the borrowed funds are put. It is irrelevant why the borrowing arrangement was structured the way that it was or, indeed, why the funds were borrowed at all.

For example, a taxpayer who borrows money at a given rate of interest and then lends the money at less than his or her borrowing cost cannot be said to be using the money for the *purpose of* earning income. The absence of an intention to earn income makes the interest non-deductible. There may be limited circumstances, however, where a person borrows money and lends it at a lower rate for the purpose of helping a major customer survive economic hardship. The courts accept the indirect purpose of such transactions.

We determine the purpose of borrowing by tracing the direct and immediate use of the borrowed funds into the income-earning process.[112] The deduction is not available where the link between the borrowed money and an eligible use is merely indirect. Interest is deductible only if there is a sufficiently direct link between the borrowed money and the current eligible use.[113]

It also does not necessarily matter if the borrowed funds are commingled with funds used for another purpose, provided that the borrowed funds can in fact be traced to a current eligible use.[114] Thus, taxpayers should borrow for income-earning activities and pay for personal consumption through savings. In *Singleton*, for example, the taxpayer, a partner in a law firm, withdrew $300,000 from his capital account in the firm to purchase his home, which he registered in the name of his wife. Later on the same day, he borrowed an identical amount in a daylight loan from the bank and replenished his capital account in the firm. The taxpayer could deduct his interest on the bank borrowing because the funds were directly traceable to the business. Tax minimization as a motive is not a bar to the deduction of an expense. Taxpayers can arrange their affairs for the sole purpose of achieving favourable tax

---

[111]*Shell Canada Ltd. v. R.*, [1999] 3 S.C.R. 622, [1999] 4 C.T.C. 313, 99 D.T.C. 5669 (Eng.) (S.C.C.).

[112]*Singleton v. R.*, [2001] 2 S.C.R. 1046, [2002] 1 C.T.C. 121, 204 D.L.R. (4th) 564, 2001 D.T.C. 5533 (Eng.) (S.C.C.).

[113]*Tennant v. R.*, [1996] 1 S.C.R. 305, [1996] 1 C.T.C. 290, 96 D.T.C. 6121 (S.C.C.).

[114]*Shell Canada Ltd. v. R.*, [1999] 3 S.C.R. 622, [1999] 4 C.T.C. 313, 99 D.T.C. 5669 (Eng.) (S.C.C.).

results.[115] Tax avoidance is not, *per se*, offensive. Absent statutory language, business transactions do not require an independent business purpose.[116]

We emphasize the form of borrowing, not its economic substance, to determine the deductibility of interest expense. Interest on debt that only indirectly earns income is not deductible for tax purposes. In *Bronfman Trust*,[117] for example, the settlor created a trust in favour of his daughter under which she would receive 50 percent of its income and such additional allocations as the trustees in their discretion might decide. The trust invested its capital in income-earning securities.

When the trustees decided to make a capital distribution of $2 million to the beneficiary, they chose to borrow the funds rather than liquidate capital to make the payment. The decision to borrow was based on business reasons. It was financially inexpedient to liquidate any portion of the trust's investments at that time because they were invested at high rates. By borrowing money for the capital distribution, the trustees preserved the high income-yielding capacity of the trust's investments. The Supreme Court held that the economic substance of the underlying transactions did not justify deduction of the interest on the borrowing. Chief Justice Dickson said:[118]

> In my view, the text of the Act requires tracing the use of borrowed funds to a specific eligible use, its obviously restricted purpose being the encouragement of taxpayers to augment their income-producing potential. This, in my view, precludes the allowance of a deduction for interest paid on borrowed funds which indirectly preserve income-earning property but which are not directly "used for the purpose of earning income from . . . property".

This principle applies equally to all taxpayers, including corporations, trusts and individuals.[119]

---

[115]See *Neuman v. Minister of National Revenue*, [1998] 1 S.C.R. 147, [1998] 2 C.T.C. 35, 98 D.T.C. 6297 (S.C.C.): "The ITA has many specific anti-avoidance provisions and rules governing the treatment of non-arm's length transactions. We should not be quick to embellish the provision at issue here when it is open for the legislator to be precise and specific with respect to any mischief to be avoided."

[116]*Stubart Investment Ltd. v. R.*, [1984] 1 S.C.R. 536, [1984] C.T.C. 294, 84 D.T.C. 6305 (S.C.C.); *Neuman v. Minister of National Revenue*, [1998] 1 S.C.R. 147, [1998] 2 C.T.C. 35 (S.C.C.) "Taxpayers can arrange their affairs in a particular way for the sole purpose of deliberately availing themselves of tax reduction devices in the ITA."

[117]*Bronfman Trust v. R.*, [1987] 1 S.C.R. 32, [1987] 1 C.T.C. 117, 87 D.T.C. 5059 (S.C.C.).

[118]*Bronfman Trust v. R.*, ibid., at 129 [C.T.C.] and 5067 [D.T.C.].

[119]*Bronfman Trust v. R.*, ibid., at 129 [C.T.C.] and 5067 [D.T.C.].

However, in *Shell Canada*,[120] the Supreme Court held that while transforming funds into a different currency changed its form and relative value, it did not change its substance — it remained money. Hence, there was no change in current use. McLachlin, J. stated:

> The mere fact that an exchange had to occur before usable money was produced is not particularly significant. Except where the borrower is a money trader, borrowed money can rarely itself produce income. It must always be exchanged for something, whether it be machinery or goods, which then produces income. The necessity of such an exchange does not mean the eventual production of income is an indirect use of the borrowed money.

g) — Expectation of Income

The deductibility of interest depends upon the intention of the borrower at the time that he or she invests the funds. The investment in business or property must have the potential to yield "income" — that is *gross* income. Thus, it is not necessary to make a taxable profit in order to deduct the interest expense. It is sufficient that the taxpayer had a reasonable expectation at the time that he invested the funds of earning an amount that would come into income for taxation purposes.[121] Moreover, it is irrelevant whether the invested funds actually produce income.[122] For example, interest on borrowed funds invested in a business venture that loses money is deductible if the taxpayer has a reasonable, albeit frustrated, expectation of earning income.

We emphasize that the intention must be to earn income from business or property and *not* from capital gains. Income from capital gains is not income from property.[123] Thus, interest expenses *solely* to earn capital gains are not deductible in computing income from business or property.[124]

---

[120]*Shell Canada Ltd. v. R.*, [1999] 3 S.C.R. 622, [1999] 4 C.T.C. 313, 99 D.T.C. 5669 (Eng.) (S.C.C.).

[121]*Ludmer c. Ministre du Revenu national*, [1999] 3 C.T.C. 601, 99 D.T.C. 5153 (Eng.) (Fed. C.A.) at para. 61; reversed [2002] 1 C.T.C. 95 (S.C.C.).

[122]See: *Lessard c. Minister of National Revenue*, [1993] 1 C.T.C. 2176, 93 D.T.C. 680 (T.C.C.) (interest on funds used to acquire shares deductible even though taxpayer was sole shareholder, because shares constituted a potential source of income).

[123]Subs. 9(3). See: *Ludmer c. Ministre du Revenue national*, [1993] 2 C.T.C. 2494, 93 D.T.C. 1351 (Eng.) (T.C.C.); affirmed [1998] 2 C.T.C. 104, 98 D.T.C. 6045 (Eng.) (Fed. T.D.); affirmed [1999] 3 C.T.C. 601, 99 D.T.C. 5153 (Eng.) (Fed. C.A.); reversed [2002] 1 C.T.C. 95, 2001 D.T.C. 5505 (Eng.) (S.C.C.); *Hugill v. R.*, [1995] 2 C.T.C. 16, 95 D.T.C. 5311 (Fed. C.A.).

[124]*Bronfman Trust v. R.*, above note 117 (". . . The fact that the loan may have prevented capital losses cannot assist the taxpayer in obtaining a deduction from income which is limited to use of borrowed money for the purpose of earning income.") See also: *Mandryk v. R.*, [1992] 1 C.T.C. 317, 92 D.T.C. 6329 (Fed. C.A.) (taxpayer not entitled to deduct interest expense to honour personal guarantees of corporate indebtedness).

h) — Current Use

It is the *current*, and not the original, use of funds that determines the deductibility of interest expense. As Jackett P. said in *Trans-Prairie*:[125]

> ... interest should be deductible for the years in which the borrowed capital is employed in the business rather than that it should be deductible for the life of a loan as long as its first use was in the business.

Similarly, in *Bronfman Trust*:[126]

> ... a taxpayer who uses or intends to use borrowed money for an ineligible purpose, but later uses the funds to earn non-exempt income from a business or property, ought not to be deprived of the deduction for the current, eligible use.

Hence, change of use can affect deductibility. For example, if a taxpayer initially borrows money to invest in bonds, and later sells the bonds and uses the money to take a vacation, the interest expense ceases to qualify as a deduction from the date of the change of use of the borrowing.[127] Conversely, interest on funds initially borrowed for personal purposes and later used for business purposes qualifies for deduction as of the date of change of use. For example, a taxpayer who borrows money to purchase a residential cottage for personal use, and then sells the cottage and uses the proceeds to buy income yielding shares, can deduct the interest on the borrowed funds as of the date of the investment.

i) — Reloaned Funds

As with initial borrowings, where an individual borrows money and then lends the money to his or her corporation, the deductibility of the interest paid by the individual depends upon the *purpose* of the lending. Where an individual borrows at a commercial rate of interest and loans at a lower rate, he or she cannot generally be borrowing for the *purpose* of earning income. Hence, any interest payable on the funds is *prima facie* not deductible. The CRA does, however allow a deduction to the extent that the individual actually earns income. In certain cases, there is a full deduction of the interest expense even though the individual loans the funds at a lower rate than the cost of his or her borrowing.[128]

---

[125]*Trans-Prairie Pipelines Ltd. v. Minister of National Revenue*, [1970] C.T.C. 537, 70 D.T.C. 6351 (Can. Ex. Ct.) at 541 [C.T.C.] and 6354 [D.T.C.]; approved by S.C.C. in *Bronfman Trust v. R.*.

[126]*Bronfman Trust v. R.*, [1987] 1 S.C.R. 32, [1987] 1 C.T.C. 117, 87 D.T.C. 5059 (S.C.C.) at 5065 [D.T.C.].

[127]Subpara. 20(1)(c)(i).

[128]See IT-533, "Interest Deductibility and Related Issues" (October 31, 2003) and *Canadian Helicopters Ltd. v. R.*, [2002] 2 C.T.C. 83, 2002 D.T.C. 6805 (Fed. C.A.).

j) — Exempt Income

Interest expense is deductible only if one incurs it to earn income from business or property and the income is taxable. Interest expense is not deductible if the taxpayer uses the funds to earn income that is exempt or to acquire a life insurance policy.[129]

k) — Compound Interest

A taxpayer can deduct interest on interest — that is, compound interest, if he or she meets all of the other conditions of deductibility.[130] Compound interest, however, is only deductible when the taxpayer actually pays it and not when it is merely payable.

l) — Bond Discounts

A bond is a legal obligation that acknowledges debt owing to a lender. Typically, the debt entitles its owner to periodic interest payments and, eventually, on a stated date to the repayment of the principal (face value) of the debt. A bond has a nominal interest rate, which is the rate that the contract specifies in relation to the face value of the debt. For example, assume that a corporation issues bonds with a face value of $1,000 and nominal interest rate of 8 percent payable annually, with the principal is repayable in 25 years. The purchaser of the bond can expect interest payments of $80 at the end of each year and a lump sum repayment of $1,000 at the end of 25 years. The nominal rate of interest is 8 percent. If the market rate of interest is also 8 percent, the present value of the bond is exactly equal to its face value ($1,000).

Present Value of future income stream is:

$80 per year × Present value* of annuity (10.6748)	=	$	854
$1,000 × Present value** of future sum	=		146
Present Value of Bond	=	$	1,000

Notes::

* Present value of a future annuity at 8 percent for 25 years equals 10.6748.

---

[129]See para. 20(1)(c). "Exempt income" is defined as property received or acquired by a person in such circumstances that it is, because of any provision in Part I, not included in computing the person's income, but does not include a dividend on a share or a support amount. See para. 248(1) "exempt income".

[130]Para. 20(1)(d).

**   Present value of a future amount at 8 percent for 25 years equals 0.1460.

The present value of the bond depends upon its annual cash flow ($80), the discount rate (8 percent), the number of years outstanding (25), and the face value of the principal amount ($1,000) payable at the end of the term. The price that a rational investor will be willing to pay for the bond today is $1,000, that is, an amount equal to the present value of its future cash flows. This is entirely logical as the nominal contractual interest rate is exactly equal to the market rate of interest.

Now assume that the market rate of interest rises to 10 percent while the nominal contractual rate of interest remains at 8 percent. The present value of the bond falls to $818.

Present Value of income stream is:

$80 per year × Present value* of annuity (9.0770)	=	$ 726
$1,000 × Present value** of future sum	=	92
Present Value of Bond	=	$ 818

Notes::

*   Present value of a future annuity at 10 percent for 25 years equals 9.0770.

**   Present value of a future amount at 10 percent for 25 years equals 0.0923.

If a new investor buys the bond for $818, his or her annual yield is $80/$818 or 9.78 percent. In addition, the investor will realize a gain of $182, that is, $1,000 minus $818 if he or she holds the bond to maturity. The combination of the interest yield and the gain provides an *effective* annual yield of 10 percent over the life of the bond. Thus, the increase in the market rate of interest causes the capital value of the bond to fall, which raises the effective rate of interest to market levels.

It is arguable that the gain of $182 is an "appreciation gain" that results from holding the asset to maturity. In economic terms, however, what we really have is an increase in the interest income that the bondholder earns to reflect the change in the market rate of interest. It is irrelevant to a bondholder who holds to maturity whether he or she earns 10 percent annually on a face value of $1,000 or 8 percent annually on a discounted value of $818 plus a lump sum gain upon maturity. In either case, the bondholder's effective yield to maturity is 10 percent. This is the inevitable result in efficient capital markets.

A discount is the amount by which the face or nominal value of a debt obligation exceeds its issue or selling price. In the above example, the bond discount is $182. The discount can arise on an initial issuance of the obligation or later in accordance with market fluctuations in interest rates. A corporation can, for example, choose to issue a $1,000 face value bond for $818 in order to increase the effective interest rate for the bondholder.

Tax law taxes capital gains at a lower rate than interest income. Thus, applying purely legal principles, form prevails over substance and the bondholder effectively converts $182 of interest income into capital gains if the corporation issues the bond at an initial discount of that amount.

The capital value of a bond also fluctuates with the time remaining to maturity. Continuing with the above example, assume that the $1,000 bond has a nominal rate of 8 percent and 20 years remaining to maturity. If the market rate of interest is 10 percent, the bond has a capital value of $830.

Present Value of income stream is:

$80 per year × Present value[*] of annuity (8.5136)	=	$ 681
$1,000 × Present value[**] of future sum (0.1486)	=	149
Present Value of Bond	=	$ 830

Notes::

[*]   Present value of a future annuity at 10 percent for 20 years equals 8.5136.

[**]   Present value of a future amount at 10 percent for 20 years equals 0.1486.

The value of the bond has increased from $818 to $830 in five years because the bond is that much closer to maturity and the eventual payout of the face value of $1000. At a price of $830 the bond has an effective yield of 10 percent. Once again, the effective yield comprises two components: the annual interest yield of 80/830 = 9.64 percent; and the capital gain of $170 over the next 20 years.

The potential for transforming fully taxable income into capital gains causes the tax authorities to regulate the treatment of initial issue bond discounts. In effect, the Act looks through the form of the initial issuance of a bond to its economic substance.

Discounts on bonds may be deductible in whole or in part in the year paid.[131] Where an issuer floats an obligation at a price of at least 97 percent of its principal amount and the obligation does not yield an amount in excess of 4/3 of the nominal interest rate, the entire amount of the discount is deductible in computing income. In contrast, where the issuer floats a bond for an amount less than 97 percent of its face amount, or its yield exceeds 4/3 of its nominal interest rate, only 50 percent of the discount is deductible in computing income. In the above example, the discounted price of the bond is less than 97 percent of its face value but the effective yield does not exceed 4/3 of the nominal interest rate.[132] Hence, the issuer can deduct only 50 percent of the discount as interest expense. A discount on a

---

[131]Para. 20(1)(f).

[132]The effective interest rate of 10 percent. 4/3 of 8% = 10.67%.

debt obligation that does not normally stipulate an interest rate (for example, strip coupon bonds) is considered interest if the discount is reasonable in the circumstances.

m) — Refinancing

Where a taxpayer borrows money to repay money that he or she previously borrowed, the Act deems the taxpayer to incur the second borrowing for the same purposes as the original borrowing.[133]

n) — Existence of Source

An essential requirement for the deduction of interest is that the source of income to which the interest expense relates must continue to exist.[134] Thus, interest on borrowed money must be traceable to a current eligible use in order for the expense to be deductible. For example, a taxpayer who finances the purchase of shares may claim any directly related interest expense as a deduction only if he or she continues to hold the original investment or substituted securities, even if they are worthless. However, section 20.1 allows one to deduct interest in certain limited circumstances even where borrowed money ceases to be used to earn income because the source of the income no longer exists.[135]

o) — Accrued Interest

The purchaser of a debt obligation (other than an income bond, income debenture, small business development bond, or small business bond) can deduct accrued interest (that is, interest earned but not paid) to the date of the purchase to the extent that he or she includes

---

[133]Subs. 20(3); see also ATR-4 "Exchange of Interest Rates" (November 29, 1985) (archived).

[134]*Emerson v. R.*, [1986] 1 C.T.C. 422, 86 D.T.C. 6184 (Fed. C.A.); leave to appeal refused (1986), 70 N.R. 160n (S.C.C.) (taxpayer not allowed to deduct interest on money used to purchase shares after selling shares at loss); see also *Deschenes v. Minister of National Revenue*, [1979] C.T.C. 2690, 79 D.T.C. 461 (T.R.B.); *Alexander v. Minister of National Revenue*, [1983] C.T.C. 2516, 83 D.T.C. 459 (T.R.B.); *Lyons v. Minister of National Revenue*, [1984] C.T.C. 2690, 84 D.T.C. 1633 (T.C.C.); *McKay v. Minister of National Revenue*, [1984] C.T.C. 2805, 84 D.T.C. 1699 (T.C.C.); *Botkin v. Minister of National Revenue*, [1989] 2 C.T.C. 2110, 89 D.T.C. 398 (T.C.C.); *Malik v. Minister of National Revenue*, [1989] 1 C.T.C. 316, 89 D.T.C. 5141 (Fed. T.D.); *Dockman v. Minister of National Revenue*, [1990] 2 C.T.C. 2229, 90 D.T.C. 1804 (T.C.C.); *Kornelow v. Minister of National Revenue*, [1991] 1 C.T.C. 2403, 91 D.T.C. 431 (T.C.C.).

[135]See Department of Finance examples in its technical notes to the section.

the amount as interest in computing income for the year. At the same time, the vendor of the debt includes the accrued interest in computing its income.[136]

p) — Financing Costs

A taxpayer can deduct expenses that he or she incurs in issuing shares or in borrowing money for the purpose of earning income from a business or property.[137] Financing expenses, which typically include legal and accounting fees, printing costs, commissions, etc., would otherwise be caught by the prohibition against deducting expenses not *directly* related to the income-earning process.[138] These expenses are deductible on a rateable basis over a five-year period.

q) — Capitalizing Interest

In certain circumstances, a taxpayer may prefer not to write off interest expense against current operations. For example, there may be little advantage in taking a deduction for interest expense on money borrowed to construct an asset if the asset is not producing income. Where the deduction of interest would merely create a loss that the taxpayer cannot use within the time limits allowed for carryover of losses,[139] the taxpayer may prefer to treat the interest charges as part of the cost of the asset. He or she can then write off the total cost of the asset when it begins to produce income. In other words, the taxpayer may prefer to treat interest costs as a capital expenditure rather than as a current expense. This aspect is now less of a concern since the loss carryover period is 20 years.

---

[136]Subs. 20(14); IT-410R "Debt Obligations — Accrued Interest on Transfer" (September 4, 1984) (archived). This rule only operates where there has been an assignment or transfer of title; evidence of registration of title would likely be necessary. See: *Hill v. Minister of National Revenue*, [1981] C.T.C. 2120, 81 D.T.C. 167 (T.R.B.) ("bond flip"; interest payment for carrying cost of bonds not deductible); *Smye v. Minister of National Revenue*, [1980] C.T.C. 2372, 80 D.T.C. 1326 (T.R.B.) (purchase of bonds plus accrued interest; upon sale, taxpayer deducted price for accrued interest from investment yield of bond).

[137]Para. 20(1)(e).

[138]*Montreal Light, Heat & Power Consol. v. Minister of National Revenue*, [1944] C.T.C. 94, 2 D.T.C. 654 (Canada P.C.); *R. v. Royal Trust Corp. of Canada*, [1983] C.T.C. 159, 83 D.T.C. 5172 (Fed. C.A.) (whether or not payment constitutes "commission" is a question of fact).

[139]See para. 111(1)(a) (limitation period in respect of non-capital losses).

(i) — Depreciable Property

A taxpayer who acquires depreciable property with borrowed money may elect to capitalize the interest charges.[140] However, the taxpayer may capitalize only those costs that would *otherwise have been deductible* as interest expense or as an expense of borrowing money. Interest expense to earn exempt income is not deductible and cannot be capitalized. The election is also available for costs that the taxpayer incurs in the year that he or she acquires the asset but also costs incurred in the three immediately preceding taxation years. The extension of the election to the three preceding years recognizes that large undertakings extend over many years and that a taxpayer may borrow money and incur expenses prior to the period in which he uses the money for its intended purpose of constructing a capital asset.

(ii) — Election

The taxpayer must make the election for the taxation year in which:

- He acquires the depreciable property, or

- Uses the money borrowed for exploration, development, or the acquisition of property.

Thus, a taxpayer cannot elect to capitalize interest in anticipation of the acquisition of depreciable property or the use of borrowed money for exploration or development. He can elect *only after* acquiring the property or expending the funds. Upon election, however, it becomes effective for the borrowing costs and interest of the current and the three preceding years.

The election does not have to be made in respect of the full amount of the costs of borrowing; a taxpayer may elect to capitalize only part of the interest charges and deduct the remainder as a current expense.

The portion of the interest that the taxpayer capitalizes is added to the capital cost of the depreciable property that he or she acquires. Thus, the capitalized cost will eventually be written off through capital cost allowances. The adjusted cost base of the property will also be increased for the purpose of determining capital gains upon disposition of the property.[141]

(iii) — Reassessment

---

[140]S. 21. Special restrictions on "soft costs" are discussed below; see subs. 18(3.1).

[141]S. 54 "adjusted cost base".

Where the taxpayer elects to capitalize interest charges that would otherwise have been deductible in preceding years, the Minister must reassess the taxpayer for those taxation years. Having made the election, the taxpayer may continue to capitalize interest in succeeding years if in each of those succeeding years, he or she capitalizes the *entire* amount of the interest on the property.

(iv) — Compound Interest

A taxpayer can also capitalize compound interest and the expense of raising money. For example, a taxpayer may pay a commitment fee to a financier before it advances the necessary funds. The commitment fee, or standby interest, may be capitalized as part of the cost of borrowed money.[142]

(v) — "Soft Costs"

"Soft costs" (such as interest expense, mortgage fees, property taxes, commitment fees, etc.) incurred in respect of the construction, renovation or alteration of a building, are not deductible as current expenses during construction, and must be added to the cost of the building.[143] Similarly, "soft costs" in respect of land subjacent to a building under construction must be capitalized. The restriction on the deduction of these expenses only applies in respect of outlays incurred before completion of construction, renovation or alteration of the building.

The scope of the prohibition against writing off soft costs as current expenses is very broad. Included in interest expenses are expenses incurred on borrowed money used to finance working capital if it *"can reasonably be considered"* that the borrowed money freed up other funds for the construction of the building. In other words, "indirect financing" is caught by the prohibition.[144]

r) — Limitations on Deduction

(i) — Real Estate

---

[142]*Sherritt Gordon Mines Ltd. v. Minister of National Revenue*, [1968] C.T.C. 262, 68 D.T.C. 5180 (Can. Ex. Ct.).

[143]Subs. 18(3.1). This rule does not apply to capital cost allowance, landscaping costs, disability related modifications to buildings under para. 20(1)(gg) and soft cots deductible under subsection 20(29).

[144]Subs. 18(3.2).

A taxpayer cannot deduct carrying charges (interest and property taxes) in respect of vacant land to the extent that the expenses exceed income from the land.[145] Thus, carrying charges on land are deductible only to the extent of the taxpayer's net revenues from the land. The purpose of this rule is to discourage speculation in real estate.

Land that one uses in the course of a business is exempt from the limitation in respect of carrying charges for land. However, the exemption from the rule does not apply to property developers whose business is the sale or development of land, or to land that is held, but not used, in a business.

L. — Capital Cost Allowance

a) — General Comment

We saw earlier that a taxpayer cannot deduct expenditures on account of capital outlays, depreciation, obsolescence, or depletion.[146] The prohibition against the deduction of depreciation and similar expenses flies in the face of accounting principles. The Act does, however, allow for the deduction of capital cost allowance (CCA) in lieu of such expenses. In computing income from a business or property, a taxpayer may deduct[147] ". . . such part of the capital cost to the taxpayer of property, or such amount in respect of the capital cost to the taxpayer of property, if any, as is allowed by regulation." Thus, a taxpayer cannot deduct depreciation calculated for financial statement purposes, but may claim a deduction for capital cost allowance, according to prescribed rules.[148]

The basic concept underlying the capital cost allowance system is that it is a deduction from income, which approximately allocates the cost of capital assets over their useful lives. Thus, in a sense, the CCA system is nothing more than statutory depreciation at pre-determined rates. The technical application of the capital cost allowance system is, however, extremely complex because the government uses the system as an instrument of social, economic, and political policy. The system sometimes stimulates investment through accelerated capital cost allowance; in other circumstances, the CCA system discourages particular types of investment by denying or restricting the allowance on those investments. For

---

[145]Subs. 18(2).

[146]Para. 18(1)(b).

[147]Para. 20(1)(a); Regulations Pt. XI (Regs. 1100–1107). The phrase "capital cost allowance" refers to an allowance in respect of the capital cost of depreciable property.

[148]See generally: *eBay Canada Ltd. v. Minister of National Revenue*, [2008] 1 C.T.C. 73, 2007 FC 930 (F.C.); additional reasons at [2008] 3 C.T.C. 1 (F.C.); affirmed (2008), [2009] 2 C.T.C. 141 (Fed. C.A.) (describes E-bay's activities outside the United States — relevant to demand requirements under section 231.2).

example, prior to 1988, the statute allowed for a rapid write-off of the cost of Canadian films. A taxpayer could claim 100 percent of the cost of film ownership in one year. This was intended to encourage the development of Canadian culture. In 1988, the CCA rate was reduced to a 30 percent write-off so as to discourage the use of films as tax shelters by high-income taxpayers. In both cases, the CCA rate did not relate to the life of films.

b) — Structure

(i) — Classification

We start by answering three basic questions in respect of the capital cost allowance system:

1. Is the property depreciable capital property?

2. To which class of assets does the property belong?

3. What is the rate of depreciation applicable to the particular class?

CCA allows a taxpayer to deduct the cost of depreciable assets over a period of time at a prescribed rate.[149] The rate is the same for all taxpayers with similar assets performing similar activities. The rates generally allow for generous write-offs. The deduction for tax purposes in the early years of an asset's life usually exceeds the comparable depreciation for accounting and financial statement purposes. Thus, in part at least, the capital cost allowance system compensates taxpayers for the effects of inflation on asset replacement costs. It also permits taxpayers to defer taxes because of the difference between tax and accounting depreciation.

(ii) — Permissive

The deduction of capital cost allowance is permissive: a taxpayer *may* claim capital cost allowance in a particular taxation year. The amount of capital cost allowance that a taxpayer may deduct in any year, however, is subject to prescribed upper limits. Thus, taxpayers have some flexibility in determining the amount of income they will recognize for tax purposes in any year.

An asset is eligible for capital cost allowance only if it is described in one of the classes listed in the Regulations. The classes list most tangible assets that are expected to depreciate over time. The list also includes intangible assets with limited lives (such as patents and limited life franchises).[150]

---

[149]IT-285R2, "Capital Cost Allowance — General Comments" (March 31, 1994).

[150]Regs., Part XI (1100–1107); Sched. II.

(iii) — General Structure

The CCA system operates as follows:

- A taxpayer can deduct CCA within the terms of the Act and the Regulations.

- The Regulations group eligible assets into prescribed classes that have approximately similar lives.

- The balance in each class at any point in time is its undepreciated capital cost (UCC).

- The UCC of a class is increased by acquisitions in that class.

- Each class is subject to a *maximum* percentage rate of capital cost allowance.

- The balance is reduced by dispositions and by the deduction of CCA claimed.

- A taxpayer may deduct a portion or all of the allowance prescribed, or forgo the claim in a particular year and postpone amortization of the class of assets to later years.

- CCA can be claimed only when assets are available for use.

- The diminishing balance, rather than the straight line,[151] method is used in computing the annual allowance for most classes of assets. Each year, the specified rate is applied to the UCC remaining in the class after deduction of amounts previously allowed.

- The balance remaining to be depreciated diminishes until the taxpayer acquires new assets of the class.

- Proceeds from the disposition of assets reduce the balance of the class, up to a maximum equal to the cost of the asset.

- On disposal of assets, CCA previously taken is "recaptured" to the extent that the proceeds of disposition exceed the UCC of the group of assets in the particular class.

- The UCC of a class can never be a negative amount. If the proceeds from a disposition of assets exceed the UCC of the class and reduce it below zero, the excess amount is immediately recaptured into income.

- Where the proceeds of disposition of an asset exceed its original capital cost, the excess is a capital gain.

- Upon disposal of *all* the assets in a particular class, any remaining balance of UCC for the class is deductible in the year as a "terminal loss".

- There can be no capital loss on the disposition of depreciable property.

---

[151]The straight line method may be used in a few situations, e.g., depreciation of Class 13 leasehold interests.

Example

Assume:

In Year 1 a taxpayer acquires one tangible asset on which he claims 20 percent CCA. It is the only asset in its class.

Capital cost	$	10,000
Capital cost allowance claimed	$	2,000

In Year 2 the taxpayer sells the asset. Assume, alternatively, that the taxpayer receives the following amounts:

Example (A)	$	11,000
Example (B)	$	9,000
Example (C)	$	6,000

Then:

	(A)	(B)	(C)
Capital cost	$ 10,000	$ 10,000	$ 10,000
CCA claimed	(2,000)	(2,000)	(2,000)
Undepreciated capital cost	$ 8,000	$ 8,000	$ 8,000
CCA recaptured	$ 2,000	$ 1,000	—
Capital gain	$ 1,000	—	—
Terminal loss	—	—	$ (2,000)

As the above example shows, the CCA system is designed to "recapture" an excess tax depreciation claimed in prior years. Similarly, it permits a loss for any shortfall in amounts claimed in prior years if there are no remaining assets in the class.

c) — Depreciable Property

Capital cost allowance is claimable only on depreciable property of a prescribed class.[152] "Depreciable property" is defined as "property acquired by the taxpayer in respect of which the taxpayer has been allowed, or . . . [is] entitled to, 'capital cost allowance'."[153] This circular definition is not very helpful.

However, the Act specifically excludes certain properties from the prescribed classes. For example, the following properties are *not* eligible for capital cost allowance:

- Property, the cost of which is *deductible as an* ordinary expense.[154]

- Property that is "described in" or is part of, the taxpayer's inventory.[155]

- Property not acquired for the purpose of gaining or producing income.[156]

- Property for which the taxpayer is entitled to a deduction for scientific research.[157]

- Property that is a yacht, camp, lodge, golf course, or facility if any part of the maintenance costs are not deductible because of subpara. 18(1)(l)(i).[158]

- Certain works of art created by non-residents.[159]

- Land.[160]

- Animals, trees and plants, radium, intangible assets, rights of way.[161]

- Property situated outside of Canada that belongs to a non-resident.[162]

---

[152]Reg. 1100(1)(a).

[153]Subs. 248(1) "depreciable property" and para. 13(21) "depreciable property".

[154]Reg. 1102(1)(a).

[155]Reg. 1102(1)(b). See Chapter 7, "Business Income" for distinction between income from business on sale of inventory and capital gains on sale of capital assets. See also IT-128R, "CCA — Depreciable Property" (May 21, 1985) and IT-102R2, "Conversion of Property, Other than Real Property, From or to Inventory" (July 22, 1985).

[156]Reg. 1102(1)(c).

[157]Reg. 1102(1)(d).

[158]Reg. 1102(1)(f).

[159]Reg. 1102(1)(e).

[160]Reg. 1102(2).

[161]Reg., Sched. II, Class 8, subpara. (i).

[162]Reg. 1102(3).

d) — Classes

A taxpayer may claim capital cost allowance on depreciable property of a prescribed class. Schedule II describes the principal classes of property.

Similar properties are generally placed in the same class and, therefore, are subject to the same rate of allowance. For example, all of a taxpayer's automobiles costing $30,000 (prescribed amount in 2013) or less would be in Class 10, and the capital cost allowance claimed at the rate applicable to that class. Similarly, all passenger vehicles costing more than $30,000 each[163] are grouped in Class 10.1. The prescribed amounts are adjusted periodically.

There are, however, some exceptions to the general rule. Some similar properties are segregated into separate classes. The effect of segregating similar properties into separate classes is that the provisions relating to "recapture" and "terminal loss" then apply separately to each property, rather than to the collective whole. The principal reason for maintaining separate classes is to accelerate the timing of recapture of capital cost allowance that a taxpayer might otherwise wholly or partially defer by subsequent acquisitions of similar properties. For example, each rental property having a cost of $50,000 or more constitutes a separate class of property.[164] Hence, it is not possible to defer recapture of capital cost allowance upon a disposition of a rental property by replacing it with a similar property in the same class and of the same type.

The amount of CCA on rental property depends upon the type of property (for example, Class 1, 3 or 6). A condominium unit in a building belongs to the same class as the building.

In certain circumstances, a depreciable property may satisfy the requirements of two or more classes. The CRA takes the position that where the description of two or more possible classes includes the words ". . . property not included in any other class . . ." and the property in question fits both classes, the taxpayer is entitled to choose the applicable class.[165] For example, a frame building acquired before 1979 could be included in Class 6; it is also a building for the purposes of Class 3. Since Classes 3 and 6 are both described to include "property not included in any other class", a taxpayer can choose to place the building in either Class 3 or Class 6. Note, however, that a brick building, for example, *must* be included in Class 3 since it is not described in Class 6.

---

[163]Para. 13(7)(g); Reg. 7307(1); Reg. Sched. II, classes 10 and 10.1.

[164]Regs. 1101(5b), 1101(lac).

[165]IT-285R2, "Capital Cost Allowance — General Comments" (March 31, 1994).

e) — Capital Cost of Property

(i) — General Comment

Capital cost allowance is based on the "capital cost" of an asset, that is, its laid-down acquisition cost.[166] Thus, the capital cost of an asset includes any legal, accounting, engineering, or other fees that the taxpayer incurs to acquire the property.

"Cost" is the actual cost of the property to the taxpayer, whether paid in money or some other property. Where the value of the consideration paid is not readily apparent (such as when payment is made by the issuance of shares), the taxpayer should obtain an appraisal to determine the capital cost of the property.[167]

Where a corporation acquires an asset in exchange for treasury shares in an arm's length transaction, the contract price will usually prevail. Under most Canadian corporate statutes, the corporation must add the contract price to the appropriate stated capital account.

"Cost" means the *entire laid-down cost* of equipment even though certain expensive parts of the equipment might require frequent replacement.[168] The cost of property paid for in foreign currency is its Canadian dollar equivalent as at the date of acquisition.[169]

Where a taxpayer manufactures an asset for personal use, it can include all outlays attributable to the construction of the asset in cost.[170] We determine cost according to generally accepted accounting principles.[171] For example, testing and start-up costs are part of the

---

[166]Para. 20(1)(a); IT-285R2, "Capital Cost Allowance — General Comments" (March 31, 1994), paras.8–12; see also R. M. Skinner, *Accounting Principles: A Canadian Viewpoint*, CICA (1972), at 5: "The recorded cost of a tangible capital asset should include all costs necessary to put the asset in a position to render service."

[167]*Craddock v. Zevo Finance Co.*, [1944] 1 All E.R. 566; affd. [1946] 1 All E.R. 523n (H.L.) (price paid by company *prima facie* nominal value of shares but contrary may be established in appropriate cases).

[168]*MacMillan Bloedel (Alberni) Ltd. v. Minister of National Revenue*, [1973] C.T.C. 295, 73 D.T.C. 5264 (Fed. T.D.) (taxpayer claimed cost of tires for logging equipment as current expense; practice held contrary to generally accepted accounting principles); see also *Cockshutt Farm Equipment of Canada Ltd. v. Minister of National Revenue* (1966), 41 Tax A.B.C. 386, 66 D.T.C. 544 (Can. Tax App. Bd.) ("capital cost to the taxpayer" means actual, factual, or historical cost of depreciable property at time of acquisition).

[169]IT-285R2, "Capital Cost Allowance — General Comments" (March 31, 1994).

[170]See IT-285R2, "Capital Cost Allowance — General Comments" (March 31, 1994).

[171]*B.P. Refinery (Kwinana) Ltd. v. Fed. Commr. of Taxation*, [1961] A.L.R. 52, 12 A.T.D. 204 (H.C.).

capital cost of assets.[172] In certain circumstances, a taxpayer may also capitalize interest costs as part of the capital cost of depreciable property, instead of deducting these costs as current expenses.[173]

Where a taxpayer acquires property as a gift, he or she is deemed to acquire it at a cost equal to its fair market value at that time.[174] Inherited assets are also generally deemed to be acquired at a cost equal to their fair market value at the date of the taxpayer's death.[175] However, there is a special rule when the recipient of the gift or inheritance is the spouse of the donor.[176]

(ii) — Foreign Currency Transactions

It is a fundamental principle of tax law that we measure income in local currency. Thus, we convert foreign currency transactions into Canadian dollars. Generally, the translation of foreign currency into Canadian dollars must be at the exchange rate prevailing on the date of the particular transaction. For example, where a taxpayer acquires a capital asset in the United States, the capital cost of the asset will be its purchase price translated into Canadian dollars, plus any duties, taxes, shipping charges, insurance fees, and handling costs.

Assets that are purchased and sold in foreign currencies may trigger a gain or loss in Canadian dollars. We distinguish between the portion of a gain or loss that is attributable to the intrinsic market value of the asset itself and the portion that is attributable to foreign exchange fluctuations between the time of purchase of the asset and the time of its disposition. The foreign exchange gain or loss from holding the asset is accounted for separately from

---

[172]*Weinberger v. Minister of National Revenue*, [1964] C.T.C. 103, 64 D.T.C. 5060 (Can. Ex. Ct.).

[173]Para. 21(1)(b); *Sherritt Gordon Mines Ltd. v. Minister of National Revenue*, [1968] C.T.C. 262, 68 D.T.C. 5180 (Can. Ex. Ct.) at 283 [C.T.C.] and 5193 [D.T.C.] it was stated that:

> . . . at least where the amount is significant in relation to the business of a company, it is in accordance with generally accepted business and commercial principles to charge, as a cost of construction, payments of interest in respect of the construction period on borrowed money expended by the company for such construction and to write such payments off over a period of years.

See also *Lions Equipment Ltd. v. Minister of National Revenue* (1963), 34 Tax A.B.C. 221, 63 D.T.C. 35 (Can. Tax App. Bd.) (limitation of deduction to actual source of farming income; hoped-for source excluded); *Ben-Odeco Ltd. v. Powlson* (1978), 52 Tax Cas. 459 (H.L.) (commitment fees and interest charges on loan used to acquire capital asset not included in capital cost despite accord with accounting principles); *S.I.R. v. Eaton Hall (Pty.) Ltd.* (1975), (4) S.A. 953, 37 S.A.T.C. 343 (A.D.).

[174]Para. 69(1)(c).

[175]Subs. 70(5).

[176]Para. 70(6)(c).

the purchase and sale of the asset. The foreign exchange gain or loss is not an adjustment to the cost of the property acquired or sold.

Gains and losses on account of foreign exchange transactions are capital gains (losses) or revenue gains (losses) and treated according to the rules applicable to each category. The characterization of foreign exchange gains and losses generally depends upon the nature of the property that gives rise to the gain or loss. Hence, gains and losses on account of inventory transactions are business income (losses); gains and losses on account of capital transactions are capital gains (losses).

Foreign exchange gains and losses on account of income transactions are included in the taxpayer's income according to the general rules.[177] In contrast, the capital gains rules govern foreign exchange gains and losses on account of capital transactions.[178]

(iii) — Change of Use of Property

A change of use of property is a disposition for tax purposes. Thus, where a taxpayer changes the use of depreciable property acquired for the purpose of earning income to personal use, he or she is deemed to dispose of the property for proceeds equal to its fair market value. Concurrently, the taxpayer is deemed to reacquire the property at a cost equal to its fair market value.[179] Hence, a change of use can trigger a capital gain, a recapture of capital cost allowance, or a terminal loss.

A change in use of property from personal to business purposes also triggers a deemed disposition of the property. Here, however, the rules are more complicated. The taxpayer's cost of acquisition is determined as follows:

- Where the fair market value at the time of change in use of the property is[180] less than its capital cost, the acquisition is equal to fair market value;

- Where fair market value is more than its capital cost, the acquisition cost is limited to the aggregate of the cost of the property and one-half of the excess of fair market value over its cost, to the extent that the taxpayer did not claim a capital gains exemption for that excess.

These rules also apply where there is a split between personal and business usage.

---

[177]S. 9.

[178]Subs. 39(2).

[179]Para. 13(7)(a).

[180]Para. 13(7)(b).

(iv) — Non-Arm's Length Transactions

There are special rules for determining the cost of depreciable property acquired in non-arm's length transfers. The following outlines some of the more frequently encountered non-arm's length property acquisitions:

Description	Reference
Depreciable property acquired from person or partnership	para. 13(7)(e)
Bequest of farm property to child	subs. 70(9), (9.1)
Gift of farm property to child	subs. 73(3)
Transfer to corporation from shareholder	subs. 85(1)
Transfer to corporation from partnership	subs. 85(2)
Winding up of partnership	subs. 85(3)
Amalgamation	subs. 87(2)
Winding up of 90 percent owned Canadian subsidiary	subss. 88(1)–(1.6)
Contribution of property to partnership	subs. 97(2)
Rules applicable where partnership ceases to exist	subss. 98(3), (5)

(v) — Luxury Automobiles

The maximum capital cost of passenger vehicles is limited to $30,000; exclusive of taxes.[181] The capital cost of a passenger vehicle that has an actual cost in excess of $30,000 is

---

[181] Prescribed amount effective 2013. See para. 13(7)(h) and Reg. 7307(1).

deemed to be $30,000. This amount is adjusted periodically to account for inflation and changed circumstances.[182]

Paragraph 13(7)(h) prevents the $30,000 limit on the depreciable capital cost of a passenger vehicle from being circumvented by a transfer of the vehicle between parties not dealing with each other at arm's length. Where a taxpayer acquires a passenger vehicle from a person with whom he does not deal at arm's length, the capital cost of the vehicle to the taxpayer is the least of:

- $30,000;[183]

- The fair market value of the vehicle; and

- Its undepreciated capital cost to the transferor immediately before the transfer.

(vi) — Reduction for Government Assistance

A taxpayer must reduce the capital cost of depreciable property to the extent that he or she deducts federal investment tax credits or receives or is entitled to receive governmental assistance in respect of the property.[184] This rule does not apply to governmental assistance received under an *Appropriation Act* in respect of scientific research and experimental developments ("R&D") expenditures. These items are not deducted from the capital cost of depreciable property, because they reduce the taxpayer's pool of R&D expenditures under subsection 37(1) of the Act.

f) — Exchanges of Property

The capital cost of an asset acquired in a barter transaction is generally equal to the value of the property traded or exchanged. It is the value of the asset used to purchase that determines the cost of the asset purchased. As Jackett P. said:[185]

> ... if A conveys Blackacre to B in exchange for a conveyance by B to A of Whiteacre, the cost of Whiteacre to A is the value of Blackacre (being what he gave up to get Whiteacre) and

---

[182]Amounts are prescribed by Regulations and adjusted from time to time; see Reg. 7307(1).

[183]See 7307(1) for current prescribed amount.

[184]See subs. 13(7.1).

[185]*D'Auteuil Lumber Co. v. Minister of National Revenue*, [1970] C.T.C. 122, 70 D.T.C. 6096 (Can. Ex. Ct.) at 128 [C.T.C.] and 6099 [D.T.C.] (timber cutting rights received from province in exchange for transfer of remaining timber limit; value of former in issue); see also *R. v. Canadian Pacific Ltd. (No. 1)*, [1978] C.T.C. 606, 77 D.T.C. 5383 (Fed. C.A.) (interest from subsidiary deemed to be dividends and not deductible by railway company).

the cost of Blackacre to B is the value of Whiteacre (being what he gave up in order to get Blackacre). Assuming both parties were equally skillful in their bargaining, there is a probability that the values of the two properties are about the same but this does not mean that A's "cost" is the "value" of what he acquired or that B's "cost" is the "value" of what he acquired.

In most arm's length transactions one trades property of equal values. Where, however, it is impossible to value the asset given up and the value of the asset acquired is known, it is permissible to use the latter.[186] Ultimately, the question is one of credibility and proof of cost.

g) — Undepreciated Capital Cost

The starting point in calculating capital cost allowance (CCA) is to determine the capital cost of each depreciable property. The Regulations group depreciable properties into classes with similar life expectations. When we deduct CCA from the capital cost of property, the residue is the "undepreciated capital cost" ("UCC") of the property.[187] Thus, UCC represents the as yet undepreciated cost of the class of assets. In accounting terms, this is equivalent to the net book value of an asset.

A taxpayer's "undepreciated capital cost" of a class of depreciable property is determined by adding the following:[188]

- The capital cost of depreciable property of the class;

- Government assistance repaid by the taxpayer subsequent to the disposition of property in respect of the acquisition of which he or she received assistance;

- Any amount recaptured in respect of the class; and

- Repayment of contributions and allowances the taxpayer received and that were previously deducted from the capital cost of that class;

- Next, one deducts the aggregate of:

- The total capital cost allowance and terminal losses that the taxpayer has claimed for property of the class;

- The proceeds of disposition of any property of the class disposed of (the deduction not to exceed the capital cost of the property); and

---

[186]See IT-490, "Barter Transactions" (July 5, 1982).

[187]Para. 13(21)"undepreciated capital cost"; Reg. 1100(1)(a); see subsections 248(1) and 13(21).

[188]Para. 13(21)"undepreciated capital cost"; Reg. 1100(1)(a).

- Government assistance received, or that the taxpayer is entitled to receive, as well as investment tax credits claimed, subsequent to the disposition by the taxpayer of the property to which such assistance or tax credit related.

For the purpose of calculating CCA in a year that the taxpayer acquires an asset, only 1/2 of the net additions to the class is generally added to the UCC balance.[189] The remaining 1/2 is added to the UCC after calculating CCA for the year of acquisition. The effect of this rule is that CCA on a newly acquired asset is claimable at only 1/2 of the normal rate in the year of acquisition.

The UCC of a class is updated annually by using the following formula:

UCC of the class at the beginning of the year		$	xxx
Add: purchases during the year			xxx
			xxx
Deduct: dispositions during the year at the *lesser* of:			
* capital cost	$	xxx	
* proceeds of disposition	$	xxx	(xxx)
UCC before adjustment			xxx
Deduct: 1/2 net additions to class			(xxx)
UCC before CCA			xxx
Deduct: CCA in the class for the year			(xxx)
Add: 1/2 net additions to class			xxx
UCC of the class at the end of the year		$	xxx

The UCC of a class can never be a negative amount. If the amount of the inclusions in a class is less than the amount of the deductions in the class, the negative balance becomes

---

[189]Reg. 1100(2). There are limited exceptions to this rule.

income for the year[190] and is then added back into the calculation of UCC of that class.[191] This increases the UCC balance back to zero.

Example

Alpha Ltd. acquires one Class 8 asset (depreciable at 20 percent) for $40,000 in YEAR 1, its first year of operation. In YEAR 2 *Alpha* disposes of the asset for $34,000 and acquires another Class 8 asset for $50,000. Assuming that Alpha claims the maximum CCA in each year, the UCC of the class at the end of YEAR 2 is as follows:

			Class 8
Opening UCC	$ NIL		
Add:			
50% of net additions	20,000		
Balance before CCA		$	20,000
CCA claimed			
($20,000 × 20%)			(4,000)
Balance before adjustment			16,000
Add:			
Remaining 50% of net additions			20,000
UCC at the end of YEAR 1			36,000
Add:			
Additions in YEAR 2	$	50,000	
Dispositions in YEAR 2		(34,000)	
Net additions	$	16,000	

---

[190]Subs. 13(1).

[191]Subpara. 13(21)"undepreciated capital cost" B.

	Class 8
50% × $16,000	8,000
Balance before CCA	44,000
CCA claimed (YEAR 2)	
(20% × $44,000)	(8,800)
Balance before adjustment	35,200
Add:	
Remaining 50% of net additions	8,000
UCC at the end of YEAR 2	$ 43,200

h) — Adjustments on Disposition of Assets

(i) — General Comment

The theory underlying the capital cost allowance system is that the cost of depreciable property can be written off over its useful life by applying pre-determined rates of depreciation. Subsequent events may show, however, that a taxpayer claimed insufficient or excessive capital cost allowance over a period of time. This may occur where the taxpayer voluntarily claims less than the maximum CCA allowable, or where the maximum rate applicable to a class of assets is either too restrictive or too generous.

Thus, the UCC of depreciable property may be higher or lower than its fair market value at a later date.

(ii) — Terminal Losses

Where a taxpayer disposes of the property of a class for less than its UCC, he or she suffers a shortfall in the depreciation claimed on the particular class. In these circumstances, the taxpayer is entitled to recoup the amount of the shortfall through a claim for a "terminal loss".

However, a taxpayer can claim a terminal loss only if he or she disposes of all the property of a class and owns no property of the class at the end of the taxation year. Where a taxpayer is eligible for a terminal loss, he or she must claim the loss in the year, or lose it forever. Thus, unlike a claim for CCA, the claim for a terminal loss is not flexible.

Example

Beta Ltd. has an undepreciated capital cost (UCC) Class 8 balance of $45,000 at the beginning of YEAR 1. During the year it acquires another Class 8 asset at a cost of $10,000. In YEAR 2, *Beta Ltd.* disposes of all of its Class 8 assets for $38,000. Assuming that it claims the maximum capital cost allowance in each year, *Beta's* terminal loss is determined as follows:

Opening UCC (YEAR 1)	$	45,000
Add:		
50% of net additions		5,000
Balance before CCA		50,000
CCA claimed (YEAR 1)(20% × $50,000)		(10,000)
Balance before adjustment		40,000
Add:		
Remaining 50% of net additions		5,000
UCC at the end of YEAR 1		45,000
Subtract:		
Proceeds of disposition (YEAR 2)		(38,000)
Balance in class (YEAR 2)		7,000
Terminal loss claimed (YEAR 2)		(7,000)
UCC at the end of YEAR 2		NIL

(iii) — Automobiles

Special rules apply to terminal losses on passenger vehicles. A taxpayer may not claim a terminal loss in respect of a passenger vehicle costing more than $30,000.[192] The $30,000 limit is subject to periodic adjustments.[193]

(iv) — Recapture

Just as a taxpayer may claim too little capital cost allowance on a class of assets, it is also possible that the taxpayer may have been allowed too much capital cost allowance. This may occur, for example, where the rate for a particular class of assets is deliberately set high in order to encourage economic activity in a particular sector. Thus, a sale of the assets of a class at fair market value may show that the assets were "over-depreciated" in the past. The Act "recaptures" any over-depreciated amount into income.[194]

1. — Negative Balance

As noted earlier, the undepreciated capital cost of a class of assets is calculated by adding certain amounts and deducting others. Where a class has a negative balance *at the end of the year*, the amount of the balance is recaptured into income for that year.[195] Any amount recaptured into income is then added back to the UCC of the class. This brings the asset balance of that particular class back to nil.[196]

In theory, recapture of capital cost allowance represents an adjustment for excessive claims of depreciation in earlier fiscal periods. In most cases, however, one can reduce the amount of CCA subject to recapture in any taxation year by acquiring additional property of the same class during the taxation year. Thus, it is usually possible to manipulate the amount of recapture recognized in a particular year by timing new acquisitions of depreciable capital

---

[192]Subs. 20(16.1); Reg. 7307(1) (prescribed amount). The $30,000 is exclusive of HST and provincial sales tax.

[193]See para. 13(7)(g) and Reg. 7307(1).

[194]Para. 13(21)"undepreciated capital cost"; see also para. 13(21.1)(a); *Malloney's Studio Ltd. v. R.*, [1979] 2 S.C.R. 326, [1979] C.T.C. 206, 79 D.T.C. 5124 (S.C.C.) (house demolished prior to sale of land; no part of proceeds from sale of land apportionable to demolished building).

[195]Subs. 13(1).

[196]Subpara. 13(21); IT-220R2, "Capital Cost Allowance — Proceeds of Disposition of Depreciable Property" (May 25, 1990).

assets.[197] However, this does not apply to cases where similar properties must be segregated — for example, rental properties in Classes 31 or 32 that have a cost of $50,000 or more.[198]

2. — Limited to Capital Cost

Recapture of CCA is a clawback previously claimed of excessive depreciation. Thus, the Act limits recapture to the capital cost of the particular depreciable property in the class. Proceeds of disposition in excess of the capital cost of an asset do *not* give rise to recapture of CCA. Rather, the excess of proceeds of disposition over the capital cost of an asset is a capital gain.[199] The distinction is important because recapture of CCA is fully taxable as income, whereas only one-half of capital gains are taxable.

Example

Assume:

Capital cost of asset	$ 10,000
CCA claimed	(5,000)
UCC of class	$ 5,000
Proceeds of disposition (net)	$ 8,000

Then:

UCC before disposition		$ 5,000
Deduct *lesser* of:*		
(i) Net proceeds	$ 8,000	

---

[197]Subpara. 13(21)"undepreciated capital cost".

[198]Reg. 1101(5b) and 1101(1ac).

[199]Subpara. 13(21)"undepreciated capital cost" F. Note: this rule does not apply to timber resource properties.

(ii) Capital cost $ 10,000

Lesser amount   (8,000   )

Recapture of CCA $ (3,000   )

Notes::

*   Subpara. 13(21)"undepreciated capital cost"

Example

Assume only one asset in class:

Capital cost $ 10,000

CCA claimed   (4,000   )

UCC $ 6,000

CASE:	A	B	C	D
Proceeds of disposition:	$ 4,000	$ 6,000	$ 9,000	$ 11,000
UCC	6,000	6,000	6,000	6,000
Terminal loss	$ 2,000	NIL	—	—
Recapture	—	—	$ 3,000	$ 4,000
Capital gain	—	—	—	$ 1,000

3. — *Deferral*

In certain circumstances, a taxpayer can defer the recapture of capital cost allowance. For example, a taxpayer who receives proceeds of disposition by way of insurance compensation for stolen or lost property (or by way of compensation for expropriated property) can elect to defer recognition of any recapture if he or she replaces the property with more expensive property.[200] This election is also available upon disposition of a "former business property".[201]

A "replacement property" is a property that the taxpayer acquires for the same or similar use as the property being replaced. A replacement property need only be a substitute for the original property; it need only be capable of being put to a similar use. It does *not* have to be an identical property.[202]

To obtain the deferral, the taxpayer must make an election when filing a return for the year in which he or she acquires the replacement property. Upon election, part of the proceeds of disposition of the former property are, in effect, transferred from the year in which the disposition occurs to the year in which the replacement property is acquired.

An election to defer recapture of CCA is also an automatic election to defer any capital gain triggered on the disposition.[203]

(v) — First Year Half-Rate Rule

We saw earlier that the Act limits in the first year the capital cost allowance on assets acquired during the year to one-half the allowance that is otherwise deductible.[204] This rule prevents tax avoidance by discouraging taxpayers from acquiring property at the end of a year in order to claim the full year's allowance. For example, a taxpayer might otherwise buy an asset on December 31 and claim CCA for the full year.[205]

---

[200]Subs. 13(4).

[201]Subss. 13(4); 248(1) "former business property".

[202]Subs. 13(4.1).

[203]Subs. 44(4); IT-259R4, "Exchanges of Property" (Sept. 23, 2003); *Korenowsky v. Minister of National Revenue* (1964), 35 Tax A.B.C. 86 (Can. Tax App. Bd.) (delay beyond specified periods precludes deferral).

[204]Reg. 1100(2). This rule applies only to acquisitions made subsequent to November 12, 1981. For acquisitions made prior to that date, the taxpayer was able to claim the full allowance in the year of acquisition. As to when a taxpayer acquires property, see *Minister of National Revenue v. Wardean Drilling Ltd.*, [1969] C.T.C. 265, 69 D.T.C. 5194 (Ex. Ct.).

[205]*Hewlett Packard (Canada) Ltd. v. R.*, 2004 FCA 240, [2004] 4 C.T.C. 230 (Fed. C.A.) (each year HP bought a new fleet of cars from Ford to replace the old fleet. In order to maximize its CCA, HP bought the new fleets just before, and sold the old fleets just after, its fiscal year-end. Minister argued HP was doubling up on CCA. Court disagreed and allowed CCA on the old fleet since HP retained both legal and beneficial interest until after fiscal year-end of each year).

Thus, the Act excludes from the undepreciated capital cost (UCC) of a class one-half of the net additions of property of that class in the year. The one-half that is excluded is then added back to the UCC of the class, after one determines the capital cost allowance (CCA) claim.

Example

Assume: **Class 8**   **(20%)**

UCC beginning of year $ 10,000

Acquisitions during the year $ 7,000

Proceeds from dispositions during $ 2,000
the year

Then:

Opening UCC $ 10,000

Additions during year $ 7,000

Dispositions during year   (2,000   )

Net additions $ 5,000

1/2 of net additions   2,500

UCC before allowance   12,500

CCA (20% × $12,500)   (2,500   )

                                                                                  10,000

Add:

Remaining 1/2 of net additions   2,500

UCC at end of year $ 12,500

The remaining one-half of the net additions, on which CCA is not claimed in the year of acquisition, is added back to the UCC of the class. In effect, the Act defers the capital cost allowance on this one-half to future years.

The first year half-rate rule does not apply to certain types of properties.[206] Nor does the rule apply to certain business reorganizations in which there is a change in legal title without any effective change in economic ownership.[207]

i) — Available for Use

The Act does not consider a taxpayer to have acquired a property until it is available for use, or until 24 months after he actually acquires the property.[208] The purpose of the first restriction is to match income and expenses more accurately; the second accommodates long-term construction projects. When the property becomes available for use, the half-year rule in Reg. 1100(2)(a)(i) applies.

j) — Short Taxation Year

The usual rule is that one calculates capital cost allowance on the undepreciated capital cost of assets of a class at the *end* of the taxation year. This rule is subject to the proviso noted above that a taxpayer may claim only one-half of the full CCA on an asset in the year that he or she acquires it.

Where the taxpayer's taxation year is less than 12 months, CCA is limited, in certain cases, to a proportional amount. This amount is calculated as follows:

(No. of days in the taxation year[209])/365 × Maximum CCA allowable

This rule applies to depreciable assets except Classes 14 (limited life intangibles), 15 (wood assets), and industrial mineral mines.[210]

---

[206]Most Class 12 (small items for which a 100 percent deduction is available in the year); Class 13 (leasehold interests, which are subject to special rules see Reg. 1100(1)(b)); Class 14 (patents and limited period franchises, etc.); Class 15 (timber rights); Classes 24, 27 and 34 (pollution control equipment), and Class 29 properties, are excluded.

[207]Reg. 1100(2.2).

[208]See subss. 13(26)–(32).

[209]"Number of days in the taxation year" refers to the number of days that the business is in operation, and not the period of ownership of the asset.

[210]Reg. 1100(3).

k) — Separate Classes for Similar Properties

Where a taxpayer operates more than one business, he or she must calculate capital cost allowance for *each* business separately.

Similarly, a taxpayer who has income from a business, as well as income from property, must use separate classes for the assets used to derive income from the business and the property.[211] For example, a taxpayer may own a building that he or she uses in business while also owning a rental property. Although the two buildings may be similar in all respects, each of the buildings must be placed into a separate class. This is another illustration of the strict segregation of income by source. Thus, it is quite possible that a taxpayer may trigger a recapture of capital cost allowance on the disposition of one asset when he owns a similar property, which, but for this rule, would be included in the same class.

Whether two or more business operations carried out simultaneously are part of the same business depends upon the degree of interconnection or interdependence between the operations of the various units.

l) — Rental Buildings over $50,000

Each rental building that costs $50,000 or more must be placed in a separate class.[212] The rule prevents taxpayers from artificially avoiding recapture of CCA upon the disposition of a rental property by acquiring another similar property of the same class. The rule also applies to rental properties that cost less than $50,000, but where additions increase the total capital cost above $50,000. In these circumstances, the properties must be transferred into a separate class. Where a taxpayer acquires a rental property consisting of numerous units, the cost of all of the units within the same building must be aggregated to determine whether the total cost exceeds $50,000.

The Act further limits the capital cost allowance claimable on "rental properties" that exceed $50,000 to the *net* of rental incomes and losses for the year from all such properties that the taxpayer owns. Thus, a taxpayer cannot use CCA on this class of assets to create a loss from property and shelter other sources of income.

---

[211]Reg. 1101(1); IT-206R, "Separate Businesses" (October 29, 1979); see also *Vincent v. Minister of National Revenue*, [1966] S.C.R. 374, [1966] C.T.C. 147, 66 D.T.C. 5123 (S.C.C.) (requirement that taxpayer calculate income from each source separately also applies to calculation of capital cost allowance); *Midwest Hotel Co. v. Minister of National Revenue*, [1972] C.T.C. 534, 72 D.T.C. 6440 (S.C.C.) (taxpayer who sold business then purchased another later in year subject to recapture); *Dupont Canada Inc. v. R.*, 2002 FCA 464, [2003] 1 C.T.C. 295, 2003 D.T.C. 5001 (Fed. C.A.); leave to appeal refused (2003), 320 N.R. 187 (note) (S.C.C.) (separate business concept).

[212]Reg. 1101(1ac); IT-304R2, "Condominiums" (June 2, 2000). Rental and non-rental properties must be placed in separate classes: Reg. 1101(1ae).

m) — Transfers of Property Between Classes

A taxpayer can elect to transfer all assets in Classes 2 to 12 that are used in the *same* business into Class 1.[213] Class 1 provides for a lower capital cost allowance rate than any of Classes 2 to 12. Hence, in normal circumstances, it is not to a taxpayer's advantage to transfer assets into Class 1. The transfer rules do, however, allow a taxpayer to establish a terminal loss or defer recapture of capital cost allowance. For example, a taxpayer may have a large UCC in one class but very few assets remaining in the class. The remaining assets may have a very low capital cost. If the taxpayer transferred these items out of the class into another class, she could recognize a terminal loss in the class from which she transferred the property.

Conversely, the UCC of a class may be low when the market value of the property in the class is high. If the taxpayer sold the property, he would have to recognize a recapture of CCA. The taxpayer could, however, transfer the property into another class with a lower rate of capital cost allowance. It would then be possible to defer the recognition of recapture by reducing the UCC of the class into which the taxpayer transferred the property.[214]

Example

Assume the following profile:

Class	UCC	Additions	Disposals	CCA
1	$ 100,000			$ 4,000
3	35,000		$ 75,000	(40,000)
8	12,000	$ 3,000		2,700
10	30,000			9,000
				$ (24,300)

The taxpayer faces a potential recapture of $24,300. He may either purchase a new Class 3 asset or elect to transfer all assets in Classes 3, 8 and 10 to Class 1. If he transfers the assets into Class 1, his CCA profile would appear as:

---

[213]Reg. 1103(1); The taxpayer must elect the transfer on or before the day on which she is required to file an income tax return for the year (Reg. 1103(3)).

[214]See Regs. 1103(2)-(2)(i) and subsection 13(5), which deals with the rules to transfer the components of classes of depreciable property between classes.

Example						
Class	UCC	Additions	Disposal	Adjustments	CCA	UCC
1	$ 100,000	$ 3,000	$ 75,000	$ 77,000	$ 4,200	$ 100,800

The taxpayer may claim CCA of $4,200 — that is, [(100,000 + 3,000 - 75,000 + 77,000) × 4%].

n) — Leaseholds

A taxpayer may deduct capital cost allowance from the cost of certain leasehold improvements (Class 13) in accordance with Schedule III,[215] based on the basis of the lesser of:

- 20 percent of the capital cost of any leasehold improvements, or

- The amount obtained by dividing the capital cost of leasehold improvements by the term of the lease in years, plus the term of the first option to renew, if any (not exceeding 40 years in total).

For example, the cost of a leasehold improvement made under a three-year lease with no option to renew is deductible at 20 percent of the capital cost per year. If, at the end of the three years, the taxpayer surrenders the lease and owns no other leasehold interests, he can deduct a terminal loss. If the lease is for a term of 10 years with an option to renew for five years, the capital cost is deductible in computing income at the rate of 1/15 per year. As we saw earlier, the deductible capital cost allowance in the year that the taxpayer acquires a Class 13 property is limited to one-half of the full year amount.[216]

o) — Patents, Franchises, Concessions, or Licences

A taxpayer can deduct CCA on a patent, franchise, concession, or licence if the asset has a limited life.[217] One determines the deductible CCA by prorating the cost of the asset over the life of the asset. Alternatively, where the asset is a patent, the taxpayer may claim a deduction that depends on the use of the patent.[218]

---

[215] Reg. 1100(1)(b).

[216] Reg. 1100(1)(b).

[217] Reg. 1100(1)(c); Sched. II, Class 14.

[218] Reg. 1100(9).

Patents also fall into Class 44, which uses a 25 percent declining balance method. A taxpayer can transfer these properties from Class 44 to Class 14 (see Reg. 1103(2)(h)).

p) — Works of Art

A taxpayer can claim CCA on certain types of works of art created by Canadian artists. These include:[219]

- Prints, etchings, drawings and paintings that cost more than $200; and

- Hand-woven tapestries and carpets that cost more than $215 per square meter.

A taxpayer *cannot* claim CCA on other types of works of art, such as:

- Antique furniture more than 100 years old that costs more than $1,000;

- Prints, etchings, drawings, paintings and carpets that are not the work of Canadian artists; and

- Engravings, lithographs, etchings, woodcuts or charts made before 1900.

These amounts have been fixes since 1981. The rationale of the sales is to promote "Canadian" art and discriminate against "foreign" art. However, the rule applies to all Canadian citizens, regardless where they reside and the theme of their art.

q) — Capital Cost of Automobiles

We saw earlier that, as a general rule, the capital cost of an asset is its full, laid-down cost. A special rule applies to automobiles. For tax purposes, the maximum cost on which a taxpayer can claim CCA is $30,000. This rule prevents taxpayers from writing off expensive automobiles against business income. The rule does not depend upon the legitimacy of the expenditure. Any amount in excess of the maximum (other than provincial sales tax and GST) is not eligible for capital cost allowance. Each passenger vehicle that costs more than $30,000 is segregated in a separate class (Class 10.1). Special rules apply to this class. For example, there is no recapture or terminal loss on Class 10.1 passenger vehicles.[220]

---

[219]Reg. 1102(1)(e).

[220]Dollar amounts can be adjusted by Regulation from time to time; see: para. 13(7)(g) and Reg. 7307(1).

M. — Eligible Capital Property

a) — General Comment

The CCA system deals for the most part with capital expenditures for tangible capital property. There is a different regime in respect of capital expenditures on intangible capital assets, such as goodwill, franchises, customer lists, and incorporation fees. We refer to these assets, as "eligible capital property".

Expenditures on account of eligible capital property are deductible in computing business income. The deductibility of such expenditures is, however, subject to stringent limits. Only 75 percent of such expenditures are deductible. The maximum rate of write-off is 7 percent per year on a declining balance basis. The Act includes 75 percent of the proceeds from the disposition of an eligible property in income, but only for amounts that exceed the taxpayer's "cumulative eligible capital account".[221] Thus, the regime has features of the capital gains and the capital cost allowance systems.

The general tax structure of eligible capital expenditures depends upon the operation of a notional account, the "cumulative eligible capital amount". This account functions as follows:

- 75 percent of outlays on account of eligible capital expenditures are included in the taxpayer's "cumulative eligible capital" account;[222] and

- 75 percent of the proceeds of disposition from eligible capital properties are credited to the "cumulative eligible capital" account.[223]

The balance in the "cumulative eligible capital" account at the end of the year can be amortized against business income at a maximum rate of 7 percent per year on a declining balance basis.[224] The Act recaptures any negative balance in the account as at the end of the year and includes it in the taxpayer's income for the year.[225] Thus, the tax structure for eligible capital property is a hybrid between the capital cost allowance rules (declining balance, fixed rate, recapture, etc.) and the capital gains rules of partial inclusion.

---

[221]Para. 20(1)(b), s. 14.

[222]Para. 14(5) "cumulative eligible capital".

[223]*Ibid.*

[224]Para. 20(1)(b).

[225]Subs. 14(1).

b) — Cumulative Eligible Capital

"Cumulative eligible capital" (CEC) is the amount by which the aggregate of 75 percent of the eligible capital expenditures made in respect of the business, and amounts previously included in income under subsection 14(1), exceed:

- Amounts previously deducted in computing income from the business under paragraph 20(1)(b); and

- 75 percent of the proceeds of sale, less selling expenses from a disposition of eligible capital property.[226]

---

[226]Para. 14(5) "cumulative eligible capital".

Example

Assume:

A taxpayer enters into the following transactions in respect of eligible capital properties.

Year	Transaction	Amount
1	Purchase	$53,334
2	—	—
3	Sale	$40,000
4	Sale	$13,334

The taxpayer claims the maximum 7 percent amortization each year.

Then:

	Cumulative Eligible Capital Account			
	Year 1	Year 2	Year 3	Year 4
Opening balance	NIL $	37,200 $	34,596 $	4,274
75% × purchases	$ 40,000	—	—	—
75% × sales	—	—	30,000	10,000
Balance before deduction from account	40,000	37,200	4,596	(5,726)
Amortization (7%)	2,800	2,604	322	—
Included in income	—	—	—	5,726
Ending Balance	$ 37,200	$ 34,596	$ 4,274	NIL

c) — Eligible Capital Expenditures

(i) — Meaning

An eligible *capital* expenditure is a capital expenditure of an intangible nature that a taxpayer incurs to earn income from a business, but one that is not deductible under any other provision of the Act. The Act specifically excludes the following expenditures from "eligible capital expenditures":[227]

- An outlay otherwise deductible in computing income or deductible under some provision of the Act, other than paragraph 20(1)(b);

- Outlays made specifically non-deductible by some provision of the Act, other than paragraph 18(1)(b);

- An outlay made to earn exempt income;

- The cost of tangible property or an interest therein, or the right to acquire the same;[228]

- The cost of intangible property that is depreciable property, or an interest therein, for example, leasehold interests, patents and franchises with a limited life, all of which costs would be deductible under the capital cost allowance provisions;

- The cost of property that would otherwise be deductible in computing a taxpayer's business income, or an interest therein, or the right to acquire the same;

- An amount paid to a creditor in settlement of a debt;

- An amount paid to a person in his or her capacity as a shareholder of the corporation;

- The cost, or part of the cost, of an interest in a trust, or a right to acquire the same;

- The cost, or part of the cost, of an interest in a partnership, or a right to acquire the same; and

- The cost or part of the cost of a share, bond, etc., or a right to acquire the same.

(ii) — "Eligible Capital Amount"

"Eligible capital amount" is 75 percent of the proceeds of the disposition of property (as adjusted by a formula) that would represent an eligible capital expenditure to the purchaser. That is, if the purchaser has made an eligible capital expenditure, the vendor is in receipt of

---

[227]Para. 14(5) "eligible capital expenditures".

[228]In most cases, a deduction in respect of tangible property would be available under the capital cost allowance provisions.

an eligible capital amount equal to 75 percent of that expenditure, less any outlays and expenses incurred on disposition.[229]

---

[229]Subpara. 14(5) "cumulative eligible capital"; subs. 14(1).

(iii) — "Eligible Capital Property"

"Eligible capital property" is any property that, if sold, would require the inclusion, in computing the taxpayer's income, of 75 percent of the proceeds under subsection 14(1).

(iv) — Characterization of Expenditures and Receipts

Amounts that a taxpayer incurs or receives on the purchase and sale of property are not necessarily characterized as mirror images of each other. In *Samoth*,[230] for example, the taxpayer acquired the exclusive right to sell Century 21 franchises in Canada to licensed real estate brokers. The taxpayer paid $100,000 for this right. The taxpayer acted as a trader in selling the Century 21 franchises, but maintained that the receipts from those sales were on account of eligible capital property. The Federal Court of Appeal held the receipts from the sale of the franchises to be on account of business income and not on account of capital. Hence, not being on account of capital, the receipts could not constitute amounts received on account of eligible capital property. In other words, although the purchase of the franchises might have been on account of eligible capital property, the sale of the franchises did not necessarily require a mirror image characterization of the proceeds of sale. In Justice Mahoney's words:[231]

> In applying the so-called "mirror image rule" . . . the face to be seen in the mirror by the [taxpayer] is not that of the actual purchaser of one of its franchises acquiring a capital asset but its own face, that of a trader in franchises.

d) — Exchanges of Property

Where a taxpayer disposes of an eligible capital property and acquires a replacement property[232] before the end of the first taxation year following the year of disposition, he or she may elect to defer recognition of any amount that might otherwise be recaptured.[233]

---

[230]*Samoth Financial Corp. v. R.*, [1986] 2 C.T.C. 107, 86 D.T.C. 6335 (Fed. C.A.).

[231]*Samoth Financial Corp. v. R.*, *ibid.*, at 108 [C.T.C.] and 6335 [D.T.C.].

[232]Subs. 14(7).

[233]Subss. 14(1) and (6).

e) — Goodwill

"Goodwill" is an asset. It has been described as ". . . the probability that the old customers will resort to the old place."[234] In other words, it is the advantage that accrues to a person as a result of a reputation. The reputation may rest on honest dealing, hard work or advertising.[235] In financial terms, goodwill means a premium sales price on the disposition of a business. The premium compensates for the "excess" earning power of the business because of its goodwill. Accountants define goodwill as:[236]

> . . . an intangible asset of a business when the business has value in excess of the sum of its net identifiable assets. . . . It has been said to fall into the three classes of commercial, industrial, and financial goodwill, which are the consequences of favourable attitudes on the part of customers, employees, and creditors, respectively. As to its value, the most common explanations emphasize the present value of expected future earnings in excess of the return required to induce investment.

"Goodwill" is also defined in terms of excess earning power over the "normal" rate of return of a business. For example, in *Dominion Dairies v. Minister of National Revenue*:[237]

> . . . goodwill can be viewed as the purchase of earning power in excess of a normal return on the investment. . . . This advantage evidences itself in the form of earnings in an amount greater than that expected in a typical firm in the industry with a similar capital investment.

---

[234]*Cruttwell v. Lye* (1810), 34 E.R. 129 (Eng. Ex. Ch.) at 134.

[235]*Trego v. Hunt*, [1896] A.C. 7 (H.L.).

[236]CICA, Terminology for Accountants.

[237]*Dominion Dairies Ltd. v. Minister of National Revenue*, [1966] C.T.C. 1, 66 D.T.C. 5028 (Can. Ex. Ct.) at 12-13 [C.T.C.] and 5033-34 [D.T.C.].

The determination of the existence of, and the amount attributable to, goodwill is a question of fact; it may result from location,[238] reputation,[239] brand loyalty,[240] competent management, good labour relations and trademarks.[241]

The tax system treats purchased goodwill differently from expenditures incurred in building up goodwill. A taxpayer who expends money on advertising, customer relations, employee relations, etc., may write off the expenditures on a current basis, even though the expenditures cultivate an asset. Where, however, a taxpayer purchases goodwill built up through such expenditures, the cost is an "eligible capital expenditure", which can only be amortized in the manner described above.

f) — Recapture of Negative Balances

(i) — General Rule

Where, at the end of a taxation year, the amounts required to be deducted from a taxpayer's pool of expenditures in respect of eligible capital property exceed the amounts required to be added to the pool, the excess ("negative balance") must be included in the taxpayer's income for the year.

(ii) — Individuals

Where an individual's cumulative eligible capital has a negative balance at the end of a taxation year, the amount that must be included in income is limited to that portion of the

---

[238]*R. v. Shok*, [1975] C.T.C. 162, 75 D.T.C. 5109 (Fed. T.D.) (contract specifying value of goodwill not upheld by court as appraisal differing and vendor was never consulted about allocation); *Saskatoon Drug & Stationery Co. v. Minister of National Revenue*, [1975] C.T.C. 2108, 75 D.T.C. 103 (T.R.B.) (court outlined types of goodwill as well as premium payable to succeed lease of choice location).

[239]*Canadian Propane Gas & Oil Ltd. v. Minister of National Revenue*, [1972] C.T.C. 566, 73 D.T.C. 5019 (Fed. T.D.) (proper assessment of value of goodwill is that amount assigned by opposing parties after hard bargaining); *Pepsi Cola Canada Ltd. v. R.*, [1979] C.T.C. 454, 79 D.T.C. 5387 (Fed. C.A.) (characterization of payment as on account of goodwill not termination of franchise).

[240]*Herb Payne (Transport) Ltd. v. Minister of National Revenue*, [1963] C.T.C. 116, 63 D.T.C. 1075 (Can. Ex. Ct.) (trucking business name part of goodwill; review of law on "goodwill"); *Schacter v. Minister of National Revenue*, [1962] C.T.C. 437, 62 D.T.C. 1271 (Can. Ex. Ct.) (court upheld agreement between taxpayer and vendor of accounting firm, absent contrary evidence of value of goodwill).

[241]*Morin v. Minister of National Revenue*, [1978] C.T.C. 2976, 78 D.T.C. 1693 (T.R.B.) (partnership held to have goodwill, and elements comprising goodwill); *Saskatoon Drug & Stationery Co. v. Minister of National Revenue*, above note 238; *Herb Payne (Transport) Ltd. v. Minister of National Revenue*, ante.

negative balance that represents the recapture of previous deductions claimed in respect of eligible capital property. The remainder of the negative balance is either deemed (in the case of qualified farm property) or electable (in the case of other properties) as capital gains.

(iii) — Bad Debts

Where a taxpayer has a negative balance in his or her cumulative eligible capital at the end of a taxation year, the negative balance is included in income for the year. This is so, regardless of whether or not the taxpayer has been paid for the disposition of the property that triggered the negative balance. If the amount proves uncollectible, the taxpayer may deduct 75 percent of the amount receivable upon the disposition of an eligible capital property that did not generate a taxable capital gain.[242]

N. — Home Office Expenses

There are special restrictions on the deductibility of home office expenses incurred on account of "workspace" in a domestic establishment. An individual may not deduct from business income, an amount in respect of an office in his or her home unless it is:

- The principal place of business, or

- Used by that person exclusively on a regular and continuous basis for meeting clients, customers or patients.

Home office expenses must be apportioned between business and non-business use when the above conditions are met. We calculate this on a *pro rata* basis, and it is normally based on the amount of floor space used.

Home office expenses may only be deducted to the extent of the taxpayer's income from the business for the year. Thus, an individual may not create a loss on account of such expenses. To the extent that there is a loss, however, it may be carried forward and used in the year immediately following the one in which the loss was incurred. This restriction does not apply to the computation of income from property.[243]

O. — Superficial Losses

A taxpayer in the business of lending money in Canada (for example, a financial institution) may not claim a "superficial loss" when it disposes of debt or equity securities used or held

---

[242]Subs. 20(4.2).

[243]Subs. 18(12).

by it in its business. This rule is similar to the superficial loss rules applicable to capital properties.

A superficial loss arises where a taxpayer — for example, a money lender — disposes of debt or equity and the taxpayer (or an affiliated person) reacquires the same or identical property within 30 days before and after the disposition. The taxpayer cannot claim the loss. The claim may, however, be revived on the occurrence of certain events.[244]

P. — Convention Expenses

a) — General Comment

Taxpayers who are in business or practice a profession may deduct their expenses for attending up to two conventions per year, provided the conventions are in connection with their business or profession. There are several limitations to the deduction.

b) — Territorial Scope

The convention must be at a location that can reasonably be regarded as falling within the territorial scope of the convening organization.[245] The taxpayer does not have to be a member of the sponsoring organization. An organization that is national in character may convene at any location in Canada; an organization that is international in character may convene abroad. A convention held during an ocean cruise is considered to be held outside Canada.

It is the character of the sponsoring organization, and not the nature of the taxpayer's business, that determines what is acceptable in terms of territorial scope.[246] The taxpayer's actual business may, however, reflect on the purpose of the trip.

c) — Primary Purpose

The *primary* purpose of the taxpayer's visit to the convention must be connected to business. Is the taxpayer entitled to enjoy being at the convention? Yes, provided that such personal enjoyment is incidental to, and not the *raison d'être* of, the trip.

---

[244]Subss. 18(13)–(16).

[245]Subs. 20(10).

[246]*Michayluk v. Minister of National Revenue*, [1988] 2 C.T.C. 2236, 88 D.T.C. 1564 (T.C.C.).

The question of the purpose of attendance at a convention should be determined by the relationship between the taxpayer's business and the subject matter covered at the convention.[247] The closer the relationship between the two, the easier it is to justify the business purpose of the trip. That is not to suggest, however, that a taxpayer who is expanding a business from one field into another is not entitled to attend a convention that discusses the subject matter of the new field.

d) — Blended Purposes

If a taxpayer combines a vacation with attendance at a convention, the personal portion of the trip is not deductible from income. The taxpayer should allocate, on some reasonable basis, the portion of the trip that is considered personal. A reasonable basis could be, for example, the number of days spent at the convention versus the total time spent away from home. The taxpayer is, however, entitled to deduct the entire cost of travel to and from the convention as a business expense. Thus, it is only the portion of the total expenditure that is directly attributable to the vacation portion (apart from travel expenses) that is considered non-deductible for tax purposes.

Costs incurred for taking the taxpayer's spouse and family to the convention are not usually deductible for tax purposes unless the presence of the taxpayer's spouse at the convention is *necessary* for business or professional purposes. The burden of proving the necessity of the presence of the taxpayer's spouse rests squarely, and heavily, on the taxpayer.

e) — U.S. Conventions

A special rule applies to Canadian businesses and professional organizations that are national in character and that hold conventions in the United States. In these circumstances, the *Canada-U.S. Tax Treaty* provides that expenses incurred for attending the organization's convention in the U.S. are deductible on the same basis as if the convention had been held in Canada. This special provision only applies to organizations that are "national" in character, and does not apply to regional or local organizations.[248]

f) — Intra-Company Meetings: Corporations

The limit of two conventions per year also applies to corporate taxpayers. Thus, where a corporation "attends" a convention through its officers or agents, it is subject to the maximum of two per year. The CRA does accept, however, that where a corporation has diversi-

---

[247]*Rovan v. Minister of National Revenue*, [1986] 2 C.T.C. 2337, 86 D.T.C. 1791 (T.C.C.).

[248]See Article XVII.9 Canada-U.S. Tax Convention.

fied business interests (as in the case of an integrated oil company), the limit applies separately to each of its business interests. For example, the corporation may send representatives to attend conventions held on the subjects of administration, accounting, chemistry, geology, etc., and deduct expenses for up to two conventions per subject grouping per year for each of its personnel.

Selected Bibliography to Chapter 9

General Deductions

Brooks, Neil, "The Principles Underlying the Deduction of Business Expenses", *Canadian Taxation*, Hansen, Krishna, Rendall, eds. (Toronto: Richard De Boo, 1981), chapter 5.

Cruikshank, Allan B., "Business Expenses Under the White Paper on Tax Reform", in *Proceedings of 39th Tax Conf.* 24:1 (Can. Tax Foundation, 1987).

Goodison, Don, "Allowable Business Expenditures" (May 1989) 23 CGA Magazine 14.

Hershfield, J.E., "Recent Trends in the Deduction of Expenses in Computing Income", in *Proceedings of 41st Tax Conf.* 44:1 (Can. Tax Foundation, 1989).

Lawrence J., "Income Receipts and Deductions in the Computations of Income from Employment, Business and Property", in *Proceedings of 31st Tax Conf.* 381 (Can. Tax Foundation, 1979).

Krishna, Vern, "Does Supreme Court Expand Deductibility of Business Expense in Symes?", (1994) Can. Current Tax J. 35.

McCart, Janice, "Deductibility of Business Expenses: Recent Developments", in *Proceedings of 37th Tax Conf.* 41 (Can. Tax Foundation, 1985).

Neville, Ralph T., "Deductibility of Automobiles, Meals and Entertainment and Home Office Expenses After Tax Reform", in *Proceedings of 40th Tax Conf.* 25:1 (Can. Tax Foundation, 1988).

Perry, Harvey, "Federal Individual Income Tax: Taxable Income and Tax", *Tax Paper No. 89* 58 (Can. Tax Foundation, 1990).

Verchere, Bruce, "Deductible Expenses", *Corporate Management Tax Conf.* 55 (Can. Tax Foundation, 1975).

Unreasonable Expenses

McGregor, G., "The 'Reasonable' Test for Business Expenses" (1959) 7 Can. Tax J. 318.

McIntyre, J.M., "The Deduction of Illegal Expenses" (1965) 2 U.B.C.L. Rev. 283.

Personal and Living Expenses

Hershfield, J.E., "Recent Trends in the Deduction of Expenses in Computing Income", in *Proceedings of 41st Tax Conf.* 44:1 (Can. Tax Foundation, 1989).

Perry, Harvey, "Federal Individual Income Tax: Taxable Income and Tax", *Tax Paper No. 89* 58 (Can. Tax Foundation, 1990).

Ramaseder, Brigitte, "Department Continues to Hold Restrictive View on Deductibility of Costs Related to Acquisition of New Residence" (1993) 5 Tax of Executive Compensation and Retirement 844.

Current Expense or Capital Expenditure

Cunningham, Noel B., and Deborah H. Schend, "How to Tax The House That Jack Built" (Spring 1988) 43 Tax Law Review 447.

"Distinguishing Between Capital Expenditures and Ordinary Business Expenses: A Proposal for a Universal Standard" (Spring 1986) 19 U. Mich. J.L. Ref. 711.

Spiro, D.E., "'Genuine Repair Crisis': A Gloss is Added to the Capital 'Improvement' Test for Repair Expenses" (1987) 35 Can. Tax J. 419.

Tremblay, Richard G. and Helen Aston, "The Deductibility of Environmental Clean-Up Costs" (September 1991) 3 Can. Current Tax C77.

Reserves

Champagne, Donald C., "Bad and Doubtful Debts, Mortgage Foreclosures and Conditional Sales Repossessions", in *Proceedings of 27th Tax Conf.* 682 (Can. Tax Foundation, 1975).

Dzau, Vivien, "Reserves: A Tool for Deferring Taxes" (1980) 113 CA Magazine 57.

Krishna, Vern, "Reserves" (1984) 1 Can. Current Tax J-41.

McCullogh, J.D., "Deferred Income Reserves — Improving Cash Flow" (1975) 106 CA Magazine 51.

Merrell, David L., "Bill C-139: New Reserve Provisions and the Forward Averaging Refundable Tax Rules", *Prairie Provinces Tax Conf.* 195 (Can. Tax Foundation, 1983).

Mida, Israel H., "Deductibility of Reserves: Contractors, Maintenance Contracts, Captive Insurance Arrangements", *Corporate Management Tax Conf.* 4:1 (Can. Tax Foundation, 1987).

Nitikman, Bert W., "Reserves", in *Proceedings of 25th Tax Conf.* (Can. Tax Foundation, 1973).

Smyth, "Accounting for Reserves — Tax Relationship and Gross Earnings" (1959) 75 Can. Chartered Accountant 549.

Chapter 9 — Deductions from Business and Investment Income

Interest

Arnold, Brian J., and Gordon D. Dixon, "Rubbing Salt into the Wound: The Denial of the Interest Deduction After the Loss of a Source of Income" (1991) 39 Can. Tax. J. 1473.

Atsidis, Elisabeth, "Technical Amendments to the Interest Deductibility Rules in the *Income Tax Act* as Proposed on 20 December 1991" (1993) 2 Dal. J. Leg. Studies 265.

Bale, Gordon, "The Interest Deduction Dilemma" (1973) Can. Tax J. 317.

Bankman, Joseph, and William A. Klein, "Accurate Taxation of Long-Term Debt: Taking Into Account the Term Structure of Interest" (Winter 1989) 44 Tax Law Review 335.

Berger, Sydney H., and Mark Potechin, "When is Interest Expense Deductible?" (1986) 119:5 CA Magazine 54.

Birnie, David A.G., "Consolidation of Corporate Structures", in *Proceedings of 31st Tax Conf.* 177 (Can. Tax Foundation, 1979).

Block, Cheryl D., "The Trouble with Interest: Reflections on Interest Deductions After the *Tax Reform Act of 1986*" (Fall 1988) 40 University of Florida Law Review 689.

Bouman, Donald G.H., "Debt Financing-II", *Corporate Management Tax Conf.* 88 (Can. Tax Foundation, 1974).

"Bronfman Panacea or Pandora's Box" (1990) 44 D.T.C. 7009.

Couzin, Robert, James R. Daman, Michael Hiltz and William R. Lawlor, "Tax Treatment of Interest: Bronfman Trust and the June 2, 1987 Release", *Corporate Management Tax Conf.* 10:1 (Can. Tax Foundation, 1987).

Crawford, William E., "The Deductibility of Interest", in *Proceedings of 42nd Tax Conf.* 4:10 (Can. Tax Foundation, 1990).

Crowe, Ian, "Tax — I'm Tired of Yoghurt" (June 1991) 124 CA Magazine 29.

Damji, Nazee, "Interest and Penalty Charges" (April 1990) 64 CMA Magazine 15.

"Discounts, Premiums and Bonuses and the Repeal of IT-114: What Happens Now" (1994) No. 1181 Tax Topics 1.

Drache, Arthur B.C., "Draft Interest Expense Legislation" (1992) 14 Can. Taxpayer 11.

Drache, Arthur B.C., "Interest Deductibility: Loans to Shareholders and Employees" (1983) 5 Can. Taxpayer 179.

Drache, Arthur B.C., "Interest Deductibility: Planning Still Worthwhile" (1991) 13 Can. Taxpayer 102.

Drache, Arthur B.C., "Interest Deductibility Reviewed" (1991) 13 Can. Taxpayer 189.

407

Drache, Arthur B.C., "Mortgage Interest Deductible . . . For Now" (1987) 9:4 Can. Tax-payer 29.

Edgar, Tim, and Brian J. Arnold, "Reflections on the Submission of the CBA-CICA Joint Committee on Taxation Concerning the Deductibility of Interest" (1992) 38 Can. Tax J. 847.

Edwards, Stanley E., "Debt Financing-I", *Corporate Management Tax Conf.* 70 (Can. Tax Foundation, 1974).

Ewens, Douglas S., "The Thin Capitalization Restrictions" (1994) Can. Tax J. 954.

Fox-Revett, Melissa G., "Interest Deductibility", (1993) Can. Current Tax P19.

Gagnon, Guy A., "Deducting Shareholder Interest the Hard Way" (1992) 40 Can. Tax J. 1343.

Glover, Paul, "Interest is Deductible — Isn't It?" (July-August 1987) 61 CMA Magazine 28.

Henly, K.S.M., "Late Payment Charges: Interest for the Purpose of Thin Capitalization Rules?" (1987) 35 Can. Tax J. 143.

Hickey, Paul B., "The Proposed New Interest Deductibility Regime: Strategies and Pitfalls" in *Processing of 46th Tax Conference* (Can. Tax Foundation, 1992).

Huggett, Donald R., "A Matter of Interest" (1987) 14 Can. Tax News 105.

Huggett, Donald R. (ed.), "Speculators Beware" (1980) 7 Can. Tax News 114.

"Income Tax Treatment of Interest — What's Happening" (1995) No. 1196 Tax Topics 2.

"Interest Deductibility Revisited" (1990) 44 D.T.C. 7026.

"Interest Expense Detailed" (1992) 4:11 Tax Notes Inter. 513.

Krever, Richard, "'Capital or Current': The Tax Treatment of Expenditures to Preserve a Taxpayer's Title or Interest in Assets" (1986) 12 Monash Univ. L.R. 49.

Krishna, Vern, "Deducting Interest Expenses" (1983) 17:11 CGA Magazine 21.

Krishna, Vern, "Interest Deductibility: More Form Over Substance", (1993) Can. Current Tax C17.

Krishna, Vern, "Interest Expenses" (1983) 17:7 CGA Magazine 39.

Krishna, Vern, "Is There a Choice of Methods in Accounting for Interest Expenses?" (1984) 1 Can. Current Tax C-21.

Krishna, Vern, "More Uncertainty on Deduction of Interest Expenses" [Case Comment: *Attaie v. Canada (M.N.R.)*, T-1319-85 (1987) (T.C.)] (1987–89) 2 Can. Current Tax J-59.

Latimer, W.R., "Capitalization of Interest" (1969) 17 Can. Tax J. 331.

Lavelle, P.M., "Deductibility of Interest Costs" (1981) 29 Can. Tax J. 536.

Lawlor, William B., "Interest Deductibility: Where to After Bronfman Trust?", in *Proceedings of 39th Tax Conf.* 19:1 (Can. Tax Foundation, 1987).

Lindsay, Robert F., "Tax Aspects of Real Estate Financing", *Corporate Management Tax Conf.* 258 (Can. Tax Foundation, 1983).

Loveland, Norman C., "Income Tax Aspects of Borrowing and Lending", (1986) Special Lectures LSUC 289.

McDonnell, T.E., "Without a Trace" (1993) 41 Can. Tax J. 134.

McNair, D. Keith, "Restricted Interest Expense" (1987) 35 Can. Tax J. 616.

Mitchell, George, "Current Assessing Trends" (1979) 27 Can. Tax J. 256.

Neville, Ralph T., "Tax Considerations in Real Estate Development and Construction", *Corporate Management Tax Conf.* 7:1 (Can. Tax Foundation, 1989).

Riehl, Gordon W., "Debt Instruments", in *Proceedings of 27th Tax Conf.* 764 (Can. Tax Foundation, 1975).

Shoup, Carl S., "Deduction of Homeowners' Mortgage Interest, Interest on Other Consumer Debt, and Property Taxes Under the Individual Income Tax: The Horizontal Equity Issue" (1979) 27 Can. Tax J. 529.

Smith, David W., "Supreme Court Shakes Up Interest-Deduction Rules" (April 1987) 14:4 Nat. 17.

Smith, Ronald, J., "Sales of Real Estate: Tax Planning for the Buyer", *Corporate Management Tax Conf.* 159 (Can. Tax Foundation, 1983).

Steiss, "Deductibility of Financing Charges", in *Proceedings of 24th Tax Conf.* 126 (Can. Tax Foundation, 1972).

Stikeman, H.H. (ed.), "Interest Deductibility — The Purpose Test", Canada Tax Letter, April 21, 1980 (De Boo).

Stikeman, H.H. (ed.), "The Deduction of Interest and the 'Use' of Money", Canada Tax Letter, July 10, 1974 (De Boo).

Thomas, Douglas, "As a Matter of Interest" (1978) 3 CA Magazine 84.

Ward, David A., "Arm's Length Acquisition Relating to Shares in a Public Corporation", *Corporate Management Tax Conf.* 108 (Can. Tax Foundation, 1978).

Wraggett, Cathy, "Minimizing Your Personal Tax Burden" (March 1990) 64 CMA Magazine 21.

Capital Cost Allowance

Arnold, Brian J., "Conversions of Property to and from Inventory: Tax Consequences" (1976) 24 Can. Tax J. 231.

Arnold, Brian J., "Recent Developments in the Tax Treatment of Inventory", in *Proceedings of 31st Tax Conf.* 865 (Can. Tax Foundation, 1979).

Bird, R.W., and J.R. Williamson, "Capital Cost Allowance" (1981) Can. Taxation 251.

Carter, Ronald W., "CCA and Eligible Capital Property: Tax Reform Implications", in *Proceedings of 40th Tax Conf.* 27:1 (Can. Tax Foundation, 1988).

Colley, Geoffrey M., "More on Capital Cost Allowance" (1976) 109 CA Magazine 62.

Daniels, C. Paul, "Real Estate Investment as a Tax Shelter", in *Proceedings of 28th Tax Conf.* 179 (Can. Tax Foundation, 1976).

"Distinguishing Between Capital Expenditures and Ordinary Business Expenses: A Proposal for a Universal Standard" (Spring 1986) 19 U. Mich. J.L. Ref. 711.

Harris, N.H., "Capital Cost Allowance" (1984) 1 Computer L. 26.

Harris, N.H., "Tax Aspects of Condominium Conversions and Lease Inducement Payments to Recipients", in *Proceedings of 38th Tax Conf.* 45 (Can. Tax Foundation, 1986).

Harris, N.H., "Capital Cost Allowances", in *Proceedings of 21st Tax Conf.* 200 at 231 (Can. Tax Foundation, 1968).

Harris, N.H., "Replacement Property", in *Proceedings of 29th Tax Conf.* 395 (Can. Tax Foundation, 1977).

Huggett, Donald R. (ed.), "Capital Cost Allowances" (1974) 11 Canadian Tax News 71.

Louis, David, *Canada's Best Real Estate Tax Shelters* (Toronto: Hume Pub. Co., 1985).

MacDonald, R.C., "Capital Cost Allowances" (1973) 47 Cost and Management 43.

Matheson, David I., "Acquisition and Disposition of Depreciable Assets" (1969) 17 Can. Tax J. 277.

Milrad, L.H., "Computers and the Law: The Taxation of Computer Systems — An Overview" (1984) 1 Bus. & L. 65.

Revenue Canada Round Table, *Corporate Management Tax Conf.* 601 (Can. Tax Foundation, 1979).

Revenue Canada Round Table, in *Proceedings of 36th Tax Conf.* 834-35 (Can. Tax Foundation, 1984).

Silver, Sheldon "Tax Implications of Different Forms of Holding Real Estate", in *Proceedings of 25th Tax Conf.* 425 (Can. Tax Foundation, 1973).

Sterritt, Deborah, "Partnerships and the Rental Property CCA Restriction: News to Some, Relief to Others", (1987–89) Can. Current Tax P35.

Stikeman, H.H. (ed.), "A Brave New World of Recapture", Canada Tax Letter, September 10, 1976 (De Boo).

Strain, W.J., "Capital Cost Allowances", *Corporate Management Tax Conf.* 26 (Can. Tax Foundation, 1975).

Weyman, C. David, "Manufacturing and Processing, Valuations and Business Deductions Including Capital Cost Allowances", in *Proceedings of 31st Tax Conf.* 254 (Can. Tax Foundation, 1980).

Witterick, Robert G., "Syndicated Acquisitions and Financing of Businesses", *Corporate Management Tax Conf.* 3:1 (Can. Tax Foundation, 1990).

Eligible Capital Property

Carter, Ronald W., "CCA and Eligible Capital Property: Tax Reform Implications", in *Proceedings of 40th Tax Conf.* 27:1 (Can. Tax Foundation, 1988).

Dwyer, Blair P., "Deductibility of Tenant Inducement Payments (Income Tax)" (1987–89) 2 Can. Current Tax C-53.

Grant, Carl T., "The Valuation and Tax Treatment of Goodwill", in *Proceedings of 24th Tax Conf.* 467 (Can. Tax Foundation, 1972).

Huggett, Donald R. (ed.), "Eligible Capital Expenditures" (1974) 11 Can. Tax News 46.

Johnston, Albert N., "All About Nothings" (1977) 110 CA Magazine 47.

Krishna, Vern, "Indirect Payments and Transfers of Income" (1986) 1:28 Can. Current Tax J-137.

Krishna, Vern, "Sale of Franchises: Receipts on Account of Eligible Capital Property or Income from Business?" (1986) 1 Can. Current Tax J-157.

McCallum, J.Thomas, "The Right Rollovers" (October 1991) 25 CGA Magazine 17.

McKay, Russell E., "Income Taxation of a Professional Partnership", in *Proceedings of 24th Tax Conf.* 421 (Can. Tax Foundation, 1972).

Mogan, Murray A., "Recent Developments in Federal Taxation of Income and Deductions", in *Proceedings of 29th Tax Conf.* 59 (Can. Tax Foundation, 1977).

Stikeman, H.H., "Goodwill or Illwill: When is a Nothing Something?", *Canada Tax Letter*, Feb. 19, 1975 (De Boo).

Stikeman, H.H. (ed.), "Payments for Know-How or Research", Canada Tax Letter, March 31, 1975 (De Boo).

Ward, David A., "Tax Considerations Relating to the Purchase of Assets of a Business", *Corporate Management Tax Conf.* 22 (Can. Tax Foundation, 1972).

Ward, David A. and Neil Armstrong, "Corporate Taxation: Lease Inducement Payments" (1986) 5 Legal Alert 98.

Home Office Expenses

Neville, Ralph T., "Deductibility of Automobiles, Meals and Entertainment and Home Office Expenses After Tax Reform", in *Proceedings of 40th Tax Conf.* 25:1 (Can. Tax Foundation, 1988).

Convention Expenses

Drache, Arthur B.C., "Deductible Convention Expenses" (1992) 13 Can. Taxpayer 7.

Drache, Arthur B.C., "Medical Convention Expenses" (1983) 5 The Can. Taxpayer 124.

Selected Other Deductions

"Automobile Expense Deduction Limits for 1995" (1994) No. 1185 Tax Topics 2.

Bacal, Norman, and Richard Lewin, "Once Bitten, Twice Shy? The Canadian Film Industry Revisited", in *Proceedings of 38th Tax Conf.* 46 (Can. Tax Foundation, 1986).

Colley, Geoffrey M., "Tax Relief for Overseas Employment Income" (1983) 116:11 CA Magazine 71.

Colley, Geoffrey M., "The 3% Inventory Allowance" (1978) 4 CA Magazine 106.

"Company Cars and Automobile Expense" (Toronto: Coopers & Lybrand Canada, 1991).

Corn, G., "Deductibility of Landscaping Costs" (1984) 1 Can. Current Tax J-27.

"Deductible Advertising Expenses" (1995) No. 1195 Tax Topics 3.

Drache, Arthur B.C., "Top Hat Pension Plans: A Rethink" (1983) 5 Can. Taxpayer 155.

Farwell, Peter M., "Scientific Research and Experimental Development", *Corporate Management Tax Conf.* 7:1 (Can. Tax Foundation, 1986).

Gillespie, Thomas S., "Lease Financing: An Update", in *Proceedings of 41st Tax Conf.* 24:1 (Can. Tax Foundation, 1989).

Goldstein, D.L., "Whether a Charitable Donation is Deductible as a Business Expense" [Case Comment: *Impenco Ltd. v. M.N.R.*, [1988] 1 C.T.C. 2339 (T.C.C.)] (1988) 36 Can. Tax J. 695.

Huggett, Donald R. (ed.), "Inventory Allowance" (1980) 7 Can. Tax News 98.

Huggett, Donald R., "Training Costs for Professionals and Other Independent Businessmen" (1980) 8 Canadian Tax News 26.

Krasa, Eva M., "The Income Tax Treatment of Legal Expenses" (1986) 34 Can. Tax J. 757.

Krasa, Eva M., "The Deductibility of Fines, Penalties, Damages and Contract Termination Payments" (1992) 38 Can. Tax Journal 1399.

Krishna, Vern, "Deductibility of Legal and Accounting Fees in Defending Tax Evasion Charges (IT-99R3)" (1986) 1 Can. Current Tax C-129.

Krishna, Vern, "Deducting Fines and Penalties" (September 1988) 22 CGA Magazine 35.

Langlois, Robert, et al., "Mid-Year Amalgamations", *Canada Tax Letter*, Jan. 20, 1978 (De Boo).

McDonnell, T.E., "Issue Costs of Interests in Real Estate Syndicate Deductible" (1992) 40 Can. Tax Journal 710.

Murray, Kenneth J., "The Definition of Scientific Research for Income Tax Purposes", in *Proceedings of 36th Tax Conf.* 563 (Can. Tax Foundation, 1984).

Neville, Ralph T., "Tax Considerations in Real Estate Development and Construction", *Corporate Management Tax Conf.* 7:1 (Can. Tax Foundation, 1989).

Novek, Barbara L., "Deductibility of Financing Expenses", *Corporate Management Tax Conf.* 3:1 (Can. Tax Foundation, 1992).

Pitfield, Ian H., "Prepaid Expenses and Other Deductions — Recent Developments" (1980) 14 CGA Magazine 41.

"Revenue Canada's Framework for Automobile Deductions" (1993) 5 Tax. of Executive Compensation and Retirement 839.

Shafer, Joel, "Income Tax Aspects of Real Estate Financing", *Corporate Management Tax Conf.* 1:1 (Can. Tax Foundation, 1989).

Tremblay, Richard G. and Helen Aston, "The Deductibility of Environmental Clean-up Costs", (1991) Can. Current Tax C77,

Valliere, Charles E., "Both Deduction and Capitalization Treatment Denied for Expenses with Respect to Real Estate that Produces No Income" (1991) 39 Can. Tax J. 1033.

Other

Anthony, Irene, "Franchising" (1983) 116:10 CA Magazine 20.

Beam, R.E., and S.N. Laiken, "Personal Tax Planning — Changes in Use and Non-Arm's Length Transfers of Depreciable Property" (1987) 35 Can. Tax J. 453.

Dean, Jacklyn I., "The January 15, 1987 Draft Amendments Relating to the Acquisition of Gains and Losses", *Corporate Management Tax Conf.* 2:1 (Can. Tax Foundation, 1987).

Drache, Arthur B.C., "Indirect Gifting: The Taxman's Approach" (1980) 2 Can. Taxpayer 167.

Drache, Arthur B.C., "On the Move?" (1979) 1 The Canadian Taxpayer 96.

Fairwell, Peter M., "Debt and Capital Gains Taxation" (1972) 20 Can. Tax J. 101.

Goodison, Donald, "Sex Discrimination and the *Income Tax Act*" (1979) 13 CGA Magazine 20.

O'Brien, Martin L., "Sale of Assets: The Vendor's Position", *Corporate Management Tax Conf.* 1 (Can. Tax Foundation, 1972).

Romano, Dianne L., "Reducing Immediate Tax Liabilities on Asset Disposals" (1979) 53 Cost and Management 44.

Strother, Robert C., "Transfer of Losses and Deduction Between Unrelated Taxpayers" (1987) 2 Can. Current Tax C-19.

Scace, Arthur R.A., and Michael G. Quigley, "Zero Coupon Obligations, Stripped Bonds, and Defeasance — An Update" (1984) 32 Can. Tax J. 689.

Williamson, W. Gordon, "Transfers of Assets to and from a Canadian Corporation", in *Proceedings of 38th Tax Conf.* 12 (Can. Tax Foundation, 1986).

Chapter 10 — Damages

Table of Contents

Table of Contents

I. — General Comment

The tax treatment of damages is the final product of commercial litigation that determines how much each party keeps or pays net of taxes. There is no specific provision in the Act that governs damages in general.[1] The only thing that one can say with any certainty about the taxation of damage awards is that some are taxable and others are not.

The difficulty lies in properly characterizing the underlying cause of legal action for tax purposes. Are damages income? The answer may depend on what happens at several steps in the litigation process. However, given the speed of our legal system, taxpayers may wait for twenty years to resolve the question.

The taxation of damages are determined largely by common law principles. There is no distinction between settlements and court awarded damages. Broadly speaking, damages in lieu of income that would otherwise have been taxable retain their character as such and are taxable. Thus, in order to determine the nature of damages we need to properly characterize the underlying purpose of the award. The first stage is in framing the cause of action and the claim for damages in the litigation pleadings. Unfortunately, counsel are not usually inclined to consider tax issues at this stage because they are primarily focused on establishing liability. The pleadings can, however, affect the court's assessment of damages.

The second stage is identifying the various parts of the award and the methodology that the trial judge uses for each component. Typically, damage awards breakdown into general damages, special damages, punitive damages (if any), pre-judgement and post-judgement interest. Each of these components can have different tax consequences. Of course, at the end of the long litigation journey, the plaintiff's only real concern is on the amount that he or she eventually gets to keep after all costs, fees and taxes.

The third stage is the actual calculation of the amount of damages. This is the step that is most likely to cause subsequent disputes with the tax authorities. One needs a yardstick to

---

[1]See, however, employment damages and "retiring allowance" in s. 248(1).

calculate losses and the most obvious choice is to use earnings lost as a result of the wrong done. But that does not mean that the yardstick determines the character of the underlying award. Thus, merely because the trial judge calculates the award by reference to earnings that might otherwise have been taxable does not make the damage award taxable.

We determine the *quantum* of capital by capitalizing the *income* that the capital generates. However, the fact that one uses lost profits as the reference point in the calculation of damages does not conclusively determine whether the damages are taxable or non-taxable. It is the actual nature of the settled interest that determines taxability. Thus, just as we can sometimes transform taxable profits into non-taxable capital receipts, we can crystallize an income stream of lost profits into a lump sum non-taxable capital amount.

The taxation of damage awards depends upon the fundamental character of the legal rights that give rise to the litigation. Proper characterization of each component of damages at trial of the action will reduce the uncertainty of subsequent treatment of the damages as income or capital for tax purposes. It will also prevent further prolonged litigation in the tax courts.

Spectrum of Damage Receipts

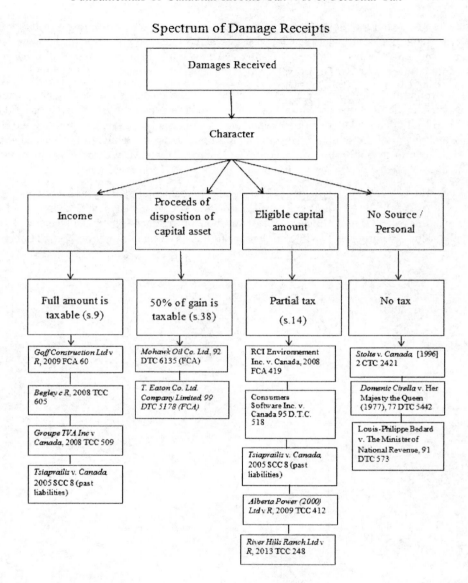

Income or capital receipt?

Full amount is taxable.

The difficulty is in characterizing the underlying nature of the damage award.[2] In *London &
Thames Haven Oil Wharves Ltd. v. Attwooll (Inspector of Taxes)*, for example, the Court
said:[3]

> Judges have from time to time been careful to say that no clear and comprehensive rule can be
> formulated, and no clear line of demarcation can be drawn, by reference to which it can be
> determined in every case whether the sum received should be regarded as a capital receipt or
> as a revenue receipt to be taken into account in arriving at the profit or gains of the recipient's
> trade. Each case must be considered on its own facts.

Therefore, we need to carefully identify the nature of the underlying claim and the cause of
action. The fundamental question is whether the payment replaces income or capital. Addi-
tionally, one must determine the character of the damage award: is the award designed to
compensate or punish the payer? Finally, if the damage award compensates one must en-
quire as to the nature of the compensation.

II. — Breach of Contract

A. — Nature of Claim

Damages for breach of contract are generally decided on the principle of compensation.
Thus, contract damages usually restore the plaintiff to the financial position he or she would
have enjoyed had the defendant performed the contract.[4] The plaintiff is entitled to the eco-

---

[2]See, for example, the 4:3 split decision of the Supreme Court of Canada in *Tsiaprailis v. R.*, [2005]
S.C.J. No. 9, 2005 CarswellNat 431, 2005 CarswellNat 432, [2005] 2 C.T.C. 1 (S.C.C.).

[3][1966] 3 All E.R. 145 at 149; reversed [1967] 2 All E.R. 124 (Eng. C.A.) [*London & Thames*].

[4]*Livingstone v. Rawyards Coal Co.* (1880), [1879-80] 5 App. Cas. 25, 28 W.R. 357 (U.K. H.L.) at 39
[App. Cas], Lord Blackburn (damages represent "that sum of money which will put the party who has
been injured, or who has suffered, in the same position as he would have been in if he had not sustained the wrong for which he is now getting his compensation or reparation"); see Street, *Principles
of the Law of Damages* (London: Sweet & Maxwell, 1962) at 3; *Yetton v. Eastwoods Froy Ltd.*, [1967]
1 W.L.R. 104, [1966] 3 All E.R. 353 (Eng. Q.B.) at 115 [W.L.R.], Blain J.; Ogus, The Law of Damages (London: Butterworths, 1973) at 17-21, 283-8; *Admiralty Commissioners v. "Susquehanna"
(The)*, [1926] A.C. 655 (U.K. H.L.) at 661 (loss to damaged ship owners not constituting lost profits
from mercantile charter where ship would not have been chartered); *Victoria Laundry (Windsor) Ltd.
v. Newman Industries Ltd.*, [1949] 2 K.B. 528, [1949] 1 All E.R. 997 (Eng. C.A.) at 539 [K.B.], As-
quith L.J. (damages for late delivery of boiler deemed foreseeable business losses); *Robinson v.
Harman* (1848), 1 Ex. 850, 154 E.R. 363 (Ex. Ct.) at 855 [Ex.], Parke B. (tenant knew lessee did not
have title to property leased; damages assessed at entire amount of loss notwithstanding); *Koufos v. C.
Czarnikow Ltd.*, [1969] 1 A.C. 350 (U.K. H.L.) at 400, Lord Morris (sugar cargo depreciated as market
price dropped while ship dallying *en route*; shipowner expected to have contemplated such result);
British Westinghouse Electric & Manufacturing Co. v. Underground Electric Railways Co. of London,

nomic value of his bargain or "expectation interest". Courts rarely award exemplary or punitive damages in contract cases.[5]

B. — The Surrogatum Principle

The general principle is that damages in lieu of receipts that would otherwise have been taxable to the taxpayer are taxable as income. Diplock L.J. stated the principle as follows:[6]

> Where, pursuant to a legal right, a trader receives from another person, compensation for the trader's failure to receive a sum of money which, if it had been received, would have been credited to the amount of profits (if any) arising in any year from the trade carried on by him at the time when the compensation is so received, the compensation is to be treated for income tax purposes in the same way as that sum of money would have been treated if it had been received instead of the compensation. The rule is applicable whatever the source of the legal right of the trader to recover the compensation. It may arise [1] from a primary obligation under a contract, such as a contract of insurance; [2] from a secondary obligation arising out of nonperformance of a contract, such as a right to damages, either liquidated, as under the demurrage clause in a charter party, or unliquidated; [3] from an obligation to pay damages for tort . . .; [4] from a statutory obligation; [5] or in any other way in which legal obligations arise.

Thus, one must determine whether the receipts, in lieu of which the damages compensate, would have been taxable. Note, however, the characterization of damages as taxable income or non-taxable capital receipts depends upon the nature of the legal right settled and not upon the method used to calculate the award.

[1912] A.C. 673, [1911-1913] All E.R. Rep. 63 (U.K. H.L.) at 689 [A.C.], Viscount Haldane L.C. (measure of damages where defective turbines replaced and replacement turbines achieved greater efficiency than the ones in question).

[5]*Addis v. Gramophone Co.*, [1909] A.C. 488, [1908-10] All E.R. Rep. 1 (Eng. H.L.) (although discredited by wrongful dismissal, employee not able to claim compensation for injured feelings or lack of notice); *Dobson v. Winton & Robbins Ltd.*, [1959] S.C.R. 775, 20 D.L.R. (2d) 164 (S.C.C.) (vendor suing on contract of sale of land entitled to specific performance or damages equal to decrease in price eventually received plus interest). See however *Jarvis v. Swan Tours Ltd.* (1972), [1973] 1 Q.B. 233, [1973] 1 All E.R. 71 (Eng. C.A.) (damages awarded against travel agent when plaintiff's holiday failed to meet advertised description).

[6]*London & Thames Haven Oil Wharves Ltd. v. Attwooll (Inspector of Taxes)*, [1967] 2 All E.R. 124 (Eng. C.A.) at 134. See also *Schwartz v. R.*, [1994] 2 C.T.C. 99, 94 D.T.C. 6249 (Fed. C.A.); reversed [1996] 1 S.C.R. 254, [1996] 1 C.T.C. 303, 96 D.T.C. 6103 (S.C.C.) (surrogatum principle also applies to employment contracts, whether anticipatory or otherwise).

C. — Nature of Legal Rights

Since damages represent compensation equal to the economic value of the underlying bargain, we usually compute them by reference to the profit lost through non-performance of the contract. However, the fact that one uses lost profits as the reference point to calculate damages does not conclusively determine whether the damages are taxable or non-taxable. It is the nature of the settled interest that determines taxability. Take a simple example. A has a contract with B that will render him a profit of $10,000 per year for the next 15 years. If B does not perform the contract, A will lose $150,000 in profits. Ignoring problems of mitigation, etc., A would usually be entitled to the present value of that amount, which at a discount rate of 8 percent is $85,595.

Whether the $85,595 is taxable as income depends upon the nature of the contract and not upon the fact that one determines the damages by reference to the annual profits. This is so even if the profits would have been taxable during the normal tenure of the contract. Destruction of an entire business, for example, will invoke compensation for capital even if one determines the capitalized value by discounting future lost profits. Thus, taxable profits may transform into non-taxable capital receipts when we crystallize an income stream into a lump-sum capital amount.

D. — Global Payments

A global payment covering several different heads of damages, for example, loss of earnings and payment on account of capital should be broken down and distributed into its taxable and non-taxable segments. The allocation is fairly easy where a court awards damages as a result of litigation and the judgment sets out the various heads of damages. An amount paid in settlement of a cause of action is more difficult to allocate and one should allocate amounts during negotiation of the settlement.

E. — Capital Receipts

Payments on account of capital are not taxable. This is so whether the payment is on account of judicially assessed damages or pursuant to a settlement. For example, a payment to compensate the plaintiff for the destruction of the entire structure of his or her income earning apparatus is a capital receipt.

The distinction between income and capital receipts is easy to state in principle. The difficulty lies in the application of the principle to the particular facts. Are damages for the cancellation of a lucrative service contract, for example, taxable in lieu of the profit that the taxpayer would have earned on the contract? What if the contract is the entire substratum of the business and its cancellation renders the enterprise a hollow shell? The difference between the two cases is essentially one of degree.[7]

F. — Non-Performance

Damages for non-performance of a service contract are usually taxable as income unless non-performance materially and substantially dislocates the taxpayer's business structure. Lord Russell explained the principle as follows:[8]

> The sum received by a commercial firm as compensation for the loss sustained by the cancellation of a trading contract or the premature termination of an agency agreement may, in the recipient's hands, be regarded either as a capital receipt or as a trading receipt forming part of the trading profit. It may be difficult to formulate a general principle by reference to which in all cases the correct decision will be arrived at since in each case the question comes to be one of circumstance and degree. When the rights and advantages surrendered on cancellation are such as to destroy or materially to cripple the whole structure of the recipient's profit-making apparatus, involving the serious dislocation of the normal commercial organization and resulting perhaps in the cutting down of the staff previously required, the recipient of the compensation may properly affirm that the compensation represents the price paid for the loss or sterilization of a capital asset and is therefore a capital and not a revenue receipt.

In *Van Den Berghs Ltd. v. Clark*,[9] for example, the taxpayer entered into an agreement with its competitor that provided for, among other things, profit-sharing, joint arrangements, control of supply, and restrictions on entering into other pooling arrangements. The parties terminated the contract following a dispute between them and the taxpayer received compensation for cancellation of its future rights under the contract. The Court considered the

---

[7]See e.g., *Schofield Oil Ltd. v. R.*, [1992] 1 C.T.C. 8, 92 D.T.C. 6022 (Fed. C.A.) ($1.37 million payment to release party from remaining 20 months of contractual obligations considered compensation for future profits and taxable as lost income).

[8]*I.R.C. v. Fleming & Co. (Machinery) Ltd.* (1951), 33 Tax Cas. 57 (Scot.) at 63.

[9][1935] A.C. 431, All E.R. Rep. 874 (U.K. H.L.). See also *Transocean Offshore Ltd. v. R.*, 2004 TCC 454, [2004] 5 C.T.C. 2133, 2004 D.T.C. 2915 (T.C.C. [General Procedure]); affirmed [2005] 2 C.T.C. 183 (Fed. C.A.); leave to appeal refused (2005), 2005 CarswellNat 3125, 2005 CarswellNat 3126 (S.C.C.) (Cdn corporation paid non-resident corporation $40 million in damages to compensate for the repudiation of a contract. *Surrogatum* principle applies: damages taxable since paid in lieu of rent which would have been taxable under Part XIII, para. 212(1)(d)).

compensation to be on account of a non-taxable capital receipt. In Lord MacMillan's words:[10]

> [T]he cancelled agreements related to the whole structure of the appellants' profit-making apparatus. They regulated the appellants' activities, defined what they might and what they might not do, and affected the whole conduct of their business. I have difficulty in seeing how money laid-out to secure, or money received for the cancellation of, so fundamental an organization of a trader's activities can be regarded as an income disbursement or an income receipt.

III. — Employment Damages

A. — Wrongful Dismissal

(a) — Nature of Claim

Damages for wrongful dismissal are in substance and effect a payment in lieu of notice of termination. Thus, where a contract is terminable on notice, damages for lost earnings are restricted to the amount payable during the period of notice.[11]

(b) — Statutory Rules

The Act treats damages for wrongful dismissal as "retiring allowances"[12] taxable as "other income" and not as employment income.[13] This is so whether the taxpayer receives the damages pursuant to a judgment or in settlement of litigation. In either case, the taxpayer must include the full amount of the payment in his or her income in the year that it is received. As with employment income, however, the payer must report damage payments and withhold tax at the prescribed rates.[14] Payments to non-residents require withholding tax of 25 percent of the amount paid.

---

[10]*Van Den Berghs Ltd. v. Clark, ibid.*, at 442 [A.C.]; see also *Barr, Crombie & Co. v. J.R.C.* (1945), 26 Tax Cas. 406 (Scot.) at 411, Lord Normand L.P.:

> In the present case, virtually the whole assets of the appellant company consisted in this agreement. When the agreement was surrendered or abandoned practically nothing remained of the company's business. It was forced to reduce its staff and to transfer into other premises, and it really started a new trading life. Its trading existence as practised up to that time had ceased with the liquidation of the shipping company.

[11]*British Guiana Credit Corp. v. Da Silva*, [1965] 1 W.L.R. 248 (England P.C.) at 259.

[12]S. 248(1)"retiring allowance".

[13]Subpara. 56(1)(a)(ii).

[14]Para. 153(1)(c).

(c) — Blended Payments

Where the damage award represents compensation for lost earnings during the period for which the employer should have given notice and also for mental suffering, one might argue that the mental suffering component is not taxable as a "retiring allowance" since it is not in respect of loss of office or employment.[15] The better view, however, is that the entire award is *in respect of* a loss of office or employment: The earnings component compensates for lack of notice and the mental anguish component compensates for the manner in which the employee lost his or her office or employment.[16] Thus, one head of the award goes to time, while the other goes to the method, but both arise from the same cause of action. They are *in respect of* improper loss of office or employment.[17]

B. — Signing Bonuses

An amount paid to an employee on account of a contractually agreed settlement (such as a "signing bonus") is taxable as income regardless of whether the employer makes the pay-

---

[15]*Specht v. Minister of National Revenue*, [1975] C.T.C. 126, 75 D.T.C. 5069 (Fed. T.D.).

[16]See e.g., the reasoning in *R. v. Savage*, [1983] 2 S.C.R. 428, [1983] C.T.C. 393, 83 D.T.C. 5409 (S.C.C.).

[17]*Young v. Minister of National Revenue*, [1986] 2 C.T.C. 2111, 86 D.T.C. 1567 (T.C.C.). As Linden J. said in *Brown v. Waterloo (Region) Commissioners of Police* (1982), 37 O.R. (2d) 277, 136 D.L.R. (3d) 49 (Ont. H.C) at 288-89 [O.R.]; reversed in part (1983), 43 O.R. (2d) 113, 150 D.L.R. (3d) 729 (Ont. C.A.):

> The aim of aggravated damages is to "soothe a plaintiff whose feelings have been wounded by the quality of the defendant's misbehavior". They are a "balm for mental distress" which is brought about by the wrongful "character of the defendant's wrongdoing". There must be evidence of damage of this type to the plaintiff. Aggravated damages are not meant to punish the defendant. (See Cooper-Stephenson and Saunders, *Personal Injury Damages in Canada* (1981) at 55; *Robitaille et al. v. Vancouver Hockey Club Ltd.* (1979), 19 BCLR 158 at 183, Esson J.; varied 124 D.L.R. (3d) 228, 16 CCLT 225, 30 BCLR 286 (C.A.)) In sum, though based on the quality of the defendant's conduct, aggravated damages are compensatory in purpose. [*cont.*]

[*cont.*] Canadian law seems to have recognized the need for something like aggravated damages in contract law by awarding damages, not only for financial losses, but also for any mental suffering incurred by the plaintiff in appropriate cases. (See *Pilon v. Peugeot Canada Ltd.* (1980), 29 OR (2d) 711, 114 D.L.R. (3d) 378, 12 B.L.R. 227 (Ont. H.C.), for example.) The purpose behind allowing such damages is to compensate for hurt feelings, anxiety and stress caused by certain types of contractual breach, where they are in contemplation of the parties. Where the conduct of a defendant which violates a contract is particularly callous, the likelihood of mental suffering would be more foreseeable to him.

ment pursuant to a legal agreement entered into before, during, or immediately after employment.[18]

C. — Arbitration Awards

Arbitration awards for breach of a collective agreement are taxable as employment income if the employer pays the amount as compensation for lost wages or other taxable benefits.[19] The gross amount of the award is income even if the employee receives only the net amount after deductions for income tax, CPP, EI, etc.

D. — Employment Insurance Benefits [para. 6(1)(f)]

Insurance payouts for disability benefits are often the product of settlements that combine past and future amount. In *Tsiaprailis*,[20] for example, the insurer settled for a lump-sum payment of $105,000 in lieu of past benefits and 75 percent of the present value of the insured's future benefits, plus interest, costs and disbursements. The majority of the Supreme Court (per Justice Charron) applied the *surrogatum* principle to the "arrears portion" of the award.

The *surrogatum* principle provides that amounts on account, or in lieu, of otherwise taxable amounts are also taxable. Thus, the determinative issue is: what is the payout intended to replace? Employment and litigation counsel should factor in the tax consequences of negotiated settlements to determine the portion of the "in lieu" amount attributable to past taxable amounts and future non-taxable amounts.

E. — Stock Options

Damages for breach of employee stock option contracts are taxable as employment income.[21]

---

[18]Subsec. 6(3); *Greiner v. R.*, [1984] C.T.C. 92, 84 D.T.C. 6073 (Fed. C.A.).

[19]*Vincent v. Minister of National Revenue*, [1988] 2 C.T.C. 2075, 88 D.T.C. 1422 (T.C.C.) (damage award restoring taxpayer to position he would have been in had wages set out in collective agreement for working on day of rest been paid); *Merrins v. Minister of National Revenue*, [1995] 1 C.T.C. 111, 94 D.T.C. 6669 (Fed. T.D.) (amount received on settlement of grievance from lay-off is retiring allowance).

[20][2005] S.C.J. No. 9, 2005 CarswellNat 431, 2005 CarswellNat 432, [2005] 2 C.T.C. 1 (S.C.C.).

[21]Para. 7(1)(b) and ss. 7(1.7).

IV. — Breach of Warranty of Authority

A. — Nature of Claim

An agent is liable for breach of warranty of authority for misrepresenting his or her authority to a person who suffers damage by acting on the strength of the misrepresentation. The law imposes the obligation because "... a person, professing to contract as an agent for another, impliedly, if not expressly, undertakes to or promises the person who enters into such contract, upon the faith of the professed agent being duly authorized, that the authority which he professes to have does in point of fact exist."[22]

B. — Damage Principles

We determine damages for breach of warranty of authority according to the usual contract rule: compensate the injured party and restore the person to the position he or she would have enjoyed had the authority claimed by the professed agent truly vested in him or her.[23]

The taxation of damages for breach of warranty of authority also follows the usual *surrogatum* rule: Damages that substitute for amounts that would have been taxable are taxable. Thus, here too, characterization for tax purposes depends upon the anterior determination as to the nature of the receipts that the damage award is intended to replace and not upon the method of calculating the amount.

In *Manley*,[24] for example, the taxpayer received damages of $587,400 in lieu of a finder's fee to which he would have been entitled if the professed agent with whom he was dealing had the authority that he claimed to have. Since the finder's fee would have constituted "profit" from an adventure in the nature of trade, the damages in lieu thereof were also taxable as income from a business:[25]

> In the present case, the [taxpayer] was a trader; he had engaged in an adventure in the nature of trade. The damages for breach of warranty of authority, which he received . . . pursuant to a legal right, were compensation for his failure to receive the finder's fee . . . .. Had the [taxpayer] received that finder's fee it would have been profit from a business required by the *Income Tax Act*, to be included in his income in the year of its receipt. The damages for breach of warranty of authority are to be treated the same way for income tax purposes.

---

[22]*Collen v. Wright* (1857), 8 E. & B. 647 (Ex. Ch.) at 657.

[23]See e.g., *Levy v. Manley* (1974), [1975] 2 S.C.R. 70, 47 D.L.R. (3d) 67 (S.C.C.) (action for commission payment turned on credibility of witnesses); *National Coffee Palace Co., Re* (1883), 24 Ch. D. 367 (Eng. C.A.) (broker purchased shares from wrong company; purchaser repudiated; outstanding purchase price exacted from broker by liquidator).

[24]*Manley v. R.*, [1985] 1 C.T.C. 186, 85 D.T.C. 5150 (Fed. C.A.) [Manley cited to C.T.C.].

[25]*Manley v. R., ibid.*, at 191 [C.T.C.].

Thus, at least in contract and agency, tax law considers damages on the *surrogatum* principle. In both cases, it is easy to justify the principle because the law almost invariably relates the damages to an income earning and profit making process.

V. — Tort Damages

A. — General Principles

Tort damages are more complex than damages in contract and agency. Although tort damages are generally taxable on the basis of the same principles that apply to other damages (include compensation for income receipts in income and exclude compensation for capital receipts), there are important differences in the manner in which the courts apply the principle to torts that involve damage to business or investments and torts that concern personal injuries or fatal accidents.

B. — Business or Investments

Compensation for tortious injury to business or property is taxable if the payment compensates for lost profits. Tort compensation is not taxable if made on account of capital receipts.[26] Hence, the taxation of damages depends upon the nature of the hole that the damage award fills. Lord Clyde illustrated the principle as follows:[27]

> Suppose someone who chartered one of the Appellant's vessels breached the charter and exposed himself to a claim of damages . . . there could, I imagine, be no doubt that the damages recovered would properly enter the Appellant's profit and loss account for the year. The reason would be that the breach of the charter was an injury inflicted on the Appellant's trading, making (so to speak) a hole in the Appellant's profits, and damages recovered could not be reasonably or appropriately put . . . to any other purpose than to fill that hole. Suppose on the other hand, that one of the taxpayer's vessels was negligently run down and sunk by a vessel belonging to some other shipowner, and the Appellant recovered as damage the value of the sunken vessel, I imagine that there could be no doubt that the damages so recovered could not enter the Appellant's profit and loss account because the destruction of the vessel would be an injury inflicted, not on the Appellant's trading, but on the capital assets of the Appellant's trade, making (so to speak) a hole in *them*, and the damages could therefore . . . only be used to fill that hole.

Thus, damages for injury to a business resulting in a loss of profits are taxable as income; compensation for destruction of an entire business is a non-taxable capital receipt. This rule

---

[26]*London & Thames Haven Oil Wharves Ltd. v. Attwooll (Inspector of Taxes)*, [1966] 3 All E.R. 145; reversed [1967] 2 All E.R. 124 (Eng. C.A.).

[27]*Burmah S.S. Co. v. I.R.C.* (1930), 16 Tax Cas. 67 (Scot.) at 71-72 (contract damages for late delivery of ship included in income as being on account of lost profits).

applies regardless of the method that one uses to estimate the loss of profits. As Lord Buck-master said:[28]

> It appears to me to make no difference whether it be regarded as the sale of the asset out and out, or whether it be treated merely as a means of preventing the acquisition of profit which would otherwise be gained. In either case the capital asset of the company to that extent has been sterilized and destroyed, and it is in respect of that action that the sum . . . was paid . . .. It is now well settled that the compensation payable in such circumstances is the full value of the minerals that are left unworked, less the cost of working, and that is of course the profit that would have been obtained were they in fact worked. But there is no relation between the measure that is used for the purpose of calculating a particular result and the quality of the figure that is arrived at by means of the application of that test.

Here too, there is no bright-line test to determine when compensation for lost earnings constitutes income or the capitalized value of earnings. It is a question of fact in each case.

C. — Depreciable Property

The Act includes compensation for damages to depreciable property in the taxpayer's income to the extent that he or she expends the money to repair the damage.[29] In effect, inclusion of the compensation in, and deduction of the repair costs from, income constitute a "wash transaction". This in effect means that the net tax effect is neutral.

D. — Capital Property

Damages for total loss or destruction of capital property are "proceeds of disposition" and go towards determining the capital gain or loss on the disposition of the property.[30] Thus, total loss or destruction of property is equivalent to a sale of the property.

E. — Eligible Capital Property

Compensation for damage to eligible capital property (for example, goodwill) is usually an eligible capital amount. If, however, the damage is so severe as to destroy the substrata of the taxpayer's business, any compensation for such damage is a capital receipt.[31]

---

[28]*Glenboig Union Fireclay Co. v. I.R.C.* (1922), 12 Tax Cas. 427 (U.K. H.L.) at 464.

[29]Para. 12(1)(f).

[30]S. 54"disposition" and "proceeds of disposition".

[31]See Interpretation Bulletin IT-182, "Compensation for Loss of Business Income, or of Property Used in a Business" (October 28, 1974).

F. — Personal Injuries

Income tax considerations are also relevant to damages for torts involving personal injuries. Here, the underlying principles are more elusive. There are two points in time when we can consider the issue of taxability:

(1) At trial when we determine liability and assess damages; and

(2) When the plaintiff receives payment of the award.

(a) — Determination of Settlement

We do not take tax factors into account in determining the amount that a defendant pays to the plaintiff in a personal injury case.[32] The theory is that we are compensating the plaintiff for the loss of his or her earning *capacity* and not for lost earnings. It does not matter that we determine the value of the plaintiff's capacity by direct mathematical reference to lost earnings. We arrive at this result by asserting our conclusion. Dickson J. explained the rule as follows:[33]

> ... an award for prospective income should be calculated with no deduction for tax which might have been attracted had it been earned over the working life of the plaintiff. This results from the fact that it is earning capacity and not lost earnings which is the subject of compensation. For the same reason, no consideration should be taken of the amount by which the income from the award will be reduced by payment of taxes on the interest, dividends, or capital gain. A capital sum is appropriate to replace the lost capital asset of earning capacity. Tax on income is irrelevant either to decrease the sum for taxes the victim would have paid on income from his job, or to increase it for taxes he will now have to pay on income from the award.

Thus, damage awards for personal injuries can be substantial where the tortfeasor renders a person who has a normal life expectancy incapable of working. In these circumstances, we capitalize the plaintiff's pre-tax earnings to determine the value of his or her lost earning capacity.

(b) — Taxation of Settlement

Damages for personal injuries are not taxable to the plaintiff when the judgment amount is received. This is so regardless of whether the amount paid is on account of special damages

---

[32]*Andrews v. Grand & Toy Alberta Ltd.*, [1978] 2 S.C.R. 229, 83 D.L.R. (3d) 452 (S.C.C.) [*Andrews* cited to D.L.R.] (plaintiff awarded $69,981 for prospective loss of earnings determined by discounting at 7 percent the sum of $564 (monthly earnings) over a period of 30.81 years (estimated working life)).

[33]*Andrews v. Grand & Toy Alberta Ltd.*, *ibid.*, at 474 [D.L.R.].

for loss of earnings up to trial, or general damages for loss of prospective earnings.[34] Here too, the damages compensate for capacity even though one measures them by reference to earnings.[35] Thus, the *surrogatum* principle does not apply in respect of damages for personal injuries.

Payments under a structured settlement that satisfy CRA's IT-365R2 are not taxable.

G. — Fatal Accidents

The theory of tort damages is quite different, however, with respect to fatal accidents. Here, we typically determine damages under fatal accident statutes on a net of tax basis by capitalizing the deceased's net take-home pay. De Grandpré J. explained this rule as follows:[36]

> It seems to me that what the widow and the child have lost in this case is the support payments made by the deceased, support payments which could only come out of funds left after deducting the cost of maintaining the husband, including the amount of tax payable on his income. I cannot see how this pecuniary loss could be evaluated on any other basis than the take-home pay, that is the net pay after deductions on many items, including income tax.

The above rule places the beneficiary in the same financial position that she would have enjoyed had the deceased lived and continued to earn income. It is, however, not possible to reconcile the rule with the theory in non-fatal personal injury settlements. The difference in

---

[34]*Cirella v. R.*, [1978] C.T.C. 1, 77 D.T.C. 5442 (Fed. T.D.).

[35]See *Graham v. Baker* (1961), 106 C.L.R. 340 (Australia H.C.); see also *Groves v. United Pacific Transport Pty. Ltd.*, [1965] Qd. R. 62 where Gibbs J. observed at 65:

> Although it is usual and convenient in an action for damages for personal injuries to say that an amount is awarded for loss of wages or other earnings, the damages are really awarded for the impairment of the plaintiff's earning capacity that has resulted from his injuries. This is so even if an amount is separately quantified and described as special damages for loss of earnings up to the time of trial. Damages for personal injuries are not rightly described as damages for loss of income.

[36]*Keizer v. Hanna*, [1978] 2 S.C.R. 342, 82 D.L.R. (3d) 449 (S.C.C.) at 371 [S.C.R.]; see also *Andrews v. Grand & Toy Alberta Ltd.*, [1978] 2 S.C.R. 229, 83 D.L.R. (3d) 452 (S.C.C.) at 474 [D.T.C.], Dickson J.:

> In contrast with the situation in personal injury cases, awards under the *Fatal Accident Act*, R.S.A. 1970, c. 138, should reflect tax considerations, since they are to compensate dependants for the loss of support payments made by the deceased. These support payments could only come out of take-home pay, and the payments from the award will only be received net of taxes.

results is perverse. Nevertheless, the Supreme Court has spoken: the capacity theory does not apply in the context of fatal accident cases.[37]

H. — Investment Income

Interest and dividends on investments acquired with a damage award are generally taxable as income from property.[38] Similarly, taxable capital gains realized on property acquired with the proceeds of a damage award are also included in income. We make an exception, however, for personal injury awards paid to, or on behalf of, persons under the age of 21. Interest and property income received from, or accrued on, the investment of a personal injury award is exempt from tax until the end of the taxation year in which the injured person attains the age of 21. Taxable capital gains from dispositions of property acquired with the proceeds of damage awards or settlements are also exempt from tax if the injured person was less than 21 years of age at any time in the year.[39] Amounts earned from the reinvestment of exempt income are also exempt.[40]

The purpose of this exception is to provide relief for young persons who have suffered personal injuries. It is unclear why the plight of young injured persons warrants preferential treatment over older persons in similar circumstances.

(a) — Interest on Special Damages

The law crystallizes tort damages as at the time of the tortious act. In determining the amount of damages it is usual to break down the award into two components: (1) Special damages up to the date of trial; and (2) General damages for future losses. The Department excludes interest on special damages from income.[41]

---

[37]*Keizer v. Hanna*, [1978] 2 S.C.R. 342, 82 D.L.R. (3d) 449 (S.C.C.) at 372 [S.C.R.], Grandpré J. ("I cannot consider that the deceased here was a capital asset").

[38]Paras. 12(1)(c) and (k).

[39]Para. 81(1)(g.1). In his 21st year, the injured person can elect to recognize any accrued capital gains; see s. 81(5).

[40]Para. 81(1)(g.2).

[41]See Interpretation Bulletin IT-365R2, "Damages, Settlements and Similar Receipts" (May 8, 1987).

(b) — Deductibility of Damages Paid

We determine the deductibility of damages by looking at the purpose of the payment. Was the payment made for the *purpose* of earning income from a business or property? The test is similar to the deduction of expenses under section 9.

Spectrum of Damage Payment

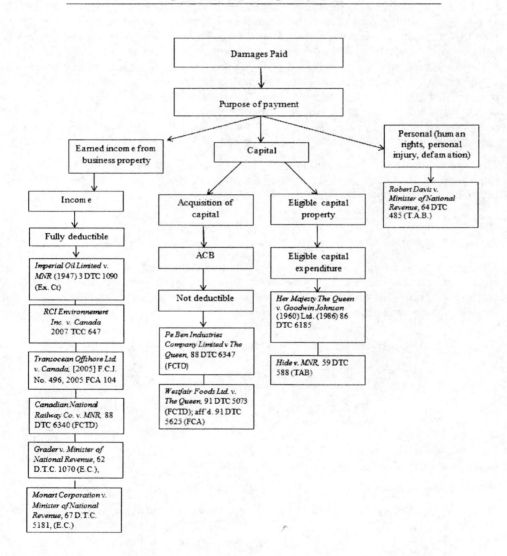

Selected Bibliography to Chapter 10

General

Bowman, D.G.H. "Tax Treatment of Payments Made in the Context of Litigation" [1986] Spec. Lect. L.S.U.C. 96.

Corn, George. "Award of Damages — Non-Taxable Capital Receipt or Taxable Reimbursement" (July 1990) 3 Can. Curr. Tax J-85.

Corn, George. "Incorrect Assessment Liability for Damages" (1986) 1 Can. Curr. Tax A-29.

Drache, A.B.C. "Tort Damages and Retiring Allowances" (1991) XIII Can. Taxpayer 79.

Harris, Peter H. "Tax Treatment of Civil Litigation and Damage Awards, Alimony and Maintenance Payments" (1985) 6 Advocates' Q. 346.

Income Tax: *Maintenance, Alimony and Employment Termination Benefits* (Audio Archives of Canada, 1984).

Krishna, Vern. "The Taxation of Damages" (1985) 1 Can. Curr. Tax C-107.

Weir, J.P. "Taxation of Prejudgment Interest: Historical and Current Developments" (1985) 33 CCLT 149.

Employment Damages and Wrongful Dismissal

Brown, Elizabeth and Julie Y. Lee. "Putting Employees on Notice: Tax Treatment of Amounts Paid on Termination of Employment" (1994) 5 Tax. of Executive Compensation and Retirement 908.

Bush, Kathryn and Caroline L. Hilbronner. "Some Tax Considerations Regarding Employment Terminations" (1994) 3 Employment and Labour L. Rev. 111.

Drache, A.B.C. "Legal Expenses in Wrongful Dismissal Not Deductible" (1988) 10 Can. Taxpayer 120.

Hugo, Sharon J. and L. Alan Rautenberg. "Damages and Settlements: Taxation of the Recipient" (1993) 41 Can. Tax J. 1.

Krishna, Vern. "Characterization of Wrongful Dismissal Awards for Income Tax" (1977) 23 McGill L.J. 43.

MacKnight, Robin J. "Termination Payments for Mental Distress and Loss of Reputation" [1993] Can. Curr. Tax P-21.

McDonnell, T.E. "Deductibility of Legal Expenses Incurred to Recover Damages for Wrongful Dismissal" [Case Comment *Lalonde v. Minister of National Revenue*, [1988] 2 C.T.C. 2032 (T.C.C.)] (1988) 36 Can. Tax J. 697.

Morgan, M.A. "Compensatory Payments Made in a Litigation Context: Tax Treatment to the Recipient" [1986] Spec. Lect. L.S.U.C. 109.

O'Brien, M.L. "Litigation Structured Settlements" [1986] Spec. Lect. L.S.U.C. 119.

Olsen, D.C. "Tax Treatment of Damages for Wrongful Dismissal" [1986] Spec. Lect. L.S.U.C. 135.

Trotter, Paul D. "Severance and Downsizing: Ongoing Tax and Benefits Issues" (1992) 5 Can. Petroleum Tax J. 21.

Chapter 11 — Capital Gains and Losses

Table of Contents

Table of Contents

Table of Contents

Table of Contents

I. — General Comment

A. — Structure

Capital gains are a separate source of income. We calculate capital gains by reference to a distinct set of rules in subdivision c of Division B. Generally, a taxpayer must include 50 percent of capital gains in income and may deduct therefrom 50 percent of capital losses.[1] Thus, strictly speaking, there is no separate tax on capital gains; capital gains, which merely

---

[1] S. 38.

expand or contract the taxable base to which tax we apply the normal tax rates. For analytical purposes, however, we consider capital gains and losses as a separate source of income subject to lower effective tax rates.

It is important to note that certain taxpayers can claim exemption from tax in respect of certain capital gains. The "capital gains exemption" is a deduction from income in computing taxable income.[2] In effect, the capital gains exemption comes into play in two steps: (1) capital gains are initially included in income;[3] then, (2) within specified limits, a taxpayer may deduct exempt gains in computing taxable income. In this chapter we look at the rules in respect of including capital gains in, and deducting capital losses from, income. We discuss the capital gains exemption in detail in "Taxable Income".

Our tax law has consistently "preferred" capital gains over other forms of income. The preferential tax rate on capital gains increases the complexity of the tax statute, the costs of tax planning, compliance and administration. Determining whether capital gains treatment is appropriate in particular circumstances absorbs more administrative time and effort than any other single feature of the tax statute. This should not be surprising given that the classification of income as a capital gain can reduce the taxable rate from 50 percent to zero.

Why should we treat capital gains preferentially? There is an intuitive notion that the appreciation of capital is not what we normally consider "income". The courts and policymakers are split on this issue. For example, the United States Supreme Court stated in 1872 that "the mere fact that property has advanced in value between the date of its acquisition and sale does not authorize the imposition of the tax on the amount of the advance. Mere advance in value in no sense constitutes the gains, profits, or income. . . . It constitutes and can be treated merely as increase of capital."[4] Even as late as 1923, United States Treasury Secretary Andrew Mellon said he "believed it would be sounder taxation policy generally not to recognize either capital gain or capital loss for purposes of income tax."

On the other hand, the Canadian *Carter Commission* (1967) favoured the theory that "a buck is a buck", regardless of its source. In Canada today one can say that there are no clearly defined *objectives* of capital gains taxation, and that our policies, both of taxation and preference, are an amalgam of intuition, political ideology, and competitive economic considerations.[5]

A capital gain is an increase in the capital value of an asset. This raises two issues: (1) when should we tax the increase? and (2) how much of the increase should we tax? In terms of

---

[2]See s. 110.6.

[3]Para. 3(b).

[4]*Gray v. Darlington* (1872), 82 U.S. 63. This position was altered by the passage of the 16th Amendment in 1913.

[5]See: Surrey, "Definitional Problems in Capital Gain Taxation" (1956) 69 Har. L. Rev. 985; Blum, "A Handy Summary of the Capital Gains Arguments" (1957) 25 Taxes 247.

finance, an increase in the value of capital reflects the increase in the discounted future cash income from the underlying investment. In the case of stocks, for example, the increment in stock values is either the enhancement in anticipated future cash flows or a reduction in the discount factor. Since we tax dividends from earnings, we must also tax capital gains to the extent that they represent the discounted present value of undistributed earnings. However, there are significant differences with respect to timing of gains, bunching of income, and inflation.

One can justify the capital gains preference as relieving the "bunching" of accrued property appreciation. Capital gains usually result from appreciation that builds up over an extended period. The gain one realizes usually extends beyond one fiscal year. For example, if one buys shares in Year 1 for $20 and sells the shares in Year 5 for $120, the realized gain of $100 reflects the unrealized accrual of gains over five years. Since the personal tax rate structure is progressive, we would penalize the investor with a higher tax rate if we included the entire gain in his or her income in Year 5. This might be unfair to the investor, particularly if we consider that the rule of realization is merely one of administrative convenience. Thus, the capital gains preference of taxing only 50 percent of the normal rate is a rough-and-ready form of mitigating the effect of progressive rates on "bunched" income. The United States Supreme Court recognized this in *Burnet v. Harmel*,[6] where it held that the purpose of the capital gains preference was to "relieve the taxpayer from . . . excessive tax burdens on gains resulting from a conversion of capital investments, and to remove the deterrent effect of those burdens on such conversions."

Of course, bunching has no effect at all on an investor whose marginal rate of tax in each of the five preceding years would have been in the top tax bracket even without the capital gain. Such an investor derives a windfall from the preference. Also, one can always relieve against the bunching effect by allowing the investor to spread back the tax on his or her entire gain at the rate that would have applied had the investor accrued the gain annually over the five-year period. Although averaging may, accidentally, yield the same approximate result as simply reducing the overall effective rate, it would be a complicated solution to the bunching problem.

The preference mitigates the "lock-in" effect of the realization rule, and makes it less costly for investors to switch investments when it is in their economic interest to do so. The "lock-in" effect also stems from the realization principle. In the above example, the investor with an unrealized gain of $100 in Year 5 may identify a better economic investment with a higher potential yield. If he sells the initial investment, however, the investor will trigger tax at, say, 40 percent, which would leave him with only $60 to reinvest. This effectively reduces the net rate of return on the new investment, and makes it less desirable. Thus, the investor might choose not to sell the original investment and defer the tax that would otherwise be payable.

---

[6] (1932), 287 U.S. 103.

The investor could defer the tax until the later of his or his spouse's death.[7] If the investor can defer the tax for 30 years, and the interest rate is 8 percent, the future value of the $40 tax that would be payable if he sells today is $403.[8] Thus, the investor can multiply his tax saving 10 times simply by not selling and locking into the original investment.

Lock-in restricts the mobility of capital and reduces its efficiency to society's overall detriment. To liquidate a poorly performing investment and reinvest in another venture, the return on the new investment must be sufficient to pay for the capital gains tax bite from the initial liquidation. The investor will only liquidate the initial investment if the return on the new opportunity is sufficiently higher to offset the tax bite. Otherwise, it is better to lock in to the initial investment. The capital gains preference reduces the deterrence effect of lock-in and allows capital to flow to its more efficient use.

If the tax on capital gains restricts the mobility of capital, one can remove the problem by allowing the investor a complete rollover of taxes if he invests the proceeds in other capital investments. We allow many such rollovers for in-kind exchanges of property.[9] The important point is that the capital gains bunching problem derives essentially from the realization principle, which is only a rule of administrative convenience. The capital gains preference is a convenient, perhaps even optimum, solution to a vexing problem.

There is another vexing aspect of the realization principle and capital gains, namely, inflation. Unlike dividends and interest income, which are taxed annually, capital gains are taxable only when we realize them. Suppose you buy a stock for $100 and sell it in a year for $140. If the capital gains tax rate is 40 percent, the tax on the gain is $16. But the gain of $40 is illusory to the extent that inflation reduces its economic value. If inflation is at 10 percent, the real economic gain in the year is only $30. This means that the effective tax rate of $16 on an economic gain of $30 is really 53 percent. Hence, tax rates rise indirectly in periods of high inflation. This doubly affects the taxpayer. The longer the holding period and the more serious the inflation rate, the higher the effective capital gains tax rate. Thus, at the very least, to avoid taxing illusory gains, we should index capital gains.

B. — Segregation of Capital Gains by Type

We bring capital gains into income according to the rules in section 3. Paragraph 3(b) includes the following gains in income:

- *Net* taxable capital gains from dispositions of property other than listed personal property ("LPP"); and

---

[7]Subs. 70(5) and (6).

[8]Future Value = $40 × 10.063.

[9]See, for example, sections 85, 86 and 87.

- Taxable *net* gains from dispositions of LPP.

"Net" refers to the excess of gains over losses.

As a rule, capital losses are deductible only against capital gains. One cannot use any excess of capital losses over capital gains to reduce income from other sources.[10] There is only one exception to this rule: business investment capital losses can be applied against "ordinary" income.

The effect of this scheme is to treat capital gains and losses as income from a separate source.

Example

Assume:

The following data applies to Alesia Ng:

Employment income (gross)	$ 64,500
Business income	15,550
Business losses	9,000
Rental income	12,500
Capital gains	4,000
Taxable listed personal property gain	5,000
Taxable listed personal property loss	7,500
Capital losses (includes BIL of $4,000)	18,000
Support payments (deductible)	5,000
Allowable business investment losses ("ABIL")	2,000

[10]See paras. 3(d)–(f).

Then: *paragraph 3(a)*:

Employment income	$ 64,500
Business income	15,550
Property income	12,500
	92,550

paragraph 3(b):

Taxable capital gains ($4,000 × 1/2)	$ 2,000	
Net LPP gains	0	
Net gains	$ 2,000	
Allowable capital losses exceeds ABIL	$ 7,000	0
		92,550

Exceeds paragraph 3(c):

Support payments	(5,000)
	87,550

Exceeds paragraph 3(d):

Business losses	$ 9,000	
ABIL	2,000	
		(11,000)
Income		$ 76,550

Notes:

- Capital losses times inclusion rate equals allowable capital losses ($18,000 × 1/2 = $9,000); minus ABIL ($2,000).

- Business investment losses (BILs) are capital losses.

- The excess of allowable capital losses (excluding ABILs) of $7,000 over taxable capital gains ($2,000) is a net capital loss deductible in computing taxable income.

II. — Capital Property

A capital gain or loss can arise only when a taxpayer disposes of "capital property". The Act defines "capital property" as property, the disposition of which will give rise to a capital gain or loss.[11] This is not a helpful definition. Thus, with the exception of specific items, the characterization of a gain or loss as being on account of income or capital is determined as a mixed question of fact and law.[12]

A. — Exclusions from Capital Gains

The Act specifically excludes the following properties from property that can give rise to a capital gain:[13]

- Property the disposition of which gives rise to income from a business, a property, or an adventure in the nature of trade;[14]

- Eligible capital property;

- Cultural property disposed of pursuant to the *Cultural Property Export and Import Act*;[15]

- Canadian and foreign resource properties, which include mineral, oil and gas rights;

---

[11]Para. 54 "capital property" (b).

[12]The CRA does not give advance rulings on the characterization of gains — see IC 70-6R5 "Advance Income Tax Ruling" (May 17, 2002).

[13]Para. 39(1)(a).

[14]S. 248(1) "business".

[15]R.S.C. 1985, c. C-51.

- Insurance policies, including life insurance policies within the meaning of section 138, except for a taxpayer's deemed interest in a related segregated fund trust;

- Timber resource properties; and

- An interest of a beneficiary under a qualifying environmental trust.

Also, dispositions of eligible capital properties, Canadian and foreign resource properties, insurance policies, and depreciable properties do not give rise to a capital loss. They are, *ipso facto*, not capital properties.[16] The disposition of a cultural property can give rise to a capital loss.[17]

To summarize: a capital gain or loss is a gain or loss that arises from the disposition of property *to the extent that* it is not ordinary income or loss. This is a circular definition since the determination of a gain or loss as being on account of income is itself a mixed question of fact and law. Thus, generally, a capital gain or loss arises from the disposition of an investment acquired for the purpose of producing income, rather than as a trading asset.

B. — Types of Capital Property

We use the terms "capital gain" and "capital loss" in a broad sense to denote a gain or loss from the disposition of a capital property. There are, however, different types of capital properties, which give rise to different types of capital gains and losses. The Act subdivides capital properties into the following categories:

- Personal-use property;[18]

- Listed personal property;[19]

- "Business investment" property;[20] and

- Other capital properties.

One calculates the gain or loss from each of these types of capital property separately, and according to the rules applicable to each category.

---

[16]Para. 54 "capital property" (b).

[17]IT-407R4, "Dispositions of cultural property to designated Canadian institutions" (Consolidated).

[18]S. 54 "personal-use property".

[19]S. 54 "listed personal property".

[20]Para. 39(1)(c); IT-484R2, "Business Investment Losses" (November 28, 1996).

C. — Deemed Capital Property

Where a person disposes of *all or substantially all* of the assets used in an active business to a corporation, any shares that she receives in consideration for the assets are her capital property.[21] Thus, a subsequent disposition of the shares will give rise to a capital gain or loss. For example, a parent corporation may transfer a business to its subsidiary and, subsequently, sell the shares of the subsidiary corporation. Any gain on the sale of the subsidiary's shares is a capital gain. Similarly, an individual might sell his business to a newly-formed corporation in exchange for its shares and then dispose of the shares of the corporation. Any gain on the sale of the shares would be a capital gain. This rule provides certainty to taxpayers who engage in business and corporate reorganizations. It is important to note, however, that the rule deems the shares to be capital property only if:

- The taxpayer disposes of "all or substantially all" of the assets of the business; and

- The business is an "active" business.

This rule does not apply to dispositions of non-business assets or in circumstances where the corporation disposes of some, but not substantially all, of its assets. Nor does the rule apply to the disposition of assets used in an adventure or concern in the nature of trade. Thus, one cannot use the rule to convert an income gain into a capital gain simply by exchanging the assets for shares and then selling the shares.

III. — Computation of Gain or Loss

A capital gain from a disposition of property is the difference between the "proceeds of disposition" ("POD") that one receives from the property and the sum of its "adjusted cost base" ("ACB") and the expenses of disposition:[22]

$$\text{Capital Gain} = \text{POD} - (\text{ACB} + \text{Expenses})$$

For present purposes, we can assume that "proceeds of disposition" means selling price and "adjusted cost base" means the cost of property. We discuss the more technical meaning of these terms later.

Example

Assume:

---

[21]S. 54.2.

[22]Para. 40(1)(a).

A taxpayer sells a capital property for $10,000. He purchased the asset for $6,000. He incurs expenses of $800 in selling the property.

Then:

Selling price		$ 10,000
Less: cost (ACB)	$ 6,000	
Selling expenses	800	(6,800)
Capital gain		$ 3,200

The taxpayer's taxable capital gain is $1,600, that is, the capital gain times the inclusion rate ($3,200 × 1/2).

Conversely, a taxpayer's capital loss from a disposition of property is the amount by which the "adjusted cost base" and selling expenses exceed the "proceeds of disposition".[23]

Example

Assume:

T sells a capital property that costs $16,000 for cash proceeds of $2,000 and incurs $80 as expenses of sale.

Then:

Proceeds of Sale		$ 2,000
Less: Cost (ACB)	$ 16,000	
Selling expenses	80	(16,080)
Capital loss		$ (14,080)

T's allowable capital loss is $7,040, that is, the capital loss times the inclusion rate ($14,080 × 1/2).

A. — Reserves

As a rule, the Act recognizes only realized capital gains and losses for tax purposes. The taxable event that gives rise to a gain or loss is the disposition of the property. A taxpayer may, however, dispose of property and not be paid the full sale price upon its sale or exchange. In these circumstances, the taxpayer realizes a capital gain, but does not collect the cash at the time of the transaction. To collect tax on uncollected gains would be a hardship for some taxpayers. The Act provides some relief and allows a taxpayer to defer recognition

---

[23]Para. 40(1)(b).

of some of the gain on his uncollected proceeds. There are, however, some restrictions that apply to the amount that the taxpayer can defer.

Where a taxpayer deducts a reserve in one year, he must bring the amount deducted into income in the following year. The taxpayer can then claim a further reserve in each of the following years to the extent that part of the proceeds of sale remain outstanding at the end of the year.[24] Where a taxpayer claims a reserve for unpaid proceeds of disposition, it cannot exceed the amount of the reserve claimed in the immediately preceding year in respect of the property. Thus, if a taxpayer claims less than the maximum allowed in one year, he cannot claim a larger reserve in respect of the same property in the next year.[25]

(a) — Limitations

The Act strictly controls the amount of reserves.[26] The maximum reserve that a taxpayer may claim in a year is limited to the *lesser* of two amounts:[27]

1. A "reasonable" amount; and

2. An amount determined by reference to a formula.

(i) — "A Reasonable Reserve"

What is reasonable is always a question of fact. The CRA does say, however, that it considers a reserve to be reasonable if it is proportional to the amount that is not payable to the taxpayer until after the end of the taxation year. Thus, one may calculate a reserve as follows:

Capital gain × (Amount not payable until after the end of the year)/(Total proceeds)

This formula is only one of many ways of calculating a reserve. A taxpayer is free to choose any other "reasonable" method.[28]

---

[24]Subpara. 40(1)(a)(iii); see also the various restrictions on claiming reserves in subs. 40(2).

[25]Subpara. 40(1)(a)(ii).

[26]Para. 18(1)(e).

[27]Subpara. 40(1)(a)(iii).

[28]*R. v. Ennisclare Corp.*, [1984] C.T.C. 286, 84 D.T.C. 6262 (Fed. C.A.).

Example

Assume:

In Year 1, T sold a capital property in an arm's length transaction. The property, which cost $63,000, was sold for $100,000, payable as $20,000 on completion of the sale and $20,000 per year for the next four years. Expenses of selling the property came to $7,000.

Then:

Proceeds of sale		$	100,000
Less: Cost (ACB)	$	63,000	
Selling expenses		7,000	(70,000)
Capital gain			30,000
Less: Reasonable reserve (see below)			(24,000)
Capital gain recognized in Year 1		$	6,000

A "reasonable" reserve may be calculated as follows:

Year	Calculation				Reserve	Capital Gain Recognized
Year 1	$30,000	×	$80,000 100,000	= $	24,000 $	6,000
Year 2	30,000	×	60,000 100,000	= $	18,000 $	6,000
Year 3	30,000	×	40,000 100,000	= $	12,000 $	6,000
Year 4	30,000	×	20,000 100,000	= $	6,000 $	6,000
Year 5			NIL		$	6,000
Total capital gain recognized					$	30,000

(ii) — Maximum Reserve

The second limitation restricts the period during which a taxpayer may claim a reserve to a maximum of five years. This limitation ensures that the cumulative amount of capital gain recognized is *not less* than 20 percent of the total gain times the number of taxation years that have elapsed since the disposition.

Example

Assume:

In Year 1, T sells a capital property to which the following data applies:

Proceeds of sale	$ 90,000
Cost of property (ACB)	$ 35,000
Selling expenses	$ 5,000

The property was sold on the basis that the purchase price was payable in five equal instalments commencing in Year 2.

Then in Year 1 the maximum reserve allowed is:

Proceeds of sale		$ 90,000
Less: Cost (ACB)	$ 35,000	
Selling expenses	5,000	(40,000)
Capital gain		50,000
Maximum reserve ($50,000 × 4/5)		(40,000)
Capital gain recognized		$ 10,000

Thus at least one-fifth of the gain is included in income in the year of sale even though the taxpayer did not receive any proceeds in that year. In contrast, a "reasonable reserve" under the first test would be $50,000.

Notes:

$$\$50,000 \times 20\% = \$10,000$$

(iii) — Special Reserves

The Act extends the maximum five-year period applicable to general reserves to 10 years if the property that the taxpayer transfers is:[29]

- Land and depreciable property used in a family farm;
- A share in a family farm corporation;
- An interest in a family farm partnership; or
- A share in a small business corporation

---

[29] Subs. 40(1.1).

and the property is transferred to the taxpayer's child.[30]

(b) — Amounts "Not Payable"

A taxpayer may claim a reserve on only the portion of the sale proceeds that are "not payable" to the taxpayer until after the end of the year. Note the distinction between "not payable" and "not collected". Fixed-maturity debt instruments are payable on the date indicated on the face of the instrument, whether or not they are actually paid or collected. A demand note is payable when the note is signed, unless the note is otherwise qualified.[31] Thus, to claim a reserve on a demand note, the note should be made payable a number of days (for example, 10 days) *after* demand for payment.

(c) — Selling Expenses

A taxpayer can deduct expenses incurred in disposing of a capital property. However, only expenses that one incurs in connection with the *disposition* of capital property are deductible in calculating a capital gain or loss. Expenses that one incurs for the purposes of earning income from a capital property are not deductible in calculating the amount of a capital gain or loss.

Expenses that one incurs in enhancing capital property into a saleable condition, or those connected directly with the disposition of the property, are also deductible from the proceeds of disposition. For example, fixing-up expenses, finder's fees, sales commissions, brokers' fees, surveyor's fees, transfer taxes, title registration fees, and legal expenses that relate to the disposition are deductible.

IV. — Dispositions

A. — General Comment

A disposition of capital property is the trigger that gives rise to a capital gain or loss.[32] A taxpayer disposes of the property when he legally alienates his rights in the property. In

---

[30]Subs. 252(1).

[31]Subpara. 40(1)(a)(iii); *R. v. Derbecker*, [1984] C.T.C. 606, 84 D.T.C. 6549 (Fed. C.A.). In the words of Parke B. in *Norton v. Ellam* (1837), 2 M & W 461 at 464: "... a promissory note, payable on demand, is a present debt, and is payable without any demand". See also *Pineo v. R.*, [1986] 2 C.T.C. 71, 86 D.T.C. 6322 (T.C.C.) (demand promissory note secured by share escrow agreement remained present debt).

[32]Subs. 39(1).

certain circumstances, however, the Act deems a taxpayer to dispose of his property even though he does not physically or legally alienate his.[33]

B. — "Property"

"Property" is defined to include real and personal property (whether corporeal or incorporeal, movable or immovable, tangible or intangible), shares, *choses in action* and timber resource properties. Indeed, the term comprises virtually every possible interest a person may have.[34]

Corporeal properties are substances that one can see or handle. In contrast, incorporeal properties are "merely an idea and abstract contemplation, though their effects and profits may frequently be objects of the bodily senses."[35]

Incorporeal property is a right issuing out of a thing corporate (whether real or personal) or concerning, annexed to or exercisable within the same. It is not the thing corporate itself (such as land, houses or jewels), but something collateral thereto, such as a rent issuing out of the land or houses. Incorporeal property includes intangibles such as reversions, remainders and executory interests in property, life interests, rights-of-way, and rights to sunlight.

C. — "Disposition"

The concept of "disposition" is one of two key elements of the capital gains system. The other is "cost". The Act does not define disposition. There is, however, a fairly comprehensive description of the types of transactions included within its meaning.

A "disposition" is any event that involves an alienation of property or a loss of ownership. The alienation may be voluntary or involuntary. However, the Act also deems dispositions in certain circumstances. Thus, for tax purposes, the word "disposition" has a much broader meaning than "sale".[36] In the simplest case, the proceeds from a disposition of property are

---

[33]See, for example, s. 45 (deemed disposition on change of use of property); subs. 50(1) (deemed disposition of bad debt); subs. 70(5) (deemed disposition on death).

[34]*Lunness, Re* (1919), 46 O.L.R. 320 (Ont. C.A.). See *Manrell v. R.*, 2003 FCA 128, [2003] 3 C.T.C. 50, 2003 D.T.C. 5225 (Fed. C.A.) for a detailed analysis of the meaning of property in the context of non-competition agreements.

[35]*Re Christmas; Martin v. Lacon* (1886), 33 Ch. D. 332 (C.A.) at 338; *Blackstone's Commentaries on the Laws of England* (1765), vol. 2, at 20.

[36]*Olympia & York Developments Ltd. v. R.*, [1980] C.T.C. 265, 80 D.T.C. 6184 (Fed. T.D.) (instalment contract; transfer of possession but not title constituted "disposition", although no "sale" until later); *Imperial General Properties Ltd. v. R.*, [1985] 1 C.T.C. 40, 85 D.T.C 5045 (Fed. C.A.); leave to

equal to the consideration or sale price that a taxpayer receives for the property. One determines the value of consideration from the terms of the contract of sale or deed. In some cases, the Act deems the amount of proceeds that the taxpayer receives — for example, fair market value in a non-arm's length transaction.

A "disposition"[37] includes any event entitling a taxpayer to "proceeds of disposition," including proceeds from:[38]

- The sale price of property;

- Compensation for stolen property;

- Compensation for property lost or destroyed;

- Compensation for expropriated property (including any interest penalty or damages that are part of the expropriation award);[39]

- Compensation for damaged property (unless funds have been expended in repairing the damage within a reasonable time);

- Mortgage settlements upon foreclosure of mortgaged property (including reductions in the liability of a taxpayer to a mortgagee as a result of the sale of mortgaged property);

- The principal amount of a debtor's claim that has been extinguished as a result of a mortgage foreclosure or conditional sales repossession;[40]

- A winding-up (or redemption) dividend, to the extent that it does not exceed the corporation's pre-1972 capital surplus on hand;

- Redemptions or cancellations of shares, bonds and other securities;

- Settlements or cancellations of any debt owing to a taxpayer;

- Conversion of shares on an amalgamation;

- Expiry of options to acquire or dispose of property; and

---

appeal refused (1985), 16 D.L.R. (4th) 615 (S.C.C.) (sale complete when conditions precedent satisfied).

[37]Subs. 248(1) "disposition".

[38]S. 54 "proceeds of disposition".

[39]*E.R. Fisher Ltd. v. R.*, [1986] 2 C.T.C. 114, 86 D.T.C. 6364 (Fed. T.D.) (interest paid pursuant to *Expropriation Act* R.S.C. 1970, c.16 (1st Supp.), as penalty, because Crown's offer inappropriate, constituted "proceeds of disposition"); *Sani Sport Inc. v. R.*, [1987] 1 C.T.C. 411, 87 D.T.C. 5253 (Fed. T.D.); affirmed [1990] 2 C.T.C. 15, 90 D.T.C. 6230 (Fed. C.A.)) (amount paid as damages for loss of business opportunity included in proceeds of disposition).

[40]See s. 79.

- Transfers of property to or by a trust (including transfers to an RRSP, DPSP, EPSP or RRIF, even if the transfer does not involve a change of beneficial ownership).

A "disposition" does *not* include any of the following:[41]

- Transfers of property to, or by, a creditor for securing or releasing a debt;

- *Issuance* by a corporation of its own bonds or debentures;

- Transfer of property without change in beneficial ownership (except transfer by resident trust to non-resident trust or transfer to a trust governed by RRSP, DPSP, EPSP, RRIF);

- *Issuance* by a corporation of its own shares;

- Amounts that represent a deemed dividend on a winding-up or share redemption; and

- Amounts deemed to be dividends paid to a non-resident person in a non-arm's length sale of shares of one Canadian corporation to another Canadian corporation.

The above list is not exhaustive.

A "disposition" includes any event that implies a loss of ownership, whether such loss occurs by voluntary action on the owner's part or the owner suffers it involuntarily. The words "disposed of" embrace every event by which property ceases to be available to the taxpayer for use in producing income, either because the property ceases to be physically accessible to the taxpayer or because it ceases to exist.[42] Thus, for tax purposes "disposition" has a

---

[41]S. 54"proceeds of disposition"; subs. 248(1) "disposition".

[42]See, generally, *Victory Hotels Ltd. v. Minister of National Revenue*, [1962] C.T.C. 614, 62 D.T.C. 1378 (Can. Ex. Ct.) (determination of disposition when documentation conflicting); *Wardean Drilling Ltd. v. Minister of National Revenue*, [1969] C.T.C. 265, 69 D.T.C. 5194 (Can. Ex. Ct.) (asset paid for in 1963, delivered in 1964; deductible in 1964, when all incidents of title passed); *Cie Immobiliere BCN Ltée v. R.*, [1979] 1 S.C.R. 865, [1979] C.T.C. 71, 79 D.T.C. 5068 (S.C.C.) (meaning of "disposed of"); *Lord Elgin Hotel Ltd. v. Minister of National Revenue* (1964), 36 Tax A.B.C. 268, 64 D.T.C. 637 (Can. Tax App. Bd.); appeal quashed [1969] C.T.C. 24, 69 D.T.C. 5059 (Can. Ex. Ct.) (winding-up of company and distribution of shares constituted "disposition" of hotel); *Malloney's Studio Ltd. v. R.*, [1979] 2 S.C.R. 326, [1979] C.T.C. 206, 79 D.T.C. 5124 (S.C.C.) (demolition of building constituted disposition of building even though taxpayer did not receive proceeds of disposition); see also *Rose v. Fed. Commr. of Taxation* (1951), 84 C.L.R. 118 (Aust. H.C.); *Gorton v. Fed. Commr. of Taxation* (1965), 113 C.L.R. 604 (Australia H.C.); *Henty House Pty. Ltd. v. Fed. Commr. of Taxation* (1953), 88 C.L.R. 141 (Australia H.C.) at 151, where the Australian High Court commented upon the meaning of the term "disposition" as follows:

> The entire expression "disposed of, lost or destroyed" is apt to embrace every event by which property ceases to be available to the taxpayer for use for the purpose of producing assessable income, either because it ceases to be his, or because it ceases to be physically accessible to him, or because it ceases to exist . . . the words "is disposed of" are wide enough to cover all

much broader meaning than "sale",[43] but does not include a transfer of legal title of property to a "bare trustee" if there is no change in its beneficial ownership.[44]

D. — Proceeds of Disposition

A taxpayer's proceeds from a disposition of property are equal to the consideration that she receives for the property, as determined by the terms of the contract of sale or deed. In some cases, this will require a valuation of the assets and liabilities acquired or sold. For example, assumption or discharge of debt obligations on a transaction can change the face value of proceeds of disposition.[45]

E. — Changes in Terms of Securities

A change in the terms or attributes of securities may be a disposition of the security. The determining factor is whether the amended security is in substance the same property as the security that underwent the change. The CRA's position is that any one of the following changes usually constitutes a disposition:[46]

Debt securities

- An interest-bearing debt becoming non-interest-bearing, or *vice versa*;

- The repayment terms or maturity date being altered significantly;

---

forms of alienation . . . and they should be understood as meaning no less than "becomes alienated from the taxpayer", whether it is by him or by another that the act of alienation is done.

[43]*Olympia & York Dev. Ltd. v. R.*, [1980] C.T.C. 265, 80 D.T.C. 6184 (Fed. T.D.) (instalment contract; transfer of possession but not title constituted "disposition", although no "sale" until later); *Imperial General Properties Ltd. v. R.*, [1985] 1 C.T.C. 40, 85 D.T.C. 5045 (Fed. C.A.); leave to appeal refused (1985), 16 D.L.R. (4th) 615n (S.C.C.) (sale complete when conditions precedent satisfied); *Attis v. Minister of National Revenue*, [1984] C.T.C. 3013, 85 D.T.C. 37 (T.C.C.) (Minister entitled to fix proceeds of disposition by reference to sale price).

[44]See ATR-1, "Transfer of Legal Title in Land to Bare Trustee Corporation — Mortgagee's Requirements Sole Reason for Transfer" (November 29, 1985).

[45]*Fradet v. R.*, [1986] 2 C.T.C. 321, 86 D.T.C. 6411 (Fed. C.A.) (proceeds reduced by difference between principal amount of debt and its fair market value).

[46]IT-448, "Dispositions — Changes in Terms of Securities" (February 21, 1994), paras. 7 and 14. See also Income Tax Technical News #14 (December 9, 1998) for additional commentary.

- The principal amount of the debt being changed;
- The addition, alteration or elimination of a repayment premium;
- A change in the debtor; or
- The conversion of a fixed interest debt into a variable interest debt, or *vice versa*.

Equity securities

- A change in voting rights that results in a change in the control of the corporation;
- The addition or elimination of, or any change in, a preferential right to share in the assets of the corporation upon winding-up;
- The addition or elimination of a right to dividends beyond a fixed preferential rate or amount; or
- The conversion of a cumulative right to dividends into a non-cumulative right, or *vice versa*.

The following changes in the terms of a share are not a disposition of the share:[47]

- The addition of a right to elect a majority of the board of directors, if the class of shares carries sufficient voting power to control the election of the board at that time;
- A change in the number of votes per share, unless the influence of a particular shareholder over the day-to-day operation of the corporation is enhanced or impaired;
- The elimination of contingent voting rights, unless the exercise of such rights would carry control of the corporation;
- A change in transfer restrictions;
- The addition of a right to redeem shares at the option of the corporation;
- A stock split or consolidation;
- The conversion of par value shares to non-par value shares, or *vice versa*;
- A change in ranking or preference features; and
- A change in the amount or rate of a fixed dividend, other than the addition or deletion of the right itself.

---

[47] *Ibid.*, at para. 15.

F. — Foreign Currencies

(a) — Characterization

Gains and losses in foreign currency transactions are taxable according to the usual rules, either as income gains (or losses) or as capital gains (or losses). Thus, the first step is to determine whether a gain or loss is on account of income or capital. The characterization of the currency gain or loss usually follows the transaction from which it results.[48] Hence, gains and losses from business transactions are income items; gains and losses from transactions in capital assets are capital gains and losses. A foreign exchange loss is not *per se* an "outlay or expense" for the purposes of determining a capital gain or loss.[49]

(b) — Method of Accounting

The general rule is that a capital gain or loss can occur for income tax purposes only if the taxpayer disposes of property.[50] This rule also applies to capital gains and losses from foreign currency transactions.

A capital gain or loss may result from fluctuations in the value of a foreign currency relative to the Canadian dollar. For example, a gain or loss may arise in respect of a cash balance in a foreign currency or on account of foreign debts. One-half of the *net* amount of such gains and losses is brought into income.

To avoid administrative and recordkeeping difficulties, however, individuals may exclude the first $200 of any *net* foreign currency gain or loss that the individual sustains in a year from the disposition of foreign currency.[51]

Example

Assume:

An individual purchased U.S. shares for $2,000 (U.S.) at a time when the U.S. dollar was worth $0.90 (Cdn.). The shares cost her $1,800 (Cdn.). She sells the shares for $3,000 (U.S.) at a time when the U.S. dollar is $1.30 (Cdn.), and receives $3,900 (Cdn.).

---

[48]*Tip Top Tailors v. Minister of National Revenue*, [1957] S.C.R. 703, [1957] C.T.C. 309, 57 D.T.C. 1232 (S.C.C.).

[49]*Avis Immobilier GMBH v. R.*, [1994] 1 C.T.C. 2204, 94 D.T.C. 1039 (T.C.C.); affirmed (1996), 97 D.T.C. 5002 (Fr.) (Fed. C.A.); leave to appeal refused (May 22, 1997), Doc. 25749 (S.C.C.).

[50]S. 39.

[51]Subs. 39(2).

Her taxable gain is calculated as follows:

Regular gain

($3,000 U.S. - $2,000 U.S.) @ $0.90 = $ 900

Currency gain

($1.30 Cdn - $0.90 Cdn) @ $3,000 U.S. = $ 1,200

Total gain

($1.30 × $3,000 - 0.90 × $2,000)   = $ 2,100

Notes:

The CRA states that subsection 39(2) applies only on an *actual* conversion of currency. See also *Rezvankhah*, 2002 D.T.C. 3928 (T.C.C.).

(c) — Determination of Cost

A taxpayer determines the cost of capital property in Canadian dollars as at the date that he acquires it, not when he disposes of it.[52] This is so even if he acquires the asset by payment in foreign currency. Thus, the capital cost of a property to a taxpayer is its actual, factual or historical cost when he acquires it.

G. — Purchase of Bonds by Issuer

We saw earlier that a taxpayer generally realizes a capital gain or loss only when she disposes of a capital property. Thus, a taxpayer who issues a bond (or similar debt obligation) does not trigger a gain or loss at the time of issuance. A purchase by the issuer of its own debt obligation may, however, trigger a capital gain or loss if the purchase is on the open market. The gain or loss is calculated as follows:[53]

Capital gain:

Issue price $ 900

---

[52]See *Gaynor v. Minister of National Revenue*, [1987] 1 C.T.C. 2359, 87 D.T.C. 279 (T.C.C.); affirmed [1988] 2 C.T.C. 163, 88 D.T.C. 6394 (Fed. T.D.); affirmed [1991] 1 C.T.C. 470 (Fed. C.A.) (capital cost of portfolio securities imported into Canada determined as at acquisition date).

[53]Subs. 39(3); see also ITAR 26(1.1) (obligations outstanding on January 1, 1972).

Less: purchase price	(600)
Capital gain	$ 300

Capital loss:

Purchase price	$ 700
Less issue price	(500)
Capital loss	$ 200

Thus, a gain results where the issue price is greater than the purchase price paid by the taxpayer. Conversely, a capital loss arises where the purchase price exceeds the greater of the principal amount and the issue price of the bond, debenture or similar obligation.[54]

H. — Deemed Dispositions

We recognize income and gains for tax purposes only when we realize them. Thus, the income tax is essentially a tax on transactions. However, the Act deems certain transactions and events to be dispositions of property. A deemed disposition is a realization that gives rise to deemed proceeds. The Act has a long list of deemed dispositions. In the following paragraphs we look at some of the more common transactions that give rise to deemed dispositions.

(a) — Change in Use of Property

(i) — Personal to Commercial

A taxpayer who acquires property for personal use is deemed to dispose of the property for proceeds equal to its fair market value if she begins to use the property for commercial purposes.[55] For example, suppose a taxpayer who owns and lives in a house that costs $100,000 begins to rent out the house at a time when its fair market value is $170,000. The act of renting out the house is a change in its use. The Act deems the taxpayer to have

---

[54]Para. 39(3)(b).

[55]Para. 45(1)(a).

disposed of, and immediately reacquired, the house for $170,000. Thus, the taxpayer realizes a capital gain of $70,000 even though she does not actually receive any funds from the change of use.

Where a taxpayer changes the use of property from personal to commercial, he may *elect* to ignore the change in use for income tax purposes. The effect of such an election is that the Act deems the taxpayer not to have begun to use the property for commercial purposes.[56] The taxpayer may rescind the election at any time. The taxpayer is deemed to have changed the use of the property on the first day of the year in which he or she rescinds the election.

A change of use can trigger adverse tax consequences. The election allows the taxpayer to defer any capital gain arising by virtue of a change in the use of the property. Thus, the election allows the taxpayer to defer payment of tax until such time as he or she disposes of the property or rescinds the election. Note, however, that during the tenure of the election the taxpayer cannot claim capital cost allowance on the property.[57]

(ii) — Commercial to Personal

The Act also deems a taxpayer who acquires property for commercial purposes to have disposed of the property at its fair market value if he begins to use it for personal purposes.[58] In the above example, if the taxpayer changes back the use of the house from commercial to personal use at a time when the fair market value of the house is $200,000, the change of use will trigger a capital gain of $30,000.

This rule does not apply where the taxpayer changes the use of property from commercial use to a principal residence if he elects in writing.[59] The deadline for the election is the earlier of two dates:

1. 90 days after the Minister demands the election; or

2. The taxpayer's filing-due date for the taxation year in which the property is actually disposed of by the taxpayer.

---

[56]Subs. 45(2).

[57]Reg. 1102(1)(c) (excludes from depreciable property any property not acquired by taxpayer for the purpose of gaining or producing income).

[58]Para. 45(1)(a); *Woods v. Minister of National Revenue*, [1978] C.T.C. 2802, 78 D.T.C. 1576 (T.R.B.) (capital gain on deemed disposition in respect of taxpayer's dwelling when he occupied it after renting it out for nine years); *Leib v. Minister of National Revenue*, [1984] C.T.C. 2324, 84 D.T.C. 1302 (T.C.C.) (change in use of principal residence deemed to be disposition despite taxpayer not receiving funds).

[59]Subss. 45(3), (4).

The effect of the election is to defer the capital gain during the period that it was rented out. The election is also available for a property that was a principle residence, then a rental, and a principle residence again.[60]

(iii) — Mixed Use Property

Where a taxpayer uses a property for both commercial and personal purposes, any change in the *proportion* of use for either of these purposes is a deemed disposition.[61] Where the change involves a decrease in the proportion of commercial use of the property, the deemed proceeds of disposition are added to the cost base of the property available for personal use.[62] In other words, the Act deems the taxpayer to reacquire that proportion of the property at a cost equal to its proportion of the fair market value for the entire property. Similarly, where the change involves an increase in the business use of the property, the deemed proceeds of disposition are added to the cost base of the property available for business use.[63]

The adjustment to the capital cost of the property under subsection 13(7) is an adjustment *solely* for the purpose of capital cost allowance and recapture. It is *not* an adjustment for capital gains purposes under subdivision c of Division B. Although the CRA may allow a taxpayer to step up the cost base of the property, the taxpayer does not have statutory authority to insist on the step-up in cost.

Example

Assume:

An individual owns a building that she uses for both business and personal use.

Cost	$	50,000
Proportion of business use		60 %
Proportion of personal use		40 %

---

[60] 2012-0433451E5.

[61] Para. 45(1)(c).

[62] Subpara. 45(1)(c)(i).

[63] Subpara. 45(1)(c)(ii) (for example, duplex that is partly rented and partly owner-occupied).

She takes over an additional 10 percent of the building for her personal use and decreases the portion occupied for business purposes to 50 percent. The fair market value at that time is $70,000.

Then, to calculate the capital gain for the 10 percent change in use:

Deemed proceeds of disposition

(10% of $70,000)	$	7,000
ACB (10% of $50,000)		(5,000)
Capital gain	$	2,000

Calculation of Revised ACB of Property:

	Business Use	Personal Use	Total
Original ACB	$ 30,000	$ 20,000	$ 50,000
Deemed disposition	(5,000)		(5,000)
Deemed acquisition		7,000	7,000
Revised ACB	$ 25,000	$ 27,000	$ 52,000

If immediately thereafter she sells the building at its fair market value of $70,000, the business and personal portions of the resulting capital gain are as follows:

	Business Portion (50%)	Personal Portion (50%)	Total
Proceeds of disposition	$ 35,000	$ 35,000	$ 70,000
Revised ACB	25,000	27,000	52,000
Capital gain	$ 10,000	$ 8,000	$ 18,000

Capital gain previously

	Business Portion (50%)	Personal Portion (50%)	Total
recognized			2,000

Total capital gain		$	20,000

Notes:

The revised ACB takes into account the capital gain resulting from the change of use:

Original cost	$	50,000
Capital gain		2,000
Revised ACB	$	52,000

Thus, the full amount of the capital gain of $20,000 ($70,000-$50,000) is eventually recognized.

(b) — Leaving Canada

(i) — "Departure Tax"

A taxpayer who ceases to be resident in Canada is deemed to dispose of virtually all of his property immediately before giving up residence. This deemed disposition may give rise to a capital gain, resulting in a "departure or exit tax" on the taxpayer.[64]

There are a few exceptions to the deemed disposition on emigration, including, for example, real property in Canada, Canadian resource properties, and timber properties. Capital property used in, and eligible capital property used in business carried on through a permanent establishment in Canada is also exempt.

(ii) — Election to Dispose

An individual (other than a trust) may elect to be considered to have disposed of real property in Canada, a Canadian resource property, a timber resource property or capital property used, eligible capital property in respect of and inventory in a business carried on

---

[64]Para. 128.1(4)(b); *R. v. Davis*, [1978] C.T.C. 536, 78 D.T.C. 6374 (Fed. T.D.); affirmed [1980] C.T.C. 88, 80 D.T.C. 6056 (Fed. C.A.).

through a PE in Canada at its fair market value and to have reacquired the property at the particular time at a cost equal to those proceeds.[65] This election is useful for departing residents who want to realize accrued capital gains to take advantage of the capital gains exemption.[66]

These two elections are available only to departing residents of Canada. Non-resident taxpayers are liable (subject to tax treaty provisions) for tax on capital gains that they realize upon disposing of their taxable Canadian property.[67]

(c) — Options

(i) — Nature

An option is a contractual right that gives its holder the power to buy or sell property at some time in the future at a fixed or otherwise determinable price.[68] A call option confers the right to buy; a put option the right to sell. Since an option is a right, it is "property" for income tax purposes.[69] An option right can be sold, exercised or allowed to expire.

(ii) — Characterization on Issuance

Granting an option may be an income transaction or a capital transaction.[70] The usual tests in characterizing gains as income gains or capital gains also apply to options. The determination depends upon the taxpayer's intention to invest or trade in the property on which the option is granted.[71] Where the taxpayer does not grant the option in the course of its business, any consideration for the option is a capital gain.

---

[65]Para. 128.1(4)(d).

[66]S. 110.6; see Chapter 14, "Taxable Income".

[67]Para. 2(3)(c).

[68]See, generally, *Day v. Minister of National Revenue*, [1971] Tax A.B.C. 1050, 71 D.T.C. 723 (Can. Tax App. Bd.) for discussion on meaning of option.

[69]Subs. 248(1) "property"; *Day v. Minister of National Revenue, ante.*

[70]See, *Western Leaseholds Ltd. v. Minister of National Revenue*, [1960] S.C.R. 10, [1959] C.T.C. 531, 59 D.T.C. 1316 (S.C.C.) (revenues from granting mineral rights options were income); *Hill-Clark-Francis Ltd. v. Minister of National Revenue*, [1963] S.C.R. 452, [1963] C.T.C. 337, 63 D.T.C. 1211 (S.C.C.).

[71]*Cook v. R.*, [1987] 1 C.T.C. 377, 87 D.T.C. 5231 (Fed. T.D.); see also *Day v. Minister of National Revenue, ante* (meaning of "option").

(iii) — Granting of Options

The Act deems a taxpayer who *grants* an option in respect of a capital property to have disposed of the property at that time.[72] The adjusted cost base of the option is nil. Thus, the issuance of an option for valuable consideration triggers a capital gain in the year in which the taxpayer issues it. This rule does not apply to options to buy or sell a principal residence, options that a corporation issues to acquire its bonds, debentures or equity capital, or options that a trust grants to acquire units of the trust. Special rules apply to employee stock options.[73]

(d) — Call Options

Where a taxpayer grants a call option (an option to purchase property), the granting of the option is a disposition of property. The statute deems the adjusted cost base of the property to be nil. The taxpayer must report the gain on the option in the year that he or she grants it.[74]

If the option is exercised, the granting of the option is retrospectively deemed not to have been a disposition of property[75] and is, in effect, retrospectively cancelled for tax purposes. The grantor then includes the price of the option in the proceeds of disposition from the property that he or she sells pursuant to the option.[76] Thus, the price of the option increases the proceeds of disposition. The purchaser includes the cost of the option in the adjusted cost base of the property that he or she acquires.[77] The grantor can retrospectively adjust the tax return for the year in which the grantor issued the option, and recalculate the earlier option gain.[78]

Example

Assume:

---

[72]Subs. 49(1).

[73]See s. 7; see Chapter 6, "Employment Income" under heading "Stock Options".

[74]Subs. 49(1).

[75]Subs. 49(3).

[76]Para. 49(3)(a).

[77]Para. 49(3)(b).

[78]Subs. 49(4).

In Year 1, *Alpha Ltd.* grants T a call option to purchase a parcel of land for $400,000. T pays $15,000 for the option, which T exercises in Year 5. The adjusted cost base ("ACB") of the land is $50,000.

Then:

1. Effect on *Alpha Ltd.* upon issuance of option:

Proceeds of disposition	$	15,000
ACB (deemed)		NIL
Capital gain	$	15,000

2. Effect on *Alpha Ltd.* upon exercise of option:

Proceeds from sale of land	$	400,000
Add: proceeds from option		15,000
Total proceeds of disposition		415,000
ACB of land		(50,000)
Capital gain	$	365,000

Alpha Ltd. may file an amended return in Year 5 to retroactively reduce its capital gain in Year 1 to nil.

3. Adjusted cost base of land to purchaser (T):

Exercise price	$	400,000
Option price		15,000
ACB	$	415,000

(e) — Put Options

Where a taxpayer issues a put option (an option to sell property), any consideration that he or she receives for the option is considered as proceeds of disposition in the year of issuance.[79] Where the option is subsequently exercised by the grantee, the Act deems the granting and exercise of the option not to have taken place. Instead, the grantor's and grantee's proceeds of disposition and cost of the property are adjusted for the price of the option.[80]

(f) — Bad Debts

Where a taxpayer establishes that his account receivable from a disposition of capital property has become uncollectible, he can elect to be deemed to have disposed of the debt.[81]

---

[79] Subs. 49(1).

[80] Subs. 49(3.1).

[81] Subs. 50(1).

Similarly, a taxpayer who establishes that a corporation in which he holds shares has become bankrupt or is subject to a winding-up order can elect to be deemed to have disposed of any shares.[82]

The taxpayer can then claim a capital loss even though he or she has not actually disposed of the shares. Where the taxpayer makes the election, he or she is deemed to have disposed of the bad debt or the shares for nil proceeds at the end of the year, and to have then acquired it for a cost of nil.

(i) — Subsequent Recovery

A taxpayer can take a deduction for bad debts arising from the sale of capital property only when he actually establishes the debt to have become bad. The Act does not permit the deduction of a reserve for doubtful accounts created from dispositions of capital property. Since a taxpayer who disposes of a bad debt can elect to do so for nil proceeds and to reacquire it for the same amount, any recovery on account of a debt previously written off is a capital gain.[83]

(ii) — Insolvent Corporations

Shareholders of a corporation that has ceased to carry on business and is insolvent can also elect to have disposed of their shares. Therefore, they may be entitled to claim a capital loss. However, a shareholder is deemed to have disposed of his or her shares in an insolvent corporation only if:[84]

- The fair market value of the shares is nil;

- It is reasonable to expect that the corporation will be wound up;

- Neither the corporation nor a corporation that it controls carries on business; and

- The shareholder elects to have the provision apply.

---

[82]Para. 50(1)(b).

[83]See also subpara. 40(2)(g)(ii).

[84]Subpara. 50(1)(b)(iii).

(g) — Death

A taxpayer who dies is deemed to have disposed of all his or her capital properties *immediately before* death.[85] The deemed disposition gives rise to proceeds of disposition, which will depend upon the type of capital property and the date of death.

(i) — Depreciable Capital Property

Upon his death, a taxpayer is deemed to have disposed of his depreciable property at its fair market value.[86] Thus, the full amount of any gain accrued on depreciable property is considered proceeds of disposition. The amount by which the deemed proceeds exceeds the adjusted cost base of the property is a capital gain. The difference between the ACB and UCC is recaptured depreciation.

A beneficiary who inherits property as a consequence of the death of a taxpayer is deemed to acquire the property at an amount equal to the deceased's (deemed) proceeds of disposition (fair market value).[87] A special rule applies, however, if the deceased's capital cost exceeds the beneficiary's deemed acquisition cost. In this circumstance, *for purposes of capital cost allowance and recapture only*, the beneficiary assumes the deceased's original cost, and any difference between this cost and the beneficiary's acquisition cost is deemed to have been claimed as capital cost allowance by the beneficiary.[88] The effect of this special rule is to bump up the beneficiary capital cost, so that the deeming provision does not obscure the true nature of the proceeds of a future disposition by the beneficiary. The bump up in the cost could result in the characterization of proceeds as recapture, rather than capital.

Example

Assume:

D dies owning a depreciable property that costs $200,000. At the time of his death, the property had a UCC of $120,000 and a fair market value ("FMV") of $320,000.

Then, D's capital gain is $120,000, calculated as follows:

Deemed proceeds	$	320,000
Original cost		(200,000)

---

[85]Para. 70(5)(a).

[86]Para. 70(5)(a).

[87]Para. 70(5)(b).

[88]Para. 70(5)(c).

Capital gain	$	120,000

D is also subject to recapture of capital cost allowance of $80,000.

Example

B inherits depreciable property from D on D's death. The following applies:

Original cost	$	200,000
UCC at death	$	120,000
FMV at death	$	180,000

Then:

Effect on D's Terminal Tax Return:		
Deemed proceeds of disposition	$	180,000
UCC at death		(120,000)
Recapture of CCA	$	60,000
Effect on B:		
Capital cost for CCA purposes	$	200,000
CCA deemed allowed to B		(20,000)
UCC to B	$	180,000
Subsequent Sale by B for $240,000:		
Deemed capital cost	$	200,000
UCC on sale		(180,000)
Recapture of CCA	$	20,000
Proceeds of disposition	$	240,000
Cost (ACB)		(200,000)
Capital gain	$	40,000

(ii) — Other Capital Property

Capital properties other than depreciable properties are also deemed to be disposed of immediately before death for proceeds equal to the fair market value of the property.[89]

---

[89]Para. 70(5)(a).

(h) — Trusts

To discourage indefinite accumulations of property in trusts, the Act provides for periodic deemed dispositions of all property held in trust. A trust is deemed to dispose of all of its capital property on the 21st anniversary of the day on which the trust was created.[90]

I. — Involuntary Dispositions

A taxpayer may involuntarily dispose of his property, for example, if it is stolen or expropriated. In these circumstances, it can cause hardship to tax the taxpayer on the full value of his deemed proceeds. To relieve against such hardship, the Act allows a taxpayer who involuntarily disposes of property to elect to defer any capital gain from the disposition,[91] provided that he replaces the property with a substitute property by the later of the end of the second taxation year and 24 months.[92]

(a) — Election to Defer Gain

The deferral is available in respect of the following types of receipts:[93]

- Compensation for property[94] that has been lost or destroyed;

- Compensation for property that is stolen;

- Compensation for property that is expropriated under statutory authority; or

- Sale proceeds from property sold under the duress of an intention to expropriate under statutory authority.

A taxpayer can defer tax only where he or she acquires a replacement for the property before the later of the end of the second taxation year and 24 months.[95] The taxpayer must acquire a capital property to replace the former property. A business asset must be replaced with a business asset.

---

[90]Subss. 104(4), (5), (5.3)–(5.8).

[91]Subs. 44(1).

[92]IT-259-R4, "Exchanges of Property".

[93]Subs. 44(1).

[94]*Sani Sport Inc. v. R.*, [1990] 2 C.T.C. 15, 90 D.T.C. 6230 (Fed. C.A.) (compensation for property includes damages suffered by business loss).

[95]Para. 44(1)(c).

(b) Proceeds of Disposition

Proceeds of an involuntary disposition are deemed to become receivable on the *earliest* of the following days:[96]

- The day when the taxpayer agrees to an amount as full compensation for property lost, stolen or destroyed;

- Where an appeal or other proceeding has been taken before a court or tribunal, the day on which the taxpayer's compensation for the property is finally determined by the court or tribunal;

- Where no such appeal or other proceeding has been taken before a court or tribunal within two years of the loss, destruction or expropriation of property, the second anniversary day of the loss, destruction or expropriation;

- The day on which the taxpayer ceases to be resident in Canada;

- The day on which the taxpayer dies; or,

- Where the taxpayer is a corporation (other than a taxable Canadian corporation that is 90 percent owned by another taxable Canadian corporation), immediately before the corporation is wound up.

Example

Assume:

Jones owns a parcel of land to which the following data applies:

ACB of land	$	80,000
Proceeds upon expropriation	$	140,000
Expenses of disposition	$	2,000
Cost of replacement land (FMV)	$	160,000

Then, Jones's capital gain is determined as follows:

Without Election:

Proceeds of disposition		$	140,000
Less: ACB of land	$ 80,000		
Expenses of disposition	2,000		(82,000)
Capital gain		$	58,000

With Election under Section 44:

---

[96]Subs. 44(2).

Capital gain otherwise determined		$ 58,000
Proceeds from former property		$ 140,000
Cost of replacement land	$ 160,000	
Expenses of disposition	2,000	162,000
Excess of proceeds over replacement cost		NIL
Deemed capital gain		NIL
ACB of Replacement Land After Election:		
Cost of replacement land		$ 160,000
Less excess of:		
Capital gain otherwise determined	$ 58,000	
Excess of proceeds over replacement cost	NIL	(58,000)
ACB of replacement land		$ 102,000

If Jones immediately sold the replacement land at its FMV of $160,000, she would realize a capital gain of $58,000 ($160,000 less $102,000), which is, in effect, the amount of the capital gain that she deferred upon the expropriation.

In general terms, a taxpayer can defer the entire capital gain that would otherwise be recognized provided that he or she replaces the disposed property with more expensive property. The deferred gain reduces the cost base of the new property.[97] In the above example, the deferred capital gain of $58,000 reduces the cost of the new property from $160,000 to $102,000. Thus, the gain on the sale of the new property will be $58,000 greater than it would otherwise have been.

V. — Adjusted Cost Base

The capital cost of a property is generally the amount that a taxpayer pays to acquire property, including the amount of any liabilities that he assumes. The "adjusted cost base" of a property means:[98]

- Where the property is depreciable property, its capital cost; and

- Where the property is any other property, the cost of the property as adjusted by section 53.

The Act does not define the terms "capital cost" and "cost". Hence, we interpret them according to their commercial usage.

---

[97]Para. 44(1)(f).

[98]S. 54 "adjusted cost base".

"Cost" refers to the price that the taxpayer gives up in order to acquire the property.[99] It includes incidental acquisition costs such as brokerage, legal, accounting, engineering and valuation fees. Carrying costs (such as interest expense) for the unpaid price of property are not part of the "cost" of the asset for purposes of the capital gains rules.[100]

There are special rules for determining the adjusted cost base of properties owned by a taxpayer at the start of the "new system" on January 1, 1972. These rules are set out in the Income Tax Application Rules (ITARs).

A. — Deemed Adjusted Cost Base

Numerous provisions of the Act *deem* the cost of a property to be a certain amount. Whenever the Act deems a disposition of property for deemed proceeds, it also deems a reacquisition of the property at a deemed cost base. Thus, every capital property always has an adjusted cost base at any point in time.

(a) — Change of Use

Where a taxpayer changes the use of a capital property from business to personal use, or *vice versa*, he or she is deemed to have acquired the property for the new purpose at a cost equal to its fair market value at the time of the change in use.[101] Thus, despite the absence of a market transaction, there is a carryover of basis from the business use to the personal use. Similarly, where a taxpayer changes the proportions of business and personal use of a capital property, the taxpayer may be deemed to have acquired the portion of the property, subject to the new use at a cost proportional to its fair market value at that time.[102]

---

[99]*R. v. Stirling*, [1985] 1 F.C. 342, [1985] 1 C.T.C. 275, 85 D.T.C. 5199 (Fed. C.A.) (interest expense on unpaid portion of price of gold bullion, and safe-keeping charges, not part of cost of bullion).

[100]*R. v. Stirling, ante*, at 343; see also *R. v. Canadian Pacific Ltd. (No. 1)*, [1978] C.T.C. 606, 77 D.T.C. 5383 (Fed. C.A.) (taxpayer not entitled to CCA on perishable product or expenditures in respect of property not owned); *Consumers' Gas Co. v. R.*, [1984] C.T.C. 83, 84 D.T.C. 6058 (Fed. C.A.) (taxpayer to add cost of pipelines to UCC without reduction for reimbursement); *Birmingham (City) v. Barnes (Inspector of Taxes)*, [1935] A.C. 292 (H.L.) (deductibility of grant received and renewal costs in determination of "actual cost" to build tramway).

[101]S. 45.

[102]Para. 45(1)(c).

(b) — Identical Properties

The cost of identical properties is their weighted average cost at any time.[103] A new average is determined each time another identical property is acquired and added to the pool. The cost of identical capital properties (other than depreciable property or an interest in a partnership) owned by a taxpayer on December 31, 1971, is also the weighted average cost of the properties.[104] However, this calculation is made separately from the one for identical properties acquired after December 31, 1971. In effect, a taxpayer must maintain two separate pools of identical properties: one for pre-1972 properties and the other for post-1971 properties.

Where a taxpayer issues debt (bonds, debentures, notes, etc.) and equity securities at different times, the securities are considered to be identical to each other if they have the same rights in all respects and differ only in the face value or principal amount of the security.[105]

(c) — Becoming a Canadian Resident

When a taxpayer becomes resident in Canada, the taxpayer is deemed to have acquire each property that he owns at a cost equal to its fair market value.[106] This rule does not apply to property that would be "taxable Canadian property".[107]

(d) — Options

When a taxpayer exercises an option to acquire property, the adjusted cost base of the property to the purchaser includes the cost of the option.[108] Upon exercise, the option and the property acquired are unified into one cost basis on their joint market values.

(e) — Conversions

Where a taxpayer acquires shares of a corporation in exchange for convertible shares, bonds, debentures or notes issued by the corporation, and the acquisition is made without any cash

---

[103]S. 47.

[104]ITAR 26(8).

[105]Subs. 248(12).

[106]Para. 128.1(1)(c).

[107]Subs. 248(1) and Para. 128.1(1)(b).

[108]Subs. 49(3).

consideration, the taxpayer's cost of the shares is deemed to be the adjusted cost base of the convertible property immediately before the exchange.[109]

(f) — Non-Arm's Length Transactions

Where a taxpayer acquires property in a non-arm's length transaction at an amount greater than its fair market value, the taxpayer is deemed to acquire the property at its fair market value at the time of acquisition.[110] If he acquires the property at less than its fair market value, the adjusted cost base of the property is his actual cost.

(g) — Prizes

A taxpayer who wins a prize in a lottery is deemed to acquire the property at a cost equal to its fair market value at the time of winning the prize.[111] Although a lottery prize is exempt from tax, a life annuity in lieu of the prize is *fully* taxable. However, under para. 60(a) the recipient may deduct the capital component of the annuity. In effect, only the investment earnings component of the annuity is taxable.

(h) — Dividends in Kind

A taxpayer who receives a dividend in kind (other than a stock dividend) is deemed to have acquired the property at its fair market value.[112]

(i) — Stock Dividends

A stock dividend includes any dividend paid by the issuance of shares of any class of a corporation.[113]

---

[109]S. 51.

[110]Para. 69(1)(a).

[111]Subs. 52(4); see *Rumack v. Minister of National Revenue*, [1984] C.T.C. 2382, 84 D.T.C. 1339 (T.C.C.); reversed [1990] 1 C.T.C. 413 (Fed. T.D.); reversed [1992] 1 C.T.C. 57, 92 D.T.C. 6142 (Fed. C.A.); leave to appeal refused (1992), 143 N.R. 393 (note) (S.C.C.).

[112]Subs. 52(2).

[113]See subs. 248(1) "dividend".

The value of a stock dividend is the amount by which the paid-up capital of the corporation paying the dividend is increased by virtue of the payment of the dividend.[114] In the case of a stock dividend that does not qualify as a "dividend", the cost is nil.[115] The cost of stock dividends received by a taxpayer will affect the adjusted cost base of all other identical shares owned by the taxpayer.[116]

A corporation that pays a stock dividend with a low paid-up capital and high fair market value and then repurchases the stock may be liable to a special corporate distributions tax.[117]

B. — Adjustments to Cost Base

(a) — General Comment

We determine the cost base of a property by reference to commercial principles and the aforementioned deeming provisions. The cost base is adjusted for various events and transactions from time to time. There are two types of adjustments to the cost base of property — *additions* to the cost base[118] and *deductions* from the cost base.[119]

Generally, a taxpayer adds to the cost base of property when he receives an amount that either has previously borne tax or was exempt from tax. Thus, additions to the adjusted cost base of property prevent double taxation of the same amount. For example, where an employee is taxed on a stock option benefit that he includes in employment income,[120] the value of the benefit is added to the cost base of his shares.[121] Without this addition, the taxpayer would be taxed again on the same gain when he disposed of the shares.

Conversely, a taxpayer deducts from the cost base of property when she has previously received an amount free of tax. The following is illustrative of some of the adjustments made to the cost base of the more common types of property.

---

[114]See para. 248(1)(c).

[115]Para. 52(3)(a.1).

[116]S. 47.

[117]Pt. II.1, (ss. 183.1, 183.2).

[118]Subs. 53(1).

[119]Subs. 53(2).

[120]S. 7; see Chapter 6, "Employment Income" under heading "Stock Options".

[121]Para. 53(1)(j).

(b) — Acquisition of Land

A taxpayer may not deduct interest on debt relating to the acquisition of vacant land to the extent that the expense exceeds any income from the land.[122] The taxpayer can, however, add the disallowed carrying charges to the cost base of the land.[123]

The phrase "interest on debt relating to the acquisition of land" includes certain interest expenses to finance the acquisition of land by another person with whom the taxpayer does not deal at arm's length.[124] For example, it includes interest on borrowed money that is used to finance the acquisition of land by a corporation of which the taxpayer is a specified shareholder, or by a partnership in which the taxpayer has at least a 10 percent interest.

(c) — Stock Dividends and Options

Stock dividends have an adjusted cost base equal to the aggregate of the value of the dividend and any amount included in the taxpayer's income as a shareholder benefit.[125]

Where an employee acquires shares of a corporation under an employee stock option plan, the employee is deemed to receive a "stock option" benefit under section 7. The amount of the benefit is added to the adjusted cost base of the shares acquired.[126]

C. — Negative Adjusted Cost Base

The adjusted cost base of a property at the time that it is disposed of cannot be less than nil.[127] If at any time the deductions from the cost of property exceed its adjusted cost and the ACB of the property becomes a negative amount, the negative balance is a capital gain from the disposition of the property. The amount of the deemed gain is then immediately added to the cost of the property, thereby raising its ACB back to nil.[128] The capital gain is eligible for the capital gains exemption under section 110.6.

---

[122]Subs. 18(2).

[123]Subpara. 53(1)(h)(i).

[124]Subs. 18(3) "interest on debt relating to the acquisition of land".

[125]Subs. 52(3); subs. 15(1.1); subs. 248(1) "stock dividend".

[126]Para. 53(1)(j).

[127]Subs. 54 "adjusted cost base" (d).

[128]Subs. 40(3).

Example

Assume:

A taxpayer owns a capital property with an adjusted cost base of $2,000. During the year, the cost base is adjusted by subsection 53(1) additions of $300 and subsection 53(2) deductions of $2,700.

Then the taxpayer's adjusted cost base is calculated as follows:

Cost of property	$ 2,000	
Subsection 53(1) additions	300	
	2,300	
Subsection 53(2) deductions	(2,700	)
Deemed capital gain	(400	)
Paragraph 53(1)(a) addition	400	
ACB of property	$ NIL	

VI. — Part Dispositions

Where a taxpayer disposes of only a part of a capital property, one calculates the adjusted cost base of that part by taking a "reasonable" proportion of the cost base of the part to the whole. The adjusted cost base of the part of the property that was disposed of is then deducted from the adjusted cost base of the whole property.[129] The balance becomes the cost base of the remaining part.[130]

Example

Assume:

A taxpayer disposes of a part of a capital property for its fair market value of $3,000, at a time when the fair market value of the entire property is $14,000. The adjusted cost base of the entire property is $7,000.

Then, (1) the ACB of the disposed property, (2) the taxpayer's capital gain, and (3) the ACB of the remaining property, are calculated as follows:

(1)   ACB of portion of property disposed of:

        $ 3,000 × $7,000

---

[129]Para. 53(2)(d).

[130]S. 43; there are special rules governing partial dispositions of personal-use property.

	$ 14,000	$	1,500
(2)	Proceeds of disposition	$	3,000
	ACB of disposed of portion		(1,500)
	Capital gain	$	1,500
(3)	ACB of entire property	$	7,000
	ACB of disposed of portion		(1,500)
	ACB of remaining portion	$	5,500

VII. — Personal-Use Property

In general terms, personal-use property refers to capital assets used primarily for the personal use or enjoyment of the taxpayer. There are special rules for determining capital gains and losses from dispositions of "personal-use property" (PUP). These rules serve two purposes. First, they eliminate the need for any record keeping in connection with the purchase and sale of low-value capital assets used primarily for the taxpayer's personal use or enjoyment. Second, they prohibit a deduction for capital losses on the disposition of this particular category of capital property.

Specifically, personal-use property includes:[131]

- Property owned by a taxpayer that is used *primarily* for the personal use or enjoyment of:

  - the taxpayer;

  - a person related to the taxpayer; or

  - if the taxpayer is a trust, a beneficiary under the trust or any person related[132] to the beneficiary;

  - A debt owing to a taxpayer in respect of the disposition of personal-use property; and

- An option to acquire property that would, if it were acquired, be personal-use property of a taxpayer or a person related to him or her.

Cars, boats, furniture, clothing, and residences are common examples of personal-use property.

A partnership may also own personal-use property. For example, where a member of a partnership, or one or more of a group of individuals consisting of a member of the partnership,

---

[131]S. 54 "personal-use property".

[132]See subs. 251(2).

or related persons, uses property primarily for personal use or enjoyment, the property is personal use property. Similarly, corporate property may be personal-use property if it is primarily for the personal use of a shareholder of the corporation.

A. — Listed Personal Property

"Listed personal property" (LPP) is a subset of personal-use property that is specifically listed and includes:[133]

- Prints, etchings, drawings, paintings, sculptures or other similar works of art;
- Jewellery;
- Rare folios, rare manuscripts or rare books;
- Stamps; and
- Coins.

An interest in, or right to, any of these items is also listed personal property. Thus, listed personal property items are assets that one acquires for dual purposes — personal consumption and investment value. Hence, gains from listed personal property are taxable; losses are deductible, but only against gains from listed personal property.[134]

B. — Computational Rules

The Act deems the *minimum* adjusted cost base and proceeds of disposition of personal-use property to be $1,000.[135] The purpose of this rule is to minimize bookkeeping for low value items of LPP. Consequently, if both the *actual* cost and the *actual* proceeds on disposition of an item of personal-use property are less than $1,000, the transaction does not give rise to any capital gain or capital loss. Thus, taxpayers do not need to keep a detailed record of low-value transactions for income tax purposes.

A special rule, however, excluding from the $1,000 minimum any property — typically art — that a taxpayer acquires with the intention of "flipping" to a charity. The rationale of the exclusion is to discourage bogus "art flips" to charities.[136]

---

[133]S. 54 "listed personal property".

[134]See para. 3(b), which includes *net* LPP gains in income.

[135]Subs. 46(1).

[136]Subs. 46(5).

Example

A taxpayer purchases and sells personal-use property for the amounts indicated. The gain or loss in each case is calculated using the $1000 rule as follows:

	A	B	C
Proceeds of disposition	$ 900	$ 1,200	$ 2,000
Cost	(600)	(600)	(1,500)
Capital gain	$ NIL	$ 200	$ 500

	D	E	F
Proceeds of disposition	$ 400	$ 800	$ 1,200
Cost	(60)	(1,500)	(1,500)
Capital loss	$ NIL	$ (500)	$ (300)

Notes:

Capital loss is deemed to be nil unless the PUP qualifies as listed personal property.

(a) — Bad Debts

Where a taxpayer establishes that a debt owing to him from a sale of PUP has become a bad debt, he may offset any prior capital gain that he recognized on the sale of the property by recognizing a capital loss when the debt becomes bad.[137]

Example

Assume:

A taxpayer sells personal-use property with an ACB of $9,000 for $10,000 in Year 1. The taxpayer receives $6,000 cash and accepts a note for $4,000. In Year 3, the debtor defaults on the note and the debt is established to have become bad.

Then:

Year 1 Proceeds of disposition	$ 10,000
ACB of property	(9,000)
Capital gain	$ 1,000
Year 3 Deemed proceeds of debt	$ 3,000

[137]Subs. 50(2).

| ACB of debt | (4,000) |
| Capital loss | $ (1,000) |

Notes:

Calculated as the amount that will give rise to a capital loss equal to the prior capital gain.

A debt from the sale of PUP is itself PUP. Subpara. 40(2)(g)(iii) deems a loss on the disposition of a PUP to be nil.[138]

C. — Part Dispositions

To prevent taxpayers from taking unfair advantage of the minimum $1,000 ACB and proceeds of disposition rule by selling sets of property in bits and pieces, a special rule requires allocation of the $1,000 whenever the various parts of a personal-use property are sold individually, or when a PUP set is sold piecemeal. The $1,000 amount is allocated proportionately, as below:

$$\$1,000 \times (\text{ACB of part disposed}) / (\text{ACB of the whole property})$$

The deemed cost and deemed proceeds of disposition rules are then applied in relation to the part of the PUP that has been disposed of on the basis of this reduced amount.[139]

The second aspect of this rule applies to dispositions of a set of personal-use properties that have an *aggregate* fair market value in excess of $1,000, and that would *ordinarily* be disposed of together. If a set of personal-use properties is sold in more than one transaction to the same person, or to a group of persons who do not deal with each other at arm's length, the set is deemed to be a single property and the $1,000 amount is proportionally reduced.[140]

D. — Capital Losses

Capital losses arising from a disposition of PUP (other than listed personal property) are deemed to be nil.[141] An additional rule provides that, where a capital gain is reduced, or a capital loss is increased, on the disposition of a share of a corporation (or an interest in a

---

[138]See, however, special carve out to which subsection 50(2) applies.

[139]Subs. 46(2). Note that these allocation rules apply only when a taxpayer disposes of a part of a PUP and retains another part. Accordingly, upon the disposition of the final remaining part, no allocation is required, since the taxpayer would not be retaining another part.

[140]Subs. 46(3).

[141]Subpara. 40(2)(g)(iii).

partnership or trust), and it may reasonably be regarded that the reduction in value of the share results from a decrease in the value of any PUP of the corporation (or partnership or trust), then the capital gain or capital loss is adjusted to the amount that it would have been if the particular PUP had not decreased in value.[142] This rule applies even if the particular PUP is listed personal property.

There are also special rules for calculating losses on listed personal property ("LPP"). The general thrust of these rules is that capital losses on LPP can be offset only against capital gains on LPP. Any remaining balance can be carried back three years and carried forward seven years; in each of those years, the LPP loss can be offset only against LPP gains.[143]

VIII. — Identical Properties

Where a taxpayer acquires a capital property identical to other properties that he or she owns, the cost of each of the properties is calculated by taking the weighted average of their adjusted cost bases. The weighted average cost of properties must be recalculated each time the taxpayer acquires another property identical to property already owned by the taxpayer.[144] The weighted average cost of identical properties is determined by dividing the aggregate of their adjusted cost bases by the number of properties owned.

Whether property acquired by a taxpayer is "identical" to property already owned by him is a question of fact. For example, corporate shares of the same class and with the same rights are identical properties, notwithstanding that they may be physically identifiable as separate properties by virtue of their serial numbers.

Bonds and debt obligations are considered similar to other debts issued by the debtor if they are identical in respect of their legal and equitable rights. This is so even if the principal amounts of the debt are different.[145]

However, land can never be an identical property for tax purposes. This is so even if the lots are adjoining lots and of the same size and quality. Each plot of land is unique.

---

[142]Subs. 46(4).

[143]Subs. 41(2) and para. 3(b).

[144]S. 47 and para. 3(b).

[145]Subs. 248(12).

Example

A taxpayer owns 100 common shares of *XYZ Co.*, which she acquired at a cost of $20 per share. The taxpayer acquires a further 200 shares of the same class and kind of the same corporation at $30 per share.

The weighted average cost of the shares is calculated as follows:

100	shares × $20/share	$	2,000
200	shares × $30/share		6,000
300		$	8,000
Weighted Average Cost per Share ($8,000/300)		$	26.67

Properties that a taxpayer owned as at December 31, 1971, are segregated in a separate pool from identical properties that the taxpayer acquired after that date. Thus, a weighted average cost is calculated for identical properties owned on December 31, 1971, and a separate average cost is calculated for properties acquired subsequently. A disposition of identical properties is deemed to be made first out of the pre-1972 pool.[146]

To summarize: identical properties are divided into two pools, one pool consisting of the properties on hand at December 31, 1971, and the other group comprising post-1971 acquisitions. The pre-1972 group is deemed to be disposed of first.

IX. — Losses Deemed to be Nil

A. — General Comment

In various circumstances, capital losses are deemed to be nil to prevent them from being deducted in computing income. The general thrust of these provisions is to prevent a taxpayer from creating or accelerating an "artificial" capital loss deduction by structuring transactions within a group of related economic entities. Sometimes the non-recognition of the capital loss is permanent; other times, the amount of the capital loss that is deemed to be nil is added to the cost base of some other property owned by the taxpayer, so that there will be a corresponding reduction in the capital gain (or increase in the capital loss) on the disposition of the other property. The underlying policy of the deeming provisions is to restrict deductions to "real" capital losses that have economic substance (see below).

---

[146]ITAR 26(8) — (8.3).

B. — Dispositions between Affiliated Persons

Section 251.1 — the affiliated person rules — control abusive transactions where taxpayers trigger losses within close economic affiliations. Such transactions, which can be quite complex, usually involve corporate or partnership structures that either inappropriately trigger unrealized losses on certain types of property or move losses from one person to another.

The stop-loss and affiliated person rules deny losses that taxpayers trigger between themselves and their spouses and common-law partners, corporations under common control, partnerships and members of partnerships who, either alone or together with other affiliated persons, are generally entitled to more than half of the partnership's earnings. They also apply to trusts and any beneficiaries who, either alone or together with certain other affiliated persons, are entitled to more than half of the trust's income or capital.

There are essentially three distinct conditions that trigger the rules. First, a person must dispose of a property at a loss. Certain types of dispositions — such as, deemed losses that occur as a result of migration from Canada — do not trigger the rules.

Second, the person who disposes of the property or someone affiliated with the person must, within a 61-day window that centres on the date of the disposition, acquire that same property or what is referred to as a "substituted property".

Third, the disposing person or a person affiliated with that person must own the property or substituted property in question on the 61st day of that same period.

In these circumstances, the rules apply to deny the loss to the disposing person.[147] There are, however, other consequences depending upon the identity of the disposing person.

If the disposing person is an individual, the loss is added to the tax cost (ACB) of the property, or substituted property, that is in the hands of the acquirer. In effect the loss can be passed from the individual to another person. If, however, the disposing person is a trust, partnership or corporation, the loss remains with the disposing party and is effectively suspended, thereby preventing such losses from moving from that trust, corporation or partnership to another person. The trust, corporation or partnership may subsequently claim the loss, generally when either the property is subsequently sold to a non-affiliated person or the parties break their affiliated connection.

For example, assume that an individual owns all of the shares of his or her corporation. The individual owns a parcel of land that is capital property. The fair market value of the land is $100,000 but its tax cost or ACB is $275,000. The individual wishes to trigger the loss to offset against his capital gains in the same year. The individual disposes of the land to his or her corporation triggering a capital loss of $175,000. Since the individual and his or her corporation are affiliated persons, the stop loss rules apply. The Act denies the individual the

---

[147]Subpara. 40(2)(g)(i) and para. 40(3.4)(a).

loss and adds it to the ACB of the land, which the corporation now owns.[148] If the corporation subsequently sells the land for $100,000 in a non-affiliated transaction, the corporation can recognize a capital loss of $175,000. In effect, the individual's loss flows to the corporation upon the subsequent sale.

If the corporation had initially owned the land and sold it to its sole shareholder, the corporation could not claim the $175,000 loss.[149] Further, since the disposing person is a corporation, there is no ACB adjustment in this case and the loss is suspended to the corporation. The corporation, however, can claim the loss when the individual sells the land in a non-affiliated transaction. The same rule applies if the disposing person is either a partnership or trust if the individual and the partnership or trust, as the case may be, are affiliated.

Similar stop-loss rules in the *Income Tax Act* to prevent the early recognition of losses on depreciable and eligible capital property.

C. — Lotteries

A taxpayer who does not win a lottery cannot claim a capital loss in respect of the cost of the ticket.[150]

D. — Superficial Losses

An individual is not allowed to claim a "superficial loss".[151] A superficial loss arises when an individual, or certain affiliated parties,[152] disposes of property and replaces it with "substituted property" within a period of 61 days.[153] This is an anti-avoidance rule that prevents individuals from claiming paper losses for tax purposes. For the purpose of this rule, the 61-day period commences 30 days before, and ends 30 days after, the day that the taxpayer disposes of the property. This rule also applies to property that certain affiliated persons may acquire during the 61 days. For example, it applies to property acquired by the individual, his spouse, common law partner, and controlled corporations.

---

[148]Subpara. 40(2)(g)(i).

[149]Para. 40(3.4)(a).

[150]Para. 40(2)(f).

[151]Subpara. 40(2)(g)(i).

[152]Subs. 251.1(1).

[153]S. 54 "superficial loss".

The taxpayer can, however, increase the cost base of the "substituted property" by the amount of his or her superficial loss.[154] Consequently, when the taxpayer disposes of the "substituted property", he or she can reduce any gain on the property. Alternatively, the taxpayer can increase the actual loss by the amount of his or her superficial loss.

The superficial loss rules do not apply in a number of situations where the Act deems a taxpayer to have disposed of, and reacquired, certain properties. For example, losses arising from the following deemed dispositions do not give rise to superficial losses:[155]

- Emigration;[156]

- A debt becoming a bad debt;[157]

- Death;[158]

- Change in use of property;[159]

- Realization by a trust under subsection 104(4); and

- An employee's profit-sharing plan as a result of an election made in accordance with subsection 144(4.1) or (4.2).

Also, the rules do not apply when an option expires.[160]

E. — Disposition of a Debt

A capital loss from a disposition, whether actual or deemed, of a debt is deemed to be nil unless the taxpayer acquired the debt for the purpose of gaining or producing income from a business or property (other than exempt income), or as consideration for the disposition of capital property to an arm's length person.[161]

---

[154]Para. 53(1)(f).

[155]S. 54 "superficial loss". Deemed dispositions under subss. 33.1(11), 138(11.3), 149(10) also do not give rise to superficial losses.

[156]S. 128.1.

[157]S. 50.

[158]S. 70.

[159]Subs. 45(1).

[160]Subs. 40(3.4).

[161]Subpara. 40(2)(g)(ii).

F. — Disposition of Personal-Use Property

A taxpayer's loss from a disposition of personal-use property is deemed to be nil unless the property qualifies as listed personal property or is a PUP debt referred to in subsection 50(2).[162] The non-recognition of the loss is permanent.

X. — Principal Residence

A Canadian resident is generally not taxable on a capital gain from his or her principal residence.[163] The entire amount of the gain is tax exempt, regardless of the value of the property sold. Thus, the principal residence exemption is the most generous exemption in the Act and is not limited by any amount. The larger the house and the richer its owner, the more generous the exemption which, in tax policy terms, is interesting.

Note, the residence does not even have to be in Canada to be eligible for the exemption.

A. — Meaning of "Principal Residence"

(a) — Minimum Requirements

There are requirements to qualify a property as a "principal residence", which address four separate criteria:[164]

1. The type of property:

    • the property may consist of a housing unit, a leasehold interest in a housing unit or a share in a co-operative housing corporation;[165]

2. Owner occupation:

    • the property must be owned by the taxpayer; and

    • the property must be "occupied" by the taxpayer during the year;[166]

---

[162]Subpara. 40(2)(g)(iii).

[163]Para. 40(2)(b).

[164]S. 54 "principal residence".

[165]*Flanagan v. Minister of National Revenue*, [1989] 2 C.T.C. 2395, 89 D.T.C. 615 (T.C.C.) (van, trailer or mobile home can qualify as housing unit eligible for exemption).

[166]*Ennist v. Minister of National Revenue*, [1985] 2 C.T.C. 2398, 85 D.T.C. 669 (T.C.C.) (24-hour occupancy of condominium not sufficient to satisfy requirement that residence be "ordinarily inhabited").

3. The period of ownership:

- the property must be ordinarily inhabited at some time during the year by the taxpayer, her spouse, former spouse, common law partner, former common law partner or child; or

- if the individual acquired the property for the purpose of gaining or producing income and the use changes to that of a principal residence, he can elect under subsection 45(3) to prevent the deemed disposal and reacquisition in subsection 45(1) from operating;

4. Designation on tax return:

- the property is designated by the taxpayer as his or her sole principal residence for the year.

(b) — Included Land

A principal residence includes the land under, and adjacent to, the housing unit provided that the land contributes to the taxpayer's use and enjoyment of the unit as a residence. The statute deems land up to 0.5 hectare to be part of the principal residence. Where the total area of land exceeds 0.5 hectare,[167] the excess does not qualify as a principal residence unless the taxpayer can establish that the excess is *necessary* for his or her use and enjoyment of the housing unit as a residence.[168] Minimum lot size restrictions and zoning laws can affect the amount of land that is exempt as part of a principal residence.[169] The severability of land is also a relevant factor in determining the value that one assigns to any portion that exceeds the exempt amount.

The principal residence exemption is anomalous and regressive. Nevertheless, it is a sacred cow. Given that the Act restricts the exemption by the physical dimensions of the residence and land, and not by its value, it is advantageous to own as much land as possible as part of

---

[167] Approx. 1.25 acres.

[168] *R. v. Yates*, [1986] 2 C.T.C. 46, 86 D.T.C. 6296 (Fed. C.A.) (minimum lot size can be used to determine amount of land necessary for use and enjoyment).

[169] *Baird v. Minister of National Revenue*, [1983] C.T.C. 2651, 83 D.T.C. 582 (T.C.C.) (taxpayer cannot make a partial disposition of principal residence); *R. v. Mitosinka*, [1978] C.T.C. 664, 78 D.T.C. 6432 (Fed. T.D.) (each half of duplex separate housing unit); *R. v. Yates*, [1983] 2 F.C. 730, [1983] C.T.C. 105 (Fed. T.D.); affirmed [1986] 2 C.T.C. 46, 86 D.T.C. 6296 (Fed. C.A.) (where taxpayer legally unable to occupy housing unit as residence on less than ten acres, excess portion necessary for taxpayer's use and enjoyment). The *Yates* decision has been accepted by the CRA: see News Release (April 9, 1987) and IT-120R6. See also, *Augart v. Minister of National Revenue*, [1993] 2 C.T.C. 34, 93 D.T.C. 5205 (Fed. C.A.) ("enjoyment" embraces the exercise of a legal right, one of which is the right of alienation. Taxpayer could not alienate less than 8.99 acres).

the residence. For example, a residence located on 0.5 hectare of land in, say, Rosedale (Toronto) will be much more valuable than one on 0.5 hectare in Moose Jaw (Saskatchewan).

(c) — Designation

A property does not qualify as a principal residence for a particular year unless the taxpayer designates it as such in his or her income tax return for the year in which he or she disposes of it. The CRA does not, however, call for the designation unless the taxpayer makes a *taxable* capital gain on the disposition of the principal residence after deducting the exempt portion of the gain.

B. — Exempt Gains

The exempt portion of a capital gain realized on the disposition of a pincipal residence is determined as follows:[170]

$$\text{Exempt Gain} = \frac{A}{B} \times \text{Capital Gain realized}$$

Where:

A = Number of taxation years ending after the acquisition date for which property was the taxpayer's principal residence and during which the taxpayer was resident in Canada plus one.

B = number of taxation years ending after the acquisition date during which the taxpayer owned the property.

A taxpayer can claim the exemption in respect of a capital gain on the disposition of a property if it was his or her principal residence *at any time* in the year. The "1 +" in the numerator of the fraction for determining the exempt portion of the capital gain ensures that a taxpayer can claim the exemption in respect of the disposition of two principal residences in the same year.

Example: Where the taxpayer owns one principal residence

Assume:

A taxpayer purchased a house in Year 1 at a cost of $50,000 and sold it in Year 7 for $200,000 (net of $10,000 selling expenses). He made no capital expenditures on the house

---

[170]Para. 40(2)(b).

during his ownership. He was resident in Canada during the relevant period, and he designated the house as a principal residence for all the years.

Then:

Proceeds of disposition		$	210,000
Less:			
Adjusted cost base	$ 50,000		
Expenses of disposition	10,000		(60,000)
Capital gain otherwise determined			150,000
Less:			
Exempt portion of capital gain			
$\dfrac{1 + 6}{7}$ × $150,000			(150,000)
Capital gain		NIL	

Example: Where there is a change in use of residence

Assume the same facts as in the above example, except that the taxpayer lived in the residence only during Years 1 through 3. The rest of the time the building was rented out to a tenant.

Then (ignoring any elections under section 45):

Proceeds of disposition		$	210,000
Less:			
ACB of property	$ 50,000		
Selling expenses	10,000		(60,000)
Capital gain otherwise determined			150,000
Less:			
Exempt portion of capital gain			
$\dfrac{1 + 3}{7}$ × $150,000			(85,714)
Capital gain		$	64,286

C. — Limits on Exemptions

A family unit living together can together designate only one principal residence per year. For the purpose of this rule, a "family unit" comprises: the taxpayer, his or her spouse, or common-law partner, children under the age of 18 who are not married or living in a common-law partnership.[171]

(a) — Two Exempt Residences

The "1+" in the numerator of the fraction, used to determine the exempt portion of the gain, allows a taxpayer to claim an exemption in respect of two principal residences in the same year. Such a situation typically arises when a taxpayer sells his or her principal residence during the course of the year and purchases another residence in the same year. In these circumstances the taxpayer would own and occupy two residences in the same year, both of which could be eligible for the principal residence exemption.

Example: Where the taxpayer owns more than one residence

A taxpayer purchased a house in Year 1 and lived in it until he sold it on February 28, Year 4. He purchased a second house on February 1, Year 4, and moved into it on March 1, Year 4, living there until he sold it on October 1, Year 4. He purchased a third house on September 30, Year 4, and moved into it on November 1, Year 4.

First House

Designate as principal residence for Years 1–3

Exempt portion of capital gain on its sale

$$\frac{1+3}{4}$$

Therefore, any capital gain is exempt.

Second House

Designate as principal residence for Year 4

Exempt portion of capital gain on its sale

$$\frac{1+0}{1}$$

Hence, any capital gain is also exempt.

If the taxpayer sold a third house also in Year 4, she could not take advantage of the principal residence exemption on both the second and third houses. This is because only one of these houses could be designated as a principal residence for Year 4. In these circumstances, however, the taxpayer may choose which house to designate for exemption. Alternatively, the taxpayer could arrange to have the closing on the third house delayed until January Year 5.

---

[171]S. 54 "principal residence".

(b) — Extended Family Unit

Where the individual claiming the principal residence exemption is an unmarried person, or under 18 years of age, the family unit is extended to include the taxpayer's mother, father and unmarried brothers and sisters under 18 years of age.[172]

(c) — "Ordinarily Inhabited"

The principal residence exemption is available only if the taxpayer, his or her spouse, former spouse, common-law partner, former common-law partner, or child ordinarily occupies the house.

The question of ordinary inhabitation of a property during the taxation year is one of fact, and depends upon the circumstances of each case. Generally, the CRA is quite generous in its interpretation of what constitutes habitation of a residence. For example, it will accept seasonal occupation of a taxpayer's vacation house (such as a cottage or ski chalet) as sufficient to qualify the premises for the entire year as a principal residence. The CRA goes even further: it will accept a seasonal residence as eligible for the exemption even where the taxpayer rents out the premises for incidental rental income. That is, provided that the rental is not a commercial or business enterprise, the taxpayer may occupy the premises for a limited portion of the season, rent it out for the remainder of the year, and still claim the exemption.

D. — Farm Houses

Special rules apply to taxpayers engaged in a farming business. An individual who disposes of land and a principal residence that he uses in a farming business is allowed to calculate the exempt portion of the capital gain attributable to the residence in one of two ways.

(a) — Alternative 1

The taxpayer can treat the property as comprising two portions, the first portion being the principal residence, and the second the balance of the farmland. Any capital gain realized from the disposition is allocated between these two portions on a reasonable basis.[173] The exempt portion of the capital gain on the principal residence is then determined in accordance with the general rules described above.

---

[172]S. 54 "principal residence" (c).

[173]Subpara. 40(2)(c)(i).

Example

Anne Jones acquired a farm in Year 1 at a cost of $145,000. The purchase price was allocated $25,000 to the farmhouse and $120,000 to the farmland. She sold the property in Year 15 for $250,000 (net of selling expenses), of which $30,000 was allocated to the farmhouse and $220,000 to the farmland. The farmhouse was the taxpayer's principal residence throughout the period. The first method applies automatically.

Gain on farmland ($220,00-120,000)	$	100,000
Gain on farmhouse ($30,000-25,000)		5,000
Less: Exempt portion		(5,000)
Capital gain	$	100,000

(b) — Alternative 2

Under the second method, the individual may elect not to allocate her proceeds between the residence and the farmland. Instead, the rule is that the exempt portion of the total capital gain realized by the taxpayer is set at $1,000, plus an additional $1,000 for each taxation year ending after the acquisition date for which the property was the taxpayer's principal residence and during which the taxpayer was resident in Canada.[174] This method applies only if the taxpayer elects to use it.

Example

Assume the same facts as in the above example.

Gain on property ($250,00-145,000)		$ 105,000
Less: Exempt portion		
• standard	$ 1,000	
• ($1,000 × 15 years)	15,000	(16,000)
Capital gain		$ 89,000

E. — Change in Use Elections

(a) — Personal to Income-Earning Use

We saw earlier that a taxpayer who changes the use of capital property from personal to income-earning use may elect under subsection 45(2) to have the change in use ignored for

---

[174]Subpara. 40(2)(c)(ii).

income tax purposes. The effect of the election is that the taxpayer is deemed not to have changed the use of the property from personal to business and not to have disposed of the property at its fair market value at that time.

(i) — Application to Principal Residence

The "change in use" election is particularly useful in respect of a principal residence. The election has two effects:

> 1. It allows the property to retain its status as a principal residence for four years (or possibly longer in the case of a work relocation) after the year in which the taxpayer moves out of the property;[175] and

> 2. The election deems the taxpayer not to have changed his or her use of the property.

Thus, where an individual elects, he may designate the property as a principal residence up to four years even though he uses the property to earn income. If the taxpayer changes use of the property again, and resumes habitation of the premises, the second change does not give rise to a deemed disposition; the taxpayer is considered never to have changed the use of the property in the first place. Thus there will be no income tax consequences when the taxpayer moves back into the property. This is because during the tenure of the election the taxpayer is *deemed* to be using the property for his own personal use (whether or not the property still qualifies as a principal residence); and when he moves back into the property, he will actually be using it for his own personal use.

(ii) — Timing of Election

An individual can elect subsection 45(2) only in respect of a change of use that occurs when she moves out of the property, that is, when she changes the use from personal to business. A taxpayer who does not make an election on moving out of the residence cannot avoid the resultant deemed disposition, and related tax consequences, on moving back into the property at a later date.

(iii) — Duration

The election continues in effect for up to four years after the year in which the taxpayer moved out or until he rescinds, at which time he is deemed to have disposed of the property.

---

[175]See subs. 45(2), subpara. 54 "principal residence"(b)(i) and para. 54 "adjusted cost base"(d).

(b) — Income-Earning Use to Principal Residence

A taxpayer who converts income property into a principal residence may elect to ignore the change in use if she has not claimed capital cost allowance on the property after 1984. This election allows the taxpayer to defer the recognition of any accrued capital gain on the property, but does not allow the taxpayer to defer recapture of capital cost allowance claimed on the property after 1984.[176]

XI. — Shares Of Small Business Corporations

Capital gains from the disposition of shares of a "qualified small business corporation" are exempt from tax up to a maximum of $800,000 (indexed). A "qualified small business corporation" (QSBC)[177] is defined as a Canadian-controlled private corporation:

> . . . that uses all or most of its assets in an active business carried on primarily in Canada and the assets of which, throughout a period of 24 months immediately preceding the disposition of shares, have not been owned by any person other than the individual who claims the exemption, or by a person or partnership related to him or her.

This exemption encourages risk-taking and stimulates investment in small businesses in Canada by providing an economic stimulus to equity participation and the development of Canadian business enterprises. As the Minister of Finance said when he introduced the exemption in 1985, it is intended to "unleash [the] full entrepreneurial dynamism of individual Canadians."[178]

The exemption is limited on three factors:

- The taxpayer's residence;

- The type of capital property that gives rise to the gain; and

- The net cumulative amount of investment income and financing expenses in the year in which the gain is realized.

The gain is generally restricted to individuals who are resident in Canada.[179] A trust may not claim the exemption, but because a trust is treated as a conduit, it may flow through its capital gains to its beneficiaries by making a special designation.

---

[176]Subss. 45(3), (4).

[177]Subs. 125(7) "Canadian-controlled private corporation"; subs. 248(1) "active business", "small business corporation".

[178]Budget speech, *House of Commons Debates* (23 May 1985) at 5014.

[179]Subs. 110.6(5).

The exemption applies only to "qualified" small business corporation shares.[180] The qualifications concern the control of the corporation, the fair market value of the assets that are attributable to use in an active business, and the carrying on of the active business primarily in Canada. These restrictions target the exemption to restrict the benefits to activities that are likely to stimulate the Canadian economy.

XII. — Capital Losses

A taxpayer's income for a taxation year is determined by aggregating income from each source on a separate basis. As a general rule, capital losses can be used only to offset capital gains.[181] Unused capital losses may, however, be carried forward indefinitely and applied against capital gains in future years; they may also be carried back three years and applied against capital gains reported in those years.[182]

A. — Current Year Losses

(a) — Listed Personal Property Losses

Capital gains and losses from listed personal property ("LPP") are calculated separately from capital gains and losses on all other types of capital properties. A taxpayer is required to include his or her "taxable *net* gain" for the year from dispositions of LPP with his or her capital gains.[183] Losses from dispositions of LPP are deductible only to the extent of gains for the same year from dispositions of LPP. In other words, if LPP losses exceed LPP gains, the excess cannot be deducted in computing the taxpayer's income for that year, even if he or she has other net taxable capital gains from dispositions of other types of capital property. LPP losses may not be deducted from capital gains on non-LPP.

(b) — Allowable Capital Losses

A taxpayer may also deduct his or her allowable capital losses (net of allowable business investment losses) from dispositions of property for the year to the extent of the taxpayer's taxable capital gains from dispositions of property and his or her taxable *net* gain from dispositions of listed personal property.

---

[180]Subs. 110.6(1) "qualified small business corporation share".

[181]Para. 3(b).

[182]Para. 111(1)(b).

[183]Para. 3(b); s. 41.

The effect of these rules is that a taxpayer may deduct his or her allowable capital losses realized on property (other than LPP) from his or her taxable net gains on listed personal property.

(c) — Allowable Business Investment Losses ("ABIL")

(i) — General Comment

A business investment loss is a special type of capital loss that receives preferential treatment for income tax purposes. A business investment loss arises on the disposition of shares or debt of a "small business corporation".[184] An allowable business investment loss is 50 percent of a business investment loss.[185]

Unlike ordinary capital losses, which a taxpayer may deduct only against capital gains, an allowable business investment loss may be deducted against income from any source — for example, from business or property income.

A taxpayer's deduction for business investment losses is restricted if he or she has previously claimed the capital gains exemption.[186]

A business investment loss arises upon the disposition of the shares or debt of a corporation that qualified as a small business corporation *at any time* within the preceding 12 months.[187] The disposition of the shares or debt may be triggered either by an actual disposition (for example, sale or transfer) or through a deemed disposition.[188]

(ii) — "Small Business Corporation"

A "small business corporation" is a Canadian-controlled private corporation that uses all or substantially all (as measured by fair market value) of its assets in an active business in Canada.[189] A corporation may also qualify as a small business corporation if all, or substantially all, of its assets are invested in shares of another small business corporation with which it is connected.

---

[184]Para. 39(1)(c).

[185]Para. 38(c).

[186]Subs. 39(9).

[187]Subs. 248(1) "small business corporation".

[188]See, for example, subs. 50(1).

[189]Subs. 248(1) "small business corporation".

(iii) — Deemed Disposition

A taxpayer is deemed to have disposed of his or her shares of a small business corporation if:

- The corporation is insolvent or bankrupt, or

- At year end, the corporation is insolvent, the FMV of its shares is nil, the corporation (or any corporation that it controls) does not carry on business and it is reasonable to expect that the corporation will be wound up or dissolved.

The term "insolvent" is not defined, but should be interpreted as the inability to pay liabilities as they come due.

B. — Unused Losses

Capital losses that are not deductible in the year in which they are sustained may be "carried over" and deducted in other years. In dealing with capital loss carry-overs, it is important to distinguish between losses from dispositions of listed personal property and losses from dispositions of property other than listed personal property.

(a) — LPP Losses

Where a taxpayer's losses for a year from LPP exceed his or her gains for the year from dispositions of LPP, the excess is the "listed personal property loss" for that year.[190] A listed personal property loss for a particular year can be deducted, in computing the "net gain", only from dispositions of listed personal property for the three preceding and the seven succeeding years.[191]

(b) — Net Capital Losses

Allowable capital losses from dispositions of property other than listed personal property which are not deductible in computing a taxpayer's income in the year in which they are sustained, become part of the taxpayer's "net capital loss".[192] A taxpayer's net capital loss for a year may be carried back and deducted in computing his or her *taxable income* for the three preceding years. Also, subject to certain limitations, the loss may be carried forward

---

[190]Subs. 41(3).

[191]Para. 41(2)(b).

[192]Subs. 111(8) "net capital loss".

indefinitely.[193] In either case, net capital losses may be deducted against only the excess of taxable gains over allowable capital losses of other years.

(i) — Change of Corporate Control

A net capital loss from an earlier year cannot be deducted by a corporation if, before the end of the year, control of the corporation changes hands and the corporation is acquired by a person who did not control it at the time when the net capital loss was sustained. This rule does not generally affect the deductibility of capital losses sustained *in the year* in which control is acquired by the new person or persons.[194]

(ii) — Death

Where a taxpayer dies with unclaimed net capital losses, the losses may be applied as follows:[195]

- Against the taxpayer's net taxable capital gains for the year of death, and

- Against the taxpayer's other sources of income in the year of death or in the immediately preceding year, to the extent that the losses exceed the taxpayer's lifetime capital gains exemption.

Thus, exemptions claimed in respect of capital gains during a taxpayer's lifetime reduce the taxpayer's unused net capital losses on death.

Example

Assume:

Net capital losses carried forward	$ 25,000
Taxable capital gains in year of death	10,000
Allowable capital losses in year of death	4,000
Capital gains exemption claimed during lifetime	15,000

Then, maximum claim in respect of net capital losses in year of death:

Taxable capital gains	$ 10,000
Less: allowable capital losses	(4,000)

---

[193]Para. 111(1)(b).

[194]Subs. 111(4).

[195]Subs. 111(2).

Net taxable capital gains			6,000
Net capital losses	$	25,000	
Prior year gains exemption		(15,000)	
Terminal year gains exemption		(6,000)	
Excess claimable			4,000
Maximum claim		$	10,000

XIII. — Transitional Rules

A. — General Comment

With the introduction of the tax on capital gains as of January 1, 1972, it became necessary to ensure that capital gains and capital losses that had accrued prior to 1972 would not be retroactively taxed. Thus, there are transitional rules to ensure smooth passage from the old system to the new. Although the rationale of the transitional rules is simple, the rules are technically complex. The essential purpose of the transitional rules is to provide a taxpayer with either a deemed cost or deemed proceeds of disposition for the capital property that was owned on December 31, 1971, so that, on selling the property, the taxpayer can calculate any gain or loss from that date.

Generally, the transitional rules apply to capital property that a taxpayer *actually* owned on December 31, 1971. In some cases, however, the person to whom the property is disposed of may be *deemed* to have owned it on December 31, 1971, so that the transitional rules will apply to the taxpayer when disposing of the property. The rules can therefore apply to dispositions of property acquired after 1971. Note, however, that the transitional rules do not apply to the property of a taxpayer who becomes resident in Canada after 1971.[196]

B. — Valuation Day

The concept of Valuation Day value is fundamental to the structure of the transitional rules for capital gains. The Valuation Day value of a capital property is its value at the beginning of the new system, when capital gains were first subjected to tax. The "V-Day value" of a property is its fair market value on Valuation Day, which was December 22, 1971, for publicly-traded shares or securities and December 31, 1971, for all other capital property.[197]

---

[196]ITAR 26(10).

[197]ITAR 24.

The fair market value of publicly-traded securities on Valuation Day is deemed to be the greater of the amount prescribed[198] in respect of the security and the fair market value of the security on December 22, 1971, "as otherwise determined." Any "other determination" of the fair market value of a publicly-traded share or security as at that date must be made by the taxpayer. If this value is greater than the prescribed amount, the taxpayer may use it for the purpose of determining the capital gain or loss realized on the disposition of the security in question.

The Valuation Day value of all other capital properties (i.e., properties other than publicly-traded securities) is their fair market value on December 31, 1971. It is the taxpayer's responsibility to determine this value for the purpose of reporting a capital gain or loss on the disposition of capital property.

C. — Depreciable Property

For depreciable property acquired by a taxpayer before 1972 and owned by him or her continuously since that time, the transitional rules eliminate any capital gain accrued as at December 31, 1971, from the total capital gain realized upon disposition of the property. There is no corresponding rule in respect of a capital loss accrued as at December 31, 1971, because a taxpayer cannot realize a capital loss on depreciable property.[199] Where depreciable property is disposed of in a non-arm's length transaction, the transitional rules preserve the tax-free character of any accrued capital gains.[200]

The transitional rules in respect of depreciable property owned on December 31, 1971 operate by deeming the proceeds of disposition of the property to be the amount determined by the following formula:

Deemed proceeds of disposition=Capital cost+Excess, if any, of actual proceeds of disposition over fair market value on Valuation Day

The transitional rules do not apply if the actual proceeds of disposition of depreciable property do not exceed the capital cost of that property, since, in this instance, a capital gain could not possibly result.

Example

Capital cost to taxpayer T of a depreciable property
acquired by him in 1970: $ 10,000

---

[198]Reg., Sched. VII.

[199]Subpara. 39(1)(b)(i).

[200]ITAR 20(1).

Fair market value of this property on Valuation Day
(December 31, 1971): $ 12,600
Selling price of the property in 1986: $ 17,200
T's deemed proceeds of disposition:
$10,000 + ($17,200 - $12,600) $ 14,600
T's capital gain is therefore:
$14,600 - $10,000 $ 4,600

Arithmetically, the capital gain equals the excess of the actual selling price of the depreciable property over its Valuation Day value, although the gain is not actually computed in this way. The capital gain of $2,600 accrued on the property as at December 31, 1971, is not subject to tax at all but would be added to the pre-1972 capital surplus on hand. In certain circumstances, this amount could be distributed tax-free on a wind-up or dissolution of the corporation. See subs. 88(2.1). Where depreciable property is disposed of after 1971 at a price greater than its original cost but less than its Valuation Day value (e.g., $12,000, in the above illustration), the transitional rules apply in the following manner:

T's deemed proceeds of disposition are:
$10,000 + ($12,000-$12,600) $ 10,000
T's capital gain is $10,000-$10,000 NIL

Since the depreciable property has been disposed of for less than its Valuation Day value, this is the result one would expect.

Notes:

The amount in the brackets cannot be less than zero.

D. — Interest in a Partnership

Transitional rules are also provided for taxpayers who were members of a partnership on December 31, 1971, and have remained so continuously since that date. These rules are provided for the purpose of computing the adjusted cost base of the partnership interest at any time after 1971. These rules affect the amount of the taxable capital gain or allowable capital loss realized by the partner when disposing of the taxpayer's interest.

These transitional rules operate by deeming the partner's cost of the partnership interest to be an amount that is the median[201] of the following three amounts:

1. Its "actual cost" to the partner;

2. His or her share of the partnership's "tax equity", subject to certain adjustments; and

---

[201]If two or more of these amounts are the same, that amount is the median.

3. The fair market value of the partnership interest, again subject to certain adjustments.

The "actual cost" of a partnership interest and the partnership's "tax equity" are both defined amounts, and all three amounts in this formula are determined as of the particular time when the deemed cost is relevant.[202] If two or more of these amounts are the same, then that amount is the median.

E. — Other Capital Property

There are also transitional rules for the purpose of computing the capital gain or loss of capital property other than the two previous examples. The effect of these rules is to deem a cost to be the taxpayer's adjusted cost base of capital property owned. The capital gain or loss of the property is then computed on the basis of this deemed cost.

There are two distinct methods of determining the deemed cost. The first of these methods is the "median rule" or "tax-free zone" method. This method applies automatically to capital property that was owned on December 31, 1971, by *any taxpayer*. The second method, known as the "Valuation Day value election", is available only to *individuals* (including trusts), and applies only to capital property *actually* owned on December 31, 1971.[203]

For individuals, the two methods for determining the deemed cost of capital property owned on December 31, 1971, are mutually exclusive alternatives. Thus an individual *either* uses the tax-free zone method to determine the deemed cost of *each and every* item of capital property that he or she owned on December 31, 1971, or makes the Valuation Day value election, in which case the taxpayer must use this method to determine the deemed cost of *each and every* item of capital property that he or she actually owned on December 31, 1971.

---

[202]ITAR 26(9)–(9.4).

[203]The tax-free zone method cannot then be used in respect of any of these properties, although it must still be used in respect of any "other capital property" that the individual taxpayer making the Valuation Day value election did not actually own on December 31, 1971, but that he is deemed by the Act to have owned on that date.

(a) — Median Rule or Tax-Free Zone Method

The median rule (tax-free zone) method operates by deeming a taxpayer's initial cost of capital property that he or she owned on December 31, 1971, to be the amount that is the median of the following three amounts:[204]

1. Its actual cost (or, if the property is an "obligation," its "amortized cost") to him or her on January 1, 1972;

2. Its fair market value on Valuation Day; and

3. The proceeds of disposition of the property, subject to certain adjustments, which are described below.

If two or more of these amounts are the same, that amount is the median.

If a particular item of capital property has been owned continuously since December 31, 1971, and it is necessary to compute its adjusted cost base at a point in time *before* it is disposed of (in which case there would be no actual proceeds of disposition), the median rule is applied by deeming the proceeds of disposition of the particular property to be its fair market value at that time.[205]

The adjustments to the proceeds of disposition of the property can be summarized as follows:

- *Add* amounts that will be deducted from the deemed cost in computing the adjusted cost base of the particular property.

- *Deduct* amounts that will be added to the deemed cost in computing the adjusted cost base of the particular property.

These adjustments are necessary for the purpose of applying the median rule to avoid double-counting of the additions and deductions that are made in computing the adjusted cost base of the property under section 53.

"Proceeds of disposition" in this context means gross proceeds before the deduction of any outlays or expenses incurred for the purpose of making the disposition. Therefore, a capital loss equal to the amount of these outlays and expenses may be realized if the deemed cost of a particular property equals the proceeds of disposition.

Example

Assume:

---

[204]ITAR 26(3).

[205]ITAR 26(4).

The actual cost of a capital property that was owned on December 31, 1971 is $4,000. Its Valuation Day value is $8,000. The proceeds of disposition of the property before deducting the sales commission of $800 are $8,000.

Then:

Applying the median rule, the deemed cost of the property is $8,000.

Proceeds of disposition		$	8,000
Deduct:			
Deemed cost	$ 8,000		
Sales commission	800		(8,800)
Capital loss		$	(800)

(b) — Valuation Day Value Election

As its name implies, the "Valuation Day value" election allows a taxpayer to determine the cost of each capital property (other than depreciable property and partnership interests) *actually* owned by the taxpayer on December 31, 1971, as its value on Valuation Day. This alternative method is administratively convenient: it provides individuals with a deemed cost for every capital property that they actually owned at the start of the new system, and accommodates taxpayers who have not maintained a record of the actual cost of their properties.[206]

XIV. — Anti-Avoidance Provisions

Several anti-avoidance provisions prevent or discourage taxpayers from artificially converting fully taxable income into income that is either non-taxable or taxable at a lower rate. Some of these provisions are quite specific and narrow in scope. For example, the rules in respect of "superficial losses" are directed squarely at preventing the creation of capital losses by transferring and immediately reacquiring properties.[207] The following additional provisions should be noted:

Subs. 55(2)	Specific provision to prevent "capital gains strips";
S. 84.1	Designed to prevent surplus stripping;
Part II.1 Tax	Prevent conversion of proceeds of disposition into exempt capital gains;

---

[206]ITAR 26(7); *Knight v. Minister of National Revenue*, [1984] C.T.C. 2643, 84 D.T.C. 1586 (T.C.C.) (failure to elect V-Day value "in prescribed manner" results in automatic application of median rule).

[207]Subpara. 40(2)(g)(i), s. 54 "superficial loss".

Subs. 110.6(7)	Intended to prevent conversion of taxable capital gains of corporations into exempt capital gains of individuals;
Subss. 110.6(8), (9)	Intended to prevent the conversion of dividend income into exempt capital gains of individuals; and
S. 245	General anti-avoidance provision ("GAAR").

Comprehensive Examples

Capital Gain or Loss of Listed Personal Properties

Assume:

A taxpayer sells the following listed personal properties in the years (all of which are subsequent to 1971) indicated:

Year	Property	ACB	Proceeds
1	A print	$ 600	$ 4,000
	A coin	1,500	600
2	A rare book	8,000	4,000
	A painting	2,000	2,500
3	Jewelry	500	2,500

Then net gain from the above is as follows:

		Actual		Deemed		

Year 1

PRINT:

		Actual		Deemed		
Proceeds		$	4,000	$	4,000	
ACB			(600)		(1,000)	
Gain						$ 3,000

COIN:

		Actual		Deemed		
Proceeds		$	600	$	1,000	
ACB			(1,500)		(1,500)	
Loss						(500)
Gain						$ 2,500
Loss carryback from Year 2						(2,500)

NET GAIN   NIL

Year 2

		Actual	Deemed	
BOOK:				
	Proceeds	$ 4,000	$ 4,000	
	ACB	(8,000)	(8,000)	
	Loss			$ (4,000)
PAINTING:				
	Proceeds	$ 2,500		
	ACB	(2,000)		
	Gain			500
	Loss			(3,500)
	Loss carryback to Year 1			2,500
NET GAIN				NIL
Year 3				
JEWELLERY:				
	Proceeds	$ 2,500	$ 2,500	
	ACB	(500)	(1,000)	
	Gain			$ 1,500
	Loss carry forward from Year 2			(1,000)
NET GAIN				$ 500

Capital Gain or Loss Where Replacement of Property

Assume:

X Ltd. owns a building to which the following data applies:

Cost	$	200,000
UCC	$	50,000

The building is expropriated under statutory authority, and X Ltd. is paid $250,000. In the same taxation year, X Ltd. acquires a substitute building in the same vicinity. The cost of the replacement property is $400,000. X Ltd. makes an election under subsection 13(4).

Then:

(a)   *Election under subsection 13(4):*

Proceeds otherwise determined minus, lesser of:	$	200,000
(i) $200,000 - 50,000 = $150,000		
(ii) $400,000		(150,000)
Elected proceeds of disposition		50,000
UCC		(50,000)

	Recapture of CCA		NIL
	Deemed capital cost of replacement of property	$	350,000
	Less: Amount of CCA deferred		(150,000)
	Deemed UCC of replacement of property	$	200,000
(b)	*Election under subsection 44(1):*		
	Proceeds of disposition	$	250,000
	Less: ACB		(200,000)
	(A) Capital gain otherwise determined	$	50,000
	Proceeds of disposition	$	250,000
	Exceeds:		
	Capital cost of replacement		400,000
	(B) Amount determined		NIL
	Capital gain (lesser of (A) and (B))		NIL
(c)	*Capital cost of replacement property:*		
	Actual capital cost of replacement property	$	400,000
	Less: capital gain deferred		(50,000)
	Deemed capital cost of replacement property	$	350,000

Notes:

Paragraph 44(1)(f).

Selected Bibliography to Chapter 11

General

Allan, J.R., et al., "The Effects of Tax Reform and Post Reform Changes in the Federal Personal Income Tax, 1972–75" (1978) 26 Can. Tax J. 1.

Barbacki, Richard, "Use It or Lose It?" (July 1989) 122 CA Magazine 43.

Bernstein, Jack, "Tax Planning for Holding Canadian Real Estate" (1984) 3:8 *Ont. Lawyers Wkly.* 8.

Binavince, E., "The Taxation of Capital Gains and Losses: General Principles," in Hansen, Krishna and Rendall, eds., *Canadian Taxation* (Toronto: De Boo, 1981) p. 297.

Bird, Richard M., "Capital Gains Taxation in Canada: A Review of a Review," in *Proceedings of 31st Tax Conf.* 525 (Can. Tax Foundation, 1980).

Birnie, David A.G., "Shareholders' Buy-Sell Agreements: Some New Opportunities," in *Proceedings of 38th Tax Conf.* 13 (Can. Tax Foundation, 1986).

Boehmer, G.C., "Personal Tax Planning — Small Business Corporations — Capital Gains Planning Opportunities and Pitfalls" (1987) 35 Can. Tax J. 987.

Boehmer, G.C., "Small Business Corporations: Capital Gains Planning Opportunities and Pitfalls" (1987) 35 Can. Tax J. 987.

Bossons, John, "Economic Effects of the Capital Gains Tax" (1981) 29 Can. Tax J. 809.

Bossons, John, "Implementing Capital Gains Reforms" (1979) 27 Can. Tax J. 145.

Broadway, Robin W., and Harry M. Kitchen, "Canadian Tax Policy," *Tax Paper No. 63* (Canadian Tax Foundation, 1980) at 71–77.

Bucovetsky, Meyer W., "Inflation and the Personal Tax Base: The Capital Gains Issue" (1977) 25 Can. Tax J. 77.

Colley, G.M., "Capital Gains Tax — A Perspective" (1981) 14 CA Magazine 63.

Corn, George, "Taxation of Gain on Appreciation of Shares: Capital Gain or Income from an Adventure in the Nature of Trade" (1994) 4 Can. Current Tax J39.

Crawford, R.W., "Sales of Real Estate: Tax Planning for the Seller," *Corporate Management Tax Conf.* 138 (Can. Tax Foundation, 1983).

Cullity, Maurice C., "The Capital Gains Exemption: Implications for Estate Planning," in *Proceedings of 37th Tax Conf.* 18 (Can. Tax Foundation, 1985).

Daly, Michael J., et al., "Toward a Neutral Capital Income Tax System" (1986) 34 Can. Tax J. 1331.

Daly, Michael J., et al., "The Taxation of Income from Capital in Canada: An International Comparison" (1987) 35 Can. Tax J. 88.

Davies, James B., and France St-Hilaire, *Reforming Capital Income Taxation in Canada: Efficiency and Distributional Effects of Alternative Options* (Economic Council of Canada, 1987).

Dean, Jacklyn I., "The January 15, 1987 Draft Amendments Relating to the Acquisition of Gains and Losses," *Corporate Management Tax Conf.* 2:1 (Can. Tax Foundation, 1987).

Drache, A.B.C., "Real Estate Capital Gains Change Raises Strategic Questions" (1992) 14 Can. Taxpayer 21.

Durnford, John W., "Profits on the Sale of Shares: Capital Gains or Business Income? A Fresh Look at Irrigation Industries" (1987) 35 Can. Tax J. 837.

Ewens, Douglas S., "The Capital Gains Exemption and the Butterfly" (1986) 34 Can. Tax J. 914.

James, Larry W., "Capital Gains Exemption, Planning Techniques," in *Proceedings of 38th Tax Conf.* 33 (Can. Tax Foundation, 1986).

James, Larry W., "Disposing of Real Estate", *Corporate Management Tax Conf.* 5:1 (Can. Tax Foundation, 1989).

Jordan, Barbara Ann, "An Economic Evaluation of the Tax Treatment of Capital Gains in Canada" (microform) (Ottawa: National Library of Canada, 1987).

Kellough, Howard J., and K. Travers Pullen, "Planning for the Lifetime Capital Gains Exemption" (1986) 3 Bus. & L. 3.

Kirby, F.P., "The Capital Gains Exemption: Other Than Qualified Small Business Shares," in *Proceedings of 40th Tax Conf.* 30:1 (Can. Tax Foundation, 1988).

Krishna, V., *The Taxation of Capital Gains* (Toronto: Butterworths, 1983).

Kroft, Edwin G., and Bruce W. Aunger, "Some Issues Relating to the Taxation of Insider Trading Transactions — Comments on Interpretation Bulletin IT-479" (1983) 31 Can. Tax J. 763.

Lawlor, William R.G., "Surplus Stripping and Other Planning Opportunities With the New $500,000 Capital Gains Exemption," in *Proceedings of 37th Tax Conf.* 8 (Can. Tax Foundation, 1985).

Maloney, Maureen A., "Capital Gains Taxation: Marching (Oh So Slowly) into the Future" (1988) 17 Man. L. J. 299.

Mayhall, "Capital Gains Taxation — The First One Hundred Years" (1980) 41 L.A. L. Rev. 81.

Messere, Kenneth C., "Capital Gains and Related Taxation in OECD Member Countries," in *Proceedings of 31st Tax Conf.* 505 (Can. Tax Foundation, 1980).

Mida, Israel H., *Capital Gains and the May 1985 Federal Budget* (C.C.H. Can., 1986).

Perry, David B., "Importance of Capital Gains and Losses in the Personal Income Tax System (The)" (1984) 32 Can. Tax J. 178.

Perry, David B., "Selected Statistics on the Evolution of the Personal Income Tax System Since 1970" (1987) 35 Can. Tax J. 207.

Quinton, Cathy, "The Additional Capital Gains Exemption" (December-January 1989) 62 CMA Magazine 47.

Richards, Gabrielle M.R., "Proceeds of Disposition of Property" (1986) 1 Can. Current Tax J-164.

Richards, Gabrielle M.R., "Quick Flips: Capital Gains or Income Treatment?" (1991) 3 Can. Current Tax C57.

Richards, Gabrielle M.R., "The Timing of Dispositions of Property" (1986) 1 Can. Current Tax C-131.

Richardson, Elinore J., "Holding Real Estate for the Production of Income," *Corporate Management Tax Conf.* 1 (Can. Tax Foundation, 1983).

Rotenberg, Charles M., "Making the Deal Work" (1991) 13 Can. Taxpayer 60.

Ruby, Stephen S., "A Glimpse at the Lifetime Capital Gains Exemption (Part I)" (1986) 3:12 Bus. & L. 93.

Ruby, Stephen S., "A Glimpse at the Lifetime Capital Gains Exemption (Part III)" (1987) 4:1 Bus. & L. 6.

Sauve, Marc, *L'imposition des gains en capital et l'égalité fiscale* (Université de Montréal, Faculté de droit, 1987).

Sheppard, Anthony F., "Capital Gains: Twenty Years Later a Buck is Still Not a Buck" in *The Quest for Tax Reform: The Royal Ciommission on Taxation Twenty Years Later* (Toronto: Carswell, 1988).

Silver, Sheldon, "Capital Gains," in *Proceedings of 23rd Tax Conf.* 68 (Can. Tax Foundation, 1971).

Stack, Thomas J., "Capital Gains and Losses on Shares of Private Corporations," in *Proceedings of 39th Tax Conf.* 17:1 (Can. Tax Foundation, 1987).

Tam, Anthony, "Capital Gains Exemption: Small Business Corporations" (1987–89) 2 Can. Current Tax P-5.

Tax Treatment of Real Estate Gains: Working Group Report (Toronto: Fair Tax Commission, 1992).

Thompson, A.E.J., and B.R. Sinclair, "Capital Gains" (1985) 13 Can. Tax News 81.

Walker, Michael A., "Perspectives on Capital Gains Taxation," in *Proceedings of 31st Tax Conf.* 535 (Can. Tax Foundation, 1980).

Ward, David A., and John M. Ulmer, "Corporate Taxation: Shares Eligible for the Capital Gains Exemption" (1986) 5 Legal Alert 81.

Warnock, Bruce A., "Income or Capital Gains on Dispositions of Property" in *Proceedings of 42nd Tax Conf.* 48:1 (Can. Tax Found., 1990).

Watchuk, Jeanne, "Are Gains on SRTC Debt Flips Capital or Income? Two Opposing Opinions" (1990) 38 Can. Tax J. 380.

Zinn, J.A., "The Taxation of Capital Gains: Selected Topics" (1981) Can. Taxation 363.

Capital Property

Drache, A.B.C., "Real Estate Capital Gains Change Raises Strategic Questions" (1992) 14 Can. Taxpayer 21.

Goodman, Wolfe D., "Charitable Gifts of Appreciated Capital Property" (1986) 8 Estates and Trusts J. 189.

Williamson, W. Gordon, "Transfers of Assets to and from a Canadian Corporation," in *Proceedings of 38th Conf.* 12 (Can. Tax Foundation, 1986).

Computation of Capital Gain or Loss

Corn, G., "Capital Gains — Calculation of Proceeds of Disposition" (1984) 1 Can. Current Tax J-24.

Dzau, Vivien, "Reserves: A Tool for Deferring Taxes" (1980) 113 CA Magazine 57.

Krishna, Vern, "Reserves" (1984) 1 Can. Current Tax J-41.

Nitikman, Bert W., "Reserves," in *Proceedings of 25th Tax Conf.* 355 (Can. Tax Foundation, 1973).

Rotenberg, Charles M., "Making the Deal Work" (1991) 13 Can. Taxpayer 60.

Stack, Thomas J., "Capital Gains and Losses on Shares of Private Corporations" in *Proceedings of 39th Tax Conf.* 17:1 (Can. Tax Foundation 1987).

Webb, K., "Escalator Clauses, Earn-Outs and Reserves," in *Proceedings of 26th Tax Conf.* 55 (Can. Tax Foundation, 1974).

Dispositions

Alliston, Paul F., "Rental of Real Estate" (1976) 109 CA Magazine 57.

Arnold, Brian J., "An Analysis of the Amendments to the FAPI and Foreign Affiliate Rules" (1983) 31 Can. Tax J. 183.

Arnold, Brian J., "Conversions of Property to and from Inventory: Tax Consequences" (1976) 24 Can. Tax J. 231.

Arnold, Brian J., and David A. Ward, "Dispositions — A Critique of Revenue Canada's Interpretation" (1980) 28 Can. Tax J. 559.

Beam, Robert E., and Stanley N. Laiken, "Personal Tax Planning — Changes in Use and Non-Arm's-Length Transfers of Depreciable Property" (1987) 35 Can. Tax J. 453.

Bittker, "Capital Gains and Losses — The 'Sale' or 'Exchange' Requirements" (1981) 32 Hastings L.J. 743.

Brown, R.D., "Can You Take It With You?" (1972) 20 Can. Tax J. 470.

Chapman, "The Time of Sale Under the *Internal Revenue Code*" (1964) 22 N.Y.U. Tax Inst. 139.

Corn, George, "Capital Gains — Calculation of Proceeds of Disposition" (1984) Can. Current Tax J-24.

Denega, M.A., "The Migrating Executive: Leaving Canada and Working Abroad", *Corp. Management Tax Conf.* 189 (Can. Tax Foundation, 1979).

Drache, A.B.C., "Foreign Exchange" (1979) 1 Can. Taxpayer 52.

Drache, A.B.C., "Real Estate Capital Gains Change Raises Strategic Questions" (1992) 14 Can. Taxpayer 21.

Ewens, Douglas S., "When Is a 'Disposition'?" in *Proceedings of 26th Tax Conf.* 515 (Can. Tax Foundation, 1974).

Goodison, Don, "Tax Forum — Not a Threat" (1990) 24 CGA Magazine 19.

Kroft, Edwin G., and Bruce W. Aunger, "Disposition of Canadian Securities" (1983) 31 Can. Tax J. 763.

Masson, Guy, et al., "The Expatriate's Departure," *Can. Tax Letter*, August 18, 1980 (De Boo).

Matheson, David I., "Taxation of Investments in Commodities Futures, Precious Metals, Options, Objects of Art, Foreign Exchange and Other Exotica," in *Proceedings of 27th Tax Conf.* 918 (Can. Tax Foundation, 1975).

Middleton, David W., "Tax Implications of Departure From Canada" (1983) 116 CA Magazine 44.

Richards, Gabrielle M.R., "Proceeds of Disposition of Property" (1986) 1 Can. Current Tax J-164.

Richards, Gabrielle M.R., "The Timing of Dispositions of Property" (1986) 1 Can. Current Tax C-131.

Richardson, Elinore, "Currency Swaps — A Canadian Perspective" (1984) 32 Can. Tax J. 345.

Tkachenko, Lorissa V., "Expropriations: The Income Tax Aspects" (1985) 33 Can. Tax J. 1.

White, Michael J., "Isolated Foreign Currency Transactions and Foreign Exchange Contracts," in *Proceedings of 30th Tax Conf.* 490 (Can. Tax Foundation, 1978).

Adjusted Cost Base

Champagne, Donald C., "Bad and Doubtful Debts, Mortgage Foreclosures and Conditional Sales Repossessions," in *Proceedings of 27th Tax Conf.* 682 (Can. Tax Foundation, 1975).

Corn, George, "Computation of Adjusted Cost Base of Shares" (December 1990) 3:12 Can. Current Tax J-59.

Couzin, Robert, "Of Arm's Length and Not Dealing Threat" (1978) 26 Can. Tax J. 271.

Crawford, William E., "Taxation of Land Developers," *Corporate Management Tax Conf.* 75 (Can. Tax Foundation, 1977).

Farwell, Peter M., "Debts and Capital Gains Taxation" (1972) 20 Can. Tax J. 101.

Goldspink, Tom, and David Allgood, "Tax Treatment of Personal Guarantees" (1983) 31 Can. Tax J. 1042.

Hogg, R.D., "Stock Option Benefits in Canadian-Controlled Private Corporations" (1978) 26 Can. Tax J. 85.

Riehl, Gordon W., et al., "Intercompany Non-Arm's Length Transactions — Income Tax Consequences," in *Proceedings of 26th Tax Conf.* 102 (Can. Tax Foundation, 1974).

Smith, David W., "Transferring the Family Business" (1979) 27 Can. Tax J. 1.

Stikeman, H.H., ed. "Stock Dividends," *Can. Tax Letter*, October 30, 1975 (De Boo).

Zinn, John A., "The Taxation of Capital Gains: Selected Topics," in Hansen, Krishna & Rendall, eds. *Canadian Taxation* (Toronto: De Boo, 1981).

Personal-Use Property

Arbuckle, J.E., "Investment in Art — For Pleasure and Profit" (1980) 54 Cost & Mgmt. 46.

Bernstein, J., "Investing in Art and Other Collectibles," in *Proceedings of 35th Tax Conf.* 124 (Can. Tax Foundation, 1983).

Dewling, A.M., "Intergenerational Transfers of Personal-use Property" (1989) 37 Can. Tax J. 1292.

Drache, A.B.C., "Real Estate Capital Gains Change Raises Strategic Questions" (1992) 14 Can. Taxpayer 21.

Edwards, S.E., "Personal Investments," (1986) Special Lectures LSUC 221.

Feingold, Fred, and Marlene F. Schwartz, "Source of Income from Sales of Personal Property" (1987) 35 Can. Tax J. 473.

Rotenberg, Charles M., "Inflation and Personal Property" (1980) 2 Can. Taxpayer 37.

Strother, Robert C., "Income Tax Implications of Personal-Use Real Estate," *Corporate Management Tax Conf.* 59 (Can. Tax Foundation, 1983).

Identical Properties

Lynch, John H., "Income Splitting Among Family Members," in *Proceedings of 32nd Tax Conf.* 752 (Can. Tax Foundation, 1980).

McDonnell, T.E.J., "Capital Gains: Tax Planning for the Individual" (1972) 20 Can. Tax J. 382.

Losses Deemed to be Nil

Brown, Robert D., and Thomas E. McDonnell, "Capital Gains Strips," in *Proceedings of 32nd Tax Conf.* 51 (Can. Tax Foundation, 1980).

Burpee, Thomas R., "Utilization of Tax Losses: A Reasonable Expectation of Profit," in *Proceedings of 37th Tax Conf.* 32:1 (Canadian Tax Foundation, 1985).

Drache, A.B.C., "Superficial Gains" (1980) 2 Can. Taxpayer 17.

Grover, Warren, "Superficial Losses" (1974) 22 Can. Tax J. 253.

Huggett, Donald R. (ed.) "Restrictions on Loss Transfers" (1987) 14:8 Can. Tax News 87.

Income Tax, Capital Gains Strips (Audio Archives of Canada, 1984).

Kirkpatrick, Paul K., "Tax Consequences of a Corporation Dealing in its Own Stock" (1964) 13 Tulane Tax Ins. 85.

Riehl, Gordon W., "Debt Instruments," in *Proceedings of 27th Tax Conf.* 764 (Can. Tax Foundation, 1975).

Stewart, E.C., "Capital Gains Considerations" (1974) 48 Cost & Mgmt. 45.

Sweet, David G., "Capital Losses," in *Proceedings of 24th Tax Conf.* 348 (Can. Tax Foundation, 1972).

Watts, David E., "Recognition of Gain or Loss to a Corporation on a Distribution of Property in Exchange for its own Stock" (1968) 22 Tax Lawyer 161.

Zimmer, Henry B., "Using Your Losses" (1974) 104 CA Magazine 58.

Principal Residence

Bergen, Rodney C., "The Tax Treatment of Principal Residences: An Update" in *Proceedings of 44th Tax Conf.* 12:1 (Can. Tax Found., 1992).

Boivin, Marc, "La 'résidence principale' lors d'un déménagement," *Recueil de fiscalité*, AQPFS, vol. 83-2, 151.

Drache, A.B.C., "The Best Investment" (1991) 13 Can. Taxpayer 134.

Drache, A.B.C., "Buying Your Student a Home" (1991) 13 Can. Taxpayer 115.

Freedman, Martin H., "The Home Owner," in *Proceedings of 25th Tax Conf.* 224 (Can. Tax Foundation, 1973); reprinted and revised in *Butterworth's Canadian Income Tax Revised* 9:5.

Fulton, Patricia, "Tax Preferences for Housing: Is There a Case for Reform?", in Thirsk and Whalley (eds.) "Tax Policy Options in the 1980s", *Tax Paper No. 66* (Can. Tax Foundation, 1982) 73.

Goldstein, D.L., "Capital Gain — Whether the Principle Residence Exemption may be taken on a Gain brought in from a Reserve" (1987) 37 Can. Tax J. 1522.

Goodison, Don, "Tax Forum — Necessary Excess" (1991) 25 CGA Magazine 14.

Gray, W.D., "When Does Land in Excess of One-half Hectare From Part of a Principal Residence?" (1989) 37 Can. Tax J. 113.

Harris, Edwin C., "A Case Study in Tax Reform: The Principal Residence" (1983) 7 Dal. L.J. 169.

Kehler, J.A., "Capitalizing on a Change of Residence or in its Use" (1985) 118 CA Magazine 12:52.

McGregor, G., "Principal Residence: Some Problems" (1973) 21 Can. Tax J. 116.

Moore, D.H., "Does a 'Principal Residence' Include Separate Buildings" (1987) 35 Can. Tax J. 702.

"Personal Tax Planning — The Principal Residence Designation Decision: The New Complexity" (1984) 32 Can. Tax J. 572.

Rotenberg, Charles M., "My Second Home" (1983) 5 Can. Taxpayer 199.

Shead, Richard G., "The Current Status of Real Estate as a Tax Shelter," in *Proceedings of 38th Tax Conf.* 48 (Can. Tax Foundation, 1986).

Simmons, Howard S., *The Family Home and Income Tax* (Toronto: Carswell, 1986).

Strother, Robert C., "Income Tax Implications of Personal-Use Real Estate," *Corporate Management Tax Conf.* 59 (Can. Tax Foundation, 1983).

Thomas, R.B., "Associated Corporations; Principal Residence," in *Proceedings of 35th Tax Conf.* 689 (Can. Tax Foundation, 1983).

William, "Private Residence: Tax Incidence and Exemptions" (1977) 41 Convey. & Prop. Lawyer 389.

Capital Losses

Arnold, Brian J., and D. Keith McNair, "The Stop-Loss Rule in Subsection 97(3): An Analysis" (1980) 28 Can. Tax J. 131.

Burpee, Thomas R., "Utilization of Tax Losses: A Reasonable Expectation of Profit," in *Proceedings of 37th Tax Conf.* 32:1 (Canadian Tax Foundation, 1985).

Cadesky, Michael, "Corporate Losses," in *Proceedings of 42nd Tax Conf.* 19:1 (Can. Tax Foundation, 1990).

Conkwright, Glen E., "The Utilization of Losses in Corporate Groups and Further Relief that Might be Taken," in *Proceedings of 31st Tax Conf.* 316 (Can. Tax Foundation, 1979).

Drache, A.B.C., "Corporate Loss Strategies" (1991) 13 Can. Taxpayer 70.

Drache, A.B.C., "New Treatment for Losses" (1983) 5 Can. Taxpayer 183.

Eaton, K.E., "The Death of the 'Profit Earning Process Test'" (1957) 5 Can. Tax J. 271.

Farwell and Mathew, "The Costs of Corporate Complexity" (1979) 112 CA Magazine 28.

Hirsch, Morley P., "The Corporate Loss Transfer System," in *Proceedings of 37th Tax Conf.* 31:1 (Canadian Tax Foundation, 1985).

Kleinman, Robert A. and Jeffrey Gerstein, "Planning to Maximize the Eligibility and Utilization of Capital Losses for Individuals" (1993) 41 Can. Tax J. 324.

Nowoselski, Barry, "Should You Buy or Sell a Company for Its Tax-Loss Carry-overs?" (1983) 116 CA Magazine 64.

Reid, Robert J., "Capital and Non-Capital Losses," in *Proceedings of 42nd Tax Conf.* 20:2 (Can. Tax Foundation, 1990).

Silver, Sheldon, "Utilization of Real Estate Losses," *Corporate Management Tax Conf.* 91 (Can. Tax Foundation, 1983).

Stacey, John A., "The Treatment of Losses," in *Proceedings of 35th Tax Conf.* 29 (Can. Tax Foundation, 1983).

Sweet, David G., "Capital Losses," in *Proceedings of 24th Tax Conf.* 348 (Can. Tax Foundation, 1972).

Wraggett, Cathy, "Accelerated Deduction of Business Losses" (1990) 64 CMA Magazine 33.

Zimmer, Henry B., "Using Your Losses" (1974) 104 CA Magazine 58.

Transitional Rules

Cadesky, Michael, "Corporate Losses," in *Proceedings of 42nd Tax Conf.* 19:1 (Can. Tax Foundation, 1990).

Reid, Robert J., "Capital and Non-Capital Losses," in *Proceedings of 42nd Tax Conf.* 20:2 (Can. Tax Foundation, 1990).

Wise, Richard M., "The V-Day Value of Publicly Traded Shares" (1980) 28 Can. Tax J. 253.

Anti-Avoidance Provisions

Goodison, Don, "Tax Forum — Not a Threat" (1990) 24 CGA Magazine 19.

Lahmer, Craig, "New Measures Against Tax Avoidance Transactions" in *Proceedings of 40th Tax Conf.* 19:1 (Can. Tax Found., 1988).

Templeton, Wendy, "Anti-Avoidance and the Capital Gains Exemption" (1986) 34 Can. Tax J. 203.

Other

Attridge, Ian, "Create Conservation Gains, Not Capital Gains" (1994) 19 Intervenor No. 6 8.

Ballon, Naomi L., "Section 68: Judicial Deference?" (1989) 2 Can. Current Tax P67.

Campbell, Ian R., "Valuation-related Issues: Tax Planning and Post-transaction Follow-up" in *Proceedings of 45th Tax Conf.* 40:1 (Can. Tax Found., 1993).

Drache, A.B.C., "Stock Dividends: Beneficial to the Few" (1981) 3 Can. Taxpayer 99.

Hanson, Suzanee I.R., "Planning for a Share Sale" in *Proceedings of 44th Tax Conf.* 27:1 (Can. Tax Foundation 1992).

Hayos, Gabriel J., "The Capital Gains Exemption: Planning Strategies to Meet the Criterial of a 'Qualified Small Business Corporation'" in *Proceedings of 40th Tax Conf.* 15:1 (Can. Tax Foundation 1988).

Krishna, Vern, "Using the Capital Gains Exemption for Matrimonial Settlement" (1993) 4 Can. Current Tax C5.

Peters, Steven, "Enhancing the Exemption" (1992) 125 CA Mag. No. 5 33.

Potvin, Jean, "The Capital Gains Deduction for Qualified Small Business Corporation Shares Revisited" in *Proceedings of 44th Tax Conf.* 5:50 (Can. Tax Foundation 1992).

Sapona, Ingrid, "Canada's Tax Treaties: A Comparison of the Treatment of Capital Gains" (1992) 40 Can. Tax J. 720.

Silver, Sheldon, "Estate Freezing With Discretion" (1978) 26 Can. Tax J. 705.

Stewart, Donald A.C., "Stock Option Plans: Bright Past, Dim Future" (1972) 20 Can. Tax J. 299.

Tam, Anthony, "Capital Gains Exemption: Small Business Corporations" (1987–89) Can. Current Tax P5.

Wise, Richard M., "Fair Market Determinations — A Few More Requirements" (1983) 31 Can. Tax J. 337.

Chapter 12 — Other Income and Deductions

Table of Contents

Table of Contents

I. — General Comment on Income

We have examined the rules governing the computation of income from the following specifically identified sources — office, employment, business, property and capital gains. Income and losses from these named sources enter into the computation of total income according to the sequence and manner set out in section 3. There are, however, certain types of income and deductions that one cannot identify as originating from, or relating to, these named sources.

The concept of income for tax purposes is less comprehensive than it is in economics. In particular, Anglo-Canadian tax law requires all income must have a source. The source theory does not, however, conveniently embrace all receipts — for example, gifts, windfall gains, and inheritances. Similarly, there are various deductions that cannot be identified with the named sources of income.

The taxable base should be broad and inclusive if we use it as the measure of a taxpayer's ability to pay. Thus, section 56 of the Act brings into income a variety of receipts that one may not necessarily include through one of the named sources of income. It is, however, important to note the opening words of section 56: *"Without restricting the generality of section 3*, there *shall* be included in computing the income of a taxpayer for a taxation year. . . ."* [Emphasis added.] Section 56 does not curtail the scope of section 3. Income from a source inside or outside Canada — that is, income from *any* source regardless of location — is included in section 3. This scope is reinforced in section 3, which provides that the named sources in that section are not to be read as an exhaustive or a restrictive list of the sources of income.

Section 56 contains a list of items to be included in income. To be included, the taxpayer must receive the amount as, or on account of, or in lieu of payment of, or in satisfaction of the items listed in para. 56(1)(a). In this chapter we look at the following:

- Pension benefits;
- Death benefits;
- Support payments;
- Indirect payments;
- Retiring allowances;
- Scholarships, bursaries, and fellowships;
- Research grants;
- Prizes; and
- Social assistance payments.

Income from the above is reportable on the cash, rather than accrual, basis.[1]

II. — Pension Benefits

Employer contributions to employee registered pension plans are not taxable as employment-source income.[2] Within specified limits, employees can also deduct contributions to a registered pension fund or plan.[3]

---

[1]*Robwaral Ltd. v. Minister of National Revenue*, [1960] C.T.C. 16 (Can. Ex. Ct.); affirmed [1964] S.C.R. vi (S.C.C.) (Dividend taxable when paid and not when declared).

[2]Subpara. 6(1)(a)(i); subs. 248(1) "superannuation or pension benefit".

[3]Para. 8(1)(m).

Pension benefits from a pension plan (not including benefits from an employee benefit plan) are taxable upon their withdrawal from the plan and are included in income in the year that the taxpayer receives the payment.[4]

An employee must include all pension benefits in income as he or she receives them. This is so whether the payments are under a formal registered plan, an unregistered plan, lump sum, or periodic. Pensions and supplementary pensions received under the *Old Age Security Act* and the *Canada Pension Plan* are also taxable as income.[5]

An individual is taxable on all receipts from a superannuation or pension plan, whether it is registered or not. Registration is of importance only in determining the deductibility of contributions to a plan; it has no bearing on the taxability of receipts out of a plan.

The source of a pension is also irrelevant to its inclusion in income. All pension income is taxable when received by a taxpayer resident in Canada. Hence, in the absence of special provisions in a tax treaty,[6] a foreign taxpayer who takes up residence in Canada is liable to tax on his or her pension income. This is so even though the taxpayer may not have been entitled to a deduction at the time that he or she contributed to the pension plan.[7]

III. — Death Benefits

A payment on account of a death benefit is included in income in the year of receipt. A "death benefit" is a payment made upon the death of an employee in recognition of service in an office or employment. A death benefit to an employee's spouse is tax-free to a maximum of $10,000.[8]

IV. — Support Payments

The statutory provisions in respect of spousal support payments are divided into two segments: (1) receipts are included in income under subdivision d; (2) deductions are permitted under subdivision e. The inclusion and deduction provisions are mirror images of each

---

[4]Subpara. 56(1)(a)(i); *Muller v. Minister of National Revenue* (1960), 26 Tax A.B.C. 295, 61 D.T.C. 246 (Can. Tax App. Bd.) (pension does not have to be related to an office or employment to be taxed).

[5]Equivalent payments under Quebec plans are also included in the taxpayer's income.

[6]See, for example, Article XVIII in the *Canada-U.S. Tax Treaty*.

[7]*R. v. Herman*, [1978] C.T.C. 442, 78 D.T.C. 6311 (Fed. T.D.).

[8]Subpara. 56(1)(a)(iii), subs. 248(1) "death benefit".

other.[9] A payment that is deductible by the payer is required to be included in income by the payee. A payment that is taxable to the recipient may be deducted by the payer.

Para. 56(1)(b) brings into income amounts that an individual receives as an allowance on a periodic basis for maintenance from a spouse, common law partner, former spouse or legal parent of the individual's child. Payments for child support are not taxable to the recipient. Thus, only spousal support is taxable.[10] The legal requirements are discussed under deductions.

V. — Retiring Allowances

A payment for the loss of employment is compensation *for the loss of* a source of income, rather than compensation *from* a source of income. Hence, individuals could structure their remuneration to avoid taxation under the source doctrine. The Act, however, specifically includes retiring allowances as income.[11]

A "retiring allowance" is a payment in recognition of long service, compensation for loss of an office or employment, or damages for wrongful dismissal.[12]

A payment pursuant to the terms of an employment contract is generally not a retiring allowance; it is remuneration.[13] In exceptional circumstances, a contractual payment to an employee upon termination of employment may be considered a "retiring allowance" if the payment is in recognition of the length of the employee's service to the company. There is generally an element of gratuitousness in the making of the payment, even though it may result from a threat of litigation.

VI. — Scholarships, Bursaries, and Fellowships

Scholarships, fellowships, bursaries, and prizes for achievement are taxable as income to the extent that the amount received in the year exceeds $500.[14] Work-related and business-related awards, prizes and similar payments do not qualify for this exemption.

---

[9]Para. 56(1)(b), s. 56.1; para. 60(b), s. 60.1. See: *Thibaudeau v. R.*, [1995] 2 S.C.R. 627, [1995] 1 C.T.C. 382, 95 D.T.C. 5273 (S.C.C.) (para. 56(1)(b)) does not impose a burden on recipient so as to attract section 15 of the *Charter*).

[10]Subsection 56.1(4).

[11]Subpara. 56(1)(a)(ii).

[12]Subs. 248(1) "retiring allowance".

[13]Para. 6(3)(b).

[14]Para. 56(1)(n), subs. 56(3).

The terms "scholarship", "fellowship" and "bursary" are often used interchangeably to mean financial assistance to selected students pursuing further education. A "prize for achievement" is an award for accomplishment. The phrase does not necessarily imply an award for victory in a competition or contest.[15] An award is only considered a "prize" if the winner of the prize is aware of the existence of, and enters, the contest.[16]

VII. — Research Grants

A fellowship, scholarship, or bursary should be distinguished from a research grant. A research grant is a sum of money given to a person to defray expenses in connection with a research project. Research grants sometimes include remuneration for the researcher.

There are two elements to a research grant: a grant for research. A grant includes any form of financial assistance to achieve an objective — a form of subsidy.[17]

"Research" generally involves a critical or scientific inquiry aimed at discovering new facts and exploring the potential for their practical application. Usually, the terms of the grant will establish that the primary purpose of the grant is the carrying out of research.

A research grant is taxable only if received directly by an individual. In other words, a payment of funds to the taxpayer's educational or research institution to finance research by the taxpayer is not taxable to the researcher.[18]

Research-related expenses are deductible from a research grant to the extent of the total value of the grant.

A taxpayer who must travel to conduct his or her research may deduct travelling expenses (including the full amount expended for meals and lodging) incurred in the carrying out of the research. The CRA takes the view, however, that a researcher who resides temporarily in a place while engaged in research is "sojourning" rather than travelling. Amounts paid for meals and lodging while the researcher is sojourning in a place are considered personal and living expenses, and are not deductible from the research grant. It is not clear how long a stay in a place converts a traveller into a sojourner.[19]

---

[15]*R. v. Savage*, [1983] 2 S.C.R. 428, [1983] C.T.C. 393, 83 D.T.C. 5409 (S.C.C.) at 400 [C.T.C.] and 5415 [D.T.C.] *per* Dickson J.

[16]*R. v. McLaughlin*, [1978] C.T.C. 602, 78 D.T.C. 6406 (Fed. T.D.).

[17]*Ghali c. R.* (2004), [2005] 4 C.T.C. 177 (Fed. C.A.).

[18]Para. 56(1)(o).

[19]Subpara. 56(1)(o)(i) IT-75R4 (June 28, 2003).

VIII. — Prizes

A prize for achievement is an award for accomplishment. Prizes are included in income in the year received[20] if the prize is for an achievement in a field of endeavour ordinarily carried on by the taxpayer. Thus, prizes won in games of chance or for athletic achievement are not taxable.[21] Certain prescribed prizes of recognition by the general public for particularly meritorious endeavours are also excluded from income.[22]

IX. — Social Assistance Payments

Most social assistance payments are not taxable. They must, however, be included in income in determining taxable income.[23] The taxpayer may then claim a deduction for the amount included in income.[24] Thus, although the net effect is that social assistance payments are not taxable, the inclusion of social assistance payments in a taxpayer's income may have other consequences. For example, it may reduce the amount of other tax incentives, such as refundable tax credits, to which the taxpayer might otherwise be entitled.

The trend in recent Canadian tax legislation is to shift the tax burden of social welfare payments to the payer with the highest rate of tax in a family. Thus, social assistance payments are taxed to the spouse with the higher marginal tax rate. This ensures that a family's access to any other income-tested tax incentives is determined by reference to the income of the spouse with the higher tax rate.

X. — Other Inclusions

Other Inclusions in Income	Statutory Reference	Comment
Amounts paid for benefit of taxpayer and/or children in taxpayer's custody	56.1	
Unemployment insurance benefits	56(1)(a)(iv)	

---

[20]Para. 56(1)(n).

[21]*R. v. Savage*, [1983] 2 S.C.R. 428, [1983] C.T.C. 393, 83 D.T.C. 5409 (S.C.C.) at 401 [C.T.C.] and 545 [D.T.C.].

[22]Reg. 7700.

[23]Para. 56(1)(u).

[24]Para. 110(1)(f).

Other Inclusions in Income	Statutory Reference	Comment
Transitional assistance benefit	56(1)(a)(v)	received by employees of automotive industry covered by the 1965 Canada-U.S. pact on automotive products
Prescribed benefit under government assistance program to extent not already included in income	56(1)(a)(vi)	
Annuity payments	56(1)(d), (d.2)	
Amount received from the disposition of an income-averaging annuity contract	56(1)(e), (f); 61(4) ("income-averaging annuity contract")	
Benefits under a supplementary unemployment benefit plan	56(1)(g); 145	
Benefits received under an RRSP or a RRIF	56(1)(h); 146	
Home buyers' plan	56(1)(h.1); 146.01	
Benefits from a deferred profit-sharing plan	56(1)(i); 147	
Amount received from the disposition of an interest in a life insurance policy	56(1)(j); 148(1), (1.1)	
Legal costs awarded by a court on an appeal for tax assessment, interest or penalties, and costs reimbursed from a decision of the Canada Employment and Immigration Commission or under the *Unemployment Insurance Act, Canada Pension Plan*	56(1)(l)	provided costs of the appeal or decision are deductible under para. 60(o)
Reimbursement of legal expenses paid to collect or establish right to a retiring allowance or pension benefit	56(1)(l.1)	
Amount received from an RESP	56(1)(q); 146.1	
Home insulation or conversion grants	56(1)(s); Regs. 5500, 5501	
Benefits from an RRIF	56(1)(t); 146.3	
Worker's compensation	56(1)(v)	

Other Inclusions in Income	Statutory Reference	Comment
Amounts received from some other person's salary deferral arrangement	56(1)(w)	amount included in income to the extent that it was not included in the other person's income
Proceeds from disposition of an interest in a RCA	56(1)(y)	
Value of benefits received or enjoyed in respect of workshops, seminars, training programs, etc.	56(1)(aa)	received by reason of membership in a registered national arts service organization

XI. — General Comments on Deductions

Just as the *Income Tax Act* includes in income various miscellaneous receipts that are not directly attributable to a particular source, it also allows for the deduction of certain expenses that are not directly related to a particular source of income. These deductions (described here as "other deductions") constitute an open category of expenses, each with its own rationale.

Certain disbursements normally considered to be personal may, however, be deductible by virtue of their intimate connection with a business. For example, meals and entertainment, travelling expenses, and the cost of special wardrobes in specialized professions sometimes have an aura of business expenditures. These types of expenditures pose difficult problems in the tax system because it is not easy to draw the line between personal and business expenditures. The distinction is not always clear cut, and the connection between the expenditure and the business purposes is sometimes tenuous.

Take, for example, the case of personal clothing. A professional lawyer or accountant is expected to dress in an appropriate manner suitable for his or her environment in the business workplace. Thus, the cost of a business suit or business dress is directly connected with the earning of business income. Nevertheless, expenditures on account of clothing are generally considered to be primarily personal expenses and, hence, not deductible in the computation of income. There comes a point, however, when clothing has only a limited and specialized purpose, and the expenditure is primarily on account of business. For example: an actor may require special-effects clothing; a doctor or surgeon may require special tunics; an auto mechanic special overalls.

XII. — Spousal and Child Support

1. — General Comment

"Spouse" includes common-law partners and same-sex (homosexual/gay/lesbian) partners. A "common-law partner" is an individual who cohabits with the taxpayer in a conjugal relationship — see subsection 248(1).

The expenses of supporting one's family are personal expenses. Hence, absent statutory authority, one would not be entitled to deduct support payments from income.

It is entirely tenable from an economic perspective that the recipient should be taxable on support, since such payments are an accretion to wealth. In law, the characterization of receipts does not usually depend on the nature of the expenditure to the payer. The tax consequences to the recipient and the payer are determined independently. For example, where an individual takes his or her family to a restaurant, the cost of the meal is a personal, non-deductible expense. The payment, however, is taxable to the owner of the restaurant as business income.

There are several reasons for varying from the theoretical norm. We allow a spouse to deduct support payments because we recognize such payments as extraordinary expenses that reduce the payer's ability to pay. Indeed, without tax relief, some spouses would find that their tax equaled, or even exceeded, their income after making support payments. Assume, for example, that an individual earns $100,000 and pays support of $35,000. Without a deduction for the support, his or her tax of approximately $36,000 would exceed the support payments. Thus, we justify the deduction for spousal support because it takes into account the taxpayer's ability to pay.

The support provisions significantly affect federal and provincial revenues. Since the payer usually has a higher marginal tax rate than the payee, the deduction for spousal support allows spouses to shift down on the rate schedule. This obviously has revenue consequences. For example, a deduction of $35,000 of spousal support has a net after-tax cost of $17,500 if the payer has a 50 percent tax rate. The treasury makes up part of the revenue loss by taxing the other spouse on the support. If the recipient spouse has a marginal rate of 25 percent, however, the tax cost to him or her is only $8,750. Thus, the treasury picks up the net loss of revenue because of the difference in marginal rates.

The statutory provisions in respect of spousal support are mirror images of each other.[25] A payment that is deductible by the payer is taxable to the payee. A payment that is taxable to the recipient is deductible to the payer. Thus, read together, the rules concern the choice of

---

[25]Para. 56(1)(b); para. 60(b). *Thibaudeau v. R.*, [1995] 2 S.C.R. 627, [1995] 1 C.T.C. 382, 95 D.T.C. 5273 (S.C.C.) (Para. 56(1)(b) is not unconstitutional under section 15 of the *Canadian Charter of Rights and Freedoms*, Part I of the *Constitution Act, 1982*, being Schedule B to the *Canada Act 1982* (U.K.), 1982, c. 11); see also, *IT-530R*, "Support Payments" (July 17, 2003).

taxable person rather than the definition of income or expense. In effect, one spouse is merely a conduit or pass-through for gross income that legally belongs to the other spouse by virtue of divorce settlement or decree.

An individual who is living separate and apart from his or her spouse or former spouse[26] because of the breakdown of their marriage can deduct spousal support payments if the payments are:[27]

- Pursuant to an order of a competent tribunal or a written agreement;

- In the nature of an allowance;

- Payable on a periodic basis; and

- For the maintenance of the recipient and/or the children.

For tax purposes, the term spouse has a broad meaning. "Spouse" includes a person of the opposite sex who is party to a void or voidable marriage. The term also includes the natural or adoptive unmarried parents of a child of the "spouses".[28] Further, "spouse" includes common-law partners, and same-sex relationships [see subsection 248(1)].

The Act limits the deduction to situations where the payer and the payee are living separate and apart from each other. It is a question of fact whether individuals are living separate and apart from each other. In certain circumstances, the law considers persons living under a common roof to be living apart from each other.[29]

---

[26]See subs. 252(3) for extended meaning of "spouse".

[27]Paras. 60(b) and 56.1(4)"support amount".

[28]Subs. 252(3).

[29]*Sanford v. R.*, [2001] 1 C.T.C. 2273, 2001 D.T.C. 12 (T.C.C. [General Procedure]); affirmed [2003] 1 C.T.C. 221, 2002 D.T.C. 7442 (Fed. C.A.). *Rushton v. Rushton* (1968), 66 W.W.R. 764 (B.C. S.C.) ("separate" means having withdrawn from marriage with intent to destroy bond; "apart" means physically separate); *Rousell v. Rousell* (1969), 69 W.W.R. 568 (Sask. Q.B.) (essence of evidence of separation being cessation of marital relationship); *Galbraith v. Galbraith* (1969), 69 W.W.R. 390 (Man. C.A.) (examination of law on cruelty as grounds for separation though couple living in same dwelling); *Minister of National Revenue v. Longchamps*, [1986] 2 C.T.C. 2231, 86 D.T.C. 1694 (T.C.C.) at 2233 [C.T.C.] and 1695 [D.T.C.] ("the termination of all rapport between a husband and his wife of the kind evidenced in this appeal is certainly in my opinion within the meaning that must be attributed to the expression, 'living apart'"; "there was no communication between them, no socializing whatsoever, each attending to his or her own affairs without consultation between them"); *Boos v. Minister of National Revenue* (1961), 27 Tax A.B.C. 283, 61 D.T.C. 520 (Can. Tax App. Bd.) (husband so withdrawn and separated from wife and children as to be in desertion, though still occupying same home).

A payment qualifies as spousal support only if the order or agreement clearly identifies it as being *solely* for the support of the spouse or former spouse.[30] Thus, the default rule is that silence makes support payments to be child support, which are neither deductible nor taxable if the order or agreement is silent as to their character.[31]

There is no Canadian tax payable if the recipient is not resident in Canada. Tax treaties will usually attempt to prevent juridical double taxation.[32]

2. — Order or Written Agreement

(a) — Payments Prior to Agreement

A payment is deductible only if it is pursuant to an order of a competent tribunal or a written agreement. The CRA does not accept anything less than a decree from a competent tribunal. Amounts that a taxpayer pays *before* the court order requires him or her to do so, or *before* the spouse enters into a written agreement, are deductible[33] only if the order or agreement incorporates the payments. The parties must ensure that they have an order or agreement before the end of the year following the payments.[34]

(b) — Written Agreement

A "written agreement" is a document signed by both parties to the agreement. It is not enough that the parties exchange correspondence with each other or that their lawyers or accountants exchange correspondence and discuss draft agreements.[35] The CRA will not

---

[30]Subs. 56.1(4)"child support amount".

[31]Para. 56(1)(b).

[32]*Studer v. R*, 2011 TCC 322, [2011] 6 C.T.C. 2224 (T.C.C. [Informal Procedure]).

[33]See *IT-530R*, "Support Payments" (July 17, 2003); *Hardtman v. R.*, [1977] C.T.C. 358, 77 D.T.C. 5219 (Fed. T.D.) (although Court able to distinguish between sham and equitable maintenance, even prior to any agreement, Court without such equitable jurisdiction); *Pezet v. Minister of National Revenue*, [1974] C.T.C. 2315, 74 D.T.C. 1246 (T.R.B.) (no retroactivity of deductibility where payments made prior to agreement, unless legislation provides otherwise); *Gagné v. Minister of National Revenue*, [1976] C.T.C. 2163, 76 D.T.C. 1125 (T.R.B.) (husband's letter listing expenses that he would pay did not constitute "agreement", since no evidence of consent); *Brooks v. Minister of National Revenue*, [1977] C.T.C. 2048, 77 D.T.C. 38 (T.R.B.) (amounts paid prior to agreement and order not deductible; even amount of arrears paid pursuant to order not deductible).

[34]Subs. 60.1(3).

[35]*Feinstein v. R.*, [1979] C.T.C. 329, 79 D.T.C. 5236 (Fed. T.D.) (agreement destroyed by fire in attorney's office; payments not deductible in these exceptional circumstances); *Chamberland v.*

accept anything less than a clear-cut "written agreement" signed by both parties. An exchange of correspondence may, however, crystallize into a "written agreement" in the same way that one can enter into a contract through an exchange of letters.[36]

(c) — Paid Under an Agreement

A payment is *made under* an order or agreement if it complies with the legal obligation created in the agreement.[37] Thus, only those amounts that are actually set out in the court order or written agreement are deductible by the payer and taxable to the payee. Voluntary payments in excess of the agreed-upon amounts are not "made under" the order or agreement. Conversely, payments that are made under a court order or agreement are taxable as income to the recipient even though the order or agreement might stipulate that the amounts are to be paid on a "tax-free" basis.[38]

3. — "Allowance"

An allowance is a pre-determined sum of money that the recipient can use for his or her own benefit. The amount must be:[39]

- Limited and pre-determined;

Minister of National Revenue, [1981] C.T.C. 2302, 81 D.T.C. 288 (T.R.B.) (agreement in principle, signed by one spouse is insufficient even if payments actually made); *Ardley v. Minister of National Revenue*, [1980] C.T.C. 2126, 80 D.T.C. 1106 (T.R.B.) (legal fees for separation agreement paid, but no proof of execution of agreement); *Hardy v. Minister of National Revenue*, [1978] C.T.C. 3120, 78 D.T.C. 1802 (T.R.B.) (and cases cited therein) (payments made pursuant to a written agreement that the payer refused to sign not deductible); *Andrychuck v. Minister of National Revenue*, [1986] 2 C.T.C. 2214, 86 D.T.C. 1667 (T.C.C.) (informal correspondence between spouses does not constitute "written agreement"; wife's letter requesting $300 support per month insufficient); *Jacoby v. Minister of National Revenue*, [1981] C.T.C. 2935, 81 D.T.C. 824 (T.R.B.) (unsigned written agreement insufficient); *Jaskot v. Minister of National Revenue*, [1992] 1 C.T.C. 2145, 92 D.T.C. 1102 (T.C.C.) (increase in support payments not deductible as only written evidence in correspondence of recipient's solicitor).

[36]*Burgess v. R.*, [1991] 1 C.T.C. 163, 91 D.T.C. 5076 (Fed. T.D.).

[37]*R. v. Sills*, [1985] 1 C.T.C. 49, 85 D.T.C. 5096 (Fed. C.A.); leave to appeal refused (1986), 68 N.R. 320 (note) (S.C.C.).

[38]*R. v. Sigglekow*, [1985] 2 C.T.C. 251, 85 D.T.C. 5471 (Fed. T.D.); additional reasons at 85 D.T.C. 5594 (Fed. T.D.).

[39]*Gagnon v. R.*, [1986] 1 S.C.R. 264, [1986] 1 C.T.C. 410, 86 D.T.C. 6179 (S.C.C.) ($360 paid to spouse pursuant to divorce decree, for purpose of paying two mortgages and interest was "allowance"); *R. v. Pascoe*, [1975] C.T.C. 656, 75 D.T.C. 5427 (Fed. C.A.).

- Paid on account of maintenance; and

- At the complete discretion of the person to whom it is paid.

In addition, subsection 56.1(4) requires that the amount must be within the complete discretion of the recipient. Amounts over which the recipient does not have discretion do not qualify as spousal support.

4. — Payable on a Periodic Basis

One of the troublesome questions in interpreting support agreements is the distinction between support payments and property settlements. Spousal support is deductible by the payer, and taxable to the payee, but only if it is payable on a periodic basis. Thus, the obligation to pay support is an annual charge against one of the spouse's pre-tax income, and entails a redirection of that income to his or her spouse. The amount payable on a periodic basis is deductible even if the payment is a lump sum, whether in arrears or in advance, if all other conditions are satisfied.[40]

The Act confines the deduction to spousal expenses. There is no deduction for property settlements. Property settlements are a division between the husband and wife of the family's after-tax savings. Capital payments to extinguish support are not deductible as an expense.[41] For example, the present value of an agreement to pay 60 monthly payments of $1,000 is equal to a lump sum of $49,272 if we assume an interest rate of 8 percent. The lump sum and the periodic payments are mathematically equal present-value amounts at that rate. Nevertheless, the lump sum is not deductible for tax purposes because it is the capitalized value of the annual expenses.[42] Thus, form prevails over economic substance in this situation.

"Periodic" means recurring at fixed or regular intervals. The payment must be *payable* on a periodic basis and the periodicity requirement must be in the court order or the written agreement.[43] It is not enough that the taxpayer actually pays on a periodic basis. The statutory requirement is that the payment be *payable* on a periodic basis, not that it actually be

---

[40]See *Ostrowski v. R.*, 2002 FCA 299, [2002] 4 C.T.C. 196, 2002 D.T.C. 7209 (Fed. C.A.)

[41]There are other provisions that allow for tax-free capital settlements: see, e.g., subs. 73(1).

[42]*Minister of National Revenue v. Armstrong*, [1956] S.C.R. 446, [1956] C.T.C. 93, 56 D.T.C. 1044 (S.C.C.).

[43]Para. 60(b).

paid periodically.[44] Thus, the obligation to pay at periodic intervals must not be left to the discretion of the payer.[45]

Some of the earlier jurisprudence interpreted "periodic" to mean that payments be on at least a monthly basis. The CRA is now more flexible. Even annual payments sometimes qualify as periodic.[46] It would, however, be quite unusual for payments that recur less frequently than annually to qualify as periodic payments.

The distinguishing characteristics of spousal support and property settlements are usually clear. Support is paid in cash and recognizes one of the spouse's legal support obligations. It is paid at regular intervals and, in most cases, continues for a stipulated period or until the other spouse's death. Thus, the deduction and inclusion regime is appropriate for spousal support, because the payments are of an income nature and the spouse merely acts as the conduit for his or her legal obligations. In contrast, property settlements are usually executed over a brief period and may include non-cash assets. Property settlements are not contingent upon subsequent events such as remarriage. A spouse is entitled to a share of the marital property, even if he or she remarries immediately after the settlement. The deduction inclusion system is inappropriate for capital settlements.

Difficulties arise because complex and sizable agreements have elements of both spousal support and property settlements. There is also the danger of lump-sum property settlements masquerading as spousal support because of the advantage to the paying spouse (normally the husband), who will usually have the higher marginal rate. Thus, the use of inappropriate language in an agreement can effectively convert spousal support into a property settlement.

An allowance for spousal support is a limited, pre-determined sum of money that one pays to enable the recipient to provide for certain kinds of expenses. Its amount is determined in advance and, once paid, it is at the complete discretion of the recipient. A lump-sum payment also represents a limited, pre-determined sum of money. Thus, the distinction between an allowance and a lump-sum payment blurs if the lump-sum payment is also payable in equal instalments on a periodic basis. The problem is essentially one of formal legal characterization, rather than underlying economic substance. One must distinguish between where

---

[44]*R. v. Sills*, [1985] 1 C.T.C. 49, 85 D.T.C. 5096 (Fed. C.A.); leave to appeal refused (1986), 68 N.R. 320 (note) (S.C.C.) (lump-sum payments for arrears of periodic alimony characterized as periodic notwithstanding tardiness and manner of payment); *James v. R.*, [1985] 1 C.T.C. 239, 85 D.T.C. 5173 (Fed. T.D.) (recipient taxable on payments made pursuant to order even though payments were late and amounts less than specified in order).

[45]*Jones v. Ogle* (1872), 8 Ch. App. 192 (Eng. Ch. Div.) at 198 (in construction of will, partnership profits did not come within meaning of "periodical payment in the nature of income"); *No. 427 v. Minister of National Revenue* (1957), 57 D.T.C. 291 (Can. Tax App. Bd.) (single $5,000 payment, which was one of several of increasing value to be paid over 12 years, was periodic in nature).

[46]*Hanlin v. R.*, [1985] 1 C.T.C. 54, 85 D.T.C. 5052 (Fed. T.D.) (three annual payments held to be part of series of payments payable on periodic basis).

support stops and property settlement begins. For example, what is the distinction between spousal support of $1,000 per month, payable for 10 years, despite remarriage and a property settlement, that pays one spouse his or her share of $120,000 at a rate of $1,000 per month over 10 years? What if the spousal support is front-end loaded, that is, one spouse receives an allowance of $1,500 per month for the first five years and only $500 per month for the last five years? What if the front-end load is $1,800 per month for five years and $200 per month for the last five years? At what point does the spousal support convert into a property settlement?

(a) — Periodic vs. Lump Sum Payments

The distinction between lump-sum amounts and periodic allowances reflects the underlying difference between income and capital. The *Income Tax Act* taxes income, not capital receipts. Similarly, one may deduct expenses from income, but not capital expenditures.

A lump sum payable in instalments is a capital amount and is neither deductible nor taxable. An obligation to pay a lump sum is a finite capital debt. The debt is assignable by the creditor and survives his or her life. Hence, the debt can pass to the estate. The critical element in determining the deductibility of maintenance payments (as opposed to capital settlements) is whether the payments were *payable* on a *periodic* basis. Thus, lump sum payments, whether in arrears or in advance, may be deductible if they are on account of maintenance.[47]

The following criteria are relevant, but not conclusive, in distinguishing between spousal support and property settlements.[48]

Indicia	Spousal support	Property settlement
Frequency of payments	Weekly, Monthly, Annually	More than annually
Ratio of payment in relation to income and living standards	Low Small percentage of annual income of payer	High In excess of annual income of payer
Interest payments prior to due date	None	Yes

---

[47]See, for example, *Ostrowski v. R.*, 2002 FCA 299, [2002] 4 C.T.C. 196, 2002 D.T.C. 7209 (Fed. C.A.).

[48]See, generally, *McKimmon v. Minister of National Revenue*, [1990] 1 C.T.C. 109, 90 D.T.C. 6088 (Fed. C.A.).

Indicia	Spousal support	Property settlement
Acceleration by payee as penalty on default	No	Yes
Prepayment at option of payer	No	Yes
Amount allows for significant capital accumulation by recipient	No	Yes
Liability to pay is for definite and fixed time	No	Yes
Payments for indefinite period or until some identifiable family event (e.g., age of child)	Yes	No
Assignability of payments	No	Yes
Survival of obligation to pay after death of payer	No	Yes
Release from future obligations to pay	No	Yes

(i) — Frequency of Payments

Periodicity implies an obligation to pay at fixed intervals and not at variable times. Moreover, the payments should be payable on a reasonably regular basis, whether weekly, monthly, or quarterly. Payments made at intervals of greater than one year warrant scrutiny to be considered to be allowances on account of maintenance.

(ii) — Amount Paid in Relation to Living Standards

Spousal support is on account of maintenance, and not for the accumulation of capital. Thus, a payment that is a very substantial portion of the payer's income is unlikely an allowance for maintenance. On the other hand, a payment that maintains the recipient's standard of living qualifies as an allowance for maintenance. There is no hard-and-fast rule as to what constitutes maintenance. The answer depends upon the lifestyle of the parties and their standard of living. The courts are fairly strict, and have denied taxpayers deductions for educational expenses, medical expenses, camping expenses, hospital insurance premiums, and life insurance premiums.[49]

(iii) — Interest

Maintenance payments do not typically bear interest. Payments that bear interest are more likely lump-sum settlements payable by instalments, rather than a true allowance for maintenance.

(iv) — Acceleration Clauses

Pre-payment and acceleration clauses are generally associated with lump-sum capital settlements. An acceleration clause in a settlement contract suggests that the debt is a non-deductible capital obligation, rather than an amount paid on account of periodic maintenance.

(v) — Accumulation of Capital

The quantum of payments is important: maintenance payments are for the recipient's living costs. They are not intended to allow for an accumulation of capital over a short period of time. It is accepted, however, that modest payments on account of capital accumulation may qualify as maintenance. For example, blended monthly mortgage principal and interest payments allow for a modest accumulation of capital over time. Mortgages are a normal living expense even though they contain an element of capital payment.

---

[49] *Urichuk v. R.*, [1993] 1 C.T.C. 226, 93 D.T.C. 5120 (Fed. C.A.) (characterization in separation agreement of instalment payments as additional maintenance does not prevent a contrary finding); *Golightly v. Minister of National Revenue*, [1979] C.T.C. 2997, [1970] Tax A.B.C. 161, 70 D.T.C. 1120 (Can. Tax App. Bd.) (various payments, including insurance, university room and board, tuition and medical insurance paid directly to institution pursuant to separation agreement were not "maintenance"); *Ivey v. Minister of National Revenue*, [1982] C.T.C. 2034, 82 D.T.C. 1083 (T.R.B.) (payments of school fees, summer camp fees and medical expenses for child with cystic fibrosis outside meaning of "maintenance"); *Shaw v. Minister of National Revenue*, [1978] C.T.C. 3230, 79 D.T.C. 26 (T.R.B.) (payment by taxpayer of spouse's income tax on maintenance payments and spouse's moving expenses not "alimony" or "maintenance"); *Evans v. Minister of National Revenue*, [1960] S.C.R. 391, [1960] C.T.C. 69, 60 D.T.C. 1047 (S.C.C.) (car payments made for spouse not "maintenance" although car highly useful).

(vi) — Term of Payments

Spousal support is either payable for an indefinite or unspecified period of time. Where time is specified, the payments generally relate to a significant event in the life of the parties. For example, spousal support payments may depend upon the coming of age of a child, because one anticipates such an event to cause a material change in the recipient's financial needs. In contrast, a lump sum generally represents a finite debt between the parties, and payments on account thereof are expected to continue for a fixed and specified term.

(vii) — Assignment of Obligation

Maintenance allowances are personal and non-assignable. The allowance is not assignable to third parties, and terminates upon the death of the recipient. In contrast, lump sum capital settlements are assignable debts, and form part of the recipient's estate.

(viii) — Release from Future Obligations

An agreement that releases the payer from all future obligations to pay maintenance is a lump-sum settlement and not a payment on account of maintenance. The consideration for the release from future maintenance is the capitalized present value of the payments that would have been made on account of future maintenance. The capital payment may be in cash, or the payer may assume a liability (such as a mortgage) on the recipient's behalf. For example, one spouse may assume a mortgage on the other spouse's property in exchange for his or her release from further liability for maintenance.

(b) — Rollovers

Capital settlements between spouses and ex-spouses are subject to a different tax regime than are periodic payments. Section 73 allows an individual two choices when transferring capital property to his or her spouse or ex-spouse. The spouse may:

1. Rollover the property to the other spouse on a tax-free basis, or

2. Elect to realize any capital gain accrued up to the date of the transfer.

In either case, the recipient takes the property at a cost equal to the transferor's proceeds of disposition. If the transferor elects a rollover, the recipient assumes the property at the transferor's cost; if the transferor realizes a capital gain, the recipient acquires the property at its fair market value.

Fundamentals of Canadian Income Tax Vol 1: Personal Tax

(c) — Arrears

Payments payable on a periodic basis do not change in character merely because they are not made on time. The test for deductibility is whether the payments are *payable* on a periodic basis, and not whether they are actually paid on a periodic schedule.[50] Thus, payments on account of arrears are deductible and taxable if they are identifiable under the terms of the agreement.[51]

5. — Child Support

Child support is not deductible by the payer where the payments are made under a written agreement or court order on or after May 1, 1997. Similarly, child support is not taxable to the recipient.[52]

Child support means any support the court order or written agreement does not identify as being *solely* for the support of the taxpayer's spouse or former spouse. For example, where an agreement provides for a global support amount for the spouse and children, the entire amount is child support and, therefore, not deductible and not taxable. Similarly, if a court order or written agreement provides for the payment of amounts to a third party, the entire amount is child support if the order or agreement does not clearly specify otherwise.

The term "children" has the same meaning that the term "child" has in other provisions of the Act.[53] For the purposes of paragraphs 56(1)(b) and 60(b), the payer must be the legal parent of a child of the recipient.[54]

Where a payer must make both spousal and child support payments, the presumption is that the payments go first towards child support and then for spousal support. Thus, in the event that the payer defaults, the recipient receives the payments first on a non-taxable basis. The payer cannot deduct any portion on account of spousal support until he fully satisfies his child support obligations.

---

[50]*R. v. Pascoe*, [1975] C.T.C. 656, 75 D.T.C. 5427 (Fed. C.A.).

[51]*R. v. Sills*, [1985] 1 C.T.C. 49, 85 D.T.C. 5096 (Fed. C.A.); leave to appeal refused (1986), 68 N.R. 320 (note) (S.C.C.).

[52]*IT-530R*, "Support Payments" (July 17, 2003).

[53]Subs. 252(1).

[54]Subs. 56.1(4) "child support amount".

6. — Third-Party Payments

Spousal support payments are usually structured as tax-deductible to the payer and taxable to the recipient. In most cases, this allows taxpayers to rate-shift and reduce their overall tax obligations. As noted above, payments are deductible if they are paid on a periodic basis by a person to his spouse or former spouse.

There are circumstances, however, when it is financially prudent to pay some or all of the support payments directly to a third party for the benefit of the spouse or children. Subsection 60.1(1) deems amounts that otherwise qualify for deduction to be deductible even if they are paid directly to a third party. The provision also ensures that the parties can take into account third-party amounts payable for child support in determining the deduction for spousal support.

Third-party support payments are deductible where the payments are:[55]

- Paid pursuant to either a judicial order of a competent tribunal or a written agreement, which stipulates that subsections 56.1(2) and 60.1(2) apply;

- For the maintenance of the payer's spouse, former spouse, an individual of the opposite sex who is the legal parent of a child of the taxpayer, and/or children;

- Incurred at a time when the payer and the recipient were living separate and apart; and

- In respect of support expenses incurred either in the year or in the preceding taxation year.

Subsection 60.1(2) deems such payments to be payable on a periodic basis.[56] There are additional requirements if the payment to a third party is in respect of mortgage payments on the family home. In these circumstances a payment is deductible only if:[57]

- The payer does not reside in the family home;

- The payment is not in respect of the purchase of tangible property; and

- The payment for principal and interest is not in excess of 20 percent of the original amount of the loan incurred to finance the home.

The Act is oppressively strict in limiting third party payments. In order for a third-party payment to be deductible, the judicial order or written agreement must *specifically* provide that subsections 60.1(2) and 56.1(2) of the Act apply to the payments. Failure to enumerate the subsections in the terms of settlement disqualifies the payments for deduction. This re-

---

[55]Subs. 60.1(2).

[56]See also, *IT-530R*.

[57]Subs. 60.1(2).

quirement, which the CRA enforces zealously, traps many taxpayers. Some courts[58] have blunted the severity of this harsh approach and accepted an oblique reference in the minutes of settlement as sufficient to satisfy the statutory requirement. It is better, however, to specify in the minutes of settlement that the subsections apply.

(a) — Deemed Allowance

The Act *deems* spousal support payments paid to a third party to have been paid as an allowance. Such payments are deductible by the payer and taxable in the hands of the person for whose benefit the payments are made.

Typically, third-party payments are made on account of, for example, medical and dental bills, mortgage payments, tuition fees, household utilities, camp fees and condominium maintenance fees. Of these expenses, mortgage fees, utilities and tangible property associated with medical, dental, or educational requirements can easily be made tax-deductible.

It is less clear, however, whether condominium maintenance expenses (common area charges) paid directly to the condominium corporation are deductible for tax purposes. Expenditures incurred on account of the family home are deductible in respect of the *acquisition* or *improvement* of the home to the extent that they do not exceed 20 percent of the original cost of financing the home. Condominium fees cannot be considered to qualify as either an acquisition or an improvement cost. Hence, it is generally better to include condominium fees as part of the negotiated allowance that is paid directly to the spouse.

(b) — Prior Payments

Support payments made prior to obtaining a judicial order or entering into a written agreement are also tax-deductible if the order or agreement *specifically* so provides.[59] In effect, the order or agreement can retroactively render the payments deductible even though they were not paid *under* the order or agreement.

XIII. — Child Care Expenses

Child care is one of the basic functions of family life. Expenses on account of child care have escalated in the last 40 years as more mothers go out of the home to work. Unlike some

---

[58]See, e.g., *Cottrell v. Minister of National Revenue*, [1990] 2 C.T.C. 2031, 90 D.T.C. 1581 (T.C.C.) (payments deductible where minutes of settlement referred to payments in issue); *Bishop v. Minister of National Revenue*, [1993] 1 C.T.C. 2333, 93 D.T.C. 333 (T.C.C.) (payment of support arrears to welfare authorities neither taxable nor deductible; payment constituted discharge of indebtedness).

[59]Subs. 60.1(3).

personal expenses such as food and shelter, which one must incur whether one works or not, child care can have an element of business purpose. If, for example, we assume that the mother is unemployed and cannot work without the child care, then any *incremental* cash outlay for child care that she incurs to work is clearly related to a business purpose. Thus, we can justify the deduction of the incremental expenses of earning a living, as opposed to the basic expenses of just living.

This rationale is different from the "but for" test: *but for* the child care expenditure, the parent could not earn income. *Ergo*, the expenditure should be fully deductible for tax purposes. If carried to the extreme, the "but for" line of reasoning extends to justifying virtually any type of personal expenditure as a business expense. However, the "but for" line of reasoning can also be unduly restrictive.

The Act allows a measure of tax relief to parents who incur such expenses so that they may pursue financial gain outside of the home.[60] However, the deduction is strictly controlled and constrained by numerous rules. The original theory was to allow working mothers some tax relief for child care. However, the Act restricts the deduction to the lower income person.[61] To qualify, the taxpayer must incur the child care expenses to permit one parent (or a supporting person of the child) to pursue employment, business, research or educational activities. The maximum yearly deduction is the least of:

- The amount actually paid for child care;
- 2/3 of the taxpayer's earned income for the year; and
- $7,000 for each eligible child under seven years of age and $4,000 for each child between seven and 16 years of age at the end of the year.

The deduction is increased to $10,000 for severely impaired children. In most cases, the deduction for child care expenses is available only to working mothers. Only in extremely rare situations may a father claim a deduction for child care expenses.

---

[60]S. 63; see also, *IT-495R2*, "Child Care Expenses" (January 13, 1997).

[61]See, for example, *Planetta v. Minister of National Revenue*, [1987] 2 C.T.C. 2258 (T.C.C.) (taxpayer with higher net income than her spouse not allowed to deduct.)

1. — Definition of "Child Care Expense"

The Act defines "child care expense" restrictively. One must satisfy the following additional conditions to qualify for expenditure as a "child care expense":[62]

- The child care services must be provided in Canada;[63]

- The services must be provided by a Canadian resident (other than the child's parents) for whom the taxpayer or his or her spouse does not claim a dependency credit; and

- The person providing the service must not be under 18 years of age if he or she is related to either the taxpayer or his or her spouse.

Advertising expenses, agency placement fees, and transportation expenses to locate, interview or bring to Canada a care-giver qualify as "child care expenses".

Subsection 63(4) provides another exception to the "in Canada" rule for child care services. Where a taxpayer resides in Canada near the Canada-U.S. border, the child care services may be provided in the United States rather than in Canada. However, the U.S. facility must be closer to the Canadian taxpayer's place of residence by a reasonably accessible route than any place in Canada where such child care services are available. Therefore, assuming these conditions are met, if a Canadian resident pays for child care services at a centre in the U.S. or to an individual in the U.S., the payments are deductible as if the child care was provided in Canada. If the child care is provided by an individual in the U.S., the taxpayer need not provide the individual's social insurance number when claiming the deduction. This exception does not apply to expenses paid for a child to attend a boarding school or camp in the U.S.

2. — Deductible Limits

(a) — Claim by Lower-Income Parent

In two-parent families, child care expenses are generally deductible only by the spouse with the lower income. In exceptional circumstances, the higher-income spouse is entitled to the

---

[62]Subs. 63(3) "child care expense".

[63]However, section 64.1 allows individuals who are absent from Canada, but still resident in Canada for tax purposes, to deduct payments for child care services provided outside of Canada.

child care deduction.[64] The parent with the lower income may claim a deduction equal to the lesser of:[65]

- The aggregate of

  - $7,000 multiplied by the number of eligible children under seven years of age (or $10,000 if the child is eligible for disability tax credit) for whom child care expenses have been paid; and

  - $4,000 per other eligible child over 6 and under 16 years of age (or over 15 years of age with physical or mental impairment) for whom child care expenses have been paid; or

- 2/3 of the taxpayer's "earned income" for the year.

(b) — Claim by Higher-Income Parent

The higher-income parent (usually the father) may make a claim for child care expenses, but only if the other parent (usually the mother) is:[66]

- In full-time attendance at a designated educational institution;

- Certified in writing by a medical doctor to be either mentally or physically ill and incapable of looking after children;

- Certified in writing by a doctor to be mentally or physically ill to the extent that the person is confined to a bed or wheelchair, or is a patient in a hospital for a period of at least two weeks in the year;

- Imprisoned for at least two weeks in the year; or

- Living apart from the taxpayer for at least 90 days that began in the year by reason of marriage breakdown.

In these circumstances the amount deductible by the higher-income parent is restricted to the *least* of the following amounts:

- The aggregate of

  - $7,000 per eligible child under seven years of age (or $10,000 if the child is eligible for disability tax credit) for whom child care expenses have been paid; and

---

[64]Subs. 63(2).

[65]Subs. 63(1).

[66]Para. 63(2)(b).

- $4,000 per other eligible child over 6 and under 16 years of age (or over 15 years of age with physical or mental impairment) for whom child care expenses were incurred;

- 2/3 of the taxpayer's "earned income" for the year;

- The number of weeks the taxpayer was eligible to make the claim multiplied by the total periodic child care expenses incurred with respect to an eligible child.

Subsection 63(3) defines "periodic child care expense" to mean 1/40 of the $4,000, $7,000 and $10,000 amounts as $100, $175 and $250 (respectively) weekly.

(c) — Nil Income

In most cases where a husband and wife have child care expenses, the child care expenses are deductible by the spouse with the lower income. However, the Act deems a taxpayer with no income to have an income of zero.[67] This rule effectively prevents the sole bread-winner from claiming child care expenses if only one parent works outside the home.[68]

XIV. — Moving Expenses

1. — General Comment

Moving expenses also have a dual flavour of personal and business-related expenditures. Prior to section 62, if an employer transferred his or her employee from one location to another and paid the moving expenses, the expenses were deductible to the employer and were not considered income to the employee. An employee could not, however, take a deduction for moving expenses if he or she paid for the move.

Mobility of labour is an important and necessary part of the Canadian economy. Labour mobility reduces unemployment and increases productive capacity. Given the size of the country, taxpayers often incur substantial moving expenses in connection with employer-related relocations. The statutory deduction for moving expenses in section 62 recognizes the importance of labour mobility. The deduction also recognizes that employees who pay their own expenses and are not reimbursed by their employers should be placed on an equal

---

[67]Para. 3(f).

[68]Para. 3(f) was enacted after court decisions held that where one spouse had no income at all, the spouse with income could deduct the child care expenses since there was only one income. See: *Fiset v. Minister of National Revenue*, [1988] 1 C.T.C. 2335, 88 D.T.C. 1226 (Eng.) (T.C.C.); *McLaren v. Minister of National Revenue*, [1988] 1 C.T.C. 2371, 88 D.T.C. 1259 (T.C.C.); See *Fromstein v. R.*, [1993] 2 C.T.C. 2214, 93 D.T.C. 726 (T.C.C.) concerning the same issue, after the enactment of paragraph 3(f).

footing with self-employed persons who move to a new work location. Thus, the Act generally regards employment-related moving expenses as a cost of earning income and permits the deduction of such expenses, subject, however, to stringent statutory conditions.

Moving expenses are deductible where the taxpayer:[69]

- Commences employment in Canada;

- Commences business in Canada; or

- Commences full-time studies at a post-secondary educational institution.

Moving expenses may be deducted in the year of the move *or any subsequent year* to the extent that the taxpayer has employment or business income at a new work location against which the moving expenses can be applied.[70]

Moving expenses are not deductible against investment income.[71]

2. — *Eligibility for Deduction*

An individual who moves to a place in Canada for the purpose of employment or to carry on a business may deduct moving expenses if he or she satisfies three conditions:[72]

1. Both the old residence and the new residence are in Canada;

2. The new residence is at least 40 km closer to the new employment or business location than was the old residence;[73] and

3. The move is *related to* the commencement of the business, employment or studies.[74]

Students may deduct expenses of moving into or out of Canada. The change in the taxpayer's residence must be by *reason* of the commencement of his or her business, employment, or studies.

---

[69]See subs. 248(1) "eligible relocation"; see also, *IT-178R3*, "Moving Expenses" (Consolidated).

[70]*Moodie v. R.*, 2004 TCC 462, [2004] 4 C.T.C. 2329 (T.C.C. [Informal Procedure]).

[71]*Schultz v. R.*, [1988] 2 C.T.C. 293, 88 D.T.C. 6468 (Fed. T.D.).

[72]Subs. 62(1); subs. 248(1) "eligible relocation".

[73]*Cameron v. Minister of National Revenue*, [1993] 1 C.T.C. 2745, 93 D.T.C. 437 (T.C.C.) (40 kms is measured "as the crow flies"); *Haines v. Minister of National Revenue*, [1984] C.T.C. 2422, 84 D.T.C. 1375 (T.C.C.) (distance to be measured in straight line).

[74]*Kubryk v. Minister of National Revenue*, [1987] 1 C.T.C. 2125, 87 D.T.C. 75 (T.C.C.).

3. — Definition of "Moving Expenses"

The Act does not define "moving expenses". Thus, any expenses that fall within the common understanding of "moving expenses" are deductible. One looks at the economic substance of the expenditure to determine whether it constitutes a "moving expense".

The following expenditures, however, are specifically included as deductible "moving expenses":[75]

- Travelling costs, including reasonable expenses for meals and lodging, incurred in the course of the move;

- Movers' costs, including storage charges;

- The cost of meals and lodging either near the old residence or near the new residence, for a period not exceeding 15 days;

- The cost of cancelling a lease;

- Selling costs[76] to dispose of the old residence;

- Legal expenses, registration, and land transfer taxes in respect of the acquisition of a new residence in the new location, if the taxpayer sells the old residence;

- Interest, property taxes, insurance premiums, and the cost of heating and utilities in respect of the old residence, to the extent of the lesser of $5,000 and the total of such expenses; and

- The cost of revising legal documents to reflect the address of the new residence, of replacing drivers' licences and non-commercial vehicle permits, and of connecting or disconnecting utilities.

Expenditures not listed above are also deductible as "moving expenses" if they qualify under the general understanding of that phrase.

The following expenditures are not deductible:[77]

- Expenses reimbursed to the taxpayer by the employer;

- Expenses paid directly by the individual's employer;

- Expenses that are deductible under any other section of the Act;

---

[75]Subs. 62(3).

[76]*Collin v. Minister of National Revenue*, [1990] 2 C.T.C. 92, 90 D.T.C. 6369 (Fed. T.D.) (lump sum paid by vendor to reduce purchaser's effective mortgage rate constituted "cost of selling property").

[77]Subs. 62(1).

- Expenses in excess of the individual's income in the year of the move from employment or business at the new location; and

- Where the taxpayer is a student, any expenses in excess of the taxable portion of scholarships, fellowships, bursaries, and research grants.

Moving expenses are generally deductible only in the year in which the move occurs. Expenses in excess of the deductible limit for a year may, however, be carried over and deducted against income in the following year. To be deductible in the year following the move, the expenses must not have been *deductible* in the year in which they were incurred. Thus, deductible moving expenses that are not claimed by the taxpayer in the year of the move are forever lost.[78]

Example

Horace Rumpole graduated from the University of Ottawa in Year 1 and found a job as a barrister in Vancouver. He commenced his job on November 1, Year 1, at a starting salary of $30,000 per year.

As part of his contract of employment, his new employers reimbursed Horace $2,000 to defray the cost of his move to Vancouver.

On October 1, Year 1, Horace moved out of his Ottawa apartment and into a hotel, where he stayed for seven days. As a consequence of his move to Vancouver, Horace incurred the following expenditures:

		$
•	Lease cancellation costs on his apartment in Ottawa	400
•	Hotel and meal expenses in Ottawa and Vancouver 21 days)	2,100
•	Airfare and ground transportation	600
•	Movers' charges	3,500
•	Storage charges	600
•	Legal fees re acquisition of house in Vancouver	1,400
•	Airfare for house-hunting trip in September Year 1 and associated living costs	850

Unfortunately for Horace, there was a fire in his mover's premises in Vancouver, where his furniture and belongings were being stored. The storage company did not carry sufficient insurance, and Horace's goods, worth $7,000, were destroyed.

---

[78]Para. 62(1)(b).

The maximum deduction available to Horace for Year 1 is calculated as follows:

	$
Eligible moving expenses under subsection 62(3):	
Lease cancellation costs	400
15 days hotel and meal expenses	
15/21 × $2,100	1,500
Airfare and ground transportation	600
Movers' charges	3,500
Storage charges	600
	6,600
Reimbursed amount	(2,000)
Net moving expenses	4,600
Income at new job	
2/12 × $30,000	5,000
Maximum deduction	4,600

Note:

1. The legal fees ($1,400) for the acquisition of the new house in Vancouver are not deductible as moving expenses, because the taxpayer did not dispose of a residence at his old location: paragraph 62(3)(f).

2. The "income at new job" limits deductibility of expenses: paragraph 62(1)(c). Horace worked for November and December, Year 1, for 2/12 of his annual salary.

XV. — Other Deductions

Other deductions include the following:

Type of Deduction	Statutory References
Capital element of each annuity payment, if paid under a contract, will or trust	para. 60(a)
Support payments	para. 60(b); *IT-530R*
Repayment of support payments	para. 60(c.2); *IT-530R*

Type of Deduction	Statutory References
Annual interest accruing on succession duties, inheritance taxes or estate taxes	para. 60(d); *IT-533*
Premium or payment under registered retirement savings plan	para. 60(i); *IT-124R6*
Transfer of superannuation benefits	para. 60(j); *IT-528*
Transfer of surplus under a defined benefit provision of a registered pension plan	para. 60(j.01)
Certain payments to registered pension plan	para. 60(j.02)
Repayment under prescribed statutory provision of pension benefits included in income	para. 60(j.03), 60(j.04)
Transfer of retiring allowances	para. 60(j.1); *IT-337R4*
Transfer to a spousal RRSP	para. 60(j.2)
Transfer of refund of a premium under a registered retirement savings plan	para. 60(l); *IT-528*
Estate tax applicable to property to which the taxpayer is the successor	para. 60(m)
Succession duties payable on property to which the taxpayer is the successor	para. 60(m.1)
Amount of overpayment of pension or benefits received by the taxpayer to the extent repaid by him or her	para. 60(n)
Amount in respect of fees or expenses in the preparation, institution or prosecution of an objection or an appeal regarding certain decisions	para. 60(o); *IT-99R5*

Type of Deduction	Statutory References
Amount in respect of legal fees to collect or establish a right to pension benefits	para. 60(o.1); *IT-99R5*
Refund of income payments in an arm's length transaction	para. 60(q); *IT-340R*
Repayment in respect of a policy loan under a life insurance policy, to the extent the amount was included in income and not otherwise deductible	para. 60(s)
Certain amount included in income in respect of a retirement compensation arrangement	para. 60(t)
Amount included in income as proceeds from a disposition of an interest in a retirement compensation arrangement	para. 60(u)
Contribution to a provincial pension plan	para. 60(v)
Repayment of unemployment insurance benefit to the extent not otherwise deductible	para. 60(v.1)
Tax on old age security benefits	para. 60(w)
Refund of undeducted additional voluntary contributions to a registered pension plan in respect of services rendered	para. 60.2
Payments made as consideration for an income-averaging annuity contract	subs. 61(1)
Moving expenses	s. 62
Child care expenses	s. 63
Disability Supports Deduction	s. 64.1; *IT-519R2*

Selected Bibliography to Chapter 12

Superannuation or Pension Benefits

Baston, Paul F., "Individual Pension Plans Revisited: Are they Really Worthwhile" (1994) 6 Tax. of Exec. Compensation and Retirement 19.

Bauslaugh, Randy V., "Past Service Enhancement and the Subsection 8503(15) Anti-avoidance Rule" (1994) 5 Tax. of Exec. Compensation and Retirement 899.

Broley, John A., "Overcoming Benefit Limitations for Executives Through Design and Use of Pension and Nonstatutory Arrangements", in *Proceedings of 33rd Tax Conf.* 869 (Can. Tax Foundation, 1981).

Bush, Kathryn M., "Executive Compensation: Supplemental Pension Plans" (1991) 8 Bus. L. 46.

Dutka, Randall J., et al., *Pensions and Retirement Income Planning 1993: Tax Rules and Strategies* (Toronto: CCH Canadian, 1993).

Johnston, William, "Taxation of Non-registered Pension Plans", *Corp. Mgmt. Tax Conf.* 9:1 (Can. Tax Foundation, 1991).

Krasa, Ewa M., "Recent Developments in Retirement Savings and Deferred Compensation: A Potpourri", in *Proceedings of 44th Tax Conf.* 18:1 (Can. Tax Foundation, 1992).

Muto, Alexander D., "Recent Changes to the *Income Tax Regulations* on Retirement Savings" (1994) 5 Tax. of Exec. Compensation and Retirement 942.

Pensions: Significant Issues and Developments (Toronto: Law Society of Upper Canada, Dpt. of Education, 1990).

Solursh, John M. and Jeremy J. Forgie, "Tax-assisted Retirement Savings: An Overview of the New System and its Application to Registered Pension Plans", *Corp. Mgmt Tax Conf.* 7:1 (Can. Tax Foundation, 1991).

Theroux, Marcel and Brad Rowse, "The Individual Pension Plan: A Complete Guide", *Corp. Mgmt. Tax Conf.* 8:1 (Can. Tax Foundation, 1991).

Wolpert, Michael, "Pension Plans and the *Income Tax Act*: The Other Side of the Equation" (1992) 2 Can Corp. Counsel 10.

Death Benefits

Atnikov, D., "Stock Options, Stock Purchase Plans, and Death Benefits", *Prairie Provinces Tax Conf.* 1 (Can. Tax Foundation, 1980).

Support Payments

"Alimony and Maintenance Trusts" (1993) 8 Money and Family Law 81.

"Alimony Insurance could be Tax Deductible" (1992) 7 Money and Family Law 36.

Arnold, Brian J., "Income Tax Consequences of Separation and Divorce", in *Proceedings of 29th Tax Conf.* 193 (Can. Tax Foundation, 1977).

Barnett, Jim, "Alimony and Maintenance Payments" (1979) 112 CA Magazine 65.

Bowman, Stephen W., et al., "The Taxability of Child Support Payments and the Charter of Rights and Freedoms" (1994) Can. Tax J. 907.

Corn, George, "Child Care Expenses — Deductibility as Business Expenses or Personal Living Expenses" (1991) 3 Can. Current Tax J-91.

Douglas, Kristen, "Child Support: Quantum, Enforcement and Taxation" (Ottawa: Library of Parliament, Research Branch, 1994).

Drache, A.B.C., "Reducing Expenses is Not Gaining Income" (1991) 13 Can. Taxpayer 156.

Drache, A.B.C., "Support Payments: All Tax Aspects Should Be Considered" (1991) 13 Can. Taxpayer 160.

Drache, A.B.C., "*Tax Act* Creates Problems in Joint Custody" (1992) 14 Can. Taxpayer 31.

Drache, A.B.C., "Written Separation Agreements" (1991) 13 Can. Taxpayer 61.

Durnford, John W. and Stephen J. Troope, "Spousal Support in Family Law and Alimony in the Law of Taxation" (1994) 42 Can. Tax J. 1.

Freedman, Andrew J., "Arrears Payments: To Tax or Not to Tax?" (1993) 8 Money and Family Law 61.

Goodison, Don, "Tax Forum — Not a Business Expense" (1991) 25 CGA Magazine 17.

Harris, J., "Alimony and Maintenance Payments: Unexpected Results" (1988) 2 Can. Current Tax P-25.

Harris, Peter H., "Tax Treatment of Civil Litigation and Damage Awards, Alimony and Maintenance Payments" (1985) 6 Advocate's Q. 346.

Income Tax and Costs: Setting Aside Separation Agreements: Appeals, Choosing the Right Forum (Audio Archives of Canada, 1984).

Income Tax: Maintenance, Alimony and Employment Termination Benefits (Audio Archives of Canada, 1984).

Klein, William A., "Tax Effects of Nonpayment of Child Support" (1990) 45 Tax Lawyer 259.

Krishna, Vern, "To Love, Honor or Pay" (1990) 24 CGA Magazine 28.

McCallum, J. Thomas, "Deferring the Inevitable" (1990) 24 CGA Magazine 23.

"Post-Marital Trusts" (1984) 6 Can. Taxpayer 15.

Raich, Robert, "Characterization of Income and Third Party Alimony Receipts", in *Proceedings of 32nd Tax Conf.* 238 (Can. Tax Foundation, 1980).

Richards, Gabrielle M.R., "Support Payments: An Update" (1992) 3 Can. Current Tax J-115.

Shillington, Richard and Ellen Zweibel, "Child Support Policy: Income Tax Treatment and Child Support Guidelines" (Toronto: Policy Research Centre on Children, Youth and Families, 1993).

Shultz, Clayton G., "Income Tax Law and Policy Applicable to Periodic Maintenance and Division of Matrimonial Assets" (1987) 1 Can. Fam. L. Q. 293.

"Taxation of Support Payments Received from Non-residents" (1994) 9 Money and Family Law 78.

"Taxation of Support Payments Simplified?" (1992) 7 Money and Family Law 75.

Retiring Allowances

Colley, Geofferey, M., "Retirement and Termination" (1980) 113 CA Magazine 57.

Fisher, G.B., "Early Retirement Tax Considerations" (1983) 31 Can. Tax J. 828.

Income Tax: Maintenance, Alimony and Employment Termination Benefits (Audio Archives of Canada, 1984).

Levine, Risa, "Retiring Allowances Part 1: How Do You Know if You Have One?" (1994) 2 RRSP Plan. 125.

Matheson, D.I., "Termination of Employment", *Corporate Management Tax Conf.* 219 (Can. Tax Foundation, 1979).

Murill, Raymond F., "Easing the Pain of Severance Pay" (1984) 117 CA Magazine 38.

Novek, Barbara L., "Retiring Allowances are subject to Administrative Guidelines" (1991) 3 Tax. of Exec. Compensation and Retirement 523.

Rayside J.W., "Retirement Planning for Owner-Managers" (1982) 30 Can. Tax J. 83.

"Retiring Allowance Reasonableness" (1980) 2 Can. Taxpayer 205.

Other

Duncan, Garry R., "Passing the Hat (The Orderly Succession of a Business to a Worthy Heir)" (Jan/Feb 1989) 122 CA Magazine 39.

Finkelstein, David N., "Tax Problems in Estate Planning for the Corporate Executive", in *Proceedings of 33rd Tax Conf.* 952 (Can. Tax Foundation, 1981).

Harris, Peter H., "Tax Treatment of Civil Litigation and Damage Awards, Alimony and Maintenance Payments" (1985) 6 Advocate's Q. 346.

Wakeling, Audrey A., "Tax Planning with Trusts", in *Proceedings of 42nd Tax Conf.* 35:1 (Can. Tax Foundation, 1990).

Selected Bibliography to Deductions

General

Drache, A.B.C., "Charter Offers No Tax Breaks" (1991) 13 Can. Taxpayer 188.

Ross, David W., "Income Tax Consequences of Property Transfers and Payments Made as a Result of Marriage Breakdown and Divorce", in *Proceedings of 41st Tax Conf.* 12:1 (Can. Tax Foundation, 1989).

Support Payments

"Alimony and Maintenance Trusts" (1993) 8 Money and Family Law 81.

Arnold, Brian J., "Income Tax Consequences of Separation and Divorce", in *Proceedings of 29th Tax Conf.* 193 (Can. Tax Foundation, 1977).

Arnold, Brian J., "Tax Aspects of Alimony and Maintenance", 9:7 *Tax Planning and Management of Canadian Income Tax, Revised* (Toronto: Butterworth and Co. (Canada) Ltd., 1975).

Benotto, Mary Lou, "An Income Tax Checklist", (1993) Special Lectures LSUC, 297.

Barnett, Jim, "Alimony and Maintenance Payments" (1979) 112 CA Magazine 65.

Bowman, Stephen W. *et al.*, "The Taxability of Child Support Payments and the Charter of Rights and Freedoms" (1994) 42 Can. Tax J. 907.

Brahmst, Oliver C., "A Definition for the Term 'Spouse': Far-reaching Changes on the Horizons" (1993) 4 Can. Current Tax P1.

Cole, Stephen R. and Andrew J. Freeman, *Property Valuation and Income Tax Implications of Marital Dissolution* (Toronto: Thomson Professional Publishing Canada, 1991).

Coleman, Gene C. and Gary S. Opolsky, "Alimony Insurance Could Be Tax Deductible" (1992) 7 Money and Family Law 36.

Drache, A.B.C., "Post-Marital Trusts" (1984) 6 Can. Taxpayer 15.

Drache, A.B.C., "Reducing Expenses is Not Gaining Income" (1991) 13 Can. Taxpayer 156.

Drache, A.B.C., "Support Payments: All Tax Aspects Should Be Considered" (1991) 13 Can. Taxpayer 160.

Drache, A.B.C., "Tax Act Creates Problems in Joint Custody" (1992) 14 Can. Taxpayer 31.

Durnford, John W. and Stephen J. Trope, "Spousal Support in Family Law and Alimony in the Law of Taxation" (1994) 42 Can. Tax J. 1.

Financial Implications of Child Support Guidelines: Research Report (Ottawa: Department of Justice, Federal/Provincial Territorial Family Law Committee)

Goldstein, D. Lisa, "Until Death Do Us Part" (1991) 39 Can. Tax J. 513.

Goodison, Don, "Taxation of Maintenance Income" (1988) 22 CGA Magazine 18.

Goodison, Don, "Tax Forum — Deduction Denied" (1991) 25 CGA Magazine 17.

Harris, P.H., "Tax Treatment of Civil Litigation and Damage Awards, Alimony and Maintenance Payments" (1985) 6 Advocates' Q. 346.

Income Tax: Maintenance, Alimony and Employment Termination Benefits, Audio Archives of Canada, 1984.

Income Tax and Costs: Setting Aside Separation Agreements: Appeals, Choosing the Right Forum, Audio Archives of Canada, 1984.

Klein, William A., "Tax Effects of Nonpayment of Child Support" (1990) 45 Tax Lawyer 259.

Krishna, V., "Alimony and Maintenance, 'Payable on a Periodic Basis?'; Paragraphs 56(b), (c), (c.1) and *60(b)*, (c) and (c.1)" (1985), 1 Can. Current Tax J-83.

Krishna, V., "Spousal Payments" (1989) 23 CGA Magazine 44.

Krishna, V., "Structuring Matrimonial Settlements" (1990) 3:3 Can. Current Tax J-19.

Krishna, V., "To Love, Honor or Pay" (1990) 24 CGA Magazine 28.

Krishna, Vern, "Using the Capital Gains Exemption for Matrimonial Settlement" (1993) 4 Can. Current Tax C5.

Kroft, E.G., "Some Income Tax Considerations Relating to Support Payments Made After 1983" (1985) 4 Can. J. Fam. L. 499.

Maisel, Neil and Steve Z. Ranot, "Who Pays the Tax on Tax?" (1992) 7 Money and Family Law 93.

McCue, David J., "Maintenance and Alimony Payments" (1979) 13 CGA Magazine 27.

McGivney, Evelyn L., "Just the Tax Ma'am, Just the Tax!" (1991) 13 Advocates Quarterly 129.

McGregor, Gwyneth, "Alimony and Maintenance Payments" (1983) 5 Can. Taxpayer 169.

Penner, Michael S. and Neil Maisel, "Understanding Capital Gains and the Capital Gains Exemption" (1992) 7 Money and Family Law 9.

Penner, Michael S. and Steve Z. Ranot, "When is Alimony Paid?" (1992) 7 Money and Family Law 65.

Richards, Gabrielle M.R., "Support Payments: An Update" (1992) 3 Can. Current Tax J-115.

Roher, Bruce, "Transferring Shares to a Separated Spouse: Who Pays the Tax?" (1994) 9 Money & Family Law 75.

Sandler, Daniel, "Family Law and the Family Jewels" (1991) 39 Can. Tax J. 513.

Sands, H., and A. Zylberlicht, "The Tax Consequences of Support Payments" (1985) 118:6 CA Magazine 56.

"Second Time Around (The): How Much Does It Cost?", *Can. Tax Letter*, May 10, 1976.

"Sections *60(b)* and (c) — A Trap for the Unwary" (1990) 44 D.T.C. 7035.

Sherman, David M., "Till Tax Do Us Part: The New Definition of 'Spouse'" in *Report of Proceedings of 44th Tax Conf.* 20:1 (Canada Tax Foundation, 1992).

Shillington, Robert and Ellen Zweibel, *Child Support Policy: Income Tax Treatment and Child Support Guidelines* (Toronto: Policy Research Centre on Children, Youth and Families, 1993).

Shultz, Clayton G., "Income Tax Law and Policy Applicable to Periodic Maintenance and Division of Matrimonial Assets" (1987) 1 Can. Fam. L.Q. 293.

"Spousal Trust Rollovers" (1990) 44 D.T.C. 7040.

"Taxation of Support Payments Simplified?" (1992) 7 Money and Family Law 75.

"The Written Separation Agreement: Not Quite Dead Yet!" (1993) 18 Money and Family Law 89.

Child Care Expenses

Arnold, B.J., "Section *63*: The Deduction for Child Care Expenses" (1973) 21 Can. Tax J. 176.

Bittker, "A Comprehensive Tax Base As A Goal of Income Tax Reform" (1967) 80 Harvard L.R. 925.

Buckley, Melina, "Symes v. The Queen" (1993) 2 National No. 437.

Drache, Arthur B.C., "Child Care Expenses: Planning Leeway" (1983) 5 Can. Taxpayer 3.

Drache, Arthur B.C., "Sexism, Human Rights and Tax" (1979) 1 Can. Taxpayer 114.

Goodison, Don, "Child Care Expenses Deduction" (1988) 22 CGA Magazine 5.

Goodison, Don, "Nanny Means Business" (1989) 23 CGA Magazine 15.

Goodison, Don, "Tax Forum — Not a Business Expense" (1991) 25 CGA Magazine 20.

MacGowan, J.M., "The Tax Consequences of Marriage", in *Proceedings of 26th Tax Conf.* 275 (Can. Tax Foundation, 1974).

McAllister, Debra M., "The Supreme Court in Symes: Two Solitudes" (1994) 4 N.J.C.L. 248.

Young, Claire F.L., "Child Care: A Taxing Issue?" (1994) 39 McGill Law J. 539.

Young, Claire F.L., "Child Care and the Charter: Privileging the Privileged" (1994) 2 Rev. Constit. Studies 20.

Moving Expenses

Finlay, Joe, "Staggered Relocations May Disqualify Moving Expenses" (1991) 49 Advocate 358.

Goodison, Donald, "It's Your Move" (1979) 13 CGA Magazine 16.

Goodison, Donald, "Moving On" (1981) 15 CGA Magazine 37.

Hugget, Donald R., "Moving Employees" (1991) 19 Can. Tax News 44.

"Interest-Free Loans to Employees and Shareholders", Can. Tax Letter, November 10, 1977.

Lemon, K.W., "Tax Considerations Arising from Household Relocation" (1981) 46 Bus. Q. 86.

"On the Move?" (1979) 1 Can. Taxpayer 96.

"Reimbursement of Moving Expenses for Same City Move Could Be Tax Free" (1992) 4 Tax. of Exec. Comp. and Retirement 667.

Schnek, M., "Employee Relocation" (1981) 29 Can. Tax J. 71.

"Student Moving Expenses" (1983) 5 Can. Taxpayer 151.

Thomas, Richard B., "A Hole That You Could Drive a Moving Van Through" (1990) 38 Can. Tax J. 937.

Other Deductions

Beach, Wayne G., "Tax Aspects of Registered Retirement Savings Plans", 9:30 *Tax Planning and Management of Canadian Income Tax, Revised* (Toronto: Butterworth and Co. (Canada) Ltd., 1978).

Boyle, "The Treatment of RRSP Proceeds on Maturity" (1979) 27 Can. Tax J. 68.

Budd, John S., "Two Unlikely Havens from Capital Gains Tax" (1979) 112 CA Magazine 70.

Clare, James L., and Paul F. Della Penna, "Tax Aspects of Employee's Pension Plans", 9:28 *Tax Planning and Management of Canadian Income Tax, Revised* (Toronto: Butterworths and Co. (Canada) Ltd., 1977).

Colley, Geoffrey M., "What's New in Personal Investment" (1977) 110 CA Magazine 63.

Connors, Raymond J., "DPSPs — The Ideal Tax Shelter for Employers and Employees" (1982) 115:2 CA Magazine 50.

Dancey, Kevin J., "Specific Expenditures: Timing and Deductibility", Corp. Mgmt. Tax Conf. 116 (Can. Tax Foundation, 1981).

Drache, Arthur B.C., "Estate Planning: Depreciable Property" (1980) 2 Can. Taxpayer 22.

Drache, Arthur B.C., "Religious School Decision" (1981) 3 Can. Taxpayer 33.

Drache, Arthur B.C., "Single Premium Deferred Annuities" (1981) 3 Can. Taxpayer 27.

Drache, Arthur B.C., "Tax Planning for Higher Education" (1981) 3 Can. Taxpayer 44.

Drache, Arthur B.C., "Tuition Fee Deductibility" (1980) 2 Can. Taxpayer 208.

Eng, Susan, and Goodman, "Education Trusts and Other Provisions for Education Expenses" (1979–81) 5 E. & T.Q. 246.

Farres, Alan E., "RRSPs: The Tax Shelter That Wasn't Meant To Be" (1982) 115:4 CA Magazine 48.

Finkelstein, David N., "Tax Problems in Estate Planning for the Corporate Executive", in *Proceedings of 33rd Tax Conf.* 952 (Can. Tax Foundation, 1981).

Fisher, G.B., "Early Retirement Tax Considerations" (1983) 31 Can. Tax J. 828.

Griffith, Thomas D., "Theories of Personal Deductions in Income Tax" (January 1989) 40 Hastings L. J. 343.

Jarman, Robert E., "Administrative and Tax Problems with Self-Administered RRSP's" (1975) 2 E. & T.Q. 105.

Knechtel, Ronald C., "Federal Income Taxation of Life Insurance Policyholders under the Present Law and under the Current Proposals", in *Proceedings of 29th Tax Conf.* 612 (Can. Tax Foundation, 1977).

Krishna, V., "Registered Retirement Savings Plans (RRSP's) — Availability of Funds for Judgment Creditors" (1984) 1 Can. Current Tax J-43.

Lengvari, George F., "Deferred Annuities as Tax Shelters" (1978) 111 CA Magazine 90.

Le Rossignol, Dan G., "Stock Dividends and Stock Options" (1979) 112 CA Magazine 67.

MacNaughton, Alan, "New Income Tax Rules for Holders of Life Insurance Policies and Annuities" (1983) 31 Can. Tax J. 921.

McGregor, Gwyneth, "Forward Averaging" (1983) 5 Can. Taxpayer 7.

McReynolds, D. Shawn, "Sheltering RRSP Assets from Creditors on Death" (1982–84) 6 E. & T.Q. 106.

Murray, L.C., "Statutory Deferred Income Plans", *Corp. Mgmt. Tax Conf.* Management Tax Conf. 121 (Can. Tax Foundation, 1979).

"*1979 Year-End Planning for Individuals*", Can. Tax Letter, November 30, 1979.

Rea, Samuel A., "Registered Retirement Savings Plans as a Tax Expenditure" (1980) 28 Can. Tax J. 459.

Schmidt, Rosemary, "Students and Taxation" (1991) 39 Can. Tax J. 673.

Young, Clair F.L., "Deductibility of Entertainment and Home Office Expenses: New Restrictions To Deal with Old Problems?" (1989) 37 Can. Tax J. 227.

Chapter 13 — Family Transactions

Table of Contents

I. — General Comment

Although an individual considers his or her immediate family (spouse and minor children) as an economic unit, the general rule in income tax law is that each member of the family is a separate taxpayer. Each individual has an independent status and is liable for tax on his or her personal income.

The Act uses a broad concept of spouse to include common-law partners and same-sex married relationships.[1]

The individual income tax structure is progressive.[2] This means that as an individual receives more income, his or her taxes increase at a progressive rate. Additional increments to

---

[1] See subs. 248(1) "common-law partner".

[2] See s. 117.

income are taxable at higher marginal rates than their predecessors. This means that a family whose income is taxed to only one member (for example, the mother) will pay higher taxes than another family with an identical income that is taxable to two members — say, the father and mother. Thus, high-income taxpayers have an incentive to reduce their taxes by shifting income to members of their family in lower tax brackets. The more that one can sprinkle income amongst family members, the lower the overall family taxes. Thus, in tax law, one plus one is not equal to two in after-tax dollars.

Potential savings from income splitting are a powerful inducement to shift income from high marginal rate taxpayers to lower marginal rates. For example, a father with income of $200,000 and a marginal tax rate of 50 percent might transfer part of his portfolio of securities to his minor daughter to reduce his investment income and potential future capital gains. If his daughter's tax rate is only 15 percent, he saves 35 percentage points of tax. The problem is exacerbated if the father can retrieve the securities at any time from his daughter and have title revert to him.

Professionals and entrepreneurs can split business income through a corporation. For example, an individual can incorporate a company and have it issue different classes of shares to each member of his or her family. The corporation can then sprinkle dividends amongst the family members according to their financial circumstances. For example:

> *Operating company with four classes of shares*

Dividend-sprinkling would reduce each family member's marginal rate of tax and the overall family tax burden.

In a slightly more sophisticated variation one might interpose a trust between the corporation and each member of the family and have the trustee sprinkle the dividends according to each member's financial circumstances. For example:

> *Operating company with four classes of shares — Trust for family*

The Act contains various anti-avoidance rules that prevent certain forms of income-splitting amongst the immediate family and in certain non-arm's length relationships. These rules protect the integrity of the progressive tax rate structure by preventing downward rate-shifting from high-rate taxpayers to their children. The rules do not affect the underlying property and commercial rights of the parties in the property transfer. In the above example, the transfer of securities by the father to his daughter is valid for purposes of commercial and property law, which come within the constitutional jurisdiction of the provinces. The federal tax rules apply only for tax purposes. Apart from the specific attribution rules, however, there is no general scheme in tax law to prevent income-splitting.[3] Indeed, the Act even promotes income-splitting in certain cases.[4] Thus, we need to evaluate each income-splitting structure on its own facts and in the context of the general anti-avoidance rule (GAAR) to ensure that the arrangement is within the policy of the stautute.

II. — Indirect Payments

A taxpayer who transfers income or property to another taxpayer may be deemed to have constructively received the diverted income or property.[5] For example, an individual who directs his employer to deposit his pay cheque directly into his spouse's savings account is liable for tax on the salary, even though the taxpayer relinquishes actual ownership and control over the property. For tax purposes, the taxpayer retains constructive ownership of the property. This rule prevents taxpayers from artificially reducing their taxable income by diverting funds to family members with lower marginal tax rates.

The constructive ownership doctrine does not apply where a taxpayer directs that a portion of his or her Canada Pension Plan be paid to the taxpayer's spouse.[6]

The doctrine of constructive receipt of income applies where a taxpayer transfers property:[7]

1. To a person;

2. At the taxpayer's direction, or with the taxpayer's concurrence;

3. For the benefit of the taxpayer or a person whom he or she wishes to benefit, *and*

4. The payment or transfer is of a type that would ordinarily have been included in the taxpayer's income if he or she received it directly.

In these circumstances, the Act deems the transferor to receive the payment or transfer directly.[8]

---

[3]*Neuman v. Minister of National Revenue*, [1998] 3 C.T.C. 177, 98 D.T.C. 6297, [1998] 1 S.C.R. 770 (S.C.C.).

[4]See, for example, the rules permitting deductions to spousal RRSPs (para. 74.5(12)(a) and subs. 146(5.1)).

[5]Subs. 56(2); see also *IT-335R2*, "Indirect Payments" (September 11, 1989).

[6]Including a prescribed provincial pension plan (see regulation 7800).

[7]Subs. 56(2). *IT-335R2*, "Indirect Payments" (September 11, 1989).

[8]*Neuman v. Minister of National Revenue*, [1998] 1 S.C.R. 770, [1998] 3 C.T.C. 177, 98 D.T.C. 6297 (S.C.C.); *McClurg v. Minister of National Revenue*, [1990] 3 S.C.R. 1020, [1991] 1 C.T.C. 169, 91 D.T.C. 5001 (S.C.C.) (income not attributed to director of corporation for participating in declaration of corporate dividend); *Boardman v. R.*, [1986] 1 C.T.C. 103, 85 D.T.C. 5628 (Fed. T.D.) (shareholder

The doctrine does not normally apply to corporate dividends. Directors of a corporation who declare a dividend do so in their capacity as directors and fiduciaries. The fourth condition requires that the taxpayer would have received the dividend if it had not been paid to the shareholder of record. An unpaid dividend remains in the corporation's retained earnings if it is not paid to the shareholder of record. Thus, subsection 56(2) cannot apply to dividends if the fourth test is not satisfied.[9] In a closely held family corporation, for example, dividends to the taxpayer's spouse on his or her shareholdings do not come within the doctrine of constructive receipt. This is so even if the taxpayer waives his or her right to receive a dividend, because the waived dividend merely remains in the corporation's retained earnings. The situation is different, however, if the shareholder of record *directs* the corporation to pay his or her dividend to another person.

Subsections 56(2), (4) and (4.1) do not apply in respect of amounts included in a minor's split income. Thus, amounts taxed as split income in the hands of a minor child are not also attributable to another person.[10]

---

taxable on diversion of corporate assets to settle financial obligations on divorce); *Minister of National Revenue v. Bronfman*, [1965] C.T.C. 378, 65 D.T.C. 5235 (Can. Ex. Ct.) (directors of corporation liable for taxes on account of gifts to relatives in need of financial assistance; combining subss. 15(1) and 56(2)); *Reininger v. Minister of National Revenue*, 58 D.T.C. 608 (corporate loan to wife of principal shareholder taxable to him under subss. 15(2) and 56(2)); *Perrault v. R.*, [1978] C.T.C. 395, 78 D.T.C. 6272 (Fed. C.A.) (waiver of dividend by majority shareholder in favour of minority shareholder was dividend income); *New v. Minister of National Revenue*, [1970] Tax A.B.C. 700, 70 D.T.C. 1415 (Can. Tax App. Bd.) (controlling shareholder in receipt of income for benefit conferred on son through rental of corporate property to son at less than fair market value).

[9]*Neuman v. Minister of National Revenue*, [1998] 1 S.C.R. 770, [1998] 3 C.T.C. 177, 98 D.T.C. 6297 (S.C.C.) (dividends paid to controlling shareholder's spouse not taxable in his hands despite absence of any "contribution" by spouse). *McClurg v. Minister of National Revenue*, [1988] 1 C.T.C. 75, 88 D.T.C. 6047 (Fed. C.A.); affirmed [1991] 1 C.T.C. 169, 91 D.T.C. 5001 (S.C.C.), *per* Urie J.:

> The language of the subsection [56(2)] creating the essential ingredients required in its application, viewed in light of its purpose, is simply not apt, in my opinion, to encompass the acts of a director when he participates in the declaration of a corporate dividend unless it is read in its most literal sense. To do so ignores the existence of the corporate entity. Only the most explicit language, which is not present in subs. 56(2), would justify the notion that a director acting as such could be seen as directing a corporation to divert a transfer or payment for his own benefit or the benefit of another person, absent bad faith, breach of fiduciary duty or acting beyond the powers conferred by the share structure of the corporation, none of which bases have been alleged here. [*cont.*] See also: Vern Krishna and J. Anthony VanDuzer, "Corporate Share Capital Structures and Income Splitting: *McClurg v. Canada*" (1992-93), 21 Can. Bus. L.J. 335 at 367.

[10]Subs. 56(5).

1. — *Transfers of Rights to Income*

The doctrine of constructive receipt also applies where a taxpayer transfers *rights to receive income* (as opposed to the income itself) to another individual.[11] The essence of this type of transfer is that the individual transfers the right to all future income but not the ownership of the income-generating property. Thus, the transferee then owns the *right to all future income or revenues* that the property may yield, but does not own the property itself.

2. — *Interest-Free or Low-Interest Loan*

A taxpayer can also shift his or her tax burden by loaning money at rates lower than the commercial rate of interest. For example, in the simplest case, an individual can make an interest-free loan. Where the purpose of the loan is to reduce or avoid tax in a non-arm's length transaction, the Act deems the borrower's income from the loan to be the income of the lender.[12] Any income from property substituted for the loan, and income from property purchased with the loan, is also included in the lender's income.

Example

Jane loans $50,000 to her spouse who earns 10 percent by depositing the money in a GIC. Jane is taxable on the $5,000 interest income for the year.

Mark loans $100,000 to his niece at 5 percent interest per year. The niece purchases an investment certificate yielding 8 percent per year. Mark is taxable on the *net* income of $3,000 from the investment certificate.

3. — *Transfers/Loans to Spouse*

An individual who transfers or loans property, directly or indirectly, to his spouse, or to a person who becomes his spouse after the transfer or loan of property, is taxable on any income from the property or from any property substituted for the transferred property. The Act attributes any income or loss from the property to the transferor during his lifetime if the transferor resides in Canada and lives with his spouse.[13] The transferor is also taxable on any taxable capital gains or allowable capital losses from dispositions of the transferred or

---

[11] Subs. 56(4).

[12] Subs. 56(4.1).

[13] Subs. 74.1(1). *Kieboom v. Minister of National Revenue*, [1992] 2 C.T.C. 59, 92 D.T.C. 6382 (Fed. C.A.) (income from taxpayer's gift of non-voting shares to wife and children subject to attribution).

loaned property.[14] Thus, in both cases, the Act deems the transferor to have constructively received the transferred income (loss) or taxable gain (loss). These rules apply only to income and losses from *property*, and do not apply to income and losses from a business.[15]

The attribution rules do not apply if the spouses are living separate and apart by reason of a breakdown of their marriage.[16] In the case of capital gains, however, the parties must file a joint election not to have the rules apply.

Similarly, the attribution rules in respect of transfers to corporations (other than small business corporations)[17] in which a spouse has a direct or indirect interest generally do not apply to the period during which the spouses are living separate and apart by reason of a breakdown of their marriage.[18]

4. — *Transfers/Loans to Persons Under 18 Years of Age*

An individual who transfers or loans property to a person under 18 years of age who is the transferor's niece or nephew or does not deal at arm's length with the transferor, is taxable on any income earned on the property.[19] Thus, income and losses realised by the recipient of the transferred property are attributed to the person who transferred or loaned the property.

---

[14]Subs. 74.2(1).

[15]See *Robins v. Minister of National Revenue*, [1963] C.T.C. 27, 63 D.T.C. 1012 (Can. Ex. Ct.) where Noel J. had this to say about the predecessor sections to s. 74.1:

> Section 21 as well as Sections 22 and 23 are designed to prevent avoidance of tax by transfer of income producing property to persons who are normally in close relationship with the transferor. But what is deemed to be the income of the transferor, and this is clearly stated, is income from property only. Indeed there is no mention of income from a business such as we have here and, therefore, this section can be of no assistance in determining whether the business profit resulting from a real estate transaction is taxable as income of the appellant or of his wife.

See, also, *Wertman v. Minister of National Revenue*, [1964] C.T.C. 252, 64 D.T.C. 5158 (Can. Ex. Ct.) (spouses' joint investment in building with funds from community property); *Minister of National Revenue v. Minden*, [1963] C.T.C. 364, 63 D.T.C. 1231 (Can. Ex. Ct.) (lawyer advanced money to spouse for investments without documentation, interest or security). For the distinction between income from business and income from property see Chapter 7 "Business Income".

[16]Para. 74.5(3)(a).

[17]Para. 74.4(2)(c).

[18]Subs. 74.5(4).

[19]Subs. 74.1(2).

III. — Non-Arm's Length Loans

The two rules discussed above (loans and transfers to spouses and to certain persons under 18 years of age) prevent taxpayers from engaging in the more blatant forms of income-splitting.

There is, however, an additional rule that is even broader: income from any property (for example, money) loaned to a non-arm's length borrower may be attributed and taxed to the lender if one of the main purposes of the loan is to reduce or avoid tax, for example, by income-splitting.[20] This rule is considerably broader in scope than the more specific attribution rules in that it applies to low-cost or interest-free loans to any individual with whom the lender does not deal at arm's length. This rule does not apply to transfers of property; it only applies to loaned property.

Unlike the more specific attribution rules, the non-arm's length rule applies only if the lender loans the property for the purposes of reducing or avoiding tax on income that he or she would otherwise have earned on the property. There is no attribution of income if the lender does not lend the money for the purposes of tax reduction or avoidance (for example, a loan to a relative or friend for altruistic reasons). Further, the attribution rules do not apply to loans at "commercial" rates of interest if the borrower pays the interest no later than 30 days after the end of the taxation year in which the interest is due.[21]

IV. — Interpretation and Application

The following aspects of the attribution rules warrant particular attention:

- The term "transfer" includes any divestiture of property from one person to another and includes gifts. In *Fasken Estate*, for example, the courts said:[22]

    ... the word "transfer" is not a form of art and has not a technical meaning. It is not necessary to a transfer of property from a husband to his wife that it should be made in any particular form or that it should be made directly. All that is required is that the husband should so deal with the property as to divest himself of it and vest it in his wife,

---

[20]Subs. 56(4.1).

[21]Subs. 56(4.2). The Act prescribes the appropriate rate of interest each quarter according to commercial market rates (Reg. 4301).

[22]*Fasken Estate v. Minister of National Revenue*, [1948] C.T.C. 265, 49 D.T.C. 491 (Can. Ex. Ct.) at 279 [C.T.C.] and 497 [D.T.C.]; see also *St. Aubyn v. Attorney General*, [1952] A.C. 15 (H.L.) at 53, *per* Lord Radcliffe:

    If the word "transfer" is taken in its primary sense, a person makes a transfer of property to another person if he does the act or executes the instrument which divests him of the property and at the same time vests it in that other person.

that is to say, pass the property from himself to her. The means by which he accomplishes this result, whether direct or circuitous, may properly be called a transfer.

- The attribution applies to income and losses from *property*, and not to income and losses from a business.[23]

- The attribution rules do not generally apply to sales at fair market value if the purchaser pays the vendor for the property.[24]

- The attribution rules apply to loans, other than loans that bear a commercial rate of interest. A loan is considered to bear a commercial rate of interest if the rate charged is at least equal to the prescribed rate or the arm's length market rate.[25]

- In the case of a transfer or loan to a person under the age of 18, income attribution continues until the person reaches 18 years of age.

- The attribution rules do not apply to a parent (or other transferor) on amounts that the Act taxes as split income[26] in the hands of a minor child.[27]

- The liability for tax from the application of the attribution rules is joint and several.[28]

---

[23]See *Robins v. Minister of National Revenue*, [1963] C.T.C. 27, 63 D.T.C. 1012 (Can. Ex. Ct.) where Noel J. said the following about the predecessor sections to s. 74.1:

> Section 21 as well as Sections 22 and 23 are designed to prevent avoidance of tax by transfer of income producing property to persons who are normally in close relationship with the transferor. But what is deemed to be the income of the transferor, and this is clearly stated, is income from property only. Indeed, there is no mention of income from a business such as we have here and, therefore, this section can be of no assistance in determining whether the business profit resulting from a real estate transaction is taxable as income of the appellant or his wife.

See, also, *Wertman v. Minister of National Revenue*, [1964] C.T.C. 252, 64 D.T.C. 5158 (Can. Ex. Ct.) (spouses' joint investment in building with funds from community property); *Minister of National Revenue v. Minden*, [1963] C.T.C. 364, 63 D.T.C. 1231 (Can. Ex. Ct.) (lawyer advanced money to spouse for investments without documentation, interest or security).

[24]Subs. 74.5(1).

[25]Subs. 74.5(2).

[26]S. 120.4.

[27]Subs. 74.5(13).

[28]Para. 160(1)(d).

- The income attribution rules apply to spouses only during the period that they are married *and* living together. The rules do not apply upon divorce or separation by reason of matrimonial breakdown.[29]

- There is no attribution of capital gains and losses following divorce or separation pursuant to matrimonial breakdown[30] if the parties file a joint election precluding attribution. The parties may file the election in the year after they begin to live separate and apart.

V. — The "Kiddie Tax"

Although the attribution rules apply to transfers of property to minor children, they do not prevent income-splitting between family members. Since dividends are eligible for the dividend tax credit, minor children could avoid paying tax on some dividends. The purpose of the "kiddie tax" is to prevent income-splitting with minor children under 18 years of age through dividend sprinkling.[31] The "kiddie tax" is a special 29 percent tax that applies to certain forms of passive income of individuals under the age of 18 years. Generally, the tax applies to:[32]

- Taxable dividends and other shareholder benefits[33] on unlisted shares of Canadian and foreign companies;

- Capital gains that a minor realizes from a disposition of unlisted shares to a person with whom he does not deal at arm's length; and

- Income from a partnership or trust where the partnership or trust derives the income from the business of providing goods or services to a business that a relative of the child carries on or in which the relative participates.

Twenty-nine percent is the highest rate of federal tax and it is applied at a flat rate. This tax prevents some of the more blatant forms of income-splitting.[34] Any income that is taxable as "split income" is deductible from the individual's income from business or property for the

---

[29]Para. 74.5(3)(a).

[30]Para. 74.5(3)(b).

[31]See for example, *Neuman v. Minister of National Revenue*, [1998] 3 C.T.C. 177 (S.C.C.), which rejected the application of subsection 56(2) to dividend sprinkling structures.

[32]S. 120.4.

[33]See s. 15.

[34]See, for example, *Ferrel v. R.*, [1999] 2 C.T.C. 101, 99 D.T.C. 5111 (Fed. C.A.), which rejected the application of subsection 56(2) to a management services structure involving a trust.

year. Hence, the regular income tax does not apply to any portion of the split income. Liability for the tax is joint and several.[35]

The only amounts deductible from the tax are the dividend tax credit and the foreign tax credit in respect of amounts that the minor includes in his or her split income. Thus, the tax has a substantial bite in that it effectively applies to gross income at the highest marginal tax rate.

The "kiddie tax" does not apply to:

- Income paid to individuals over 18 years of age;

- Reasonable remuneration to minors; or

- Interest income.

Thus, income-splitting is still permissible, unless the Act specifically prohibits it in particular circumstances. For example, income-splitting with spouses is in a corporate business context still possible.

VI. — Transfers and Loans to Corporations

In certain circumstances, an individual who transfers or loans property to a corporation may be taxable on investment income attributed to him from the transfer or loan. In the case of equity investments, the Act attributes to the transferor 5/4ths of any dividends that he or she receives on shares issued for the transfer. In the case of a loan, the amount attributed is the amount by which interest at the prescribed rate on the loan exceeds the total of any interest that he or she actually receives on the loan. In both cases, the attribution rules apply only if one of the main purposes of the transfer is to reduce the transferor's income and benefit a person who is his spouse, common-law partner, a related person under 18 years of age, or niece or nephew.[36]

These attribution rules do not apply if the transferee corporation is a small business corporation. This is an important exclusion that allows income-splitting in many cases. A small business corporation[37] is a Canadian-controlled private corporation that uses all or substantially all of its assets in an "active business"[38] that it carries on primarily in Canada. A corporation also qualifies as a small business corporation if a related corporation uses the assets in an active business in Canada.

---

[35]Subs. 160(1.2).

[36]Subs. 74.5(5).

[37]Subs. 248(1) "small business corporation".

[38]Subs. 125(7) "active business carried on by a corporation".

The CRA interprets the phrase "all or substantially all" as 90 percent of the corporation's assets. Hence, if a corporation permanently uses more than 10 percent of its total assets for investment purposes, it does not qualify as a small business corporation. The CRA interprets "primarily" as being more than 50 percent in respect of the business.

VII. — Artificial Transactions

Taxpayers can sometimes structure transactions to take advantage of the attribution rules and trigger "reverse attribution". For example, an individual might guarantee his or her high-income spouse's borrowing from a bank and argue that the income from the borrowed funds is attributable to the individual.[39] Subsection 74.5(11) is a specific anti-avoidance provision that prevents the attribution rules from applying if "one of the main reasons" for the transfer or loan is to reduce the tax payable on income or gains from loaned or transferred property.

In *Lipson*, for example, the taxpayers engaged in an elaborate three-step financing structure, the ultimate effect of which was to attribute net losses (net of personal home mortgage interest) to the higher income spouse. Notwithstanding the specific anti-avoidance attribution rule, the Supreme Court (Rothstein J dissenting) used the general anti-avoidance rule to strike down the structure.

---

[39]See subs. 74.5(7).

Selected Bibliography to Chapter 13

Indirect Payments

Davidson, A. Barrie, "Personal Service and Professional Corporations Incorporating Employment and Professional Income", in *Proceedings of 32nd Tax Conf.* 212 (Can. Tax Foundation, 1980).

Desaulniers, Claude P., "Choix d'une structure du capital", *J. d'études fiscales* 79 (Can. Tax Foundation, 1981).

Drache, A.B.C., "Controlling a Company Without Shares" (1992) 14 Can. Taxpayer 56.

Drache, A.B.C., "Gifting Without a Transfer" (1991) 13 Can. Taxpayer 164.

Drache, A.B.C., "Income Splitting 'Loophole' Closed" (1992) 14 Can. Taxpayer 21.

Drache, A.B.C., "McClurg Obiter Creates Problems" (1992) 14 Can. Taxpayer 47.

Drache, A.B.C., "Technical Hitches Ruin Income Split" (1991) 13 Can. Taxpayer 62.

"Estate Planning Time Bomb" (1983) 5 Can. Taxpayer 42.

Grafton, S., "Income-Splitting" (1985) 13 Can. Tax News 88.

Graschuk, Harry S., "The Professional Corporation in Alberta" (1977) 25 Can. Tax J. 109.

Harris, Neil H., "Tax Aspects of Condominium Conversions and Lease Inducement Payments to Recipients", in *Proceedings of 38th Tax Conf.* 45 (Can. Tax Foundation, 1986).

Innes, William I., "The Taxation of Indirect Benefits: An Examination of Subsections 56(2), 56(3), 56(4), 245(2) and 245(3) of the *Income Tax Act*", in *Proceedings of 38th Tax Conf.* 42 (Can. Tax Foundation, 1986).

Krishna, Vern, "Corporate Share Capital Structures and Income Splitting" (1991) 3 Can. Current Tax C-71.

Krishna, Vern, "Corporate Share Structures and Estate Planning" (1983) 6 E. & T.Q. 168.

Krishna, Vern, "Designing Share Capital Structures for Income Splitting" (1984) 1 Can. Current Tax C-51.

Krishna, Vern, "Indirect Payments and Transfer of Income" (1986) 1 Can. Current Tax J-137.

Kroft, E.G., "Income Splitting" (1983) 17 CGA Magazine 28.

Kwan, Stanley P.W., and Kenneth J. Murray, "Remuneration Planning for the Owner-Manager" (1982) 29 Can. Tax J. 603.

Levine, Risa, "Incorporation and the Taxation of a Private Corporation", *British Columbia Tax Conf.* 1 (Can. Tax Foundation, 1980).

Zaytsoff, J.J., "Accountant's Comment: Innovative Share Capital Structures to Split Income Effectively" (1984) 42 Advocate (Van.) 177.

Non-Arm's Length Loans

Brahmst, Oliver C., "Beware of the Breadth of Subsection 56(4.1)" (1991) 3 Can. Current Tax P-43.

Brahmst, Oliver C., "Subsection 56(4.1) — An Update" (1992) 3 Can. Current Tax P-47.

Drache, A.B.C., "Income Splitting Needs Advance Planning" (1991) 13 Can. Taxpayer 181.

Drache, A.B.C., "Income Splitting Through Lending" (1991) 13 Can. Taxpayer 174.

Chapter 14 — Taxable Income

Table of Contents

Table of Contents

I. — General Comment

To this point, we have looked at the rules for calculating net income. Now, we look at the rules that determine "taxable income" or the taxable base.[1] In the next chapter we will review the computation of tax payable.

A taxpayer is taxable on his or her taxable income. Canadian residents are taxable on their *worldwide taxable income* for the year.[2] Subject to income tax treaty provisions, non-residents are taxable only on their Canadian source taxable income during a taxation year.[3]

There are two principle issues in designing an appropriate structure to determine the taxable base:

1. What relief, if any, should we provide for individual and personal circumstances?

2. Should the relief take the form of a deduction from income or a credit against taxes payable?

1. — "Taxable Income"

How should we account for individual and family circumstances? "Taxable income" is a mathematical measure of the taxable base. A resident's "taxable income" is his or her net income plus or minus the adjustments and deductions in Division C. Thus, "taxable income" is the mathematical residue of net income adjusted by various items in Division C.

Income is the measure of a taxpayer's net realized gains attributable to a source of income recognized in law. Income, which for tax purposes represents the net realized increment to wealth, is not, however, always the most appropriate measure of a taxpayer's ability to pay tax, because it does not take into account personal and individual circumstances. In this chapter we look at some of the adjustments that the tax system makes for individual circumstances. We also see, once again, how we use the system to engineer behaviour by providing incentives for particular behaviour, for example, charitable giving.

Taxable income is a fairer measure of a taxpayer's ability to pay tax than net economic loss. In the case of individuals, for example, it is easy to see that taxpayers who have the same amount of net income do not necessarily have equal amounts of disposable income with which to pay their tax. For example, consider two individuals, each of whom earns $50,000: an unmarried person with no dependants and a married person with a family of six, one of whom is seriously ill and requires expensive medication. These two individuals have differ-

---

[1]Subs. 2(2); Div. C (ss. 110-114.2).

[2]Subs. 2(1).

[3]Subs. 2(3). A non-resident's taxable income is determined by reference to the rules in Div. D (ss. 115-116).

ent abilities to pay tax. Should we allow the individual with substantial financial responsibilities a measure of tax relief to ease the burden of his or her responsibilities? Should the amount of relief be related to the taxpayer's income, or should it be determined as a blanket amount regardless of the particular circumstances? If relief is to be income-tested, should we test by reference to the individual's income or his or her family income? How do we determine "family" for the purposes of income testing? These questions are difficult and, sometimes, politically controversial. How do we adjust for the "lumpiness" of income in different tax years?

The adjustments in Division C are of three types: (1) those available only to individuals; (2) those available only to corporations; and (3) those available to both individuals and corporations.

2. — Deduction or Credit?

The second issue concerns the mode of adjustment for personal circumstances. Should we provide relief for persons in different financial circumstances through tax deductions or tax credits?

A tax deduction is a deduction from income in computing taxable income. We measure the saving that results from a deduction by multiplying the deduction by the taxpayer's marginal tax rate. For example, a deduction of $1,000 reduces tax by $450 if the taxpayer's marginal rate is 45 percent, and by $300 if the tax rate is 30 percent. Thus, the higher the marginal tax rate, the more valuable the deduction to the taxpayer and the greater the revenue loss to the public treasury. We use deductions to measure net income to determine the net increment to wealth.

A tax credit also reduces the tax that would otherwise be payable. The savings resulting from a tax credit, however, are constant, regardless of the taxpayer's marginal tax rate. For example, a tax credit of $500 reduces tax by that amount, no matter whether the taxpayer's marginal tax rate is 45 percent or 30 percent. Hence, tax credits have a more equal distributive impact. However, unless a tax credit is refundable, it is of value only to those taxpayers who would otherwise have to pay tax. Most tax credits do not assist a taxpayer who does not have any tax payable.[4] We use tax credits to accommodate personal circumstances that might affect a taxpayer's ability to pay tax.

We subtract a tax credit directly from the amount of tax payable, rather than from income. Thus, each individual achieves the same saving regardless of his or her income level or marginal tax rate. For example, the basic personal tax credit applies to all individuals regard-

---

[4]Governments sometimes create "refundable" tax credits for the purpose of furthering a particular tax policy objective. This type of tax credit will entitle the taxpayer to a tax credit even where no taxes are payable. Hence, a taxpayer could receive money back even when he or she has paid no tax.

less of their income level. The credit is granted for being alive. Hence, a person earning $100,000 per year receives the same basic credit as a person earning $8,000 per year.

II. — Charitable Donations

1. — General Comment

The tax system provides financial incentives for taxpayers, who contribute to charitable, philanthropic, and public service organizations. These incentives encourage private financial support of philanthropic activities that are considered beneficial to the community. We justify the incentives on the basis of social policy, but they cost the federal and provincial treasuries, and, therefore, require strict control. The incentives have also led to numerous abusive schemes that have resulted in class action litigation.

The nature and extent of the incentives depend upon the type of taxpayer.

2. — Individuals

An individual can claim a tax credit for charitable donations at 29 percent, which translates into provincial-federal rate equivalent to approximately 46 percent (depending upon province of residence).

3. — Corporations

A corporation is entitled to a *deduction* for its charitable donations. Gifts to charitable and certain other organizations are deductible by a corporation up to an annual maximum of 75 percent of its income for the year.[5] Donations in excess of 75 percent of net income may be carried forward for five years and, in any of those years, deducted to the extent that they were not deducted in a previous year.

There are two substantive criteria for determining the deductibility of a donation:

    1. Is the contribution a gift? and

    2. Was the gift to a registered charity or other public service organization?

---

[5]Para. 110.1(1)(a).

(a) — What Constitutes a Gift?

At common law, a gift is a voluntary transfer of property for no consideration or material advantage. As Deane J. said:[6]

> The word "gift" . . . is intended to bear the meaning which it bears as a matter of ordinary language. . . . [I]t is not to be assumed that its ambit can properly be defined, with a lawyer's or logician's precision, by reference to a number of unqualified propositions or tests. . . .

Generally, a "gift" is a voluntary and gratuitous transfer of property from one person to another; it may be conditional but, once the condition is satisfied, it is not revocable.[7] A transfer of property is a gift where it is made:[8]

- By way of benefaction;[9]

---

[6]*Leary v. Federal Commissioner of Taxation* (1980), 32 A.L.R. 221 (Australia Fed. Ct.) at 241.

[7]"Gift" is defined in *Halsbury's Laws of England*, 4th ed., Vol. 20, §1 as follows:

> A gift *inter vivos* may be defined shortly as the transfer of any property from one person to another gratuitously while the donor is alive and not in expectation of death. . . .

In *Black's Law Dictionary*, 4th ed., (1968), "gift" is defined as:

> [a] voluntary transfer of personal property without consideration.

and:

> [b] parting by owner with property without pecuniary consideration . . .

The *Shorter Oxford Dictionary* defines "giving" as:

> . . . [a] transfer of property in a thing, voluntarily and without any valuable consideration. . . .

See also *Commr. of Taxation (Cth.) v. McPhail* (1968), 41 A.L.R. 346 (Australia H.C.) at 348, where Owen J. said,

> . . . but it is, I think, clear that to constitute a "gift," it must appear that the property transferred was transferred voluntarily and not as the result of a contractual obligation to transfer it and that no advantage of a material character was received by the transferor by way of return. . . .

This definition was approved by the Federal Court in *R. v. Zandstra*, [1974] C.T.C. 503, 74 D.T.C. 6416 (Fed. T.D.).

[8]*Leary v. Federal Commissioner of Taxation, ante,* at 243 (quoted with approval by the Federal Court of Appeal in *McBurney v. R.*, [1985] 2 C.T.C. 214, 85 D.T.C. 5433 (Fed. C.A.); leave to appeal refused (1986), 65 N.R. 320n (S.C.C.).

[9]*Collector of Imposts (Vic.) v. Cuming Campbell Invt. Pty. Ltd.* (1940), 63 C.L.R. 619 (Australia H.C.) (transfer by way of benefaction being "essential idea" of gift, *per* Dixon, J. at 642). Some courts speak of a "detached and disinterested generosity"; see, e.g., *Commissioner v. LoBue* (1956), 351 U.S. 243 at 246 (gift of affection, respect, admiration, charity or like impulses); *Robertson v. U.S.* (1952), 343 U.S.

- Without exchange for material reward or advantage; and

- Without contractual obligation.

The essence of a gift is that it is a transfer without *quid pro quo*, a contribution motivated by detached and disinterested generosity.[10]

Subsection 248(30) modifies the common law meaning of "gift" for tax purposes to include donations that confer an advantage[11] on the donor, provided that the value of the donated property exceeds the value of the advantage that the donor receives. A person is not considered to make a gift if he or she receives valuable consideration equal to his or her "donation".[12] For example, payment for a dinner organized by a charity may involve both charitable and non-charitable elements.[13] Regardless of the form and documentation of the arrangements, it is the substance of the contribution that determines whether the taxpayer makes a gift or a disguised payment for services. There is no litmus paper test: one must look to the substance of the contribution. The creativity of promoters to disguise the purchase of tax credits as gifts led to a good deal of litigation.[14]

Although a payment pursuant to a contractual obligation to the donee is not a gift, the absence of a contractual obligation does not necessarily imply that the payment is a gift. Note also, a contractual obligation between the donor and a third party does not necessarily deprive a payment of its character as a gift. For example, a contract between A and B that each

---

711 (U.S., Utah) at 714; *C.I.R. v. Duberstein* (1960), 363 U.S. 278 at 285; see also, *Savoy Overseers v. Art Union of London*, [1896] A.C. 296 (H.L.) at 308 and 312 (charitable donation made where donor not looking "for any return in the shape of direct personal advantage," *per* Lord McNaghten); *Collector of Imposts (Vic.) v. Cuming Campbell Investments Pty. Ltd.*, *ante*, at 641.

[10]*Tite v. Minister of National Revenue*, [1986] 2 C.T.C. 2343, 86 D.T.C. 1788 (T.C.C.).

[11]Para. 248(31)(a).

[12]*Tite v. Minister of National Revenue*, above note 10 (taxpayer's claim for charitable donation denied where evidence demonstrated that payment to acquire print equal to value of work).

[13]*Burns v. Minister of National Revenue*, [1988] 1 C.T.C. 201, 88 D.T.C. 6101 (Fed. T.D.); affirmed [1990] 1 C.T.C. 350 (Fed. C.A.) (taxpayer's payments to amateur athletic association not "gifts" because taxpayer expected and received benefit in return for payments).

[14]See, e.g., *C.I.R. v. Duberstein*, above note 9, at 289, *per* Justice Brennan:

Decision of the issue presented in these cases must be based ultimately on the application of the fact-finding tribunal's experience with the mainsprings of human conduct to the totality of the facts of each case. The nontechnical nature of the statutory standard, the close relationship of it to the data of practical human experience, and the multiplicity of relevant factual elements, with their various combinations, creating the necessity of ascribing the proper force to each, confirm us in our conclusion that primary weight in this area must be given to the conclusions of the trier of fact.

will contribute an equal amount to a registered charity does not *per se* disqualify their contributions as gifts.

(b) — Blended Payments

Blended contributions should be broken down into their component parts. For example, the admission price to a charity event may cover the costs of goods and services (such as food and entertainment) and a premium intended as a gift.[15] Similarly, a global payment to a charity that offers both religious and secular education might comprise a payment for tuition fees and a gift for charitable purposes. The tuition component is a personal expenditure; the gift for charitable purposes is deductible as a donation. The allocation between the deductible and the non-deductible portions is always a question of fact.[16]

(c) — Eligible Organizations

Donations to the following organizations are deductible to the extent of the annual maximum limit:[17]

- Registered charities;

- Registered Canadian amateur athletic associations;

- Resident housing corporations that provide low-cost housing accommodations for the aged;

- Canadian municipalities;

- The United Nations and its agencies;

- Prescribed foreign universities that admit Canadian students;[18] and

- Certain foreign charitable organizations to which the federal government has contributed in the year or in the preceding year.

---

[15]*Aspinall v. Minister of National Revenue*, [1970] Tax A.B.C. 1073, 70 D.T.C. 1669 (Can. Tax App. Bd.).

[16]*McBurney v. R.*, [1985] 2 C.T.C. 214, 85 D.T.C. 5433 (Fed. C.A.); leave to appeal refused (1986), 65 N.R. 320n (S.C.C.).

[17]Para. 110.1(1)(a).

[18]Reg. 3503.

The deduction for charitable donations is available only if the taxpayer provides receipts that disclose prescribed information.[19]

(d) — Charities

A "charity" can be either a charitable organization or charitable foundation.[20] A "charitable organization" is an organization that devotes itself to charitable activities[21] and a "charitable foundation" is, more specifically, a trust or corporation that operates exclusively for charitable purposes.[22]

(i) — Charitable Purposes

An organization qualifies as a charity under section 149.1 of the *Income Tax Act* if:[23]

1. Its purposes are charitable, and the purposes define the scope of the activities that it engages in, and

2. It devotes all of its resources to these activities.[24]

The *Pemsel*[25] test determines what is "charitable"[26] and comprises four divisions:

1. Trusts for the relief of poverty;

2. Trusts for the advancement of education;

3. Trusts for the advancement of religion; and

4. Trusts for other purposes beneficial to the community.

---

[19]Reg. 3501.

[20]Subs. 149.1(1) "charity".

[21]Subs. 149.1(1) "charitable organization".

[22]Subs. 149.1(1) "charitable foundation".

[23]*Vancouver Society of Immigrant & Visible Minority Women v. Minister of National Revenue*, [1999] 1 S.C.R. 10, 169 D.L.R. (4th) 34 (S.C.C.).

[24]Unless the organization falls within the specific exemptions of subss. 149.1(6.1) and (6.2).

[25]*Pemsel v. Special Commissioners of Income Tax*, [1891] A.C. 531 (H.L.) at 583. These categories are well accepted in Canadian law; see *Towle Estate v. Minister of National Revenue*, [1967] S.C.R. 133, [1966] C.T.C. 755, 67 D.T.C. 5003 (S.C.C.) at 141 [S.C.R.], 759 [C.T.C.] and 5005 [D.T.C.].

[26]*Vancouver Society of Immigrant & Visible Minority Women v. Minister of National Revenue*, [1999] 1 S.C.R. 10, 169 D.L.R. (4th) 34 (S.C.C.).

In addition to complying with one or more of these categories, the organization must also have a charitable purpose that is within "the spirit and intendment" of the preamble to the *Charitable Uses Act 1601*.[27]

At first blush, the fourth division appears to be a broad and inclusive category for all sorts of beneficent activities. In fact, it is not that easy to qualify under this division because of the requirement that the charitable purpose must meet the spirit and intendment of the *Charitable Uses Act*, a statute enacted in 1601. Stated in modern English, but reflecting social perceptions of a bygone era, the statute's list of charitable purposes is as follows:[28]

> The relief of aged, impotent, and poor people; the maintenance of sick and maimed soldiers and mariners, schools of learning, free schools, and scholars in universities; the repair of bridges, ports, havens, causeways, churches, seabanks, and highways; the education and preferment of orphans; the relief, stock, or maintenance of houses of correction; marriage of poor maids; supportation, aid, and help of young tradesmen, handicraftsmen, and persons decayed; the relief or redemption of prisoners or captives; and the aid or ease of any poor inhabitants concerning payment of fifteens, setting out of soldiers, and other taxes.

Only activities that are beneficial to the community *and* that come within the spirit and intendment of the above preamble are recognized as "charitable".[29] Thus, the double-headed aspect of the qualification causes difficulty for organizations that seek registration as a charity.

The CRA typically applies the tests in a rigid and dogmatic manner, without accommodation or adaptation to the nuances of modern Canadian society. But, as Lord Wilberforce said,

---

[27] 1601 (43 Eliz. I, c. 4).

[28] *Per* Slade J. in *McGovern v. Attorney General*, [1982] Ch. 321 (Eng. Ch. Div.) at 332.

[29] See, e.g., *National Anti-Vivisection Society v. Inland Revenue Commissioners*, [1948] A.C. 31 (H.L.) (main object political; unclear whether public benefit advanced if such scientific research curtailed); *Strakosch, Re*, [1949] Ch. 529 (C.A.) (gift must be beneficial to community in way law regards as charitable).

"the law of charity is a moving subject." The preamble should not be read literally but in the context of contemporary society.[30] As Lord Upjohn put it:[31]

> This so-called fourth class is incapable of further definition and can to-day hardly be regarded as more than a portmanteau to receive those objects which enlightened opinion would regard as qualifying for consideration under the second heading.

However, that despite some relaxation of the rules for registration, the basic focus remains: are the activities of a public character or are they "member-oriented"?[32]

In *Vancouver Society*,[33] the Supreme Court of Canada set out the test to assess whether an organization's purposes are beneficial in a way the law regards as charitable. In assessing an organization's purposes, one must:

1. Consider the trend of decisions that establish certain objects as charitable under this heading, and determine whether, by reasonable extension or analogy, the facts fit within the earlier decisions;[34]

2. Examine certain accepted anomalies to see whether they fairly cover the objects under consideration; and

3. Ask whether, consistent with the declared objects, the income and property in question can be applied for purposes clearly falling outside the scope of charity.

Under the Pemsel test, an organization is not considered to be charitable if its activities are illegal or contrary to public policy. There must be a definite and somehow officially declared and implemented policy for an activity to be considered "contrary to public policy".

---

[30]See, for example, *Native Communications Society of British Columbia v. Minister of National Revenue*, [1986] 2 C.T.C. 170, [1986] 4 C.N.L.R. 79 (Fed. C.A.); *Vancouver Regional FreeNet Assn. v. Minister of National Revenue*, [1996] 3 F.C. 880, 137 D.L.R. (4th) 206 (Fed. C.A.) (non-profit network establishing a free community computer that would provide free access to information on the Internet granted charitable organization status).

[31]*Scottish Burial Reform & Cremation Society v. Glasgow (City)*, [1968] A.C. 138 (Scotland H.L.) at 150.

[32]*National Model Railroad Assn., Seventh Division, Pacific Northwest Region v. Minister of National Revenue*, [1989] 1 C.T.C. 300, (sub nom. *Seventh Div., Pac. N.W. Region, Nat. Model Railroad Assn. v. Minister of National Revenue*) 89 D.T.C. 5133 (Fed. C.A.).

[33]*Vancouver Society of Immigrant & Visible Minority Women v. Minister of National Revenue*, [1999] 1 S.C.R. 10, 169 D.L.R. (4th) 34 (S.C.C.).

[34]See, also, *Vancouver Regional FreeNet Assn. v. Minister of National Revenue*, [1996] 3 F.C. 880, 137 D.L.R. (4th) 206, [1996] 3 C.T.C. 102, 96 D.T.C. 6440 (Fed. C.A.) (the provision of free access to information and to a means of communication was a type of purpose similar to those that had been held to be charitable in previous case law).

An entity will not be denied charitable status on the basis that its objects are politically controversial.[35]

(ii) — Tax-Exempt Status

A registered charity is a tax-exempt organization. Thus, the tax subsidy in respect of registered charities is double-barrelled: the charity is tax-exempt and its benefactors obtain a tax deduction or credit.

We justify the tax exemption on the basis that it encourages private organizations to engage in philanthropic activities that would otherwise fall to the public purse. The subsidy is expensive. Thus, to control the cost of the subsidy, the Act has stringent registration and annual accounting requirements.

(iii) — Political Activities

An organization is not a charity if its main or principal object is political.[36] For example, tenants and ratepayer groups that merely lobby governments to act in support of societal change do not qualify as charitable organizations if their primary focus is political activity.[37] Similarly, anti-pornography groups that are, in effect, "political" organizations lobbying for legislative change under the guise of education do not qualify as charitable organizations.[38]

However, charities that engage in non-partisan political activities that are "ancillary and incidental" to their charitable purposes or activities can maintain registration as tax-exempt

---

[35]*Everywoman's Health Centre Society (1988) v. Minister of National Revenue*, [1992] 2 F.C. 52, [1991] 2 C.T.C. 320, 92 D.T.C. 6001 (Fed. C.A.) (abortion counselling and medical services registered as a charity). See also *Canadian Magen David Adom for Israel / Magen David Adom Canadien pour Israël v. Minister of National Revenue*, 2002 FCA 323, [2002] 4 C.T.C. 422, 2002 D.T.C. 7353 (Fed. C.A.) (medical and ambulance services offered in occupied territory not registered as a charity on other grounds).

[36]*Patriotic Acre Fund, Re*, [1951] 2 D.L.R. 624 (Sask. C.A.):

> . . . the Court has no means of judging whether a proposed change in the law will or will not be for the public benefit and therefore cannot say that a gift to secure the change is a charitable gift.

[37]*Notre Dame de Grâce Neighbourhood Assn. v. Minister of National Revenue*, [1988] 2 C.T.C. 14, 88 D.T.C. 6279 (Fed. C.A.) (tenants' association denied registration as charity).

[38]*Positive Action Against Pornography v. Minister of National Revenue*, [1988] 1 C.T.C. 232, 88 D.T.C. 6186 (Fed. C.A.).

organizations.[39] For example, a charity can use mass mailings or media campaigns to influence public opinion or government policy. More active involvement in partisan political activities, however, endangers a charity's registration.[40]

It is not always easy to draw the line between political activity and public education. Generally, there is a reluctance to recognize organizations that merely engage in lobbying for legislative change. The following activities are "political":[41]

- The furthering of the interests of a particular political party;

- The procuring of changes to the laws of the country;

- The procuring of changes to the laws of a foreign country;

- The procuring of a reversal of government policy or of particular decisions of governmental authorities in the country; or

- The procuring of a reversal of government policy or of particular decisions of governmental authorities in a foreign country.

(e) — Donations of Capital Property

Where a person donates capital property to a registered charity, he or she can designate the value of the gift at any amount between its fair market value and its adjusted cost base. The designated value then becomes the taxpayer's proceeds of disposition. Thus, a taxpayer has some flexibility in determining the amount of the capital gain on the disposition of the property.[42]

---

[39]Subs. 149.1(6.1).

[40]Para.149.1(6.1)(c); *Action des Chrétiens pour l'Abolition de la Torture (L'A.C.A.T.) c. R.*, 2003 FCA 499, [2003] C.T.C. 121, (sub nom. *Action by Christians for the Abolition of Torture (ACAT) v. R.*) 2003 D.T.C. 5394 (Eng.) (Fed. C.A.); leave to appeal refused (2003), 2003 CarswellNat 2040, 2003 CarswellNat 2041 (S.C.C.) (exercise of moral pressure on governments held to be a political rather than charitable purpose); *Alliance for Life v. Minister of National Revenue*, [1999] 3 C.T.C. 1, 99 D.T.C. 5228 (Fed. C.A.) (pro-life organization did not qualify for exemption under subsection 149.1(6.2) because materials were political and not ancillary and incidental to their charitable activities); *Human Life International In Canada Inc. v. Minister of National Revenue*, [1998] 3 F.C. 202, [1998] 3 C.T.C. 126, 98 D.T.C. 6196 (Fed. C.A.); leave to appeal refused [1998] S.C.C.A. No. 246 (S.C.C.) (Minister allowed to revoke organization's charitable status as the organization was primarily concerned with swaying public opinion).

[41]*McGovern v. Attorney General*, [1982] Ch. 321, [1982] 2 W.L.R. 222 (Ch. D.).

[42]Subs. 110.1(3) and 118.1(6). A non-resident can also make the designation in respect of certain types of real property situated in Canada.

4. — *Valuation*

(a) — *Fair Market Value*

Once we determine that a contribution to an eligible organization qualifies as a gift, the next task is to attach a value to it. We generally value gifts at their fair market value at the time that the donor transfers the property to the donee. The fair market value of an asset is its exchange value.[43] Where there is a regular and efficient market for the asset (for example, widely-held shares on a stock exchange), its trading price is probably the best, though not necessarily the only, measure of its fair market value.[44] Where there is no efficient market for the asset, it is necessary to determine fair market value through other criteria, such as, earnings value, liquidation value, replacement value, etc.

The "fair market value" of an asset for tax purposes is the highest price that it "might reasonably be expected to bring if sold by the owner in the normal method applicable to the asset in question, in the ordinary course of business in a market not exposed to any undue stresses, and composed of willing buyers and sellers dealing at arm's length and under no compulsion to buy or sell."[45] Thus, the focus of the determination of fair market value is on an efficient, normal and knowledgeable market.

(b) — *Expert Evidence*

The best and usually most accurate measure of a property's value is its fair market value at the time that the taxpayer donates it to the charity. We can determine fair market value with precision if there is an active and open market for the property. For example, one can determine the value of publicly traded shares by reference to the trading price of a share at a particular time on a particular day.

Where there is no active market, however, one must rely upon the opinion of experts to determine the value of the property. A non-arm's length expert opinion can be a reliable guide to value, but only if the expert is truly independent. In recent years, we have seen clever "buy-low, donate-high" arrangements that gave taxpayers a substantial tax benefit for rapid turnover of art.

Valuation is a sophisticated art that calls for the expertise and judgment of people trained in its discipline. It is also an art that is vulnerable to manipulation and one should consider carefully the expert testimony of professional valuators. Expert evidence should, in Lord

---

[43]See generally, *Mann, Re*, [1972] 5 W.W.R. 23 (B.C. S.C.); affirmed [1973] 4 W.W.R. 223 (B.C. C.A.); affirmed [1974] 2 W.W.R. 574 (S.C.C.).

[44]*Mann, Re, ante*, at 27.

[45]*Henderson v. Minister of National Revenue*, [1973] C.T.C. 636, 73 D.T.C. 5471 (Fed. T.D.); affirmed [1975] C.T.C. 485, 75 D.T.C. 5332 (Fed. C.A.).

Wilberforce's words, ". . . be, and should be seen to be, the independent product of the expert, uninfluenced as to form or content by the exigencies of litigation."[46] Unfortunately, some experts have a propensity for moulding their opinions to identify with, and accommodate, their client's positions. As Adrian Keane says in the *Modern Law of Evidence*:[47]

> . . . the danger is particularly acute in the case of opinions expressed by expert witnesses, of whom it has been said, not without some sarcasm, "it is quite often surprising to see with what facility and to what extent, their views can be made to correspond with the wishes or the interests of the parties who call them."

Experts, particularly lawyers, owe a duty to the court to be independent and objective. Valuation and accounting experts find it equally difficult to distance themselves from the purse-strings that determine their livelihood. As Professor Bonbright said:[48]

> . . . few, if any, appraisers can take an unbiased position when they take the witness stand under an engagement from one of the contesting parties . . . a court must choose between the tremendous errors implicit in a capitalization of audited reported earnings, and the tremendous errors implicit in a capitalization of prejudiced prophecies.

In *Klotz*,[49] for example, the taxpayer participated in a program called "Art for Education" (AFE). Under the AFE program, the program's sponsors would acquire prints for a modest cost, generally under $50 per print. The sponsors would then sell the prints to individuals for approximately $300 per print. The taxpayer purchased 250 such "limited edition" prints on December 28 and donated them two days later to Florida State University. The taxpayer obtained a charitable donation receipt for $258,400, the alleged market value, supported by the expert valuation of an art dealer and appraiser.

Motive is irrelevant in the determination of value. The taxpayer was entitled to take advantage of the tax law provided that all the transactions were proper and appropriately valued. To be sure, the taxpayer did not appear to be preoccupied with broadening the cultural or intellectual horizons of the students at FSU. Indeed, he donated the prints without ever having seen them or having them in his possession. The Tax Court said: "His sole concern was that he get a charitable receipt." Altruistic motivation, however, is not a prerequisite to a charitable gift.

The expert art dealer and appraiser valued most of the prints at $1,000 each, which was significant because the *Income Tax Act* deems the *minimum* cost and proceeds of personal use property to be $1,000. Thus, if the prints qualified as personal use property, there would

---

[46]*Whitehouse v. Jordan*, [1981] 1 W.L.R. 246 (H.L.) at 256.

[47]Keane, *Modern Law of Evidence* (London: Butterworths, 1985), at 377.

[48]Bonbright, *Valuation of Property* (New York: McGraw-Hill, 1937), vol. 1, at 251.

[49]*Klotz v. R.*, 2004 TCC 147, [2004] 2 C.T.C. 2892, 2004 D.T.C. 2236 (T.C.C. [General Procedure]); affirmed [2005] 3 C.T.C. 78 (Fed. C.A.); leave to appeal refused (2006), 2006 CarswellNat 930, 2006 CarswellNat 931 (S.C.C.).

be no capital gain on the donation to FSU. This would leave the taxpayer with only the deduction for the charitable gift, without any corresponding inclusion in income for the gain realized on the gift.

Klotz is also remarkable in that the CRA did not call any expert witnesses in a valuation dispute involving millions of dollars. Instead, the Minister relied on the presumption that his assessment is deemed correct, unless upset by the taxpayer. The Tax Court of Canada did not accept the expert valuation opinions of the taxpayer. To be sure, a court is not bound to accept any expert's opinion and, ultimately, must make its own determination of value on the evidence. Nevertheless, it shows the heavy burden of proof that the taxpayer carries in tax cases that the Minister does not even need to introduce expert testimony in a valuation dispute to win the case.

After a careful and thorough analysis of the expert testimony of the art dealer and appraiser, the Tax Court of Canada rejected the expert's opinion on value. The court said:

> It is one thing serendipitously to pick up for $10 a long lost masterpiece at a garage sale and give it to an art gallery and receive a receipt for its true value. It is another for [the promoter] to buy thousands of prints for $50, create a market at $300 and then hold out the prospect of a tax write-off on the basis of a $1,000 valuation.

Notwithstanding the failure of the tax arrangements in *Klotz*, Finance, with its penchant for detailed statutory rules, amended the *Income Tax Act* to limit the value of a gift for charitable donation purposes to the donor's cost of the property if the donor donates the property within three years of acquiring it. The new rules deem the fair market value of a gifted property to be the lesser of its fair market value as otherwise determined and its costs basis if the holding period of the property is less than three years. This is intended to prevent escalating valuations.[50]

However, the statutory rules go even further and introduce a motive test to determine the value of a gift. Even if the taxpayer holds the gifted property for more than three years, he or she may not be eligible to claim any real enhancement in fair market value if the taxpayer acquired the property initially for the purpose of gifting it. For example, assume that a taxpayer purchases a renowned artist's work, knowing full well that it will appreciate in value and that he or she will ultimately donate it to his or her alma mater some years down the road. In these circumstances, the new rules will restrict the fair market value of the gift to its cost basis.

5. — Registration as Charity

Only registered charities receive the benefits of tax-exempt status. To secure or maintain its registration, a registered charity must operate exclusively for charitable purposes and must

---

[50]See subs. 248(35) to (38).

not carry on any other unrelated business. Otherwise, the Minister may revoke the registration of the charitable organization.[51] A "related business", however, includes ". . . a business that is unrelated to the objects of the charity if substantially all of the people employed by the charity in the carrying on of that business are not remunerated for such employment."[52]

Where a charity carries on a business, there are, in effect, two separate tests that must be satisfied in order to acquire or maintain its registration: (1) the taxpayer must operate exclusively for charitable purposes, and (2) the business must be a "related business".

(a) — Related Business

We determine whether a business is related to the charitable organization by looking at the use of the profits of the business. It remains unclear, however, how far we can apply the use of funds test.[53]

In *AIMR*, for example, Heald J., speaking for the majority, said:[54]

> [W]here *all* of the monies received are dedicated to the charitable purposes for which the appellant was incorporated and where the business aspect of the operation is merely incidental to the attainment of its charitable objects, the appellant can, indeed, be said to be operating exclusively for charitable purposes.

The majority favoured the destination of funds test as ". . . the clear intention of Parliament to recognize the contemporary reality insofar as the fundraising activities of modern charita-

---

[51]Para. 149.1(2)(a).

[52]Subs.149.1(1) "related business"; see also, *Alberta Institute on Mental Retardation v. R.*, [1987] 2 C.T.C. 70, 87 D.T.C. 5306 (Fed. C.A.); leave to appeal refused (1988), 87 N.R. 397 (note) (S.C.C.).

[53]*Alberta Institute on Mental Retardation v. R.*, [1987] 2 C.T.C. 70, 87 D.T.C. 5306 (Fed. C.A.); leave to appeal refused (1988), 87 N.R. 397 (note) (S.C.C.). See *British Launderers' Research Assn. v. Hendon Rating Authority (Borough)*, [1949] 1 K.B. 462 (Eng. C.A.); followed by Supreme Court of Canada in *Towle Estate v. Minister of National Revenue*, [1967] S.C.R. 133, [1966] C.T.C. 755, 67 D.T.C. 5003 (S.C.C.).

[54]*Alberta Institute on Mental Retardation v. R.*, *ibid.*, at 75 [C.T.C.] and 5310 [D.T.C.].

ble organizations are concerned."[55] The concept of charity must be kept moving with changing social needs.[56] In Justice Heald's words:[57]

> If the operation of a cafeteria on the premises of an art gallery or the operation of a parking lot adjacent to and on premises owned by a hospital, for example, can be said to be related businesses even though the cafeteria and the parking lot may be operated by concessionaires for profit, then surely an activity such as that of this [taxpayer] must be in the same category.

Thus, charities may carry on any type of business so long as the profits of the business are ultimately diverted to charitable purposes.

III. — Residents of Remote Regions

Individuals who reside in prescribed isolated posts in the near and far north can claim special deductions when computing taxable income.[58] These deductions subsidize the personal costs of taxpayers who live in remote regions.

Thus, the subsidies also indirectly subsidize northern businesses by reducing labour costs. The deduction is the lesser of:

- 20 percent of the taxpayer's net income for the year, and

- $7.50 multiplied by the number of days in the year that the individual resided in the area plus an additional $7.50 for each day that the taxpayer maintained a dwelling in the area.

Individuals who work in a prescribed area are also entitled to special deductions in respect of travel expenses. These deductions are of two types: (1) travel for medical purposes, and (2) general travel. Travel for trips to obtain medical services is deductible where such services are not available locally. Employees may claim a deduction for up to two trips per calendar year for other purposes.[59]

Only residents of the "prescribed northern zone" can claim the maximum deductions. Residents of the "prescribed intermediate zone" receive only 50 percent of the deductions.

---

[55]*Alberta Institute on Mental Retardation v. R.*, *ibid.*, at 77 [C.T.C.] and 5306 [D.T.C.].

[56]*Native Communications Society of British Columbia v. Minister of National Revenue*, [1986] 2 C.T.C. 170, [1986] 4 C.N.L.R. 79 (Fed. C.A.).

[57]*Alberta Institute on Mental Retardation v. R.*, [1987] 2 C.T.C. 70, 87 D.T.C. 5306 (Fed. C.A.) at 77 [C.T.C.].

[58]S. 110.7. In certain circumstances, the deduction may apply to residents of any isolated or sparsely populated area of the country.

[59]Para. 110.7(1)(a); subs. 110.7(3).

IV. — Losses

1. — General Comment

We measure income for a period of time. We refer to this period as the "fiscal year". The fiscal year is the calendar year for individuals and partnerships and any 53-week period for corporations. The fiscal year as the unit of time to measure income creates problems for taxpayers whose incomes fluctuate between years. For example, a taxpayer who earns income in one year and suffers an equal loss in the next would, in the absence of relieving provisions, face financial hardship as a result of paying tax in the first year without relief in the second. Consider the following alternatives:

Taxpayer	Year 1	Year 2	Year 3	Total
A	$ 120,000	$ (40,000)	$ (80,000)	NIL
B	(80,000)	120,000	(40,000)	NIL
C	(40,000)	(80,000)	120,000	NIL

The economic well-being of all three taxpayers is identical over the three-year period. There are, however, important differences if we tax them on an annual basis. Taxpayer A must pay tax on income of $120,000 in Year 1, Taxpayer B in Year 2, and Taxpayer C in Year 3. Thus, we cannot measure a taxpayer's "true" income until the end of his or her economic existence.

On the other hand, a tax system cannot wait until the end of an individual's life or the termination of a business enterprise to collect revenues for its annual expenditures. Instead, we allow taxpayers to shift their losses between fiscal periods. In the absence of provisions that allow for the shifting of losses from one period to another, taxpayers could end up paying tax on illusory income.

A taxpayer can offset his or her losses from one source against income from other sources in the same year.[60] There are, however, several restrictions. For example, capital losses may be offset only against capital gains; listed personal property losses may be used only against listed personal property gains.[61] Losses from a decline in value of household durables (for example, cars, furniture, etc.) are personal losses and deemed to be nil.[62] Where a taxpayer

---

[60]S. 3.

[61]Para. 3(b); subs. 41(2).

[62]Subpara. 40(2)(g)(iii).

does not use his or her losses in the year in which they occur, the taxpayer may, within certain limits, use them to offset income in other years.[63]

2. — *Types of Losses*

The tax loss rules are complicated by three factors. First, economic losses are forced to fit into the annual accounting requirement. Second, in the absence of consolidated corporate reporting, we must confine losses within corporate entities and control any spillover between corporations. Third, given the compartmentalized structure of the source of income in the Act, the characterization of losses is as important as the characterization of income. There are different rules for each type and sub-type of loss.

Some losses (such as non-capital losses) are more valuable to a taxpayer than others (such as capital losses) because the entire loss may be written off against all sources of income. But capital losses have a longer shelf life than non-capital losses and can be more valuable in certain circumstances. Thus, the first step in determining the tax treatment of a loss is to determine the nature and character of the loss.

There are five major categories of losses:

1. Non-capital losses;

2. Net capital losses;

3. Restricted farm losses;

4. Farm losses; or

5. Limited partnership losses.

We subdivide capital losses into three categories:

1. Personal-use property losses;

2. Listed personal property losses; and

3. Business investment losses.

The loss application rules dictate the order in which a taxpayer can claim losses in the current taxation year and in other tax years.

A taxpayer's loss from a source first offsets other sources of income for the purpose of calculating *income* for the current year. Losses that we cannot use in the current year to reduce income from other sources may, subject to various limitations, be carried back or

---

[63]*Burleigh v. R.*, 2004 TCC 197, [2004] 2 C.T.C. 2797, 2004 D.T.C. 2399 (T.C.C. [General Procedure]) (losses can be carried forward/back whether or not they were reported in an income tax return in the year they were incurred).

forward to other years and deducted in computing the taxpayer's *taxable income* for those years. Thus, current year losses are deductible in the computation of net income. Losses carried over to other years (whether prior or subsequent) are deductible only in the computation of taxable income.

(a) — Non-Capital Losses

A non-capital loss (which we loosely refer to as a "business loss") is deductible from income in any of the three taxation years preceding, and the 20 taxation years following, the year in which we incur the loss.[64] Thus, we can use non-capital losses to offset income over a period of 24 years: the year of the loss, three years prior to the loss, and 20 years subsequent to the loss. These carry back and forward rules allow some flexibility and ease the rigidity of the annual accounting requirement.

(i) — Meaning

A taxpayer's non-capital loss includes the following amounts:[65]

- A loss from any business (including losses from a farming or fishing business);

- A loss from the ownership of any property;

- A loss from any office or employment;

- An allowable business investment loss for the year;

- Any used portion of the deduction for Part VI.1 special taxes on dividends;

- An amount deductible by a life insurer in computing taxable income in respect of taxable dividends received from taxable Canadian corporations;[66]

- 1/2 of the amount included in the taxpayer's income as an employee benefit in respect of the exercise or disposition of prescribed shares;[67]

- 1/2 of the amount included in the taxpayer's income as an employee benefit in respect of a stock option plan issued by a Canadian-controlled private corporation;[68]

---

[64]Para. 111(1)(a).

[65]Subs. 111(8)"non-capital loss".

[66]Subs. 138(6).

[67]Para. 110(1)(d); increased from 1/4 in Budget 2000.

[68]Para. 110(1)(d.1); increased from 1/4 in Budget 2000.

- 1/2 of the amount included in the taxpayer's income as prospectors' shares;[69]

- An amount deductible by a corporation in computing its taxable income in respect of dividends received from other corporations;[70]

- 1/2 of the amount included in the taxpayer's income in respect of certain deferred profit-sharing benefits;[71]

- An amount deducted from taxable income in respect of a home relocation loan;[72]

- An amount claimed as a capital gains exemption;[73]

- Certain amounts deducted under paragraph 110(1)(f), such as amounts exempt under a tax convention, social assistance payments, and workers' compensation; and

- Amounts added to a corporation's taxable income for foreign tax deductions.[74]

Then, we deduct the following amounts from the aggregate of the above:[75]

- The amount determined under paragraph 3(c);

- The taxpayer's farm loss;

- An amount deducted under subsection 111(10) (fuel tax rebate); and

- The amount by which non-capital loss must be reduced under section 80 (debt forgiveness).

Thus, we initially apply a taxpayer's losses from non-capital sources against income in the *current* year. The residue less any portion that is a farm loss becomes the taxpayer's non-capital loss. There are special rules for farm losses.[76]

A taxpayer cannot increase his or her non-capital loss by the deductions permitted under subdivision e of Division B (sections 60–66.8). These deductions may, however, reduce other income in the year. For example, an individual who suffers a business loss in a particular year cannot increase his or her loss carryforward by including in the non-capital loss

---

[69]Para. 110(1)(d.2); increased from 1/4 in Budget 2000.

[70]S. 112; subs. 113(1).

[71]Para. 110(1)(d.3); increased from 1/4 in Budget 2000.

[72]Para. 110(1)(j).

[73]S. 110.6.

[74]S. 110.5.

[75]Subs. 111(8)"non-capital loss".

[76]Para. 111(1)(d).

amounts paid as support. If, however, the individual was also employed in the same year, he or she could use any support payments to reduce or eliminate his or her employment income and carry forward the business loss.

(ii) — Non-Residents

A non-resident taxpayer may not include as a non-capital loss any losses from businesses that are not carried on in Canada.[77] Also, a resident taxpayer may not deduct non-capital losses incurred while he or she was a non-resident and had no Canadian source of income.[78] Thus, a corporation that becomes resident in Canada cannot import its non-capital losses accumulated while it was a non-resident corporation and had no Canadian income source.

Section 111 of the Act also restricts a non-resident from applying a business or property loss incurred in Canada in a preceding year from a treaty-exempt source against taxable income earned in Canada in a subsequent year that is not treaty-exempt. These losses cannot be utilized to offset taxable income.

(iii) — Order of Deductions

A taxpayer must deduct his or her non-capital losses in the order in which the taxpayer incurs them.[79]

(iv) — Transfer of Losses

A loss is generally deductible only by the taxpayer who incurs it. For example, where an individual incurs a non-capital loss, the loss cannot be claimed by another taxpayer to whom the business is sold. Similarly, a sole proprietor cannot transfer the losses of the proprietorship on selling his or her business to a corporation. This is so even if the individual owns all the shares of the corporation that acquires the business.

Since a corporation is a legal entity in its own right, any losses that it incurs belong to it. It is only in very rare circumstances that another corporation can use its losses. However, even though a corporation owns its losses, a change of control of the corporation may extinguish its non-capital losses.[80]

---

[77]Subs. 111(9).

[78]*Oceanspan Carriers Ltd. v. R.*, [1987] 1 C.T.C. 210, 87 D.T.C. 5102 (Fed. C.A.).

[79]Subpara. 111(3)(b)(i).

[80]Subs. 111(5).

(b) — Net Capital Losses

Allowable capital losses may only offset taxable capital gains. Listed personal property losses may be used only to offset gains on listed personal property, and not against other capital property.[81]

A taxpayer's "net capital loss" is made up of:[82]

- The excess of its allowable capital losses over taxable capital gains, and

- Any unutilized allowable business investment losses previously included in its non-capital losses in respect of which the carryover period expired in the year.

Net capital losses may be carried back three years and carried forward indefinitely. Hence, they have an unlimited life. They may, however, be applied only against capital gains in other years.[83]

(c) — Farm Losses

Farm losses can be on account of:

1. Business farm losses;

2. Restricted farm losses; or

3. Hobby farm losses.

The Act controls farming losses strictly because of the propensity of "gentlemen farmers" to use such losses to offset their professional income.

Where a taxpayer in the *business* of farming incurs a "farm loss", the loss is subject to the rules generally applicable to business losses.[84] A taxpayer's "farm loss" is the excess of his

---

[81]Para. 3(b).

[82]Subs. 111(8)"net capital loss". The taxpayer's net capital loss is also reduced as required by s. 80 (debt forgiveness). Capital losses that also qualify as "allowable business investment losses" are initially treated as non-capital losses and may be written off against income from any source. If they cannot be used as non-capital losses within the ten–year carry forward period, they are added to net capital losses and may be carried forward indefinitely.

[83]Para. 111(1)(b).

[84]Para. 111(1)(d) and subs. 111(8) "farm loss"; *Brown v. R.*, [1975] C.T.C. 611, 75 D.T.C. 5433 (Fed. T.D.). In both *Kroeker v. R.*, 2002 FCA 392, [2003] 1 C.T.C. 183, 2002 D.T.C. 7436 (Fed. C.A.) and *Taylor v. R.*, 2002 FCA 425, [2003] 1 C.T.C. 318, 2002 D.T.C. 7596 (Fed. C.A.) farming losses were fully deductible even though taxpayers had full time jobs; sufficient time, labour and capital were devoted to farm.

or her losses from farming and fishing over any income from these sources.[85] A taxpayer may carry back the farm losses three years and forward 20 years and apply the losses against income from any source.[86] Thus, it is necessary to distinguish between unrestricted and restricted farm losses.

Section 31 limits the amount by which a taxpayer's income may be reduced by farming operations conducted as a secondary business. A "restricted farm loss" is a farming loss that results from a combination of farming and some other source of income.

The factors to consider are the capital invested in farming and the second source of income, the income derived from each source, the time spent on the two sources of income, and the taxpayer's mode of living. A taxpayer who places significant emphasis on each of the farming business and other earning activity is not subject to the restriction of subsection 31(1).[87]

A taxpayer whose chief source of income is neither farming nor a combination of farming and some other source of income cannot deduct more than $8,750 in any year for "farming losses".[88] Any loss in excess of this limit becomes the taxpayer's "restricted farm loss" for the year. The taxpayer can carry forward his or her restricted farm loss to future years.[89]

A restricted farm loss may be carried back three years and forward 20 years.[90] The amount of a restricted farm loss that is deductible in any year is limited to the amount of the taxpayer's income from farming for the year.[91]

Where a farmer disposes of farmland and has unclaimed restricted farm losses that were not deductible in prior years, the farmer may add the unclaimed losses to the adjusted cost base of the land. Thus, he or she can reduce any capital gain on the eventual disposition of the land by the amount of the unclaimed losses.[92]

---

[85]Subs. 111(8) "farm loss". For the meaning of "farm loss", see *Craig v. R*, [2012] 5 C.T.C. 205 (S.C.C.) (lawyer who spent significant time and capital on a horse racing business not subject to restricted farm loss even though his primary source of income was from law).

[86]Para. 111(1)(d).

[87]See *Craig v. R*, [2012] 5 C.T.C. 205 (S.C.C.) at para. 45; see also *Gunn v. R.*, [2006] 5 C.T.C. 191 (F.C.A.).

[88]Subs. 31(1).

[89]Subs. 31(1.1).

[90]Para. 111(1)(c).

[91]Para. 111(1)(c).

[92]Para. 53(1)(i).

A hobby farm loss is a loss from a farming operation that is conducted without a profit motive or a reasonable expectation of profit.[93] Hobby farm losses are not deductible at all since they are not income from a source.[94]

(d) — Allowable Business Investment Losses

A "business investment loss" is a hybrid loss,[95] a particular type of capital loss that is deductible from income from *any* source.

(i) — Capital Loss

Characterization of a loss as a capital loss is a necessary precondition to its characterization as a business investment loss. A capital loss that is deemed to be nil (for example, a superficial loss) cannot give rise to a business investment loss.[96]

A "business investment loss" is a loss that a taxpayer incurs on a disposition of capital property under the following conditions:[97]

- The capital property is a share of a "small business corporation" or a debt owed to the taxpayer by such a corporation;

- Where the taxpayer is a corporation and the capital property is a debt, the debtor corporation is at arm's length from the taxpayer; and

- The shares or debt are, unless subsection 50(1) applies, disposed of to a person dealing with the taxpayer at arm's length.

(ii) — Hybrid Nature of Loss

An allowable business investment loss has features of both business and capital losses: it results from a disposition of capital property, but it may be used to offset income from *any*

---

[93]See *Sobon v. R.*, 2004 TCC 2, [2004] 3 C.T.C. 2347 (T.C.C. [Informal Procedure]); reversed (2006), 2006 CarswellNat 1885, [2006] 5 C.T.C. 83 (Fed. C.A.) (taxpayer not entitled to deduct farm losses in excess of $8,750 per year; ostrich farm sustained losses in all 10 years of its operation and could not generate a profit as it was currently run).

[94]See the guidelines that the Supreme Court set out in the *Stewart* and *Walls* decisions.

[95]Para. 39(1)(c); subs. 111(8)"non-capital loss".

[96]Para. 40(2)(g).

[97]Para. 39(1)(c); see also subs. 248(1)"small business corporation".

source.[98] Any unused portion of an allowable business investment loss is a non-capital loss. Thus, one can apply unused allowable business losses against income from any source.

Since an unused allowable business loss is treated as a non-capital loss, it has a limited life. It may be carried back three years and carried forward for only 20 years.[99] In contrast, net capital losses may be carried back three years and carried forward indefinitely.

An allowable business loss that is not used within the 20-year carry forward period applicable to non-capital losses reverts to a net capital loss.[100] Thereafter, it may be carried forward indefinitely, but applied only against taxable capital gains.

(e) — Net Capital Losses in Year of Death

A taxpayer's net capital losses may be deducted against net taxable capital gains in the year of death and in the immediately preceding year. Unused capital losses can be carried back and written off against income in the year before the taxpayer's death, but only to the extent that such losses exceed any capital gains exemption claimed by that person in his or her lifetime.[101]

Capital losses in excess of capital gains realized by a deceased's estate within its first taxation year may also be written off *as if* they had been realized by the deceased in the year of death. Thus, the deceased's estate is given credit for the amount of income tax that the deceased would have saved in the year of death if the excess capital losses had been sustained by the deceased rather than by the estate.

This relief is available only where the legal representative of the deceased makes an election and designates the amount of the excess capital losses to be carried back. The amount designated is deemed not to have been a capital loss of the estate.[102] The representative must file an amended return for the deceased taxpayer for the year in which he or she died.

---

[98]S. 3.

[99]Para. 111(1)(a), subs. 111(8)"non-capital loss".

[100]Subs. 111(8)"net capital loss".

[101]Subs. 111(2).

[102]Subs. 164(6).

(f) — Limited Partnership Losses

A taxpayer may carry forward limited partnership losses indefinitely and apply them against income from any source. The Act restricts the deduction for limited partnership losses, however, to the amount that the taxpayer is "at risk" in the partnership in the year.[103]

3. — Change of Corporate Control

(a) — General Comment

The Act discourages taxpayers from trading in "loss companies", that is, corporations with accumulated losses purchased and sold primarily for the sake of tax, rather than business, advantages. It does this by streaming the carryforward of losses when control of a corporation changes hands.[104] In the absence of these rules, a taxpayer could purchase a "loss company", inject a new profitable business into it and shelter the profits of the new business from tax.

(b) — Meaning of "Control"

(i) — De Jure Control

"Control" implies ownership of sufficient shares to carry with them the ability to cast a majority of the votes on election of a board of directors. Thus, at common-law, control means *de jure* and not *de facto* control. As Jackett P. said in *Buckerfield's*:[105]

> [M]any approaches might conceivably be adopted in applying the word "control" in a statute such as the *Income Tax Act* . . .
>
> It might, for example, refer to control by "management," where management and the Board of Directors are separate, or it might refer to control by the Board of Directors. The kind of control exercised by management officials of the Board of Directors is, however, clearly not intended by [s. 256] when it contemplates control of one corporation by another as well as control of a corporation by individuals. . . . The word "control" might conceivably refer to *de facto* control by one or more shareholders whether or not they hold a majority of the shares. I am of the view, however, that in [s. 256 of] the *Income Tax Act*, the word "controlled" con-

---

[103]Para. 111(1)(e).

[104]Subss. 111(4), 111(5).

[105]*Buckerfield's Ltd. v. Minister of National Revenue*, [1964] C.T.C. 504, 64 D.T.C. 5301 (Can. Ex. Ct.) at 507 [C.T.C.] and 5303 [D.T.C.]; *Duha Printers (Western) Ltd. v. R.*, [1998] 1 S.C.R. 795, [1998] 3 C.T.C. 303, 98 D.T.C. 6334 (S.C.C.).

templates the right or control that rests in ownership of such a number of shares as carries with it the right to a majority of the votes in the election of the Board of Directors.

The lack of power to elect a majority of the board of directors, however, does not necessarily imply a lack of control; control can also be determined by other tests, such as the power to wind up the corporation.[106]

(ii) — Statutory Exceptions

There are circumstances, however, in which the Act deems control of a corporation not to have changed. For example, the Act deems a person who acquires shares of a corporation *not* to have acquired control by virtue of the acquisition, redemption or cancellation of shares, if immediately before such transaction he or she was related to the acquired corporation.[107]

(iii) — Restrictions on Losses

In the absence of consolidated corporate reporting for tax purposes, the Act applies stringent restrictions on the use of accumulated losses following a change of corporate control. The general thrust of these rules is to limit transfers of losses between unrelated corporate taxpayers and to discourage business arrangements that are nothing more than "loss-trading" or "loss-offset" transactions. For example, in the typical "loss-trading" transaction, a taxpayer would sell property with an accrued gain and use an intermediary corporation with accumulated losses as a conduit. Any gain from the transaction could then be offset against the intermediary's losses to reduce taxable income. Generally, the loss-transfer rules do not allow for migration of losses between corporations. There are, however, several exceptions.

(iv) — Non-Capital Losses

A corporation may carry forward its non-capital and farm losses following a change of control if it satisfies two conditions: prior year's losses are deductible against income from the *same* business, but only if the corporation that sustained the loss continues to carry on that same business for profit or with a reasonable expectation of profit. The corporation must carry on the acquired business with a reasonable expectation of profit *throughout the year* following the time of its acquisition.[108]

---

[106]*R. v. Imperial General Properties Ltd.*, [1985] 2 S.C.R. 288, [1985] 2 C.T.C. 299, 85 D.T.C. 5500 (S.C.C.).

[107]Para. 256(7)(a).

[108]Subpara. 111(5)(a)(i).

The acquired business by which the losses were originally sustained must be continuously maintained for profit or with a reasonable expectation of profit. The substitution of a new or similar, but more profitable, business does not satisfy this requirement.

Following a change of control, a corporation may only deduct its non-capital and farm losses from prior years to the extent of the aggregate of:[109]

- Its income for the year from the acquired business; and,

- Any other business income substantially derived from the sale, lease, rental, or development of properties, or the rendering of services, which are similar to those properties sold, leased, rented, or developed or the services rendered, as the case may be, in the course of carrying on the *particular* business in question, prior to the change in control.

(v) — Deemed Year-End

The Act deems a corporation to have a year-end immediately before its control changes hands.[110] Any losses incurred in the year in which control changes are subject to the restrictions on loss carryovers. Thus, a change of corporate control can speed up the timetable for the use of losses.

(vi) — Capital Losses

The restrictions on capital losses are even more stringent than for non-capital losses. Net capital losses for preceding years may not be deducted in computing its income for the year of change of control or in any subsequent year. Further, losses incurred in years subsequent to the change of control cannot be carried back to offset income earned in the years prior to the change of control.[111]

Following a change of corporate control, the Act deems a corporation to have realized any losses accrued on its *non-depreciable* capital properties.[112] Its deemed capital losses then become subject to the restrictions on the carryover of capital losses. The Act also reduces the adjusted cost base of the non-depreciable capital properties by the amount of the capital

---

[109]Subpara. 111(5)(a)(ii); *Yarmouth Industrial Leasing Ltd. v. R.*, [1985] 2 C.T.C. 67, 85 D.T.C. 5401 (Fed. T.D.) ("control" includes both direct and indirect control).

[110]Subs. 249(4).

[111]Subs. 111(4).

[112]Para. 111(4)(d). Other provisions — such as, subs. 111(5.1) — apply to properties such as depreciable property.

loss.[113] The purpose of these rules is to make it less attractive to trade in corporations that are pregnant with capital losses.

V. — Capital Gains Exemption

1. — Purpose

Canada did not tax capital gains until 1972 when it introduced a rule that effectively taxed capital gains at 50 percent of the tax on ordinary income. Since 1972 we have seen the tax on capital gains climb to an effective rate of 75 percent of the tax on ordinary income and then fall back to 50 percent in 2001. The capital gains exemption was introduced in 1985. The exemption is intended to encourage risk-taking and to stimulate investment in small businesses while assisting farmers and broadening the participation of individuals in the equity markets. In short, the exemption was intended to ". . . unleash the full entrepreneurial dynamism of individual Canadians."[114]

2. — Structure

The $800,000 (indexed as of 2014) lifetime capital gains exemption is available in respect of two categories of capital properties:

1. "Qualified farm property";[115] and

2. Shares of qualified small business corporations.[116]

An individual's exemption depends upon three principal factors:

1. The individual's residence;

2. The type of capital property that gives rise to the gain; and

3. The net cumulative amount of the individual's investment income and financing expenses in the year in which he or she realizes the gain.

These three factors determine who is eligible for the exemption and how much of the gain the individual may shelter from tax in a particular year.

---

[113]Para. 53(2)(b.2).

[114]Budget speech, May 23, 1985.

[115]Subs. 110.6(2).

[116]Subs. 110.6(2.1).

3. — *Eligible Taxpayers*

(a) — *Residents*

Only individuals resident in Canada may claim the exemption. An individual can claim the exemption if he or she is resident in Canada:

- *Throughout* the year; or

- For part of the year, if the individual was resident in Canada throughout the year preceding, or the year following, the year in which he or she realized the gain.[117]

A trust cannot claim the exemption. A trust may, however, flow through its capital gain to its beneficiaries by making a special designation.[118]

A spouse trust may claim a deduction in respect of its eligible taxable capital gains in the year in which the spouse dies.[119]

(b) — *Deemed Residents*

For the purposes of the exemption, the Act deems an individual who was resident in Canada at any time in a taxation year to have been resident in Canada throughout the year if he or she was resident in Canada throughout either the year immediately preceding, or the year immediately following, the taxation year.[120] Thus, a person who becomes a non-resident in a particular year can claim the exemption if he or she was resident in Canada throughout the year immediately preceding it.

An immigrant may claim the exemption on becoming resident in Canada if he or she remains a resident throughout the following year.

4. — *Eligible Properties*

The exemption is available in respect of capital gains from the disposition of shares of a "qualified small business corporation" or "qualified farm property".

---

[117]Subs. 110.6(5).

[118]Subs. 104(21) and 104(21.2).

[119]Subs. 110.6(12), paras. 104(4)(a), (a.1).

[120]Subs. 110.6(5).

5. — Restrictions

Generally, an individual (other than a trust) resident in Canada may claim an exemption equal to the least of the following three amounts:

1. The individual's unused capital gains exemption limit;

2. The individual's annual gains limit for the year; and

3. The individual's cumulative gains limit at the end of the year.

6. — Farm Property

The general purpose of the farm property rules is to limit the exemption to taxpayers who are engaged in the business of farming for a minimum stipulated period of time and to circumstances in which farming constitutes the taxpayer's main source of income.

(a) — "Qualified Farm Property"

A taxpayer is entitled to the exemption in respect of "qualified farm property". The phrase "qualified farm property" refers to farm property held personally or through a partnership or family farm corporation.

More specifically, an individual's "qualified farm property" includes any real property that has been used by:[121]

- The individual;

- His or her spouse or common-law partner;

- His or her child or parent;

- The individual's family farm corporation in which he or she owns shares; or

- A family farm partnership in which he or she has an interest.

The property must have been used to carry on the business of farming in Canada. The business may be, or may have been, carried on by the individual who owns the farm property, that person's spouse or children, a family farm corporation, or family farm partnership in which the individual, or the spouse, children, or parents have an interest. For the purposes of these rules, grandchildren qualify as children.[122]

---

[121] Subs. 110.6(1)"qualified farm property".

[122] Para. 110.6(1)"child".

(b) — The Business of Farming

To qualify as farm property eligible for the exemption, the property must be used, or must have been used, in the course of carrying on the business of farming in Canada. What constitutes "the business of farming" is a question of fact.

(c) — Additional Tests

The following two tests must also be met:[123] (1) the property must have been owned by the individual, the spouse, common-law partner, children or parents, a family farm partnership, or a personal trust *throughout* the 24 months immediately preceding its disposition; and (2) during a period of at least two years while the property was so owned, the individual's gross revenue from the property used in farming must have exceeded his or her income from all other sources for the year.

7. — Small Business Corporation Shares

The exemption is also available in respect of capital gains that a taxpayer realizes from the disposition of qualified small business corporation ("QSBC") shares.

The Act defines a "small business corporation" as:[124]

- A Canadian-controlled private corporation in which all or most of the fair market value of the assets is attributable to assets used principally in an active business carried on primarily in Canada; and

- A Canadian-controlled private corporation in which the assets, throughout a period of 24 months immediately preceding the corporation's disposition, have not been owned by any person other than the individual claiming the exemption, or by a person or partnership related to the individual.

Shareholders of newly incorporated small business corporations can, however, claim the exemption, even where the corporation has existed for less than 24 months. Thus, a sole proprietor can dispose of his or her active business by transferring all of the business to a corporation and then selling the shares of the corporation rather than the assets of the business.

There is a risk that the CRA may attack a quick flip of shares after a rollover to a corporation as an income transaction that is not eligible for the capital gains exemption.[125]

---

[123]Subs. 110.6(1)"qualified farm property".

[124]Subs. 248(1); see also, subs. 110.6(1)"qualified small business corporation share".

[125]See, for example, *Fraser v. Minister of National Revenue*, [1964] S.C.R. 657, [1964] C.T.C. 372, 64 D.T.C. 5224 (S.C.C.).

8. — Reporting Requirements

A taxpayer who claims a capital gains exemption must disclose the amount claimed on his or her tax return for the year. In other words, a taxpayer may not simply omit net taxable capital gains from income on the basis that they are not, in effect, subject to tax. Failure to file an income tax return within one year of its due date or failure to report the capital gain in income may nullify the exemption.[126] The Minister can deny the exemption only if it can be established that failure to file the return or to disclose the amount of the capital gain was attributable to the taxpayer's gross negligence or that the taxpayer "knowingly" failed to conform to the reporting requirements.

9. — Anti-Avoidance Rules

The capital gains exemption is a generous tax preference. Thus, taxpayers have an incentive to convert income that would be otherwise taxable into non-taxable capital gains. Hence, there are several anti-avoidance provisions in place in anticipation of such manoeuvres. Some of the provisions are very specific, while others are broad provisions that cast a wide net. Indeed, in some cases, the net has been cast so widely that it is impossible to determine the types of transactions it might catch.

The primary focus of the anti-avoidance provisions, however, is the prevention of three types of tax avoidance:

1. Conversion of capital gains earned by corporations into capital gains earned by individuals ("Type A");

2. Conversion of dividend income into capital gains ("Type B"); and

3. Disproportionate allocations of gains between taxpayers.

(a) — Type A Conversions

As already noted, only individuals can claim the exemption in respect of capital gains. Consequently, there is every incentive to convert potential corporate capital gains into gains attributable to individual shareholders.

An individual cannot claim the exemption for a gain realized as a consequence of a corporation or partnership's acquisition of property at a price that is significantly less than its fair market value.[127] For example, where a corporation disposes of a property by transferring it to another corporation for less than its fair market value, any capital gain from a sale of the

---

[126]Subs. 110.6(6).

[127]Para. 110.6(7)(b).

shares of either corporation is not eligible for the exemption if the dispositions of property are part of a series of transactions. This rule applies where the transformed gain *results* from a "series of transactions or events".[128] It is not necessary to establish any intention or purpose on the part of the taxpayer to transform the gain. The sequence of events must, however, be sufficiently connected to constitute a "series of transactions".

(b) — Type B Conversions

The second category of anti-avoidance provisions is concerned with the conversion of dividend income into capital gains. In the simplest case, the value of shares may be enhanced by restricting the dividend payout on the shares. (See, for example, Berkshire Hathway, which has never paid a dividend.) In these circumstances, the CRA may deny the taxpayer's claim for an exemption in respect of the gain from a disposition of the shares.[129]

More specifically, an individual may not claim the capital gains exemption in respect of gains realized on shares where:[130]

- It is reasonable to conclude that a significant part of the gain is attributable to non-payment of dividends on the shares; or

- The dividends paid in the year *or in any preceding taxation year* were less than 90 percent of the average annual rate of return on the shares for that year.

The individual need not have an intention to convert dividend income into capital gains. It is sufficient that there is a causal connection between significant enhancement in the value of the shares and inadequacy of the payment of dividends. The Minister's assumption is presumed to be correct unless the taxpayer can "demolish" it through contrary evidence. The onus shifts the individual to provide an alternative explanation for the enhanced value of the shares.

This rule does not apply to prescribed shares.[131] A "prescribed share" is one that is commonly referred to as a "common share", that is, a share not restricted to a maximum dividend, or to a maximum amount upon winding up of the corporation. Shares issued as part of an estate freeze[132] and shares issued by mutual fund corporations are also prescribed for the purposes of this rule.[133]

---

[128]See subs. 248(10) (defining "series of transactions").

[129]Subs. 110.6(8).

[130]*Ibid.*

[131]Reg. 6205.

[132]Reg. 6205(2)(a).

[133]Reg. 6205(2)(b).

The average annual rate of return on a share is the rate of return that a "knowledgeable and prudent investor" would expect to receive on such a share.[134] Here too, the taxpayer must incur the cost of establishing what a knowledgeable and prudent investor would expect. In determining the rate, any delay, postponement, or failure to pay dividends in respect of the shares should be ignored. Variations in the amount of dividends payable from year to year should also be ignored.

Finally, the return is to be determined on the assumption that the shares may only be disposed of for proceeds equal to their issue price. These assumptions are intended to provide a nearly mechanical formula for determining a rate of return, without regard to all the factual financial nuances that might otherwise influence the return on shares.

---

[134]Subs. 110.6(9).

Selected Bibliography to Chapter 14

General

McQuillan, Peter E., "Computation of Income for Tax Purposes", in *Proceedings of 44th Tax Conf.* 5:27 (Canada Tax Foundation, 1992).

Swanson, Julie Anne, "The Alternative Minimum Tax" (Toronto: CCH Canadian, 1991).

Charitable Donations, Medical Expenses, etc.

Anderson, Alec R., "The Statutory Non-charitable Purpose Trust: Estate Planning in the Tax Havens" in *Equity, Fiduciaries and Trusts* (Toronto: Carswell, 1993).

Arbuckle, J.E., "Investment in Art — For Pleasure and Profit" (1980) 54 Cost & Mgt. 46.

Bale, G., "Construing a Taxing Statute or Tilting at Windmills: Charitable Donation Deduction and the Charter of Rights and Freedoms" (1985) 19 E.T.R. 55.

Bromley, E. Blake, "A Response to 'A Better Tax Administration in Support of Charities'" (1991) 10 Philanthrop. No. 3 3.

Bromley, E. Blake, "Parallel Foundations and Crown Foundations" (1993) 11 Philanthrop. No. 4 37.

"Charity Lotteries" (1983) 5 Can. Taxpayer 112.

"Corporate Donations" A Double Winner" (1980) 2 Can. Taxpayer 200.

Dickson, M.L., and Lawrence C. Murray, "Recent Tax Developments" (1985) 5 Philanthrop. 50, 52.

Dickson, M.L., and Laurence C. Murray, "Recent Tax Developments" (1986) 6 Philanthrop. 40, 59.

Dickson, M.L., and Lawrence C. Murray, "Recent Tax Developments (Charitable Organizations)" (1985) 5 Philanthrop. 56.

Dickson, M.L., and Lawrence C. Murray, "Recent Tax Developments" (1991) 10 Philanthrop. 42.

Drache, A.B.C., "Abortion Clinic Recognized as Charitable" (1992) 14 Can. Taxpayer 18.

Drache, A.B.C., *Canadian Tax Treatment of Charities and Charitable Donations* (Toronto: De Boo, 1978).

Drache, A.B.C., *Canadian Taxation of Charities and Donations* (Toronto: Carswell, 1994).

Drache, A.B.C., "Complaints Against 'Charitable Business'" (1992) 14 Can. Taxpayer 20.

Chapter 14 — Taxable Income

Drache, A.B.C., "Residual Gift to Charity Recognized" (1992) 14 Can. Taxpayer 15.

Drache, A.B.C., "Tax Exempt Organizations" (1991) 13 Can. Taxpayer 165.

Erlichman, Harry, "Profitable Donations: What Price Culture?" (1992) Philanthrop. No. 2 3.

Farrow, Trevor C.W., "The Limits of Charity: Redefining the Boundaries of Charitable Trust Law" (1994) 13 Estates and Trusts J. 306.

Finkelstein, David N., "Tax Problems in Estate Planning for the Corporate Executive," in *Proceedings of 33rd Tax Conf.* 952 (Can. Tax Foundation, 1981).

Forster, George V., "Tax-effective Compensation for the Employees of Charitable Organizations" (1986) 6 Philanthrop. 24.

Goldstein, Lisa D., "Non-profit Organization Can Be Profitable" (1993) 41 Can. Tax J. 720.

Goodison, Don, "Tax Deductible Donations" (1988) 22 CGA Magazine 11.

Goodman, Wolfe D., "Charitable Gifts of Appreciated Capital Property" (1986) 8 Estates & Trusts Q. 189.

Goodman, Wolfe D., "The Impact of Taxation on Charitable Giving: Some Very Personal Views" (1984) 4 Philanthrop. 5.

Gotlieb, Maxwell, *Charities and the Tax Man and More* (Toronto: Canadian Bar Association — Ontario, Continuing Legal Education, 1990).

Gotlieb, Maxwell, "Taxation of, and Tax Planning for, Charitable Donations" (1993) 11 Philanthrop. No. 4 3.

Haney, Mary-Anne, "Abortion Too Controversial for Revenue Canada" (1992) 40 Can. Tax J. 171.

Innes, William I., "Gifts of Cultural Property by Artists" (1993) 12 Estates and Trusts J. 219.

Juneau, Carl D., "Some Major Issues Affecting Evaluation of the Charities Tax Incentive" (1990) 9 Philanthrop. No. 4 3.

Krishna, Vern, "Advantages des dons de charité au Canada (Les)" (soc. canadienne du cancer, 1984).

Krishna, Vern, "Charitable Donations: What Constitutes a 'Gift'?" (1985) 1 Can. Current Tax J107.

Krishna, Vern, "Charitable Donations: What is a Charitable Purpose?" (1986) 1 Can. Current Tax C159.

Law, Tax, and Charities: The Legislative and Regulatory Environment for Charitable and Non-profit Organizations (Toronto: The Canadian Centre for Philanthropy, 1990).

615

Midland, Christina H., "Limitations on Charities Under the *Income Tax Act*" (1992) 44 E.T.R. 111.

Monaco, Joseph C., *Charitable Donations: "Gifts in Kind"* (Hamilton, Ont.: Thorne Ernst and Whinney, 1989).

"Personal Tax Planning: Charitable Giving" (1987) 35 Can. Tax J. 182.

Pintea, Hans O., "Taxation of Ongoing Partnership Operations," in *Proceedings of 33rd Tax Conf.* 195 (Can. Tax Foundation, 1981).

"Private Religious Schools in Jeopardy" (1980) 2 Can. Taxpayer 203.

"Religious School Problem: Final Resolution" (1982) 4 Can. Taxpayer 83.

Schusheim, Pearl E., "Charities and the Federal Income Tax Provisions: Getting and Staying Registered" (1986) 6 Philanthrop. 11.

Senecal, David, "The Tax Sleepers: Charitable and Nonprofit Organizations" (1975) 107 CA Magazine 52.

"Special Fund-Raising Events" (1983) 5 Can. Taxpayer 196.

Stephen, Peter R., "Charitable Giving" (1987) 35 Can. Tax J. 182.

Tamagno, Edward, "The Medical Expenses Deduction" (1979) 1 Can. Taxation 58.

Watson, Rod, "Charity and the Canadian Income Tax: An Erratic History" (1985) 5 Philanthrop. 3.

Zweibel, Ellen B., "A Truly Canadian Definition of Charity and a Lesson in Drafting Charitable Purposes: A Comment on *Native Communications Society of B.C. v. M.N.R.*" (1987) 26 E.T.R. 41.

Zweibel, Ellen B., "Looking the Gift Horse in the Mouth: An Examination of Charitable Gifts Which Benefit the Donor" (1986) 31 McGill L.J. 417.

Zweibel, Ellen B., "Registration as Charity — Political Activities (case comment on *Scarborough Community Legal Services v. R.*)" (1985) 1 Can. Current Tax A20.

Interest and Dividend Income

Alter, Dr. A., "Different Techniques for Adjusting Taxable Income Under Inflationary Conditions" (1986) Br. Tax Rev. 347.

Birnie, David A.G., "Shareholders' Buy-Sell Agreements: Some New Opportunities" in *Proceedings of the 38th Tax Conf.* 13 (Can. Tax Foundation, 1986).

Boultbee, Jack, "Tax Gimmicks", in *Proceedings of 33rd Tax Conf.* 300 (Can. Tax Foundation, 1981).

Colley, Geoffrey M., "Is Indexing a Necessary Evil?" (1986) 119 CA Magazine 52.

Colley, Geoffrey M., "Personal Tax Planning and You" (1976) 109 CA Magazine 45.

Colley, Geoffrey M., "Planning Ahead for Your Tax Exemption" (1981) 14 CA Magazine 59.

Colley, Geoffrey M., "What's New in Personal Investment?" (1977) 110 CA Magazine 63.

Communications Directorate, Revenue Canada Taxation, "Application for Registration: A Revenue Canada Taxation Perspective" (1986) 6 Philanthrop. 4.

Gould, Lawrence I., and Stanley N. Laiken, "Dividends vs. Capital Gains under Share Redemptions" (1979) 27 Can. Tax J. 161.

Gould, Lawrence I., and Stanley N. Laiken, "Effects of the Investment Income Deduction on Investment Returns" (1982) 30 Can. Tax J. 228.

Guilbault, P., "Individuals" (1985) 13 Can. Tax News 97.

"Interest Deductibility" (1979) 1 Can. Taxpayer 20.

"Juggling Dividends" (1980) 2 Can. Taxpayer 27.

Kennedy, James F., "The Use of Trust in Tax and Estate Planning," in *Proceedings of 33rd Tax Conf.* 577 (Can. Tax Foundation, 1981).

McNair, D. Keith, *Taxation of Farmers and Fishermen* (Toronto: De Boo, 1986).

Pintea, Hans O., "Taxation of Ongoing Partnership Operations," in *Proceedings of 33rd Tax Conf.* 195 (Can. Tax Foundation, 1981).

Pipes, Sally, and Michael Walker, with Douglas Wills, *Tax Facts 5: The Canadian Consumer Tax Index and You* (Vancouver: Fraser Institute, 1986).

Thomas, Douglas, "As A Matter of Interest" (1978) 111 CA Magazine 84.

Miscellaneous Deductible Losses

Amighetti, Leopole, "Income Tax Events Triggered by Death, an Examination of Selected Problems," in *Proceedings of 31st Tax Conf.* 652 (Can. Tax Foundation, 1979).

Blom, J., "Deductions for Personal Expenditures (Subdivision e and Divison C)" (1981) Can. Taxation 473.

Cadesky, Michael, "Corporate Losses," in *Proceedings of 42nd Tax Conf.* (Can. Tax Foundation, 1990).

Burpee, Thomas R., "Utilization of Tax Losses: "A Reasonable Expectation of Profit'," in *Proceedings of 37th Tax Conf.* 32:1 (Can. Tax Foundation, 1985).

Clarkson Gordon Foundation, *Policy Options for the Treatment of Tax Losses in Canada* (Scarborough, Ont.: Clarkson Gordon Foundation, 1991).

Dean, Jacklyn I., "The January 15, 1987 Draft Amendments Relating to the Acquisition of Gains and Losses" (1987) Corporate Management Tax Conf. 2:1.

Dunbar, Alisa E., "Sale of Stock Plan Shares May Produce Freely Deductible Loss" (1991) 3 Tax. of Exec. Compensation and Retirement 499.

Farden, Eric N., "Income Tax for Farmers" (Sask.: E.N. Farden, 1985).

Flynn, Gordon W., "Tax Planning for Corporations with Net Capital and Noncapital Losses," *Corporate Management Tax Conf.* 208 (Can. Tax Foundation, 1981).

Foster, David R., "Restoration of Non-capital Losses" (1992) 3 Can. Current Tax A7.

Hirsch, Morley P., "The Corporate Loss Transfer System", in *Proceedings of 37th Tax Conf.* 31 (Can. Tax Foundation, 1985).

Krishna, Vern, "Farm Losses; Subsection 31(1); 'Chief Source of Income'" (1985) 1 Can. Current Tax J-91.

LePan, Nicholas, "Federal and Provincial Issues in the Corporate Loss Transfer Proposal," in *Proceedings of 37th Tax Conf.* 13 (Can. Tax Foundation, 1985).

Neville, Ralph J., "Acquisition of Control and Corporate Losses" in *Proceedings of 44th Tax Conf.* 25:25 (Can. Tax Foundation, 1992).

"New Treatment for Losses" (1983) 5 Can. Taxpayer 183.

Nowoselski, Barty, "Should You Buy or Sell a Company for Its Tax-Loss Carryovers?" (1983) 116 CA Magazine 64.

Pearson, Hugh, "Farming and the *Income Tax Act*" (1993) 41 Can. Tax J. 1135.

Reid, Robert J., "Capital and Non-capital Losses," in *Proceedings of 42nd Tax Conf.* 20:1 (Can. Tax Foundation, 1990).

Richardson, Stephen R., "A Corporate Loss Transfer System for Canada: Analysis of Proposals," in *Proceedings of 37th Tax Conf.* 12 (Can. Tax Foundation, 1985).

Silver, Sheldon, "Utilization of Real Estate Losses," *Corporate Management Tax Conf.* 91 (Can. Tax Foundation, 1983).

Slutsky, Sam, "Insolvency: A Refresher from a Taxation Perspective" (1982) 30 Can. Tax J. 528.

Swirsky, Benjamin, "Utilization of Losses," *Corporate Management Tax Conf.* 213. (Can. Tax Foundation, 1978).

Thomas, Richard B., "A Farm Loss with a Difference: The Farmer is Successful" (1993) Can. Tax J. 513.

Ward, David A., "Arm's Length Acquisitions Relating to Shares in a Public Corporation," *Corporate Management Tax Conf.* 108 (Can. Tax Foundation, 1978).

Wilson, Michael H., *A Corporate Loss Transfer System for Canada*, Dept. of Finance, Canada, 1985.

Wise, Richard M., "Fair Market Determinations — A Few More Requirements" (1983) 31 Can. Tax J. 337.

Wraggett, Cathy, "Accelerated Deduction of Business Losses" (1990) 64 CMA Magazine 33.

Capital Gains Exemption

Attridge, Ian, "Create Conservation Gains, Not Capital Gains" (1994) 19 Intervenor No. 6 8.

Barbacki, Richard, "Use It or Lose It?" (1989) 122 CA Magazine 43.

Colley, G.M., "What Price the Capital Gains Exemption?" (1985) 118 CA Magazine 10:75.

Cullity, Maurice C., "The Capital Gains Exemption: Implications for Estate Planning," in *Proceedings of 37th Tax Conf.* 18 (Can. Tax Foundation, 1985).

Goodison, Don, "Business Losses" (1987) 21 CGA Magazine 6.

Goodman, S.H., and N.C. Tobias, "The Proposed $500,000 Capital Gains Exemption" (1985) 33 Can. Tax J. 721.

Hayos, Gabriel J., "The Capital Gains Exemption: Planning Strategies to Meet the Criteria of a Qualified Small Business Corporation," in *Proceedings of 40th Tax Conf.* 15:1 (Can. Tax Foundation, 1988).

James, Larry W., "Capital Gains Exemption: Planning Techniques," in *Proceedings of 38th Tax Conf.* 33 (Can. Tax Foundation, 1986).

Kellough, Howard J., and K. Travers Pullen, "Planning for the Lifetime Capital Gains Exemption" (1986) 3 Bus. & L. 3.

Kirby, F.P., "The Capital Gains Exemption: Other Than Qualified Small Business Shares," in *Proceedings of 40th Tax Conf.* 30:1 (Can. Tax Foundation, 1988).

Lawlor, W.R., "Surplus Stripping and Other Planning Opportunities with the New $500,000 Capital Gains Exemption" (1986) 34 Can. Tax J. 49.

Peters, Steven, "Enhancing the Exemption" (1992) 125 CA Magazine No. 5 33.

Potvin, Jean, "The Capital Gains Deduction for Qualified Small Business Corporation Shares Revisited," in *Proceedings of 44th Tax Conf.* (Can. Tax Foundation, 1992).

Quinton, Cathy, "The Additional Capital Gains Exemption" (1989) 62 CMA Magazine 34.

Rotenberg, Charles M., "Making the Deal Work" (1991) 13 Can. Taxpayer 60.

Ruby, Stephen S., "A Glimpse at the Lifetime Capital Gains Exemption (Part I)" (1986) 3 Bus. & L. 93.

Ruby, Stephen S., "A Glimpse at the Lifetime Capital Gains Exemption (Part III)" (1987) 4 Bus. & L. 6.

Stack, Thomas J., "Capital Gains and Losses on Shares of Private Corporations," in *Proceedings of 39th Tax Conf.* 17:1 (Can. Tax Foundation, 1987).

Tam, Anthony, "Capital Gains Exemption: Small Business Corporations" (1987–89) 2 Can. Current Tax P-5.

"Taxation of Corporate Reorganizations (The): New Measures to Restrict Netting of Gains and Shelter" (1987) 35 Can. Tax J. 198.

Templeton, Wendy, "Anti-Avoidance and the Capital Gains Exemption" (1986) 34 Can. Tax J. 203.

Templeton, Wendy, "The Taxation of Corporate Reorganizations: Anti-Avoidance and the Capital Gains Exemption" (1986) 34 Can. Tax J. 203.

Templeton, Wendy, "The Taxation of Corporate Reorganizations: Anti-Avoidance and the Capital Gains Exemptions: Part 2" (1986) 34 Can. Tax J. 446.

Chapter 15 — Computation of Tax

Table of Contents

Fundamentals of Canadian Income Tax Vol 1: Personal Tax

Table of Contents

Chapter 15 — Computation of Tax

Table of Contents

I. — General Comment

The preceding chapters have focused on the computation of income and taxable income, i.e., determination of the taxable base upon which we calculate the tax payable. We now turn to the second variable in determining a taxpayer's liability for income tax: tax rates.

Setting of an appropriate tax rate(s) is a complex matter that requires us to consider several factors. First, we must set the rate at a level that generates sufficient government revenues. However, rates and revenues are not always positively correlated. Indeed, excessively high rates foster tax avoidance and can lead to reduced revenues. Second, we must harmonize individual, trust, and corporate rates in order that the tax system is reasonably neutral among different forms of organization. For example, if the corporate tax rate is substantially lower than individual rates, there is an incentive to incorporate, earn and accumulate income in the corporation. Third, rates — particularly corporate tax rates — must be competitive in the international marketplace. For example, Canadian corporate tax rates must take into account U.S. rates, or risk losing business and investments if our rates are substantially higher than our principle trading partner. Uneven corporate tax rates lead to flight of capital to low tax jurisdictions through transfer pricing and other tax avoidance measures. Fourth, political considerations affect tax rates, particularly if the government is vulnerable in an election year.

We determine tax payable is a multi-step process that involves more than the application of a single rate to taxable income. Once we determine the basic tax by applying a rate to taxable income, we apply various credits, surtaxes, and reductions.

Division E of Part I of the Act, which deals with the calculation of tax payable, has three parts:

1. Rules applicable to individuals;

2. Rules applicable to corporations; and

3. Rules applicable to all taxpayers.

As we will see, the computation takes into account several tax rates, surtaxes, and tax credits in balancing the competing needs of revenue generation, fairness and equity, economic efficiency, and political considerations.

II. — Individuals

Individuals are entitled to personal tax credits — that is, deductions from tax liability, as opposed to exemptions from income. The overall effect is that every individual, regardless of income level, gets to reduce his or her taxes by the same amount. Thus, although high income individuals pay taxes at progressively higher marginal rates, their tax credits are fixed, generally at the lowest marginal rate of 15%.

1. — Basic Tax Rate

(a) — General Rates

Section 117 sets out the federal tax rates applicable to individuals. The general basic tax rates for 2014 are as follows:

Taxable Income	Rate
$1–43,953	15%
$43,953–87,907	22%
$87,907–136,270	26%
$136,270 and over	29%

These tax rates are indexed by a formula linked to the Consumer Price Index ("CPI").[1]

(b) — Provincial Taxes

The rates in section 117 are the federal rates. In addition to the federal tax, Canadian residents are also liable for provincial income tax. Provinces that have a tax collection agreement with the federal government ("participating provinces") may elect to calculate their income taxes using one of two methods: the "tax on tax" method or the "tax on income" method. All of the participating provinces have adopted the new tax on income method.

The "tax on tax" method calculates the provincial income tax by applying the provincial rate of tax to the *federal tax payable*. This method is inflexible and limits the ability of the provinces to raise revenues and set provincial income tax policies. In response to the prov-

[1] S. 117.1.

inces' desire for more control over how their income taxes are levied, the "tax on income" method was introduced.[2]

The "tax on income" method calculates the provincial income tax by reference to taxable *income* rather than to federal tax payable. As such, it allows the provinces to determine their own unique income tax brackets and rates and to create their own distinct block of non-refundable tax credits,[3] which gives the provinces greater flexibility in setting their tax policy. However, in order to ensure a common tax base, the provinces and the federal government use a common definition of "taxable income".

Quebec is the only province that does not have a tax collection agreement with the federal government. It also calculates the provincial income tax by reference to "taxable income".

The combined federal and provincial marginal income tax rates (including surtaxes) at the top end of the rate schedule are set out in Figure 1.

Figure 1 — Federal/Provincial Top Income Tax Rates (2014)

Resident of:	Percent
Alberta	39.0
British Columbia	45.8
Manitoba	46.4
New Brunswick	46.84
Newfoundland	42.3
Nova Scotia	50.0
Ontario	49.5
Prince Edward Island	47.4

---

[2]See generally the Department of Finance's *Federal Administration of Provincial Taxes*, October 1998, Report prepared by the Federal-Provincial Committee on Taxation for presentation to Ministers of Finance, online: <http://www.fin.gc.ca/fapt/fapt3e.html.>

[3]Subject to restrictions on minimums; see *ibid.* at Design and Operation.

Figure 1 — Federal/Provincial Top Income Tax Rates (2014)

Quebec	50.0
Saskatchewan	44.0
Northwest Territories	43.0
Yukon Territory	42.4
Nunavut	40.5

As Figure 1 shows, individuals pay taxes at different rates depending on where they live. Thus, the tax burden does not always reflect an individual's ability to pay. A part of the price of federalism is that individuals bear differential tax burdens depending on where they live.

Apart from the indexing of tax brackets, the basic rate schedule is fairly stable. Instead, governments increase or decrease taxes by adjusting deductions and by imposing or removing surtaxes, or by allowing for special tax credits.

2. — Surtaxes

The disparity of tax rates does not stop at the basic provincial rate. There are further adjustments to tax rates through surtaxes (often labelled as "temporary") or tax credits. A surtax is a tax calculated by reference to another tax, usually the basic federal tax.

3. — Tax Credits

Once we determine an individual's tentative tax liability before adjustments, he or she may also be entitled to certain personal and other tax credits. A tax credit reduces the tax that would otherwise be payable by the individual. In general, tax credits depend on:

1. Status;

2. Source of income;

3. Type of expenditure; and

4. Location of source of income.

For example, a taxpayer can claim a credit for:

• Personal tax credits;

- Pension income;

- Dividends from taxable Canadian corporations;

- Tuition and education;

- Medical expenses;

- Charitable donations;

- Eligible children;

- Overseas employment; or

- Foreign taxes.

We calculate these according to a formula that applies a percentage to the aggregate of the claimable amounts. The credits are indexed and, as such, are partially adjusted each year to reflect inflationary increases as measured by the Consumer Price Index.

Some of the credits are refundable — that is, the taxpayer receives a cash refund if the credits exceed his or her income for the year. Others are non-refundable, and the taxpayer loses the credit if he or she cannot deduct it from tax otherwise payable for the year.

Tax credits are available at both the federal and provincial levels. Each province has the flexibility (subject to some restrictions) to choose which tax credits it will offer and to set the amount of those credits. Thus, tax credits vary from province to province.

The following tax credits are credits under the federal tax statute.

(a) — Personal Tax Credits

A taxpayer can claim tax credits on account of:

- Single status;

- Spousal and common law partner status;

- Equivalent-to-spouse status;

- Dependants; and

- Age.

These credits are not refundable. References to spouse in this chapter include, where appropriate, common-law partners.

627

A common law partner of an individual is a person of the same or opposite sex who has cohabitated with the taxpayer in a conjugal relationship[4] for a continuous period of at least one year or they share parenthood of a child.

Whether persons are living in a conjugal relationship is a question of fact, including how the couple present themselves in public and register for benefit plans.

(i) — Method of Calculation

A taxpayer claims a credit by aggregating the dollar value of all the amounts that he or she is entitled to claim, and then multiplying this value by the "appropriate percentage" for the year.[5] The "appropriate percentage" for a taxation year is the *lowest* marginal tax rate applicable in the particular year.[6]

Provinces determine their own unique income tax brackets and rates and create their own distinct block of non-refundable tax credits.[7] As a result, provincial tax credits are often different than the federal tax credits. Provinces have the flexibility to supplement federal credits or add any additional unique provincial credits. They are also not required to follow any federal increases in a credit except in the case of expenditure-based credits. For expenditure-based credits (e.g., CPP, EI, tuition fees, medical expenses, charitable donations), provinces may increase credits beyond the level of the gross federal credit, but may not fall below the federal level.

(ii) — Single Status

Every individual is entitled to $11,138 (2014) as their personal federal claim.[8] This amount is multiplied by the "appropriate percentage". For example, in 2014 the credit for a single person is $1,670 that is, 15 percent of $11,138. In addition, there is a parallel provincial claim.

---

[4]For meaning of "conjugal relationship" see *Moldowich v. Penttinen* (1980), 17 R.F.L. (2d) 376 (Ont. Dist. Ct.) cited in *M v. H* (S.C.C.).

[5]Subs. 118(1).

[6]Subs. 248(1) "appropriate percentage"; subs. 117(2).

[7]See generally the Department of *Finance's Federal Administration of Provincial Taxes*, October 1998, Report prepared by the Federal-Provincial Committee on Taxation for presentation to Ministers of Finance, online: <http://www.fin.gc.ca/fapt/fapt3e.html.>

[8]Para. 118(1)(c).

(iii) — Spousal Status

An individual who supports his or her spouse or a common-law partner can claim an additional amount as a federal tax credit. In 2014, for example, the additional amount was $11,138. Thus, in the simplest case, an individual is entitled to claim a total of $22,276, which converts to a credit of $3,341, that is, 15 percent of $22,276.

A person is "married" if he or she undergoes a form of marriage recognized by the laws of Canada and is not a widow or widower, or divorced.[9] Subsection 252(3) expands the meaning of

"spouse" to include individuals who are party to a void or voidable marriage.

"Income" means *net* income. The spouse's or common law partner's income for the entire year is taken into account in determining whether the supporting taxpayer is entitled to the additional claim.[10] Where the individual was living apart from his or her spouse at the end of the year by reason of marriage breakdown, the spouse's income for the period during the year in which the parties were not separated is taken into account in determining the claim.[11]

(iv) — Wholly-Dependent Persons

A person who is not entitled to the spousal status credit, but who supports a person who depends upon him can claim the credit for a wholly-dependent person (also referred to as the "equivalent-to-spouse credit").[12] The amount claimable under this provision is equivalent to the amount that a married person whose spouse does not earn more than the total threshold amount can claim.

The equivalent-to-spouse credit is available only to an individual who maintains (either alone or jointly with another person), and lives in, a self-contained domestic establishment and actually supports therein the dependent person. For example, a single parent supporting a child would qualify for the credit under this provision.

There are two additional qualifications for the claim on account of wholly-dependent persons. First, except where the claim is in respect of the taxpayer's child, the credit is available

---

[9]*R. v. Scheller*, [1975] C.T.C. 601, 75 D.T.C. 5406 (Fed. T.D.); *McPhee v. Minister of National Revenue*, [1980] C.T.C. 2042, 80 D.T.C. 1034 (T.R.B.); *R. v. Taylor*, [1984] C.T.C. 244, 84 D.T.C. 6234 (Fed. T.D.).

[10]*Johnston v. Minister of National Revenue*, [1948] S.C.R. 486, [1948] C.T.C. 195, 3 D.T.C. 1182 (S.C.C.) (husband considered to support his wife if contributing to her support, even though she may supply some money towards meeting expenses of household).

[11]Para. 118(1)(a).

[12]Para. 118(1)(b).

only in respect of dependants who reside in Canada.[13] A taxpayer is not entitled to the credit in respect of foreign resident dependants. This discriminatory provision is based on the convenience of the CRA to audit the claim for the credit.

Second, except in the case of a claim for a parent or grandparent, a taxpayer cannot claim an amount in respect of a dependant who is 18 years of age or older, unless the person's dependency is because of mental or physical infirmity.[14]

(v) — Dependants

A taxpayer may also claim an amount in respect of individuals who depend on him or her for support. The claim depends upon five criteria:[15]

1. Dependency;

2. Relationship between the taxpayer and the individual claimed as a dependant;

3. Residence;

4. Age; and

5. Mental or physical infirmity of dependant.

1. — Dependency

Whether an individual is dependent on a taxpayer is a question of fact in each case. In the event that a person is partially dependent on two or more taxpayers, their aggregate claim in respect of that dependant cannot exceed the maximum amount that would be deductible in respect of a claim by one taxpayer. Where the supporting individuals cannot agree on the portion of the total that each is to deduct, the Minister may allocate the amount between them.

2. — Relationship

The term "dependant" in respect of a taxpayer or his or her spouse means:[16]

• Their children or grandchildren;

---

[13]Cl. 118(1)(b)(ii)(A).

[14]Cl. 118(1)(b)(ii)(D).

[15]Para. 118(1)(d).

[16]Subs. 118(6).

- Their nieces or nephews, if resident in Canada;
- Their brothers or sisters, if resident in Canada; and
- Their parents, grandparents, aunts or uncles, if resident in Canada.

3. — Residence

Except in respect of a claim for the taxpayer's, or his or her spouse's, children or grandchildren, the dependency deduction is available only for the support of dependants who reside in Canada. This distinction between the various categories of dependants reflects the concerns of the tax authorities with the authenticity of dependency claims.

4. — Age

The infirm dependent deduction is available only in respect of dependants over the age of 18. The amount claimable in any year depends upon the amount fixed for the year less the excess of the dependant's income over a stipulated amount for that year.

5. — Mental or Physical Infirmity

A taxpayer can claim the dependency deduction for individuals over the age of 18 only if they depend upon him or her because of mental or physical infirmity.[17]

6. — Senior Citizen Credit

An individual who is 65 years of age or older can claim an additional federal amount.[18] The maximum amount claimable is 15 percent of $6,916 (2014; indexed),[19] — that is, $1,037.

For individuals whose income exceeds $34,562 (2014; indexed),[20] the maximum amount claimable is reduced by 15 percent of income over that amount. Thus, there is no credit available when net income exceeds $34,873 (2014).

---

[17]Subpara. 118(1)(d)(ii).

[18]Subs. 118(2).

[19]See 117.1.

[20]*Ibid.*

7. — Pension Income

The pension income credits provide some relief from inflation, particularly for individuals who have to live on fixed incomes. The credit depends on two factors: the source of the pension and the recipient's age.

An individual who is 65 years of age or older may claim a credit in respect of pension income. We determine the claim by applying the appropriate percentage (15 percent in 2014) to the lesser of $2,000 (unindexed) and the pension income in the year.[21] For example, in 2014, the maximum federal credit in respect of pension income is $300, that is, 15 percent of $2,000 (not indexed) plus a parallel provincial credit.

"Pension income" includes:[22]

• Life annuity payments out of a superannuation or pension fund;

• Annuity payments out of registered retirement savings plans;

• Payments out of registered retirement income funds;

• Payments out of deferred profit-sharing plans; and

• Accrued income on an annuity or life insurance policy included in income.

Lump-sum payments out of pension plans and deferred income plans are not eligible for the pension income credit. We determine the credit by reference to *annuity* payments out of these plans.

Pensions under the *Old Age Security Act*, the Canada Pension Plan or the Quebec Pension Plan, retirement allowances, death benefits, exempt income, and payments out of an employee benefit plan, an employee trust, a salary deferral arrangement, or a retirement compensation arrangement do not qualify for the credit.

The concept of "qualified pension income" is much narrower than "pension income". "Qualified pension income" includes:[23]

• Life annuities paid out under a superannuation or pension fund plan; and

• Amounts paid as a consequence of the death of a taxpayer's spouse, on account of registered retirement savings plans, registered retirement income funds, deferred profit-sharing plans, or certain annuity payments.

---

[21]Para. 118(3)(a).

[22]Subs. 118(7) "pension income".

[23]Subs. 118(7) "qualified pension income".

For example, where an individual takes out a guaranteed term annuity under a registered retirement savings plan and designates his spouse as a beneficiary under the plan, any payments made under the guaranteed term of the plan to the beneficiary on his death are eligible for the pension income credit.

(c) — Tuition Fees

Tuition fees on account of education are generally personal capital expenditures. Tuition fees may be business expenses where an employer pays the fees for business purposes. Thus, an individual could not, without specific authorization, claim a deduction or a credit for tuition fees. For social policy reasons, however, the tax system allows individuals a tax credit for tuition fees paid to certain educational institutions.

There are two different sets of conditions that regulate the credit for tuition fees: the first deals with students attending educational institutions in Canada, the second with those attending educational institutions outside Canada. The rules in respect of the former category are considerably less stringent than those in respect of the latter.

(i) — Institutions in Canada

A student may claim a credit for fees paid to attend:[24]

- A post-secondary educational institution; or

- An institution certified by the Minister of Human Resources Development to provide courses that furnish or improve occupational skills.

We determine the credit by applying the "appropriate percentage" to the eligible tuition fees paid in the year. The credit is available only if the total fees exceed $100.[25]

(ii) — Deemed Residence

A student who is deemed to be a resident of Canada[26] can claim the credit even if he or she attends an educational institution outside Canada. The credit is available on the same terms and conditions as if the student were attending an institution in Canada.[27]

---

[24]Para. 118.5(1)(a).

[25]Subs. 118.5 (1.1).

[26]S. 250.

[27]Subs. 118.5(2).

(iii) — Transfer of Unused Credits

A student can transfer the tuition tax credit to his or her spouse.[28] Where a student is unmarried, or a married student's spouse does not claim a personal tax credit for him or her, the education and tuition tax credit may be transferred to the student's parents or grandparents.[29]

The maximum amount the student can transfer each year is $5,000 minus the amount he or she uses that year.

(iv) — Fees Paid by Employer

Tuition fees paid by a student's employer are also creditable by the student, but only to the extent that the student includes the fees in income. The employer may deduct the fees as a business expense if the fees are paid for business purposes.[30]

(v) — "Tuition Fees"

Tuition fees include:

- Admission fees;
- Charges for the use of a library, or laboratory fees;
- Exemption fees;
- Examination fees;
- Application fees;
- Confirmation fees;
- Charges for a certificate, diploma or degree;
- Membership or seminar fees specifically related to an academic program and its administration;
- Mandatory computer service fees; and
- Academic fees.

---

[28] S. 118.8.

[29] S. 118.9.

[30] S. 9.

Fees for student activities (whether social or athletic), medical care fees, transportation and parking charges, board and lodging, equipment costs of a capital nature, and initiation or entrance fees to professional organizations are not creditable for tax purposes.

(vi) — Books

Although the cost of books does not usually qualify as a tuition fee, a student may claim a credit for such costs if he or she is enrolled in a correspondence course and the cost of the books is an integral part of the fee paid for the course.

(vii) — Period Covered by Fees

Only tuition fees paid *in respect of a particular year*[31] are creditable in that year. Fees paid to cover tuition for an academic session that straddles the calendar year are eligible for the tax credit only for the year to which they relate. For example, where the academic year is from September in one year to May of the next year, the tuition tax credit must be allocated so that the portion from September to December is claimable in one year and the portion from January to May is claimable in the subsequent year.

(viii) — Educational Institutions Outside Canada

A full-time student enrolled at a university outside Canada can claim a credit by applying the "appropriate percentage" to the amount of eligible tuition fees paid in respect of the year to the university.[32]

The qualifications to claim the tuition fee credit for attending a university outside Canada are considerably more stringent than those for institutions in Canada. The credit is available only if the student satisfies the following conditions:

- The student attends a course that is of not less than 13 consecutive weeks' duration;
- The program of study leads to a *degree* (not a diploma) from the institution;
- The institution that the student attends is a *university*, not a college or other educational institution; and
- The student attends on a full-time basis.

Students are considered to be in "full-time attendance" at a university if the institution regards them to be full-time students for academic purposes. A certificate from a university

---

[31]Subs. 118.5(1).

[32]Para. 118.5(1)(b).

stating that a student was in full-time attendance, in a particular academic year or semester, is acceptable for tax purposes. Hence, a student who holds a full-time job and takes a full course load at a university is considered to be in full-time attendance at the educational institution for tax purposes.

The CRA interprets the 13 consecutive weeks' attendance requirement quite liberally. For example, a student satisfies the requirement if he or she drops out of the course before completing the program of studies, the particular academic term falls a little short of 13 weeks, or the term is broken by official holidays.

(ix) — Post-Graduate Studies

A student who enrolls in a post-graduate program of studies on a regular basis is considered to be in "full-time attendance" if he or she is registered for the regular academic year. This is so even if the requirements for attendance in class are minimal. For example, a registered post-graduate student who spends most of his or her time in a laboratory or a library engaged in research, whether on or off campus, is usually considered to be in full-time attendance. Similarly, a post-graduate student who holds a full-time job is not necessarily precluded from claiming the tuition tax credit.

(x) — Commuting to United States

A Canadian resident who commutes to a post-secondary level educational institution in the United States can claim the tax credit for tuition fees.[33] This credit is available only to students who reside throughout the year near the Canada-U.S. border.

(d) — Education Credit

In addition to the tuition fee credit, a student can also claim an "education credit" if he or she enrolls in a qualifying educational program in a designated educational institution.[34]

As with the other tax credits, we determine the education tax credit by applying the "appropriate percentage" for the year to the number of months of full-time attendance at the institution, multiplied by $400. For example, the credit for a student who attended a university for eight months in 2014 is 400×8 months $\times 15$ percent — that is, $480.[35] Part-time students may claim an education credit of 15 percent of $120 per month of part-time attendance.

---

[33]Para. 118.5(1)(c).

[34]S. 118.6.

[35]Subs. 118.6(2).

Part-time attendance is defined as attendance at a program lasting at least three consecutive weeks and involving a minimum of 12 hours of courses each month.

(e) — Medical Expenses

Medical expenditures are personal expenses and, therefore, would usually not be deductible for tax purposes. The Act does, however, provide some relief for "extraordinary" medical expenses over a minimum threshold limit to reflect the burden that such expenditures may have on one's ability to pay. The statute attempts, with limited success, to balance the social policy of providing relief for extraordinary medical expenses, but within stringent revenue constraints. There are over 300 expenses itemized in the Medical Expense Quick Reference Table. See CRA Guide RC 4064 ad Income Tax Folio 51-F1-C1: Medical Expense Tax Credit.

(i) — Computation of Credit

We determine the medical expense credit by applying the "appropriate percentage" (15 percent in 2014) to the sum of the taxpayer's medical expenses in excess of a threshold amount.[36] The threshold amount is the lesser of $1,813 (as indexed) and three percent of the individual's income from the year. The threshold amount is $2,171 in 2014.

Thus, the first step is to determine the taxpayer's total medical expenses for any 12 month period ending in the year. The second step is to deduct from the total medical expenses the *lesser* of $2,171 (2014) and three percent of the taxpayer's income for the year. The final step is to determine the medical expense credit by applying the appropriate percentage (15% - the lowest tax rate) to the amount by which the medical expenses exceed the threshold.

(ii) — Meaning of "Medical Expenses"

A taxpayer may deduct medical expenses incurred on behalf of:[37]

- himself;

- his spouse;

- his children, or his spouse's children, who depend on the taxpayer for support; or

- his or his spouse's parent, grandparent, brother, sister, uncle, aunt, niece, or nephew who reside in Canada and depend on the taxpayer for support.

---

[36]Subs. 118.2(1).

[37]Subss. 118.2(2), 118(6).

The taxpayer must support his or her claim for the credit by filing receipts with the return for the year.

"Medical expenses" means expenses paid to a medical practitioner, dentist, nurse, public or licensed private hospital. At first glance, the phrase "medical expenses" appears to include any expenditures that an individual may incur as a consequence of disability or illness. In fact, the phrase is circumscribed by several restrictive conditions. The list of eligible medical expenses is regularly reviewed and expanded in light of new technologies.

Payments for full-time nursing care in a nursing home or group home and payments for a full-time attendant to look after an individual qualify as medical expenses if the individual who requires the care is suffering from severe and prolonged mental or physical impairment.[38] A person is considered to be suffering from severe and prolonged impairment if his or her disability markedly restricts daily activities and can be expected to last for a continuous period of at least 12 months.[39] Reasonable expenses can also be claimed that were incurred to train an individual to care for a relative having a physical or mental infirmity. This relative must live with or be dependant on the individual.

Payments for a part-time attendant to look after an individual also qualify as medical expenses to the extent that the total paid does not exceed $10,000 (or $20,000, where the individual died in the year). Therapy administered by a person other than a qualified therapist or medical practitioner (e.g., audiologists and psychologists) to persons who are eligible for the disability tax credit also qualify. Finally, tutoring services that are supplementary to the primary education of persons with learning disabilities is a qualifying medical expense.

The restrictions on eligible medical expenses are long and detailed. It is important to note that an individual must satisfy all of the requirements before he or she can claim the credit. The courts used to be very strict in permitting a claim for medical expenses. They applied the statutory rules rigidly, sometimes excessively so, regardless of the underlying purpose of the deduction.[40] Recently, some courts have become a little more liberal in their interpretation of the provisions following the Supreme Court of Canada's guidelines that the *Income Tax Act* should be read in context and that *ambiguous* provisions should be interpreted according to the "object and spirit" of the rule.[41] See, for example, Judge Bowman's comments in *Radage*, 96 D.T.C. 1615 (T.C.C.): "The court must, while recognizing the narrow-

---

[38]See paras. 118.2(2)(b), (b.1).

[39]Subs. 118.4(1).

[40]See, e.g., *Witthuhn v. Minister of National Revenue* (1959), 17 Tax A.B.C. 33, 57 D.T.C. 174 (Can. Tax App. Bd.) (board denied claim for medical expenses for amounts paid to attendant to look after infirm spouse; taxpayer claimed expenses on basis that spouse was confined to bed or wheelchair; spouse in fact did not own wheelchair because she could not afford one. Instead, she sat in a special rocking chair; claim denied as rocking chair not a "wheelchair").

[41]*Stubart Investments Ltd. v. R.*, [1984] 1 S.C.R. 536, [1984] C.T.C. 294, 84 D.T.C. 6305 (S.C.C.).

ness of the tests . . . construe the provisions liberally, humanely and compassionately and not narrowly and technically."[42]

(f) — Mental or Physical Impairment

An individual with a severe and prolonged mental or physical impairment may claim a tax credit.[43] The credit is 15 percent of $6,000 (indexed after 2001). The claim must be supported by a doctor's certificate in prescribed form certifying the impairment. A person is considered to have a "severe and prolonged . . . impairment" only if he or she is markedly restricted all or substantially all of the time in the ability to perform a basic activity of daily living and the impairment lasts but for therapy that is essential to sustain a vital function of the individual that is required to be administered at least three times each week for a total period averaging not less than 14 hours per week, or can reasonably be expected to last, for a continuous period of at least 12 months.[44] The Act defines the basic activities of daily living.[45]

4. — Dividend Tax Credit

(a) — Tax Integration

Since corporations are legal entities separate and apart from their owners, corporate income is vulnerable to economic double taxation — first at the corporate level and then again at the shareholder level. Double taxation is inefficient and unfair and we should avoid it as much as possible. The Act provides a measure of relief by partially integrating corporate and personal shareholders taxation through a dividend tax credit mechanism.

In an ideal system, we would perfectly integrate corporate and personal taxes. However, that is not possible where we have thirteen different provincial tax rates. An individual who receives a taxable dividend from a corporation resident in Canada must include a grossed up value of the dollar amount of the dividend in income.[46] In other words, the cash value of the dividend is "grossed-up" by a percentage that depends upon the nature of the underlying dividend. Thus, initially one calculates the tax payable on the dividend by reference to a figure that is higher than the actual income. In theory, the gross-up reflects the underlying

---

[42]See also, *Crockart v. R.*, [1999] 2 C.T.C. 2409, 99 D.T.C. 3493 (T.C.C.) (meaning of a "hospital bed").

[43]S. 118.3.

[44]S. 118.4.

[45]Paras. 118.4(1)(c), (d).

[46]Para. 12(1)(j) and 82(1)(b).

corporate tax (at an assumed rate) paid by the corporation. The individual may, however, claim a dividend tax credit against the amount of federal tax that the gross-up imputes to the corporation.[47]

This two-step process of "grossing up" taxable dividends, followed by a tax credit, is a structural device that prevents, to a limited extent, double taxation of corporate income. The tax credit integrates the tax paid by corporations resident in Canada with the tax paid by individual shareholders on dividends so that the individual can claim a partial credit against his or her tax payable.

Individuals who receive eligible taxable dividends from taxable Canadian corporations must gross-up the dividend by 38 percent (para. 82(1)(b)). Individuals receive dividends other than eligible dividends (ineligible dividends) must gross-up by 18 percent.

A dividend is considered to have been "received" on the actual date of receipt and not when it is declared or the record date.[48]

The theory of the gross-up is to increase the amount to the corporate pre-tax level.

"Eligible dividends" are generally dividends from public corporations resident in Canada[49] paid to individuals who are Canadian residents.

The rationale of the dividend gross-up and tax credit is to prevent double taxation of Canadian corporate income. The gross-up restores, in theory, and approximately, income to the level that the corporation could have paid as a dividend if it had not paid corporate tax on its income. The dividend tax credit represents, in theory and approximately, the corporate income tax paid. Hence, the individuals end up paying tax on their dividends at their personal marginal rate on the corporation's notional income.

The remainder of the dividend tax structure simply fine tunes the rates to accommodate varying corporate tax rates and types of corporations. Hence, there are two levels of dividends: eligible and "other".

Eligible dividends are grossed-up by 38 percent and are eligible for a federal tax credit equal to 6/11 of the gross-up which is equivalent to 15 percent of the grossed up amount. The remaining 5/11 is, in theory, provided by the provincial portion of the tax credit.

---

[47]S. 121.

[48]*Horkoff v. R.*, [1996] 3 C.T.C. 2737 (T.C.C.).

[49]Para 89(1) "eligible dividend".

Example

Jane receives $100 of eligible dividends in 2014. Then:

Actual dividend	$100
Gross-up by 38 percent	$38
Grossed-up amount	$138

Federal dividend tax credit	
@ 6/11 × $38	$20.73
or 15 percent × $138	$20.70
(Difference due to rounding)	

"Other dividends" are also grossed-up and eligible for tax credit, but at different rates. The gross-up is at 25 percent of the actual dividend and the federal tax credit is equal to 2/3 of the 1/4 gross-up, or 13.33 percent of the taxable amount of the dividend.

Example

Harry receives $100 of "other dividends" in 2014. Then:

Actual dividend	$100
Gross-up by 25 percent	$25
Grossed-up amount	$125

Federal dividend tax credit	
@ 2/3 of $25	$16.67
or 13.33% × $125	$16.67

Thus, we see that although eligible dividends are grossed-up by a higher percentage than that for "other dividends", the dividend tax credit for eligible dividends is actually larger. These mathematical gyrations simply reflect assumptions of the underlying corporate tax rates of public versus private companies. Hence, when corporate rates change, so too then do the gross-up and dividend tax credit rates adapt.

(b) — Federal Credit

The dividend tax credit is equal to two-thirds of the value of the dividend gross-up. For example, an individual who receives a dividend of $800 is taxable on $1,000 and may claim a federal dividend tax credit of $133 (2/3 × $200).

(c) — Provincial Credit

Most provinces calculate the provincial dividend tax credit in the same manner as the federal tax credit. The provincial credit is often expressed as a percentage of the taxable amount rather than a percentage of the gross-up. For example, if the provincial credit is 25.5 percent of the gross-up, the CRA will often refer to the credit as 5.1 percent of the taxable amount.

5. — Overseas Employment Tax Credit

As a rule, Canadian residents are liable for tax on their worldwide income.[50] We refer to this as a system of full tax liability. An individual employed on an overseas (including the United States) contract may be entitled to a special tax credit. The credit is available only in limited circumstances, but it is extremely generous. We justify the credit on the basis that it allows Canadian businesses employing Canadian workers to compete in international markets with other countries that offer similar tax relief to their residents.

The credit is available only to an individual who is employed by a *specified* employer, and then only if the employee works overseas for a period of at least six consecutive months in certain *approved* activities. Thus, the statute limits the credit in four ways:[51]

- The taxpayer must work for a "specified employer";
- The employer must engage in an approved activity;
- The employee must work abroad for more than six consecutive months; and
- The amount of the credit is subject to a ceiling.

A "specified employer" is generally an employer resident in Canada.[52] The employer must engage in an approved activity such as construction, exploration for, and exploitation of, natural resources, or an agricultural project.

The amount of the credit is subject to a ceiling of $40,000 (2014) and $20,000 (2015).[53] The credit is equal to that portion of the tax otherwise payable that the *lesser* of $80,000 and 80 percent of the employee's net overseas employment income is of his or her total income. The credit is being phased out and will be eliminated by 2016.

---

[50]Subs. 2(1).

[51]Subs. 122.3(1); *IT-497R4*, "Overseas Employment Tax Credit" (May 14, 2004).

[52]Subs. 122.3(2) "specified employer".

[53]Paras. 122.3(1)(c), (d).

6. — Alternative Minimum Tax

High-income taxpayers may be subject to an "alternative minimum tax" ("AMT"), even though they do not have any taxable income.[54] The federal alternative minimum tax is payable at a flat rate of 15 percent on "adjusted taxable income".

The alternative minimum tax applies only to individuals and to certain trusts; it does not apply to corporations. AMT is an alternative tax. Thus, it applies only if the amount computed under it exceeds the individual's regular tax calculated on regular taxable income. The AMT is a substitute for the regular tax and is targeted at high income individuals who use "tax preference", such as the capital gains exemption.

Generally, a taxpayer's "adjusted taxable income" for the alternative minimum tax is his or her regular taxable income plus certain addbacks in respect of tax preference items.[55] These tax preference items are deductions that might be used to shelter income. For example, 60 percent of the exempt portion of capital gains, writeoffs for resource expenses, Canadian films, and a portion of the stock option deductions are added back into taxable income.

The AMT applies if the individual's "regular tax" is less than the minimum tax threshold calculated by removing preferential deductions. Any excess AMT over the regular basic tax is available for carryover for seven years. In computing "adjusted taxable income" for AMT purposes, a taxpayer is entitled to a basic exemption of $40,000.[56]

III. — Rules: Corporations

The rules that deal with the computation of tax payable by corporations are more detailed and complex than the rules applicable to individuals. This is because corporate taxation depends upon numerous variables: (1) type and size of the corporation; (2) ownership structure; (3) type and source of income; and (4) amount of income earned in a year. The federal tax system also takes into account the provincial need for taxes. Ultimately, the total corporate tax depends upon the corporation's residence and places of business. In this chapter, we look at the general rules applicable to all corporations. There are also special rates applicable to certain types of corporations (small business), forms of income (investment), and types of industry (mining, oil, and gas).

---

[54]Subss. 127.5–127.55.

[55]S. 127.52.

[56]S. 127.53.

1. — General Tax Rate

The general basic rate of federal tax payable by a corporation is 38 percent,[57] which is reduced by a rate abatement of 10 percent to provide room for provincial taxes. The general rate reduction does not apply to the income upon which a CCPC claims the small business deduction.[58] There is a special reduction for CCPCs. Income that is not attributable to a province is taxable at the full rate of 38 percent.

The 28 percent (after tax abatement) corporate rate is reduced further by a general reduction of 13 percent. Hence, the net general corporate tax rate before special deductions and credits is 15 percent (2014).

2. — Tax Adjustments

Few, if any, corporations actually pay tax at the general rate. The adjustments to the basic corporate tax include the following:

- Provincial tax credit;
- Foreign tax credit;
- Small business deduction;
- Manufacturing and processing profits deduction;
- Logging tax deduction;
- Investment tax credit; and
- Political contributions credit.

Also, the Act taxes certain types of corporations at special rates because of their special status.[59]

3. — Provincial Tax Credit

A corporation can claim a tax credit of 10 percent of its taxable income earned in a province.[60] The provincial tax credit vacates part of the income tax field to the provinces so that they may levy a corporate tax of their own. Where a province imposes a corporate tax of 10

---

[57]Para. 123(1)(a).

[58]Subs. 123.4(2).

[59]For example, investment corporations are subject to the special rules in s. 130.

[60]S. 124(1).

percent, the total general corporate tax (ignoring special tax adjustments) is 25 percent taking into account the general rate reduction of 13 percent. Where, however, a province imposes a provincial corporate tax in excess of 10 percent, the effective corporate tax burden (ignoring special tax adjustments) exceeds 25 percent (as adjusted by the general rate reduction). For example, Ontario's corporate tax rate is 11.5 percent (July 2014); British Columbia's rate is 11 percent; and Nova Scotia's is 16 percent.

The provincial tax credit is applicable only to a corporation's "taxable income earned . . . in a province." We determine this amount by allocating the corporation's total taxable income to its "permanent establishment[s]" in the provinces.[61] Thus, the calculation of a corporation's provincial tax credit involves four steps:

1. Determine whether the corporation has a "permanent establishment" in one or more provinces;

2. Allocate the taxable income of the corporation to the various provinces in accordance with the prescribed formulae;

3. Calculate the provincial tax abatement as 10 percent of the amount of "taxable income earned" in the provinces; and

4. Deduct the provincial tax abatement from the corporation's "tax otherwise payable".

The Act does not define "tax otherwise payable". It means the tax that is payable after the deduction of *all* permissible deductions.

(a) — "Permanent Establishment"

A "permanent establishment" is a fixed place of business of a corporation. A fixed place of business includes:[62]

- An office;
- A branch;
- A mine;
- An oil well;
- A farm;
- Timberland;
- A factory;

---

[61]Regs. 401, 402.

[62]Reg. 400(2).

- A workshop; or

- A warehouse.

Where a corporation does not have a fixed place of business, the term "permanent establishment" means the principal place in which the corporation conducts its business.[63]

The Act sometimes deems a corporation to have a permanent establishment in a particular place.

For example:

- Where a corporation carries on business in a particular place through an employee (or agent) who has general authority to contract or who has a stock of merchandise owned by his or her employer or principal, from which he or she regularly fills orders, that place is a permanent establishment.[64]

- Where a corporation that *otherwise* has a permanent establishment in Canada also owns land in a province, such land is a permanent establishment.[65]

- Where a corporation uses substantial machinery or equipment in a particular place *at any time in a taxation year*, it has a permanent establishment in that place.[66]

- An insurance corporation registered or licensed to do business in a province has a permanent establishment in that province.[67]

The mere fact, however, that a corporation's subsidiary does business in a particular place does not necessarily mean that the parent corporation has a permanent establishment in that same place.[68] Similarly, the maintenance of an office solely for the purchase of merchandise does not *necessarily* imply the presence of a permanent establishment in that location.[69]

---

[63]Reg. 400(2)(a).

[64]Reg. 400(2)(b).

[65]Reg. 400(2)(d).

[66]Reg. 400(2)(e).

[67]Reg. 400(2)(c).

[68]Reg. 400(2)(g).

[69]Reg. 400(2)(f).

(b) — Allocation of Taxable Income

Once we determine that a corporation has one or more permanent establishments, the next step is to allocate its taxable income to the provinces in which it maintains the establishments. The allocation is as follows:[70]

- Where a corporation has only one permanent establishment, we allocate its entire taxable income to the province in which it has that permanent establishment; and

- Where the corporation has a permanent establishment in more than one province, we allocate its taxable income on the basis of the following formula:

$$1/2 \text{ [(Provincial Gross Revenue) / (Total Gross Revenue) +}$$
$$\text{(Provincial Salary \& Wages) / (Total Salary \& Wages)]} \times \text{Taxable Income}$$

The Act *deems* a Canadian resident corporation that has only one permanent establishment in Canada and no other permanent establishment outside Canada to have earned its entire taxable income in that province.[71]

(c) — Computation of Provincial Tax Credit

The final step in the determination of the provincial tax credit is to calculate 10 percent of its total taxable income allocated to the provinces in which the corporation has permanent establishments. This amount is deducted from the federal tax otherwise payable.

The provincial tax credit applies only to taxable income that a corporation earns in a province. It does not apply to taxable income that it earns in a foreign jurisdiction. Foreign-source income that a corporation earns is taxable at the full corporate tax rate. The corporation may however, claim foreign tax credits.

4. — Small Business Deduction

A Canadian-controlled private corporation ("CCPC") that earns active business income in Canada can claim a special annual tax credit (the "small business deduction") equal to 17 percent of the first $500,000 of its active business income.[72] Thus, in effect, a CCPC pays federal tax at a rate of 13.11 percent on the first $500,000 of its business income. The prov-

---

[70]Reg. 402. The phrase "gross revenue" is defined in subs. 248(1), and detailed rules are prescribed for determining the gross revenue attributable to a permanent establishment.

[71]Reg. 402(1).

[72]S. 125.

inces and territories also have special small business rates. For example, Ontario taxes small business at 4.5 percent (July 2014); Manitoba at nil; British Columbia at 2.5 percent.

Example	General	CCPC
	%	
Basic federal rate	38	38
Less provincial abatement	(10)	(10)
Federal rate before surtax	28	28
General reduction	(13)	(17)
Net federal rate	*15*	*11*

The purpose of the "small business deduction" (which is actually a tax credit) is to allow small Canadian companies to generate capital for business operations.

IV. — Rules: All Taxpayers

1. — Foreign Tax Credit

(a) — General Comment

Canadian residents are subject to full tax liability on their worldwide income. Hence, a taxpayer may be subject to double taxation: to a foreign government for his income taxed at source, and to Canada on the basis of his residence. A resident taxpayer may, however, claim a credit against Canadian tax for taxes paid to a foreign government.[73] The purpose of the credit is to relieve Canadian residents from double taxation of income earned outside Canada. The foreign tax credit, which one calculates separately in respect of *each* country, only relieves juridical double taxation, but does not provide any relief from double taxation.[74] For example, if company A in Canada owns 5 percent of company B in the United

---

[73]S. 126; S5-F2-C1 (February 6, 2014).

[74]Subs. 126(6).

States, income earned by the U.S. company is taxable there. The foreign tax credit merely provides relief from the tax imposed on any dividends paid to company A, and not on the underlying U.S. corporate tax.

The tax credit is available only in respect of obligatory taxes paid to a foreign government. Discretionary foreign taxes levied by a foreign government that would not have been imposed if the taxpayer were not entitled to a Canadian foreign tax credit are not eligible for credit in Canada.[75] The rationale for this rule is that the Canadian government does not want to finance foreign governments by encouraging them to levy taxes on Canadians resident in their country in the expectation that the taxpayers will receive a rebate for the tax under Canadian tax law.

The foreign tax credit rules deal with three different circumstances:

- Foreign taxes paid by a resident on non-business income;
- Foreign taxes paid by a resident on business income; and
- Taxes paid by non-residents in respect of certain capital gains.

The foreign tax credit rules may operate independently or in conjunction with Canada's tax treaties, which are also intended to prevent double taxation.

The general effect of the foreign tax credit rules is to limit the foreign credit to a maximum of the equivalent Canadian tax if the taxpayer earned the income in Canada. Thus, the taxpayer ends up paying the higher of the foreign tax paid and the equivalent Canadian tax.

(b) — Non-Business-Income Tax

A resident taxpayer may deduct from "tax otherwise payable" under Part I an amount equal to the non-business-income taxes[76] paid to a foreign jurisdiction. The tax credit cannot exceed the amount of Canadian tax that would have been payable on the foreign income had that income been earned in Canada.[77]

---

[75]Subs. 126(4).

[76]Subs. 126(7) "non-business-income tax".

[77]This is the effect of the formula in subs. 126(1).

(i) — Definition

"Non-business-income tax" generally means taxes paid to a foreign jurisdiction, whether a foreign country or a subdivision of a foreign country. It does not include:[78]

- Amounts included in calculating the taxpayer's "business income tax" (the credit for business income taxes is calculated separately);[79]

- Taxes in respect of which the taxpayer has already taken a *deduction* in computing income;[80]

- Taxes attributable to income eligible for the overseas employment tax credit;[81]

- Taxes payable to a foreign country based solely on the taxpayer being a citizen of that country if the taxes are attributable to income earned in Canada;[82]

- Taxes relating to an amount that is refunded to any person or partnership;[83]

- Taxes reasonably attributable to a taxable capital gain for which the taxpayer or a spouse has claimed a deduction;[84]

- Taxes reasonably attributable to a loan received or receivable by the taxpayer;[85] and

- Taxes relating to an amount that was exempt by treaty.[86]

---

[78]Subs. 126(7) "non-business-income tax".

[79]Subs. 126(7) "non-business-income tax" (a).

[80]Subs. 20(11) (deduction for tax in excess of 15 percent paid to foreign government on income from property, other than real property); subs. 20(12) (deduction for tax paid to foreign government in respect of income from business or property, other than, where the taxpayer is a corporation, from shares of a foreign affiliate, to the extent of the "non-business-income" tax paid by taxpayer); subs. (recalculation of trust's foreign tax); subs. 126(7) "non-business-income tax" (b) & (c).

[81]See subs. 122.3(1).

[82]Subs. 126(7) "non-business-income tax" (d); for example, a United States citizen who pays U.S. tax on employment income earned in Canada is not entitled to the foreign tax credit for the U.S. taxes.

[83]Subs. 126(7) "non-business-income tax" (e); some countries, such as Brazil, refund taxes withheld from payments to foreigners to the local payer; the purpose of these refunds is to subsidize domestic operations and borrowings.

[84]Subs. 126(7) "non-business-income tax" (g); s. 110.6.

[85]Subs. 126(7) "non-business-income tax" (h); subs. 33.1(1).

[86]Subs. 126(7) "non-business-income tax" (i); subpara. 110(1)(f)(i).

The credit is available only for foreign taxes *actually paid* by the taxpayer *for the year.* Hence, tax refunded by a foreign government in a subsequent year because of a loss carryback necessitates a recalculation of the foreign tax credit for the year to which the refund applies.[87]

The credit is available only in respect of "income or profits" taxes paid to a foreign government. A corporate taxpayer cannot claim a credit for foreign taxes on income from a share in a foreign affiliate.[88]

(ii) — Limits

The foreign tax credit is subject to a limit calculated according to the following formula:

$$\text{(Amount of foreign non-business income)/(Income from all sources)} \times \text{Canadian tax otherwise payable}$$

The effect of this formula is that the credit for Canadian income tax purposes cannot exceed a rate that is higher than the rate that would have been payable by the taxpayer had the income been earned in Canada rather than in the foreign jurisdiction.[89]

(iii) — No Carryover

There is no carryover for non-business-income tax.

(c) — Business-Income Tax

The credit for foreign business income tax benefits Canadian resident taxpayers who have branch operations in foreign countries.

(i) — Definition

"[B]usiness-income tax" means tax paid by the taxpayer that may reasonably be regarded as a tax in respect of the income of the taxpayer from any business carried on by him in a foreign country.[90]

---

[87]*Icanda Ltd. v. Minister of National Revenue*, [1972] C.T.C. 163, 72 D.T.C. 6148 (Fed. T.D.).

[88]Para. 126(1)(a).

[89]Para. 126(1)(b).

[90]Subs. 126(7) "business-income tax".

(ii) — Separate Calculation

As with the tax credit for non-business-income tax, the tax credit for business-income taxes must be calculated separately for each country in which the taxpayer carries on business.

(iii) — Carryover

Business-income taxes paid to a foreign jurisdiction may exceed the amount that the taxpayer can claim as a credit against Canadian taxes. Any excess may be carried forward as an "unused foreign tax credit" for 10 years and carried back for three years.[91] The foreign tax credit in respect of the current year must be claimed before any unused credits from other years.[92]

(iv) — Limits

The credit in respect of business-income tax is limited to the amount of tax that would have been payable on a comparable amount of income earned in Canada.[93] Non-business-income tax credits are to be deducted before business-income tax credits.[94]

(d) — Employees of International Organizations

Employees of international organizations are usually exempt from income tax levied by the country in which they are stationed. Some of these organizations (for example, the United Nations) impose a levy upon their employees for the purpose of defraying the expenses of the organization. The levy is calculated in the same manner as an income tax.

Since a Canadian resident working abroad is subject to Canadian income tax on his or her worldwide income, the imposition of this additional levy constitutes double taxation of the income. To prevent double taxation, Canadian residents employed by international agencies are allowed either a deduction or a credit for foreign income.

An employee of a *prescribed* international organization may deduct his or her employment income in calculating taxable income.[95]

---

[91] Para. 126(2)(a), subs. 126(7) "unused foreign tax credit".

[92] Subs. 126(2.3).

[93] Para. 126(2)(b), subs. 126(2.1).

[94] Para. 126(2)(c).

[95] Subpara. 110(1)(f)(iii).

Employees of other international organizations may claim a tax credit for foreign taxes paid to the organization.[96]

2. — Political Contributions Credit

Contributions to political parties and to candidates for political office are not deductible from income for tax purposes.[97] The rationale is that such expenses are not incurred to earn income even though they may well enhance future political appointments and income. The Act does, however, allow a credit for political contributions *against tax payable*.[98] The theory of the credit is to encourage taxpayers to support the democratic process.

The credit is available in respect of contributions to a "registered party" or to an "officially nominated candidate" in a federal election. Some of the provinces also allow for a credit against provincial taxes for contributions to provincial political parties and officially nominated candidates in provincial elections.

The amount of the federal credit is restricted on a sliding scale. The percentage claimable declines as the amount of the contribution increases.

	Contribution	Tax Credit
On the first	$ 400	75%
On the next	$ 350	50%
On the next	$ 525	33 1/3%
On any excess over	$ 1,275	nil

Thus the maximum credit $650 (2014). The theory of the sliding scale is to encourage small contributions with no credit for amounts above $1,275. Corporations cannot make political contributions under the *Canada Elections Act*. A claim for the credit must be supported by filing an official receipt signed by a registered agent of the party or candidate. The receipt must disclose certain prescribed information.[99]

---

[96]Subs. 126(3).

[97]Para. 18(1)(n); *Stasiuk v. Minister of National Revenue*, [1986] 2 C.T.C. 346 (Fed. T.D.) (taxpayer denied deduction for amounts expended on publicizing her political views).

[98]Subs. 127(3).

[99]Reg. 2000.

3. — Other Tax Credits

There are other special tax credits available to taxpayers who derive income from particular types of activities.

(a) — Logging Tax Credit

Subsection 127(1) allows a credit for "logging taxes" paid by a taxpayer to a province in respect of logging operations.[100]

(b) — Investment Tax Credit

An investment tax credit is available for most current and capital expenditures on account of research and development carried on in Canada.[101]

The investment tax credit is intended to stimulate investment in certain types of activities and in certain regions of the country.

Generally, the credit is available to a taxpayer in respect of acquisitions of depreciable property used by the taxpayer in Canada primarily for the purpose of:[102]

- Manufacturing or processing of goods for sale or lease;
- Operating an oil or gas well;
- Processing heavy crude oil recovered from a natural reservoir in Canada to a stage that is not beyond the crude oil stage or its equivalent;
- Extracting minerals from a resource;
- Processing ore (other than iron or tar sands) to the prime metal stage or its equivalent;
- Exploring or drilling for petroleum or natural gas;
- Prospecting or exploring for, or developing, a mineral resource;
- Logging;
- Farming or fishing;
- Storing grain;

---

[100]British Columbia and Quebec impose logging taxes.

[101]Subs. 127(5).

[102]Subs. 127(9) "qualified property".

- Producing industrial minerals;
- Canadian field processing;
- Producing or processing electrical energy or steam;
- Harvesting peat;
- Processing iron ore to the pellet stage; or
- Processing tar sands to the crude oil stage.

The amount of the credit depends upon the type of investment made by the taxpayer, the region in which the investment is made, whether the property is "available for use" and, in certain cases, the taxpayer's status.

The investment tax credit is deductible against taxes otherwise payable. Unused credits may be carried back three years and carried forward for 10 years.[103]

---

[103]Subs. 127(9) "investment tax credit" (c).

Selected Bibliography to Chapter 15

Individuals

Beam, Robert E., and Karen Wensley, "Personal Tax Planning: Alternative Minimum Tax — The Political Tax" (1986) 34 Can. Tax J. 174.

Dart, Robert J., "A Critique of an Advance Corporate Tax System for Canada" (1990) 38 Can. Tax J. 1245.

Erlichman, Harry, "Profitable Donations: What Price Culture?" (1992) 11 Philanthrop. 3.

Huggett, Donald R., "Alternative Minimum Tax (A Fiscal Albatross)" (1986) 13 Can. Tax News 109.

Huggett, Donald R., "Minimum Income Tax (A)", in *Proceedings of 37th Tax Conf.* 10:1 (Can. Tax Foundation, 1985).

Huggett, Donald R., "Minimum Tax (The)" (1985) 13 Can. Tax News 75.

Jenkins, Glenn P., "The Role and Economic Implications of the Canadian Dividend Tax Credit", *Discussion Paper No. 307* (Ottawa: Economic Council of Canada, June 1986).

Low Income Tax Relief Working Group of Fair Tax Commission, *Working Group Report* (Toronto: Fair Tax Commission, 1992).

Newman, Eric J., "Tax Indexing — What Does It Mean to You?" (1974) 105:5 CA Magazine 54.

Novek, Barbara L., "Sector Specific Tax Relief for Canadian Residents Working Overseas" (1993) 5 Tax. of Exec. Compensation and Retirement 808.

Sherbeniuk, Douglas J., "Future Trends in Tax Policy: Focus on the Alternative Minimum Tax and the Corporate Income Tax Discussion Papers," (1986) Special Lectures L.S.U.C. 425.

Smith, Roger S., "Rates of Personal Income Tax: The Carter Commission Revisited" (1987) 35 Can. Tax J. 1226, and in *The Quest for Tax Reform*, W. Neil Brooks, ed., (Toronto: Carswell, 1988) at 173.

Wilson, Michael H., *A Minimum Tax for Canada*, Dept. of Finance, Canada, 1985.

Rules: Corporations

Blais, A., and F. Vaillancourt, "The Federal Corporate Income Tax: Tax Expenditures and Tax Discrimination in the Canadian Manufacturing Industry, 1972–1981" (1986) 34 Can. Tax J. 1122.

Dale, Michael, "A Comparison of Effective Marginal Tax Rates on Income Capital in Canadian Manufacturing" (1985) 33 Can. Tax J. 1154.

Horne, Barry D. and Tim S. Wach, "Canadian Taxation of Foreign Sourced Income: The Foreign Tax Credit" (1991) 3 Imm. & Cit. 4.

Huggett, Donald R., "Temporary Surtax" (1985) 13 Can. Tax News 97.

Lahmer, Craig, "Recent Developments in Manufacturing and Processing" in *Proceedings of 44th Tax Conf.* (Can. Tax Found., 1992) 52:1.

McDonnell, T.E., "Manufacturing and Processing Profits: Some Interpretive Questions" (1994) 40 Can. Tax J. 929.

Sennema, James R., "Temporary Business Operations as 'Permanent Establishments'" (1992) 5 C.U.B.L.R. 171.

Vytas, Nalaitas, "Large Corporation's Tax" (1990) 64 CMA Magazine 34.

Rules: All Taxpayers

Tremblay, Richard G., "Foreign Tax Credit Planning" (1993) Corp. Mgmt. Tax Conf. 3:1.

INDEX

659

Index

660

Index

Moving expenses

- defined, 548–550
- eligibility for deduction, 547
- generally, 546-547

Musicians, 250

N

Net worth basis, 179-180

Neutrality principle, 23

Nexus, *see* Taxable nexus

Non-arm's length transactions, 186–188

- cost of property, 376
- deemed fair market value, 475
- loans, 569

Non-business income tax, 649–651

Non-residents, liability for tax, 92-93

O

Options

- call options, 465-466
- characterization on issue, 464
- granting of, 465
- put options, 466

Other sources of income

- death benefits, 524

- other inclusions, 527–529
- pension benefits, 523-524
- prizes, 527
- research grants, 526
- retiring allowances, 525
- scholarships, bursaries, fellowships, 525-526
- social assistance payments, 527
- support payments, 524-525

Overseas employment tax credit, 642

P

Partnerships

- defined, 91
- limited losses, 604
- residence, 91

Penalties, levies, and fines, 326

Pension benefits income, 523-524

Pension income tax credit, 632-633

Permanent establishment, 84-85, 645-646

Personal and living expenses

- allowance from employment, 226-227
- as compared to business expense, 339-340
- generally, 332-333
- purpose test, 333–337

670

Index

Tax treaties

• interpretation, 51

• residence, *see under* Residence

Taxable benefits, 224

Taxable income, defined, 579-580

Taxable nexus

• generally, 64–66

• residence, *see* Residence

• who is taxable, 66–8

Taxpayers, identified, 9

Tort damages

• business or investments, 427-428

• eligible capital property, 428

• fatal accidents, 430-431

• generally, 427

• investment income, 431-432

• personal injuries settlements, 429-430

• property, capital and depreciable, 428

Travelling expenses, 247-248

• inadequate compensation, 247

• meals, 248

• motor vehicles and aircraft, 248

Trusts

• deemed dispositions, 470

• defined, 89

• residence, 89-90

Tuition fees tax credit, 633–636

V

Valuation day

• depreciable property, 502-503

• election, 506

• generally, 501-502

• median-rule or tax-free zone method, 505-506

• other capital property, 504–506

• partnership interest, 503-504

W

Who is taxable, *see under* Taxable nexus

Windfall gains, 136-137

Wrongful dismissal, 423-424